Fundamentals of Corporate Finance

Robert Parrino
David S. Kidwell

Custom Edition for use in FIR 3410

University of Memphis

Copyright © 2010 by John Wiley & Sons, Inc.

All rights reserved.

No part of this publication may be reproduced, stored in a retrieval system or transmitted in any form or by any means, electronic, mechanical, photocopying, recording, scanning or otherwise, except as permitted under Sections 107 or 108 of the 1976 United States Copyright Act, without either the prior written permission of the Publisher, or authorization through payment of the appropriate per-copy fee to the Copyright Clearance Center, Inc., 222 Rosewood Drive, Danvers, MA 01923, website www.copyright.com. Requests to the Publisher for permission should be addressed to the Permissions Department, John Wiley & Sons, Inc., 111 River Street, Hoboken, NJ 07030-5774, (201) 748-6011, fax (201) 748-6008, website http://www.wiley.com/go/permissions.

To order books or for customer service, please call 1(800)-CALL-WILEY (225-5945).

Printed in the United States of America.

ISBN 978-0-470-54364-1

Printed and bound by Integrated Book Technology.

10 9 8 7 6 5 4 3 2 1

Fundamentals of Corporate Finance

Robert Parrino
Lamar Savings Centennial Professor of Finance
University of Texas at Austin

David S. Kidwell
Professor of Finance and Dean Emeritus
University of Minnesota

WILEY
John Wiley & Sons, Inc.

ASSOCIATE PUBLISHER	Judith Joseph
SENIOR DEVELOPMENTAL EDITOR	Marian D. Provenzano
EXECUTIVE MARKETING MANAGER	Amy Scholz
SENIOR PRODUCTION EDITOR	William A. Murray
ASSOCIATE EDITOR	Brian Kamins
SENIOR ILLUSTRATION EDITOR	Sigmund Malinowski
ASSOCIATE PHOTO EDITOR	Sheena Goldstein
SENIOR MEDIA EDITOR	Allie K. Morris
SENIOR DESIGNER	Kevin Murphy
INTERIOR DESIGN	Nancy Field
COVER DESIGN	David Levy
COVER PHOTO	Bill Frymire/Masterfile

The CFA Institute Materials used in this book are reproduced and republished from the CFA Program Materials with permission from the CFA Institute. The authors and publisher are grateful for permission to use this material.

This book was set in Times Ten Roman by Aptara®, Inc. and printed and bound by R.R. Donnelley.

This book is printed on acid free paper. ∞

Copyright © 2009 John Wiley & Sons, Inc. All rights reserved. No part of this publication may be reproduced, stored in a retrieval system, or transmitted in any form or by any means, electronic, mechanical, photocopying, recording, scanning or otherwise, except as permitted under Sections 107 or 108 of the 1976 United States Copyright Act, without either the prior written permission of the Publisher, or authorization through payment of the appropriate per-copy fee to the Copyright Clearance Center, Inc., 222 Rosewood Drive, Danvers, MA 01923 (Web site: www.copyright.com). Requests to the Publisher for permission should be addressed to the Permissions Department, John Wiley & Sons, Inc., 111 River Street, Hoboken, NJ 07030-5774, (201) 748-6011, fax (201) 748-6008, or online at: www.wiley.com/go/permissions.

To order books or for customer service please call 1-800-CALL WILEY (225-5945).

ISBN 978-0-471-27056-0

Printed in the United States of America

10 9 8 7 6 5 4 3 2 1

Contents

Part 1 Introduction

CHAPTER 1 The Financial Manager and the Firm 1

Part 2 Foundations

CHAPTER 2 The Financial Environment and the Level of Interest Rates 27

CHAPTER 3 Financial Statements, Cash Flows, and Taxes 53

CHAPTER 4 Analyzing Financial Statements 85

Part 3 Valuation of Future Cash Flows and Risk

CHAPTER 5 The Time Value of Money 131

CHAPTER 6 Discounted Cash Flows and Valuation 167

CHAPTER 7 Risk and Return 209

CHAPTER 8 Bond Valuation and the Structure of Interest Rates 249

CHAPTER 9 Stock Valuation 281

Part 4 Capital Budgeting Decisions

CHAPTER 10 The Fundamentals of Capital Budgeting 312

CHAPTER 11 Cash Flows and Capital Budgeting 355

CHAPTER 12 Evaluating Project Economics and Capital Rationing 396

CHAPTER 13 The Cost of Capital 426

APPENDIX A Present Value and Future Value Tables 727

APPENDIX B Solutions to Selected Questions and Problems 737

GLOSSARY 743

SUBJECT INDEX 751

COMPANY INDEX 766

Selected Abbreviations and Notation

β =		beta (a measure of systematic risk)
Δ =		change (e.g., ΔP = change in price level, ΔS = change in sales level)
ρ =		correlation
$\sigma^2\,(\sigma)$ =		variance (standard deviation)
x =		fractional weight of investment or component of capital
Add WC =		addition to working capital
APR =		annual percentage rate
ARR =		accounting rate of return
C =		coupon payment (bond)
Cap Exp =		capital expenditures
CF =		cash flow
CF Opns =		cash flow from operations
CIP =		call interest premium
CO =		crossover level of unit sales
COGS =		cost of goods sold
CV =		coefficient of variation
D =		dividend (stock)
D&A =		depreciation and amortization
DOL =		degree of operating leverage
DPO =		days' payables outstanding
DRP =		default risk premium
DSI =		days' sales in inventory
DSO =		days' sales outstanding
E(•) =		expected value (E(R) = expected return, etc.)
EAC =		equivalent annual cost
EAR = EAY =		effective annual rate (yield)
EBIT =		earnings before interest and taxes
EBITDA =		earnings before interest, taxes, depreciation, and amortization
EBT =		earnings before taxes
EFN =		external funding needed
EOQ =		economic order quantity
EROA =		EBIT return on assets
F =		face value (bond)
FC =		fixed costs
FCF =		free cash flows
FCFE =		free cash flow to equity
FCFF =		free cash flow from the firm
FV =		future value

FVA_n =	future value of an annuity
FXR =	foreign exchange or currency risk premium
g =	growth rate
i =	nominal rate of interest
IGR =	internal growth rate
IRR =	internal rate of return
k =	cost of capital (debt or equity)
m =	number of payments per year
MAT =	maturity adjustment to cost of a loan
MRP =	marketability risk premium
MV =	market value
n =	number of periods
NCF =	net cash flow
NCFOA =	net cash flow from operating activities
NOPAT =	net operating profits after tax
NPV =	net present value
NWC =	net working capital
OC =	operating cycle
Op Ex =	cash operating expenses
p =	probability
P =	price (P_0 = price at time zero, etc.)
P/E ratio =	price/earnings ratio
PB =	payback period
PI =	profitability index
PR =	prime rate
PV =	present value
PV annuity factor =	present value of annuity factor
PVA_n =	present value of an annuity
r =	real rate of interest
R =	return (R_{rf} = risk free, R_i, $R_{Portfolio}$, etc.)
ROA =	return on assets
ROE =	return on equity
SGR =	sustainable growth rate
t =	tax rate
TV =	terminal value
V =	value (e.g., $V_{Firm} = V_{Assets} = V_{Debt} + V_{Equity}$)
VC =	variable costs
WACC =	weighted average cost of capital

THE FINANCIAL MANAGER AND THE FIRM

CHAPTER 1

LEARNING OBJECTIVES

1. Identify the key financial decisions facing the financial manager of any business firm.

2. Identify the basic forms of business organization used in the United States, and review their respective strengths and weaknesses.

3. Describe the typical organization of the financial function in a large corporation.

4. Explain why maximizing the current value of the firm's stock is the appropriate goal for management.

5. Discuss how agency conflicts affect the goal of maximizing stockholder value.

6. Explain why ethics is an appropriate topic in the study of corporate finance.

©AP/Wide World Photos

On February 25, 2007, TXU Corporation, a Texas-based electric utility company, announced that a group of investors had offered to acquire the company in a leveraged buyout—a transaction in which the purchaser uses a lot of debt. The investor group, led by the leveraged buyout firms Kohlberg Kravis Roberts & Co. (KKR) and Texas Pacific Group (TPG), was offering $69.25 per share for all of the outstanding shares of TXU. Only a month earlier, the stock had been trading at $54.30 per share. The price offered by KKR and TPG represented a 27.5 percent premium over this recent market price. With a total value of $46 billion, this was the largest leveraged buyout announced up to that point in time.

How did KKR and TPG arrive at this high offering price, and how could they justify it? Surely they did not make the offer planning to lose money. In fact, even though they were paying $69.25 per share, KKR and TPG still expected to earn more than 20 percent per year on their investment over the following five years. By focusing TXU's investment activities, increasing the efficiency of operations, and using a great deal of debt financing, the new owners planned to increase the value of the cash flows TXU would generate.

Investors in leveraged buyouts use many of the concepts covered in this chapter and elsewhere in this book to create the most possible value. They begin by structuring the compensation of firm managers to provide them with incentives to focus on value creation. Managers create value by investing only in projects whose benefits exceed their costs, managing the assets of the company as efficiently as possible, and financing the company with the least expensive combination of debt and equity. This chapter introduces you to the key financial aspects of these activities, and the remainder of the book fills in many of the details.

CHAPTER PREVIEW

This book provides an introduction to corporate finance. In it we focus on the responsibilities of the financial manager, who oversees the accounting and treasury functions and sets the overall financial strategy for the firm. We pay special attention to the financial manager's role as a decision maker. To that end, we emphasize the mastery of fundamental finance concepts and the use of a set of financial tools, which will result in sound financial decisions that create value for stockholders. These financial concepts and tools apply not only to business organizations but also to other venues, such as government entities, not-for-profit organizations, and sometimes even your own personal finances.

We open this chapter by discussing the three major types of decisions that a financial manager makes. We then describe common forms of business organization. After next discussing the major responsibilities of the financial manager, we explain why maximizing the price of the firm's stock is an appropriate goal for a financial manager. We go on to describe the conflicts of interest that can arise between stockholders and managers and the mechanisms that help align the interests of these two groups. Finally, we discuss the importance of ethical conduct in business.

1.1 The Role of the Financial Manager

LEARNING OBJECTIVE 1

wealth
the economic value of the assets someone possesses

The financial manager is responsible for making decisions that are in the best interests of the firm's owners, whether the firm is a start-up business with a single owner or a billion-dollar corporation owned by thousands of stockholders. The decisions made by the financial manager or owner should be one and the same. In most situations this means that the financial manager should make decisions that maximize the value of the owners' stock. This helps maximize the owners' **wealth**. Our underlying assumption in this book is that most people who invest in businesses do so because they want to increase their wealth. In the following discussion, we describe the responsibilities of the financial manager in a new business in order to illustrate the types of decisions that such a manager makes.

Stakeholders

stakeholder
anyone other than an owner (stockholder) with a claim on the cash flows of a firm, including employees, suppliers, creditors, and the government

Before we discuss the new business, you may want to look at Exhibit 1.1, which shows the cash flows between a firm and its owners (in a corporation, the stockholders) and various stakeholders. A **stakeholder** is someone other than an owner who has a claim on the cash flows of the firm: *managers*, who want to be paid salaries and performance bonuses; *creditors*, who want to be paid interest and principal; *employees*, who want to be paid wages; *suppliers*, who want to be paid for goods or services; and the *government*, which wants the firm to pay taxes. Stakeholders may have interests that differ from those of the owners. When this is the case, they may exert pressure on management to make decisions that benefit them. We will return to these types of conflict of interest later in the book. For now, though, we are primarily concerned with the overall flow of cash between the firm and its stockholders and stakeholders.

It's All about Cash Flows

productive assets
the tangible and intangible assets a firm uses to generate cash flows

To produce its products or services, a new firm needs to acquire a variety of assets. Most will be long-term assets or **productive assets**. Productive assets can be tangible assets, such as equipment, machinery, or a manufacturing facility, or intangible assets, such as patents, trademarks, technical expertise, or other types of intellectual capital.

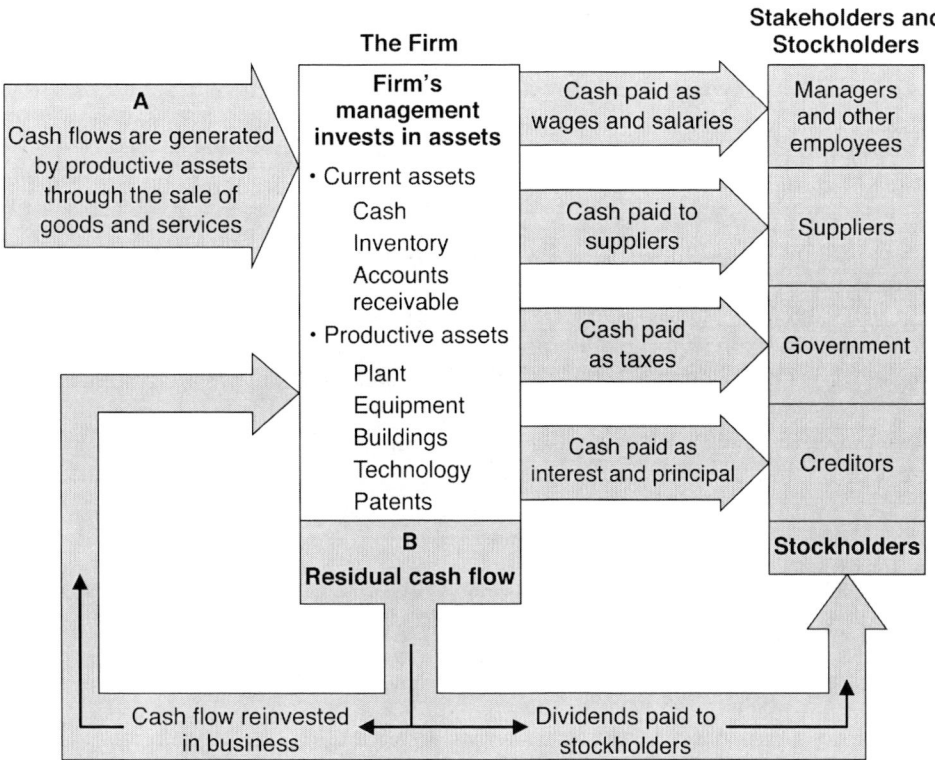

Exhibit 1.1
Cash Flows Between the Firm and Its Stakeholders and Owners
A. Making business decisions is all about cash flows, because only cash can be used to pay bills and buy new assets. Cash initially flows into the firm as a result of the sale of goods or services. The firm uses these cash inflows in a number of ways: to invest in assets, to pay wages and salaries, to buy supplies, to pay taxes, and to repay creditors.
B. Any cash that is left over (residual cash flows), can be reinvested in the business or paid as dividends to stockholders.

Regardless of the type of asset, the firm tries to select assets that will generate the greatest profits. The decision-making process through which the firm purchases long-term productive assets is called *capital budgeting*, and it is one of the most important decision processes in a firm.

Once the firm has selected its productive assets, it must raise money to pay for them. *Financing decisions* are concerned with the ways in which firms obtain and manage long-term financing to acquire and support their productive assets. There are two basic sources of funds: debt and equity. Every firm has some equity because equity represents ownership in the firm. It consists of capital contributions by the owners plus earnings that have been reinvested in the firm. In addition, most firms borrow from a bank or issue some type of long-term debt to finance productive assets.

After the productive assets have been purchased and the business is operating, the firm will try to produce products at the lowest possible cost while maintaining quality. This means buying raw materials at the lowest possible cost, holding production and labor costs down, keeping management and administrative costs to a minimum, and seeing that shipping and delivery costs are competitive. In addition, the firm must manage its day-to-day finances so that it will have sufficient cash on hand to pay salaries, purchase supplies, maintain inventories, pay taxes, and cover the myriad of other expenses necessary to run a business. The management of current assets, such as money owed by customers who purchase on credit, inventory, and current liabilities, such as money owed to suppliers, is called *working capital management*.[1]

A firm generates cash flows by selling the goods and services it produces. A firm is successful when these cash inflows exceed the cash outflows needed to pay operating expenses, creditors, and taxes. After meeting these obligations, the firm can pay

---

[1]From accounting, *current assets* are assets that will be converted into cash within a year; and *current liabilities* are liabilities that must be paid within one year.

residual cash flows
the cash remaining after a firm has paid operating expenses and what it owes creditors and in taxes; can be paid to the owners as a cash dividend or reinvested in the business

the remaining cash, called **residual cash flows**, to the owners as a cash dividend, or it can reinvest the cash in the business. The reinvestment of residual cash flows back into the business to buy more productive assets is a very important concept. If these funds are invested wisely, they provide the foundation for the firm to grow and provide larger residual cash flows in the future for the owners. The reinvestment of cash flows (earnings) is the most fundamental way that businesses grow in size. Exhibit 1.1 illustrates how the revenue generated by productive assets ultimately becomes residual cash flow.

A firm is unprofitable when it fails to generate sufficient cash inflows to pay operating expenses, creditors, and taxes. Firms that are unprofitable over time will be forced into **bankruptcy** by their creditors if the owners do not shut them down first. In bankruptcy the company will be reorganized or the company's assets will be liquidated, whichever is more valuable. If the company is liquidated, creditors are paid in a priority order according to the structure of the firm's financial contracts and prevailing bankruptcy law. If anything is left after all creditor and tax claims have been satisfied, which usually does not happen, the remaining cash, or residual value, is distributed to the owners.

bankruptcy
legally declared inability of an individual or a company to pay its creditors

BUILDING INTUITION

Cash Flows Matter Most to Investors

Cash is what investors ultimately care about when making an investment. The value of any asset—stocks, bonds, or a business—is determined by the future cash flows it will generate. To understand this concept, just consider how much you would pay for an asset from which you could never expect to obtain any cash flows. Buying such an asset would be like giving your money away. It would have a value of exactly zero. Conversely, as the expected cash flows from an investment increase, you would be willing to pay more and more for it.

Three Fundamental Decisions in Financial Management

Based on our discussion so far, we can see that financial managers are concerned with three fundamental decisions when running a business:

1. *Capital budgeting decisions:* Identifying the productive assets the firm should buy.

2. *Financing decisions:* Determining how the firm should finance or pay for assets.

3. *Working capital management decisions:* Determining how day-to-day financial matters should be managed so that the firm can pay its bills, and how surplus cash should be invested.

Exhibit 1.2 shows the impact of each decision on the firm's balance sheet. We briefly introduce each decision here and discuss them in greater detail in later chapters.

CAPITAL BUDGETING DECISIONS

A firm's capital budget is simply a list of the productive (capital) assets management wants to purchase over a budget cycle, typically one year. The capital budgeting decision process addresses which productive assets the firm should purchase and how much money the firm can afford to spend. As shown in Exhibit 1.2, capital budgeting decisions affect the asset side of the balance sheet and are concerned with a firm's long-term investments. Capital budgeting decisions, as we mentioned earlier, are

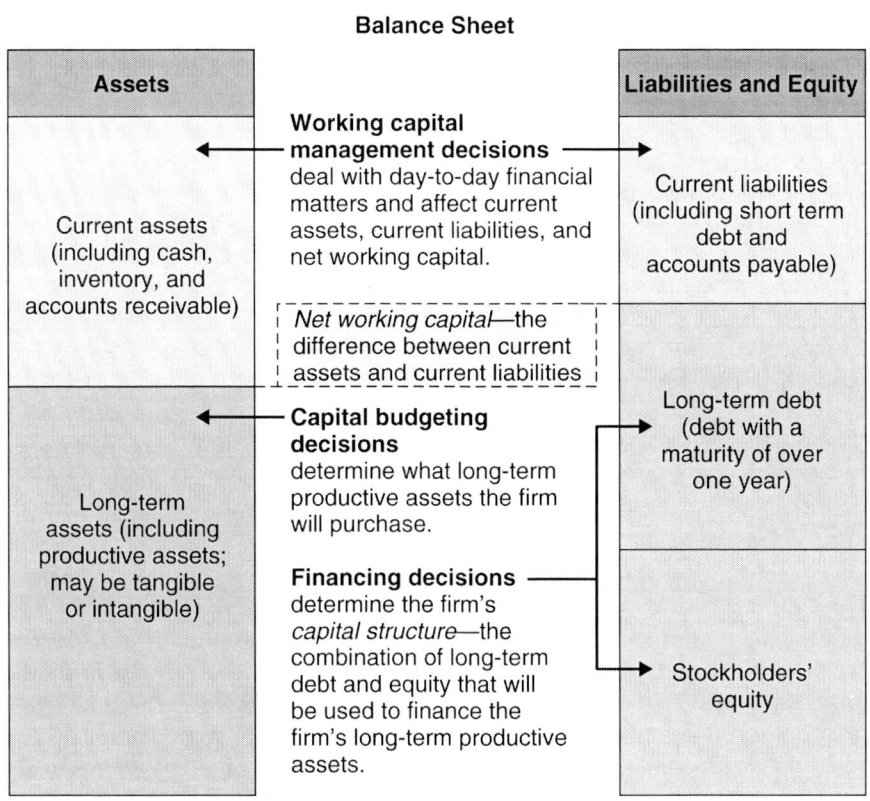

Exhibit 1.2
How the Financial Manager's Decisions Affect the Balance Sheet
Financial managers are concerned with three fundamental types of decisions: capital budgeting decisions, financing decisions, and working capital management decisions. Each type of decision has a direct and important effect on the firm's balance sheet—in other words, on the firm's profitability.

among management's most important decisions. Over the long run, they have a large impact on the firm's success or failure. The reason is twofold. First, capital assets generate most of the cash flows for the firm. Second, capital assets are long term in nature. Once they are purchased, the firm owns them for a long time, and they may be hard to sell without taking a financial loss.

The fundamental question in capital budgeting is this: Which productive assets should the firm purchase? A capital budgeting decision may be as simple as a movie theater's decision to buy a popcorn machine or as complicated as Boeing's decision to invest more than $6 billion to design and build the 7E7 *Dreamliner* passenger jet. Capital investments may also involve the purchase of an entire business, such as IBM's purchase of PricewaterhouseCoopers' (PwC) management consulting practice.

Regardless of the project, a good capital budgeting decision is one in which the benefits are worth more to the firm than the cost of the asset. For example, IBM paid around $3.5 billion for PwC's consulting practice. Presumably, IBM expects that the investment will produce a stream of cash flows worth more than that. Suppose IBM estimates that in terms of the current market value, the future cash flows from the PwC acquisition are worth $5 billion. Is the acquisition a good deal for IBM? The answer is yes because the value of the cash flow benefits from the acquisition exceeds the cost by $1.5 billion ($5.0 billion − $3.5 billion). If the PwC acquisition works out as planned, the value of IBM will be increased by $1.5 billion!

Not all investment decisions are successful. Just open the business section of any newspaper on any day, and you will find stories of bad decisions. For example, Walt Disney Studios' uninspiring movie *The Country Bear* turned out to be a dog. The film cost $40 million to make and took in about $5 million on its opening weekend. With a box office flop, it is unlikely that the movie's overall cash flow will be worth more than its $40 million cost. When, as in this case, the cost exceeds the value of the future cash flows, the project will decrease the value of the firm by that amount.

> **BUILDING INTUITION**
>
> ## Sound Investments Are Those Where the Value of the Benefits Exceeds Their Costs
>
> Financial managers should invest in a capital project only if the value of its future cash flows exceeds the cost of the project (benefits > cost). Such investments increase the value of the firm and thus increase stockholders' (owners') wealth. This rule holds whether you're making the decision to purchase new machinery, build a new plant, or buy an entire business.

FINANCING DECISIONS

Financing decisions concern how firms raise cash to pay for their investments, as shown in Exhibit 1.2. Productive assets, which are long term in nature, are financed by long-term borrowing, equity investment, or both. Financing decisions involve trade-offs between advantages and disadvantages to the firm.

A major advantage of debt financing is that debt payments are tax deductible for many corporations. However, debt financing increases a firm's risk because it creates a contractual obligation to make periodic interest payments and, at maturity, to repay the amount that is borrowed. Contractual obligations must be paid regardless of the firm's operating cash flow, even if the firm suffers a financial loss. If the firm fails to make payments as promised, it defaults on its debt obligation and could be forced into bankruptcy.

In contrast, equity has no maturity, and there are no guaranteed payments to equity investors. In a corporation, the board of directors has the right to decide whether dividends should be paid to stockholders. This means that if the board decides to omit or reduce a dividend payment, the firm will not be in default. Unlike interest payments, however, dividend payments to stockholders are not tax deductible.

The mix of debt and equity on the balance sheet is known as a firm's **capital structure**. The term *capital structure* is used because long-term funds are considered capital, and these funds are raised in **capital markets**—financial markets where equity and debt instruments with maturities greater than one year are traded.

capital structure
the mix of debt and equity that is used to finance a firm

capital markets
financial markets where equity and debt instruments with maturities greater than one year are traded

> **BUILDING INTUITION**
>
> ## Financing Decisions Affect the Value of the Firm
>
> How a firm is financed with debt and equity affects the value of the firm. The reason is that the mix between debt and equity affects the taxes the firm pays and the probability that the firm will go bankrupt. The financial manager's goal is to determine the combination of debt and equity that minimizes the cost of financing the firm.

WORKING CAPITAL MANAGEMENT DECISIONS

Management must also decide how to manage the firm's current assets, such as cash, inventory, and accounts receivable, and its current liabilities, such as trade credit and accounts payable. The dollar difference between current assets and current liabilities is called **net working capital**, as shown in Exhibit 1.2. As mentioned earlier, working capital management is the day-to-day management of the firm's short-term assets and liabilities. The goals of managing working capital are to ensure that the firm has enough money to pay its bills and to profitably invest any spare cash to earn interest.

The mismanagement of working capital can cause a firm to default on its debt and go into bankruptcy, even though, over the long term, the firm may be profitable. For example, a firm that makes sales to customers on credit but is not diligent about collecting the accounts receivable can quickly find itself without enough cash to pay its

net working capital
the dollar difference between current assets and current liabilities

bills. If this condition becomes chronic, trade creditors can force the firm into bankruptcy if the firm cannot obtain alternative financing.

A firm's profitability can also be affected by its inventory level. If the firm has more inventory than it needs to meet customer demands, it has too much money tied up in nonearning assets. Conversely, if the firm holds too little inventory, it can lose sales because it does not have products to sell when customers want them. The firm must therefore determine the optimal inventory level.

> **Before You Go On**
>
> 1. What are the three most basic types of financial decisions managers must make?
> 2. Why are capital budgeting decisions among the most important decisions in the life of a firm?
> 3. Explain why you would accept an investment project if the value of the expected cash flows exceeds the cost of the project.

1.2 Forms of Business Organization

LEARNING OBJECTIVE 2

In this section we look at the way firms organize to conduct their business activities. The owners of a business usually choose the organizational form that will help management to maximize the value of the firm. Important considerations are the size of the business, the manner in which income from the business is taxed, the legal liability of the owners, and the ability to raise cash to finance the business.

Most start-ups and small businesses operate as either sole proprietorships or partnerships because of their small operating scale and capital requirements. Large businesses in the United States, such as Procter and Gamble, are most often organized as corporations. As a firm grows larger, the benefits to organizing as a corporation become greater and are more likely to outweigh any disadvantages.

Sole Proprietorships

A **sole proprietorship** is a business owned by one person. About 75 percent of all businesses in the United States are sole proprietorships, typically consisting of the proprietor and a handful of employees. A sole proprietorship offers several advantages. It is the simplest type of business to start, and it is the least regulated. In addition, sole proprietors keep all the profits from the business and do not have to share decision-making authority. Finally, profits from a sole proprietorship are subjected to lower income taxes than are those from the most common type of corporation.

On the downside, a sole proprietor is responsible for paying all the firm's bills and has unlimited liability for all business debts and other obligations of the firm. This means that creditors can look beyond the assets of the business to the proprietor's personal wealth for payment. Another disadvantage is that the amount of equity capital that can be invested in the business is limited to the owner's personal wealth, which may restrict the possibilities for growth. Finally, it is difficult to transfer ownership of a sole proprietorship because there is no stock or other such interest to sell. The owner must sell the company's assets, which can reduce the price that the owner receives for the business.

sole proprietorship
a business owned by a single individual

Partnerships

A **partnership** consists of two or more owners who have joined together legally to manage a business. Partnerships are typically larger than sole proprietorships, and about 10 percent of all businesses in the United States are organized in this manner. To form a

partnership
two or more owners who have joined together legally to manage a business and share in its profits

partnership, the owners enter into an agreement that details how much capital each partner will contribute to the partnership, what their management roles will be, how key management decisions will be made, how the profits will be divided, and how ownership will be transferred in case of specified events, such as the retirement or death of a partner.

A *general partnership* has the same basic advantages and disadvantages as a sole proprietorship. A key disadvantage of a general partnership is that all partners have unlimited liability for the partnership's debts and actions, regardless of what proportion of the business they own or how the debt or obligations were incurred. The problem of unlimited liability can be avoided in a *limited partnership*, which consists of *general* and *limited* partners. Here, one or more general partners have unlimited liability and actively manage the business, while each limited partner is liable for business obligations only up to the amount of capital he or she contributed to the partnership. In other words, the limited partners have **limited liability**. To qualify for limited partner status, a partner cannot be actively engaged in managing the business.

> **limited liability**
> the legal liability of a limited partner or stockholder in a business, which extends only to the capital contributed or the amount invested

> **corporation**
> a legal entity formed and authorized under a state charter; in a legal sense, a corporation is a "person" distinct from its owners

Corporations

Most large businesses are corporations. A **corporation** is a legal entity authorized under a state charter. In a legal sense, it is a "person" distinct from its owners. Corporations can sue and be sued, enter into contracts, issue debt, borrow money, and own assets, such as real estate. They can also be general or limited partners in partnerships, and they can own stock in other corporations. Although only 15 percent of all businesses are incorporated, corporations hold nearly 90 percent of all business assets, generate nearly 90 percent of revenues, and account for about 80 percent of all business profits in the United States. The owners of a corporation are its stockholders.

Starting a corporation is more costly than starting a sole proprietorship or partnership. Those starting the corporation, for example, must create articles of incorporation and by-laws that conform to the laws of the state of incorporation. These documents spell out the name of the corporation, its business purpose, its intended life span (it can be forever), the amount of stock to be issued, and the number of directors and their responsibilities.

> Visit the Web sites of the NYSE and NASDAQ at www.nyse.com and www.nasdaq.com to get more information about market activity.

A major advantage of the corporate form of business organization is that stockholders have limited liability for debts and other obligations of the corporation. The "corporate veil" of limited liability exists because corporations are "legal persons" that borrow in their own names, not in the names of any individual owners. A major disadvantage of the most common corporate form of organization, compared with sole proprietorships and partnerships, is the way they are taxed. Because the corporation is a legal "person," it must pay taxes on the income it earns. If the corporation then pays a cash dividend, the stockholders pay taxes on that dividend as income. Thus, the owners of corporations are subject to double taxation—first at the corporate level and then at the personal level when they receive dividends.[2]

> **public markets**
> markets regulated by the Securities and Exchange Commission in which large amounts of debt and equity are publicly traded

Corporations can be classified as public or private. Most large companies prefer to operate as public corporations, which can sell their debt or equity in the public markets, because large amounts of capital can be sold in these markets at a relatively low cost. **Public markets**, such as the New York Stock Exchange (NYSE) and NASDAQ, are regulated by the federal Securities and Exchange Commission (SEC). Although firms whose securities are publicly traded are technically called public corporations, they are generally referred to simply as corporations. We will follow that convention.

> **privately held corporations**
> corporations whose stock is not traded in public markets; also called *closely held corporations*

In contrast, **privately held**, or **closely held**, corporations are typically owned by a small number of investors, and their shares are not traded publicly. When a corporation is first formed, the common stock is often held by a few investors, typically the founder, a small number of key managers, and financial backers. Over time, as the

---

[2]In recent years, businesses have increasingly been organizing as Subchapter S corporations. The key advantage of an S corporation is that stockholders receive all the organizational benefits of a corporation while escaping the double taxation. They are taxed like the partners in a partnership. A major limitation is that a Subchapter S corporation cannot have more than 75 shareholders.

[3]We examine the public and private markets in more detail in Chapters 2 and 15.

company grows in size and needs larger amounts of capital, management may decide that the company should "go public" in order to gain access to the public markets. Not all privately held corporations go public, however.

Hybrid Forms of Business Organization

Historically, law firms, accounting firms, investment banks, and other professional groups were organized as sole proprietorships or partnerships. For partners in these firms, all income was taxed as personal income, and general partners had unlimited liability for all debts and other financial obligations of the firm. It was widely believed that in professional partnerships, such as those of attorneys, accountants, or physicians, the partners should be liable individually and collectively for the professional conduct of each partner. This structure gave the partners an incentive to monitor each other's professional conduct and discipline poorly performing partners, resulting in a higher quality of service and greater professional integrity. Financially, however, misconduct by one partner could result in disaster for the entire firm. For example, a physician found guilty of malpractice exposes every partner in the medical practice to financial liability, even though the others never treated the patient in question.

In the early 1980s, because of sharp increases in the number of professional malpractice cases and large damages awards in the courts, professional groups began lobbying state legislators to create a hybrid form of business organization. These organizations, known as **limited liability partnerships (LLPs)**, are now permitted in most states. An LLP combines the limited liability of a corporation with the tax advantage of a partnership—there is no double taxation. In general, income to the partners of an LLP is taxed as personal income, the partners have limited liability for the business, and they are not personally liable for other partners' malpractice or professional misconduct. Other more recent organizational forms that are essentially equivalent to LLPs include limited liability companies (LLCs) and professional corporations (PCs).

limited liability partnerships (LLPs)
hybrid business organizations that combine some of the advantages of corporations and partnerships; in general, income to the partners is taxed only as personal income, but the partners have limited liability

Before You Go On

1. Why are many businesses operated as sole proprietorships or partnerships?
2. What are some advantages and disadvantages of operating as a public corporation?
3. Explain why professional partnerships such as physicians' groups organize as limited liability partnerships.

1.3 Managing the Financial Function

As we discussed earlier in the chapter, financial managers are concerned with a firm's investment, financing, and working capital management decisions. The senior financial manager holds one of the top executive positions in the firm. In a large corporation, the senior financial manager usually has the rank of vice president or senior vice president and goes by the title of **chief financial officer**, or **CFO**. In smaller firms, the job tends to focus more on the accounting function, and the top financial officer may be called the controller or chief accountant. In this section we focus on the financial function in a large corporation.

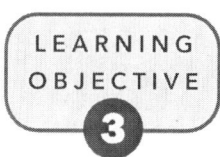

chief financial officer (CFO)
the most senior financial manager in a company

Organization Structure

Exhibit 1.3 shows a typical organizational structure for a large corporation, with special attention to the financial function. As shown, the top management position in the firm is the chief executive officer (CEO), who has the final decision-making authority

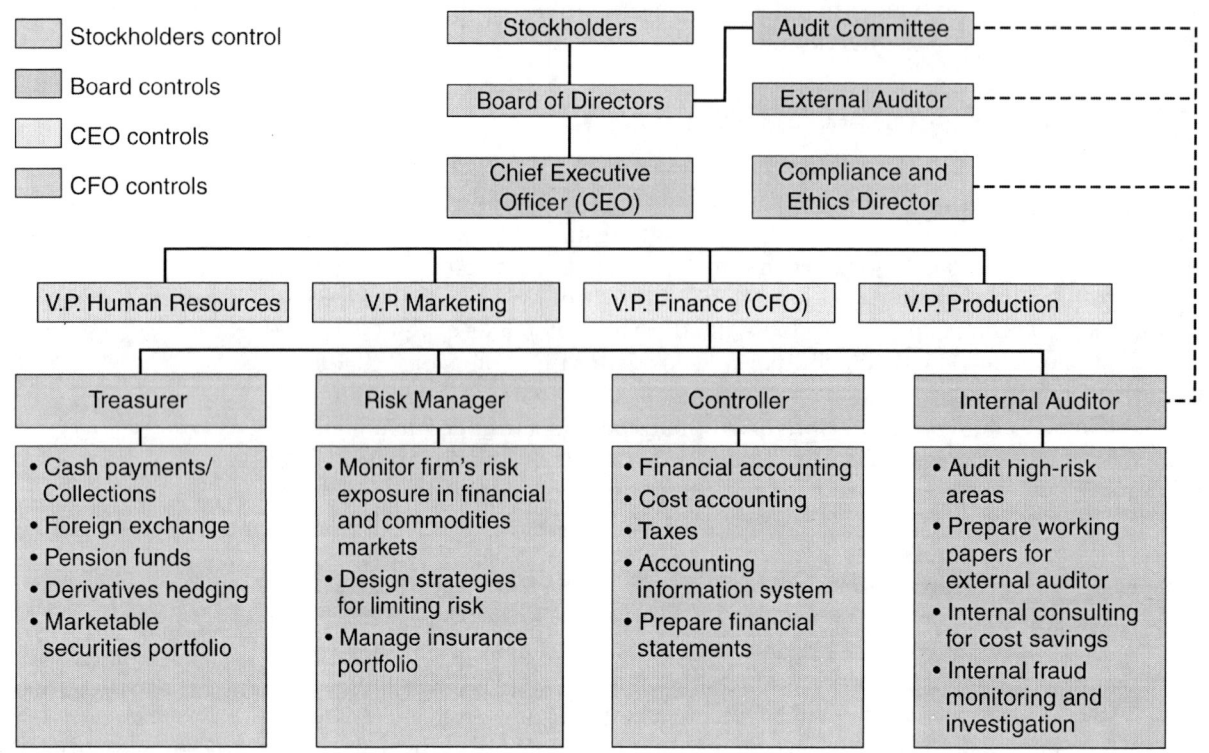

Exhibit 1.3
Simplified Corporate Organization Chart
The firm's top finance and accounting executive is the CFO, who reports directly to the CEO. Positions that report directly to the CFO include the treasurer, risk manager, and controller. The internal auditor reports both to the CFO and to the audit committee of the board of directors. The external auditor and the ethics director also are ultimately responsible to the audit committee.

Go to www.cfo.com to get a better idea of the responsibilities of a CFO.

among all the firm's executives. The CEO's most important responsibilities are to set the strategic direction of the firm and see that the management team executes the strategic plan. The CEO reports directly to the board of directors, which is accountable to the company's stockholders. The board's responsibility is to see that the top management makes decisions that are in the best interest of the stockholders.

The CFO reports directly to the CEO and focuses on managing all aspects of the firm's financial side, as well as working closely with the CEO on strategic issues. A number of positions report directly to the CFO. In addition, the CFO often interacts with people in other functional areas on a regular basis because all senior executives are involved in financial decisions that affect the firm and their areas of responsibility.

Positions Reporting to the CFO

Exhibit 1.3 also shows the positions that typically report to the CFO in a large corporation and the activities managed in each area.

- The *treasurer* looks after the collection and disbursement of cash, investing excess cash so that it earns interest, raising new capital, handling foreign exchange transactions, and overseeing the firm's pension fund managers. The

treasurer also assists the CFO in handling important Wall Street relationships, such as those with investment bankers and credit rating agencies.
- The *risk manager* monitors and manages the firm's risk exposure in financial and commodity markets and the firm's relationships with insurance providers.
- The *controller* is really the firm's chief accounting officer. The controller's staff prepares the financial statements, maintains the firm's financial and cost accounting systems, prepares the taxes, and works closely with the firm's external auditors.
- The *internal auditor* is responsible for identifying and assessing major risks facing the firm and performing audits in areas where the firm might incur substantial losses. The internal auditor reports to the board of directors as well as the CFO.

External Auditors

Nearly every business hires a licensed certified public accounting (CPA) firm to provide an independent annual audit of the firm's financial statements. Through this audit the CPA comes to a conclusion as to whether the firm's financial statement presents fairly, in all material respects, the financial position of the firm and results of its activities. In other words, whether the financial numbers are reasonably accurate, accounting principles have been consistently applied year to year and do not significantly distort the firm's performance, and the accounting principles used conform to those generally accepted by the accounting profession. Creditors and investors require independent audits, and the SEC requires publicly traded firms to supply audited financial statements.

The Audit Committee

The audit committee, a powerful subcommittee of the board of directors, has the responsibility of overseeing the accounting function and the preparation of the firm's financial statements. In addition, the audit committee oversees or, if necessary, conducts investigations of significant fraud, theft, or malfeasance in the firm, especially if it is suspected that senior managers in the firm may be involved.

External auditors report directly to the audit committee to help ensure their independence from management. On a day-to-day basis, however, they work closely with the CFO staff. The internal auditor, too, reports to the audit committee so that the position more independent from management, and his or her ultimate responsibility is to the audit committee. On a day-to-day basis, however, the internal auditor, like the external auditors, works closely with the CFO staff.

The Compliance and Ethics Director

The SEC requires that all publicly traded companies have a compliance and ethics director who oversees three mandated programs: (1) a compliance program that ensures that the firm complies with federal and state laws and regulations, (2) an ethics program that promotes ethical conduct among executives and employees, and (3) a compliance hotline, which must include a whistleblower program. Like the internal auditor, the compliance director reports to the audit committee to ensure independence from management, though on a day-to-day basis the director typically reports to the firm's legal counsel.

> Before You Go On
>
> 1. What are the major responsibilities of the CFO?
> 2. Identify three financial officers who typically report to the CFO and describe their duties.
> 3. Why does the internal auditor report to both the CFO and the board of directors?

1.4 The Goal of the Firm

For business owners, it is important to determine the appropriate goal for financial management decisions. Should the goal be to try to keep costs as low as possible? or to maximize sales or market share? or to achieve steady growth and earnings? Let's look at this fundamental question more closely.

What Should Management Maximize?

Suppose you own and manage a pizza parlor. Depending on your preferences and tolerance for risk, you can set any goal for the business that you want. For example, you might have a fear of bankruptcy and losing money. To avoid the risk of bankruptcy, you could focus on keeping your costs as low as possible, paying low wages, avoiding borrowing, advertising minimally, and remaining reluctant to expand the business. In short, you will avoid any action that increases your firm's risk. You will sleep well at night, but you may eat poorly because of meager profits.

Conversely, you could focus on maximizing market share and becoming the largest pizza business in town. Your strategy might include cutting prices to increase sales, borrowing heavily to open new pizza parlors, spending lavishly on advertising, and developing exotic menu items such as *pizza de foie gras*. In the short run, your high-risk, high-growth strategy will have you both eating poorly and sleeping poorly as you push the firm to the edge. In the long run, you will either become very rich or go bankrupt! There must be a better operational goal than either of these extremes.

Why Not Maximize Profits?

One goal for financial decision making that seems reasonable is *profit maximization*. After all, don't stockholders and business owners want their companies to be profitable? Although profit maximization seems a logical goal for a business, it has some serious drawbacks.

One problem with profit maximization is that it is hard to pin down what is meant by "profit." To the average businessperson, profits are just revenues minus expenses. To an accountant, however, a decision that increases profits under one set of accounting rules can reduce it under another. This is the origin of the term *creative accounting*. A second problem is that accounting profits are not necessarily the same as cash flows. For example, many firms recognize revenues at the time a sale is made, which is typically before the cash payment for the sale is received. Ultimately, the owners of a business want cash because only cash can be used to make investments or to buy goods and services.

Yet another problem with profit maximization as a goal is that it does not distinguish between getting a dollar today and getting a dollar some time in the future. In finance, the timing of cash flows is extremely important. For example, the longer you go without paying your credit card balance, the more interest you must pay the bank for the use of the money. The interest accrues because of the *time value of money;* the longer you have access to money, the more you have to pay for it. The time value of money is one of the most important concepts in finance and is the focus of Chapters 5 and 6.

> **BUILDING INTUITION**
>
> **The Timing of Cash Flows Affects Their Value**
>
> A dollar today is worth more than a dollar in the future because if you have a dollar today, you can invest it and earn interest. For businesses, cash flows can involve large sums of money, and receiving money one day late can cost a great deal. For example, if a bank has $100 billion of consumer loans outstanding and the average annual interest payment is 5 percent, it would cost the bank $13.7 million if every consumer decided to make an interest payment one day later.

Finally, profit maximization ignores the uncertainty, or risk, associated with cash flows. A basic principle of finance is that there is a trade-off between expected return and risk. When given a choice between two investments that have the same expected returns but different risk, most people choose the less risky one. This makes sense because most people do not like bearing risk and, as a result, must be compensated for taking it. The profit maximization goal ignores differences in value caused by differences in risk. We return to the important topics of risk, its measurement, and the trade-off between risk and return in Chapter 7. What is important at this time is that you understand that investors do not like risk and must be compensated for bearing it.

> **BUILDING INTUITION**
>
> ### The Riskiness of Cash Flows Affects Their Value
>
> A risky dollar is worth less than a safe dollar. The reason is that investors do not like risk and must be compensated for bearing it. For example, if two investments have the same return—say 5 percent—most people will prefer the investment with the lower risk. Thus, the more risky an investment's cash flows, the less it is worth.

In sum, it appears that profit maximization is not an appropriate goal for a firm because the concept is difficult to define and does not directly account for the firm's cash flows. What we need is a goal that looks at a firm's cash flows and considers both their timing and their riskiness. Fortunately, we have just such a measure: the market value of the firm's stock.

Maximize the Value of the Firm's Stock

The underlying value of any asset is determined by the future cash flows generated by that asset. This principle holds whether we are buying a bank certificate of deposit, a corporate bond, or an office building. Furthermore, as we will discuss in Chapter 9, when security analysts and investors on Wall Street determine the value of a firm's stock, they consider (1) the size of the expected cash flows, (2) the timing of the cash flows, and (3) the riskiness of the cash flows. Notice that the mechanism for determining stock values overcomes all the cash flow objections we raised with regard to profit maximization as a goal.

Thus, an appropriate goal for financial management is to maximize the current value of the firm's stock. By maximizing the current stock price, the financial manager will be maximizing the value of the stockholders' shares. Notice that maximizing share value is an unambiguous objective, and it is easy to measure. We simply look at the market value of the stock in the newspaper on a given day to determine the value of the stockholders' shares and whether it went up or down. Publicly traded securities are ideally suited for this task because public markets are wholesale markets with large numbers of buyers and sellers where securities trade near their true value.

What about firms whose equity is not publicly traded, such as private corporations and partnerships? The total value of the stock in such a company is equal to the value of the stockholders' equity. *Thus, our goal can be restated for these firms as this: maximize the current value of owner's equity.* The only other restriction is that the entities must be for-profit businesses.

> **BUILDING INTUITION**
>
> ### The Financial Manager's Goal Is to Maximize the Value of the Firm's Stock
>
> The goal for financial managers is to make decisions that maximize the firm's stock price. By maximizing stock price, management will help maximize stockholders' wealth. To do this, managers must make investment and financing decisions so that the total value of cash inflows exceeds the total value of cash outflows by the greatest possible amount (benefits > costs). Notice that the focus is on maximizing the value of cash flows, not profits.

Can Management Decisions Affect Stock Prices?

An important question is whether management decisions actually affect the firm's stock price. Fortunately, the answer is yes. As noted earlier, a basic principle in finance is that the value of an asset is determined by the future cash flows it is expected to generate. As shown in Exhibit 1.4, a firm's management makes numerous decisions that affect its cash flows. For example, management decides what type of products or services to produce and what productive assets to purchase. Managers also make decisions concerning the mix of debt to equity, debt collection policies, and policies for paying suppliers, to mention a few. In addition, cash flows are affected by how efficient management is in making products, the quality of the products, management's sales and marketing skills, and the firm's investment in research and development for new products. Some of these decisions affect cash flows over the long term, such as the decision to build a new plant, and other decisions have a short-term impact on cash flows, such as launching an advertising campaign.

Of course, the firm also must deal with a number of external factors over which it has little or no control, such as economic conditions (recession or expansion), war or

Exhibit 1.4
Major Factors Affecting Stock Prices
The firm's stock price is affected by a number of factors, and management can control only some of them. Managers exercise little control over external conditions (blue boxes), such as the general economy, although they can closely observe these conditions and make appropriate changes in strategy. Also, managers make many other decisions that directly affect the firm's expected cash flows (green boxes)—and hence the price of the firm's stock.

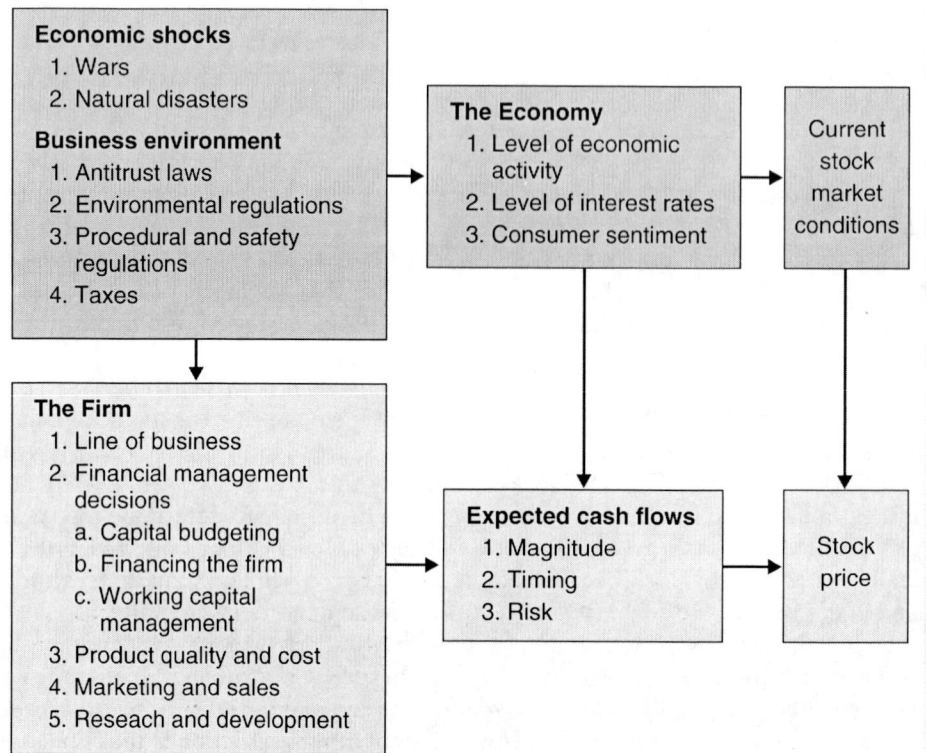

peace, and new government regulations. External factors are constantly changing, and management must weigh the impact of these changes and adjust its strategy and decisions accordingly.

The important point here is that, over time, management makes a series of decisions when executing the firm's strategy that affect the firm's cash flows and, hence, the price of the firm's stock. Firms that have a better business strategy, are more nimble, make better business decisions, and can execute their plans well will have a higher stock price than similar firms that just can't get it right.

> **Before You Go On**
>
> 1. Why is profit maximization an unsatisfactory goal for managing a firm?
> 2. Explain why maximizing the current market price of a firm's stock is an appropriate goal for the firm's management.
> 3. What is the fundamental determinant of an asset's value?

1.5 Agency Conflicts: Separation of Ownership and Control

LEARNING OBJECTIVE 5

We turn next to an important issue facing stockholders of large corporations: the separation of ownership and control of the firm. In a large corporation, ownership is often spread over a large number of stockholders who may effectively have little control over management. Management may therefore make decisions that benefit their own interests rather than those of the stockholders. In contrast, in smaller firms owners and managers are usually one and the same, and there is no conflict of interest between owners and managers. As you will see, this self-interested behavior may affect the value of the firm.

Ownership and Control

To illustrate, let's continue with our pizza parlor example. As the owner of a pizza parlor, you have decided your goal is to maximize the value of the business, and thereby your ownership interest. There is no conflict of interest in your dual roles as owner and manager because your personal and economic self-interest is tied to the success of the pizza parlor. The restaurant has succeeded because you have worked hard and have focused on customer satisfaction.

Now suppose you decide to hire a college student to manage the restaurant. Will the new manager always act in your interest? Or could the new manager be tempted to give free pizza to friends now and then or, after an exhausting day, leave early rather than spend time cleaning and preparing for the next day? From this example, you can see that once ownership and management are separated, managers may be tempted to pursue goals that are in their own self-interest rather than the interests of the owners.

Agency Relationships

The relationship we have just described between the pizza parlor owner and the student manager is an example of an agency relationship. An agency relationship arises whenever one party, called the *principal,* hires another party, called the *agent,* to perform some service on behalf of the principal. The relationship between stockholders and management is an agency relationship. Legally, managers (who are the agents) have a fiduciary duty to the stockholders (the principals), which means managers are obligated to put the interests of the stockholders above their own. However, in these and all other agency relationships, the potential exists for a conflict of interest between the principal and the agent. These conflicts are called **agency conflicts**.

> **agency conflicts**
> conflicts of interest between a principal and an agent

Do Managers Really Want to Maximize Stock Price?

It is not difficult to see how conflicts of interest between managers and stockholders can arise in the corporate setting. In most large corporations, especially those that are publicly traded, there is a significant degree of separation between ownership and management. For example, General Motors Corporation (GMC) has more than two million stockholders. As a practical matter, it is not possible for all of the stockholders to be active in the management of the firm or to individually bear the high cost of monitoring management. The bottom line is that stockholders own the corporation, but managers control the money and have the opportunity to use it for their own benefit.

How might management be tempted to indulge itself and pursue its own self-interest? We need not look far for an answer to this question. Corporate excesses are legion, but high on the list are palatial office buildings, corporate hunting and fishing lodges in exotic places, expensive corporate jets, extravagant expense-account dinners kicked off with bottles of Dom Perignon and washed down with 1953 Margaux—and, of course, a king's compensation package.[4] Besides economic nest feathering, corporate managers may focus on maximizing market share and their industry prestige, job security, and so forth.

Needless to say, these types of activities and spending conflict with the goal of maximizing a firm's stock price. The costs of these activities are called *agency costs*. **Agency costs** are the costs incurred because of conflicts of interest between a principal and an agent. Examples are the cost of the lavish dinner mentioned earlier and the cost of a corporate jet for executives. However, not all agency costs are frivolous. The cost of hiring an external auditor to certify financial statements is also an agency cost.

> **agency costs**
> the costs arising from conflicts of interest between a principal and an agent; for example, between a firm's owners and its management

Aligning the Interests of Management and Stockholders

If the linkage between stockholder and management goals is weak, a number of mechanisms can help to better align the behavior of managers with the goals of corporate stockholders. These include (1) management compensation, (2) managerial labor markets, (3) board of directors, (4) other managers, (5) large stockholders, (6) the takeover market, and (7) the legal and regulatory environment.

MANAGEMENT COMPENSATION

The most effective means of aligning the interests of managers with those of stockholders is a well-designed compensation (pay) package that rewards managers when they do what stockholders want them to do and penalizes them when they do not. This type of plan is effective because a manager will quickly internalize the benefits and costs of making good and bad decisions and, thus, will be more likely to make the decisions that stockholders want. Therefore, there is no need for some outside monitor, such as the board of directors, to try to figure out whether the managers are making the right decisions. The information that outside monitors have is not as good as the managers' information, so these outside monitors are always at a disadvantage in trying to determine whether a manager is acting in the interest of stockholders.

Most corporations have management compensation plans that tie compensation to the performance of the firm. The idea behind these plans is that if compensation is

---

[4] A favorite premeal "quaffing" champagne of young investment bankers on Wall Street is Dom Perignon, known as the "Domer," which is priced in the range of $250 a bottle. Senior partners who are more genteel are reported to favor a 1953 Margaux, a French Bordeaux wine from Château Margaux; 1953 is considered a stellar vintage year, and Margaux 1953 is an excellent but very pricey (about $1,300 per bottle wholesale in 2006) choice.

sensitive to the performance of the firm, managers will have greater incentives to make decisions that increase the stockholders' wealth. Although these incentive plans vary widely, they usually include (1) a base salary, (2) a bonus based on the accounting performance, and (3) some compensation that is tied to the firm's stock price.[5] The base salary assures the executive of some minimum compensation as long as he or she remains with the firm, and the bonus and stock price–based compensation are designed to align the manager's incentives with those of the stockholders. The trick in designing such a program is to choose the right mix of these three components so that the manager has the right incentives and the overall package is sufficiently appealing to attract and retain high-quality managers at the lowest possible cost.

MANAGERIAL LABOR MARKET

The managerial labor market also provides managers with incentives to act in the interests of stockholders. Firms that have a history of poor performance or a reputation for "shady operations" or unethical behavior have difficulty hiring top managerial talent. Individuals who are top performers have better alternatives than to work for such firms. Therefore, to the extent that managers want to attract high-quality people, the labor market provides incentives to run a good company.

Furthermore, studies show that executives who "manage" firms into bankruptcy or are convicted of white-collar crimes can rarely secure equivalent positions after being fired for poor performance or convicted for criminal behavior. Thus, the penalty for extremely poor performance or a criminal conviction is a significant reduction in the manager's lifetime earnings potential. Managers know this, and the fear of such consequences helps keep them working hard and honestly.[6]

BOARD OF DIRECTORS

A corporation's board of directors has a legal responsibility to represent stockholders' interests. The board's duties include hiring and firing the CEO, setting his or her compensation, and monitoring his or her performance. The board also approves major decisions concerning the firm, such as the firm's annual capital budget or the acquisition of another business. These responsibilities make the board a key mechanism for ensuring that managers' decisions are aligned with those of stockholders.

How well boards actually perform in this role has been questioned in recent years. As an example, critics point out that some boards are unwilling to make hard decisions such as firing the CEO when a firm performs poorly. Other people believe that a lack of independence is a reason that boards are not as effective as they might be. For example, the CEO typically chairs the board of directors. This dual position can give the CEO undue influence over the board, as the chairperson sets the agenda for and chairs board meetings, appoints committees, and controls the flow of information to the board. Also inhibiting board independence in the past was the practice that allowed any number of the companies' own executives to serve on the board. Before passage of the Sarbanes-Oxley Act, discussed later in this chapter, these *inside directors* could actually outnumber *outside directors*, who were not employees of the firm.

OTHER MANAGERS

Competition among managers within firms also helps provide incentives for management to act in the interests of stockholders. Managers compete to attain the CEO position and in doing so try to attract the board of directors' attention by acting in the stockholders' interests. Furthermore, even when a manager becomes CEO, he or she is always looking over his or her shoulder because other managers covet that job.

---

[5]This component, which may include stock options, will increase and decrease with the stock price.

[6]Nonquantifiable costs of convictions for crimes are the perpetrators' personal embarrassment and the embarrassment of their families and the effect it may have on their lives. On average, the overall cost of such convictions is higher than even that suggested by the labor market argument.

LARGE STOCKHOLDERS

All stockholders obviously have a strong interest in providing managers with incentives to maximize stockholder value. After all, that is what stockholders want, and it is an appropriate goal for management. We single out stockholders who own a lot of shares because they have enough money at stake—and enough power—to make it worthwhile to actively monitor managers and try to influence their decisions.

THE TAKEOVER MARKET

The market for takeovers provides incentives for managers to act in the interests of stockholders. When a firm performs poorly because management is doing a poor job, an opportunity arises for astute investors, so-called corporate raiders, to make money by buying the company at a price that reflects its poor performance and replacing the current managers with a top-flight management team. If the investors have evaluated the situation correctly, the firm will soon be transformed into a strong performer, its stock price will increase, and investors can sell their stock for a significant profit. The possibility that a firm might be discovered by corporate raiders provides incentives for management to perform.

THE LEGAL AND REGULATORY ENVIRONMENT

Finally, the laws and regulations that firms must adhere to limit the ability of managers to make decisions that harm the interests of stockholders. An example is federal and state statutes that make it illegal for managers to steal corporate assets. Similarly, regulatory reforms such as the Sarbanes-Oxley Act, discussed next, limit the ability of managers to mislead stockholders.

Sarbanes-Oxley and Other Regulatory Reforms

To find out more about current ethics issues in corporate America, visit www.sarbanes-oxley.com.

A series of accounting scandals and ethical lapses by corporate officers shocked the nation in the early years of the twenty-first century. A case in point was WorldCom's bankruptcy filing in 2002 and the admission that its officers had "cooked the books" by misstating $7.2 billion of expenses, which allowed WorldCom to report "profits" when the firm had actually lost money. The accounting fraud at WorldCom followed similar scandals at Enron, Global Crossing, Tyco, and elsewhere. These scandals—and the resulting losses to stockholders—resulted in a set of far-reaching regulatory reforms passed by Congress in 2002.[7] Relevant to our discussion is the Sarbanes-Oxley Act of 2002, which focuses on (1) reducing agency costs in corporations, (2) restoring ethical conduct within the business sector, and (3) improving the integrity of accounting reporting system within firms.

Overall, the new regulations require all public corporations to implement five overarching strategies. (Private corporations and partnerships are not required to implement these measures.)

1. **Ensure greater board independence.** Firms must restructure their boards so that the majority of the members are outside directors. Furthermore, it is recommended that the positions of chair and CEO be separated. Finally, Sarbanes-Oxley makes it clear that board members have a fiduciary responsibility to represent and act in the interest of stockholders, and board members who fail to meet their fiduciary duty can be fined and receive jail sentences.

2. **Establish internal accounting controls.** Firms must establish internal accounting control systems to protect the integrity of the accounting systems and safeguard the firms' assets. The internal controls are intended to improve the reliability of accounting data and the quality of financial reports and to reduce the likelihood that individuals within the firm engage in accounting fraud.

---

[7]The major laws passed by Congress in this area in 2002 were the Public Accounting Reform and Investor Protection Act and the Sarbanes-Oxley Act.

3. **Establish compliance programs.** Firms must establish corporate compliance programs that ensure that the firms comply with important federal and state regulations. For example, a compliance program would document whether a firm's truck drivers complied with all federal and state truck and driver safety regulations, such as the number of hours one can drive during the day and the gross highway weight of the truck.

4. **Establish an ethics program.** Firms must establish ethics programs that monitor the ethical conduct of employees and executives through a compliance hotline, which must include a whistleblower protection provision. The intent is to create an ethical work environment so that employees will know what is expected of them and their relationships with customers, suppliers, and other stakeholders. If fraud is detected, the programs should provide an established procedure to follow.

5. **Expand the audit committee's oversight powers.** The external auditor, the internal auditor, and the compliance/ethics officer owe their ultimate legal responsibilities to the audit committee, not to the firm. These reporting lines give the audit committee deep tentacles into the firm to discover financial improprieties. In addition, the audit committee has the unconditional power to probe and question any person in the firm, including the CEO, regarding any matter that might materially impact the firm or its financial statements.

Exhibit 1.5 summarizes some of the recent regulatory changes that significantly expand the board of directors' powers.

Exhibit 1.5 Corporate Governance Regulations That Reduce Agency Costs

Board of Directors
- Board has a fiduciary responsibility to represent the best interest of the firm's owners.
- Majority of the board must be outside independent directors.
- Firm is required to have code of ethics, which has to be approved by the board.
- Firm must establish an ethics program that has a complaint hotline and a whistleblower protection provision which is approved by the board of directors.
- Separation of chairman and CEO positions is recommended.
- Board memebers can be fined or receive jail sentences if they fail to fulfill their fiduciary responsibilities.

Audit Committee
- External auditor, internal auditor, and compliance officer's fiduciary (legal) responsibilities are to the audit committee.
- Audit committee approves the hiring, firing, and fees paid to external auditors.
- CEO and CFO must certify financial statements.
- All audit committee members must be outside independent directors.
- One member must be a financial expert.

External Auditors
- Lead partner must change every five years.
- There are limits on consulting (nonaudit) services that external auditors can provide.

Source: Sarbanes-Oxley Act, the Public Accounting Reform and Investor Protection Act, and NYSE and NASDAQ new listing requirements.

Recent regulatory changes have significantly expanded the powers of corporate boards of directors. The most important changes resulted from the Sarbanes-Oxley Act, passed by Congress in 2002. The act was aimed at reducing agency costs, promoting ethical conduct, and improving the integrity of accounting reporting systems.

It is too early to tell how effective the new regulations will be. Indications are, however, that a noticeable shift has occurred in the behavior of board members and management. Boards appear much more serious about monitoring firms' performance and ratifying important decisions by management. Audit committees, with their new independence and investigative powers, are providing greater oversight in the preparation of financial statements. Stronger internal accounting controls systems, compliance programs, and ethics programs are improving the integrity of the accounting systems and reducing the likelihood of fraud and other illegal activities. Thus, the Sarbanes-Oxley Act does appear to be having an effect. The major complaint from business has been the cost of compliance, which averaged $5 million to $8 million per firm in 2004 but declined to $4.7 million in 2006.

> Before You Go On
>
> 1. What are agency conflicts?
> 2. What are corporate raiders?
> 3. List the three main objectives of the Sarbanes-Oxley Act.

1.6 The Importance of Ethics in Business

We have just seen that Congress included ethics program requirements in the Sarbanes-Oxley Act. Why are ethics important to business?

Business Ethics

The term *ethics* describes a society's ideas about what actions are right and wrong. Ethical values are not moral absolutes, and they can and do vary across societies. Regardless of cultural differences, however, if we think about it, all of us would probably prefer to live in a world where people behave ethically—where people try to do what is right.

In our society, ethical rules include considering the impact of our actions on others, being willing to sometimes put the interests of others ahead of our own interests, and realizing that we must follow the same rules we expect others to follow. The golden rule—"Do unto others as you would have done unto you"—is an example of a widely accepted ethical norm.[8]

The site www.web-miner.com/busethics.htm offers a wide range of articles on the role of ethics in business today.

Are Business Ethics Different from Everyday Ethics?

Perhaps business is a dog-eat-dog world where ethics do not matter. People who take this point of view link business ethics to the "ethics of the poker game" and not to the ethics of everyday morality. Poker players, they suggest, must practice cunning deception and must conceal their strengths and their intentions. After all, they are playing the game to win. How far does one go to win?

In 2002, investors learned the hard way about a number of firms that had been behaving according to the ethics of the poker game: cunning deception and concealment of information were the order of the day at WorldCom, Enron, Global Crossing, Tyco, and a host of other firms. The market's reaction to their concealment and deception was to wipe out $2.3 trillion of stockholder value.

---

[8]The golden rule can be stated in a number of ways. One version, in the Gospel of Matthew, states, "In everything do to others as you would have them do to you." A less noble version you occasionally hear in business is "He who has the gold makes the rules."

We believe that those who argue that ethics do not matter in business are mistaken. Indeed, most academic studies on the topic suggest that traditions of morality are very relevant to business and to financial markets in particular. The reasons are practical as well as ethical. Corruption in business creates inefficiencies in an economy, inhibits the growth of capital markets, and slows a country's rate of economic growth.

For example, as Russia made the transition to a market economy, it had a difficult time establishing a stock market and attracting foreign investment. The reason was a simple one. Corruption was rampant in local government and in business. Contractual agreements were not enforceable, and there was no reliable financial information about Russian companies. Not until the mid-1990s did some Russian companies begin to display enough honesty and financial transparency to attract investment capital.[9]

Types of Ethical Conflicts in Business

We turn next to a consideration of the ethical problems that arise in business dealings. Most problems involve three related areas: agency costs, conflicts of interest, and informational asymmetry.

AGENCY COSTS

As we discussed earlier in this chapter, many relationships in business are agency relationships. Agents can be bound both legally and ethically to act in the interest of the principal. Financial managers have agency obligations to act honestly and to see that subordinates act honestly with respect to financial transactions. Of all the corporate officers, financial managers, when they are guilty of misconduct, present among the most serious danger to stockholder wealth. A product recall or environmental offense may cause temporary declines in stock prices. However, revelations of dishonesty, deception, and fraud in financial matters have a huge impact on the stock price. If the dishonesty is flagrant, the firm may go bankrupt, as we saw with the bankruptcies of Enron and WorldCom.

CONFLICTS OF INTEREST

Conflicts of interest often arise in agency relationships. A conflict of interest in such a situation can arise when the agent's interests are different from those of the principal. For example, suppose you're interested in buying a house and a local real estate agent is helping you find the home of your dreams. As it turns out, the dream house is one for which your agent is also the listing agent. Your agent has a conflict of interest because her professional obligation to help you find the right house at a fair price conflicts with her professional obligation to get the highest price possible for the client whose house she has listed.

Organizations can be either principals or agents and, hence, can be parties to conflicts of interest. In the past, for example, many large accounting firms provided both consulting services and audits for corporations. This dual function may compromise the independence and objectivity of the audit opinion, even though the work is done by different parts of the firm. For example, if consulting fees from an audit client become a large source of income, is the auditing firm less likely to render an adverse audit opinion and thereby risk losing the consulting business?

Conflicts of interest are typically resolved in one of two ways. Sometimes complete disclosure is sufficient. Thus, in real estate transactions, it is not unusual for the same lawyer or realtor to represent both the buyer and the seller. This practice is not considered unethical as long as both sides are aware of the fact and give their consent. Alternatively, the conflicted party can withdraw from serving the interests of one of the parties. Sometimes the law mandates this solution. For example, recent legislation requires that public accounting firms stop providing certain consulting services to their audit clients.

---

[9]In economics, *transparency* refers to openness and access to information.

INFORMATION ASYMMETRY

information asymmetry
the situation in which one party in a business transaction has information that is unavailable to the other parties in the transaction

Information asymmetry occurs when one party in a business transaction has information that is unavailable to the other parties in the transaction. The existence of information asymmetry in business relationships is commonplace. For example, suppose you decide to sell your 10-year-old car. You know much more about the real condition of the car than does the prospective buyer. The moral issue is this: How much should you tell the prospective buyer? In other words, to what extent is the party with the information advantage obligated to reduce the amount of information asymmetry?

Decisions in this area often center on issues of fairness. Consider the insider trading of stocks based on confidential information not available to the public. Using insider information is considered morally wrong and, as a result, has been made illegal. The rationale for the notion is ethical fairness. The central idea is that investment decisions should be made on a "level playing field."

What counts as fair and as unfair is somewhat controversial, but there are a few ways to determine fairness. One relates to the golden rule and the notion of impartiality that underlies it. You treat another fairly when you "do unto others as you want them to do unto you." Another test of fairness is whether you are willing to publicly advocate the principle behind your decision. Actions based on principles that do not pass the golden rule test or that cannot be publicly advocated are not likely to be fair.

The Importance of an Ethical Business Culture

Some economists have noted that the legal system and market forces impose substantial costs on individuals and institutions that engage in unethical behavior. As a result, these forces provide important incentives that foster ethical behavior in the business community. The incentives include financial losses, legal fines, jail time, and destruction of companies (bankruptcy). Ethicists argue, however, that laws and market forces are not enough. For example, the financial sector is one of the most heavily regulated areas of the U.S. economy. Yet despite heavy regulation, the sector has a long and rich history of financial scandals.

In addition to laws and market forces, then, it is important to create an ethical culture in the firm. Why is this important? An ethical business culture means that people have a set of principles—a moral compass, so to speak—that help them identify moral issues and make ethical judgments without being told what to do. The culture has a powerful influence on the way people behave and the way they make decisions.

The people at the top of a company determine whether or not the culture of that company is ethical. At Enron, for example, top officers promoted a culture of aggressive risk taking and willingness, at times, to cross over ethical and even legal lines. Once this type of culture is established at the top, people in the organization think it is acceptable to step over legal and ethical boundaries themselves.

More than likely, you will be confronted with ethical issues during your professional career. Knowing how to identify and deal with ethical issues is thus an important part of your professional "survival kit." Exhibit 1.6 presents a framework for making ethical judgments.

Serious Consequences

In recent years the "rules" have changed, and the cost of ethical mistakes can be extremely high. In the past, the business community and legal authorities often dismissed corporate scandals as a "few rotten apples" in an otherwise sound barrel. This is no longer true today. In 2005, for instance, Bernard J. Ebbers, the 63-year-old CEO of WorldCom, was found guilty of fraud and theft and was sentenced to 25 years in prison. Judge Barbara S. Jones, acknowledging that Ebbers would probably serve the rest of his days in jail, said "I find a sentence of anything less would not reflect the seriousness of the crime." In the past, sentences for white-collar crimes were minimal; even for serious crimes, there often was no jail time at all. Clearly, business ethics is a topic of high interest and increasing importance in the business community, and it is a topic that will be discussed throughout the book.

Exhibit 1.6   A Framework for the Analysis of Ethical Conflicts

The first step toward ethical behavior is to recognize that you face a moral issue. In general, if your actions or decisions will cause harm to others, you are facing a moral issue. When you find yourself in this position, you might ask yourself the following questions:

1. What does the law require? When in doubt, consult the legal department.
2. What do your role-related obligations require? What is your station, and what are its duties? If you are a member of a profession, what does the code of conduct of your profession say you should do in these circumstances?
3. Are you an agent employed on behalf of another in these circumstances? If so, what are the interests and desires of the employing party?
4. Are the interests of the stockholders materially affected? Your obligation is to represent the best interests of the firm's owners.
5. Do you have a conflict of interest? Will full diclosure of the conflict be sufficient? If not, you must determine what interest has priority.
6. Are you abusing information asymmetry? Is your use of the information asymmetry fair? It probably is fair if you would make the same decision if the roles of the parties were reversed or if you would publicly advocated the principle behind your decision.
7. Would you be willing to have your action and all the reasons that motivated it reported in the *Wall Street Journal*?

Dealing with ethical conflicts is an inescapable part of professional life for most people. An analytical framework can be helpful in understanding and resolving such conflicts.

Before You Go On

1. What is a conflict of interest in a business setting?
2. How would you define an ethical business culture?

Summary of Learning Objectives

1. **Identify the key financial decisions facing the financial manager of any business firm.**

   In running a business, the financial manager faces three basic decisions: (1) which productive assets the firm should buy (capital budgeting), (2) how the firm should finance the productive assets purchased (financing decision), and (3) how the firm should manage its day-to-day financial activities (working capital decisions). The financial manager should make these decisions in a way that maximizes the current value of the firm's stock.

2. **Identify the basic forms of business organization used in the United States, and review their respective strengths and weaknesses.**

   A business can organize in three basic ways: as a sole proprietorship, a partnership, or a corporation (public or private). The owners of a firm select the form of organization that they believe will best allow management to maximize the value of the firm. Most large firms elect to organize as public corporations because of the ease of raising money; the major disadvantage is double taxation. Smaller companies tend to organize as sole proprietorships or partnerships. The advantages of these forms of organization include ease of formation and taxation at the personal income tax rate. The major disadvantage is the owners' unlimited personal liability.

3. **Describe the typical organization of the financial function in a large corporation.**

   In a large corporation, the financial manager generally has the rank of vice president and goes by the title of chief financial officer. The CFO reports directly to the firm's CEO. Positions reporting directly to the CFO generally include the treasurer, the risk manager, the controller, and the internal auditor. The audit committee of the board of directors is also important in the financial function. The committee hires the external auditor for the firm, and the internal auditor, external auditor, and compliance officer all report to the audit committee.

4. **Explain why maximizing the current value of the firm's stock is the appropriate goal for management.**

   The goal of the financial manager is to maximize the current value of the firm's stock. Maximizing stock value is an appropriate goal because it forces management to focus on decisions that will generate the greatest amount of wealth for stockholders. Since the value of a share of stock (or any asset) is determined by its cash flows, management's decisions must consider the size of the cash flow (larger is better), the timing of the cash flow (sooner is better), and the riskiness of the cash flow (given equal returns, lower risk is better).

5. **Discuss how agency conflicts affect the goal of maximizing stockholder value.**

   In most large corporations, there is a significant degree of separation between management and ownership. As a result, stockholders have little control over corporate managers, and management may thus be tempted to pursue its own self-interest rather than maximizing the wealth of the owners. The resulting conflicts give rise to agency costs. Ways of reducing agency costs include developing compensation agreements that link employee compensation to the firm's performance and having independent boards of directors monitor management.

6. **Explain why ethics is an appropriate topic in the study of managerial finance.**

   If we lived in a world without ethical norms, we would soon discover that it would be difficult to do business. As a practical matter, the law and market forces provide important incentives that foster ethical behavior in the business community, but they are not enough to ensure ethical behavior. An ethical culture is also needed. In an ethical culture, people have a set of moral principles—a moral compass—that helps them identify ethical issues and make ethical judgments without being told what to do.

Self-Study Problems

1.1 Give an example of a financing decision and a capital budgeting decision.

1.2 What is the decision criterion for financial managers when selecting a capital project?

1.3 What are some ways to manage working capital?

1.4 Which one of the following characteristics does not pertain to corporations?
   a. can enter into contracts
   b. can borrow money
   c. are the easiest type of business to form
   d. can be sued
   e. can own stock in other companies

1.5 What are typically the main components of an executive compensation package?

Solutions to Self-Study Problems

1.1 Financing decisions determine how a firm will raise capital. Examples of financing decisions would be securing a bank loan or selling debt in the public capital markets. Capital budgeting involves deciding which productive assets the firm invests in, such as buying a new plant or investing in a renovation of an existing facility.

1.2 Financial managers should select a capital project only if the value of the project's future cash flows exceeds the cost of the project. In other words, firms should only take on investments that will increase their value and thus increase the stockholders' wealth.

1.3 Working capital is the day-to-day management of a firm's short-term assets and liabilities. It can be managed through maintaining the optimal level of inventory, keeping track of all the receivables and payables, deciding to whom the firm should extend credit, and making appropriate investments with excess cash.

1.4 The answer that does *not* pertain to corporations is (c) are the easiest type of business to form.

1.5 The three main components of an executive compensation package are: base salary, bonus based on accounting performance, and some compensation tied to the firm's stock price.

Critical Thinking Questions

1.1 Describe the cash flows between a firm and its stakeholders.

1.2 What are the three fundamental decisions the financial management team is concerned with, and how do they affect the firm's balance sheet?

1.3 What is the difference between stockholders and stakeholders?

1.4 Suppose that a group of accountants wants to start their own accounting company. What organizational form of business would they choose, and why?

1.5 What does double taxation in the corporate setting mean?

1.6 Explain why profit maximization is not the best goal for a company. What is an appropriate goal?

1.7 In determining the price of a firm's stock, what are some of the external and internal factors that affect price? What is the difference between these two types of variables?

1.8 Identify the sources of agency costs. What are some ways a company can control these factors?

1.9 What is the Sarbanes-Oxley Act, and what are its main goals that affect the board of directors?

1.10 Give an example of a conflict of interest in a business setting other than the one involving the real estate agent discussed in the text.

Questions and Problems

1.1 Capital: What are the two basic sources of funds for all businesses?

1.2 Management role: What is working capital management?

1.3 Cash flows: Explain the difference between profitable and unprofitable firms.

1.4 Management role: What three major decisions are of most concern to financial managers?

1.5 Cash flows: What is the general decision rule for a firm considering undertaking a project? Give a real-life example.

1.6 Management role: What is capital structure, and why is it important to a company?

1.7 Management role: What are some of the working capital decisions that a financial manager faces?

1.8 Organizational form: What are the three basic forms of business organization discussed in this chapter?

1.9 Organizational form: What are the advantages and disadvantages of a sole proprietorship?

1.10 Organizational form: What is a partnership, and what is the biggest disadvantage of this form of business organization? How can this disadvantage be avoided?

1.11 Organizational form: Who are the owners of a corporation, and how is their ownership represented?

1.12 Organizational form: Explain what is meant by stockholders' limited liability.

1.13 Organizational form: What is double taxation?

1.14 Organizational form: What is the business organization form preferred by most physicians, lawyers, and accountants, and why?

1.15 Finance function: What is the most important governing body within a business organization? What responsibilities does it have?

1.16 Finance function: Almost all public companies hire a certified public accounting firm to perform an independent audit of the financial statements. What exactly does an audit mean?

1.17 Firm's goal: What are some of the drawbacks to setting profit maximization as the main goal of a company?

1.18 Firm's goal: What is the appropriate goal of financial managers? Can managers' decisions affect this goal in any way? If so, how?

1.19 Firm's goal: What are the major factors affecting stock price?

1.20 Agency conflicts: What is an agency relationship, and what is an agency conflict? How can agency conflicts be reduced in a corporation?

1.21 Firm's goal: What can happen if a firm is poorly managed and its stock price falls substantially below its maximum?

1.22 Agency conflicts: What are some of the regulations that pertain to boards of directors that were put in place to reduce agency conflicts?

1.23 Business ethics: How could business dishonesty and low integrity cause an economic downfall? Give an example.

1.24 Agency conflicts: What are some possible ways to resolve a conflict of interest?

1.25 Business ethics: What ethical conflict does insider trading present?

Sample Test Problems

1.1 Why is value maximization superior to profit maximization as a goal for the firm?

1.2 The major advantage of debt financing is
   a. it allows a firm to use creditors' money.
   b. interest payments are more predictable than dividend payments.
   c. interest payments are not required when a firm is not doing well.
   d. interest payments are tax deductible.

1.3 Identify three fundamental decisions that a financial manager has to make in running a firm.

1.4 What are agency costs? Explain.

1.5 Identify four of the seven mechanisms that align the goals of managers with those of stockholders.

THE FINANCIAL ENVIRONMENT AND THE LEVEL OF INTEREST RATES

CHAPTER 2

LEARNING OBJECTIVES

1. Discuss the primary role of the financial system in the economy, and describe the two basic ways in which fund transfers take place.

2. Discuss direct financing and the important role that investment banks play in this process.

3. Describe the primary and secondary markets, and explain why secondary markets are so important to businesses.

4. Explain why money markets are important financial markets for large corporations.

5. Discuss the most important stock market exchanges and indexes.

6. Explain how financial institutions serve consumers and small businesses that are unable to participate in the direct financial markets and describe how corporations use the financial system.

7. Explain how the real rate of interest is determined in the economy, differentiate between the real rate and the nominal rate of interest, and be able to compute the nominal or real rate of interest.

©AP/Wide World Photos

One of the most important institutional players in the financial system is the Federal Reserve System (called the Fed). In fact, it is sometimes said that the chairman of the Federal Reserve Board is the second most powerful person in the United States—second only to the president. Where does all of this power come from?

It comes from the Fed's role as the nation's central bank—the institution that controls the money supply. The Fed "manages" the nation's economy by conducting monetary policy, which affects how much money is available in the economy. One way it does this is by setting a target short-term interest rate at which large money center banks lend to each other (called the federal funds rate) and by buying and selling Treasury and federal agency securities to achieve this rate. Increases in the money supply put downward pressure on short-term interest rates. Over time, this can lead to increases in the level of economic activity, along with higher inflation. Conversely, decreases in the money supply put upward pressure on short-term interest rates. This can lead to a lower level of economic activity and lower inflation.

Small wonder that when the Fed speaks, everyone stops and listens. Ben Bernanke, the current Fed chairman, described the effects of Fed announcements on the stock market as follows:

Normally, the [Federal Open Market Committee, or] FOMC, the monetary policymaking arm of the Federal Reserve, announces its interest rate decisions at around 2:15 p.m. following each of its eight regularly scheduled meetings each year. An air of expectation reigns in financial markets in the few minutes before to the announcement. If you happen to have access to a monitor that tracks key market indexes, at 2:15 p.m. on an announcement day you can watch those indexes quiver as if trying to digest the information in the rate decision and the FOMC's accompanying statement of explanation. Then the black line representing each market index moves quickly up or down, and the markets have priced the FOMC action into the aggregate values of U.S. equities, bonds, and other assets.[1]

As you can see, the Fed's policy actions are transmitted quickly through the financial system and ultimately affect the economic well-being of nearly all consumers and businesses. This chapter provides a basic explanation of how the financial system works and discusses interest rates and their movements.

CHAPTER PREVIEW

Chapter 1 identified three kinds of decisions that financial managers make: *capital budgeting decisions*, which concern the purchase of capital assets; *financing decisions*, which concern how assets will be paid for; and *working capital management decisions*, which concern day-to-day financial matters. Making sound decisions in any of these areas requires knowledge of financial markets and services.

In making capital budgeting decisions, financial managers should select projects whose cash flows increase the value of the firm. The financial models used to evaluate these projects require an understanding of financial markets and interest rates. In making financing decisions, financial managers naturally want to obtain capital at the lowest possible cost, which means that they need to understand how financial markets work and what financing alternatives are available. Finally, working capital management is concerned with whether a firm has enough money to pay its bills and how it invests its spare cash to earn interest. Making decisions in these areas requires knowledge of money markets and financial services.

Clearly, then, financial managers need a working knowledge of financial markets and financial institutions. This chapter provides a quick overview of the financial sector and the services it provides to businesses. We will revisit many of the topics covered here in later chapters.

We begin the chapter by looking at how the financial system facilitates the transfer of money from those who have it to those who need it. Then we describe direct financing, through which large business firms finance themselves by issuing debt and equity, and the important role that investment banks play in the process. Next we explain why smaller firms and consumers must finance themselves indirectly by borrowing from financial institutions such as commercial banks. We then examine other types of services that financial institutions provide large and small businesses. Finally, we discuss the factors that determine the general level of interest rates in the economy and explain why interest rates vary over the business cycle.

2.1 The Financial System

LEARNING OBJECTIVE 1

The financial system consists of financial markets and financial institutions. *Financial market* is a general term that includes a number of different types of markets for the creation and exchange of financial assets, such as stocks and bonds. *Financial institutions* are firms such as commercial banks, credit unions, insurance companies, pension funds, and finance companies that provide financial services to the economy. The distinguishing feature of financial institutions is that they invest their funds in financial assets, such as business loans, stocks, and bonds, rather than real assets, such as plants and equipment.

The critical role of the financial system in the economy is to gather money from people and businesses with surplus funds to invest and channel money to those who

---

[1]Ben S. Bernanke, "Remarks at the Fall 2003 Banking and Finance Lecture," Widener University, Chester, Pennsylvania, October 2, 2003.

need it. Businesses need money to invest in new productive assets to expand their operations and increase the firm's cash flow, which should increase the value of the firm. Consumers, too, need money, which they use to purchase things such as condos, cars, and boats—or to pay college tuition bills. Some of the players in the financial system are household names such as the New York Stock Exchange, Bank of America, Merrill Lynch, and State Farm Insurance. Others are lesser-known but important firms, such the multinational giant GE Capital.

A well-developed financial system is critical for the operation of a complex industrial economy such as that of the United States. Highly industrialized countries cannot function without a competitive and sound financial system that efficiently gathers money and channels it into the best investment opportunities. Let's look at a simple example to illustrate how the financial system channels money to businesses.

The Financial System at Work

Suppose you are a college student. At the beginning of the school year, you receive a $10,000 student loan to help pay your expenses for the year, but you need only $5,000 for the first semester. You wisely decide to invest the remaining $5,000 to earn some interest income. After shopping at several banks near campus, you decide that the best deal is a $5,000 consumer certificate of deposit (CD) that matures in three months and pays 5 percent interest. (CDs are debt instruments issued by a bank that pay interest and are insured by the federal government.)

The bank pools your money with funds from other CDs and uses this money to make business and consumer loans. In this case, the bank makes a loan to the pizza parlor near campus: $30,000 for five years at a 9 percent interest rate. The bank decides to make the loan because of the pizza parlor's sound credit rating and because it expects the pizza parlor to generate enough cash flows to repay the loan. The pizza parlor owner wants the money to invest in additional earning assets to earn greater profits (cash flows) and thereby increase the value of the firm. During the same week, the bank makes loans to other businesses and also rejects a number of loan requests because the borrowers have poor credit ratings or the proposed projects have low rates of return.

From this example, we can draw some important inferences about financial systems:

- If the financial system is *competitive,* the interest rate the bank pays on CDs will be at or near the highest rate that you can earn on a CD of similar maturity and risk. At the same time, the pizza parlor and other businesses will have borrowed at or near the lowest possible interest cost, given their risk class. Competition among banks for deposits will drive CD rates up and loan rates down.

- The bank gathers money from you and other consumers in small dollar amounts, aggregates it, and then makes loans in much larger dollar amounts. Saving by consumers in small dollar amounts is the origin of much of the money that funds large business loans in the economy.

- An important function of the financial system is to direct money to the best investment opportunities in the economy. If the financial system works properly, only business projects with high rates of return and good credit are financed. Those with low rates of return or poor credit will be rejected. Thus, financial systems contribute to higher production and efficiency in the overall economy.

- Finally, note that the bank has earned a tidy profit from the deal. The bank has borrowed money at 5 percent by selling CDs to consumers and has lent money to the pizza parlor and other businesses at 9 percent. Thus, the bank's gross profit is 4 percent (9 − 5), which is the difference between the bank's lending and borrowing rates. Banks earn much of their profits from the spread between the lending and borrowing rates.

How Funds Flow through the Financial System

We have seen that the financial system plays a critical role in the economy. The system moves money from *lender-savers* (whose income exceeds their spending) to *borrower-spenders* (whose spending exceeds their income), as shown schematically in Exhibit 2.1.[2] The largest lender-savers in the economy are households, but some businesses and many state and local governments at times have excess funds to lend to those who need money. The largest borrower-spenders in the economy are businesses, followed by the federal government.

The arrows in Exhibit 2.1 show that there are two basic mechanisms by which funds flow through the financial system: (1) funds can flow *directly* through financial markets (the route at the top of the diagram) and (2) funds can flow *indirectly* through financial institutions (the route at the bottom of the diagram). In the following sections, we look more closely at the direct flow of funds and at the financial markets. After that, we discuss financial institutions and the indirect flow of funds.

> **Before You Go On**
> 1. What essential economic role does the financial system play in the economy?
> 2. What are the two basic ways in which funds flow through the financial system from lender-savers to borrower-spenders?

Exhibit 2.1 The Flow of Funds Through the Financial System
The role of the financial system is to gather money from people and businesses with surplus funds and channel it ot those who need it. Money flows through the financial system in two basic ways: *directly*, through wholesale financial markets, as shown in the top route of the diagram, and *indirectly*, through financial institutions, as shown in the bottom route.

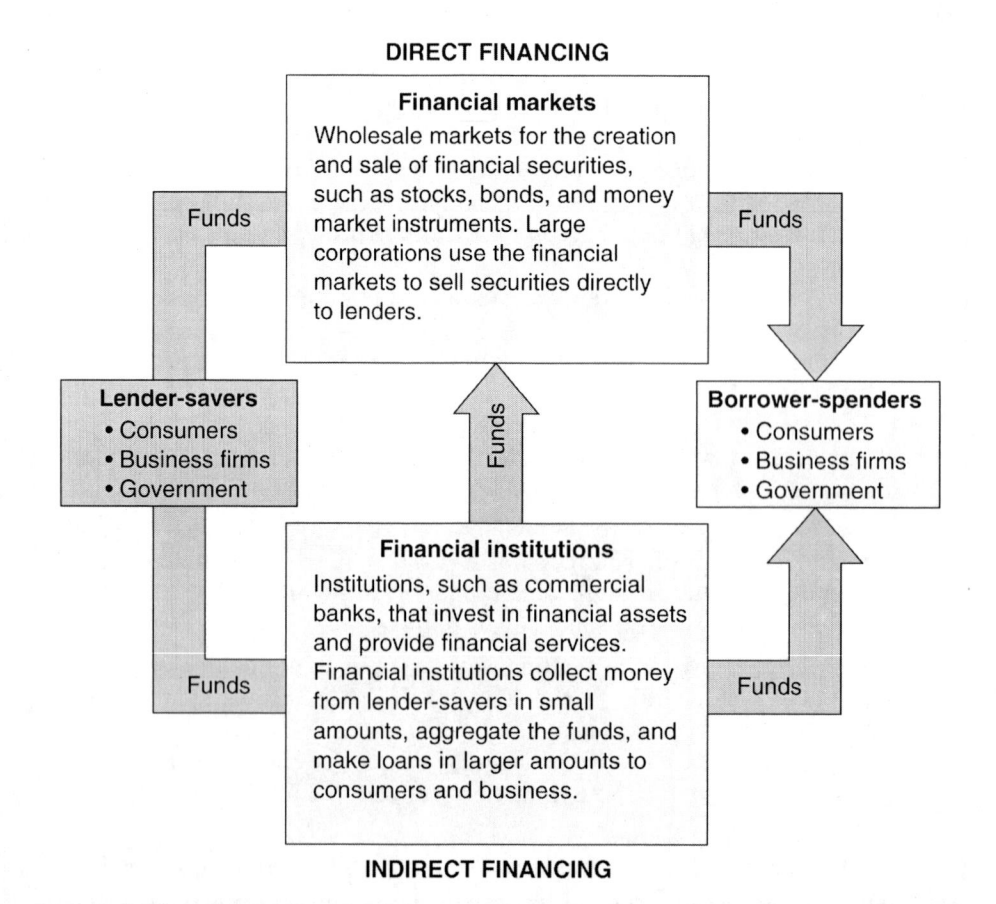

DIRECT FINANCING

Financial markets
Wholesale markets for the creation and sale of financial securities, such as stocks, bonds, and money market instruments. Large corporations use the financial markets to sell securities directly to lenders.

Lender-savers
- Consumers
- Business firms
- Government

Borrower-spenders
- Consumers
- Business firms
- Government

Financial institutions
Institutions, such as commercial banks, that invest in financial assets and provide financial services. Financial institutions collect money from lender-savers in small amounts, aggregate the funds, and make loans in larger amounts to consumers and business.

INDIRECT FINANCING

---

[2]Lender-savers are also called surplus spending units (SSU), and borrower-spenders are also called deficit spending units (DSU).

2.2 Direct Financing

In this section we turn our attention to direct financing, in which funds flow directly through financial markets. In direct transactions, the lender-savers and the borrower-spenders deal "directly" with one another; borrower-spenders sell securities, such as stocks and bonds, to lender-savers in exchange for money. These securities represent claims on the borrowers' future income or assets. A number of different interchangeable terms are used to refer to securities, including *financial instruments* and *financial claims*.

The financial markets where direct transactions take place are wholesale markets with a typical minimum transaction size of $1 million. For most business firms, these markets provide funds at the lowest possible cost. The major buyers and sellers of securities in the direct financial markets are commercial banks; other financial institutions, such as insurance companies and business finance companies; large corporations; the federal government; hedge funds; and some wealthy individuals. It is important to note that financial institutions are major buyers of securities in the direct financial markets. For example, life and casualty insurance companies buy large quantities of corporate bonds and stocks for their investment portfolios. In Exhibit 2.1 the arrow leading from financial institutions to financial markets depicts this flow.

Although few individuals participate in direct financial markets, individuals can gain access to many of the financial products produced in these markets through retail channels at investment banking firms or financial institutions such as commercial banks (the lower route in Exhibit 2.1). For example, individuals can buy or sell stocks and bonds in small dollar amounts at Merrill Lynch, an investment banking firm, or from Bank of America's retail brokerage business. We discuss indirect financing through financial institutions later in this chapter.

A Direct Market Transaction

Let's look at a typical direct market transaction. When managers decide to engage in a direct market transaction, they often have a specific capital project in mind that needs financing, such as building a new manufacturing facility. Suppose that Apple Computer needs $20 million to build a new facility and decides to fund it by selling long-term bonds with a 15-year maturity. Say that Apple contacts a group of insurance companies, which express an interest in buying Apple's bonds. The insurance companies will buy Apple's bonds only after determining that they are priced fairly for their level of risk. Apple will sell its bonds to the insurance companies only after shopping the market to be sure the investors are offering a competitive price.

If Apple and the insurance companies strike a deal, the flow of funds between them will be as shown below:

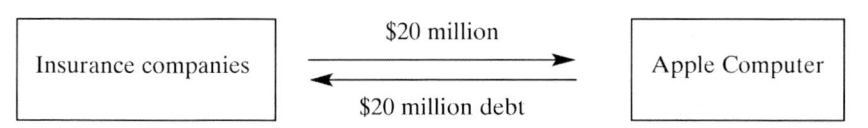

```
                    $20 million
┌───────────────────┐ ──────────────→ ┌───────────────┐
│ Insurance companies│                │ Apple Computer │
└───────────────────┘ ←────────────── └───────────────┘
                   $20 million debt
```

Apple sells its bonds to the insurance group for $20 million and gets the use of the money for 15 years. For Apple, the bonds are a liability, and it pays the bondholders interest for use of the money. For the insurance companies, the bonds are assets that earn interest.

Investment Banks and Direct Financing

Two important players that deliver critical services to firms transacting in the direct financial markets are investment banks and money center banks. **Investment banks** specialize in helping companies sell new debt or equity, although they also provide other services, such

investment banks
firms that underwrite new security issues and provide broker-dealer services

money center banks
large commercial banks that transact in both the national and international financial markets

To get a better idea of all the lines of business in which large investment banking firms engage, go to Merrill Lynch's home page at www.ml.com.

as the broker and dealer services discussed later. **Money center banks** are large commercial banks located in major financial centers. Since 1999 these large banks have been allowed to engage in investment banking activities.[3] Today money center banks such as Citicorp and Bank of America successfully compete head-to-head against traditional Wall Street investment banks. When investment bankers help firms bring new debt or equity securities to market, they perform three tasks: origination, underwriting, and distribution.

ORIGINATION

Origination is the process of preparing a security issue for sale. During the origination phase, the investment banker may help the client company determine the feasibility of the project being funded and the amount of capital that needs to be raised. Once this is done, the investment banker helps secure a credit rating, if needed, determines the sale date, obtains legal clearances to sell the securities, and gets the securities printed. If securities are to be sold in the public markets, the issuer must also file a registration statement with the SEC. Securities sold in the private markets are not required by the SEC to file a registration statement.

UNDERWRITING

Underwriting is the process by which the investment banker helps the company sell its new security issue. In the most common type of underwriting arrangement, called *firm-commitment underwriting,* the investment banker assumes the risk of buying the new securities from the issuing company and reselling them to investors. Note that the investment banker guarantees to buy the entire security issue from the company at a fixed price. The guaranteed price is important to the issuing company. The company likely needs a certain amount of money to pay for a particular project or to fund operations, and getting anything less than this amount will pose a serious problem. As you would expect, financial managers almost always prefer to have their new security issues underwritten on a firm-commitment basis.[4]

Once the investment bankers buy the securities from the issuer, they immediately offer to resell individual securities to institutional investors and the public at a specified offering price. The underwriters hope to be able to sell the offering at the market-clearing price, which is the price that will allow the entire security issue to be sold during the first day of sale. Underwriting involves considerable risk because it is difficult to estimate the price that will clear the market. The risk is that the investment bank may eventually have to sell the securities at a price below the guaranteed price that it paid to the issuing company. If this happens, the investment bank suffers a financial loss.

The investment banker's compensation is called the *underwriting spread*. It is the difference between the price the investment banker pays for the security issue and the offering price. The underwriting spread is one of the costs to the firm of selling new securities issues.

DISTRIBUTION

Distribution is the process of marketing and reselling the securities to investors. Because security prices can take large, unexpected swings, a quick resale of all the securities is important. To that end, the underwriters often form large sales syndicates, consisting of a number of different investment banking firms, to sell the securities. If the securities are not sold within a few days, the syndicate is disbanded, and the individual syndicate members sell the unsold securities at whatever price they can get.

---

[3]The Financial Services Modernization Act of 1999 allows money center banks to engage in investment banking. Banks had been barred from investment banking following the Great Depression (1929–1933) because it was believed that these activities were too risky for banks. It was believed that excessive risk taking by commercial banks had resulted in a large number of bank failures, which precipitated the Great Depression. Recent research has exonerated the banking system of this charge.

[4]If the risk of underwriting a new security issue is high, investment bankers may refuse to underwrite the securities for a guaranteed price. Instead, they will underwrite the new issue on a *best-effort basis,* which means that they will sell the securities for the highest price that investors are willing to pay. These issues are discussed in more detail in Chapter 15.

LEARNING BY DOING APPLICATION 2.1

Underwriter's Compensation

Problem: Dairy Queen needs to raise $5 million for expansion and decides to issue long-term bonds. The financial manager hires an investment banking firm to help design the bond issue and underwrite it. The issue consists of 5,000 bonds, and the investment banker agrees to purchase the entire issue for $5 million. The investment banker then resells the bonds to individual investors at the offering price. The sale totals $5.2 million. What is the underwriter's compensation?

Approach: The underwriter's compensation is the underwriting spread, which is the difference between the price at which the bonds were resold to individual investors and the price the underwriter paid for the issue. The underwriting spread per bond is then calculated by dividing the total spread by the number of bonds that are issued.

Solution:

Underwriting spread: $5,200,000 − $5,000,000 = $200,000

Underwriting spread per bond: $200,000/5,000 = $40

Notice that the issuer gets a check from the underwriter for $5.0 million regardless of the price at which the bonds are resold because of the guarantee.

Before You Go On

1. Why is it difficult for individuals to participate in direct financial markets?
2. Why might a firm prefer to have a security issue underwritten by an investment banking firm?

2.3 Types of Financial Markets

We have seen that direct flows of funds occur in financial markets. However, as already mentioned, *financial market* is a very general term. A complex industrial economy such as ours includes many different types of financial markets, and not all of them are involved in direct financing. Next, we examine some of the more important ways to classify financial markets. Note that these classifications overlap to a large extent. Thus, for example, the New York Stock Exchange fits into several different categories.

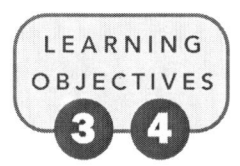

Primary and Secondary Markets

A **primary market** is any market where companies sell new security issues (debt or equity). For example, Hewlett-Packard (HP) needs to raise $100 million for business expansion and decides to raise the money through the sale of common stock. The company will sell the new equity issue in the primary market for corporate stock—probably with the help of an underwriter, as discussed in Section 2.2. The primary markets are not well known to the general public because they are wholesale markets and the sales take place outside of the public view.

primary market
a financial market in which new security issues are sold by companies directly to investors

secondary market
a financial market in which the owners of outstanding securities can sell them to other investors

A **secondary market** is any market where owners of outstanding securities can sell them to other investors. Secondary markets are like used-car markets in that they allow investors to buy or sell second-hand, or previously owned, securities for cash. These markets are important because they enable investors to buy and sell securities as frequently as they want. As you might expect, investors are willing to pay higher prices for securities that have active secondary markets. Secondary markets are important to corporations as well because investors are willing to pay higher prices for securities in primary markets if the securities have active secondary markets. Thus, companies whose securities have active secondary markets enjoy lower funding costs than similar firms whose securities do not have active secondary markets.

MARKETABILITY VERSUS LIQUIDITY

marketability
the ease with which a security can be sold and converted into cash

An important characteristic of a security to investors is its marketability. **Marketability** is the ease with which a security can be sold and converted into cash. A security's marketability depends in part on the costs of trading and searching for information, so-called *transaction costs*. The lower the transaction costs, the greater a security's marketability. Because secondary markets make it easier to trade securities, their presence increases a security's marketability.

liquidity
the ability to convert an asset into cash quickly without loss of value

A term closely related to marketability is **liquidity**. Liquidity is the ability to convert an asset into cash quickly without loss of value. In common use, the terms *marketability* and *liquidity* are often used interchangeably, but they are different. Liquidity implies that when the security is sold, its value will be preserved; marketability does not carry this implication.

BROKERS VERSUS DEALERS

brokers
market specialists who bring buyers and sellers together, usually for a commission

Two types of market specialists facilitate transactions in secondary markets. **Brokers** are market specialists who bring buyers and sellers together when a sale takes place. They execute the transaction for their client and are compensated for their services with a commission fee. They bear no risk of ownership of the securities during the transactions; their only service is that of "matchmaker."

dealers
market specialists who "make markets" for securities by buying and selling from their own inventories

Dealers, in contrast, "make markets" for securities and do bear risk. They make a market for a security by buying and selling from an inventory of securities they own. Dealers make their profit, just as retail merchants do, by selling securities at a price above what they paid for it. The risk that dealers bear is *price risk,* which is the risk that they will sell a security for less than they paid for it.

Exchanges and Over-the-Counter Markets

Financial markets can be classified as either "organized" markets (more commonly called exchanges) or over-the-counter markets. Traditional exchanges, such as the New York Stock Exchange (NYSE), provide a physical meeting place and communication facilities for members to buy and sell securities or other assets (such as commodities) under a specific set of rules and regulations. Members are individuals who represent securities firms as well as people who trade for their own accounts. Only members can use the exchange.

Securities not listed on an exchange are bought and sold in the over-the-counter (OTC) market. The OTC market differs from organized exchanges in that the "market" has no central trading location. Instead, investors can execute OTC transactions by visiting or telephoning an OTC dealer or by using a computer-based electronic trading system linked to the OTC dealer. Traditionally, stocks traded over the counter have been those of small and relatively unknown firms, most of which would not qualify to be listed on a major exchange. However, electronic trading has become much more important in recent years, as you will see later in the chapter when we discuss NASDAQ.

Money and Capital Markets

Money markets are global markets where short-term debt instruments, which have maturities of less than one year, are sold. Money markets are wholesale markets in which the minimum transaction is $1 million and transactions of $10 million or $100 million are not uncommon. Money market instruments are lower in risk than other securities because of their high liquidity and low default risk. In fact, the term "*money*" *market* is used because these instruments are close substitutes for cash. The most important and largest money markets are in New York City, London, and Tokyo. Exhibit 2.2 lists the most common money market instruments and the dollar amounts outstanding.

Large companies use money markets to adjust their liquidity positions. Liquidity, as mentioned, is the ability to convert an asset into cash quickly without loss of value. Liquidity problems arise because companies' cash receipts and expenditures are rarely perfectly synchronized. To manage liquidity, a firm can invest idle cash in money market instruments; then, if the firm has a temporary cash shortfall, it can raise cash overnight by selling money market instruments from its portfolio.

Recall from Chapter 1 that capital markets are global markets where intermediate-term and long-term debt and corporate stocks are traded. In these markets, large firms finance capital assets such as plants and equipment. The New York Stock Exchange, as well as the London and Tokyo stock exchanges, are capital markets. Exhibit 2.2 also lists the major U.S. capital market instruments and the dollar amounts outstanding. Compared with money market instruments, capital market instruments are less marketable, carry more default risk, and have longer maturities.

money markets
markets where short-term financial instruments are traded

Public and Private Markets

Public markets are organized financial markets where the general public buys and sell securities through their stockbrokers. The New York Stock Exchange, for example,

public markets
financial markets where securities registered with the SEC are sold

Exhibit 2.2 Selected Money Market and Capital Market Instruments, March 2007 ($ billions)

Money market instruments		
Treasury bills		$ 783
Other marketable short-term securities		487
Bank negotiable CDs		128
Commercial paper		1,782
	Total	$ 3,180
Capital market instruments		
Treasury notes		$ 2,420
Treasury bonds		803
State and local government bonds		2,062
Corporate and foreign bonds		10,097
Corporate stock (at market value)		20,809
Mortgages		13,549
	Total	$49,740

Source: Board of Governors, Federal Reserve System, Flow of Funds Accounts.

The exhibit shows the size of the U.S. market for each of the most important money market and capital market instruments. Notice that the largest security market is the market for corporate bonds, followed by those for corporate stock, mortgage debt, and, a distant fourth, money market instruments. Compared with money market instruments, capital market instruments are less marketable, have higher default risk, and have longer maturities.

is a public market. The SEC regulates public securities markets in the United States.[5] This agency is responsible for overseeing the securities industry and regulating all primary and secondary markets in which securities are traded. Most corporations want access to the public markets because they are wholesale markets where issuers can sell their securities at the lowest possible funding cost. The downside for corporations selling in the public markets is the cost of complying with the various SEC regulations.

In contrast to public market, *private market* involves direct transactions between two parties. Transactions in private market are often called **private placements**. In private market, a company contacts investors directly and negotiates a deal to sell them all or part of a security issue. Larger firms may be equipped to handle these transactions themselves. Smaller firms are more likely to use the services of an investment bank, which will help locate investors, help negotiate the deal, and handle the legal aspects of the transaction. Major advantages of a private placement are the speed at which funds can be raised and low transaction costs. Downsides are that privately placed securities cannot legally be sold in the public markets because they lack SEC registration and the dollar amounts that can be raised tend to be smaller.

> **private placement**
> the sale of an unregistered security directly to an investor, such as an insurance company

Futures and Options Markets

Markets also exist for trading in futures and options. Perhaps the best known futures markets are the New York Board of Trade and the Chicago Board of Trade. The Chicago Board Options Exchange is a major options market.

Futures and options are often called *derivative securities* because they derive their value from some underlying asset. Futures contracts are contracts for the future delivery of such assets as securities, foreign currencies, interest cash flows, or commodities. Corporations use these contracts to reduce (hedge) risk exposure caused by fluctuation in things such as foreign exchange rates or commodity prices. We discuss this use of futures contracts further in Chapter 21.

Options contracts call for one party (the option writer) to perform a specific act if called upon to do so by the option buyer or owner. Options contracts, like futures contracts, can be used to hedge risk in situations where the firm faces risk from price fluctuations. Options are discussed in more detail in Chapter 20.

> **Before You Go On**
> 1. What is the difference between primary and secondary markets?
> 2. How and why do large business firms use money markets?
> 3. What are capital markets, and why are they important to corporations?

2.4 The Stock Market

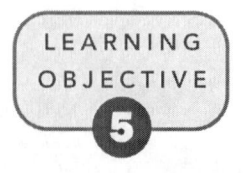

LEARNING OBJECTIVE 5

We noted earlier that secondary markets are important to corporations because companies whose securities trade in active secondary markets enjoy lower funding costs than firms whose securities do not. Here, we discuss a particularly important secondary market: the large, public market in which corporate stocks are bought and sold.

---
[5] The SEC was established in 1933 following the stock market crash of 1929.

The New York Stock Exchange

Recall that a traditional securities exchange is an organized market that provides a physical meeting place and communication facilities for members to buy and sell securities under a specific set of rules and regulations. The oldest, largest, and best-known exchange of this kind in the United States is the New York Stock Exchange, which was founded in 1792. The exchange lists the common and preferred stocks of more than three thousand companies, as well as eight hundred bonds. Collectively, the companies whose securities are traded on the NYSE have a market capitalization (total stock value) of about $16 trillion.

Stocks that are traded on an exchange are said to be *listed* on that exchange. For a firm's stocks to be listed on an exchange, the firm must pay a fee and meet the exchange's requirements for membership. Requirements include a minimum asset size, total stock value, a minimum number of shares of stock outstanding, and a minimum number of stockholders. Because of the prestige associated with being listed on the "big board," as the NYSE is known, it has the most stringent listing requirements. As a result, companies listed on the NYSE tend to be large, well-known firms.

> Learn more about the NYSE by visiting its Web site at www.nyse.com.

NASDAQ

The NASDAQ (pronounced "Naz-dak") is the world's largest electronic stock market, listing nearly four thousand companies. NASDAQ was created in 1971 by the National Association of Securities Dealers (NASD), and its odd name is an acronym for National Association of Securities Dealers Automated Quotation (NASDAQ) system.

NASDAQ fits our earlier definition of an OTC market because it does not have a physical location where trading takes place. Nevertheless, NASDAQ has achieved the stature of a major exchange. In fact, thanks to its sophisticated electronic trading system, NASDAQ is the second largest stock market in the United States in terms of the dollar volume of trading; only the NYSE is larger. Although the OTC market has generally traded in the stocks of small firms that would not qualify to be listed on a major exchange, only 20 percent of the firms traded on NASDAQ are considered small.

> Find out about over-the-counter markets and NASDAQ at www.nasdaq.com.

Stock Market Indexes

Stock market indexes are used to measure the performance of the stock market—whether stock prices on average are moving up or down. The indexes are watched closely not only to track economic activity but also to measure the performance of specific firms. A wide variety of general and specialized indexes is available. Here, we discuss some of the better-known indexes.

> The Web site www.bigcharts.com offers a real-time summary of all the major market indexes.

- *Dow Jones Industrial Average.* The most widely published stock market index is the Dow Jones Industrial Average (DJIA), which was first published in 1896. The index consists of 30 companies that represent about 20 percent of the market value of all U.S. stocks. Dow Jones also publishes specialized indexes for industrial, transportation, and utility companies. These specialized indexes tell us how stocks in a particular segment of the economy are performing.
- *New York Stock Exchange Index.* The New York Stock Exchange composite index, published since 1966, includes all of the common and preferred stocks listed on the New York Stock Exchange. The index provides information on the performance of the largest and most well-known firms in the economy.
- *Standard and Poor's 500 Index.* The Standard and Poor's 500 Index, which consists of 500 stocks, was created in 1926 and is regarded as the best index for measuring the performance of the largest companies in the U.S. economy. The stocks in the S&P 500 are selected by the Standard and Poor's Index

Committee and represent more than 70 percent of the total market capitalization of all stocks traded in the United States.

- *NASDAQ Composite Index.* The NASDAQ Composite Index consists of all of the common stocks listed on the NASDAQ stock exchange. Currently, the index includes more than three thousand firms, many of which are in the technology sector of the economy. Thus, the NASDAQ Composite Index is considered a barometer of performance in the high-tech sector.

> **Before You Go On**
>
> 1. What is NASDAQ?
> 2. List the major stock market indexes, and explain what they tell us.

2.5 Financial Institutions and Indirect Financing

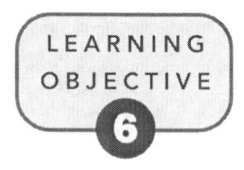

LEARNING OBJECTIVE 6

financial intermediation
conversion of securities with one set of characteristics into securities with another set of characteristics

As we mentioned earlier, many business firms are too small to sell their debt or equity directly to investors. They have neither the expert knowledge nor the money to transact in wholesale markets. When these companies need funds for capital investments or for liquidity adjustments, their only choice may be to borrow in the *indirect* market from a financial institution. These financial institutions act as intermediaries, converting financial securities with one set of characteristics into securities with another set of characteristics. This process is called **financial intermediation**. The hallmark of indirect financing is that a financial institution—an intermediary—stands between the lender-saver and the borrower-spender. This route is shown at the bottom of Exhibit 2.1.

Indirect Market Transactions

We worked through an example of indirect financing at the beginning of the chapter. In that situation, a college student had $5,000 to invest for three months. A bank sold the student a three-month consumer CD for $5,000, pooled this $5,000 with the proceeds from other CDs, and used the money to make small-business loans, one of which was a $30,000 loan to our pizza parlor owner. Following is a schematic diagram of that transaction:

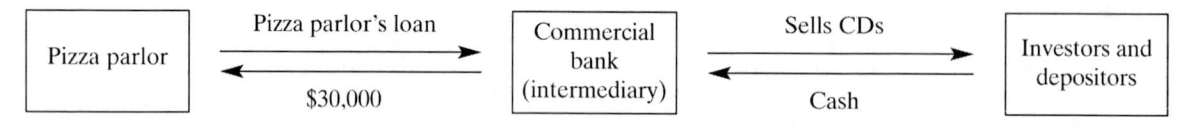

```
                 Pizza parlor's loan                    Sells CDs
 ┌─────────────┐ ──────────────────→ ┌──────────────┐ ──────────────→ ┌─────────────┐
 │ Pizza parlor│                     │  Commercial  │                 │ Investors and│
 │             │ ←────────────────── │     bank     │ ←────────────── │  depositors  │
 └─────────────┘     $30,000         │(intermediary)│     Cash        └─────────────┘
                                     └──────────────┘
```

The bank raises money by selling services such as checking accounts, savings accounts, and consumer CDs and then uses the money to make loans to businesses or consumers.

On a larger scale, insurance companies provide much of the long-term financing in the economy through the indirect credit market. These companies invest heavily in corporate bonds and equity securities using funds they receive when they sell insurance policies to individuals and businesses. The schematic diagram for intermediation by an insurance company is as follows:

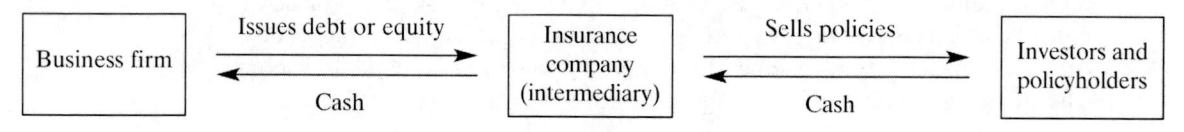

```
                 Issues debt or equity                  Sells policies
 ┌─────────────┐ ──────────────────→ ┌──────────────┐ ──────────────→ ┌───────────────┐
 │Business firm│                     │   Insurance  │                 │ Investors and │
 │             │ ←────────────────── │    company   │ ←────────────── │ policyholders │
 └─────────────┘        Cash         │(intermediary)│      Cash       └───────────────┘
                                     └──────────────┘
```

Notice an important difference between the indirect and direct financial markets. In the direct market, as securities flow between lender-savers and borrower-spenders, the form of the securities remains unchanged. In the indirect market, however, as securities flow between lender-savers and borrower-spenders, they are repackaged, and their form is changed. In the example above, money from the sale of insurance policies becomes investments in corporate debt or equity. By repackaging securities, financial intermediaries tailor-make a wide range of financial products and services that meet the needs of consumers, small businesses, and large corporations. Their products and services are particularly important for smaller businesses that do not have access to direct financial markets.

Somewhat surprisingly, the indirect markets are a much larger and more important source of financing to businesses than the more newsworthy direct financial markets. This is true not only in the United States, but in all industrial countries.

Financial Institutions and Their Services

We have briefly discussed the role of financial institutions as intermediaries in the indirect financial market. Next, we look at various types of financial institutions and the services they provide to small businesses as well as large corporations. We discuss only financial institutions that provide a significant amount of services to businesses.

COMMERCIAL BANKS

Commercial banks are the most prominent and largest financial intermediaries in the economy and offer the widest range of financial services to businesses. Nearly every business, small or large, has a significant relationship with a commercial bank—usually a checking or transaction account and some type of credit or loan arrangement. For businesses, the most common type of bank loan is a line of credit (often called revolving credit), which works much like a credit card. A line of credit is a commitment by the bank to lend a firm an amount up to a predetermined limit, which can be used as needed. Banks also make term loans, which are fixed-rate loans with a maturity of one year to ten years. In addition, banks do a significant amount of equipment lease financing. A lease is a contract that gives a business the right to use an asset, such as a truck or a computer mainframe, for a period of time in exchange for payments.

For an example of the range of services provided by commercial banks to businesses, visit the small-business section of www.pncbank.com.

LIFE AND CASUALTY INSURANCE COMPANIES

Two types of insurance companies are important in the financial markets: (1) life insurance companies and (2) casualty insurance companies, which sell protection against loss of property from fire, theft, accidents, and other predictable causes. The cash flows for both types of companies are fairly predictable. As a result, they are able to provide funding to corporations through the purchase of stocks and bonds in the direct credit markets as well as funding for private corporations through private placement financing. Businesses of all sizes purchase life insurance programs as part of their employee benefit packages and purchase casualty insurance policies to protect physical assets such as automobiles, truck fleets, equipment, and entire plants.

PENSION FUNDS

Pension funds invest retirement funds on behalf of businesses or government agencies that provide retirement programs for their employees. Pension funds obtain money from employee and employer contributions during the employee's working years, and they provide monthly cash payments upon retirement. Because of the predictability of these cash flows, pension fund managers invest in corporate bonds and equity securities purchased in the direct financial markets and participate in the private placement market.

INVESTMENT FUNDS

Investment funds such as mutual funds sell shares to investors and use the funds to purchase a wide variety of direct and indirect financial instruments. As a result, they are an important source of business funding. For example, mutual funds may focus on purchasing (1) equity or debt securities; (2) securities of small or medium-sized corporations; (3) securities of companies in a particular industry, such as energy, computer, or information technology; or (4) foreign investments.

BUSINESS FINANCE COMPANIES

Business finance companies obtain the majority of their funds by selling short-term debt, called commercial paper, to investors in direct credit markets. These funds are used to make a variety of short- and intermediate-term loans and leases to small and large businesses. The loans are often secured by accounts receivable or inventory. Business finance companies are typically more willing than commercial banks to make loans and leases to firms with higher levels of default risk.

Corporations and the Financial System

We began this chapter by saying that financial managers need to understand the financial system in order to make sound decisions. We now follow up on that statement by briefly describing how corporations operate within the financial system. The interaction between the financial system and a large public corporation is shown in Exhibit 2.3. The arrows show the major cash flows for a firm over a typical operating cycle. These cash flows relate to some of the key decisions that the financial manager must make. As you know, those decisions involve three major areas: capital budgeting, financing, and working capital management.

Let's work through an example using Exhibit 2.3 to illustrate how corporate businesses use the financial system. Suppose you are the CFO of a new high-tech firm with business ties to 3M Corporation. The new venture has a well-thought-out business plan, owns some valuable technology, and has one manufacturing facility. The company is large enough to have access to public markets. The company plans to use its core

Exhibit 2.3
Cash Flows between the Firm and the Financial System
This exhibit shows how the financial system helps businesses finance their activities. The arrows in the exhibit indicate the major cash flows into and out of a firm over a typical operating cycle. Money obtained from the financial system, combined with reinvested cash from operations, enables a firm to make necessary investments and fund any other requirements.

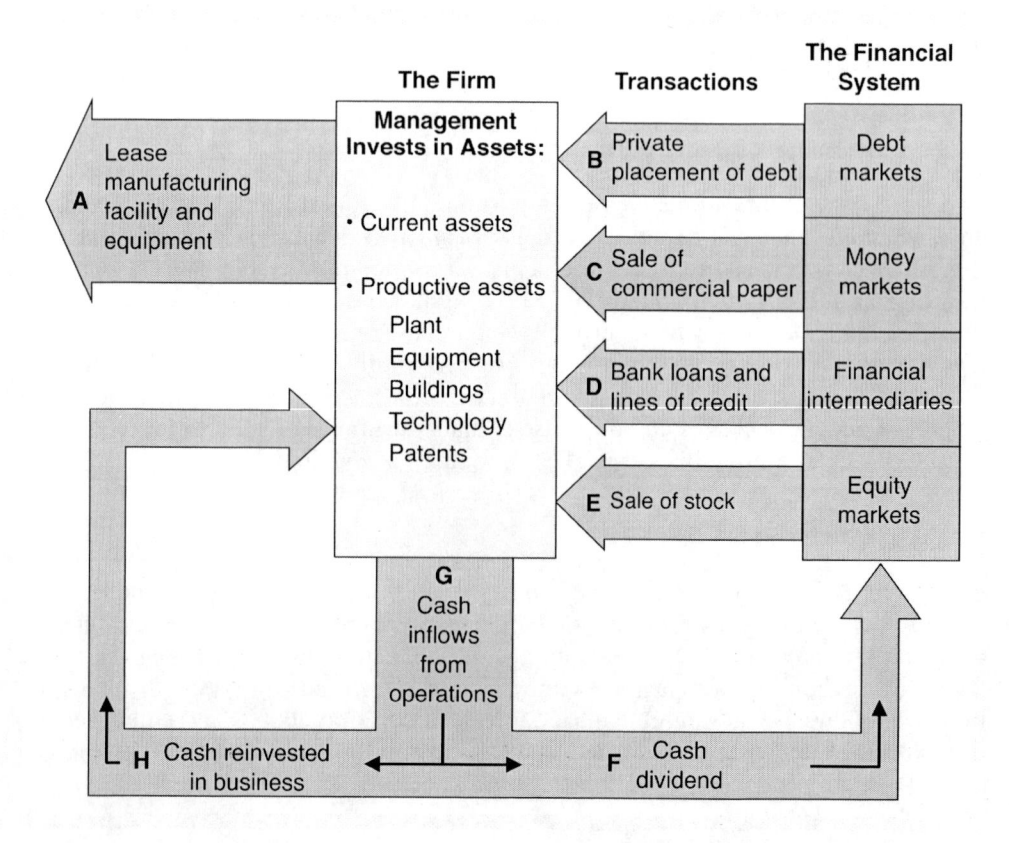

technology to develop and sell a number of new products that the marketing department believes will generate a strong market demand.

To start the new company, management's first task is to sell equity and debt to finance the expansion of the firm. 3M and the senior management team will provide 40 percent of the equity, and the balance will come from an **initial public offering (IPO)** of common stock. An IPO is a corporation's first offering of its stock to the public. For example, management hires Morgan Stanley as its investment bank to underwrite the new securities. After the deal is underwritten, the new venture receives the proceeds from the stock sale, less Morgan Stanley's fees (see arrow E in the exhibit).[6]

In addition to the equity financing, 30 percent of the firm's total funding will come from the sale of long-term debt through a private placement deal with a large insurance company (see arrow B). Management decided to use a private placement because the lender is willing to commit to lend the firm additional money in the future if the firm meets certain performance goals. Since management has ambitious growth plans, locking in a future source of funds is important.

Once the funds from the debt and equity sales are in hand, they are deposited in the firm's checking account at a commercial bank. Management then decides to lease the existing manufacturing facility and equipment to manufacture the new high-technology products; the cash outflow is represented by arrow A.

To begin manufacturing, the firm needs to raise working capital and does this by (1) selling commercial paper in the money markets (arrow C) and (2) getting a line of credit from a bank (arrow D). As the firm becomes operational, it generates cash inflows from its earning assets (arrow G). Some of this cash inflow is reinvested in the firm (arrow H), and the remainder is used to pay a cash dividend to stockholders (arrow F).

> **initial public offering (IPO)**
> the first offering of a corporation's stock to the public

> **Before You Go On**
>
> 1. What is financial intermediation, and why is it important?
> 2. What are some services that commercial banks provide to businesses?
> 3. What is an IPO, and what role does an investment banker play in the process?

2.6 The Determinants of Interest Rate Levels

We conclude this chapter by examining the factors that determine the general level of interest rates in the economy and describing how interest rates vary over the business cycle. Understanding interest rates is important because the financial instruments and most of the financial services discussed in this chapter are priced in terms of interest rates. We will continue our study of interest rates in Chapter 8, where we discuss the structure of interest rates and explain why different firms have different borrowing costs.

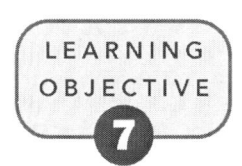

LEARNING OBJECTIVE 7

The Real Rate of Interest

One of the most important economic variables in the economy is the **real rate of interest**—an interest rate determined in the absence of inflation. *Inflation* is the amount by which aggregate price levels rise over time. The real rate of interest measures the inflation-adjusted return earned by lender-savers and represents the inflation-adjusted cost incurred by borrower-spenders when they borrow to finance capital goods. We focus on capital investments because they are the productive assets that create economic wealth in the economy.

The real rate of interest is rarely observable because most industrial economies operate with some degree of inflation, and periods of zero inflation are not common.

> **real rate of interest**
> the interest rate that would exist in the absence of inflation

---
[6]Chapter 15 contains a detailed discussion of the IPO process.

nominal rate of interest
the rate of interest unadjusted for inflation

The rate that we actually observe in the marketplace at a given time is called the **nominal rate of interest**. The factors that determine the real rate of interest, however, are the underlying determinants of all interest rates we observe in the marketplace. For this reason, an understanding of the real rate is important.

DETERMINANTS OF THE REAL RATE OF INTEREST

The fundamental determinants of interest rates are the return earned on capital investments (productive assets) and individuals' time preference for consumption. Let's examine how these two factors interact to determine the real rate of interest.

Return on Investment. Recall from Chapter 1 that businesses invest in capital projects that are expected to generate positive cash flows by producing additional real output—cars, machinery, computers, and video games.[7] The output generated by the capital projects constitutes the return on investment, which is usually measured as a percentage. For example, if a capital investment project with a one-year life costs $1,000 and produces $180 in cash flows, the project's return on investment is 18 percent ($180/$1,000). The higher the return on investment, the more likely a particular project will be undertaken by a firm.

For a capital project to be accepted, its return on investment must exceed the firm's cost of funds (debt and equity); otherwise, the project will be rejected. Intuitively, this decision rule makes sense because if an investment earns a return greater than the firm's cost of funding, it should be profitable and thus should increase the value of the firm. For example, if a firm's average cost of funding—often called the *cost of capital*—is 15 percent, the one-year capital project mentioned above would be accepted (18 percent > 15 percent). If the capital project was expected to earn only 13 percent, though, the project would be rejected (13 percent < 15 percent). The firm's cost of capital is the minimum acceptable rate of return on capital projects.

DECISION-MAKING EXAMPLE 2.1

Capital Budgeting Preview

Situation: Sonic Manufacturing Company's capital budget includes six projects that management has identified as having merit. The CFO's staff computed the return on investment for each project. The firm's average cost of funding is 10 percent. The projects are as follows:

Project	Return on Investment
A	13.0%
B	12.0
C	10.9
D	10.5
E	9.8
F	8.9

Which capital projects should the firm undertake?

Decision: The firm should accept all projects with a return on investment greater than the firm's average cost of funding, which is 10 percent. These projects are A, B, C, and D. As noted in the text, this decision-making principle makes intuitive sense because all projects with a return on investment greater than the cost of funds will increase the value of the firm. In Chapters 10 through 13, we will delve much more deeply into capital budgeting, and you will find out a great deal more about how these decisions are made.

---

[7]Note that *business investment* is just a formal name that economists give to business spending.

2.6 The Determinants of Interest Rate Levels

Time Preference for Consumption. All other things being equal, most people prefer to consume goods today rather than tomorrow. This is called a positive time preference for consumption. For example, most people who want to buy a new car prefer to have it now rather than wait until they have earned enough cash to make the purchase. When people consume today, however, they realize that their future consumption may be less because they have forgone the opportunity to save and earn interest on their savings.

Given people's positive time preference for consumption, the interest rate offered on financial instruments determines how much people will save. At low rates of interest, it hardly makes sense to save, so most people will continue to spend money on cars and TV sets rather than put money aside in savings. To coax people to postpone current spending, interest rates must be raised.

Equilibrium Condition. We have just seen that people save more and spend less when interest rates are higher. Also, higher interest rates choke off business investment (or spending) because fewer business projects can earn a high enough return on investment to cover the added interest cost. Thus, at higher interest rates, people want to spend less on consumer purchases, and businesses want to finance fewer investment projects. At the same time, lender-savers would like to lend more money. The real rate of interest depends on the interaction between these two opposing factors. Using a supply-and-demand framework, Exhibit 2.4 shows that the equilibrium rate of interest (r) is the point where the desired level of lending (L) by lender-savers equals the desired level of borrowing (B) by people and businesses to finance capital projects.[8]

FLUCTUATIONS IN THE REAL RATE

In the supply-and-demand framework discussed above, any economic factor that causes a shift in desired lending or desired borrowing will cause a change in the equilibrium rate of interest. For example, a major breakthrough in technology should cause a shift to

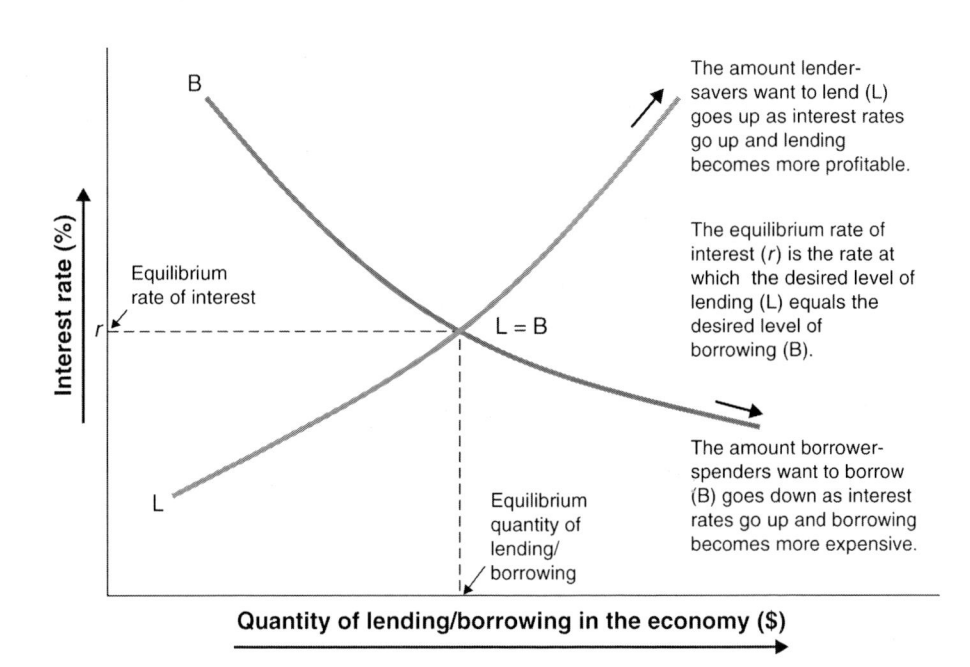

Exhibit 2.4
The Determinants of the Equilibrium Rate of Interest
The equilibrium rate of interest is a function of supply and demand. Lender-savers are willing to supply more funds as interest rates go up, but borrower-spenders demand fewer funds at higher interest rates. The interest rate at which the supply of funds equals the demand for those funds is the equilibrium rate.

---

[8] The model presented here is based on the loanable funds theory of market equilibrium. Saving (or giving up current consumption) is the source of loanable funds, and business spending (or investment) is the use of funds.

the right in the desired level of borrowing schedule, thus increasing the real rate of interest. This makes intuitive sense because the new technology should spawn an increase in investment opportunities, increasing the desired level of borrowing. Similarly, a reduction in the corporate tax rate should provide businesses with more money to spend on investments, which should increase the desired level of borrowing schedule, causing the real rate of interest to increase.

One factor that would shift the desired level of lending to the right, and hence lead to a decrease in the real rate of interest, would be a decrease in the tax rates for individuals. Another would be monetary policy action by the Federal Reserve Bank to increase the money supply.

Other forces that could affect the real rate of interest include growth in population, demographic variables such as the age of the population, and cultural differences. In sum, the real rate of interest reflects a complex set of forces that control the desired level of lending and borrowing in the economy. The real rate of interest has historically been around 3 percent for the U.S. economy, but has varied between 2 and 4 percent because of changes in economic conditions.

Loan Contracts and Inflation

The real rate of interest ignores inflation, but in the real world, price-level changes are a fact of life, and these changes affect the value of a loan contract or, for that matter, any financial contract. For example, if prices rise (inflation) during the life of a loan contract, the purchasing power of the dollar decreases because the borrower repays the lender with inflated dollars—dollars with less buying power.[9]

To see the impact of inflation on a loan, let's look at an example. Suppose that you lend a friend $1,000 for one year at a 4 percent interest rate. Furthermore, you plan to buy a new surfboard for $1,040 in one year when you graduate from college. With the $40 of interest you earn ($1,000 × 0.04), you will have just enough money to buy the surfboard. At the end of the year, you graduate, and your friend pays off the loan, giving you $1,040. Unfortunately, the rate of inflation during the year was an unexpected 10 percent, and your surfboard now will cost 10 percent more, or $1,144 ($1,040 × 1.10). You have experienced a 10 percent decrease in your purchasing power due to the unanticipated inflation. The loss of purchasing power is $104 ($1,144 − $1,040).

The Fisher Equation and Inflation

How do we write a loan contract that provides protection against loss of purchasing power due to inflation? We have no crystal ball to tell us what the actual rate of inflation will be when the loan contract is written. However, market participants collectively (often called "the market") have expectations about how prices will change during the contract period.

To incorporate these "inflation expectations" into a loan contract, we need to adjust the real rate of interest by the amount of inflation that is expected during the contract period. The mathematical formula used to adjust the real rate of interest for the expected rate of inflation is as follows:

$$1 + i = (1 + r) \times (1 + \Delta P_e)$$
$$1 + i = 1 + r + \Delta P_e + r\Delta P_e$$
$$i = r + \Delta P_e + r\Delta P_e$$
(2.1)

---

[9] Recall from economics two important relationships: (1) the value of money is its purchasing power—what you can buy with it and (2) there is a negative relation between changes in price level and the value of money. As the price level increases (inflation), the value of money decreases, and as the price level decreases (deflation), the value of money increases. This makes sense because when we have rising prices (inflation), our dollars will buy less.

where:

i = nominal (or market) rate of interest
r = real rate of interest
ΔP_e = expected annualized price-level change
$r\Delta P_e$ = adjustment of the interest rate for expected price-level change

Equation 2.1 is called the Fisher equation. It is named after Irving Fisher, who first developed the concept and is considered by many to be one of America's greatest economists.

Applying Equation 2.1 to our earlier example, we can find out what the nominal rate of interest should be if the expected inflation rate is 10 percent and the real rate of interest is 4 percent:

$$i = r + \Delta P_e + r\Delta P_e$$
$$= 0.04 + 0.10 + (0.04 \times 0.10)$$
$$= 0.1440, \text{ or } 14.40\%$$

Looking at Equation 2.1, notice that ΔP_e is the *expected* price-level change and not the *realized* (actual) rate of inflation. Thus, to properly determine the nominal rate of interest, it is necessary to predict prices over the life of the loan contract. Also, recall that the nominal rate of interest is the market rate of interest—the rate actually observed in financial markets. The real and nominal rates of interest are equal only when the expected rate of inflation over the contract period is zero ($\Delta P_e = 0$).[10]

When either r or ΔP_e is a small number, or when both are small, then $r\Delta P_e$ is very small and is approximately equal to zero. In these situations, it is common practice to write the Fisher equation as a simple additive function, where the nominal rate of interest is divided into two parts: (1) the real rate of interest and (2) the anticipated percent change in the price level over the life of the loan contract. The simplified Fisher equation can be written as follows:

$$i = r + \Delta P_e \tag{2.2}$$

Thus, for our one-year loan example:

$$i = 0.04 + 0.10 = 0.1400, \text{ or } 14.00\%$$

The difference in the contract loan rates between the two variations of the Fisher equation is 0.40 percent (14.40 − 14.00), a difference of less than 3 percent (0.40/14.40 = 0.0278, or 2.78 percent). Thus, dropping $r\Delta P_e$ from the equation makes the equation easier to understand without creating a significant computational error.

LEARNING BY DOING
APPLICATION 2.2

Calculating a New Inflation Premium

Problem: The current one-year Treasury rate is 4.5 percent. On the evening news, several economists at leading investment and commercial banks predict that the annual inflation rate is going to be 0.25 percent higher than originally expected. The

(continued)

---

[10] In economics the terms *nominal* and *real* are frequently used as modifiers, as in *nominal GNP* and *real GNP*. *Nominal* means that the data are from the marketplace; thus, the values may contain price-level changes due to inflation. *Real* means the data are corrected for changes in purchasing power.

higher inflation forecasts reflect unexpectedly strong employment figures released by the government that afternoon. What is the current inflation premium? When the market opens tomorrow, what should happen to the Treasury rate? (Assume that the real rate of interest is 3.0 percent.)

Approach: You must first estimate the current inflation premium using Equation 2.2. You should then adjust this premium to reflect the economists' revised beliefs. Finally, this revised inflation premium can be used in the Fisher equation to estimate what the Treasury rate will be tomorrow morning.

Solution:
Current inflation premium:

$$i = r + \Delta P_e$$
$$\Delta P_e = i - r$$
$$= 4.5\% - 3.0\%$$
$$= 1.5\%$$

New inflation premium:

$$\Delta P_e = 1.5\% + 0.25\% = 1.75\%$$

The opening Treasury rate in the morning:

$$i = r + \Delta P_e = 3.0\% + 1.75\% = 4.75\%$$

LEARNING BY DOING APPLICATION 2.3

International Consulting Experience

Problem: You are a financial manager at a manufacturing company that is going to make a one-year loan to a key supplier in another country. The loan will be made in the supplier's local currency. The supplier's government controls the banking system, and there is no reliable market data available. For this reason, you have spoken with five economists who have some knowledge about the economy. Their predictions for inflation next year are 30, 40, 45, 50, and 60 percent.

What rate should your firm charge for the one-year business loan if you are not concerned about the possibility that your supplier will default? You recall from your managerial finance course that the real rate of interest is, on average, 3 percent.

Approach: Although the sample of economists is small, it should provide a reasonable estimate of the expected rate of inflation (ΔP_e). This value can be used in Equation 2.2 to calculate the nominal rate of interest.

Solution:

$$\Delta P_e = (30\% + 40\% + 45\% + 50\% + 60\%)/5$$
$$= 225\%/5$$
$$= 45\%$$

Nominal rate of interest:

$$i = r + \Delta P_e$$
$$= 3\% + 45\%$$
$$= 48\%$$

This number is a reasonable estimate, given that you have no market data.

Cyclical and Long-Term Trends in Interest Rates

Now let's look at some market data to see how interest rates have actually fluctuated over the past five decades in the United States. Exhibit 2.5 plots the interest rate yield on 10-year government bonds since 1960 to represent interest rate movements. In addition, the exhibit plots the annual rate of inflation, represented by the annual percent change in the consumer price index (CPI). The CPI is a price index that measures the change in prices of a market basket of goods and services that a typical consumer purchases. Finally, the shaded areas on the chart indicate periods of recession. Recession occurs when real output from the economy is decreasing and unemployment is increasing. Each shaded area begins at the peak of the business cycle and ends at the bottom (or trough) of the recession. From our discussion of interest rates and an examination of Exhibit 2.5, we can draw two general conclusions:

1. *The level of interest rates tends to rise and fall with changes in the actual rate of inflation.* The positive relation between the rate of inflation and the level of interest rates is what we should expect given Equation 2.1. Thus, we feel comfortable concluding that inflationary expectations have a major impact on interest rates.

   Our findings also explain in part why interest rates can vary substantially between countries. For example, during July 2007 the rate of inflation in the United States was 2.7 percent; during the same period, the rate of inflation in Russia was 8.5 percent. If the real rate of interest is 3.0 percent, the short-term

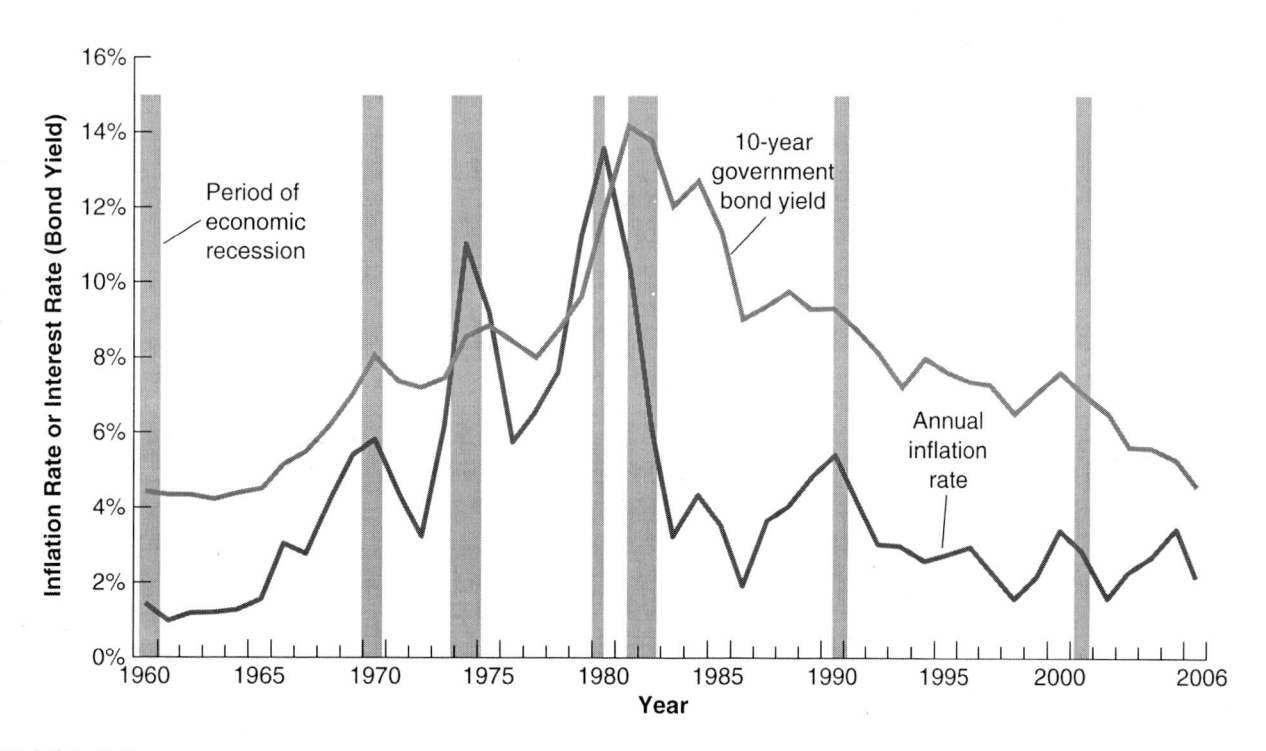

Exhibit 2.5
Relation between Annual Inflation Rate and Long-Term Interest Rate (1960–2006)
Based on the graph shown in the exhibit, we can draw two important conclusions about interest rate movements. First, the level of interest rates tends to rise and fall with the actual rate of inflation—a conclusion also supported by the Fisher Equation, which suggests that interest rates rise and fall with the *expected* rate of inflation. Second, the level of interest rates tends to rise during periods of economic expansion and decline during periods of economic contraction.

interest rate in the United States should have been around 5.7 percent (2.7 + 3.0) and the Russian interest rate should have been around 11.5 percent (3.0 + 8.5). In fact, during that period the U.S. short-term interest rate was 5.3 percent and the Russian rate was 10.0 percent. Though hardly scientific, this analysis illustrates the point that countries with higher rates of inflation or expected rates of inflation will have higher interest rates than countries with lower inflation rates.

2. *The level of interest rates tends to rise during periods of economic expansion and decline during periods of economic contraction.* It makes sense that interest rates should increase during years of economic expansion. The reasoning is that as the economy expands, businesses begin to borrow money to build up inventories and to invest in more production capacity in anticipation of increased sales. As unemployment begins to decrease, the economic future looks bright, and consumers begin to buy more homes, cars, and other durable items on credit. As a result, the demand for funds by both businesses and consumers increases, driving interest rates up. Also, near the end of expansion, the rate of inflation begins to accelerate, which puts upward pressure on interest rates. At some point, the Federal Reserve System (the Fed) becomes concerned over the increasing inflation in the economy and begins to tighten credit, which further raises interest rates, slowing the economy down. The higher interest rates in the economy choke off spending by both businesses and consumers.

During a recession, the opposite takes place; businesses and consumers rein in their spending and their use of credit, putting downward pressure on interest rates. To stimulate demand for goods and services, the Fed will typically begin to make more credit available. The result is to lower interest rates in the economy and encourage business and consumer spending.

Also notice in Exhibit 2.5 that periods of business expansion tend to be much longer than periods of contraction (recessions). Since the end of the Great Depression (1929–1933), the average period of economic expansion has lasted three to four years, and the average period of contraction, about nine months. Keep in mind that the numbers given are averages and that actual periods of economic expansion and contraction can vary widely from averages. For example, the last period of business expansion lasted about 10 years (1990–2001), and the last recession lasted eight months (March 2001 to November 2001).

Planning Ahead by Financial Managers

It is important for a financial manager to understand what factors determine the level of interest rates and what causes interest rates to vary over the business cycle. The financial manager's goal is to obtain funds at the lowest possible cost so that the firm's management can achieve its strategic objectives. The lower the firm's overall cost of funds, the greater the value of the firm.

> Before You Go On
>
> 1. Explain how the real rate of interest is determined.
> 2. How are inflationary expectations accounted for in the nominal rate of interest?
> 3. Explain why interest rates follow the business cycle.

Summary of Learning Objectives

1. **Discuss the primary role of the financial system in the economy, and describe the two basic ways in which fund transfers take place.**

   The primary role of the financial system is to gather money from people and businesses with surplus funds to invest (lender-savers) and channel money to businesses and consumers who need to borrow money (borrower-spenders). If the financial system works properly, only investment projects with high rates of return and good credit are financed and all other projects are rejected. Money flows through the financial system in two basic ways: (1) directly, through financial markets, or (2) indirectly, through financial institutions.

2. **Discuss direct financing and the important role that investment banks play in this process.**

   Direct markets are wholesale markets where large public corporations transact. These corporations sell securities, such as stocks and bonds, directly to investors in exchange for money, which they use to invest in their businesses. Investment banks are important in the direct markets because they help firms sell their new security issues. The services provided by investment bankers include origination, underwriting, and distribution.

3. **Describe the primary and secondary markets, and explain why secondary markets are so important to businesses.**

   Primary markets are markets in which new securities are sold for the first time. Secondary markets provide the aftermarket for securities previously issued. Not all securities have secondary markets. Secondary markets are important because they enable investors to convert securities easily to cash. Business firms whose securities are traded in secondary markets are able to issue new securities at a lower cost than they otherwise could because investors are willing to pay a premium price for securities that have secondary markets.

4. **Explain why money markets are important financial markets for large corporations.**

   Large corporations use money markets to adjust their liquidity because cash inflows and outflows are rarely perfectly synchronized. Thus, on the one hand, if cash expenditures exceed cash receipts, a firm can borrow short-term in the money markets or, if the firm holds a portfolio of money market instruments, it can sell some of these securities for cash. On the other hand, if cash receipts exceed expenditures, the firm can temporarily invest the funds in short-term money market instruments. Businesses are willing to invest large amounts of idle cash in money market instruments because of their high liquidity and their low default risk.

5. **Discuss the most important stock market exchanges and indexes.**

   A traditional stock exchange is an organized market that provides a physical meeting place and communication facilities for members to buy and sell securities under a specific set of rules and regulations. The oldest, largest, and best-known exchange of this kind in the United States is the New York Stock Exchange. Second only to the NYSE in dollar trading volume is NASDAQ, a sophisticated electronic trading system. Indexes are used to measure the performance of the stock market. The major stock market indexes include the Dow Jones Industrial Average, New York Stock Exchange Index, Standard and Poor's 500 Index, and NASDAQ Composite Index.

6. **Explain how financial institutions serve consumers and small businesses that are unable to participate in the direct financial markets and describe how corporations use the financial system.**

   One problem with direct financing is that it takes place in a wholesale market. Most small businesses and consumers do not have the expert skills or the money to transact in this market. In contrast, a large portion of the indirect market focuses on providing financial services to consumers and small businesses. For example, commercial banks collect money from consumers in small dollar amounts by selling them checking accounts, savings accounts, and consumer CDs. They then aggregate the funds and make loans in larger amounts to consumers and businesses. The financial services bought or sold by financial institutions are tailor-made to fit the needs of the market they serve. Exhibit 2.3 illustrates how corporations use the financial system.

7. **Explain how the real rate of interest is determined in the economy, differentiate between the real rate and the nominal rate of interest, and be able to compute the nominal or real rate of interest.**

   The real rate of interest is the interest rate in the economy in the absence of inflation. It is determined by the interaction of (1) the rate of return that businesses can expect to earn on capital goods and (2) individuals' time preference for consumption. The interest rate we observe in the marketplace is called the nominal rate of interest. The nominal rate of interest is composed of two parts: (1) the real rate of interest and (2) the expected rate of inflation. Equations 2.1 and 2.2 are used to compute the nominal (real) rate of interest when you have the real (nominal) rate and the inflation rate.

Summary of Key Equations

Equation	Description	Formula
2.1	Fisher equation	$i = r + \Delta P_e + r\Delta P_e$
2.2	Fisher equation simplified	$i = r + \Delta P_e$

Self-Study Problems

2.1 Economic units that need to borrow money are said to be:
  a. Lender-savers
  b. Borrower-spenders
  c. Balanced budget keepers
  d. None of the above

2.2 Explain what marketability of a security means and how it is determined.

2.3 What are over-the-counter markets (OTCs), and how do they differ from organized exchanges?

2.4 What effect does an increase in demand for business goods and services have on the real interest rate? What other factors can affect the real interest rate?

2.5 How does the business cycle affect the interest rate and inflation rate?

Solutions to Self-Study Problems

2.1 Such units are said to be (b) borrower-spenders.

2.2 Marketability refers to the ease with which a security can be sold and converted into cash. The level of marketability depends on the cost of trading the security and the cost of searching for information. The lower these costs are, the greater the security's marketability.

2.3 Securities that are not listed on an organized exchange are sold OTC. An OTC market differs from an organized exchange in that there is no central trading location. Security transactions are made via phone or computer as opposed to on the floor of an exchange.

2.4 An increase in the demand for business goods and services will cause the borrowing schedule to shift to the right, thus increasing the real rate of interest. Other factors that can affect the real interest rate are increases in productivity, changes in technology, or changes in the corporate tax rate. Demographic factors, such as growth or age of the population, and cultural differences can also affect the real rate of interest.

2.5 Both the nominal interest and inflation rates follow the business cycle; that is, they rise with economic expansion and fall during a recession.

Critical Thinking Questions

2.1 Explain why total financial assets in the economy must equal total financial liabilities.

2.2 Why don't small businesses make greater use of the direct credit markets since these markets enable firms to finance their activities at a very low cost?

2.3 Explain the economic role of brokers and dealers. How does each make a profit?

2.4 Why were commercial banks prohibited from engaging in investment banking activities beginning in the 1930s?

2.5 What are the two basic services that investment banks provide in the economy?

2.6 Many large corporations sell commercial paper as a source of funds. From time to time, some of these firms find that they are unable to issue commercial paper. Why is this true?

2.7 How do large corporations adjust their liquidity in the money markets?

2.8 Shouldn't the nominal rate of interest (Equation 2.1) be determined by the actual rate of inflation (ΔP_a), which can be easily measured, rather than by the expected rate of inflation (ΔP_e)?

2.9 How does Exhibit 2.5 help explain why interest rates were so high during the early 1980s as compared to the relatively low interest rates in the early 1960s?

2.10 When determining the real interest rate, what happens to businesses that find themselves with unfunded capital projects whose rate of return exceeds the firms' cost of capital?

Questions and Problems

2.1 Financial System: What is the role of the financial system, and what are the two major components of the financial system?

2.2 Financial System: What does a competitive financial system imply about interest rates?

2.3 Financial System: What is the difference between saver-lenders and borrower-spenders, and who are the major representatives of each group?

2.4 Financial Markets: List the two ways in which a transfer of funds takes place in an economy. What is the main difference between these two?

2.5 Financial Markets: Suppose you own a security that you know can be easily sold in the secondary market, but the security will sell at a lower price than you paid for it. What would this mean for the security's marketability and liquidity?

2.6 Financial Markets: Why are direct financial markets also called wholesale markets?

2.7 Financial Markets: Trader Inc. is a $300 million company, as measured by asset value, and Horst Corp. is a $35 million company. Both are privately held corporations. Explain which firm is more likely to go public and register with the SEC, and why.

2.8 Primary Markets: What is a primary market? What does IPO stand for?

2.9 Primary Market: Identify whether the following transactions are primary market or secondary market transactions.
   a. Jim Hendry bought 300 shares of IBM through his brokerage account.
   b. Peggy Jones bought $5,000 of IBM bonds from the firm.
   c. Hathaway Insurance Company bought 500,000 shares of Trigen Corp. when the company issued stock.

2.10 Investment Banking: What does it mean to "underwrite" a new security issue? What compensation does an investment banker get from underwriting a security issue?

2.11 Investment Banking: Cranjet Inc. is issuing 10,000 bonds, and its investment banker has guaranteed a price of $985 per bond. The investment banker sells the entire issue to investors for $10,150,000.
   a. What is the underwriting spread for this issue?
   b. What is the percentage underwriting cost?
   c. How much did Cranjet raise?

2.12 Financial Institutions: What are some of the ways in which a financial institution or intermediary can raise money?

2.13 Financial Institutions: How do financial institutions act as "intermediaries" to provide services to small businesses?

2.14 Financial Institutions: Which financial institution is usually the most important to businesses?

2.15 Financial Markets: What is the main difference between money markets and capital markets?

2.16 Stock Market Index: What is a stock market index? List three stock market indexes.

2.17 Stock Market Index: What is the Dow Jones Industrial Average?

2.18 Stock Market Index: What does NASDAQ represent?

2.19 Money Markets: What are U.S. Treasury bills?

2.20 Money Markets: Besides U.S. Treasury bills, what are other money market instruments?

2.21 Money Markets: What is the primary role of money markets? Explain how money markets work.

2.22 Capital Markets: How do capital market instruments differ from money market instruments?

2.23 Interest Rates: What are the major differences between public and private markets?

2.24 Financial Instruments: What are the two risk-hedging instruments discussed in the chapter?

2.25 Interest Rates: What is the real rate of interest, and how is it determined?

2.26 Interest Rates: How does the nominal rate of interest vary over time?

2.27 Interest Rates: What is the Fisher equation, and how is it used?

2.28 Interest Rates: Imagine you borrow $500 from your roommate, agreeing to pay her back $500 plus 7 percent nominal interest in one year. Assume inflation over the life of the contract is expected to be 4.25 percent. What is the total dollar amount you will have to pay her back in a year? What percentage of the interest payment is the result of the real rate of interest?

2.29 Interest Rates: Your parents have given you $1,000 a year before your graduation so that you can take a trip when you graduate. You wisely decide to invest the money in a bank CD that pays 6.75 percent interest. You know that the trip costs $1,025 right now and that inflation for the year is predicted to be 4 percent. Will you have enough money in a year to purchase the trip?

2.30 Interest Rates: When are the nominal and real interest rates equal?

Sample Test Problems

2.1 How are brokers different from dealers?

2.2 What is the S&P 500 Index?

2.3 Identify what type of transactions (direct or indirect) the following are:
   a. You buy 200 shares of Fidelity Growth Mutual Fund.
   b. Roger buys a bank CD for $5,000.
   c. Bank of America makes a $25,000 loan to Leila's Coffee Shop.
   d. Nora buys $3,000 of Xerox bonds from a new issue.

2.4 If the nominal rate of interest is 7.5 percent and the real rate is 4 percent, what is the expected inflation premium?

2.5 What is the relationship between business cycles and the general level of interest rates?

FINANCIAL STATEMENTS, CASH FLOWS, AND TAXES

CHAPTER 3

LEARNING OBJECTIVES

1. Discuss generally accepted accounting principles (GAAP) and their importance to the economy.
2. Know the balance sheet identity, and explain why a balance sheet must balance.
3. Describe how market-value balance sheets differ from book-value balance sheets.
4. Identify the basic equation for the income statement and the information it provides.
5. Explain the difference between cash flows and accounting income.
6. Explain how the four major financial statements discussed in this chapter are related.
7. Discuss the difference between average and marginal tax rates.

Suzi Altman/NewsCom

The new millennium has been a difficult period for the accounting profession. A case in point is the bankruptcy filing of WorldCom, whose officers had misstated $7.2 billion of expenses in the firm's financial statements. As accounting misconduct cases mounted in the early 2000s, investors and creditors became more and more concerned about the reliability and integrity of the financial statements of U.S.-based firms. To restore investor confidence and protect U.S. financial markets, Congress and federal regulators tightened accounting standards and oversight of the accounting profession. Passage of the Sarbanes-Oxley Act, discussed in Chapter 1, is an example of these steps.

There are many reasons for the accounting scandals that plagued the U.S. economy in the early years of this century. Many observers, however, place some of the blame on Wall Street's obsession with the earnings estimates set by financial analysts. Analysts estimate how much firms should earn in a particular reporting period, and firms that fail to meet these estimates can be severely punished by falling stock prices—and their CEOs can find themselves out of a job. These intense pressures led some firms to engage in a questionable practice called "backing in." It works as follows: Instead of starting by calculating sales and subtracting expenses and taxes to get profits, they work backward—that is, they start with the profits that analysts are expecting and then manipulate sales and expenses to make sure the numbers work out.

Clearly, the correct preparation of financial statements is crucial. In this chapter and the next, we focus on the preparation, interpretation, and limitations of financial statements. As you will see, the preparation of financial statements is not a cut-and-dried affair but involves considerable professional judgment, which can and does lead to variations in financial statements.

CHAPTER PREVIEW

In Chapter 1 we noted that all businesses have stakeholders—managers, creditors, suppliers, and the government, among others—who have some claim on the firms' cash flows. The stakeholders in a firm, along with the stockholders, need to monitor the firm's progress and evaluate its performance. Financial statements enable them to do these things. The accounting system is the framework that gathers information about the firm's business activities and translates the information into objective numerical financial reports.

Most firms prepare financial statements on a regular basis and have independent auditors certify that the financial statements have been prepared in accordance with generally accepted accounting principles and contain no material misstatements. The audit increases the confidence of the stakeholders that the financial statements prepared by management present a "fair and accurate" picture of the firm's financial condition at a particular point in time. In fact, it is difficult to get any type of legitimate business loan without audited financial statements.

This chapter reviews the basic structure of a firm's financial statements and explains how the various statements fit together. We examine the preparation of the balance sheet, the income statement, the statement of retained earnings, and the statement of cash flows. As you read through this part of the chapter, pay particular attention to the differences between (1) cash flows and accounting income and (2) book value and market value. Understanding the differences between these two sets of concepts is necessary to avoid serious analytical and decision-making errors. The last part of the chapter discusses essential features of the federal tax code for corporations. In finance we make most decisions on an after-tax basis, so understanding the tax code is very important.

3.1 Financial Statements and Accounting Principles

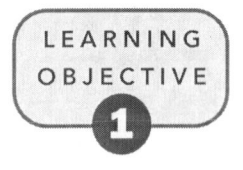

LEARNING OBJECTIVE 1

Before we can meaningfully interpret and analyze financial statements, we need to understand some accounting principles that guide their preparation. Thus, we begin the chapter with a discussion of generally accepted accounting principles, which guide firms in the preparation of financial statements. First, however, we briefly discuss the annual report.

Annual Reports

To see samples of annual reports from a variety of companies, visit http://www.zpub.com/sf/arl.

The *annual report* is the most important report that firms issue to their stockholders and make available to the general public. Historically, annual reports were dull, black-and-white publications that presented the firm's audited financial statements. Today some annual reports, especially those of large public companies, are slick, picture-laden, glossy "magazines" in full color with orchestrated media messages exalting the deeds of top management.

Annual reports typically are divided into three distinct sections. First are the financial tables, which contain financial information about the firm and its operations for the year, and an accompanying summary explaining the firm's performance over the past year. For example, the summary might explain that sales and profits were down because of lost sales in the Gulf States due to Hurricane Katrina in 2005. Often, there is a letter from the chairman or CEO that provides some insights into the reasons for the firm's performance, a discussion of new developments, and a high-level view of the firm's strategy and future direction. It is important to note that the financial tables are historical records reflecting past performance of the firm and do not necessarily indicate what the firm will do in the future.

The second part of the report is often a corporate public relations piece discussing the firm's product lines, its services to its customers, and its contributions to the communities in which it operates.

The third part of the annual report presents the audited financial statements: the balance sheet, the income statement, the statement of retained earnings, and the statement of cash flows. Overall, the annual report provides a good overview of the firm's operating and financial performance and states why, in management's judgment, things turned out the way they did.

Generally Accepted Accounting Principles

In the United States, accounting statements are prepared in accordance with **generally accepted accounting principles (GAAP)**, a set of widely agreed-upon rules and procedures that define how companies are to maintain financial records and prepare financial reports. These principles are important because without them, financial statements would be less standardized. Accounting standards such as GAAP make it easier for analysts and management to make meaningful comparisons of a company's performance against that of other companies.

Accounting principles and reporting practices for U.S. firms are promulgated by the Financial Accounting Standards Board (FASB), a not-for-profit body that operates in the public interest. FASB derives its authority from the Securities and Exchange Commission (SEC). GAAP and reporting practices are published in the form of FASB statements, and certified public accountants are required to follow these statements in their auditing and accounting practices.

> **generally accepted accounting principles (GAAP)**
> a set of rules that defines how companies are to prepare financial statements

> You can find more information about FASB at www.fasb.org.

Fundamental Accounting Principles

To better understand financial statements, it is helpful to look at some fundamental accounting principles embodied in GAAP. These principles determine the manner of recording, measuring, and reporting company transactions. As you will see, the practical application of these principles requires professional judgment, which can result in considerable differences in financial statements.

THE ASSUMPTION OF ARM'S-LENGTH TRANSACTIONS

Accounting is based on the recording of economic transactions that can be quantified in dollar amounts. It assumes that the parties to a transaction are economically rational and are free to act *independently* of each other. To illustrate, let's assume that you are preparing a personal balance sheet for a bank loan on which you must list all your assets. You are including your BMW 325 as an asset. You bought the car a few months ago from your father for $3,000 when the retail price of the car was $15,000. You got a good deal. However, the price you paid, which would be the number recorded on your balance sheet, was not the market price. Since you did not purchase the BMW in an arm's-length transaction, your balance sheet would not reflect the true value of the asset.

THE COST PRINCIPLE

Generally, the value of an asset that is recorded on a company's "books" reflects its historical cost. The historical cost is assumed to represent the fair market value of the item at the time it was acquired and is recorded as the **book value**. Over time, it is unlikely that an asset's book value will be equal to its market value because market values tend to change over time. The major exception to this principle is marketable securities, such as the stock of another company, which are recorded at their current market value.

> **book value**
> the net value of an asset or liability recorded on the financial statements—normally reflects historical cost

It is important to note that accounting statements are records of past performance; they are based on historical costs, not on current market prices or values. Accounting statements translate the business's past performance into dollars and cents, which helps management and investors better understand how the business has performed in the past.

THE REALIZATION PRINCIPLE

Under the realization principle, revenue is recognized only when the sale is virtually completed and the exchange value for the goods or services can be reliably determined. As a practical matter, this means that most revenues are recognized at the time of sale whether or not cash is actually received. At this time, if a firm sells to its customers on credit, an account receivable is recorded. The firm receives the cash only when the customer actually makes the payment. Although the realization principle concept seems straightforward, there can be considerable ambiguity in its interpretation. For example, should revenues be recognized when goods are ordered, when they are shipped, or when payment is received from the customer?

THE MATCHING PRINCIPLE

Accounting tries to match revenue on the income statement with the expenses used to generate the revenue. In practice, this principle means that revenue is first recognized (according to the realization principle) and then is matched with the costs associated with producing the revenue. For example, if we manufacture a product and sell it on credit (accounts receivable), the revenue is recognized at the time of sale. The expenses associated with manufacturing the product—expenditures for raw materials, labor, equipment, and facilities—will be recognized at the same time. Notice that the actual cash outflows for expenses may not occur at the same time the expenses are recognized. It should be clear that the figures on the income statement more than likely will not correspond to the actual cash inflows and outflows during the period.

THE GOING CONCERN ASSUMPTION

The going concern assumption is the assumption that a business will remain in operation for the foreseeable future. This assumption underlies much of what is done in accounting. For example, suppose that Kmart has $4.6 billion of inventory on its balance sheet, representing what the firm actually paid for the inventory in arm's-length transactions. If we assume that Kmart is a going concern, the balance sheet figure is a reasonable number because in the normal course of business we expect Kmart to be able to sell the goods for its cost plus some reasonable markup.

However, suppose Kmart declares bankruptcy and is forced by its creditors to liquidate its assets. If this happens, Kmart is no longer a going concern. What will the inventory be worth then? We cannot be certain, but 50 cents on the dollar might be a high figure. The going concern assumption allows the accountant to record assets at cost rather than their value in a liquidation sale, which is usually much less.

You can see that the fundamental accounting principles just discussed leave considerable professional discretion to accountants in the preparation of financial statements. As a result, financial statements can and do differ because of honest differences in professional judgments. Of course, there are limits on "honest professional differences," and at some point, an accountant's choices can cross a line and result in "cooking the books."

International GAAP

Accounting is often called the language of business. Just as there are different dialects within languages, there are different international "dialects" in accounting. For example, the set of generally accepted accounting principles in the United Kingdom is called

U.K. GAAP. With the emergence of the European Union (EU), member countries are moving toward a "European GAAP." In other parts of the world, the accounting system used often depends on a country's history. For example, Hong Kong and India, which were once colonies of England, use a variant of the British accounting system.

The good news is that it is not difficult for accountants to adjust financial statements so that meaningful comparisons can be made between statements based on differing accounting principles. At the same time, these adjustments represent an economic inefficiency that adds a cost to international business transactions.

As more businesses operate internationally and world economies become more integrated, maintaining and translating between different accounting systems makes less and less economic sense. Economic and political pressures are thus building in both the United States and Europe to develop a unified accounting system. As of now, the adoption of a common accounting standard by the United States and Europe is not around the corner. How soon it will occur depends on the political climate between the two economic powers and the continued globalization of commerce.

Illustrative Company: Diaz Manufacturing

In the next part of the chapter, we turn to a discussion of four fundamental financial statements: the balance sheet, the income statement, the statement of retained earnings, and the statement of cash flows. To more clearly illustrate these financial statements, we use data from Diaz Manufacturing Company, a fictional Houston-based provider of petroleum and industrial equipment and services worldwide.[1] Diaz Manufacturing was formed in 2003 as a spin-off of several divisions of Cooper Industries. The firm specializes in the design and manufacturing of systems used in petroleum production and has two divisions: (1) Diaz Energy Services, which sells oil and gas compression equipment, and (2) Diaz Manufacturing, which makes valves and related parts for energy production.

In 2008 Diaz Manufacturing's sales increased to $1.56 billion, an increase of 12.8 percent from the previous year. A letter to stockholders in the 2008 annual report stated that management did not expect earnings in 2009 to exceed the 2008 earnings. The reason for caution was that Diaz's earnings are very susceptible to changes in the political and economic environment in the world's energy-producing regions, and in 2008 the environment in the Middle East was highly unstable. Management reassured investors, however, that Diaz had the financial strength and the management team needed to weather any economic adversity.

> **Before You Go On**
>
> 1. What types of information does a firm's annual report contain?
> 2. What is the realization principle, and why may it lead to a difference in the timing of when revenues are recognized on the books and cash is collected?

3.2 The Balance Sheet

The **balance sheet** reports the firm's financial position at a particular point in time. Exhibit 3.1 shows the balance sheets for Diaz Manufacturing on December 31, 2007 and December 31, 2008. The left-hand side of the balance sheet identifies the firm's assets, most of which are listed at book value. These assets are owned by the firm and

LEARNING OBJECTIVE 2

---

[1] Although Diaz Manufacturing Company is not a real firm, the financial statements and situations presented are based on a composite of actual firms.

Exhibit 3.1 Diaz Manufacturing Balance Sheets as of December 31 ($ millions)

Assets	2008	2007	Liabilities and Stockholders' Equity	2008	2007
Cash[a]	$ 288.5	$ 16.6	Accounts payable and accruals	$ 349.3	$ 325.0
Accounts receivable	306.2	268.8	Notes payable	10.5	4.2
Inventories	423.8	372.7	Accrued taxes	18.0	16.8
Other current assets	21.3	29.9	Total current liabilities	$ 377.8	$ 346.0
Total current assets	$1,039.8	$ 688.0	Long-term debt	574.0	305.6
Plant and equipment	911.6	823.3	Total liabilities	$ 951.8	$ 651.6
Less: Accumulated depreciation	512.2	429.1	Preferred stock[b]	—	—
Net plant and equipment	$ 399.4	$ 394.2	Common stock (54,566,054 shares)[c]	50.0	50.0
Goodwill and other assets	450.0	411.6	Additional paid-in capital	842.9	842.9
			Retained earnings	67.8	(50.7)
			Treasury stock (571,320 shares)	(23.3)	—
			Total stockholders' equity	$ 937.4	$ 842.2
Total assets	$1,889.2	$1,493.8	Total liabilities and equity	$1,889.2	$1,493.8

[a]Cash includes marketable securities.
[b]10,000,000 preferred stock shares authorized.
[c]150,000,000 common stock shares authorized.

The left-hand side of the balance sheet lists the assets that the firm has at a particular point in time, while the right-hand side shows how the firm has financed those assets.

---

balance sheet
financial statement that shows a firm's financial position (assets, liabilities, and equity) at a point in time

Go to the EDGAR database at www.sec.gov, the Web site of the SEC, to see the financial statements of any publicly traded company.

are used to generate income. The right-hand side of the balance sheet includes liabilities and stockholders' equity, which tell us how the firm has financed its assets. Liabilities are obligations of the firm that represent claims against its assets. These claims arise from debts and other obligations to pay creditors, employees, or the government. In contrast, stockholders' equity represents the residual claim of the owners on the remaining assets of the firm after all liabilities have been paid.[2] The basic balance sheet identity can thus be stated as follows:[3]

$$\text{Total assets} = \text{Total liabilities} + \text{Total stockholders' equity} \quad (3.1)$$

Since stockholders' equity is the residual claim, stockholders would receive the residual value if the firm decided to sell off all of its assets and use the money to pay its creditors. That is why the balance sheet always balances. Simply put, if you total what the firm owns and what it owes, then the difference between the two is the total stockholders' equity:

$$\text{Total stockholders' equity} = \text{Total assets} - \text{Total liabilities}$$

Notice that total stockholders' equity can be positive, negative, or equal to zero.

Next, we examine some important balance sheet accounts of Diaz Manufacturing as of December 31, 2008 (see Exhibit 3.1). As a matter of convention, accountants divide assets and liabilities into short-term (or current) and long-term parts. We will start by looking at current assets and liabilities.

---

[2]The terms *owners' equity, stockholders' equity, shareholders' equity, net worth,* and *equity* are used interchangeably to refer to the ownership of a corporation's stock.

[3]An *identity* is an equation that is true by definition; thus, a balance sheet must balance.

Current Assets and Liabilities

Current assets are assets that can reasonably be expected to be converted into cash within one year. Besides cash, which includes marketable securities, other current assets are accounts receivable, which are typically payable within 30 to 45 days, and inventory, which is money invested in raw materials, work-in-process inventory, and finished goods. Diaz's current assets total $1,039.8 million.

Current liabilities are obligations payable within one year. Typical current liabilities are accounts payable, which arise in the purchases of goods and services from vendors and are normally paid within 30 to 60 days; notes payable, which are formal borrowing agreements with a bank or some other lender that have a stated maturity; and accrued taxes from federal, state, and local governments, which are taxes Diaz owes but has not yet paid. Diaz's total current liabilities equal $377.8 million.

NET WORKING CAPITAL

Recall from Chapter 1 that the dollar difference between total current assets and total current liabilities is the firm's net working capital:

$$\text{Net working capital} = \text{Total current assets} - \text{Total current liabilities} \quad (3.2)$$

Net working capital is a measure of a firm's liquidity, which is the ability of the firm to meet its obligations as they come due. One way that firms maintain their liquidity is by holding assets that are highly liquid. Recall that the liquidity of an asset is how quickly it can be converted into cash without loss of value. Thus, an asset's liquidity has two dimensions: (1) the speed and ease with which the asset can be sold and (2) whether the asset can be sold without loss of value. Of course, any asset can be sold easily and quickly if the price is low enough.

For Diaz Manufacturing, total current assets are $1,039.8 million, and total current liabilities are $377.8 million. The firm's net working capital is thus:

$$\begin{aligned}\text{Net working capital} &= \text{Total current assets} - \text{Total current liabilities} \\ &= \$1{,}039.8 \text{ million} - \$377.8 \text{ million} \\ &= \$662.0 \text{ million}\end{aligned}$$

To interpret this number, if Diaz Manufacturing took its current stock of cash and liquidated its marketable securities, accounts receivables, and inventory at book value, it would have $1,039.8 million with which to pay off its short-term liabilities of $377.8 million, leaving $662.0 million of "cushion." As a short-term creditor, such as a bank, you would view the net working capital position as positive because Diaz's current assets exceed current liabilities by almost three times ($1,039.8/$377.8 = 2.75).

ACCOUNTING FOR INVENTORY

Inventory, as noted earlier, is a current asset on the balance sheet, but it is usually the least liquid of the current assets. The reason is that it can take a long time for a firm to convert inventory into cash. For a manufacturing firm, the inventory cycle begins with raw materials, continues with goods in process, proceeds with finished goods, and finally concludes with selling the asset for cash or an account receivable. For a firm such as The Boeing Company, for example, the inventory cycle in manufacturing an aircraft can be nearly a year.

An important decision for management is the selection of an inventory valuation method. The most common methods are FIFO (first in, first out) and LIFO (last in, first out). During periods of changing price levels, how a firm values its inventory affects both its balance sheet and its income statement. For example, suppose that prices have been rising (inflation). If a company values its inventory using the FIFO method, when the firm makes a sale, it assumes the sale is from the oldest, lowest-cost inventory—first in, first out. Thus, during rising prices, firms using FIFO will have the lowest cost of goods sold, the highest net income, and the highest inventory value. In contrast, a company using the LIFO method assumes the sale is from the newest, highest-cost inventory—last in, first out. During a period of inflation, firms using LIFO will have the highest cost of goods sold, the lowest net income, and the lowest inventory value.

Because inventory valuation methods can have a significant impact on both the income statement and the balance sheet, when financial analysts compare different companies, they make adjustments to the financial statements for differences in inventory valuation methods. Although firms can switch from one inventory valuation method to another, this type of change is an extraordinary event and cannot be done frequently.

Diaz Manufacturing reports inventory values in the United States using the LIFO method. The remaining inventories, which are located outside the United States and Canada, are calculated using the FIFO method. Diaz's total inventory is $423.8 million.

Long-Term Assets and Liabilities

The remaining assets on the balance sheet are classified as long-term assets. Typically, these assets are financed by long-term liabilities and stockholders' equity.

LONG-TERM ASSETS

Long-term or productive assets are the assets that the firm uses to generate most of its income. Long-term assets may be tangible or intangible. Tangible assets are balance sheet items such as land, mineral resources, buildings, equipment, machinery, and vehicles that are used over an extended period of time. In addition, tangible assets can include other businesses that a firm wholly or partially owns, such as foreign subsidiaries. Intangible assets are items such as patents, copyrights, licensing agreements, technology, and other intellectual capital the firm owns.

Goodwill is an intangible asset that arises only when a firm purchases another firm. Conceptually, goodwill is a measure of how much the value of the acquired firm exceeds the sum of the values of its individual assets. This additional value is created by the way in which those assets are being used. For example, if Diaz Manufacturing paid $2.0 million for a company that had individual assets with a total fair market value of $1.9 million, the goodwill premium paid would be $100,000 ($2.0 million − $1.9 million).

Diaz Manufacturing's long-term assets comprise net plant and equipment of $399.4 million and intangible and other assets of $450.0 million, as shown in Exhibit 3.1. The term *net plant and equipment* indicates that accumulated depreciation has been subtracted to arrive at the net value. That is, net plant and equipment equals total plant and equipment less accumulated depreciation; accumulated depreciation is the total amount of depreciation expense taken on plant and equipment up to the balance sheet date. For Diaz Manufacturing, the above method yields the following result:

Net plant and equipment = Total plant and equipment − Accumulated depreciation
= $911.6 million − $512.2 million
= $399.4 million

ACCUMULATED DEPRECIATION

depreciation
allocation of the cost of an asset over its estimated life to reflect the wear and tear on the asset as it is used to produce the firm's goods and services

When a firm acquires a tangible asset that deteriorates with use and wears out, accountants try to allocate the asset's cost over its useful life. The matching principle requires that the cost be expensed against the period in which the firm benefited from use of the asset. Thus, **depreciation** allocates the cost of a limited-life asset to the periods in which the firm is assumed to benefit from the asset. Tangible assets with an unlimited life, such as land, are not depreciated. Depreciation affects the balance sheet through the accumulated depreciation account; we discuss its effect on the income statement in Section 3.4.

A company can elect whether to depreciate its assets using straight-line depreciation or one of the approved accelerated depreciation methods. Accelerated depreciation methods allow for more depreciation expense in the early years of an asset's life than straight-line depreciation.

Diaz Manufacturing uses the straight-line method of depreciation. Had Diaz elected to use accelerated depreciation, the value of its depreciable assets would have been written off to the income statement more quickly (higher depreciation expense), resulting in a lower "net plant and equipment" account on its balance sheet and a lower net income for the period.

LONG-TERM LIABILITIES

Long-term liabilities include debt instruments due and payable beyond one year as well as other long-term obligations of the firm. They include bonds, bank term loans, mortgages, and other types of liabilities, such as pension obligations and deferred compensation. Typically, firms finance long-term assets with long-term liabilities. Diaz Manufacturing has a single long-term liability of $574.0 million, which is a long-term debt.

Equity

We have summarized the types of assets and liabilities that appear on the balance sheet. Now we look at the equity accounts. Diaz Manufacturing's total stockholders' equity at the end of 2008 is $937.4 million and is made up of four accounts—common stock, additional paid-in capital, retained earnings, and treasury stock—which we discuss next. We conclude with a discussion of preferred stock. Although preferred stock appears on Diaz Manufacturing's balance sheets, the company has no shares of preferred stock outstanding.

THE COMMON STOCK ACCOUNTS

The most important equity accounts are those related to the common stock, which represent the true ownership of the firm. Certain basic rights of ownership typically come with common stock; those rights are as follows:

1. The right to vote on corporate matters such as the election of the board of directors or important actions such as the purchase of another company.

2. The preemptive right, which allows stockholders to purchase any additional shares of stock issued by the corporation in proportion to the number of shares they currently own. This allows common stockholders to retain the same percentage of ownership in the firm, if they choose to do so.

3. The right to receive cash dividends if they are paid.

4. If the firm is liquidated, the right to all remaining corporate assets after all creditors and preferred stockholders have been paid.

A common source of confusion is the number of different common stock accounts, each of which identifies a source of the firm's equity. The *common stock account* identifies the initial funding from investors that was used to start the business and is priced at a par value. The par value is an arbitrary number set by management, usually a nominal amount such as $1.

Clearly, par value has little to do with the market value of the stock. The *additional paid-in capital account* is the amount of capital received for the common stock in excess of par value. Thus, if the new business is started with $40,000 in cash and the firm decides to issue 1,000 shares of common stock with a par value of $1, the owners' equity account looks as follows:

Common stock (1,000 shares @ $1 par value)	$ 1,000
Additional paid-in capital	39,000
Total paid-in capital	$40,000

Note the money put up by the initial investors: $1,000 in total par value (1,000 shares of common stock with a par value of $1) and $39,000 additional paid-in capital, for a total of $40,000.

As you can see in Exhibit 3.1, Diaz manufacturing has 54,566,054 shares of common stock with a par value of 91.63 cents, for a total value of $50.0 million (54,566,054 shares × 91.63 cents). The additional paid-in capital is $842.9 million. Thus, Diaz's total paid-in capital is $892.9 million ($50.0 + $842.9).

RETAINED EARNINGS

The retained earnings account represents earnings that have been retained and reinvested in the business over time rather than being paid out as cash dividends. Diaz Manufacturing's retained earnings account is only $67.8 million, compared with the total paid-in capital of $892.9 million. Reading the annual report, we learn that in the recent past the company "wrote down" a substantial amount of assets. This transaction, which will be discussed later in the chapter, reduced the size of the retained earnings account.

Note that retained earnings are not the same as cash. In fact, a company can have a very large retained earnings account and no cash. Conversely, it can have lots of cash and a very small retained earnings account. Because retained earnings appear on the liability side of the balance sheet, they do not represent an asset, as cash and marketable securities do.

TREASURY STOCK

treasury stock
stock that the firm has repurchased from investors

The **treasury stock** account represents stock that the firm has purchased back from investors. Publicly traded companies can simply buy shares of stock from stockholders on the market at the prevailing price. Typically, repurchased stock is held as "treasury stock," and the firm can reissue it in the future if it desires. Diaz Manufacturing has spent a total of $23.3 million to repurchase the 571,320 shares of common stock it currently holds as treasury stock. The company has had a policy of repurchasing common stock, which has been subsequently reissued to senior executives under the firm's stock-option plan.

You may wonder why a firm's management would repurchase its own stock. This is a classic finance question, and it has no simple answer. The conventional wisdom is that when a company has excess cash and management believes its stock price is undervalued, it makes sense to purchase stock with the cash.

However, it is not obvious that management can beat the market over the long term when buying and selling company stock. A case in point is Hewlett-Packard (HP), the computer equipment giant, which spent $6.4 billion to purchase its own shares from November 1998 to July 2000 at an average price per share of $53.60. At the time, HP's public relations department said the shares were a "bargain." But as of March 15, 2007, about seven years later, the "bargain" shares traded for about $40.22 per share. Furthermore, bear in mind that the company could have used those funds to pay down debt, finance new products and development, or finance strategic acquisitions or could simply have kept the cash for a rainy day.

PREFERRED STOCK

Preferred stock is a cross between common stock and long-term debt. Preferred stock pays dividends at a specified fixed rate, which means that the firm cannot increase or decrease the dividend rate, regardless of whether the firm's earnings increase or decrease. However, like common stock dividends, preferred stock dividends are declared by the board of directors, and in the event of financial distress, the board can elect not to pay a preferred stock dividend. If preferred stock dividends are missed, the firm is typically required to pay dividends that have been skipped in the past before they can pay dividends to common stockholders. In the event of bankruptcy, preferred stockholders are paid before common stockholders but after bondholders and other creditors. As shown in Exhibit 3.1, Diaz Manufacturing has no preferred stock outstanding, but the company is authorized to issue up to 10 million shares of preferred stock.

> Before You Go On
>
> 1. What is net working capital? Why might a low value for this number be considered undesirable?
> 2. Explain the accounting concept behind depreciation.
> 3. What is treasury stock?

3.3 Market Value versus Book Value

Although accounting statements are helpful to analysts and managers, they have a number of limitations. One of these limitations, mentioned earlier, is that accounting statements are historical—they are based on data such as the cost of a building that was built years ago. Thus, the value of assets on the balance sheet is what the firm paid for them and not their current **market value**—the amount they are worth today.

Investors and management, however, care about how the company will do in the future. The best information concerning how much a company's assets can earn in the future, as well as how much of a burden its liabilities are, comes from the current market value of those assets and liabilities. Accounting statements would therefore be more valuable if they measured current value. The process of recording assets at their current market value is often called *marking to market*.

In theory, everyone agrees that it is better to base financial statements on current information. Marking to market provides decision makers with financial statements that more closely reflect a company's true financial condition; thus, they have a better chance of making the correct economic decision, given the information available. For example, providing current market values means that managers can no longer conceal a failing business or hide unrealized gains on assets.

On the downside, the current value of some assets can be hard to estimate, and accountants are reluctant to make estimates. Critics also point out that some of the valuation models used to estimate market values are complicated to apply and the resulting numbers are potentially open to abuse. For example, Enron manipulated its forecasts of energy prices to maximize the value of long-term gas and electric contracts on its books.

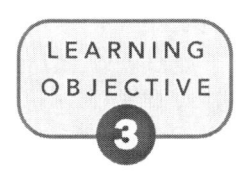

LEARNING OBJECTIVE 3

market value
the price at which an item can be sold

An article in *Business Week Online* offers a perspective on market-value accounting; go to www.businessweek.com/magazine/content/02_10/b3773103.htm.

A More Informative Balance Sheet

To illustrate why market value provides better economic information than book value, let's revisit the balance sheet components discussed earlier. Our discussion will also help you understand why there can be such large differences between some book-value and market-value balance sheet accounts.

ASSETS

For current assets, market value and book value may be reasonably close. The reason is that current assets have a short life cycle and typically are converted into cash quickly. Then, as new current assets are added to the balance sheet, they are entered at their current market price.

In contrast, fixed assets have a long life cycle, and their market value and book value are not likely to be equal. In addition, if an asset is depreciable, the amount of depreciation shown on the balance sheet does not necessarily reflect actual loss of economic value. As a general rule, the longer the time that has passed since an asset was acquired, the more likely it is that the current market value will differ from the book value.

For example, suppose a firm purchased land for a trucking depot in Atlanta, Georgia, 30 years ago for $100,000. Today the land is nestled in an expensive suburban area and is worth around $5.5 million. The difference between the book value of $100,000 and the market value is $5.4 million. In another example, say an airline company decided to replace its aging fleet of aircraft with new fuel-efficient jets in the late 1990s. Following the September 11, 2001, terrorist attack, airline travel declined dramatically; and during 2003 nearly one-third of all commercial jets were "mothballed." In 2003 the current market value of the replacement commercial jets was about two-thirds their original cost. Why the decline? Because the expected cash flows from owning a commercial aircraft had declined a great deal.

LIABILITIES

The market value of liabilities can also differ from their book value, though typically by smaller amounts than is the case with assets. For liabilities, the balance sheet shows the amount of money that the company has promised to pay. This figure is generally close to the actual market value for short-term liabilities.

For long-term debt, however, book value and market value can differ substantially. The market value of debt with fixed interest payments is affected by the level of interest rates in the economy. More specifically, after long-term debt is issued, if the market rate of interest increases, the market price of the debt will decline. Conversely, if interest rates decline, the value of the debt will increase. For example, assume that a firm has $1 million of 20-year bonds outstanding. If the market rate of interest increases from 5 to 8 percent, the price of the bonds will decline to around $700,000.[4] Thus, changes in interest rates can have an important effect on the market values of long-term liabilities, such as corporate bonds. Even if interest rates do not change, the market value of long-term liabilities can change if the performance of the firm declines and the probability of default increases.

STOCKHOLDERS' EQUITY

The book value of the firm's equity is one of the least informative items on the balance sheet. The book value of equity, as suggested earlier, is simply a historical record. As a result, it says very little about the market value of the stockholders' stake in the firm.

In contrast, on a balance sheet where both assets and liabilities are marked to market, the firm's equity is more informative to management and investors. *The difference between the market values of the assets and liabilities provides a better estimate of the market value of stockholders' equity than the difference in the book values.* Intuitively, this makes sense because if you know the "true" market value of the firm's assets and liabilities, the difference must equal the market value of the stockholders' equity.

You should be aware, however, that the difference between the sum of the market values of the individual assets and total liabilities will not give us an exact estimate of the market value of stockholders' equity. The reason is that the true total value of a firm's assets depends on how these assets are utilized. By utilizing the assets efficiently, management can make the total value greater than the simple sum of parts. We will discuss this concept in more detail in Chapter 18.

Finally, if you know the market value of the stockholders' equity and the number of shares of stock outstanding, it is easy to compute the stock price. Specifically, the price of a share of stock is the market value of the firm's stockholders' equity divided by the number of shares outstanding.

---

[4]We will discuss precisely how changes in interest rates affect the market price of debt in Chapter 8, so for now, don't worry about the numerical calculation.

A Market-Value Balance Sheet

Let's look at an example of how a market-value balance sheet can differ from a book-value balance sheet. Marvel Airline is a small regional carrier that has been serving the Northeast for five years. The airline has a fleet of short-haul jet aircrafts, most of which were purchased over the past two years. The fleet has a book value of $600 million. Recently, the airline industry has suffered substantial losses in revenue due to price competition, and most carriers are projecting operating losses for the foreseeable future. As a result, the market value of Marvel's aircraft fleet is only $400 million. The book value of Marvel's long-term debt is $300 million, which is near its current market value. The firm has 100 million shares outstanding. Using these data, we can construct two balance sheets, one based on historical book values and the other based on market values:

Marvel Airlines
Market-Value versus Book-Value Balance Sheets ($ millions)

Assets	Book	Market	Liabilities and Stockholders' Equity	Book	Market
Aircraft	$ 600	$ 400	Long-term debt	$ 300	$ 300
			Stockholders' equity	300	100
Total	$ 600	$ 400		$ 600	$ 400

Based on the book-value balance sheet, the firm's financial condition looks fine; the book value of Marvel's aircraft at $600 million is near what the firm paid, and the stockholders' equity account is $300 million. But when we look at the market-value balance sheet, a different story emerges. We immediately see that the value of the aircraft has declined by $200 million and the stockholders' equity has declined by $200 million!

Why the decline in stockholders' equity? Recall that in Chapter 1 we argued that the value of any asset—stocks, bonds, or a firm—is determined by the future cash flows the asset will generate. At the time the aircraft were purchased, it was expected that they would generate a certain amount of cash flows over time. Now that hard times plague the industry, the cash flow expectations have been lowered, and hence the decline in the value of stockholders' equity.

The Market-Value Balance Sheet

**LEARNING BY DOING
APPLICATION 3.1**

Problem: Grady Means and his four partners in Menlo Park Consulting (MPC) have developed a revolutionary new continuous audit program that can monitor high-risk areas within a firm and identify abnormalities so that corrective actions can be taken. The partners have spent about $300,000 developing the program. The firm's bookkeeper carries the audit program as an asset valued at cost, which is $300,000. To launch the product, the four partners recently invested an additional $1 million, and the money is currently in the firm's bank account. At a recent trade show, a number of accounting and financial consulting firms tried to buy the new continuous product—the highest offer being $15 million. Assuming these are MPC's only assets and liabilities, prepare the firm's book-value and market-value balance sheet and explain the difference between the two.

Approach: The main differences between the two balance sheets will be the treatment of the $300,000 already spent to develop the program and the $15 million offer. The book-value balance sheet is a historical document, which means all assets are valued at what it cost to put them in service, while the market-value balance sheet reflects the value of the assets if they were sold under current market conditions. The differences between the two approaches can be considerable.

(continued)

Solution: The two balance sheets are as follows:

Menlo Park Consulting
Market-Value versus Book-Value Balance Sheets ($ thousands)

Assets	Book	Market	Liabilities and Stockholder's Equity	Book	Market
Cash in bank	$ 1,000	$ 1,000	Long-term debt	$ —	$ —
Intangible assets	300	15,000	Stockholders' equity	1,300	16,000
Total	$ 1,300	$ 16,000		$ 1,300	$ 16,000

The book-value balance sheet provides little useful information. The book value of the firm's total assets is $1.3 million, which consists of cash in the bank and the cost of developing the audit program. Since the firm has no debt, total assets must equal the book value of stockholders' equity. The market value tells a dramatically different story. The market value of the audit program is estimated to be $15.0 million; thus, the market value of stockholders' equity is $16.0 million and not $1.3 million as reported in the book-value balance sheet.

> **Before You Go On**
>
> 1. What is the difference between book value and market value?
> 2. What are some objections to the preparation of marked-to-market balance sheets?

3.4 The Income Statement and the Statement of Retained Earnings

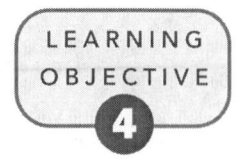

LEARNING OBJECTIVE 4

In the previous sections, we examined a firm's balance sheet, which is like a financial snapshot of the firm at a point in time. In contrast, the income statement is like a video clip showing how profitable a firm is between two points in time.

The Income Statement

income statement
a financial statement that reports a firm's revenues, expenses, and profits or losses over a period of time

The **income statement** summarizes the revenues, expenses, and the profitability (or losses) of the firm over some period of time, usually a month, a quarter, or a year. The basic equation for the income statement can be expressed as follows:

$$\text{Net income} = \text{Revenues} - \text{Expenses} \tag{3.3}$$

Let's look more closely at each element in this equation.

REVENUES

A firm's revenues arise from the products and services it creates through its business operations. For manufacturing and merchandising companies, revenues come from the sale of merchandise. Service companies, such as consulting firms, generate fees for the services they perform. Other kinds of businesses earn revenues by charging interest or collecting rent. Regardless of how they earn revenues, most firms either receive cash or create an account receivable for each transaction, which increases their total assets.

EXPENSES

Expenses are the various costs that the firm incurs to generate revenues. Broadly speaking, expenses are (1) the value of long-term assets consumed through business operations, such as depreciation expense; and (2) the costs incurred in conducting business, such as labor, utilities, materials, and taxes.

NET INCOME

The firm's net income reflects its accomplishments (revenues) relative to its efforts (expenses) during a time period. If revenues exceed expenses, the firm generates net income for the period. If expenses exceed revenues, the firm has a net loss. Net income is often referred to as profits, as income, or simply as the "bottom line," since it is the last item on the income statement. Net income is often reported on a per-share basis and is then called **earnings per share (EPS)**, where EPS equals net income divided by the number of common shares outstanding. A firm's earnings per share tell a stockholder how much the firm has earned (or lost) for each share of stock outstanding.

Income statements for Diaz Manufacturing for 2007 and 2008 are shown in Exhibit 3.2. You can see that in 2008 total revenues from all sources (sales) were $1,563.7 million. Total expenses for producing and selling those goods were $1,445.2 million—the total of the amounts for cost of goods sold, selling and administrative expenses, depreciation, interest expense, and taxes.[5]

> **earnings per share (EPS)**
> net income divided by the number of common shares outstanding

Exhibit 3.2 — Diaz Manufacturing Income Statements for Year Ending December 31 ($ millions)

	2008	2007
Net sales[a]	$1,563.7	$1,386.7
Cost of goods sold	1,081.1	974.8
Selling and administrative expenses	231.1	197.4
Earnings before Interest, taxes, depreciation, and amortization (EBITDA)	$ 251.5	$ 214.5
Depreciation and amortization	83.1	75.3
Earnings before interest and taxes (EBIT)	$ 168.4	$ 139.2
Interest expense	5.6	18.0
Earnings before taxes (EBT)	$ 162.8	$ 121.2
Taxes	44.3	16.1
Net income	$ 118.5	$ 105.1
Common stock dividend	—	—
Addition to retained earnings	$ 118.5	$ 105.1
Per-share data:		
Common stock price		
Earnings per share (EPS)	$ 2.17	$ 1.93
Dividends per share (DPS)	—	—
Book value per share (BVPS)	—	—
Cash flow per share (CFPS)	$ 3.69	$ 3.31

[a]Net sales is defined as total sales less all sales discounts and sales returns and allowances.

> The income statement shows the sales, expenses, and profits earned by the firm over a specific period of time.

---

[5] Looking at Exhibit 3.2, we find that the total expenses (in millions) are as follows: $1,081.1 + $231.1 + $83.1 + $5.6 + $44.3 = $1,445.2.

Using Equation 3.3, we can use these numbers to calculate Diaz Manufacturing's net income for the year:

$$\text{Net income} = \text{Revenues} - \text{Expenses}$$
$$= \$1{,}563.7 \text{ million} - \$1{,}445.2 \text{ million} = \$118.5 \text{ million}$$

Since Diaz Manufacturing had 54,566,054 common shares outstanding at year's end, its EPS was $2.17 per share ($118.5 million/54.566 million).

A CLOSER LOOK AT SOME EXPENSE CATEGORIES

Next, we take a closer look at some of the expense items on the income statement. We discussed depreciation earlier in relation to the balance sheet, and we now look at the role of depreciation in the income statement.

Depreciation Expense. An interesting feature of financial reporting is that companies are allowed to prepare two sets of financial statements: one for tax purposes and one for managing the company and for financial reporting to the SEC and investors. For tax purposes, most firms elect to accelerate depreciation as quickly as is permitted under the tax code. The reason is that accelerated depreciation results in a higher depreciation expense to the income statement, which in turn results in a lower net income and a lower tax liability in the first few years after the asset is acquired. The good news about accelerating depreciation for tax purposes is that the firm pays lower taxes but does not actually write a bigger check for depreciation expense. The depreciation method does not affect the cost of the asset. In contrast, straight-line depreciation results in lower depreciation expenses to the income statement, which results in higher net income and higher tax payments. Firms generally use straight-line depreciation in the financial statements they report to the SEC and investors because it makes their earnings look better.

It is important to understand that the company does not take more total depreciation under accelerated depreciation methods than under the straight-line method; the total amount of depreciation expensed to the income statement over the life of an asset is the same. Total depreciation cannot exceed the price paid for the asset. Accelerating depreciation only alters the timing of when the depreciation is expensed.

Amortization Expense. Amortization is the process of writing off expenses for intangible assets—such as patents, licenses, copyrights, and trademarks—over their useful life. Since depreciation and amortization are very similar, they are often lumped together on the income statement. Both are noncash expenses, which means that an expense is recorded on the income statement, but the associated cash does not necessarily leave the firm in that period. For Diaz Manufacturing, the depreciation and amortization expense for 2008 was $83.1 million.

At one time, goodwill was one of the intangible assets subject to amortization. As of June 2001, however, goodwill could no longer be amortized. The value of the goodwill on a firm's balance sheet is now subject to an annual *impairment test*. This test requires that the company annually value the businesses that were acquired in the past to see if the value of the goodwill associated with those businesses has declined below the value at which it is being carried on the balance sheet. If the value of the goodwill has declined (been impaired), management must write off the amount of the impairment. This write-off reduces the firm's reported net income.

Extraordinary Items. Other items reported separately in the income statement are extraordinary items, which are reserved for nonoperating gains or losses. Extraordinary items are unusual and infrequent occurrences, such as gains or losses from floods, fires, or earthquakes. For example, in 1980 the volcano Mount St. Helens erupted in Washington state, and Weyerhaeuser Company reported an extraordinary loss of $67 million to cover the damage to its standing timber, buildings, and equipment. Diaz Manufacturing has no extraordinary expense item during 2008.

STEP BY STEP TO THE BOTTOM LINE

You probably noticed in Exhibit 3.2 that Diaz Manufacturing's income statement showed income at several intermediate steps before reaching net income, the so-called bottom line. These intermediate income figures, which are typically included on a firm's income statement, provide important information about the firm's performance and help identify what factors are driving the firm's income or losses.

EBITDA. The first intermediate income figure is EBITDA, or earnings before interest, taxes, depreciation, and amortization. The importance of EBITDA is that it shows what is earned purely from operations and reflects how efficiently the firm can manufacture and sell its products without taking into account the cost of the productive asset base (plant and equipment and intangible assets). For Diaz Manufacturing, EBITDA was $251.5 million in 2008.

EBIT. Subtracting depreciation and amortization from EBITDA yields the next intermediate figure, EBIT, or earnings before interest and taxes. EBIT for Diaz Manufacturing was $168.4 million.

EBT. When interest expense is subtracted from EBIT, the result is EBT, or earnings before taxes. Diaz Manufacturing had an EBT of $162.8 million in 2008.

Net Income. Finally, taxes are subtracted from EBT to arrive at net income. For Diaz Manufacturing, as we have already seen, net income in 2008 was $118.5 million.

In Chapter 4 you will see how to use these intermediate income figures to evaluate the firm's financial condition. Next, we look at the statement of retained earnings, which provides detailed information about how management allocated the $118.5 million of net income earned during the period.

The Statement of Retained Earnings

Corporations often prepare a statement of retained earnings, which identifies the changes in the retained earnings account from one accounting period to the next. During any accounting period, two events can affect the retained earnings account balance:

1. When the firm reports net income or loss
2. When the board of directors declares and pays a cash dividend

Exhibit 3.3 shows the activity in the retained earnings account for 2008 for Diaz Manufacturing. The beginning balance is a negative $50.7 million. The firm's annual report explains that the retained earnings deficit resulted from a $441 million writedown of assets that occurred when Diaz Manufacturing became a stand-alone business in June 2003. As reported in the 2008 income statement (Exhibit 3.2), the firm earned $118.5 million that year, and the board of directors elected not to declare any dividends. Retained earnings consequently went from a negative $50.7 million to a positive balance of $67.8 million, an increase of $118.5 million.

Exhibit 3.3 Diaz Manufacturing Statement of Retained Earnings for the Year Ending December 31, 2008 ($ millions)

Balance of retained earnings, December 31, 2007	$ (50.7)
Add: Net income, 2008	118.5
Less: Dividends to common stockholders	—
Balance of retained earnings, December 31, 2008	$ 67.8

The statement of retained earnings accompanies the balance sheet and shows the beginning balance of retained earnings, the adjustments made to retained earnings during the year, and the ending balance.

Before You Go On

1. How do you compute net income?
2. What is EBITDA, and what does it measure?
3. What accounting events trigger changes to the retained earnings account?

3.5 Cash Flows

LEARNING OBJECTIVE 5

As we discussed in Chapter 1, the concept of cash flows is an important one in financial management. Financial managers are concerned with maximizing the value of stockholders' shares, which means making decisions that will maximize the value of the firm's future cash flows. It is important to recognize that the revenues, expenses, and net income reported in a firm's income statement do not necessarily reflect cash flows. We must therefore distinguish between a company's net income and the cash flows it generates.

Net Income versus Cash Flows

net cash flow
a firm's actual cash receipts less cash payments in a given period

As we explained earlier, net income is equal to revenues minus expenses. **Net cash flow** is the cash that a firm generates in a given period (cash receipts less cash payments). Why is net income different from net cash flow? The reason is that when accountants prepare financial statements, they do not count the cash coming in and the cash going out. Under GAAP, they recognize revenues at the time a sale is substantially completed, not when the customer pays. In addition, because of the matching principle, accountants match revenues with the costs of producing the revenues. Finally, capital expenditures are paid for at the time of purchase, but the expense for the use of the capital asset is spread out over the asset's useful life through depreciation and amortization. As a result of these accounting rules, typically a significant lag in time exists between when revenues and expenses are recorded and when the cash is actually collected (in the case of revenue) or paid (in the case of expenses).[6]

Though neither method is precise, two "rough and ready" ways can be used to convert accounting profits into net cash flows from operating activities. The first method adjusts the firm's net income for all noncash revenue and noncash expenses. Net cash flow from operating activities (NCFOA) is:

$$\text{NCFOA} = \text{Net income} - \text{Noncash revenues} + \text{Noncash expenses} \quad (3.4)$$

For most businesses, the largest noncash expenses are depreciation and amortization. These two items are deducted from revenues on the income statement, but no cash is paid out. The cash outflows took place when the assets were purchased. Other noncash items include the following:

- Depletion charges, which are like depreciation but which apply to extractive natural resources, such as crude oil, natural gas, timber, and mineral deposits (noncash expense)
- Deferred taxes, which are the portion of a firm's income tax expense that is postponed because of differences in the accounting policies adopted for management financial reporting and for tax reporting (noncash expense)
- Prepaid expenses that are paid in advance, such as for rent and insurance (noncash expense)
- Deferred revenues, which are revenues received as cash but not yet earned. An example of deferred revenue would be prepaid magazine subscriptions to a publishing company (noncash revenue)

The second method simply recognizes the fact that depreciation and amortization are usually the largest noncash charges and assumes that the remaining noncash revenues or charges cancel one another. The result is a simplified version of Equation 3.4:

$$\text{NCFOA} = \text{Net income} + \text{Depreciation and amortization} \quad (3.5)$$

---

[6]The accounting practice of recognizing revenues and expenses as they are earned and incurred, and not when cash is received or paid, is called accrual accounting.

Equation 3.5 provides satisfactory estimates of NCFOA for many finance problems, unless there are significant noncash items beyond depreciation and amortization. To illustrate, we can use the data from Diaz Manufacturing's 2008 income statement (Exhibit 3.2):

$$\text{NCFOA} = \$118.5 + \$83.1 = \$201.6 \text{ million}$$

Diaz Manufacturing's net cash flow is much larger than its net income, illustrating the point that profits and net cash flow are not the same. However, as a cautionary warning, note that neither Equation 3.4 nor Equation 3.5 adjusts for changes in the working capital accounts, such as inventory levels and accounts payable, and if changes in these accounts are significant, the equations cannot be used. We consider these adjustments next.

The Statement of Cash Flows

There are times when the financial manager wants to know in detail all the cash flows that have taken place during the year and reconcile the beginning-of-year and end-of-year cash balances. The reason for the focus on cash flows is very practical. There is ample evidence from practice that business firms can post significant earnings (net income) but still have inadequate cash to pay wages, suppliers, and other creditors. On occasion, these firms have had to file for bankruptcy. The problem, of course, lies in the fact that profits (net income) are not the same as cash flows.

SOURCES AND USES OF CASH

The **statement of cash flows** shows the company's cash inflows (receipts) and cash outflows (payments) for a period of time. We derive these cash flows by looking at changes in balance sheet accounts from the end of one accounting period to the end of next and at the firm's net income for the period. In analyzing the cash flow statement, it is important to understand that changes in the balance sheet accounts reflect cash flows. More specifically, increases in assets or decreases in liabilities and equity are uses of cash, while decreases in assets or increases in liabilities and equity are sources of cash, as explained in the following:

> **statement of cash flows**
> a financial statement that shows a firm's cash receipts and cash payments for a period of time

- *Working capital.* An increase in current assets (such as accounts receivable and inventory) is a use of cash. For example, if a firm increases its inventory, it must use cash to purchase the additional inventory. Conversely, the sale of inventory increases a firm's cash position. An increase in current liabilities (such as accounts and notes payable) is a source of cash. For example, if during the year a firm increases its accounts payable, it has effectively "borrowed" money from suppliers and increased its cash position.
- *Fixed assets.* An increase in fixed assets is a use of cash. If a company purchases fixed assets during the year, it decreases cash because it must use cash to pay for the purchase. If the firm sells a fixed asset during the year, the firm's cash position will increase.
- *Long-term liabilities and equity.* An increase in long-term debt (bonds or private placement) or equity (common and preferred stock) is a source of cash. The retirement of debt or the purchase of treasury stock requires the firm to pay out cash, reducing cash balances.
- *Dividends.* Any cash dividend payment decreases a firm's cash balance.

ORGANIZATION OF THE STATEMENT OF CASH FLOWS

The statement of cash flows is organized around three business activities—operating activities, investing activities, and financing activities—and the reconciliation of the cash account. We discuss each of these elements next and illustrate them with reference to the statement of cash flows for Diaz Manufacturing, which is shown in Exhibit 3.4.

Exhibit 3.4 Diaz Manufacturing Statement of Cash Flows for the Year Ending December 31, 2008 ($ millions)

Operating Activities	
Net income	$118.5
Additions (sources of cash)	
Depreciation and amortization	83.1
Increase in accounts payable	24.3
Decrease in other current assets	8.6
Increase in accrued income taxes	1.2
Subtractions (uses of cash)	
Increase in accounts receivable	(37.4)
Increase in inventories	(51.1)
Net cash provided by operating activities	$147.2
Long-Term Investing Activities	
Property, equipment, and other assets	$ (88.3)
Increase in goodwill and other assets	(38.4)
Net cash used in investing activities	($126.7)
Financing Activities	
Increase in long-term debt	$268.4
Purchase of treasury stock	(23.3)
Increase in notes payable	6.3
Net cash provided by financing activities	$251.4
Cash Reconciliation[a]	
Net increase in cash and marketable securities	$271.9
Cash and securities at beginning of year	16.6
Cash and securities at end of year	$288.5

[a] Cash includes marketable securities.

The statement of cash flows shows the sources of the cash that has come into the firm during a period of time and the ways in which this cash has been used.

Operating Activities. Cash flows from operations are the net cash flows that are related to a firm's principal business activities. The most important items are the firm's net income, depreciation expense, and working capital accounts (other than cash and short-term debt obligations, which are classified elsewhere).

In Exhibit 3.4, the first section of the statement of cash flows for Diaz Manufacturing shows the cash flow from operations. The section starts with the firm's net income of $118.5 million for the year ending December 31, 2008. Depreciation expense ($83.1 million) is added because it is a noncash expense on the income statement.

Next come changes in the firm's working capital accounts that affect operating activities. Note that working capital accounts that involve financing (bank loans and notes payable) and cash reconciliation (cash and marketable securities) will be classified separately. For Diaz, the working capital accounts that are *sources* of cash are: (1) increase in accounts payable of $24.3 million ($349.3 − $325.0), (2) decrease in other current assets of $8.6 million ($29.9 − $21.3), and (3) increase in accrued income taxes of $1.2 million ($18.0 − $16.8). Changes in working capital items that are *uses* of cash are: (1) increase in accounts receivable of $37.4 million ($306.2 − $268.8) and (2) increase in inventory of $51.1 million ($423.8 − $372.7). The total cash provided to the firm from operations is $147.2 million.

To clarify why changes in working capital accounts affect the statement of cash flows, let's look at some of the changes. Diaz had a $37.4 million increase in accounts receivable, which is subtracted from net income as a use of cash. The increase in accounts receivable is a use of cash because the number represents sales that were included in the income statement but for which no cash has been collected. Diaz provided financing for these sales to its customers. The $24.3 million increase in accounts payable represents a source of cash because goods and services the company purchased were received but no cash was paid out.

Investing Activities. Cash flows from investment activities relate to the buying and selling of long-term assets. The primary investment activities for manufacturing and service firms are the purchase or sale of land, buildings, and plant and equipment.

In Exhibit 3.4, the second section shows the cash flows from long-term investing activities. Diaz Manufacturing made long-term investments in two areas, which resulted in a cash outflow of $126.7 million. They were as follows: (1) the purchase of plant and equipment, totaling $88.3 million ($911.6 − $823.3) and (2) an increase in goodwill and other assets of $38.4 ($450.0 − $411.6). Diaz's investments in property, equipment, and other assets resulted in a cash outflow of $126.7 million.

Financing Activities. Cash flows from financing come from activities in which cash is obtained from or repaid to creditors or owners (stockholders). Typical financing activities involve cash received from owners as they invest in the firm by buying common stock or preferred stock, as well as cash from bank loans, notes payable, and long-term debt. Cash payments of dividends to stockholders and cash purchases of treasury stock reduce a company's cash position.

Diaz Manufacturing's financing activities include the sale of bonds for $268.4 million ($574.0 − $305.6), which is a source of cash and the purchase of treasury stock for $23.3 million, which is a use of cash. The firm's notes payable position was also increased by $6.3 million ($10.5 − $4.2). Overall, Diaz had a net cash inflow from financing activities of $251.4 million.

Cash Reconciliation. The final part of the statement of cash flows is a reconciliation of the firm's beginning and ending cash positions. For Diaz Manufacturing, these cash positions are as shown on the 2007 and 2008 balance sheets. The first step in reconciling the company's beginning and ending cash positions is to add together the amounts from the first three sections of the statement of cash flows: (1) the net cash inflows from operations of $147.2 million, (2) the net cash outflow from long-term investment activities of − $126.7 million, (3) and the net cash inflow from financing activities of $251.4 million. Together, these three items represent a total net increase in cash to the firm of $271.9 million ($147.2 − $126.7 + $251.4). Finally, we add this amount ($271.9 million) to the beginning cash balance of $16.6 million to obtain the ending cash balance for 2008 of $288.5 million ($271.9 + $16.6).

Additional Cash Flow Calculations

This section has introduced cash flow calculations. We will return to the topic of cash flows in Chapters 11 and 18. In those chapters we will develop more precise measures of cash flows that will allow us to determine (1) the incremental cash flows necessary to estimate the value of a capital project and (2) the free cash flows needed to estimate the value of a firm.

> **Before You Go On**
>
> 1. What is the difference between accounting profits and net cash flows?
> 2. Should a firm consider only depreciation and amortization expenses when calculating the net cash flow? Explain.
> 3. Explain the difference between financing and investing activities.

3.6 Tying the Financial Statements Together

LEARNING OBJECTIVE 6

Up to this point, we have treated a firm's financial statements as if they were independent of one another. As you might suspect, though, the four financial statements presented in this chapter are related. Let's see how.

Recall that the balance sheet summarizes what assets the firm has at a particular point in time and how the firm has financed those assets with debt and equity. From

Income Statement, 12/31/08

Revenues	$1,563.7
Expenses	(1,312.2)
Net income	118.5

Balance Sheet, 12/31/07

Cash	$ 16.6
Current assets (less cash)	671.4
Fixed assets	805.8
Current liabilities (less notes)	341.8
Long-term debt and notes	309.8
Capital stock	892.9
Retained earnings	(50.7)

Statement of Cash Flows, 12/31/08

Net Income	$118.5
Depreciation and amortization	83.1
Net working capital investment (excluding cash)	(54.4)
Operating activities	$147.2
Investing activities	(126.7)
Financing activities	251.4
Net increase in cash	$271.8

Balance Sheet, 12/31/08

Cash	$288.5
Current assets (less cash)	751.3
Fixed assets	849.4
Current liabilities (less notes)	367.3
Long-term debt and notes	584.5
Capital stock	869.6
Retained earnings	67.8

Statement of Retained Earnings 12/31/08

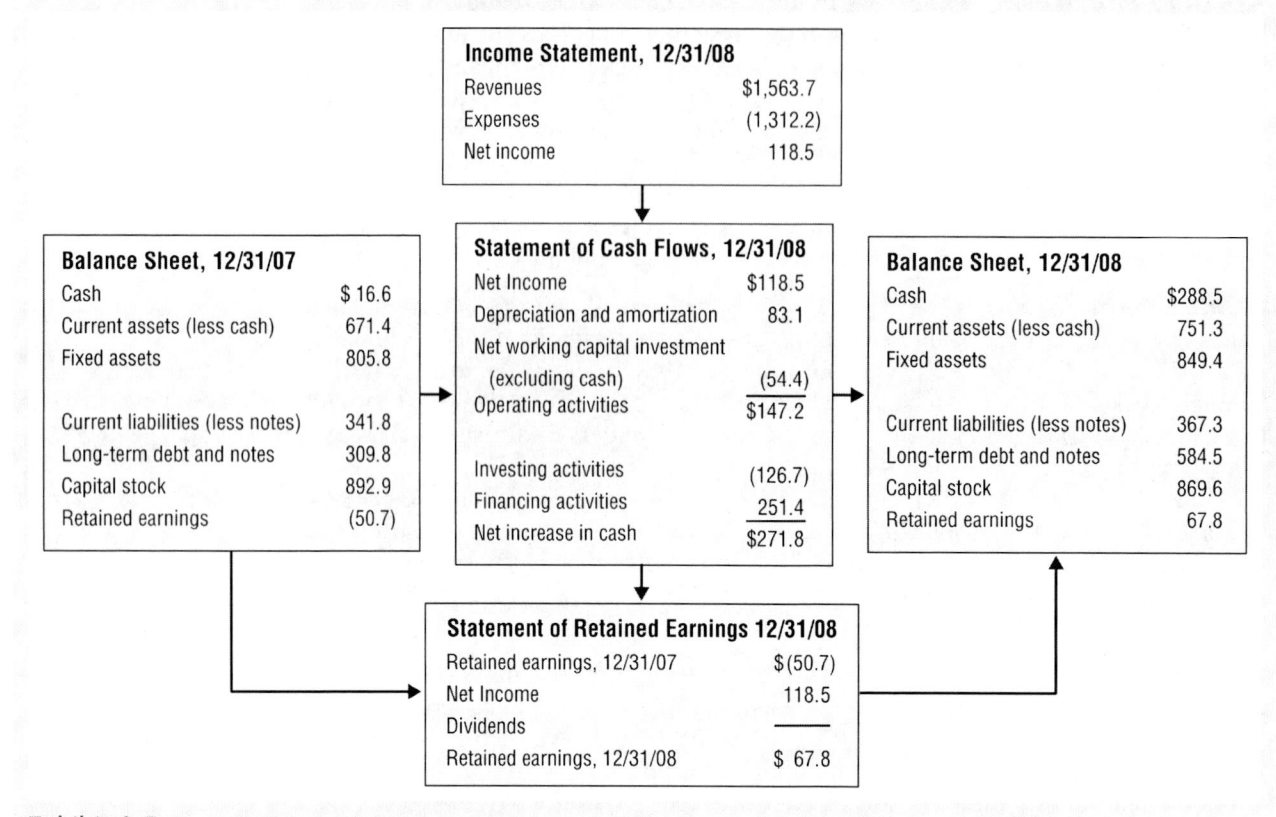

Retained earnings, 12/31/07	$ (50.7)
Net Income	118.5
Dividends	
Retained earnings, 12/31/08	$ 67.8

Exhibit 3.5
The Interrelations among the Financial Statements: Illustrated Using Diaz Manufacturing Financial Results

The statement of cash flows ties together the income statement with the balance sheets from the beginning and the end of the period. The statement of retained earnings shows how the retained earnings account has changed from the beginning to the end of the period.

---

one year to the next, the firm's balance sheet will change because the firm will buy or sell assets and the dollar value of the debt and equity financing will change. These changes are exactly the ones presented in the statement of cash flows. In other words, the statement of cash flows presents a summary of the changes in a firm's balance sheet from the beginning of a period to the end of that period.

This concept is illustrated in Exhibit 3.5, which presents summaries of the four financial statements for Diaz Manufacturing for the year 2008. The exhibit also presents the balance sheet for the beginning of that year, which is dated December 31, 2007. If you compare the changes in the balance sheet numbers from the beginning of the year to the end of the year, you can see that these changes are in fact summarized in the statement of cash flows. For example, the change in the cash balance of $271.8 ($288.5 − $16.6) appears at the bottom of the statement of cash flows. Similarly, excluding cash, the change in net working capital from the beginning to the end of 2008 is $54.4, which is calculated as follows: [($751.3 − $367.3) − ($671.4 − $341.8)] = ($384.0 − $329.6) = $54.4.[7] This number is equal to the net working capital investment reflected in the statement of cash flows. Note, too, that the net working capital investment in Diaz's statement of cash flows is just the total change in the firm's investment in the working capital accounts—accounts payable, other current assets, accrued income taxes, accounts receivable, and inventories. You can also see in Exhibit 3.5 that the change in fixed assets, which includes net property plant and equipment, goodwill, and other assets, is $43.6 ($849.4 − $805.8). This number is equal to the sum of the cash flows from invest-

---

[7]From the 2008 balance sheet: (1) working capital less cash = $1,039.8 − $288.5 = $751.3, and (2) current liabilities − notes payable = $377.8 − $10.5 = $367.3. The calculations are similar for the 2007 balance

depreciation and amortization, $-\$126.7 + \$83.1 = -\$43.6$, in the statement of cash flows. We add depreciation to investing activities in the latter calculation because the fixed asset accounts in the balance sheet are net of depreciation.

Turning to the liability and equity side of the balance sheet, notice the change in the amount of debt plus equity that the firm has sold in 2008, which is represented by the sum of the long-term liabilities and notes and capital stock in the balance sheet. This sum equals the value of the financing activities in the statement of cash flows. The change in the balance sheet values is calculated as follows: $[(\$584.5 + \$869.6) - (\$309.8 + \$892.9)] = (\$1,454.1 - \$1,202.7) = 251.4$.[8] Finally, since Diaz did not pay a dividend in 2008, the change in retained earnings of $118.5, which equals $67.8 - (-\$50.7)$, exactly equals the company's net income, which appears on the top line of the statement of cash flows.

Again, the important point here is that the statement of cash flows summarizes the changes in the balance sheet. How do the other financial statements fit into the picture? Well, the income statement calculates the firm's net income, which is used to calculate the retained earnings at the end of the year and is included as the first line in the statement of cash flows. The income statement provides an input that is used in the balance sheet and the statement of cash flows. The statement of retained earnings just summarizes the changes to the retained earnings account a little differently than the statement of cash flows. This different format makes it simpler for managers and investors to see why retained earnings changed as it did.

> **Before You Go On**
>
> 1. Explain how the four financial statements are related.

3.7 Federal Income Tax

LEARNING OBJECTIVE 7

We conclude the chapter with a discussion of corporate income taxes. Taxes take a big bite out of the income of most businesses and represent one of their largest cash outflows. For example, as shown in the income statement (Exhibit 3.2) for Diaz Manufacturing, the firm's earnings before interest and taxes (EBIT) in 2008 amounted to $168.4 million, and its tax bill was $44.3 million, or 26.3 percent of EBIT ($44.3/168.4)—not a trivial amount by any standard. Because of their magnitude, taxes play a critical role in most business financial decisions.

As you might suspect, corporations spend a considerable amount of effort and money deploying tax specialists to find legal ways to minimize their tax burdens. The tax laws are complicated, continually changing, and at times seemingly bizarre—in part because the tax code is not an economically rational document, but reflects the political and social values of Congress and the President.

If you work in the finance or accounting area, a tax specialist will advise you on the tax implications of most decisions in which you will be involved as a businessperson. Consequently, we will not try to make you a tax expert, but we will present a high-level view of the major portions of the federal tax code that have a significant impact on the operations of corporations and their business decision making.

Corporate Income Tax Rates

Exhibit 3.6 shows the 2007 federal income tax schedule for corporations. As you can see, the marginal tax rate varies from 15 percent to 39 percent. In general, smaller companies with lower taxable incomes have lower tax rates than larger companies with

---

[8] From the 2008 balance sheet, note the following: debt = $574.0 (long-term debt) + $10.5 (notes payable) = $584.5 and equity = $50.0 (common stock) + $842.9 (additional paid-in capital) − $23.3 (treasury stock) = $869.6. The calculations for 2007 are made in a similar manner.

Exhibit 3.6 Corporate Tax Rates for 2007

(1) Corporations' Taxable Income	(2) Pay This Amount on the Base of the Bracket	(3) Marginal Tax Rate: Tax Rate on the Excess over the Base	(4) Average Tax Rate at Top of Bracket
$0–$50,000	$ 0	15%	15.0%
50,001–75,000	7,500	25	18.3
75,001–100,000	13,750	34	22.3
100,001–335,000	22,250	39	34.0
335,001–10,000,000	113,900	34	34.0
10,000,001–15,000,000	3,400,000	35	34.3
15,000,001–18,333,333	5,150,000	38	35.0
More than 18,333,333	6,416,667	35	35.0

The federal corporate marginal tax rate varies from 15 to 39 percent. Generally speaking, smaller companies with lower taxable income have lower tax rates than larger companies with higher taxable incomes. Smaller businesses are given preferential treatment to encourage new business formation.

The U.S. Department of the Treasury provides a comprehensive tax information site at www.irs.gov.

higher taxable incomes. Historically, the federal income tax code has given preferential treatment to small businesses and start-up companies as a means of stimulating new business formation. In addition, the federal system is a progressive income tax system; that is, as the level of income rises, the tax rate rises. Under the current tax code, which has its origins in the Tax Reform Act of 1986, marginal tax rates do not increase continuously through the income brackets, however. As you can see in Exhibit 3.6, marginal tax rates rise from 15 percent to 39 percent for incomes up to $335,000; they decrease to 34 percent, then increase to 38 percent for incomes up to $18.3 million; and they ultimately rest at 35 percent for all taxable income above $18.3 million.

Average versus Marginal Tax Rates

average tax rate
total taxes paid divided by taxable income

marginal tax rate
the tax rate paid on the last dollar of income earned

The difference between the average tax rate and the marginal tax rate is an important consideration in financial decision making. The **average tax rate** is simply the total taxes paid divided by taxable income. In contrast, the **marginal tax rate** is the tax rate that is paid on the last dollar of income earned. Exhibit 3.6 shows the marginal tax rates (column 3) and average tax rates (column 4) for corporations.

A simple example will clarify the difference between the average and marginal tax rates. Suppose a corporation has a taxable income of $150,000. Using the data in Exhibit 3.6, we can determine the firm's federal income tax bill, its marginal tax rate, and its average tax rate. The firm's total tax bill is computed as follows:

$$
\begin{aligned}
0.15 \times \$50,000 &= \$\ 7,500 \\
0.25 \times (\$75,000 - \$50,000) &= 6,250 \\
0.34 \times (\$100,000 - \$75,000) &= 8,500 \\
0.39 \times (\$150,000 - \$100,000) &= \underline{19,500} \\
& \quad\ \$41,750
\end{aligned}
$$

The firm's average tax rate is equal to the total taxes divided by the firm's total taxable income; thus, the average tax rate is $41,750/$150,000 = 0.278, or 27.8 percent. The firm's marginal tax rate is the rate paid on the last dollar earned, which is 39 percent.

LEARNING BY DOING APPLICATION 3.2

The Difference between Average and Marginal Tax Rates

Problem: Taxland Corporation has taxable corporate income of $90,000. What is the firm's federal corporate income tax liability? What are the firm's average and marginal tax rates?

Approach: Use Exhibit 3.6 to calculate the firm's tax bill. To calculate the average tax rate, divide the total amount of taxes paid by the $90,000 of taxable income. The marginal tax rate is the tax rate paid on the last dollar of taxable income.

Solution:

$$\text{Tax bill} = (0.15 \times \$50,000) + [0.25 \times (\$75,000 - \$50,000)] \\ + [0.34 \times (\$90,000 - \$75,000)] \\ = \$7,500 + \$6,250 + \$5,100 \\ = \$18,850$$

Average tax rate = $18,850/$90,000 = 0.209, or 20.9%
Marginal tax rate = 34%

When you are making investment decisions for a firm, the relevant tax rate to use is usually the marginal tax rate. The reason is that new investments (projects) are expected to generate new cash flows, which will be taxed at the firm's marginal tax rate. Thus, the marginal tax rate is used to compute the project's tax bill.

To simplify calculations throughout the book, we will generally specify a single tax rate for a corporation, such as 40 percent. The rate may include some payment for state and local taxes, which will add an upward adjustment to the total tax rate firms pay. We use different corporate tax rates to emphasize that taxes change over time and may differ from one location to another.

Unequal Treatment of Dividends and Interest Payments

An interesting anomaly in the tax code is the unequal treatment of interest expense and dividend payments. For the most common type of corporation, interest paid on debt obligations is a tax-deductible business expense. Dividends paid to common or preferred stockholders are not deductible, however. Because of this difference, a firm must generate more earnings to support a $100 payment of dividends than a $100 payment of interest. For example, if a firm pays $100 in interest, it must generate $100 of earnings before interest and taxes (EBIT) to support this payment. However, for the $100 of dividends, the firm will need more than $100 of EBIT because the dividends are not tax deductible. More specifically, if the average tax rate is 40 percent, the firm will need to generate $166.70 to cover the cash dividend.[9]

The unequal treatment of interest expense and dividend payments is not without consequences. In effect, it lowers the cost of debt financing compared with the cost of an equal amount of common or preferred stock financing. Thus, there is a tax-induced bias toward the use of debt financing, which we discuss more thoroughly in later chapters.

---

[9]To find the amount of EBIT necessary to support the cash dividend, simply divide the amount by 1 minus the average tax rate $(1 - t)$. If the average tax rate (t) is 40 percent, the necessary EBIT to support $100 of cash dividends is as follows: EBIT necessary = $100/(1 - 0.40) = $100/0.60 = $166.70.

> **Before You Go On**
>
> 1. Why is it important to consider the consequences of taxes when financing a new project?
> 2. Which type of tax rate, marginal or average, should be used in analyzing the expansion of a product line, and why?
> 3. What are the tax implications of a decision to finance a project using debt rather than new equity?

Summary of Learning Objectives

1. **Discuss generally accepted accounting principles (GAAP) and their importance to the economy.**

   GAAP are a set of authoritative guidelines that define accounting practices at a particular point in time. The principles determine the rules for how a company maintains its accounting system and how it prepares financial statements. Accounting standards are important because without them, each firm could develop its own unique accounting practices, which would make it difficult for anyone to monitor the firm's true performance or compare the performance of different firms. The result would be a loss of confidence in the accounting system and the financial reports it produces. Fundamental accounting principles include that transactions are arms-length, the cost principle, the realization principle, the matching principle, and the going concern assumption.

2. **Know the balance sheet identity, and explain why a balance sheet must balance.**

   A balance sheet provides a summary of a firm's financial position at a particular point in time. The balance sheet identifies the productive resources (assets) that a firm uses to generate income, as well as the sources of funding from creditors (liabilities) and owners (stockholders' equity) that were used to buy the assets. The balance sheet identity is: Total assets = Total liabilities + Total stockholders' equity. Stockholders' equity represents ownership in the firm and is the residual claim of the owners after all other obligations to creditors, employees, and vendors have been paid. The balance sheet must always balance because the owners get what is left over after all creditors have been paid—that is Total stockholders' equity = Total assets − Total liabilities.

3. **Describe how market-value balance sheets differ from book-value balance sheets.**

   Book value is the amount a firm paid for its assets at the time of purchase. The current market value of an asset is the amount that a firm would receive for the asset if it were sold on the open market (not in a forced liquidation). Most managers and investors are more concerned about what a firm's assets can earn in the future than in what the assets cost in the past. Thus, balance sheets marked to market are more helpful in showing a company's true financial condition than balance sheets based on historical costs. Of course, the problem with marked-to-market balance sheets is that it is difficult to estimate market values for some assets and liabilities.

4. **Identify the basic equation for the income statement and the information it provides.**

   An income statement is a video clip of the firm's profit or loss for a period of time, usually a month, quarter, or year. The income statement identifies the major sources of revenues generated by the firm and the corresponding expenses needed to generate those revenues. The equation for the income statement is Net income = Revenues − Expenses. If revenues exceed expenses, the firm generates a net profit for the period. If expenses exceed revenues, the firm generates a net loss. Net profit or income is the most comprehensive accounting measure of a firm's performance.

5. **Explain the difference between cash flows and accounting income.**

   Cash flows represent the movement of cash within the firm. Cash flows are important in finance because the value of any asset—stocks, bonds, or a business—is determined by the future cash flows generated by the asset. Accounting profits, in contrast, are calculated according to GAAP to determine taxes and to report to stakeholders in a consistent manner. Accounting profits include noncash revenues (such as revenue booked by a manufacturer when products are shipped on credit) and noncash expenses (such depreciation), whereas cash flows do not include these items.

6. **Explain how the four major financial statements discussed in this chapter are related.**

   The four financial statements discussed in the chapter are the balance sheet, the income statement, the statement of cash flows, and the statement of retained earnings. The key financial statement that ties the other three statements together is the statement of cash flows, which summarizes changes in the balance sheet from the beginning of the year to the end. These changes reflect the information in the income statement and in the statement of retained earnings.

7. **Discuss the difference between average and marginal tax rates.**

   The average tax rate is computed by dividing the total taxes by taxable income. It takes into account the taxes paid at all levels of income and will normally be lower than the marginal tax rate, which is the rate that is paid on the last dollar of income earned. However, for very high income earners, these two rates can be equal. When companies are making financial investment decisions, they use the marginal tax rate because new projects are expected to generate additional cash flows, which will be taxed at the firm's marginal tax rate.

Summary of Key Equations

Equation	Description	Formula
3.1	Balance sheet identity	Total assets = Total liabilities + Total stockholders' equity
3.2	Net working capital	Net working capital = Total current assets − Total current liabilities
3.3	Income Statement identity	Net income = Revenues − Expenses
3.4	Net cash flow from operating activities	NCFOA = Net income − Noncash revenues + Noncash expenses
3.5	Net cash flow from operating activities	NCFOA = Net income + Depreciation and amortization

Self-Study Problems

3.1 The *going concern assumption* of GAAP implies that the firm:
   a. is going under and needs to be liquidated at historical cost.
   b. will continue to operate and its assets should be recorded at historical cost.
   c. will continue to operate and that all assets should be recorded at their cost rather than at their liquidation value.
   d. is going under and needs to be liquidated at liquidation value.

3.2 The Ellicott City Ice Cream Company management has just completed an assessment of its assets and liabilities and has come up with the following information. It has total current assets worth $625,000 at book value and $519,000 at market value. In addition, its long-term assets include plant and equipment valued at market for $695,000, while their book value is $940,000. The company's total current liabilities are valued at market for $543,000, while their book value is $495,000. Both the book value and the market value of its long-term debt is $350,000. If the company's total assets are equal to a market value of $1,214,000 (book value of $1,565,000), what are the book value and market value of its stockholders' equity?

3.3 Depreciation and amortization expenses are:
   a. part of current assets on the balance sheet.
   b. after-tax expenses that reduce a firm's cash flows.
   c. long-term liabilities that reduce a firm's net worth.
   d. noncash expenses that cause a firm's after-tax cash flows to exceed its net income.

3.4 You are given the following information about Clarkesville Plumbing Company. The company's annual report on December 31, 2008, showed that during the year its revenues totaled $896, current assets $121, current liabilities $107, depreciation expenses $75, costs of goods sold $365, and interest expenses $54. The company is in the 34 percent tax bracket. Calculate its net income by setting up an income statement.

3.5 The Huntington Rain Gear Company had $633,125 in taxable income in the year ending September 30, 2007. Calculate the company's tax using the tax schedule in Exhibit 3.6.

Solutions to Self-Study Problems

3.1 One of the key assumptions under GAAP is the *going concern assumption*, which states that the firm (c) will continue to operate and that all assets should be recorded at their cost rather than at their liquidation value.

3.2 The book value and market value are as follows (in thousands of dollars):

Assets	Book Value	Market Value	Liabilities	Book Value	Market Value
Total current assets	$ 625	$ 519	Total current liabilities	$ 495	$ 543
Fixed assets	940	695	Long-term debt	350	350
			Stockholders' equity	720	321
Total assets	$1,565	$1,214	Total liabilities and equity	$1,565	$1,214

3.3 Depreciation and amortization expenses are (d) noncash expenses that cause a firm's after-tax cash flows to exceed its net income.

3.4 Clarkesville's income statement and net income are as follows:

Clarkesville Plumbing Company
Income Statement for Year Ending December 31, 2008

	Amount
Revenues	$ 896.00
Costs	365.00
EBITDA	$ 531.00
Depreciation	75.00
EBIT	$ 456.00
Interest	54.00
EBT	$ 402.00
Taxes (34%)	136.68
Net income	$ 265.32

3.5 Huntington's tax bill is calculated as follows:

Tax rate	Income	Tax
15%	$50,000	$ 7,500
25	(75,000 − 50,000)	6,250
34	(100,000 − 75,000)	8,500
39	(335,000 − 100,000)	91,650
34	(633,125 − 335,000)	101,363
	Total taxes payable	$ 215,263

Critical Thinking Questions

3.1 What is a major reason for the accounting scandals in recent years? How do firms sometimes attempt to meet Wall Street analysts' projection of earnings?

3.2 Why are taxes and the tax code important for managerial decision making?

3.3 Identify the five fundamental principles of GAAP, and explain briefly their importance.

3.4 Explain why firms prefer to use accelerated depreciation methods over the straight-line method for tax purposes.

3.5 What is treasury stock? Why do firms have treasury stock?

3.6 Define book-value accounting and market-value accounting.

3.7 Compare and contrast depreciation expense and amortization expense.

3.8 Why are retained earnings not considered an asset of the firm?

3.9 How does net cash flow differ from net income, and why?

3.10 What is the statement of cash flows, and what is its role?

Questions and Problems

3.1 Balance sheet: Given the following information about Elkridge Sporting Goods, Inc., construct a balance sheet for the period ending June 30, 2008. The firm had cash and marketable securities of $25,135, accounts receivable of $43,758, inventory of $167,112, net fixed assets of $325,422, and other assets of $13,125. It had accounts payables of $67,855, notes payables of $36,454, long-term debt of $223,125, and common stock of $150,000. How much retained earnings does the firm have?

BASIC

3.2 Inventory accounting: Differentiate between FIFO and LIFO.

3.3 Inventory accounting: Explain how the choice of FIFO versus LIFO can affect a firm's balance sheet and income statement.

3.4 Market-value accounting: How does the use of market-value accounting help managers?

3.5 Working capital: Laurel Electronics reported the following information at its annual meetings: The company had cash and marketable securities worth $1,235,455, accounts payables worth $4,159,357, inventory of $7,121,599, accounts receivables of $3,488,121, short-term notes payable worth $1,151,663, and other current assets of $121,455. What is the company's net working capital?

3.6 Working capital: The financial information for Laurel Electronics referred to in Problem 3.5 is all book value. Suppose marking to market reveals that the market value of the firm's inventory is 20 percent below its book value and its receivables are 25 percent below its book value. The market value of its current liabilities is identical to the book value. What is the firm's net working capital using market values? What is the percentage change in net working capital?

3.7 Income statement: The Oakland Mills Company has disclosed the following financial information in its annual reports for the period ending March 31, 2008: sales of $1.45 million, costs of goods sold to the tune of $812,500, depreciation expenses of $175,000, and interest expenses of $89,575. Assume that the firm has a tax rate of 35 percent. What is the company's net income? Set up an income statement to answer the question.

3.8 Cash flows: Describe the organization of the statement of cash flows.

3.9 Cash flows: During 2008 Towson Recording Company increased its investment in marketable securities by $36,845, funded fixed-assets acquisitions of $109,455, and had marketable securities of $14,215 mature. What is the net cash used in investing activities?

3.10 Cash flows: Caustic Chemicals identified the following cash flows as significant in its meeting with analysts: During the year it had repaid existing debt of $312,080 and raised additional debt capital of $650,000. It also repurchased stock in the open market for a total of $45,250. What is the net cash provided by financing activities?

3.11 Cash flows: Identify and explain the noncash expenses that a firm may incur.

3.12 Tax: Define average tax rate and marginal tax rate.

3.13 Tax: What is the relevant tax rate to use when making financial decisions? Explain why.

3.14 Tax: Manz Property Management Company announced that in the year ended June 30, 2008, its earnings before taxes amounted to $1,478,936. Calculate its taxes using Exhibit 3.6.

INTERMEDIATE

EXCEL

3.15 Balance sheet: Tim Dye, the CFO of Blackwell Automotive, Inc., is putting together this year's financial statements. He has gathered the following information: The firm had a cash balance of $23,015, accounts payable of $163,257, common stock of $313,299, retained earnings of $512,159, inventory of $212,444, goodwill and other assets equal to $78,656, net plant and equipment of $711,256, and short-term notes payable of $21,115. It also had accounts receivable of $141,258 and other current assets of $11,223. What amount of long-term debt does Blackwell Automotive have?

3.16 Balance sheet: Refer to the information for Blackwell Automotive in Problem 3.15. What level of net working capital does Blackwell Automotive have?

3.17 Working capital: Mukhopadhya Network Associates has a current ratio of 1.60, where the current ratio is defined as follows: current ratio = current assets/current liabilities. The firm's current assets are equal to $1,233,265, its accounts payables are $419,357, and its notes payables are $351,663. Its inventory is currently at $721,599. The company plans to raise funds in the short-term debt market and invest the entire amount in additional inventory. How much can their notes payable increase without lowering their current ratio below 1.50?

3.18 Market value: Reservoir Bottling Company reported to stockholders the following information: total current assets worth $237,513 at book value and $219,344 at market value. In addition, its long-term assets include plant and equipment valued at market for $343,222, while their book value is $362,145. The company's total current liabilities are valued at market for $134,889, while their book value is $129,175. Both the book value and the market value of its long-term debt is $144,000. If the company's total assets are equal to a market value of $562,566 (book value of $599,658), what is the difference in the book value and market value of its stockholders' equity?

3.19 Income statement: Nimitz Rental Company provided the following information to its auditors: for the year ended March 31, 2009, the company had revenues of $878,412, general and administrative expenses of $352,666, depreciation expenses of $131,455, leasing expenses of $108,195, and interest expenses equal to $78,122. If the company's tax rate is 34 percent, what is its net income after taxes?

3.20 Income statement: Sosa Corporation recently reported an EBITDA of $31.3 million and net income of $9.7 million. The company has $6.8 million interest expense, and the corporate tax rate is 35 percent. What was its depreciation and amortization expense?

3.21 Income statement: Fraser Corporation has announced that its net income for the year ended June 30, 2008, is $1,353,412. The company had an EBITDA of $4,967,855, and its depreciation and amortization expense was equal to $1,112,685. The company's tax rate is 34 percent. What is the amount of interest expense for Fraser Corporation?

EXCEL

3.22 Income statement: Carmichael Hobby Shop has an EBITDA of $512,725.20, EBIT of $362,450.20, and a cash flow of $348,461.25. What is this firm's net income after taxes?

3.23 Retained earnings: Columbia Construction Company earned $451,888 during the year ended June 30, 2008. After paying out $225,794 in dividends, the balance went into retained earnings. If the firm's total retained earnings were $846,972, what was the level of retained earnings on its balance sheet on July 1, 2007?

3.24 Cash flows: Refer to the information given in Problem 3.19. What is the cash flow for Nimitz Rental?

3.25 Tax: Mount Hebron Electrical Company's financial statements indicated that the company had earnings before interest and taxes of $718,323. Its interest rate on debt of $850,000 was 8.95 percent. Calculate the amount of taxes the company is likely to owe. What are the marginal and average tax rates for this company?

ADVANCED

EXCEL

3.26 The Centennial Chemical Corporation announced that for the period ending March 31, 2008, it had earned income after taxes worth $5,330,275 on revenues of $13,144,680. The company's costs (excluding depreciation and amortization) amounted to 61 percent of sales, and it had interest expenses of $392,168. What is the firm's depreciation and amortization expense if its tax rate is 34 percent?

3.27 Eau Claire Paper Mill, Inc., had, at the beginning of the fiscal year, April 1, 2007, retained earnings of $323,325. During the year ended March 31, 2008, the company produced net income after taxes of $713,445 and paid out 45 percent of its net income as dividends. Construct a statement of retained earnings and compute the year-end balance of retained earnings.

3.28 Menomonie Casino Company earned $23,458,933 before interest and taxes for the fiscal year ending March 31, 2008. If the casino had interest expenses of $1,645,123, calculate its tax burden using Exhibit 3.6. What are the marginal tax rate and the average tax rate for this company?

3.29 Vanderheiden Hog Products Corp. provided the following financial information for the quarter ending June 30, 2008:   EXCEL®
   Net income: $189,425
   Depreciation and amortization: $63,114
   Increase in receivables: $62,154
   Increase in inventory: $57,338
   Increase in accounts payable: $37,655
   Decrease in other current assets: $27,450
   What is this firm's cash flow from operating activities during this quarter?

3.30 Cash flows: Analysts following the Tomkovick Golf Company were given the following information for the year ended June 30, 2008:   EXCEL®

Assets	2008	2007
Cash and marketable securities	$ 33,411	$ 16,566
Accounts receivable	260,205	318,768
Inventory	423,819	352,740
Other current assets	41,251	29,912
Total current assets	$ 758,686	$ 717,986
Plant and equipment	1,931,719	1,609,898
Less: Accumulated depreciation	(419,044)	(206,678)
Net plant and equipment	$ 1,512,675	$ 1,403,220
Goodwill and other assets	382,145	412,565
Total assets	$ 2,653,506	$ 2,533,771

Liabilities and Equity	2008	2007
Accounts payable and accruals	$ 378,236	$ 332,004
Notes payable	14,487	7,862
Accrued income taxes	21,125	16,815
Total current liabilities	$ 413,848	$ 356,681
Long-term debt	679,981	793,515
Total liabilities	$ 1,093,829	$ 1,150,196
Preferred stock	—	—
Common stock (10,000 shares)	10,000	10,000
Additional paid-in capital	975,465	975,465
Retained earnings	587,546	398,110
Less: Treasury stock	13,334	—
Total common equity	$ 1,559,677	$ 1,383,575
Total liabilities and equity	$ 2,653,506	$ 2,533,771

In addition, it was reported that the company had a net income of $3,155,848 and that depreciation expenses were equal to $212,366.
a. Construct a cash flow statement for this firm.
b. Calculate the net cash provided by operating activities.
c. What is the net cash used in investing activities?
d. Compute the net cash provided by financing activities.

Sample Test Problems

3.1 Drayton, Inc., has current assets of $256,312 and total assets of $861,889. It also has current liabilities of $141,097, common equity of $200,000, and retained earnings of $133,667. How much long-term debt does the firm have?

3.2 Ellicott Testing Company produced revenues of $745,000 in 2008. It has expenses (excluding depreciation) of $312,640, depreciation of $65,000, and interest expense of $41,823. It pays a marginal tax rate of 34 percent. What is the firm's net income after taxes?

3.3 Tejada Enterprises reported an EBITDA of $7,300,125 and $3,328,950 of net income for the fiscal year ended September 30, 2008. The company has $1,155,378 interest expense, and the corporate tax rate is 35 percent. What was the company's depreciation and amortization expense?

3.4 In the year ended June 30, 2008, Tri King Company increased its investment in marketable securities by $234,375, funded fixed-assets acquisition by $1,324,766, and sold $77,215 of long-term debt. In addition, the firm had a net inflow of $365,778 from selling certain assets. What is the net cash used in investing activities?

3.5 Triumph Soccer Club has the following cash flows during this year: It repaid existing debt of $875,430, while raising additional debt capital of $1,213,455. It also repurchased stock in the open markets for a total of $71,112. What is the net cash provided by financing activities?

ANALYZING FINANCIAL STATEMENTS

CHAPTER 4

REUTERS/Peter Jones

LEARNING OBJECTIVES

1. Explain the three perspectives from which financial statements can be viewed.

2. Describe common-size financial statements, explain why they are used, and be able to prepare and use them to analyze the historical performance of a firm.

3. Discuss how financial ratios facilitate financial analysis, and be able to compute and use them to analyze a firm's performance.

4. Describe the DuPont system of analysis, and be able to use it to evaluate a firm's performance and identify corrective actions that may be necessary.

5. Explain what benchmarks are, describe how they are prepared, and discuss why they are important in financial statement analysis.

6. Identify the major limitations in using financial statement analysis.

Today the largest U.S. airlines are struggling to compete against smaller, more nimble carriers that feature low-cost fares with no-frills service. As a result, several large airlines have been forced into bankruptcy, while a number of smaller carriers, such as Southwest Airlines and AirTran, have achieved rapid growth and profitability.

Just how do analysts compare the performance of companies like those named above? One approach is to compare the accounting data from the financial statements that the companies file with the SEC. Below are selected accounting data for Southwest Airlines (SWA), a successful low-cost carrier, and American Airlines (AA), the largest U.S. airline, for the fiscal year ending in December 2006:

	SWA ($ millions)	AA ($ millions)
Total sales	$ 9,086	$ 22,563
Net income	499	231

The accounting numbers by themselves do not provide much insight, and they are difficult to analyze because of the size difference between the two firms. However, if we compute one of the profitability ratios discussed in this chapter, the net profit margin, we see a dramatic difference in performance between the two airlines. The net profit margins (Net income/Total sales) for SWA and AA are 5.49 percent and 1.02 percent, respectively. This means that for every $100 in revenues, SWA is able to generate $5.49 of profit, whereas AA can only squeeze out $1.02. As this example illustrates, one advantage of using ratios is that they make direct comparisons possible by adjusting for size differences.

This chapter focuses on financial ratio analysis (or financial statement analysis), which involves the calculation and comparison of ratios derived from financial statements. These ratios can be used to draw useful conclusions about a company's financial condition, its operating efficiency, and the attractiveness of its securities as investments.

CHAPTER PREVIEW

In Chapter 3 we reviewed the basic structure of financial statements. This chapter explains how financial statements are used to evaluate a company's overall performance and assess its strengths and shortcomings. The basic tool used to do this is financial ratio analysis. Financial ratios are computed by dividing one number from a firm's financial statements by another such number in order to allow for meaningful comparisons between firms or areas within a firm.

Management can use the information from this type of analysis to help maximize the firm's value by identifying areas where performance improvements are needed. For example, the analysis of data from financial statements can help determine why a firm's cash flows are increasing or decreasing, why a firm's profitability is changing, and whether a firm will be able to pay its bills next month.

We begin the chapter by discussing some general guidelines for financial statement analysis, along with three different perspectives on financial analysis: those of the stockholder, manager, and creditor. Next, we describe how to prepare common-size financial statements, which allow us to compare firms that differ in size and to analyze a firm's financial performance over time. We then explain how to calculate and interpret key financial ratios and discuss the DuPont system, a diagnostic tool that uses financial ratios. After a discussion of benchmarks, we conclude with a description of the limitations of financial statement analysis.

4.1 Background for Financial Statement Analysis

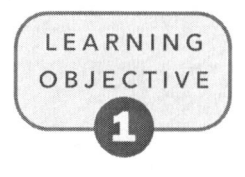

LEARNING OBJECTIVE 1

financial statement analysis
the use of financial statements to evaluate a company's overall performance and assess its strengths and shortcomings

This chapter will guide you through a typical **financial statement analysis**, which involves the use of financial ratios to analyze a firm's performance. We start with some general background. First, we look at the different perspectives we can take when analyzing financial statements; then we present some helpful guidelines for financial statement analysis.

Perspectives on Financial Statement Analysis

Stockholders and stakeholders may differ in the information they want to gain when analyzing financial statements. In this section, we discuss three perspectives from which we can view financial statement analysis: those of (1) stockholders, (2) managers, and (3) creditors. Although members of each of these groups view financial statements from their own point of view, the perspectives are not mutually exclusive.

STOCKHOLDERS' PERSPECTIVE

Stockholders are primarily concerned with the value of their stock and with how much cash they can expect to receive from dividends and/or capital appreciation. Therefore, stockholders want financial statements to tell them how profitable the firm is, what the return on their investment is, whether the firm can pay a dividend and, if so, how much, and how much cash is available for stockholders, both in total and on a per-share basis. Ultimately, stockholders are interested in how much a share of stock is worth in the market and whether the market is pricing the stock correctly. We address pricing issues in detail in Chapter 9, but financial analysis is a key step in valuing a company's stock.

MANAGERS' PERSPECTIVE

Broadly speaking, management's perspective of financial statement analysis is similar to that of stockholders. The reason is that stockholders own the firm and managers have a fiduciary responsibility to make decisions that are in the owners' best interests. Thus, managers are interested in the same performance measures as stockholders; profitability, dividends, capital appreciation, return on investment, and the like.

Managers, however, are also responsible for running the business on a daily basis and must make decisions that will maximize stockholder wealth in the long run. Maximizing stockholder wealth is not a single "big decision," but a series of day-to-day decisions. Thus, managers need feedback on the short-term impact these decisions have on the firm's financial statements and the current stock price. For example, managers can track trends in sales and can determine how well they are controlling expenses and how much of each sales dollar goes to the bottom line. In addition, managers can see the impact of their investment, financing, and working capital decisions reflected in the financial statements. Keep in mind that managers, as insiders, have access to much more detailed financial information than those outside the firm. Generally, outsiders have access to only published financial statements for publicly traded firms.

CREDITORS' PERSPECTIVE

The primary concern of creditors is whether and when they will receive the interest payments they are entitled to and when they will be repaid the money they loaned to the firm. Thus, a firm's creditors, including long-term bondholders, closely monitor how much debt the firm is currently using, whether the firm is generating enough cash to pay its day-to-day bills, and whether the firm will have sufficient cash in the future to make interest and principal payments on long-term debt *after* satisfying obligations that have a higher legal priority, such as paying employees' wages. Of course, the firm's ability to pay ultimately depends on cash flows and profitability; hence, creditors—like stockholders and managers—are interested in those aspects of the firm's financial performance. When millions or billions of dollars are at stake, you can bet that banks, insurance companies, and other creditors will examine the financial statements closely to uncover potential future problems.

Guidelines for Financial Statement Analysis

We turn now to some general guidelines that will help you when analyzing a firm's financial statements. First, make sure you understand which perspective you are adopting to conduct your analysis: stockholder, manager, or creditor. The perspective will dictate the type of information you need for the analysis and may affect the actions you take based on the results.

Second, always use audited financial statements, if they are available. As we discussed in Chapter 1, an audit means that an independent accountant has attested that the financial statements were correctly prepared and fairly represent the firm's financial condition at a point in time. If the statements are unaudited, you may need to make an extra effort. For example, if you are a creditor considering making a loan, you will need to make an especially diligent examination of the company's books before closing the deal. It would also be a good idea to make sure you know the company's management team and accountant very well. This will provide additional insight into the credit worthiness of the firm.

Third, use financial statements that cover three to five years, or more, to conduct your analysis. This enables you to perform a **trend analysis**, which involves looking at historical financial statements to see how various ratios are increasing, decreasing, or staying constant over time.

trend analysis
analysis of trends in financial data

Fourth, when possible, it is always best to compare a firm's financial statements with those of competitors that are roughly the same size and that offer similar products and services. If you compare firms of disparate size, the results may be meaningless because the two firms may have very different infrastructures, sources of financing, production capabilities, product mixes, and distribution channels. For example, comparing The Boeing Company's financial statements with those of Piper Aircraft, a firm that manufactures small aircraft, makes no sense whatsoever, although both firms manufacture aircraft. You will have to use your judgment as to whether relevant comparisons can be made between firms with large size differences. In general, the greater the size disparity, the less likely the comparisons between firms in the same business will be relevant.

In business it is common to **benchmark** a firm's performance, as discussed in the previous paragraph. The most common type of benchmarking involves comparing a firm's performance with the performance of similar firms that are relevant competitors. For example, Ford Motor Company may want to benchmark itself against General Motors and Toyota, its major competitors in the North American market. Firms can also benchmark against themselves—comparing this year's performance with last year's, for example—or compare against a goal, such as a 10 percent growth in sales. We discuss benchmarking in more detail later in the chapter.

benchmark
a standard against which performance is measured

Before You Go On

1. Why is it important to look at a firm's historical financial statements?
2. What is the primary concern of a firm's creditors?

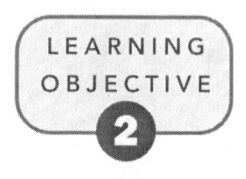

4.2 Common-Size Financial Statements

common-size financial statement
a financial statement in which each number is expressed as a percent of a base number, such as total assets or total revenues

Common-size financial statement analysis is one of the most basic forms of financial statement analysis. A **common-size financial statement** is one in which each number is expressed as a percentage of some base number, such as total assets or total revenues. For example, each number on a balance sheet may be divided by total assets. Dividing numbers by a common base to form a ratio is called *scaling*. It is an important concept, and you will read more about it later in the chapter, in the discussion of financial ratios. Financial statements scaled in this manner are also called *standardized financial statements*.

Common-size financial statements allow you to make meaningful comparisons between the financial statements of two firms that are different in size. For example, in the oil and gas field equipment market, Schlumberger Limited is the major competitor of Diaz Manufacturing, the illustrative firm introduced in Chapter 3. However, Schlumberger has $19.4 billion in total assets while Diaz Manufacturing's assets are only $1.9 billion. Without common-size financial statements, comparisons of these two firms would be difficult to interpret. Common-size financial statements are also useful for analyzing trends within a single firm over time, as you will see.

Common-Size Balance Sheets

To create a *common-size balance sheet,* we divide each of the asset accounts by total assets. We also divide each of the liability and equity accounts by total assets since Total assets = Total liabilities + Total equity. You can see the common-size balance sheet for Diaz Manufacturing in Exhibit 4.1. Assets are shown in the top portion of the exhibit, and liabilities and equity in the lower portion. The calculations are simple. For example,

Exhibit 4.1 Common-Size Balance Sheets for Diaz Manufacturing on December 31 ($ millions)

	2008	% of Total	2007	% of Total	2006	% of Total
Assets:						
Cash and marketable securities	$ 288.5	15.3	$ 16.6	1.1	$ 8.2	0.6
Accounts receivable	306.2	16.2	268.8	18.0	271.5	19.4
Inventories	423.8	22.4	372.7	24.9	400.0	28.6
Other current assets	21.3	1.1	29.9	2.0	24.8	1.8
Total current assets	$1,039.8	55.0	$ 688.0	46.1	$ 704.5	50.4
Plant and equipment (net)	399.4	21.1	394.2	26.4	419.6	30.0
Goodwill and other assets	450.0	23.8	411.6	27.6	273.9	19.6
Total assets	$1,889.2	100.0	$1,493.8	100.0	$1,398.0	100.0
Liabilities and Stockholders' Equity:						
Accounts payable and accruals	$ 349.3	18.5	$ 325.0	21.8	$ 395.0	28.3
Notes payable	10.5	0.6	4.2	0.3	14.5	1.0
Accrued income taxes	18.0	1.0	16.8	1.1	12.4	0.9
Total current liabilities	$ 377.8	20.0	$ 346.0	23.2	$ 421.9	30.2
Long-term debt	574.0	30.4	305.6	20.5	295.6	21.1
Total liabilities	$ 951.8	50.4	$ 651.6	43.6	$ 717.5	51.3
Common stock (54,566,054 shares)	0.5	0.0	0.5	0.0	0.5	0.0
Additional paid in capital	892.4	47.2	892.4	59.7	892.4	63.8
Retained earnings	67.8	3.6	(50.7)	(3.4)	(155.8)	(11.1)
Less: treasury stock	(23.3)	(1.2)	—	—	(56.6)	(4.0)
Total stockholders' equity	$ 937.4	49.6	$ 842.2	56.4	$ 680.5	48.7
Total liabilities and equity	$1,889.2	100.0	$1,493.8	100.0	$1,398.0	100.0

In common-size balance sheets, such as those in this exhibit, each asset account and each liability and equity account is expressed as a percentage of total assets. Common-size statements allow financial analysts to compare firms that are different in size and to identify trends within a single firm over time.

on the asset side in 2008, cash and marketable securities were 15.3 percent of total assets ($288.5/$1,889.2), and inventory was 22.4 percent of total assets ($423.8/$1,889.2). Notice that the percentages of total assets add up to 100 percent. On the liability side, accounts payable are 18.5 percent of total assets ($349.3/$1,889.2), and long-term debt is 30.4 percent ($574.0/$1,889.2). To test yourself, see if you can re-create the percentages in Exhibit 4.1 using your calculator. Make sure the percentages add up to 100, but realize that you may obtain slight variations from 100 because of rounding.

What kind of information can Exhibit 4.1 tell us about Diaz Manufacturing's operations? Here are some examples. Notice that in 2008, inventories accounted for 22.4 percent of total assets, down from 24.9 percent in 2007 and 28.6 percent in 2006. In other words, Diaz Manufacturing has been steadily reducing the proportion of its money tied up in inventory. This is probably good news because it is usually a sign of more efficient inventory management.

Now look at liabilities and equity, and notice that in 2008 total liabilities represent 50.4 percent of Diaz Manufacturing's total liabilities and equity. This means that common stockholders have provided 49.6 percent of the firm's total financing and that creditors have provided 50.4 percent of the financing. In addition, you can see that from 2006 to 2008, Diaz Manufacturing substantially increased the proportion of financing from long-term debt holders. Long-term debt provided 21.1 percent ($295.6/$1.398.0) of the financing in 2006 and 30.4 percent ($574.0/$1,889.2) in 2008.

A good source for financial statements is http://finance.yahoo.com.

Overall, we can identify the following trends in Diaz Manufacturing's common-size balance sheet. First, Diaz Manufacturing is a growing company. Its assets increased from $1,398.0 million in 2006 to $1,889.2 million in 2008. Second, the percentage of total assets held in current assets grew from 2006 to 2008, a sign of increasing liquidity. Recall from Chapter 2 that assets are liquid if they can be sold easily and quickly for cash without a loss of value. Third, the percentage of total assets in plant and equipment declined from 2006 to 2008, a sign that Diaz Manufacturing is becoming more efficient because it is using fewer long-term assets in producing sales (below you will see that sales have increased over the same period). Finally, as mentioned, Diaz Manufacturing has significantly increased the percentage of its financing from long-term debt. Generally, these are considered signs of a solidly performing company, but we have a long way to go before we can confidently reach that conclusion. We will now turn to Diaz Manufacturing's common-size income statement.

Common-Size Income Statements

The most useful way to prepare a *common-size income statement* is to express each account as a percentage of net sales, as shown for Diaz Manufacturing in Exhibit 4.2. *Net sales* are defined as total sales less all sales discounts and sales returns and allowances. You should note that when looking at accounting information and "sales" numbers as reported, they almost always mean net sales, unless otherwise stated. We will follow this convention in the book. Again, the percent calculations are simple. For example, in 2008 selling and administrative expenses are 14.8 percent of sales ($231.1/$1,563.7), and net income is 7.6 percent of sales ($118.5/$1,563.7). Before proceeding, make sure that you can verify each percentage in Exhibit 4.2 with your calculator.

Interpreting the common-size income statement is also straightforward. As you move down the income statement, you will find out exactly what happens to each dollar of sales that the firm generates. For example, in 2008 it cost Diaz Manufacturing 69.1 cents in cost of goods sold to generate one dollar of sales. Similarly, it cost 14.8 cents in selling and administrative expenses to generate a dollar of sales. The government takes 2.8 percent of sales in the form of taxes.

Exhibit 4.2 Common-Size Income Statements for Diaz Manufacturing for Fiscal Years Ending December 31 ($ millions)

	2008	% of Total	2007	% of Total	2006	% of Total
Net sales	$1,563.7	100.0	$1,386.7	100.0	$1,475.1	100.0
Cost of goods sold	1,081.1	69.1	974.8	70.3	1,076.3	73.0
Selling and administrative expenses	231.1	14.8	197.4	14.2	205.7	13.9
Earnings before interest, taxes, depreciation, and amortization (EBITDA)	$ 251.5	16.1	$ 214.5	15.5	$ 193.1	13.1
Depreciation	83.1	5.3	75.3	5.4	71.2	4.8
Earnings before interest and taxes (EBIT)	$ 168.4	10.8	$ 139.2	10.0	$ 121.9	8.3
Interest expense	5.6	0.4	18.0	1.3	27.8	1.9
Earnings before taxes (EBT)	$ 162.8	10.4	$ 121.2	8.7	$ 94.1	6.4
Taxes	44.3	2.8	16.1	1.2	27.9	1.9
Net income	$ 118.5	7.6	$ 105.1	7.6	$ 66.2	4.5
Dividends	—		—		—	
Addition to retained earnings	$ 118.5		$ 105.1		$ 66.2	

Common-size income statements express each account as a percentage of net sales. These statements allow financial analysts to better compare firms of different sizes and to analyze trends in a single firm's income statement accounts over time.

The common-size income statement can tell us a lot about a firm's efficiency and profitability. For example, in 2006, Diaz Manufacturing's cost of goods sold and selling and administrative expenses totaled 86.9 percent of sales (73.0 + 13.9). By 2008, these expenses declined to 83.9 percent of sales (69.1 + 14.8). This might mean that Diaz Manufacturing is negotiating lower prices from its suppliers or is more efficient in its use of materials and labor. Or it could mean that the company is getting higher net prices for its products, perhaps by offering fewer discounts or rebates. The important point, however, is that more of each sales dollar is contributing to net income.

Examination of the trends in the income statement and balance sheet suggests that Diaz Manufacturing is improving along a number of dimensions. The real question, however, is whether Diaz Manufacturing is performing well, as compared with other firms in the same industry. For example, the fact that 7.6 cents of every sales dollar reaches the bottom line may not be a good sign if we find out that Diaz Manufacturing's competitors average 10 cents of net income for every sales dollar.

> This CNBC Web site offers lots of financial information, including ratios of firms of your choice: moneycentral.msn.com/investor/research/welcome.asp.

Before You Go On

1. Why does it make sense to standardize financial statements?
2. What are common-size, or standardized, financial statements, and how are they prepared?

4.3 Financial Statement Analysis

In addition to the common-size ratios we have just discussed, other specialized financial ratios help analysts interpret the myriad of numbers in financial statements. In this section we examine financial ratios that measure a firm's liquidity, efficiency, leverage, profitability, and market value, using Diaz Manufacturing as an example. Keep in mind that for ratio analysis to be most useful, it should also include trend and benchmark analysis, which we discuss in more detail later in the chapter.

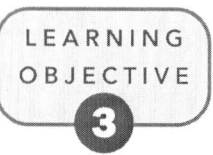

LEARNING OBJECTIVE 3

Why Ratios Are Better Measures

A **financial ratio** is simply one number from a financial statement that has been divided by another financial number. Like the percentages in common-size financial statements, ratios eliminate problems arising from differences in size because size is effectively "divided out"; more precisely, the denominator of the ratio adjusts, or scales, the numerator to a common base.

Here's an example. Suppose you want to assess the profitability of two firms. Firm A's net income is $5, and firm B's is $50. Which firm had the best performance? You really cannot tell because you have no idea what asset base was used to generate the income. In this case, a relevant measure of financial performance might be net income scaled by the firm's stockholders' equity—that is, the return on equity (ROE):

> Another source of financial statements for publicly held firms is the U.S. Securities and Exchange Commission at www.sec.gov.

financial ratio
A number from a financial statement that has been scaled by dividing by another financial number

$$\text{ROE} = \frac{\text{Net income}}{\text{Stockholders' equity}}$$

If firm A's total stockholders' equity is $25 and firm B's stockholders' equity is $5,000, the ROE for each firm is as follows:

Company	ROE Calculation	ROE Ratio	ROE
Firm A	$5/$25	0.20	20%
Firm B	$50/$5,000	0.01	1%

As you can see, the ROE for firm A is 20 percent—much larger than the ROE for firm B at 1 percent. Even though firm B had the higher net income in absolute terms ($50 versus $5), its stockholders had invested more money in the firm ($5,000 versus

$25), and it generated less income per dollar of invested equity than firm A. Clearly, firm A's performance is better than firm B's, given its smaller equity investment.

The bottom line is that accounting numbers are more easily compared and interpreted when they are scaled. This is why, for example, consumer groups pressured grocery stores to provide unit pricing. When comparing a bottle of Mel's Picante Sauce with four other brands, all in different-sized bottles, you need to know the cost per ounce, not the cost per bottle. The same is true in business. Common-size financial statements, for example, allow us to compare the financial data of large and small firms with the effect of size held constant.

CHOICE OF SCALE IS IMPORTANT

An important decision is your choice of the "size factor" for scaling. The size factor you select must be relevant and make economic sense. For example, suppose you want a measure that will enable you to compare the productivity of employees at a particular plant with the productivity of employees at other plants that make similar products. Your assistant makes a suggestion: divide net income by the number of parking spaces available at the plant. Will this ratio tell you how productive labor is at a plant? Clearly, the answer is no.

Your assistant comes up with another idea: divide net income by the number of employees. This ratio makes sense as a measure of employee productivity. A higher ratio indicates that employees are more productive because, on average, each employee is generating more income. In business, the type of variable most commonly used for scaling is a measure of size, such as total assets or total net sales. Other scaling variables are used in specific industries where they are especially informative. For example, in the airline industry, a key measure of performance is revenue per available seat mile; in the steel industry, it is sales or cost per ton; and in the automobile industry, it is cost per car.

OTHER COMMENTS ON RATIOS

The ratios we present in this chapter are widely accepted and are almost always included in any financial workup. However, you will find that different analysts will compute many of these standard ratios slightly differently. Modest variations in how ratios are computed are not a problem as long as the analyst carefully documents the work done and discloses the ratio formula. These differences are particularly important when you are comparing data from different sources.

Short-Term Liquidity Ratios

Liquid assets have active secondary markets and can be sold quickly for cash without a loss of value. Some assets are more liquid than others. For example, short-term marketable securities are very liquid because they can be easily sold in the secondary market at or near the original purchase price. In contrast, plant and equipment can take months or years to sell and often must be sold substantially below the cost of building or acquiring them.

When we examine a company's *liquidity position,* we want to know whether the firm can pay its bills when cash from operations is insufficient to pay short-term obligations, such as payroll, invoices from vendors, and maturing bank loans. As the name implies, *short-term liquidity ratios* focus on whether the firm has the ability to convert current assets into cash quickly without loss of value. As we have noted before, even a profitable business can fail if it cannot pay its current bills on time. The inability to pay debts when they are due is known as **insolvency.** Thus, liquidity ratios are also known as *short-term solvency ratios.* The two most important liquidity ratios are the current ratio and the quick ratio.

insolvency
the inability to pay debts when they are due

THE CURRENT RATIO

To calculate the current ratio, we divide current assets by current liabilities.[1] The formula appears in the following, along with a calculation of the current ratio for Diaz Manufacturing for 2008 based on balance sheet account data from Exhibit 4.1:

---
[1]This calculation involves dividing total current assets by total current liabilities. We drop the word "total" in the interest of brevity.

$$\text{Current ratio} = \frac{\text{Current assets}}{\text{Current liabilities}} \qquad (4.1)$$

$$= \frac{\$1{,}039.8}{\$377.8}$$

$$= 2.75$$

Diaz Manufacturing's current ratio is 2.75, which should be read as "2.75 times." What does this number mean? If Diaz Manufacturing were to take its current supply of cash and add to it the proceeds of liquidating its other current assets—such as marketable securities, accounts receivable, and inventory—it would have $1,039.8 million. This $1,039.8 million would cover the firm's short-term obligations of $377.8 million approximately 2.75 times, leaving a "cushion" of $662.0 million ($1,039.8 − $377.8).

Now turn to Exhibit 4.3, which shows the ratios discussed in this chapter for Diaz Manufacturing for the three-year period 2006–2008. The exhibit will allow us to identify important trends in the company's financial statements. Note that Diaz Manufacturing's current ratio has been steadily increasing over time. What does this trend mean? From the perspective of a potential creditor, it is a positive sign. To a potential creditor, more liquidity is better because it means that the firm will have the ability, at least in the short term, to make payments. From a stockholder's perspective, however, too much liquidity is not necessarily a good thing. If we were to discover that Diaz Manufacturing has a much higher current ratio than its competitors, it could mean that management is being too conservative by keeping too much money tied up in low-risk and low-yield assets, such as marketable securities. Generally, more liquidity is better and is a sign of a healthy firm. Only a benchmark analysis can tell us the complete story, however.

THE QUICK RATIO

The quick ratio is similar to the current ratio except that inventory is subtracted from current assets in the numerator. This change reflects the fact that inventory is often much less liquid than other current assets. Inventory is the most difficult current asset to convert to cash without loss of value. Of course, the liquidity of inventory varies with the industry. For example, inventory of a raw material commodity, such as gold or crude oil, is more likely to be sold with little loss in value than inventory consisting of perishables, such as fruit, or fashion items, such as basketball shoes. Another reason for excluding inventory in the quick ratio calculation is that the book value of inventory may be significantly more than its market value because it may be obsolete, partially completed, spoiled, out of fashion, or out of season.

To calculate the quick ratio—or *acid-test ratio*, as it is sometimes called—we divide current assets, less inventory, by current liabilities. The calculation for Diaz Manufacturing for 2008 is as follows, based on balance sheet data from Exhibit 4.1:

$$\text{Quick ratio} = \frac{\text{Current assets} - \text{Inventory}}{\text{Current liabilities}} \qquad (4.2)$$

$$= \frac{\$1{,}039.8 - \$423.8}{\$377.8}$$

$$= 1.63$$

The quick ratio of 1.63 times means that if we exclude inventory, Diaz Manufacturing had $1.63 of current assets for each dollar of current liabilities. You can see from Exhibit 4.3 that Diaz Manufacturing's liquidity position, as measured by its quick ratio, has been improving over time; this is generally a sign of good financial health.

Note that the quick ratio is almost always less than the current ratio, as it was for Diaz Manufacturing in 2008.[2] The quick ratio is a very conservative measure of liquidity because the calculation assumes that the inventory is valued at zero, which in most cases is not a realistic assumption. Even in a bankruptcy "fire sale," the inventory can be sold for some small percentage of its book value, generating at least some cash.

---

[2] The quick ratio will always be less than the current ratio for any firm that has inventory.

Exhibit 4.3 Ratios for Time-Trend Analysis for Diaz Manufacturing for Fiscal Years Ending December 31

Financial Ratio	2008	2007	2006
Liquidity Ratios:			
Current ratio	2.75	1.99	1.67
Quick ratio	1.63	0.91	0.72
Efficiency Ratios:			
Inventory turnover	2.55	2.62	2.69
Day's sales in inventory	143.14	139.31	135.69
Accounts receivable turnover	5.11	5.16	5.43
Day's sales outstanding	71.43	70.74	67.22
Total asset turnover	0.83	0.93	1.06
Fixed asset turnover	3.92	3.52	3.52
Leverage Ratios:			
Total debt ratio	0.50	0.44	0.51
Debt-to-equity ratio	1.02	0.77	1.05
Equity multiplier	2.02	1.77	2.05
Times interest earned	30.07	7.73	4.38
Cash coverage	44.91	11.92	6.95
Profitability Ratios:			
Gross profit margin	30.86 %	29.70 %	27.04 %
Operating profit margin	10.77 %	10.04 %	8.26 %
Net profit margin	7.58 %	7.58 %	4.49 %
EBIT return on assets	8.91 %	9.32 %	8.72 %
Return on assets	6.27 %	7.04 %	4.74 %
Return on equity	12.64 %	12.48 %	9.73 %
Market-Value Indicators:			
Price-earnings ratio	22.40	18.43	14.29
Earnings per share	$ 2.17	$ 1.93	$ 1.21

Note: Numbers may not add up because of rounding.

Comparing how financial ratios, such as these ratios for Diaz Manufacturing, change over time enables financial analysts to identify trends in company performance.

DECISION-MAKING EXAMPLE 4.1

The Liquidity Paradox

Situation: You are asked by your boss whether Wal-Mart or H&R Block is more liquid. You have the following information:

	Wal-Mart	H&R Block
Current ratio	0.92	1.20
Quick ratio	0.21	1.20

You also know that Wal-Mart carries a large inventory and that H&R Block is a service firm that specializes in income-tax preparation. Which firm is the most liquid? Your boss asks you to explain the reasons for your answers, and also to explain why H&R Block's current and quick ratios are the same.

> **Decision:** H&R Block is much more liquid than Wal-Mart. Looking at the difference between the quick ratios—0.21 versus 1.20—pretty much tells the story. Inventory is the least liquid of all the current assets. Because H&R Block does not manufacture or sell goods, it has no inventory; hence, the current and quick ratios are equal. Wal-Mart has a lot of inventory relative to the rest of its current assets, and that explains the large numerical drop between the current and quick ratios.

Efficiency Ratios

Now we turn to a group of ratios, called *efficiency ratios* or *asset turnover ratios,* that measure how efficiently a firm uses its assets to generate sales. These ratios are most useful to managers, who use them to identify inefficiencies in operations, and to creditors, who use them to find out how quickly inventory can be turned into receivables and ultimately into cash that can be used to satisfy debt obligations.

INVENTORY TURNOVER AND DAYS' SALES IN INVENTORY

We measure inventory turnover by dividing the cost of goods sold from the income statement by inventory from the balance sheet (see Exhibits 4.1 and 4.2). The formula for inventory turnover and its value for Diaz Manufacturing in 2008 are:

$$\text{Inventory turnover} = \frac{\text{Cost of goods sold}}{\text{Inventory}} \quad (4.3)$$

$$= \frac{\$1,081.1}{\$423.8}$$

$$= 2.55$$

The firm "turned over" its inventory 2.55 times during the year. Looking back at Exhibit 4.3, you can see that this ratio remained about the same over the period covered.

What exactly does "turning over" inventory mean? Consider a simple example. Assume that a firm starts the year with an inventory worth $100 and replaces the inventory when it is all sold; that is, the inventory goes to zero. Over the course of the year, the firm sells the inventory and replaces it three times. For the year, the firm has an inventory turnover of three times.

As a general rule, turning over inventory faster is a good thing because it means that the firm is doing a good job of minimizing its investment in inventory. Nevertheless, like all ratios, inventory turnover can be either too high or too low. Too high an inventory turnover ratio may signal that the firm has too little inventory and could be losing sales as a result. If the firm's inventory turnover level is too low, it could mean that management is not managing the firm's inventory efficiently or that an unusually large portion of the inventory is obsolete or out of date and has not yet been written off. In sum, inventory turnover that is significantly lower or significantly higher than that of competitors calls for further investigation.[3]

Based on the inventory turnover figure, and using a 365-day year, we can also calculate the *days' sales in inventory,* which tells us how long it takes a firm to turn over its inventory on average. The formula for days' sales in inventory, along with a calculation for Diaz Manufacturing, is as follows:

---

[3]Some financial analysts compute inventory turnover using sales rather than cost of goods sold in the numerator. On the one hand, this alternative calculation (Inventory turnover = Sales/Inventory) makes sense if the analyst wants to know the amount of sales generated per dollar of inventory. On the other hand, the calculation can be misleading if the firm generates a significant amount of revenues from activities that are not associated with inventory, such as providing services.

$$\text{Day's sales in inventory} = \frac{365 \text{ days}}{\text{Inventory turnover}} \quad (4.4)$$

$$= \frac{365 \text{ days}}{2.55}$$

$$= 143.14 \text{ days}$$

Note that inventory turnover in the formula is computed from Equation 4.3. On average, Diaz Manufacturing takes about 140 days to turn over its inventory. Generally speaking, the smaller the number, the more efficient the firm is at moving its inventory.

ALTERNATIVE CALCULATION FOR INVENTORY TURNOVER

Normally, we determine inventory turnover by dividing cost of goods sold by the inventory level at the end of the period. However, if a firm's inventory fluctuates widely or is growing (or decreasing) over time, some analysts prefer to compute inventory turnover using the average inventory value for the time period. In this case, the inventory turnover is calculated in two steps:

1. We first calculate average inventory by adding beginning and ending inventory and dividing by 2:

$$\text{Average inventory} = \frac{\text{Beginning inventory} + \text{Ending inventory}}{2}$$

2. We then divide the cost of goods sold by average inventory to find inventory turnover:

$$\text{Inventory turnover} = \frac{\text{Cost of goods sold}}{\text{Average inventory}}$$

LEARNING BY DOING APPLICATION 4.1

Alternative Calculations for Efficiency Ratios

Problem: For Diaz Manufacturing, compute the inventory turnover based on the average inventory. Then compare that value with 2.55, the turnover ratio based on Equation 4.3. Why do you think the two values differ?

Approach: Use the alternative calculation described above. In comparing the two values, you want to consider fluctuations in inventory over time.

Solution:

1. $\text{Average inventory} = \dfrac{\text{Beginning inventory} + \text{Ending inventory}}{2}$

   $= \dfrac{\$372.7 + \$423.8}{2}$

   $= \$398.3$

2. $\text{Inventory turnover} = \dfrac{\text{Cost of goods sold}}{\text{Average inventory}}$

   $= \dfrac{\$1,081.1}{\$398.3}$

   $= 2.71$

The inventory turnover computed with average inventory, 2.71 times, is slightly higher than 2.55 because the inventory increased during the year.

ACCOUNTS RECEIVABLE TURNOVER AND DAYS' SALES OUTSTANDING

Many firms make sales to their customers on credit, which creates an account receivable on the balance sheet. It does not do the firm much good to ship products or provide the services on credit if it cannot ultimately collect the cash from its customers. A firm that collects its receivables faster is generating cash faster. We can measure the speed at which a firm converts its receivables into cash with a ratio called accounts receivable turnover; the formula and calculated values for Diaz Manufacturing in 2008 are as follows:

$$\text{Accounts receivable turnover} = \frac{\text{Net sales}}{\text{Accounts receivable}} \qquad (4.5)$$

$$= \frac{\$1,563.7}{\$306.2}$$

$$= 5.11$$

The data to compute this ratio is from Diaz's balance sheet and income statement (Exhibits 4.1 and 4.2). Roughly, this ratio means that Diaz Manufacturing loans out and collects an amount equal to its outstanding accounts receivable 5.11 times over the course of a year.

In most circumstances, higher accounts receivable turnover is a good thing—it means that the firm is collecting cash payments from its credit customers faster. As shown in Exhibit 4.3, Diaz's collection speed slowed down slightly from 2006 to 2008. This may be a cause for management concern, for at least three reasons. First, Diaz's system for collecting accounts receivable may be inefficient. Second, the firm's customers may not be paying on time because their businesses are slowing down due to industry or general economic conditions. Finally, Diaz may be extending credit to customers that are poor credit risks. Making a determination of the cause would require us to compare Diaz's accounts receivable turnover with corresponding figures from its competitors.

You may find it easier to evaluate a firm's credit and collection policies by using days' sales outstanding, often referred to as DSO, which is calculated as follows:

$$\text{Days' sales outstanding} = \frac{365 \text{ days}}{\text{Accounts receivable turnover}} \qquad (4.6)$$

$$= \frac{365 \text{ days}}{5.11}$$

$$= 71.43 \text{ days}$$

Note that accounts receivable turnover is computed from Equation 4.5. The DSO for Diaz Manufacturing means that, on average, the company converts its credit sales into cash in 71.43 days. DSO is commonly called the *average collection period*.

Generally, faster collection is better. Whether 71.43 days is fast enough really depends on industry norms and on the credit terms Diaz Manufacturing extends to its customers. For example, if the industry average DSO is 77 days and Diaz Manufacturing gives customers 90 days to pay, then a DSO of 71.43 days is an indication of good management. If, in contrast, Diaz gives customers 60 days to pay, the company has a problem, and management needs to determine why customers are not paying on time.

ASSET TURNOVER RATIOS

We turn next to a discussion of some broader efficiency ratios. In this section we discuss two ratios that measure how efficiently management is using the firm's assets to generate sales.

Total asset turnover measures the dollar amount of sales generated with each dollar of total assets. Generally, the higher the total asset turnover, the more efficiently management is using total assets. Thus, if a firm increases its asset turnover, management is squeezing more sales out of a constant asset base. When a firm's asset turnover ratio is high for its industry, the firm may be approaching full capacity. In such a situation, if management wants to increase sales, it will need to make an investment in additional fixed assets.

The formula for total asset turnover and the calculation for Diaz Manufacturing's turnover value in 2008 (based on data from Exhibits 4.1 and 4.2) are as follows:

$$\text{Total asset turnover} = \frac{\text{Net sales}}{\text{Total assets}} \qquad (4.7)$$

$$= \frac{\$1,563.7}{\$1,889.2}$$

$$= 0.83$$

Total asset turnover for Diaz Manufacturing is 0.83 times. In other words, in 2008, Diaz Manufacturing generated $0.83 in sales for every dollar in assets. In Exhibit 4.3 you can see that Diaz Manufacturing's total asset turnover has declined slightly since 2006. This does not necessarily mean that the company's management team is performing poorly. The decline could be part of a typical industry sales cycle, or it could be due to a slowdown in the business of Diaz Manufacturing's customers. As always, getting a better fix on potential problems requires comparing Diaz Manufacturing's total asset turnover with comparable figures for its close competitors.

The turnover of total assets is a "big picture" measure. In addition, management may want to see how particular types of assets are being put to use. A common asset turnover ratio measures sales per dollar invested in fixed assets (plant and equipment). The fixed asset turnover formula and the 2008 calculation for Diaz are:

$$\text{Fixed asset turnover} = \frac{\text{Net sales}}{\text{Net fixed assets}} \qquad (4.8)$$

$$= \frac{\$1,563.7}{\$399.4}$$

$$= 3.92$$

Diaz Manufacturing generates $3.92 of sales for each dollar of fixed assets in 2008, which is an increase over the 2007 value of $3.52. This means that the firm is generating more sales for every dollar in fixed assets. In a manufacturing firm that relies heavily on plant and equipment to generate output, the fixed asset turnover number is an important ratio. In contrast, in a service-industry firm with little plant and equipment, *total* asset turnover is more relevant.

DECISION-MAKING EXAMPLE 4.2

Ranking Firms by Fixed Asset Turnover

Situation: Different industries use different amounts of fixed assets to generate their revenues. For example, the airline industry is capital intensive, with large investments in airplanes, whereas firms in service industries use more human capital (people) and have very little invested in fixed assets. As a financial analyst, you are given the following fixed asset turnover ratios: 0.79, 4.42, and 15.10. You must decide which ratios match up with three firms: Delta Air Lines, H&R Block, and Wal-Mart. Make this decision, and explain your reasoning.

Decision: At the extremes, Delta is a capital-intensive firm, and H&R Block is a service firm. We would expect firms with large investments in fixed assets (Delta) to have lower asset turnover than service-industry firms, which have few fixed assets. Wal-Mart is the middle-ground firm, with fixed asset holdings primarily in stores and land. Thus, the firms and their respective fixed asset turnovers are: Delta = 0.79, Wal-Mart = 4.42, and H&R Block = 15.10.

Leverage Ratios

Leverage ratios measure the extent to which a firm uses debt rather than equity financing and indicate the firm's ability to meet its long-term financial obligations, such as interest payments on debt and lease payments. The ratios are also called *long-term solvency ratios*. They are of interest to the firm's creditors, stockholders, and managers. Many different leverage ratios are used in industry; in this chapter we present some of the most widely used.

FINANCIAL LEVERAGE

The term **financial leverage** refers to the use of debt in a firm's capital structure. When a firm uses debt financing, rather than only equity financing, the returns to stockholders may be magnified. This so-called leveraging effect occurs because the interest payments associated with debt are fixed, regardless of the level of the firm's operating profits. On the one hand, if the firm's operating profits increase from one year to the next, debt holders continue to receive only their fixed-interest payments, and all of the increase goes to the stockholders. On the other hand, if the firm falls on hard times and suffers an operating loss, debt holders receive the same fixed-interest payment (assuming that the firm does not go bankrupt), and the loss is charged against the stockholders' equity. Thus, debt increases the returns to stockholders during good times and reduces the returns during bad times. In Chapter 16 we discuss financial leverage in greater depth and present a detailed example of how debt financing creates the leveraging effect.

> **financial leverage**
> the use of debt in a firm's capital structure; the more debt, the higher the financial leverage

The use of debt in a company's capital structure increases the firm's **default risk**—the risk that it will not be able to pay its debt as it comes due. The explanation is, of course, that debt payments are a fixed obligation and debt holders must be paid the interest and principal payments they are owed, regardless of whether the company earns a profit or suffers a loss. If a company fails to make an interest payment on the prescribed date, the company defaults on its debt and could be forced into bankruptcy by creditors.

> **default risk**
> the risk that a firm will not be able to pay its debt obligations as they come due

DEBT RATIOS

We next look at three leverage ratios that focus on how much debt, rather than equity, the firm employs in its capital structure. The more debt a firm uses, the higher its financial leverage, the more volatile its earnings, and the greater its risk of default.

Total Debt Ratio. The total debt ratio measures the extent to which the firm finances its assets from sources other than the stockholders. The higher the total debt ratio, the more debt the firm has in its capital structure. The total debt ratio and a calculation for Diaz Manufacturing for 2008 based on data from Exhibit 4.1 appear as follows:

$$\text{Total debt ratio} = \frac{\text{Total debt}}{\text{Total assets}} \quad (4.9)$$
$$= \frac{\$951.8}{\$1,889.2}$$
$$= 0.50$$

How do we determine the figure to use for total debt? Many variations are used, but perhaps the easiest is to subtract total equity from total assets. In other words, total debt is equal to total liabilities. Using Exhibit 4.1, we can calculate total debt for Diaz Manufacturing in 2008 as follows:

$$\text{Total debt} = \$1,889.2 - \$937.4 = \$951.8$$

As you can see from Equation 4.9, the total debt ratio for Diaz Manufacturing is 0.50, which means that 50 percent of the company's assets are financed with debt.

Looking back at Exhibit 4.3, we find that Diaz Manufacturing increased its use of debt from 2007 to 2008. The current total debt ratio of 50 percent appears relatively high, raising questions about the company's financing strategy. Whether a high or low value for the total debt ratio is good or bad, however, depends on how the firm's capital structure affects the value of the firm. We explore this topic in greater detail in Chapter 16.

We turn next to two common variations of the total debt ratio: the debt-to-equity ratio and the equity multiplier.

Debt-to-Equity Ratio. The *total debt ratio* tells us the amount of debt for each dollar of total assets. The *debt-to-equity ratio* tells us the amount of debt for each dollar of equity. Based on data from Exhibit 4.1, Diaz Manufacturing's debt-to-equity ratio for 2008 is 1.02:

$$\text{Debt-to-equity ratio} = \frac{\text{Total debt}}{\text{Total equity}} \quad (4.10)$$

$$= \frac{\$951.8}{\$937.4}$$

$$= 1.02$$

The total debt ratio and the debt-to-equity ratio are directly related by the following formula, shown with a calculation for Diaz Manufacturing:

$$\text{Total debt ratio} = \frac{\text{Debt-to-equity ratio}}{1 + \text{Debt-to-equity ratio}}$$

$$= \frac{1.02}{1 + 1.02}$$

$$= 0.50$$

As you can see, once you know one of these ratios, you can compute the other. Which of the two ratios you use is really a matter of personal preference.

Equity Multiplier. The equity multiplier tells us the amount of assets that the firm has for every dollar of equity. Diaz Manufacturing's equity multiplier ratio is 2.02, as shown here:

$$\text{Equity multiplier} = \frac{\text{Total assets}}{\text{Total equity}} \quad (4.11)$$

$$= \frac{\$1,889.2}{\$937.4}$$

$$= 2.02$$

Notice that the equity multiplier is directly related to the debt-to-equity ratio:

$$\text{Equity multiplier} = 1 + \text{Debt-to-equity ratio}$$

This is no accident. Recall the balance sheet identity: Total assets = Total liabilities (debt) + Total stockholders' equity. This identity can be substituted into the numerator of the equity multiplier formula (Equation 4.11):

$$\text{Equity multiplier} = \frac{\text{Total assets}}{\text{Total equity}}$$

$$= \frac{\text{Total equity} + \text{Total debt}}{\text{Total equity}}$$

$$= \frac{\text{Total equity}}{\text{Total equity}} + \frac{\text{Total debt}}{\text{Total equity}}$$

$$= 1 + \frac{\text{Total debt}}{\text{Total equity}}$$

$$= 1 + \frac{\$951.8}{937.4}$$
$$= 1 + 1.02$$
$$= 2.02$$

Therefore, all three of these leverage ratios (Equations 4.9–4.11) are related by the balance sheet identity, and once you know one of the three ratios, you can compute the other two ratios. All three ratios provide the same information.

> **LEARNING BY DOING**
> **APPLICATION 4.2**
>
> ### Finding a Leverage Ratio
>
> **Problem:** A firm's debt-to-equity ratio is 0.5. What is the firm's total debt ratio?
>
> **Approach:** Use the equation that relates the total debt ratio to the debt-to-equity ratio.
>
> **Solution:**
>
> $$\text{Total debt ratio} = \frac{\text{Debt-to-equity ratio}}{1 + \text{Debt-to-equity ratio}}$$
> $$= \frac{0.5}{1 + 0.5}$$
> $$= 0.33$$

> **LEARNING BY DOING**
> **APPLICATION 4.3**
>
> ### Solving for an Unknown Using the Debt-to-Equity Ratio
>
> **Problem:** You are given the follow information about H&R Block's year-end balance sheet. The firm's debt-to-equity ratio is 1.83, and its total equity is $1.90 billion. Determine the book (accounting) values for H&R Block's total debt and total assets.
>
> **Approach:** We know that the debt-to-equity ratio is 1.83 and that total equity is $1.90 billion. We also know that the debt-to-equity ratio (Equation 4.10) is equal to total debt divided by total equity, and we can use this information to solve for total debt. Once we have a figure for total debt, we can use the basic accounting identity to solve for total assets.
>
> **Solution:**
>
> $$\text{Total debt} = \text{Debt-to-equity ratio} \times \text{Total equity}$$
> $$= 1.83 \times \$1.90$$
> $$= \$3.48 \text{ billion}$$
>
> $$\text{Total assets} = \text{Total debt} + \text{Total equity}$$
> $$= \$3.48 + \$1.90$$
> $$= \$5.38 \text{ billion}$$

COVERAGE RATIOS

A second type of leverage ratio measures the firm's ability to service its debts, or how easily the firm can "cover" debt payments out of earnings or cash flow. What does "coverage" mean? If your monthly take-home pay from your part-time job is $400 and the rent on your apartment is $450, you are going to be in some financial distress because your income does not "cover" your $450 fixed obligation to pay the rent. If, on the other hand, your take-home pay is $900, your monthly coverage ratio with respect to rent is $900/$450 = 2 times. This means that for every dollar of rent you must pay, you earn two dollars of revenue. The higher your coverage ratio, the less likely you will default on your rent payments.

Times Interest Earned. Our first coverage ratio is times interest earned, which measures the extent to which operating profits (earnings before interest and taxes, or EBIT) cover the firm's interest expenses. Creditors prefer to lend to firms whose EBIT is far in excess of their interest payments. The equation for the times-interest-earned ratio and a calculation for Diaz Manufacturing from its income statement (Exhibit 4.2) for 2008 are:

$$\text{Times interest earned} = \frac{\text{EBIT}}{\text{Interest expense}} \quad (4.12)$$
$$= \frac{\$168.4}{\$5.6}$$
$$= 30.07$$

Diaz Manufacturing can cover its interest charges about 30 times with its operating income. This is an extremely large figure, which appears to point to a good margin of safety for creditors. In general, the larger the times interest earned figure, the more likely the firm is to meet its interest payments.

Cash Coverage. As we have discussed before, depreciation is a noncash expense, and as a result, no cash goes out the door when depreciation is deducted on the income statement. Thus, rather than asking whether operating profits (EBIT) are sufficient to cover interest payments, we might ask how much cash is available to cover interest payments. The cash a firm has available from operations to meet interest payments are better measured by EBIT plus depreciation and amortization (EBITDA).[4] Thus, the cash coverage ratio for Diaz Manufacturing in 2008 is:

$$\text{Cash coverage} = \frac{\text{EBITDA}}{\text{Interest expense}} \quad (4.13)$$
$$= \frac{\$251.5}{\$5.6}$$
$$= 44.91$$

For a firm with depreciation or amortization expenses, which includes virtually all firms, EBITDA coverage will be larger than times interest earned coverage.

Profitability Ratios

Profitability ratios measure management's ability to efficiently use the firm's assets to generate sales and manage the firm's operations. These measurements are of interest to stockholders, creditors, and managers because they focus on the firm's earnings. The profitability ratios presented in this chapter are among a handful of ratios used by virtually all stakeholders when analyzing a firm's performance. In general, the higher the profitability ratios, the better the firm is performing.

GROSS PROFIT MARGIN

The gross profit margin measures the percentage of net sales remaining after the cost of goods sold is paid. It captures the firm's ability to manage the expenses directly

---

[4] EBITDA can differ from actual cash flows because of the accounting accruals discussed in Chapter 3.

associated with producing the firm's products or services. Next we show the gross profit margin formula, along with a calculation for Diaz Manufacturing in 2008, using data from Exhibit 4.2:

$$\text{Gross profit margin} = \frac{\text{Net sales} - \text{Cost of goods sold}}{\text{Net sales}} \quad (4.14)$$

$$= \frac{\$1,563.7 - \$1,081.1}{\$1,563.7}$$

$$= 30.86\%$$

Thus, after paying the cost of goods sold, Diaz Manufacturing has 30.86 percent of the sales amount remaining to pay other expenses. From Exhibit 4.3, you can see that Diaz Manufacturing's gross profit margin has been increasing over the past several years, which is good news.

OPERATING PROFIT MARGIN AND EBITDA MARGIN

Moving farther down the income statement, you can measure the percentage of sales that remains after payment of cost of goods sold and all other expenses, except for interest and taxes. Operating profit is typically measured as EBIT. The operating profit margin, therefore, gives an indication of the profitability of the firm's operations, independent of its financing policies or tax management strategies. The operating profit margin formula, along with Diaz Manufacturing's 2008 operating profit margin calculated from Exhibit 4.2, is as follows:

$$\text{Operating profit margin} = \frac{\text{EBIT}}{\text{Net sales}} \quad (4.15)$$

$$= \frac{\$168.4}{\$1,563.7}$$

$$= 10.77\%$$

Many Wall Street stock analysts are concerned with cash flows generated by operations rather than operating earnings and will use EBITDA in the numerator instead of EBIT. Calculated in this way, the operating profit margin is known as the EBITDA margin.

NET PROFIT MARGIN

The net profit margin indicates the percentage of sales remaining after all of the firm's expenses, including interest and taxes, have been paid. The net profit margin formula is shown here, along with the calculated value for Diaz Manufacturing in 2008, using data from the firm's income statement (Exhibit 4.2):

$$\text{Net profit margin} = \frac{\text{Net income}}{\text{Net sales}} \quad (4.16)$$

$$= \frac{\$118.5}{\$1,563.7}$$

$$= 7.58\%$$

As you can see from Exhibit 4.3, Diaz Manufacturing's net profit margin improved dramatically from 2006 to 2008. This is good news. The question remains, however, whether 7.58 percent is a good profit margin in an absolute sense. Answering this question requires that we compare Diaz Manufacturing's performance to the performance of its competitors, which we will do later in this chapter. What qualifies as a good profit margin varies significantly across industries. Generally speaking, the higher a company's profit margin, the better the company's performance.

RETURN ON ASSETS

So far, we have examined profitability as a percentage of sales. It is also important that we analyze profitability as a percentage of investment, either in assets or in equity. First, let's look at return on assets. In practice, return on assets is calculated in two different ways.

One approach provides a measure of operating profit (EBIT) per dollar of assets. This is a powerful measure of return because it tells us how efficiently management utilized the assets under their command, independent of financing decisions and taxes. It can be thought of as a measure of the pre-tax return on the total net investment in the firm from operations. The formula for this version of return on assets, which we call EBIT return on assets (EROA), is shown next, together with the calculated value for Diaz Manufacturing in 2008, using data from Exhibits 4.1 and 4.2:

$$\text{EROA} = \frac{\text{EBIT}}{\text{Total assets}} \qquad (4.17)$$
$$= \frac{\$168.4}{\$1,889.2}$$
$$= 8.91\%$$

Exhibit 4.3 shows us that, unlike the other profitability ratios, Diaz Manufacturing's EROA did not really improve from 2006 to 2008. The very similar EROA values for 2006 and 2008 indicate that assets increased at approximately the same rate as operating profits.

Some analysts calculate return on assets (ROA) as:

$$\text{Return on assets} = \frac{\text{Net income}}{\text{Total assets}} \qquad (4.18)$$
$$= \frac{\$118.5}{\$1,889.2}$$
$$= 6.27\%$$

Although it is a common calculation, we advise against using the calculation in Equation 4.18 unless you are using the DuPont system, which we discuss shortly. The ROA calculation divides a measure of earnings available to stockholders (net income) by total assets (debt plus equity), which is a measure of the investment in the firm by both stockholders and creditors. Constructing a ratio of those two numbers is like mixing apples and oranges. The information that this ratio provides about the efficiency of asset utilization is obscured by the financing decisions the firm has made and the taxes it pays. You can see this in Exhibit 4.3, which shows that, in contrast to the very small change in EROA, ROA increases substantially for 2006 to 2008. This increase in ROA is due not to improved efficiency but rather to a large decrease in interest expense (see Exhibit 4.2).

The key point is that EROA surpasses ROA as a measure of how efficiently assets are utilized in operations. Dividing a measure of earnings to both debt holders and stockholders by a measure of how much both debt holders and stockholders have invested gives us a clearer view of what we are trying to measure.

In general, when you calculate a financial ratio, if you have a measure of income to stockholders in the numerator, you want to make sure that you have only investments by stockholders in the denominator. Similarly, if you have a measure of total profits from operations in the numerator, you want to divide it by a measure of total investments by both debt holders and stockholders.

RETURN ON EQUITY

Return on equity (ROE) measures net income as a percentage of the stockholders' investment in the firm. The return on equity formula and the calculation for Diaz Manufacturing in 2008 based on data from Exhibits 4.1 and 4.2 are as follows:

$$\text{Return on equity} = \frac{\text{Net income}}{\text{Total equity}} \qquad (4.19)$$

$$= \frac{\$118.5}{\$937.4}$$

$$= 12.64\%$$

ALTERNATIVE CALCULATION OF ROA AND ROE

As with efficiency ratios, the calculation of ROA and ROE involves dividing an income statement value, which relates to a period of time, by a balance sheet value from the end of the time period. Some analysts prefer to calculate ROA and ROE using the average asset value or equity value, where the average value is determined as follows:

$$\text{Average asset or equity value} = \frac{\text{Beginning value} + \text{Ending value}}{2}$$

LEARNING BY DOING APPLICATION 4.4

Alternative Calculations for EROA and ROE Ratios

Problem: Calculate the EROA and ROE for Diaz Manufacturing using average balance sheet values, compare the results with the calculations based on Equations 4.17 and 4.19, and explain why some analysts might prefer the alternative calculation.

Approach: To make the calculations, first find average values for the asset and equity accounts using data in Exhibit 4.1. Then use these values to calculate the EROA and ROE. In explaining why some analysts might prefer the alternative calculation, consider possible fluctuations of assets or equity over time.

Solution:

$$\text{Average asset or equity value} = \frac{\text{Beginning value} + \text{Ending value}}{2}$$

$$\text{Average asset value} = \frac{\$1{,}493.8 + \$1{,}889.2}{2}$$

$$= \$1{,}691.5$$

$$\text{Average equity value} = \frac{\$842.2 + \$937.4}{2}$$

$$= \$889.8$$

$$\text{EROA} = \frac{\text{EBIT}}{\text{Total assets}} = \frac{\$168.4}{\$1{,}691.5}$$

$$= 9.96\%$$

$$\text{ROE} = \frac{\text{Net income}}{\text{Total equity}} = \frac{\$118.5}{\$889.8}$$

$$= 13.32\%$$

Both EROA (9.96 percent versus 8.91 percent) and ROE (13.32 percent versus 12.64 percent) are higher when the average values are used. The reason is that Diaz's total assets grew from $1,493.8 million in 2007 to $1,889.2 million in 2008 and its equity grew from $842.2 million to $937.4 million during the same period. We could argue in favor of using the average asset or equity value by pointing out that the earnings for the one-year period are earned with the average value of assets or equity over the period.

Market-Value Indicators

The ratios we have discussed so far rely solely on the firm's financial statements, and we know that much of the data in those statements are historical and do not represent current market value. Also, as we discussed in Chapter 1, the appropriate objective for the firm's management is to maximize stockholder value, and the market value of the stockholders' claims is the value of the *cash flows* that they are entitled to receive, which is not necessarily the same as accounting income. To find out how the stock market evaluates a firm's liquidity, efficiency, leverage, and profitability, we need ratios based on market values.

Over the years, financial analysts have developed a number of ratios, called *market-value ratios,* which combine market-value data with data from a firm's financial statements. Here we examine the most commonly used market-value ratios: earnings per share and the price-earnings ratio.

EARNINGS PER SHARE

Dividing a firm's net income by the number of shares outstanding yields earnings per share (EPS). At the end of 2008, Diaz Manufacturing had 54,566,054 shares outstanding (see Exhibit 3.1 in Chapter 3) and net income of $118.5 million (Exhibit 4.2). Its EPS at that point is thus calculated as follows:

$$\text{Earning per share} = \frac{\text{Net income}}{\text{Shares outstanding}} \qquad (4.20)$$

$$= \frac{\$118,500,000}{54,566,054} = \$2.17 \text{ per share}$$

PRICE-EARNINGS RATIO

The price-earnings (P/E) ratio relates earnings per share to price per share. The formula, with a calculation for Diaz Manufacturing for the end of 2008, is as follows:

$$\text{Price-earnings ratio} = \frac{\text{Price per share}}{\text{Earnings per share}} \qquad (4.21)$$

$$= \frac{\$48.61}{\$2.17} = 22.4$$

Price per share on a given date can be obtained from listings in the *Wall Street Journal* or from an online source, such as Yahoo! Finance.

What does it mean for a firm to have a price-earnings ratio of 22.4? It means that the stock market places a value of $22.40 on every $1 of net income. Why are investors willing to pay $22.40 for a claim on $1 of earnings? The answer is that the stock price does not only reflect the earnings this year. It reflects all future cash flows from earnings, and the especially high P/E ratio can indicate that investors expect the firm's earnings to grow in the future. Alternatively, a high P/E ratio might be due to unusually low earnings in a particular year and investors might expect earnings to recover to a normal level soon. We will discuss how expected growth affects P/E ratios in detail in later chapters. As with other measures, to understand whether the P/E ratio is too high or too low, we must compare the firm's P/E ratio with those of competitors and also look at movements in the firm's P/E ratio relative to market trends.

Concluding Comments on Ratios

We could have covered many more ratios, but that is enough for now; we will introduce additional ratios as we need them in future chapters. However, the group of ratios presented in this chapter is a fair representation of the ratios needed to analyze the performance of a business. When using ratios, it is important that you consider each ratio and ask yourself, "What does this ratio mean, or what is it measuring?" rather than trying to memorize a definition. Good ratios make good economic sense when you look at them.

> **Before You Go On**
>
> 1. What are the efficiency ratios, and what do they measure? Why, for some firms, is the total asset turnover more important than the fixed asset turnover?
> 2. List the leverage ratios discussed in this section, and explain how they are related.
> 3. List the profitability ratios discussed in this section, and explain how they differ from each other.

4.4 The DuPont System: A Diagnostic Tool

LEARNING OBJECTIVE 4

By now, your mind may be swimming with ratios. Fortunately, some enterprising financial managers at the DuPont Company developed a system in the 1960s that ties together some of the most important financial ratios and provides a systematic approach to financial ratio analysis.

An Overview of the DuPont System

The DuPont system of analysis is a diagnostic tool that uses financial ratios to evaluate a company's financial health. The process has three steps. First, management assesses the company's financial health using the DuPont ratios. Second, if any problems are identified, management corrects them. Finally, management monitors the firm's financial performance over time, looking for differences from ratios established as benchmarks by management.

Under the DuPont system, management is charged with making decisions that maximize the firm's return on equity (ROE) as opposed to maximizing the value of the stockholders' shares. The system is primarily designed to be used by management as a diagnostic and corrective tool, though investors and other stakeholders have found its diagnostic powers of interest.

The DuPont system is derived from two equations that link the firm's return on assets (ROA) and return on equity (ROE). The system identifies three areas where management should focus its efforts in order to maximize the firm's ROE: (1) how much profit management can earn on sales, (2) how efficient management is in using the firm's assets, and (3) how much financial leverage management is using. Each of these areas is monitored by a single ratio, and together the ratios comprise the *DuPont equation*. We now develop the DuPont equation and discuss its managerial implications. We start by looking at the equation for ROA.

The ROA Equation

The ROA equation links the firm's return on assets with its total asset turnover and net profit margin. We derive this relationship from the ROA equation as follows:

$$ROA = \frac{\text{Net income}}{\text{Total assets}}$$

$$= \frac{\text{Net income}}{\text{Total assets}} \times \frac{\text{Net sales}}{\text{Net sales}}$$

$$= \frac{\text{Net income}}{\text{Net sales}} \times \frac{\text{Net sales}}{\text{Total assets}}$$

$$= \text{Net profit margin} \times \text{Total asset turnover}$$

As you can see, we start with the ROA formula presented earlier as Equation 4.18. Then we multiply ROA by net sales divided by net sales. In the third line, we rearrange the terms, coming up with the expression ROA = (Net income/Net sales) × (Net sales/Total assets). You may recognize the first ratio in the third line as the firm's net profit margin (Equation 4.16) and the second ratio as the firm's total asset turnover (Equation 4.7). Thus, we end up with the final equation for ROA, which is restated as Equation 4.22:

$$\text{ROA} = \text{Net profit margin} \times \text{Total asset turnover} \quad (4.22)$$

Equation 4.22 says that a firm's ROA is determined by two factors: (1) the firm's net profit margin and (2) the firm's total asset turnover. Let's look at the managerial implications of each of these terms.

Net Profit Margin. The net profit margin ratio can be written as follows:

$$\text{Net profit margin} = \frac{\text{Net income}}{\text{Net sales}} = \frac{\text{EBIT}}{\text{Net sales}} \times \frac{\text{EBT}}{\text{EBIT}} \times \frac{\text{Net income}}{\text{EBT}}$$

As you can see, the net profit margin can be viewed as the product of three ratios: (1) the operating profit margin (EBIT/Net sales), which is Equation 4.15, (2) a ratio that measures the impact of interest expenses on profits (EBT/EBIT), and (3) a ratio that measures the impact of taxes on profits (Net income/EBT). Thus, the profit margin focuses on management's ability to generate profits from sales by efficiently managing the firm's (1) operating expenses, (2) interest expenses, and (3) tax expenses.

Total Asset Turnover. Total asset turnover, which is defined as Net sales/Total assets, measures how efficiently management uses the assets under its command—that is, how much output management can generate with a given asset base. Thus, total asset turnover is a measure of *asset use efficiency*.

PROFIT MARGINS VERSUS ASSET TURNOVER

The ROA equation provides some very interesting managerial insights. It says that if management wants to increase the firm's ROA, it can increase the net profit margin, total asset turnover, or both. Of course, every firm would like to make both terms as large as possible so as to earn the highest possible ROA. Though every industry is different, competition, marketing considerations, technology, and manufacturing capabilities, to name a few, place upper limits on asset turnover and net profit margins and, thus, ROA. However, Equation 4.22 suggests that management can follow two distinct strategies to maximize ROA. Deciding between the strategies involves a trade-off between asset turnover and profit margin.

The first management strategy emphasizes high profit margin and low asset turnover. Examples of companies that use this strategy are luxury stores, such as jewelry stores, high-end department stores, and upscale specialty boutiques. Such stores carry expensive merchandise that has a high profit margin but tends to sell slowly. The second management strategy depends on low profit margins and high turnover. Typical examples of firms that use this strategy are discount stores and grocery stores, which have very low profit margins but make up for it by turning over their inventory very quickly. A typical chain grocery store, for example, turns over its inventory more than 12 times per year.

Exhibit 4.4 illustrates both strategies. The exhibit shows asset turnover, profit margin, and ROA for four retailing firms in 2006. Nordstrom is a department store that sells expensive merchandise, and Polo Ralph Lauren stores are upscale boutiques that

Exhibit 4.4 Two Basic Strategies to Earn a Higher ROA[a]

Company	Asset Turnover	×	Profit Margin (%)	=	ROA (%)
High Profit Margin:					
Polo Ralph Lauren	1.21		8.22		9.95
Nordstrom	1.57		7.13		11.19
High Turnover:					
Whole Foods Market	2.74		3.63		9.95
Wal-Mart Stores	2.28		3.56		8.12

[a]Ratios are calculated using financial results for 2006.

To maximize a firm's ROA, management can focus more on achieving high profit margins or on achieving high asset turnover. High-end retailers like Polo Ralph Lauren and Nordstrom focus more on achieving high profit margins, while grocery and discount stores like Whole Foods Market and Wal-Mart tend to focus more on achieving high asset turnover because competition limits their ability to achieve very high profit margins.

carry expensive casual wear for men and women. At the other end of the spectrum are Wal-Mart, which is famous for its low-price, high-volume strategy, and Whole Foods Markets, a successful grocery chain based in Austin, Texas.

Notice that the two luxury-item stores (Nordstrom and Polo Ralph Lauren) have lower asset turnover and higher profit margins, while the discount and grocery stores have lower profit margins and much higher asset turnover. Whole Foods and Wal-Mart are strong financial performers in their industry sectors. Whole Foods' ROA of 9.95 percent is quite remarkable for the grocery business. Both Polo Ralph Lauren and Nordstrom are top performers in their sectors of the economy, and their high ROAs (9.95 and 11.19 percent, respectively) corroborate that fact, as well as reflecting the strength of the U.S. economy during 2006.

The ROE Equation

To derive the ROE equation, we start with the formula from Equation 4.19:

$$\text{ROE} = \frac{\text{Net income}}{\text{Total equity}}$$

$$= \frac{\text{Net income}}{\text{Total equity}} \times \frac{\text{Total assets}}{\text{Total assets}}$$

$$= \frac{\text{Net income}}{\text{Total assets}} \times \frac{\text{Total assets}}{\text{Total equity}}$$

$$= \text{ROA} \times \text{Equity multiplier}$$

Next, we multiply by total assets divided by total assets, and then we rearrange the terms so that ROE = (Net income/Total assets) × (Total assets/Total equity), as shown in the third line. By this definition, ROE is the product of two ratios already familiar to us: ROA (Equation 4.18) and the equity multiplier (Equation 4.11). The equation for ROE is shown as Equation 4.23:

$$\text{ROE} = \text{ROA} \times \text{Equity multiplier} \quad (4.23)$$

Interesting here is the fact that ROE is determined by the firm's ROA and its use of leverage. The greater the use of debt in the firm's capital structure, the greater the

ROE. Thus, increasing the use of leverage is one way management can increase the firm's ROE—but at a price. That is, the greater the use of financial leverage, the more risky the firm. How aggressively a company uses this strategy depends on management's preferences for risk and the willingness of creditors to lend money and bear the risk.

The DuPont Equation

Now we can combine our two equations into a single equation. From Equation 4.23, we know that ROE = ROA × Equity multiplier; and from Equation 4.22, we know that ROA = Net profit margin × Total asset turnover. Substituting Equation 4.22 into Equation 4.23 yields an expression formally called the DuPont equation, as follows:

$$\text{ROE} = \text{Net profit margin} \times \text{Total asset turnover} \times \text{Equity multiplier} \quad (4.24)$$

We can also express the DuPont equation in ratio form:

$$\text{ROE} = \frac{\text{Net income}}{\text{Net sales}} \times \frac{\text{Net sales}}{\text{Total assets}} \times \frac{\text{Total assets}}{\text{Total equity}} \quad (4.25)$$

To check the DuPont relationship, we will use some values from Exhibit 4.3, which lists financial ratios for Diaz Manufacturing. For 2008, Diaz's net profit margin is 7.58 percent, total asset turnover is 0.83, and the equity multiplier is 2.02. Substituting these values into Equation 4.24 yields:

ROE = Net profit margin × Total asset turnover × Equity multiplier
    = 7.58 × 0.83 × 2.02
    = 12.71 percent

With rounding error, this agrees with the value computed for ROE in Exhibit 4.3.

Applying the DuPont System

In summary, the DuPont equation tells us that a firm's ROE is determined by three factors: (1) net profit margin, which measures the firm's operating efficiency and how it manages its interest expense and taxes; (2) total asset turnover, which measures the efficiency with which the firm's assets are utilized; and (3) the equity multiplier, which measures the firm's use of financial leverage. The ROA is the product of the firm's net profit margin and total asset turnover. The schematic diagram in Exhibit 4.5 shows how the three key DuPont ratios are linked together and how they relate to the balance sheet and income statement for Diaz Manufacturing.

The DuPont system of analysis is a useful tool to help identify problem areas within a firm. For example, suppose that North Sails Group, a sailboat manufacturer located in San Diego, California, is having financial difficulty. The firm hires you to help apply the DuPont system of analysis to find out why the ship is financially sinking. The firm's CFO has you calculate the DuPont ratio values for the firm and obtain some industry averages to use as benchmarks, as shown.

DuPont Ratios	Firm	Industry
ROE	8%	16%
ROA	4%	8%
Equity multiplier	2	2
Net profit margin	8%	16%
Asset turnover	0.5	0.5

4.4 The DuPont System: A Diagnostic Tool

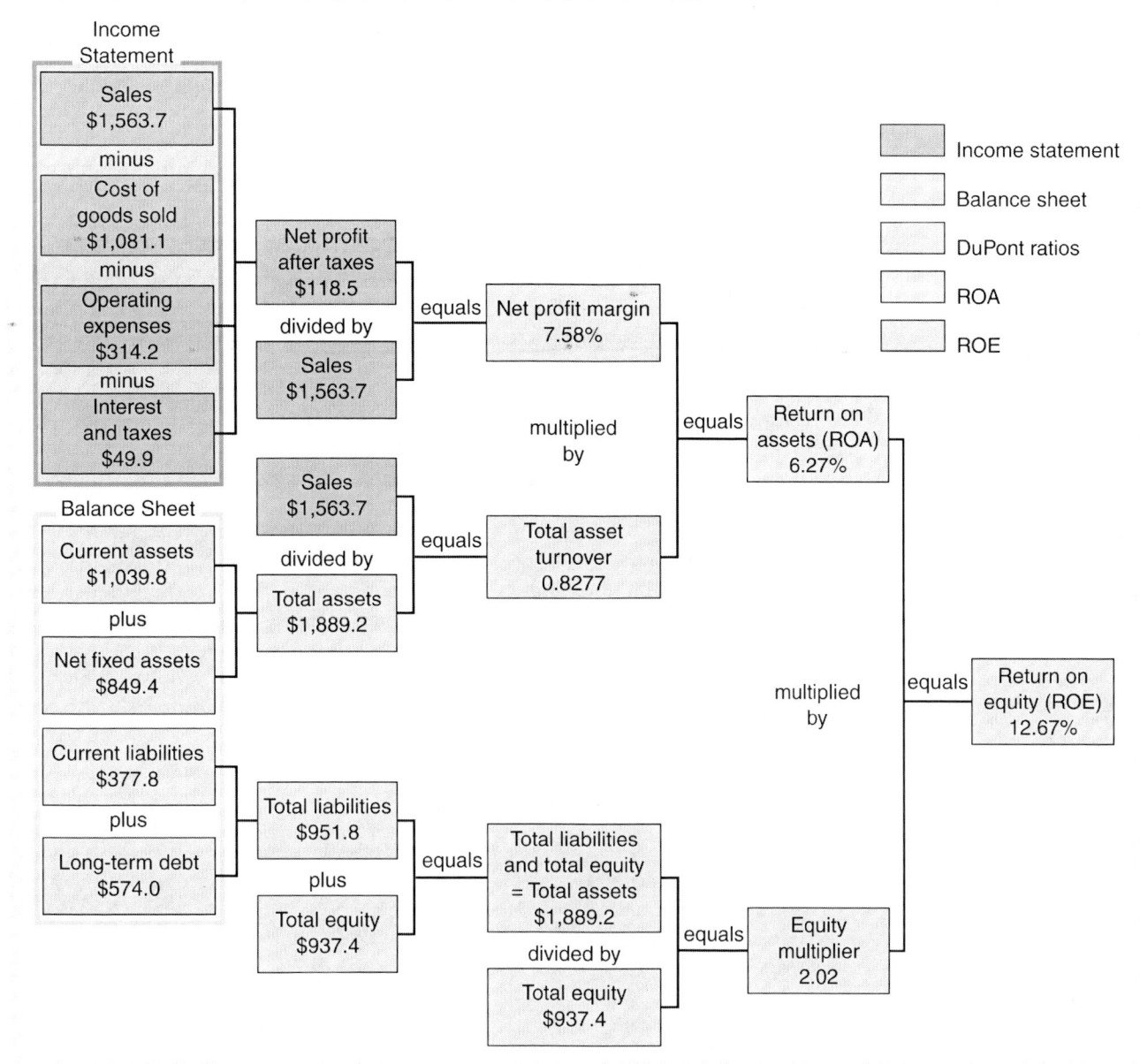

Exhibit 4.5

Relations in the DuPont System of Analysis for Diaz Manufacturing in 2008 ($ millions)

The diagram shows how the three key DuPont ratios are linked together and to the firm's balance sheet and income statement. Numbers in the exhibit are in millions of dollars and represent 2008 data from Diaz Manufacturing. The ROE of 12.67 percent differs from the 12.64 percent in Exhibit 4.3 due to rounding.

Clearly, the firm's ROE is quite low compared with the benchmark data (8 percent versus 16 percent), so without question the firm has problems. Next, you examine the values for the firm's ROA and equity multiplier and find that the firm's use of financial leverage is equal to the industry standard of 2 times but that its ROA is half that of the industry (4 percent versus 8 percent). Because ROA is the product of net profit margin and total asset turnover, you next examine these two ratios. Asset turnover does not appear to be a problem because the firm's ratio is equal to the industry standard of 0.5 times. However, the firm's net profit margin is substantially below the benchmark standard (8 percent versus 16 percent). Thus, the firm's performance problem stems from a low profit margin.

Identifying the low profit margin as an area of concern is only a first step, of course. Further investigation will be necessary to determine the underlying problem and its causes. The point to remember is that financial analysis identifies areas of concern within the firm, but rarely does such analysis tell us all we need to know.

Is Maximizing ROE an Appropriate Goal?

Throughout the book we have stressed the notion that management should make decisions that maximize the current value of the company stock. An important question is whether maximizing the value of ROE, as suggested by the DuPont system, is equivalent to wealth maximization. The short answer is that the two goals are not equivalent, but some discussion is warranted.

A major shortcoming of ROE is that it does not directly consider cash flow. ROE considers earnings, but earnings are not the same as future cash flows. Second, ROE does not consider risk. As discussed in Chapter 1, management and stockholders are very concerned about the degree of risk they face. Third, ROE does not consider the size of the initial investment or the size of future cash payments. As we stressed in Chapter 1, the essence of any business or investment decision is this: What is the size of the cash flows to be received, when do you expect to receive the cash flows, and how likely are you to receive them? More succinctly, what are the size, timing, and risk of the cash flows to be received?

In spite of these shortcomings, ROE analysis is widely used in business as a measure of operating performance. Proponents of ROE analysis argue that it provides a systematic way for management to work through the income statement and balance sheet and to identify problem areas within the firm. Furthermore, they note that ROE and stockholder value are often highly correlated. Thus, they argue, ROE is a legitimate diagnostic tool for management and focusing on maximizing ROE is an appropriate goal. We agree that ROE analysis can be a helpful diagnostic tool to help identify and correct problems within the firm. However, any investment decision should involve the analysis of current and future cash flows and the risk associated with them.

> **Before You Go On**
>
> 1. What is the purpose of the DuPont system of analysis?
> 2. What is the equation for ROA in the DuPont system, and how do the factors in that equation influence the ratio?
> 3. What are the three major shortcomings of ROE?

4.5 Selecting a Benchmark

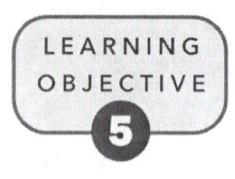

LEARNING OBJECTIVE 5

How do you judge whether a ratio value is too high or too low? Is the value good or bad? We touched on these questions several times earlier in the chapter. As we suggested, the starting point for making these judgments is selecting an appropriate benchmark—a standard that will be the basis for meaningful comparisons. Financial managers can gather appropriate benchmark data in three ways: through trend, industry, and peer group analysis.

Trend Analysis

Trend analysis uses history as its standard by evaluating a single firm's performance over time. This sort of analysis allows management to determine whether a given ratio value has increased or decreased over time and whether there has been an abrupt shift in a ratio value. An increase or decrease in a ratio value is in itself neither good nor bad. However, a ratio value that is changing typically prompts the financial manager to sort out the issues surrounding the change and to take any action that is warranted. Exhibit 4.3 shows the trends in Diaz Manufacturing's ratios. For example, the exhibit

Visit the Web site of the Risk Management Association for benchmark information: www.rmahq.org/RMA/ProductsandServices/RMABookstore/StatementStudies.

shows that Diaz's current ratio has improved, suggesting that the company is not having a problem with liquidity at the present time.

Industry Analysis

A second way to establish a benchmark is to conduct an industry group analysis. To do that, we identify a group of firms that have the same product line, compete in the same market, and are about the same size. The average ratio values for these firms will be our benchmarks. Obviously, no two firms are identical, and deciding which firms to include in the analysis is always a judgment call. If we can construct a sample of reasonable size, however, the average values provide defensible benchmarks.

Financial ratios and other financial data for industry groups are published by a number of sources—the U.S. Department of Commerce, Dun & Bradstreet, the Risk Management Association, and Standard & Poor's (S&P), to name a few. One widely used system for identifying industry groups is the **Standard Industrial Classification (SIC) System**. The SIC codes are four-digit numbers established by the federal government for statistical reporting purposes. The first two digits describe the type of business in a broad sense (for example, firms engaged in building construction, mining of metals, manufacturing of machinery, food stores, or banking). Shown in the following list are the two-digit SIC codes for some manufacturing industries. Diaz's two-digit code is 35, "Industrial and commercial machinery and computer equipment":

- 20 Food and kindred products
- 22 Textile mill products
- 28 Chemicals and allied products
- 29 Petroleum refining and related industries
- 31 Leather and leather products
- 35 Industrial and commercial machinery and computer equipment
- 37 Transportation equipment

Standard Industrial Classification (SIC) System
a numerical system developed by the U.S. Government to classify businesses according to the type of activity they perform

More than 400 companies fall into the "Industrial and commercial machinery and computer equipment" code category. To narrow the group, we use more digits. Diaz Manufacturing's four-digit code is 3533 ("oil and gas field machinery and equipment"), and there are only 35 firms in this category. Among firm's within an SIC code, financial ratio data can be further categorized by asset size or by sales, which allows for more meaningful comparisons.

In 1977, the **North American Industry Classification System (NAICS)** was introduced as a new classification system. It was intended to refine and replace the older SIC codes, but it has been slow to catch on. Industry databases still allow you to sort data by either SIC or NAICS classifications.

North American Industry Classification System (NAICS)
a classification system for businesses introduced to refine and replace the older SIC codes

Although industry databases are readily available and easy to use, they are far from perfect. When trying to find a sample of firms that are "similar" to your company, you may find the classifications too broad. For example, Wal-Mart and Nordstrom have the same SIC code, but as our brief discussion in this chapter reveals, they are very different firms. Another problem is that different industrial databases may compute ratios differently. Thus, when making benchmark comparisons, you must be careful that your calculations match those in the database, or there could be some distortions in your findings.

You can find information about SIC and NAICS at www.census.gov/epcd/www/naicstab.htm.

Peer Group Analysis

The third way to establish benchmark information is to identify a group of firms that compete with the company we are analyzing. Ideally, the firms are in similar lines of business, are about the same size, and are direct competitors of the target firm. These firms form a *peer group*. Once a peer group has been identified, management can obtain their annual reports and compute average ratio values against which the firm can compare its performance.

Exhibit 4.6 Peer Group Ratios for Diaz Manufacturing

	2008	2007	2006
Liquidity Ratios:			
Current ratio	2.10	2.20	2.10
Quick ratio	1.50	1.60	1.50
Efficiency Ratios:			
Inventory turnover	5.40	5.30	5.20
Day's sales in inventory	67.59	68.87	70.19
Accounts receivable turnover	4.90	4.20	4.10
Days' sales outstanding	76.70	89.80	90.00
Total asset turnover	0.87	0.90	0.80
Fixed asset turnover	3.50	3.30	2.40
Leverage Ratios:			
Total debt ratio	0.18	0.11	0.21
Debt-to-equity ratio	0.40	0.20	0.50
Equity multiplier	2.02	1.77	2.05
Times interest earned	7.00	5.60	1.60
Cash coverage	7.50	8.20	1.30
Profitability Ratios:			
Gross profit margin	26.80%	24.10%	19.20%
Operating profit margin	12.00%	6.90%	2.70%
Net profit margin	10.74%	3.30%	0.10%
Return on assets	9.34%	3.30%	0.80%
Return on equity	13.07%	7.00%	1.00%
Market-Value Indicators:			
Price-to-earnings ratio	18.10	38.40	44.60
Earnings per share	$1.65	$3.85	$3.78

Peer group analysis is one way to establish benchmarks for a firm. Ideally, a firm's peer group is made up of firms that are its direct competitors and are of about the same size. Diaz Manufacturing's peer group is made up of FMC Technologies, Halliburton, Hydril, Varco, and Weatherford International. The exhibit shows the average financial ratios for these companies for 2006, 2007, and 2008.

How do we determine which firms should be in the peer group? The senior management team within a company will know its competitors. If you're working outside the firm, you can look at the firm's annual report and at financial analysts' reports. Both of these sources usually identify key competitors. Exhibit 4.6 shows ratios for a five-firm peer group constructed for Diaz Manufacturing for 2006 through 2008.

We consider the peer group methodology the best way to establish a benchmark if financial data for peer firms are publicly available. We should note, however, that comparison against a single firm is acceptable when there is a clear market leader and we want to compare a firm's performance and other characteristics against those of a firm considered the best. For example, Ford Motor Company may want to compare itself directly against Toyota, which is the "best in breed" in manufacturing productivity and quality. It is worthwhile to compare a firm with the market leader to identify areas of weakness as well of possible strength.

> **Before You Go On**
>
> 1. In what three ways can a financial manager choose a benchmark?
> 2. Explain what the SIC codes are, and discuss the pros and cons of using them in financial analysis.

4.6 Using Financial Ratios

So far, our focus has been on the calculation of financial ratios. As you may already have concluded, however, the most important tasks are to *correctly interpret* the ratio values and to *make appropriate decisions* based on this interpretation. In this section we discuss using financial ratios in performance analysis.

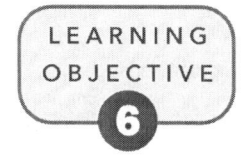

LEARNING OBJECTIVE 6

Performance Analysis of Diaz Manufacturing

Let's examine Diaz Manufacturing's performance during 2008 using the DuPont system of analysis as our diagnostic tool and the peer group sample in Exhibit 4.6 as our benchmark. For ease of discussion, Diaz's financial ratios and the benchmark data are assembled in Exhibit 4.7.

We start our analysis by looking at the big picture—the three key DuPont ratios for the firm and a peer group of firms (see Exhibit 4.7). We see that Diaz Manufacturing's ROE of 12.64 percent is below the benchmark value of 13.07 percent, a difference of 0.43 percent, which is not good news. More dramatically, Diaz's ROA is 3.07 percent below the peer group benchmark, which is a serious difference. Clearly, Diaz Manufacturing has some performance problems that need to be investigated.

Exhibit 4.7 Peer Group Analysis for Diaz Manufacturing

	(1) Diaz Ratio	(2) Peer Group Ratio	(3) Difference (Column 1 − Column 2)
DuPont Ratios:			
Return on equity (%)	12.64	13.07	(0.43)
Return on assets (%)	6.27	9.34	(3.07)
Equity multiplier (%)	2.02	1.40	0.62
Net profit margin (%)	7.58	10.74	(3.16)
Total asset turnover	0.83	0.87	(0.04)
Profit Margins:			
Gross profit margin (%)	30.86	26.80	4.06
Operating margin (%)	10.77	12.00	(1.23)
Net profit margin (%)	7.58	10.74	(3.16)
Asset Ratios:			
Current ratio	2.75	2.10	0.65
Fixed asset turnover	3.92	3.50	0.42
Inventory turnover	2.55	5.40	(2.85)
Accounts receivable turnover	5.11	4.90	0.21

Examining the differences between the ratios of a firm and its peer group is a good way to spot areas that require further analysis.

To determine the problems, we examine the firm's equity multiplier and ROA results in more detail. The equity multiplier value of 2.02, versus the benchmark value of 1.40, suggests that Diaz Manufacturing is using more leverage than the average firm in the benchmark sample. Management is comfortable with the higher-than-average leverage. Conversations with the firm's investment banker, however, indicate that although the current use of leverage is not a problem, the company's debt could become a problem if the economy deteriorated and went into a recession.

Without the higher equity multiplier and management's willingness to bear additional risk, Diaz Manufacturing's ROE would be much lower. To illustrate this point, suppose management reduced the company's leverage to the peer group average of 1.40 (see Exhibit 4.7). With an equity multiplier of 1.40, the firm's ROE would be only 8.78 percent (0.0627×1.40); this is 3.86 percent below the firm's current ROE of 12.64 percent and 4.29 percent below the peer group benchmark. Thus, the use of higher leverage has, to some extent, masked the severity of the firm's problem with ROA.

Recall that ROA equals the product of the net profit margin and total asset turnover. Diaz's net profit margin is 3.16 percent lower than the benchmark value (7.58 − 10.74), and its total asset turnover ratio is slightly below the benchmark value (0.83 versus 0.87). Thus, both ratios that comprise ROA are below the peer group benchmark standard, but the net profit margin appears to be the larger problem.

Turning to the detailed asset turnover ratios shown in Exhibit 4.7, we find that the ratios for Diaz are generally similar to the corresponding peer group ratios. An exception is inventory turnover ratio, which is substantially below the benchmark: 2.55 for Diaz versus 5.40 for the benchmark. Diaz's management needs to investigate why the inventory turnover ratio is off the mark.

Because Diaz Manufacturing's net profit margin is low, we next look at the various profit margins shown in Exhibit 4.7 to gain insight into this situation. Diaz Manufacturing's gross profit margin is 4.06 percentage points above the benchmark value (30.86 − 26.80), which is good news. Since gross profit margin is a factor of sales and the cost of goods sold, we can conclude that there is no problem with the price the firm is charging for its products or with its cost of goods sold.

Diaz's problems begin with its operating margin of 10.77 percent, which is 1.23 percentage points below the peer group benchmark of 12.00 percent (10.77 − 12.00). The major controllable expense here is selling and administrative costs, and management needs to investigate why these expenses appear to be out of line.

In sum, the DuPont analysis of Diaz Manufacturing has identified two areas that warrant detailed investigation by management: (1) the larger-than-average inventory (slow inventory turnover) and (2) the above-average selling and administrative expenses. Management must now investigate each of these areas and come up with a course of action. Management may want to give careful consideration to the firm's high degree of financial leverage and whether it represents a prudent degree of risk.

LEARNING BY DOING
APPLICATION 4.5

Ron's Jewelry Store and the Missing Data

Problem: Ron Roberts has owned and managed a profitable jewelry business in San Diego County for the past five years. He believes his jewelry store is one of the best managed in the county, and he is considering opening several new stores.

When Ron started the store, he supplied all the equity financing himself and financed the rest with personal loans from friends and family members. To open more stores, Ron needs a bank loan. The bank will want to examine his financial statements and know something about the competition he faces.

Ron has asked his brother-in-law, Dennis O'Neil, a CPA, to analyze the financials. Ron has also gathered some financial information about a company he considers the chief competition in the San Diego County market. The company has been in business for 25 years, has a number of stores, and is widely admired for its owners' management skills. Dennis organizes the available information in the following table:

Financial Ratio/Data	Ron's Store	Competitor
Sales	$240	$300
Net income	$ 6	—
ROE	13.13%	—
Net profit margin	—	5.84%
Asset turnover	1.5	1.5
Equity multiplier	—	1.5
Debt-to-equity ratio	2.5	—

Calculate the missing values for the financial data above.

Approach: Use the ratio equations discussed in the text to calculate the missing financial ratios for both Ron's store and the competitor.

Solution:

Ron's jewelry store:

1. Net profit margin $= \dfrac{\text{Net income}}{\text{Sales}} = \dfrac{\$6}{\$240} = 0.025$, or 2.5%
2. Equity multiplier $= 1 +$ Debt-to-equity ratio $= 1 + 2.5 = 3.5$

Competitor:

1. ROE = Net profit margin × Asset turnover × Equity multiplier
   $= 0.0584 \times 1.5 \times 1.5 = 0.1314$, or 13.14%
2. Net profit = Net profit margin × Net sales = $0.0584 \times \$300 = \$17.52$
3. Debt-to-equity ratio $= \dfrac{\text{Debt}}{\text{Equity}} = \dfrac{\$66.82}{\$133.1} = 0.50$
   (a) Equity $= \dfrac{\text{NI}}{\text{ROE}} = \dfrac{\$17.5}{0.1314} = \$133.18$
   (b) Assets $= \dfrac{\text{Net sales}}{\text{Asset turnover}} = \dfrac{\$300}{1.5} = \$200.0$
   (c) Debt = Assets − Equity = $\$200.0 - \$133.18 = \$66.82$

DECISION-MAKING EXAMPLE 4.3

Ron's Jewelry Store and the DuPont Analysis

Situation: Let's continue with our analysis of Ron's jewelry store, introduced in Learning by Doing Application 4.5. Brother-in-law Dennis has been asked to analyze the company's financials. He decides to use the DuPont system of analysis as a framework. He arranges the critical information as follows:

Financial Ratios	Ron's Store	Competitor
ROE	13.13%	13.14%
ROA	3.75%	8.76%
Net profit margin	2.50%	5.84%
Asset turnover	1.5	1.5
Equity multiplier	3.5	1.5
Debt-to-equity ratio	2.5	0.5
Net sales	$240	$300
Net income	$ 6.0	$ 17.5

Given the above financial ratios, what recommendations should Dennis make regarding Ron's jewelry store and its management?

(continued)

> **Decision:** The good news is that Ron is able to earn about the same ROE as his major competitor. Unfortunately for Ron, it's pretty much downhill from there. Turning to the first two DuPont system ratios, we can see that Ron's ROA of 3.75 percent is much lower than his major competitor's ROA of 8.76 percent. Ron's business is also very highly leveraged, with an equity multiplier of 3.5 times, compared with 1.5 times for the competitor. In fact, the only reason Ron's ROE is comparable to the competitor's is the high leverage.
>
> Breaking the ROA into its components, we find that Ron's asset turnover ratio is the same as the competitor's, 1.5. However, the profitability of Ron's store is extremely poor as measured by the firm's net profit margin of 2.50 percent, compared with the competitor's margin of 5.84 percent. One possible explanation is that to stimulate sales and maintain asset turnover, Ron has been selling his merchandise at too low a price.
>
> As mentioned, Ron is employing a very high degree of financial leverage. Ron's debt-to-equity ratio is 2.5, while the competitor's is only 0.5. To illustrate how big the difference is, suppose both firms have $100 in equity financing. For $100 of equity, the competitor would hold $50 in debt, and Ron would hold $250.
>
> In summary, Ron's jewelry store is not well managed. Ron needs to either increase his net profit margin or increase his inventory turnover to bring his ROA into line with that of his major competitor. Ron also needs to reduce his dependence on financial leverage. If San Diego County were to suffer a significant economic downturn, Ron's business would be a likely candidate for failure.

Financial ratio analysis is an excellent diagnostic tool. It helps management identify the problem areas in the firm—the symptoms. However, it does not tell management what the causes of the problems are or what course of action should be taken. Management must drill down into the accounting data, talk with managers in the field, and if appropriate, talk with people outside the firm, such as suppliers, to understand what is causing the problems.

Limitations of Financial Statement Analysis

Financial statement and ratio analysis as discussed in this chapter presents two major problems. First, it depends on accounting data based on historical costs. As we discussed in Chapter 3, knowledgeable financial managers would prefer to use financial statements in which all of the firm's assets and liabilities are valued at market. Financial statements based on current market values more closely reflect a firm's true economic conditions than do statements based on historical cost.

Second, there is little theory to guide us in making judgments based on financial statement and ratio analysis. That is why it is difficult to say a current ratio of 2.0 is good or bad or to say whether ROE or ROA is a more important ratio. The lack of theory explains, in part, why rules of thumb are often used as decision rules in financial statement analysis. The problem with decision rules based on experience and "common sense" rather than theory is that they may work fine in a stable economic environment but may fail when a significant shift takes place. For example, if you were in an economic environment with low inflation, you could develop a set of decision rules to help manage your business. However, if the economy became inflationary, more than likely many of your decision rules would fail.

Despite the limitations, we know that financial managers and analysts routinely use financial statements and ratio analysis to evaluate a firm's performance and to make a variety of decisions about the firm. These financial statements and the resulting analysis are the primary means by which financial information is communicated both inside and outside firms. At this time, the availability of market value data is limited for public corporations and not available for privately held firms and other entities such as government units.

Thus, we conclude that, practically speaking, historical accounting information represents the best available information. However, times are changing. As the accounting profession becomes more comfortable with the use of market data and as technology

> **Before You Go On**
>
> 1. Explain how the DuPont identity allows us to evaluate a firm's performance.
> 2. What are the limitations on traditional financial statement analysis?
> 3. List some of the problems that financial analysts confront when analyzing financial statements.

Summary of Learning Objectives

1. **Explain the three perspectives from which financial statements can be viewed.**

   Financial statements can be viewed from the owners', managers', or creditors' perspective. All three groups are ultimately interested in a firm's profitability, but each group takes a different view. Stockholders want to know how much cash they can expect to receive for their stock, what their return on investment will be, and/or how much their stock is worth in the market. Managers are concerned with maximizing the firm's long-term value through a series of day-to-day management decisions; thus, they need to see the impact of their decisions on the financial statements to confirm that things are going as planned. Creditors monitor the firm's use of debt and are concerned with how much debt the firm is using and whether the firm will have enough cash to meet its obligations.

2. **Describe common-size financial statements, explain why they are used, and be able to prepare and use them to analyze the historical performance of a firm.**

   Common-size financial statements are financial statements in which each number has been scaled by a common measure of firm size: balance sheets are expressed as a percentage of total assets, and income statements are expressed as a percentage of net sales. Common-size financial statements are necessary when comparing firms that are significantly different in size. The preparation of common-size financial statements and their use are illustrated for Diaz Manufacturing in Section 4.2.

3. **Discuss how financial ratios facilitate financial analysis, and be able to compute and use them to analyze a firm's performance.**

   Financial ratios are used in financial analysis because they eliminate problems caused by comparing two or more companies of different size or when looking at the same company over time as the size changes. Financial ratios can be divided into five categories: (1) Liquidity ratios measure the ability of a company to cover its current bills. (2) Efficiency ratios tell how efficiently the firm uses its assets. (3) Leverage ratios tell how much debt a firm has in its capital structure and whether the firm can meet its long-term financial obligations. (4) Profitability ratios focus on the firm's earnings. Finally, (5) market value indicators look at a company based on market data as opposed to historical data used in financial statements. The computation and analysis of major financial ratios are presented in Section 4.3 (also see the Summary of Key Equations that follows the Summary of Learning Objectives).

4. **Describe the DuPont system of analysis and be able to use it to evaluate a firm's performance and identify corrective actions that may be necessary.**

   The DuPont system of analysis is a diagnostic tool that uses financial ratios to assess a firm's financial strength. Once the financial ratios are calculated and the assessment is complete, management focuses on correcting the problems within the context of maximizing the firm's ROE. For analysis, the DuPont system breaks ROE into three components: net profit margin, which measures operating efficiency; total asset turnover, which measures how efficiently the firm deploys its assets; and the equity multiplier, which measures financial leverage. A diagnostic analysis of a firm's performance using the DuPont system is illustrated in Section 4.4.

5. **Explain what benchmarks are, describe how they are prepared, and discuss why they are important in financial statement analysis.**

   Once we have calculated financial ratios, we need some way to evaluate them. A benchmark provides a standard for comparison. In financial statement analysis, a number of benchmarks are used. Most often, benchmark comparisons involve competitors that are roughly the same size and that offer a similar range of products. Another form of benchmarking is time-trend analysis, which compares a firm's current financial ratios against the same ratios from past years. Time-trend analysis tells us whether a ratio is increasing or decreasing over time. The preparation and use of peer group benchmark data are illustrated in Section 4.6.

6. **Identify the major limitations in using financial statement analysis.**

   The major limitations to financial statement and ratio analysis are the use of historical accounting data and the lack of theory to guide the decision maker. The lack of theory explains, in part, why there are so many rules of thumb. Though rules of thumb are useful, and they may work under certain conditions, they may lead to poor decisions if circumstances or the economic environment have changed.

Summary of Key Equations

Equation	Description	Formula
4.1		$\text{Current ratio} = \dfrac{\text{Current assets}}{\text{Current liabilities}}$
4.2	Liquidity Ratios	$\text{Quick ratio} = \dfrac{\text{Current assets} - \text{Inventory}}{\text{Current liabilities}}$
4.3		$\text{Inventory turnover} = \dfrac{\text{Cost of goods sold}}{\text{Inventory}}$
4.4		$\text{Day's sales in inventory} = \dfrac{365 \text{ Days}}{\text{Inventory turnover}}$
4.5		$\text{Accounts receivable turnover} = \dfrac{\text{Net sales}}{\text{Accounts receivable}}$
4.6	Efficiency Ratios	$\text{Day's sales outstanding} = \dfrac{365 \text{ days}}{\text{Accounts receivable turnover}}$
4.7		$\text{Total asset turnover} = \dfrac{\text{Net sales}}{\text{Total assets}}$
4.8		$\text{Fixed asset turnover} = \dfrac{\text{Net sales}}{\text{Net fixed assets}}$
4.9		$\text{Total debt ratio} = \dfrac{\text{Total debt}}{\text{Total assets}}$
4.10		$\text{Debt-to-equity ratio} = \dfrac{\text{Total debt}}{\text{Total equity}}$
4.11	Leverage Ratios	$\text{Equity multiplier} = \dfrac{\text{Total assets}}{\text{Total equity}}$
4.12		$\text{Times interest earned} = \dfrac{\text{EBIT}}{\text{Interest expense}}$
4.13		$\text{Cash coverage} = \dfrac{\text{EBITDA}}{\text{Interest expense}}$
4.14		$\text{Gross profit margin} = \dfrac{\text{Net sales} - \text{Cost of goods sold}}{\text{Net sales}}$
4.15		$\text{Operating profit margin} = \dfrac{\text{EBIT}}{\text{Net sales}}$
4.16		$\text{Net profit margin} = \dfrac{\text{Net income}}{\text{Net sales}}$
4.17	Profitability Ratios	$\text{EBIT return on assets (EROA)} = \dfrac{\text{EBIT}}{\text{Total assets}}$
4.18		$\text{Return on assets (ROA)} = \dfrac{\text{Net income}}{\text{Total assets}}$
4.19		$\text{Return on equity (ROE)} = \dfrac{\text{Net income}}{\text{Total equity}}$
4.20	Market Value Indicators	$\text{Earning per share} = \dfrac{\text{Net income}}{\text{Shares outstanding}}$
4.21		$\text{Price-earnings ratio} = \dfrac{\text{Price per share}}{\text{Earnings per share}}$

4.22		ROA = Net profit margin × Total asset turnover
4.23		ROE = ROA × Equity multiplier
4.24	DuPont Equation	ROE = Net profit margin × Total asset turnover × Equity multiplier
4.25		$\text{ROE} = \dfrac{\text{Net income}}{\text{Net sales}} \times \dfrac{\text{Net sales}}{\text{Total assets}} \times \dfrac{\text{Total assets}}{\text{Total equity}}$

Self-Study Problems

4.1 The Abercrombie Supply Company reported the following information for the year ended June 30, 2008. Prepare a common-size income statement for the year ended June 30, 2008.

Abercrombie Supply Company
Income Statement ($ thousands)

	2008
Net sales	$ 2,110,965
Cost of goods sold	1,459,455
Selling and administrative expenses	312,044
Nonrecurring expenses	27,215
Earnings before interest, taxes, depreciation, and amortization (EBITDA)	$ 312,251
Depreciation	112,178
Earnings before interest and taxes (EBIT)	$ 200,073
Interest expense	117,587
Earnings before taxes (EBT)	$ 82,486
Taxes (35%)	28,870
Net income	$ 53,616

4.2 Prepare a common-size balance sheet from the following information for Abercrombie Supply Company.

Abercrombie Supply Company
Balance Sheet as of June 30, 2008 ($ thousands)

Assets:		Liabilities and Equity:	
Cash and marketable securities	$ 396,494	Accounts payable	$ 817,845
Accounts receivable	708,275	Notes payable	101,229
Inventories	1,152,398	Accrued income taxes	41,322
Other current assets	42,115		
Total current assets	$ 2,299,282	Total current liabilities	$ 960,396
Net plant and equipment	1,978,455	Long-term debt	1,149,520
		Total liabilities	$ 2,109,916
		Common stock	1,312,137
		Retained earnings	855,684
		Total common equity	$ 2,167,821
Total assets	$ 4,277,737	Total liabilities and equity	$ 4,277,737

4.3 Using the 2008 data for the Abercrombie Supply Company, calculate the following liquidity ratios:
  a. Current ratio
  b. Quick ratio

4.4 Refer to the balance sheet and income statement for Abercrombie Supply Company for the year ended June 30, 2008. Calculate the following ratios:
   a. Inventory turnover ratio
   b. Days' sales outstanding
   c. Total asset turnover
   d. Fixed asset turnover
   e. Total debt ratio
   f. Debt-to-equity ratio
   g. Times-interest-earned ratio
   h. Cash coverage ratio

4.5 Refer to the balance sheet and income statement for Abercrombie Supply Company for the year ended June 30, 2008. Use the DuPont equation to calculate the return on equity (ROE). In the process, calculate the following ratios: profit margin, total asset turnover, equity multiplier, EBIT return on assets, and return on assets.

Solutions to Self-Study Problems

4.1 The standardized income statement for Abercrombie Supply Company should look like the following one:

Abercrombie Supply Company
Income Statement ($ thousands)

	2008	Percent of Sales
Net sales	$ 2,110,965	100.0%
Cost of goods sold	1,459,455	69.1
Selling and administrative expenses	312,044	14.8
Nonrecurring expenses	27,215	1.3
Earnings before interest, taxes, depreciation and amortization (EBITDA)	$ 312,251	14.8%
Depreciation	112,178	5.3
Earnings before interest and taxes (EBIT)	$ 200,073	9.5%
Interest expense	117,587	5.6
Earnings before taxes (EBT)	$ 82,486	3.9%
Taxes (35%)	28,870	1.4
Net income	$ 53,616	2.5%

4.2 Abercrombie Supply's common-size balance sheet is as follows:

Assets:	2008	Percent of Total Assets	Liabilities and Equity:	2008	Percent of Total Assets
Cash and marketable sec.	$ 396,494	9.3%	Accounts payable and accruals	$ 817,845	19.1%
Accounts receivable	708,275	16.5%	Notes payable	101,229	2.4
Inventories	1,152,398	26.9%	Accrued income taxes	41,322	1.0
Other current assets	42,115	1.0%			
Total current assets	$ 2,299,282	53.7%	Total current liabilities	$ 960,396	22.4%
Net plant and equipment	1,978,455	46.2%	Long-term debt	1,149,520	26.9
			Total liabilities	$ 2,109,916	49.3%
			Common stock	1,312,137	30.7
			Retained earnings	855,684	20.0
			Total common equity	$ 2,167,821	50.7%
Total asssets	$ 4,277,737	100.0%	Total liabilities and equity	$ 4,277,737	100.0%

4.3 Abercrombie Supply's current ratio and quick ratio are calculated as follows:

a. Current ratio $= \dfrac{\$2,299,282}{\$960,396} = 2.39$

b. Quick ratio $= \dfrac{\$2,299,282 - \$1,152,375}{\$960,396} = 1.19$

4.4 The ratios are calculated as shown in the following table:

Ratio	Calculation	Value
Inventory turnover ratio	$1,459,455 / 1,152,398	1.27
Days' sales outstanding	$708,275 / ($2,110,965/365)	122.5 days
Total asset turnover	$2,110,965 / $4,277,737	0.49
Fixed asset turnover	$2,110,965 / $1,978,455	1.07
Total debt ratio	$2,109,916 / $4,277,737	0.493
Debt-to-equity ratio	$2,109,916 / $2,167,821	0.974
Times-interest-earned ratio	$200,073 / $117,587	1.7
Cash coverage ratio	$312,251 / $117,587	2.66

4.5 Following are the calculations for the ROE and associated ratios:

$$\text{Profit margin} = \dfrac{\text{Net income}}{\text{Net sales}} = \dfrac{\$53,616}{\$2,110,965} = 2.54\%$$

$$\text{EBIT ROA} = \dfrac{\text{EBIT}}{\text{Total assets}} = \dfrac{\$200,073}{\$4,277,737} = 4.68\%$$

$$\text{Return on assets} = \dfrac{\text{Net income}}{\text{Total assets}} = \dfrac{\$53,616}{\$4,277,737} = 1.25\%$$

$$\text{Equity multiplier} = \dfrac{\text{Total assets}}{\text{Total equity}} = \dfrac{\$4,277,737}{\$2,167,821} = 1.97$$

$$\text{Total asset turnover} = \dfrac{\text{Net sales}}{\text{Total assets}} = \dfrac{\$2,110,965}{\$4,277,737} = 0.49$$

DuPont identity:

$$\begin{aligned}\text{ROE} &= \text{ROA} \times \text{EM} \\ &= \text{Profit margin} \times \text{Total assets turnover ratio} \times \text{EM} \\ &= \dfrac{\text{Net income}}{\text{Net sales}} \times \dfrac{\text{Net sales}}{\text{Total assets}} \times \dfrac{\text{Total assets}}{\text{Total equity}} \\ &= 0.0254 \times 0.49 \times 1.97 \\ &= 2.45\%\end{aligned}$$

Critical Thinking Questions

4.1 What does it mean when a company's return on assets (ROA) is equal to its return on equity (ROE)?

4.2 Why is too much liquidity not a good thing?

4.3 Inventory is excluded when the quick ratio or acid-test ratio is calculated because inventory is the most difficult current asset to convert to cash without loss of value. What types of inventory are likely to be most easily converted to cash?

4.4 What does a very high inventory turnover ratio signify?

4.5 How would one explain a low receivables turnover ratio?

4.6 What additional information does the fixed assets turnover ratio provide over the total assets turnover ratio? For which industries does it carry greater significance?

4.7 How does financial leverage help shareholders?

4.8 Why do banks have a low ROA (relative to other industries) but a high ROE?

4.9 Why is the ROE a more appropriate proxy of wealth maximization for smaller firms rather than for larger ones?

4.10 Why is it not enough for an analyst to look at just the short-term and long-term debt on a firm's balance sheet?

Questions and Problems

BASIC

4.1 Liquidity ratios: Explain why the quick ratio or acid-test ratio is a better measure of a firm's liquidity than the current ratio.

4.2 Liquidity ratios: Flying Penguins Corp. has total current assets of $11,845,175, current liabilities of $5,311,020, and a quick ratio of 0.89. What is its level of inventory?

4.3 Efficiency ratio: If Newton Manufacturers has an accounts receivable turnover of 4.8 times and net sales of $7,812,379, what is its level of receivables?

4.4 Efficiency ratio: Bummel and Strand Corp. has a gross profit margin of 33.7 percent, sales of $47,112,365, and inventories of $14,595,435. What is its inventory turnover ratio?

4.5 Efficiency ratio: Sorenson Inc. has sales of $3,112,489, a gross profit margin of 23.1 percent, and inventory of $833,145. What are the company's inventory turnover ratio and days' sales in inventory?

4.6 Leverage ratios: Breckenridge Ski Company has total assets of $422,235,811 and a debt ratio of 29.5 percent. Calculate the company's debt-to-equity ratio and the equity multiplier.

4.7 Leverage ratios: Norton Company has a debt-to-equity ratio of 1.65, ROA of 11.3 percent, and total equity of $1,322,796. What are the company's equity multiplier, debt ratio, and ROE?

4.8 DuPont equation: The Rangoon Timber Company has the following relationships:

Sales/Total assets = 2.23;   ROA = 9.69%;   ROE = 16.4%

What are Rangoon's profit margin and debt ratio?

4.9 Benchmark analysis: List the ways a company's financial manager can benchmark the company's own performance.

4.10 Benchmark analysis: Trademark Corp.'s financial manager collected the following information for its peer group so that it can compare its own performance against that of its peers.

Ratios	Trademark	Peer Group
DSO	33.5 days	27.9 days
Total assets turnover	2.3	3.7
Inventory turnover	1.8	2.8
Quick ratio	0.6	1.3

a. Explain how Trademark is doing relative to its peers.
b. How do the industry ratios help Trademark's management?

4.11 Market-value ratios: Rockwell Jewelers has announced net earnings of $6,481,778 for this year. The company has 2,543,800 shares outstanding, and the year-end stock price is $54.21. What are the company's earnings per share and P/E ratio?

INTERMEDIATE

4.12 Liquidity ratios: Laurel Electronics has a quick ratio of 1.15, current liabilities of $5,311,020, and inventories of $7,121,599. What is the firm's current ratio?

4.13 Efficiency ratio: Payton Corp. has total sales of $31,115,964, inventories of $4,412,933, cash and equivalents of $2,469,050, and days' sales outstanding of 39 days. If the firm's management wanted its DSO to be 30 days, by how much will the accounts receivable have to change?

4.14 Efficiency ratio: Norwood Corp. currently has accounts receivable of $1,223,675 on net sales of $6,216,900. What are its accounts receivable turnover ratio and days' sales outstanding?

4.15 Efficiency ratio: If Norwood Corp.'s management wants to reduce the DSO from that calculated in the above problem to an industry average of 56.3 days and its net sales are expected to decline by about 12 percent, what would be the new level of receivables?

4.16 Coverage ratios: Nimitz Rental Company had depreciation expenses of $108,905, interest expenses of $78,112, and an EBIT of $1,254,338 for the year ended June 30, 2008. What are the times-interest-earned and cash coverage ratios for this company?

4.17 Leverage ratios: Conseco, Inc., has a debt ratio of 0.56. What are the company's debt-to-equity ratio and equity multiplier?

4.18 Profitability ratios: Cisco Systems has total assets of $35.594 billion, total debt of $9.678 billion, and net sales of $22.045 billion. Their net profit margin for the year is 20 percent, while the operating profit margin was 30 percent. What are Cisco's net income, EBIT ROA, ROA, and ROE?

4.19 Profitability ratios: Procter & Gamble reported the following information for year-end 2008: On net sales of $51.407 billion, the company earned a net income after taxes of $6.481 billion. It had a cost of goods sold of $25.076 billion and an EBIT of $9.827 billion. What is the company's (a) gross profit margin, (b) operating profit margin, and (c) net profit margin?

4.20 Profitability ratios: Wal-Mart, Inc., has net income of $9,054,000 on net sales of $256,329,812. The company has total assets of $104,912,112 and shareholders' equity of $43,623,445. Use the extended DuPont identity to find the return on assets and return on equity for the firm.

4.21 Profitability ratios: Xtreme Sports Innovations has disclosed the following information:

EBIT = $25,664,300   Net income = $13,054,000   Net sales = $83,125,336
Total debt = $20,885,753   Total assets = $71,244,863

Compute the following ratios for this firm using the DuPont identity: debt-to-equity ratio, EBIT ROA, ROA, and ROE.

4.22 Market-value ratios: Cisco Systems had net income of $4.401 billion and, at year end, 6.735 billion shares outstanding. Calculate the earnings per share for the company.

4.23 Market-value ratios: Use the information for Cisco Systems in the last problem. In addition, the company's EBITDA was $6.834 billion and its share price was $22.36. Compute the firm's price-earnings ratio and the price-EBITDA ratio.

4.24 DuPont equation: Carter, Inc., a manufacturer of electrical supplies, has an ROE of 23.1 percent, a profit margin of 4.9 percent, and a total asset turnover ratio of 2.6 times. Its peer group also has an ROE of 23.1 percent but has outperformed Carter with a profit margin of 5.3 percent and a total assets turnover ratio of 3.0 times. Explain how Carter managed to achieve the same level of profitability as reflected by the ROE.

4.25 DuPont equation: Grossman Enterprises has an equity multiplier of 2.6 times, total assets of $2,312,000, an ROE of 14.8 percent, and a total assets turnover of 2.8 times. Calculate the firm's sales and ROA.

4.26 Complete the balance sheet of Flying Roos Corp., given the following information: **ADVANCED**

Flying Roos Corp. Balance Sheet as of 12/31/2008

Assets:		Liabilities and Equity:	
Cash and marketable securities		Accounts payable and accruals	
Accounts receivable		Notes payable	$ 300,000
Inventories			
Total current assets		Total current liabilities	
		Long-term debt	$2,000,000
Net plant and equipment		Common stock	
		Retained earnings	$1,250,000
Total assets	$8,000,000	Total liabilities and equity	

You are also given the following information:

Debt ratio = 40%   DSO = 39 days
Current ratio = 1.5   Inventory turnover ratio = 3.375
Sales = $2.25 million   Cost of goods sold = $1.6875 million

4.27 For the year ended June 30, 2008, Northern Clothing Company has total assets of $87,631,181, ROA of 11.67 percent, ROE of 21.19 percent, and a profit margin of 11.59 percent. What are the company's net income and net sales? Calculate the firm's debt-to-equity ratio.

4.28 Blackwell Automotive's balance sheet at year-end 2007–2008 shows the following information:

Blackwell Automotive Balance Sheet as of 3/31/2008

Assets:		Liabilities and Equity:	
Cash and marketable sec.	$ 23,015	Accounts payable and accruals	$ 163,257
Accounts receivable	141,258	Notes payable	21,115
Inventories	212,444		
Total current assets	$ 376,717	Total current liabilities	$ 184,372
		Long-term debt	168,022
Net plant and equipment	711,256	Total liabilities	$ 352,394
Goodwill and other assets	89,899	Common stock	313,299
		Retained earnings	512,159
Total assets	$1,177,852	Total liabilities and equity	$1,177,852

In addition, it was reported that the firm had a net income of $156,042 on sales of $4,063,589.

a. What are the firm's current ratio and quick ratio?
b. Calculate the firm's days' sales outstanding, total asset turnover ratio, and fixed asset turnover ratio.

4.29 The following are the financial statements for Nederland Consumer Products Company for the fiscal year ended September 30, 2008.

As Reported on Annual Income Statement	9/30/08
Net sales	$51,407
Cost of products sold	25,076
Gross margin	$26,331
Marketing, research, administrative exp.	15,746
Depreciation	758
Operating income (loss)	$ 9,827
Interest expense	477
Earnings (loss) before income taxes	$ 9,350
Income taxes	2,869
Net earnings (loss)	$ 6,481

Balance Sheet as of 9/30/2008

Assets:		Liabilities and Equity:	
Cash and marketable securities	$ 5,469	Accounts payable	$ 3,617
Investment securities	423	Accrued and other liabilities	7,689
Accounts receivable	4,062	Taxes payable	2,554
Total inventories	4,400	Debt due within one year	8,287
Deferred income taxes	958		
Prepaid expenses and other receivables	1,803		
Total current assets	$17,115	Total current liabilities	$22,147
Property, plant, and equipment, at cost	25,304	Long-term debt	12,554
Less: Accumulated depreciation	11,196	Deferred income taxes	2,261
Net property, plant, and equipment	$14,108	Other noncurrent liabilities	2,808
Net goodwill and other intangible assets	23,900	Total liabilities	$39,770
Other noncurrent assets	1,925	Convertible class A preferred stock	1,526
		Common stock	2,141
		Retained earnings	13,611
		Total stockholders' equity (deficit)	$17,278
Total assets	$57,048	Total liabilites and shareholders' equity	$57,048

Calculate all the ratios (for which industry figures are available) for Nederland and compare the firm's ratios with the industry ratios.

Ratio	Industry Average
Current ratio	2.05
Quick ratio	0.78
Gross margin	23.9%
Net profit margin	12.3%
Debt ratio	0.23
Long-term debt to equity	0.98
Interest coverage	5.62
ROA	5.3%
ROE	18.8%

4.30 Refer to the preceding information for Nederland Consumer Products Company. Compute the firm's ratios for the following categories and briefly evaluate the company's performance from these numbers.
  a. Efficiency ratios
  b. Asset turnover ratios
  c. Leverage ratios
  d. Coverage ratios

4.31 Refer to the earlier information for Nederland Consumer Products Company. Using the DuPont identity, calculate the return on equity for Nederland, after calculating the ratios that make up the DuPont identity.

4.32 Nugent, Inc., has a gross profit margin of 31.7 percent on sales of $9,865,214 and total assets of $7,125,852. The company has a current ratio of 2.7 times, accounts receivable of $1,715,363, cash and marketable securities of $315,488, and current liabilities of $870,938.
  a. What is Nugent's level of current assets?
  b. How much inventory does the firm have? What is the inventory turnover ratio?
  c. What is Nugent's days' sales outstanding?
  d. If management wants to set a target DSO of 30 days, what should Nugent's accounts receivable be?

4.33 Recreational Supplies Co. has net sales of $11,655,000, an ROE of 17.64 percent, and a total asset turnover of 2.89 times. If the firm has a debt-to-equity ratio of 1.43, what is the company's net income?

4.34 Nutmeg Houseware Inc. has an operating profit margin of 10.3 percent on revenues of $24,547,125 and total assets of $8,652,352.
  a. Find the company's total asset turnover ratio and its operating profit (EBIT).
  b. If the company's management has set a target for the total asset turnover ratio to be 3.25 next year without any change in the total assets of the company, what will have to be the new sales level for the next year? Calculate change in sales necessary and the percentage sales necessary.
  c. If the operating profit margin now shrinks to 10 percent, what will be the EBIT at the new level of sales?

4.35 Modern Appliances Corporation has reported its financial results for the year ended December 31, 2008.

Income Statement for the Fiscal
Year Ended December 31, 2008

Net sales	$5,398,412,000
Cost of goods sold	3,432,925,255
Gross profit	$1,965,486,745
Selling, general, and administrative expenses	1,036,311,231
Depreciation	299,928,155
Operating income	$ 629,247,359
Interest expense	35,826,000
EBT	$ 593,421,359
Income taxes	163,104,554
Net earnings	$ 430,316,805

Consolidated Balance Sheet
Modern Appliances Corporation
December 31, 2008

Assets:		Liabilities and Equity:	
Cash and cash equivalents	$ 514,412,159	Short-term borrowings	$ 117,109,865
Accounts receivables	1,046,612,233	Trade accounts payable	466,937,985
Inventories	981,870,990	Other current liabilities	994,289,383
Other current assets	313,621,610		
Total current assets	$2,856,516,992	Total current liabilities	$1,578,337,233
Net fixed assets	754,660,275	Long-term debt	1,200,691,565
Goodwill	118,407,710	Common stock	397,407,352
Other assets	665,058,761	Retained earnings	1,218,207,588
Total asssets	$4,394,643,738	Total liabilities and equity	$4,394,643,738

Using the information from the financial statements, complete a comprehensive ratio analysis for Modern Appliances Corporation.
a. Calculate these liquidity ratios: current and quick ratios.
b. Calculate these efficiency ratios: inventory turnover, accounts receivable turnover, DSO.
c. Calculate these asset turnover ratios: total asset turnover, fixed asset turnover.
d. Calculate these leverage ratios: total debt ratio, debt-to-equity ratio, equity multiplier.
e. Calculate these coverage ratios: times interest earned, cash coverage.
f. Calculate these profitability ratios: gross profit margin, net profit margin, ROA, ROE.
g. Use the DuPont identity, and after calculating the component ratios, compute the ROE for this firm.

CFA PROBLEMS

4.36 Common-size analysis is used in financial analysis to
a. evaluate changes in a company's operating cycle over time.
b. predict changes in a company's capital structure using regression analysis.
c. compare companies of different sizes or compare a company with itself over time.
d. restate each element in a company's financial statement as a proportion of the similar account for another company in the same industry.

4.37 The TBI Company has a number of days of inventory of 50. Therefore, the TBI Company's inventory turnover is closest to
a. 4.8 times.
b. 7.3 times.
c. 8.4 times.
d. 9.6 times.

4.38 DuPont analysis involves breaking return-on-assets ratios into their
a. profit components.
b. marginal and average components.
c. operating and financing components.
d. profit margin and turnover components.

4.39 If a company's net profit margin is −5 percent, its total asset turnover is 1.5 times, and its financial leverage ratio is 1.2 times, its return on equity is closest to
a. −9.0 percent.
b. −7.5 percent.
c. −3.2 percent.
d. 1.8 percent.

Sample Test Problems

4.1 Morgan Sports Equipment Company has accounts payable of $1,221,669, cash of $677,423, inventory of $2,312,478, accounts receivable of $845,113, and net working capital of $2,297,945. What are the company's current ratio and quick ratio?

4.2 Southwest Airlines, Inc., has total operating revenues of $6.53 million on total assets of $11.337 million. Their property, plant, and equipment, including their ground equipment and other assets, are listed at a historical cost of $11.921 million, while the accumulated depreciation and amortization amount to $3.198 million. What are the airline's total asset turnover and fixed asset turnover ratios?

4.3 Haugen Enterprises has an equity multiplier of 2.5. What is the firm's debt ratio?

4.4 Centennial Chemical Corp. has a gross profit margin of 31.4 percent on revenues of $13,144,680 and EBIT of $2,586,150. What are the company's cost of goods sold and operating profit margin?

4.5 National City Bank has 646,749,650 shares of common stock outstanding, and they are currently priced at $37.55. If its net income is $2,780,955,000, what are its earnings per share and price-earnings ratio?

A Sad Tale: The Demise of Arthur Andersen

ETHICS CASE

In January 2002, there were five major public accounting firms: Arthur Andersen, Deloitte Touche, KPMG, Pricewaterhouse-Coopers, and Ernst & Young. By late fall of that year, the number had been reduced to four. Arthur Andersen became the first major public accounting firm to be found guilty of a felony (a conviction later overturned), and as a result it virtually ceased to exist.

That such a fate could befall Andersen is especially sad given its early history. When Andersen and Company was established in 1918, it was led by Arthur Andersen, an acknowledged man of principle, and the company had a credo that became firmly embedded in the culture: "Think Straight and Talk Straight." Andersen became an industry leader partly on the basis of high ethical principles and integrity.

How did a one-time industry leader find itself in a position where it received a corporate death penalty over ethical issues? First, the market changed. During the 1980s, a boom in mergers and acquisitions and the emergence of information technology fueled the growth of an extremely profitable consulting practice at Andersen. The profits from consulting contracts soon exceeded the profits from auditing, Andersen's core business. Many of the consulting clients were also audit clients, and the firm found that the audit relationship was an ideal bridge for selling consulting services. Soon the audit fees became "loss leaders" to win audits, which allowed the consultants to sell more lucrative consulting contracts.

Tension between Audit and Consulting

At Andersen, tension between audit and consulting partners broke into open and sometimes public warfare. At the heart of the problem was how to divide up the earnings from the consulting practice among the two groups. The resulting conflict ended in divorce, with the consultants leaving to form their own firm. The firm, Accenture, continues to thrive today.

Once the firm split in two, Andersen began to rebuild a consulting practice as part of the accounting practice. Consulting continued to be a highly profitable business, and audit partners were now asked to sell consulting services to other clients, a role that many auditors found uncomfortable.

Although the accountants were firmly in charge, the role of partners as salespersons compounded an already existing ethical issue—that of conflict of interest. It is legally well established that the fiduciary responsibility of a certified public accounting (CPA) firm is to the investors and creditors of the firm being audited. CPA firms are supposed to render an opinion as to whether a firm's financial statements are reasonably accurate and whether the firm has applied generally accepted accounting principles in a consistent manner over time so as not to distort the financial statements. To meet their fiduciary responsibilities, auditors must maintain independence from the firms they audit.

What might interfere with the objective judgment of the public accounting firms? One problem arises because it is the audited companies themselves that pay the auditors' fees. Auditors might not be completely objective when auditing a firm because they fear losing consulting business. This is an issue that regulators and auditors have not yet solved. But another problem arises in situations where accounting firms provide consulting services to the companies they audit. Although all of the major accounting firms were involved in this practice to some extent, Andersen had developed an aggressive culture for engaging partners to sell consulting services to audit clients.

Andersen's Problems Mount

The unraveling of Andersen began in the 1990s with a series of accounting scandals at Sunbeam, Waste Management, and Colonial Realty—all firms that Andersen had audited. But scandals involving the energy giant Enron proved to be the firm's undoing. The account was huge. In 2000 alone, Andersen received $52 million in fees from Enron, approximately 50 percent for auditing and 50 percent for other consulting services, especially tax services. The partner in charge of the account and his entire 100-person team worked out of Enron's Houston office. Approximately 300 of Enron's senior and middle managers had been Andersen employees.

Enron went bankrupt in December 2001 after large-scale accounting irregularities came to light, prompting an investigation by the Securities and Exchange Commission (SEC). It soon became clear that Enron's financial statements for some time had been largely the products of accounting fraud, showing the company to be in far better financial condition than was actually the case. The inevitable question was asked: Why hadn't the auditors called attention to Enron's questionable accounting practices? The answer was a simple one. Andersen had major conflicts of interest. Indeed, when one member of Andersen's Professional Standards Group objected to some of Enron's accounting practices, Andersen removed him from auditing responsibilities at Enron—in response to a request from Enron management.

Playing Hardball and Losing

The SEC was determined to make an example of Andersen. The Justice Department began a criminal investigation, but investigators were willing to explore some "settlement options" in return for Andersen's cooperation. However, Andersen's senior management appeared arrogant and failed to grasp the political mood in Congress and in the country after a series of business scandals that had brought more than one large company to bankruptcy.

After several months of sparring with the Andersen senior management team, the Justice Department charged Andersen with a felony offense—obstruction of justice. Andersen was found guilty in 2002 of illegally instructing its employees to destroy documents relating to Enron, even as the government was conducting inquiries into Enron's finances. During the trial, government lawyers argued that by instructing its staff to "undertake an unprecedented campaign of document destruction," Andersen had obstructed the government's investigation.

Since a firm convicted of a felony cannot audit a publicly held company, the conviction spelled the end for Andersen. But even before the guilty verdict, there had been a massive defection of Andersen clients to other accounting firms. The evidence presented at trial showed a breakdown in Andersen's internal controls, a lack of leadership, and an environment in Andersen's Houston office that fostered recklessness and unethical behavior by some partners.

In 2005, the United States Supreme Court unanimously overturned the Andersen conviction on the grounds that the jury was given overly broad instructions by the federal judge who presided over the case. But by then it was too late. Most of the Andersen partners had either retired or gone to work for former competitors, and the company had all but ceased to exist.

Discussion Questions

1. To what extent do market pressures encourage unethical behavior? Can the demise of Andersen be blamed on the fact that the market began rewarding consulting services of the kind Andersen could provide?

2. How serious are the kinds of conflicts of interest discussed in this case? Did Sarbanes-Oxley eliminate the most serious conflicts?

3. Was it fair for the government to destroy an entire company because of the misdeeds of some of its members, or had Andersen become such a serious offender that such an action on the part of the government was justified?

THE TIME VALUE OF MONEY

CHAPTER 5

LEARNING OBJECTIVES

1. Explain what the time value of money is and why it is so important in the field of finance.

2. Explain the concept of future value, including the meaning of *principal amount, simple interest,* and *compound interest,* and be able to use the future value formula to make business decisions.

3. Explain the concept of present value and how it relates to future value, and be able use the present value formula to make business decisions.

4. Discuss why the concept of compounding is not restricted to money, and be able to use the future value formula to calculate growth rates.

Alamy

When you purchase an automobile from a dealer, the decision of whether to pay cash or finance your purchase can affect the price you pay. For example, when market conditions are tough, automobile manufacturers often offer customers a choice between a cash rebate and low-cost financing. Both of these alternatives affect the cost of purchasing an automobile, but one alternative can be worth more than the other.

To see why, consider the following. In September 2007, the automobile manufacturer Chrysler wanted to increase sales of its Sebring model. The company offered consumers a choice between (1) receiving $1,500 off the base price of $25,840 if they paid cash and (2) receiving 0 percent financing on a three-year loan if they paid the base price. For someone who had enough cash to buy the car outright and did not need the cash for some other use, the decision of whether to pay cash or finance the purchase of a Sebring depended on the rate of return that they could earn by investing the cash. On the one hand, if it was possible to earn only a 3 percent interest rate by investing in a certificate of deposit at a bank, the buyer was better off paying cash. On the other hand, if it was possible to earn 5 percent, the buyer was better off taking the financing. With a 4 percent rate of return, the buyer would have been largely indifferent between the two alternatives.

As with most business transactions, a crucial element in the analysis of the alternatives offered by Chrysler is the value of the expected cash flows. Because the cash flows for the two alternatives take place in different time periods, they must be adjusted to account for the time value of money before they can be compared. A car buyer wants to select the alternative with the cash flows that have the lowest value (price). This chapter and the next provide the knowledge and tools you need to make the correct decision. You will learn that at the bank, in the boardroom, or in the showroom, money has a time value—dollars today are worth more than dollars in the future—and you must account for this when making financial decisions.

CHAPTER PREVIEW

Business firms routinely make decisions to invest in productive assets to earn income. Some assets, such as plant and equipment, are tangible, and other assets, such as patents and trademarks, are intangible. Regardless of the type of investment, a firm pays out money now in the hope that the value of the future benefits (cash inflows) will exceed the cost of the asset. This process is what *value creation* is all about—buying capital assets that are worth more than they cost.

The valuation models presented in this book will require you to compute the present and future values of cash flows. This chapter and the next one provide the fundamental tools for making these calculations.

Chapter 5 explains how to value a single cash flow in different time periods, and Chapter 6 covers valuation of multiple cash flows. These two chapters are critical for your understanding of corporate finance.

We begin this chapter with a discussion of the time value of money. We then look at future value, which tells us how funds will grow if they are invested at a particular interest rate. Next, we discuss present value, which answers the question "What is the value today of cash payments received in the future?" We conclude the chapter with a discussion of several additional topics related to time value calculations.

5.1 The Time Value of Money

LEARNING OBJECTIVE 1

In financial decision making, one basic problem managers face is determining the value of (or price to pay for) cash flows expected in the future. Why is this a problem? Consider as an example the popular Mega Millions™ lottery game, which is played in 12 states across the U.S. In Mega Millions, the jackpot continues to build up until some lucky person buys a winning ticket—the payouts for a number of jackpot winning tickets have exceeded $100 million.[1]

If you won $100 million, headlines would read "Lucky Student Wins $100 Million Jackpot!" Does this mean that your ticket is worth $100 million on the day you win? The answer is no. A Mega Millions jackpot is paid either as a series of 26 payments over 25 years or as a cash lump sum. If you win "$100 million" and choose to receive the series of payments, the 26 payments will total $100 million. If you choose the lump sum option, Mega Millions will pay you less than the stated value of $100 million. This amount was about $60 million in February 2008. Thus, the value, or market price, of a "$100 million" winning Mega Millions ticket is really about $60 million because of the time value of money and the timing of the 26 cash payments. An appropriate question to ask now is, "What is the time value of money?"

Take an online lesson on the time value of money from TeachMeFinance.com at http://teachmefinance.com/timevalueofmoney.html.

Consuming Today or Tomorrow

time value of money
the difference in value between a dollar in hand today and a dollar promised in the future; a dollar today is worth more than a dollar in the future

The **time value of money** is based on the belief that people have a positive time preference for consumption. That is, people prefer to consume goods today rather than wait to consume similar goods in the future. Most people would prefer to have a

---

[1]As of February 3, 2008, the largest Mega Million jackpot was $370 million, won in March 2007. Mega Millions is operated by a consortium of the state lottery commissions in California, Georgia, Illinois, Maryland, Massachusetts, Michigan, New Jersey, New York, Ohio, Texas, Virginia, and Washington. To play the game, a player pays one dollar and picks five numbers from 1 to 56 and one additional number from 1 to 46 (the Mega Ball number). Twice a week, a machine mixes numbered balls and randomly selects six balls (five white balls and one Mega Ball), which determines the winning combination for that drawing. There are various winning combinations, but a ticket that matches all six numbers, including the Mega Ball number, is the jackpot winner.

large-screen TV today than to have one a year from now, for example. Money has a time value because a dollar in hand today is worth more than a dollar to be received in the future. This makes sense because if you had the dollar today, you could buy something with it—or, instead, you could invest it and earn interest. For example, if you had $100,000, you could buy a one-year bank certificate of deposit paying 5 percent interest and earn $5,000 interest for the year. At the end of the year, you would have $105,000 ($100,000 + $5,000). The $100,000 today is worth $105,000 a year from today. If the interest rate was higher, you would have even more money at the end of the year.

Based on this example, we can make several generalizations. First, the value of a dollar invested at a positive interest rate grows over time. Thus, the further in the future you receive a dollar, the less it is worth today. Second, the trade-off between money today and money at some future date depends in part on the rate of interest you can earn by investing. The higher the rate of interest, the more likely you will elect to invest your funds and forgo current consumption. Why? At the higher interest rate, your investment will earn more money.

> **BUILDING INTUITION**
>
> ### The Value of Money Changes with Time
>
> The term *time value of money* reflects the notion that people prefer to consume things today rather than at some time in the future. For this reason, people require compensation for deferring consumption. The effect is to make a dollar in the future worth less than a dollar today.

In the remainder of this section, we look at two views of time value—future value and present value. First, however, we describe time lines, which are pictorial aids to help solve future and present value problems.

Time Lines as Aids to Problem Solving

Time lines are an important tool for analyzing problems that involve cash flows over time. They provide an easy way to visualize the cash flows associated with investment decisions. A time line is a horizontal line that starts at time zero (today) and shows cash flows as they occur over time. For example, Exhibit 5.1 shows the time line for a five-year investment opportunity and its cash flows. Here, as in most finance problems, cash flows are assumed to occur at the end of the period. The project involves a $10,000 initial investment (cash outflow), such as the purchase of a new machine, that is expected to generate cash inflows over a five-year period: $5,000 at the end of year 1, $4,000 at the end of year 2, $3,000 at the end of year 3, $2,000 at the end of year 4, and $1,000 at the end of year 5. Because of the time value of money, it is critical that you identify not only the size of the cash flows, but also the timing.

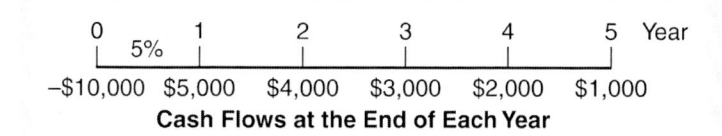

```
  0        1        2        3        4        5   Year
    5%
 -$10,000  $5,000  $4,000  $3,000  $2,000  $1,000
         Cash Flows at the End of Each Year
```

Exhibit 5.1
Five-year Time Line for a $10,000 Investment
Time lines help us to correctly identify the size and timing of cash flows—critical tasks in solving time value problems. This time line shows the cash flows generated over five years by a $10,000 investment in a situation where the relevant interest rate is 5 percent.

If it is appropriate, the time line will also show the relevant interest rate for the problem. In Exhibit 5.1 this is shown as 5 percent. Also, note in Exhibit 5.1 that the initial cash flow of $10,000 is represented by a negative number. It is conventional that cash outflows from the firm, such as for the purchase of a new machine, are treated as negative values on a time line and that cash inflows to the firm, such as revenues earned, are treated as positive values. The −$10,000 therefore means that there is a cash outflow of $10,000 at time zero. As you will see, it makes no difference how you label cash inflows and outflows as long as you are consistent. That is, if *all* cash outflows are given a negative value, then *all* cash inflows must have a positive value. If the signs get "mixed up"—if some cash inflows are negative and some positive—you will get the wrong answer to any problem you are trying to solve.

Future Value versus Present Value

We can analyze financial decisions using either future value or present value techniques. Although the two techniques approach the decision differently, both yield the same result. Both techniques focus on the valuation of cash flows received over time. In corporate finance, future value problems typically measure the value of cash flows at the end of a project, whereas present value measures the value of cash flows at the start of a project (time zero).

Exhibit 5.2 compares the $10,000 investment decision shown in Exhibit 5.1 in terms of future value and present value. When managers are making a decision about whether to accept a project, they must look at all of the cash flows associated with that project with reference to the same point in time. As Exhibit 5.2 shows, for most business decisions, that point is either the start (time zero) or the end of the project (in this example, year 5). The present value technique uses *discounting* to find the present value of each cash flow at the beginning of the project. Alternatively, the future value technique uses *compounding* to find the future value of each cash flow at the end of the project's life. We will look more closely at compounding and discounting later in the chapter.

For a discussion of simple versus compound interest, go to www.financeprofessor.com/introcorpfinnotes/simplevscompound.htm.

Compounding

```
                                                  Future
                                                  Value
 0        1        2        3        4        5 Year
 5%
−$10,000  $5,000   $4,000   $3,000   $2,000   $1,000

Present
 Value
```

Discounting

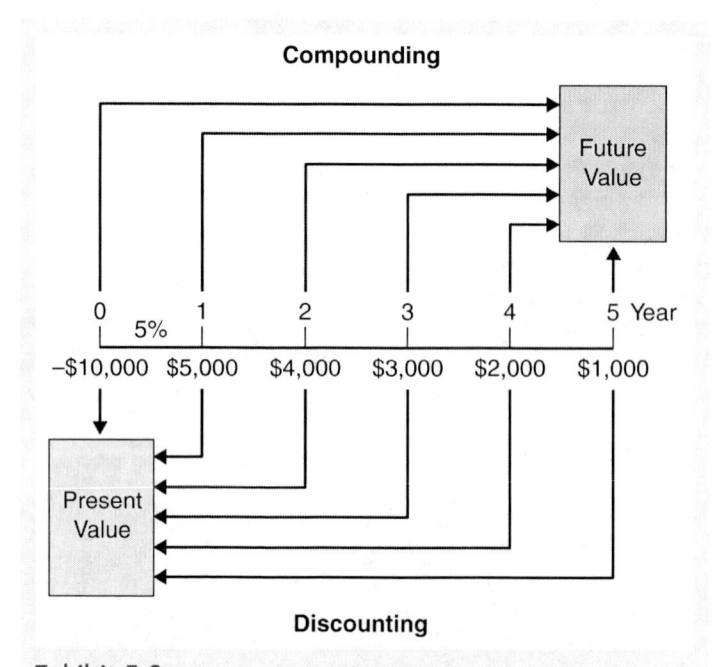

Exhibit 5.2
Future Value and Present Value Compared
Compounding converts a present value into its future value, taking into account the time value of money. Discounting is just the reverse—it converts future cash flows into their present value.

Financial Calculator

We recommend that students purchase a financial calculator for this course. A financial calculator will provide the computational tools—financial and algebraic—to solve most problems in the book. A financial calculator is just an ordinary calculator that has preprogrammed future value and present value algorithms. Thus, all the variables you need to make financial calculations exist on the calculator keys. To solve problems, all you have to do is press the proper keys. The instructions in this book are generally meant for Texas Instruments calculators, such as the TI BAII Plus. If you are using an HP or Sharp calculator, consult the user's manual for instructions.

It may sound as if the financial calculator will solve problems for you. It won't. To get the correct answer to textbook or real-world problems, you must first analyze the problem correctly and then identify the cash flows (size and timing), placing them correctly on a time line. Only then will you enter the correct inputs into the financial calculator. The calculator will, however, eliminate computation errors, save you a great deal of time, and eliminate an enormous source of frustration in your life.

To help you master your financial calculator, throughout this chapter, we provide helpful hints on how to best use the calculator. We also recognize that some professors or students may want to solve problems using one of the popular spreadsheet programs. In this chapter and a number of other chapters, we provide solutions to several problems that lend themselves to spreadsheet analysis. In solving these problems, we used Microsoft Excel™ for those using other types of spreadsheets, the analysis and basic commands are similar. We also provide spreadsheet solutions for additional problems on the book's Web site.

> **Before You Go On**
>
> 1. Why is a dollar today worth more than a dollar one year from now?
> 2. What is a time line, and why is it important in financial analysis?

5.2 Future Value and Compounding

The **future value (FV)** of an investment is what the investment will be worth after earning interest for one or more time periods. The process of converting the initial amount into future value is called *compounding*. We will define this term more precisely later. First, though, we illustrate the concepts of future value and compounding with a simple example.

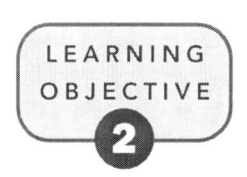

LEARNING OBJECTIVE 2

Single-Period Investment

future value (FV)
the value of an investment after it earns interest for one or more periods

Suppose you place $100 in a bank savings account that pays interest at 10 percent a year. How much money will you have in one year? Go ahead and make the calculation. Most people can intuitively arrive at the correct answer, $110, without the aid of a formula. Your calculation could have looked something like this:

$$\begin{aligned}\text{Future value at the end of year 1} &= \text{Principal} + \text{Interest earned} \\ &= \$100 + (\$100 \times 0.10) \\ &= \$100 \times (1 + 0.10) \\ &= \$100 \times (1.10) \\ &= \$110\end{aligned}$$

This approach computes the amount of interest earned ($100 × 0.10) and then adds it to the initial, or *principal,* amount ($100). Notice that when we solve the equation, we factor out the $100. Recall from algebra that if you have the equation $y = c + (c \times x)$, you can factor out the common term c as follows:

$$y = c + (c \times x)$$
$$= c \times (1 + x)$$

By doing this in our future value calculation, we arrived at the term $(1 + 0.10)$. This term can be stated more generally as $(1 + i)$, where i is the interest rate. As you will see, this is a pivotal term in both future value and present value calculations.

Let's use our intuitive calculation to generate a more general formula. First, we need to define the variables used to calculate the answer. In our example $100 is the principal amount (P_0), which is the amount of money at the beginning of the transaction (time zero); the 10 percent is the simple interest rate (i); and the $110 is the future value (FV_1) of the deposit after one year, which is one year in the future. We can write the formula for a single-period investment as follows:

$$FV_1 = P_0 + (P_0 \times i)$$
$$= P_0 \times (1 + i)$$

Looking at the formula, we more easily see mathematically what is happening in our intuitive calculation. P_0 is the principal amount invested at time zero. If you invest for one period at an interest rate of i, your investment, or principal, will grow by $(1 + i)$ per dollar invested. The term $(1 + i)$ is the *future value interest factor*—often called simply the *future value factor*—for a single period, such as one year. To test the equation, we plug in our values:

$$FV_1 = \$100 \times (1 + 0.10)$$
$$= \$100 \times 1.10$$
$$= \$110$$

Good, it works!

Two-Period Investment

We have determined that at the end of one year (one period), your $100 investment has grown to $110. Now let's say you decide to leave this new principal amount (FV_1) of $110 in the bank for another year earning 10 percent interest. How much money would you have at the end of the second year (FV_2)? To arrive at the value for FV_2, we multiply the new principal amount by the future value factor $(1 + i)$. That is, $FV_2 = FV_1 \times (1 + i)$. We then substitute the value of FV_1 (the single-period investment value) into the equation and algebraically rearrange terms, which yields $FV_2 = P_0 \times (1 + i)^2$. The mathematical steps to arrive at the equation for FV_2 are shown in the following; recall that $FV_1 = P_0 \times (1 + i)$:

$$FV_2 = FV_1 \times (1 + i)$$
$$= [P_0 \times (1 + i)] \times (1 + i)$$
$$= P_0 \times (1 + i)^2$$

The future value of your $110 at the end of the second year (FV_2) is as follows:

$$FV_2 = P_0 \times (1 + i)^2$$
$$= \$100 \times (1 + 0.10)^2$$
$$= 100 \times (1.10)^2$$
$$= \$100 \times 1.21$$
$$= \$121$$

Exhibit 5.3 Future Value of $100 at 10 Percent

(1) Year	(2) Value at Beginning of Year	(3) Simple Interest		(4) Interest on Interest		(5) Total (Compound) Interest	(6) Value at End of Year
1	$100.00	$10.00	+	$ 0.00	=	$10.00	$110.00
2	110.00	10.00	+	1.00	=	11.00	121.00
3	121.00	10.00	+	2.10	=	12.10	133.10
4	133.10	10.00	+	3.31	=	13.31	146.41
5	146.41	10.00	+	4.64	=	14.64	161.05
Five-year total	$100.00	$50.00	+	$11.05	=	$61.05	$161.05

With compounding, interest earned on an investment is reinvested so that in future periods, interest is earned on interest as well as on the principal amount. Here, interest on interest begins accruing in year 2.

Another way of thinking of a two-period investment is that it is two single-period investments back-to-back. From that perspective, based on the preceding equations, we can represent the future value of the deposit held in the bank for two years as follows:

$$FV_2 = P_0 \times (1 + i)^2$$

Turning to Exhibit 5.3, we can see what is happening to your $100 investment over the two years we have already discussed and beyond. The future value of $121 at year 2 consists of three parts. First is the initial *principal* of $100 (column 2). Second is the $20 ($10 + $10) of *simple interest* earned at 10 percent for the first and second years (column 3). Third is the $1 interest earned during the second year (column 4) on the $10 of interest from the first year ($10 × 0.10 = $1.00). This is called *interest on interest*. The total amount of interest earned is $21 ($10 + $11), which is shown in column 5 and is called *compound interest*.

We are now in a position to formally define some important terms already mentioned in our discussion. The **principal** is the amount of money on which interest is paid. In our example, the principal amount is $100. **Simple interest** is the amount of interest paid on the original principal amount. With simple interest, the interest earned each period is paid only on the original principal. In our example, the simple interest is $10 per year or $20 for the two years. **Interest on interest** is the interest earned on the reinvestment of previous interest payments. In our example, the interest on interest is $1. **Compounding** is the process by which interest earned on an investment is reinvested so that in future periods, interest is earned on the interest previously earned as well as the principal. In other words, with compounding, you are able to earn **compound interest**, which consists of both simple interest and interest on interest. In our example, the compound interest is $21.

The Future Value Equation

Let's continue our bank example. Suppose you decide to leave your money in the bank for three years. Looking back at equations for a single-period and two-period investment, you can probably guess that the equation for the future value of money invested for three years would be:

$$FV_3 = P_0 \times (1 + i)^3$$

---

principal
the amount of money on which interest is paid

simple interest
interest earned on the original principal amount only

interest on interest
interest earned on interest that is earned in previous periods

compounding
the process by which interest earned on an investment is reinvested, so in future periods interest is earned on the interest as well as the principal

compound interest
interest earned both on the original principal amount and on interest previously earned

CNNMoney's Web site has a savings calculator at cgi.money.cnn.com/tools/savingscalc/savingscalc.html.

With this pattern clearly established, we can see that the general equation to find the future value after any number of periods is as follows:

$$FV_n = PV \times (1 + i)^n \tag{5.1}$$

where:
FV_n = future value of investment at the end of period n
PV = original principal (P_0) or the present value
i = the rate of interest per period, which is often a year
n = the number of periods; a period is typically a year but can be a quarter, a month, a day, or some other unit of time
$(1 + i)^n$ = the future value factor

Let's test our general equation. Say you leave your $100 invested in the bank savings account at 10 percent interest for five years. How much would you have in the bank at the end of five years? Applying Equation 5.1 yields the following:

$$\begin{aligned} FV_5 &= \$100 \times (1 + 0.10)^5 \\ &= \$100 \times (1.10)^5 \\ &= \$100 \times 1.6105 \\ &= \$161.05 \end{aligned}$$

Exhibit 5.3 shows how the interest is earned on a year-by-year basis. Notice that the total compound interest earned over the five-year period is $61.05 (column 5) and that it is made up of two parts: (1) $50.00 of simple interest (column 3) and (2) $11.05 of interest on interest (column 4). Thus, the total interest can be expressed as follows:

$$\begin{aligned} \text{Total compound interest} &= \text{Total simple interest} + \text{Total interest on interest} \\ &= \$50.00 + \$11.05 \\ &= \$61.05 \end{aligned}$$

The simple interest earned is ($100 × 0.10) = $10.00 per year, and thus, the total simple interest for the five-year period is $50.00 (5 years × $10.00). The remaining balance of $11.05 ($61.05 − $50.00) comes from earning interest on interest.

A helpful equation for calculating the simple interest can be derived by using the equation for a single-period investment and solving for the term $FV_1 - P_0$, which is equal to the simple interest.[2] The equation for the simple interest earned (SI) is:

$$SI = P_0 \times i$$

where:
i = the simple interest rate for the period, usually one year
P_0 = the initial or beginning principal amount

Thus, the calculation for simple interest is:[3]

$$SI = P_0 \times i = \$100 \times 0.10 = \$10.00$$

Exhibit 5.4 shows graphically how the compound interest in Exhibit 5.3 grows. Notice that the simple interest earned each year remains constant at $10 per year but that the amount of interest on interest increases every year. The reason, of course, is

---

[2] The formula for a single-period investment is $FV_1 = P_0 + (P_0 \times i)$. Solving the equation for $FV_1 - P_0$ yields the simple interest, SI.

[3] Another helpful equation is the one which computes the total simple interest over several periods (TSI): TSI = Number of periods × SI = Number of periods × ($P_0 \times i$).

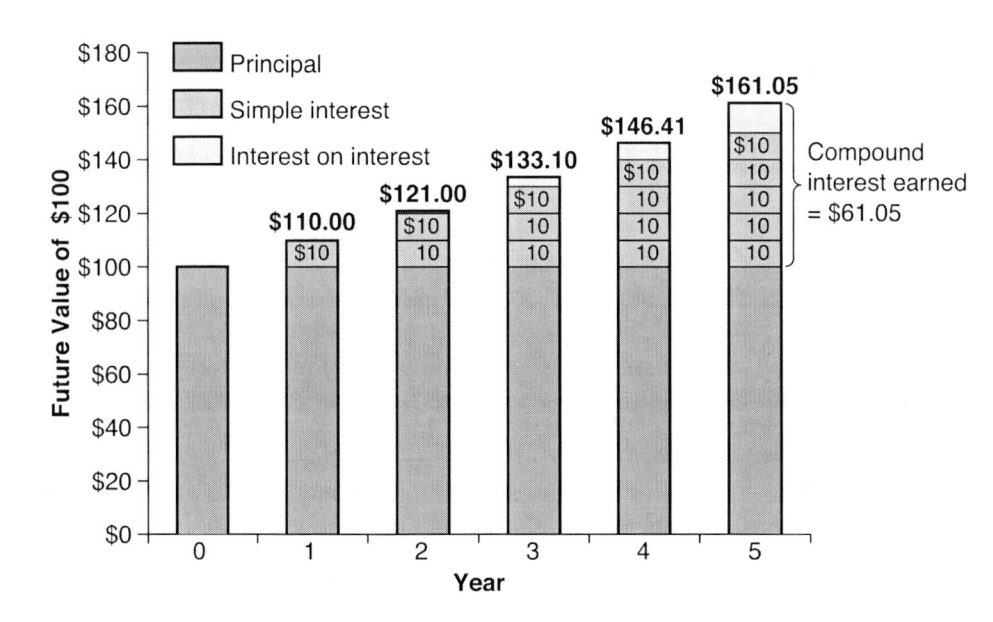

Exhibit 5.4
How Compound Interest Grows on $100 at 10 Percent

The amount of simple interest earned on $100 invested at 10 percent remains constant at $10 per year, but the amount of interest earned on interest increases each year. As more and more interest builds, the effect of compounding accelerates the growth of the total interest earned.

that interest on interest begins to build every time you compound. As more and more interest builds, the effect of compounding accelerates the growth of the total interest earned.

An interesting observation about Equation 5.1 is that the higher the interest rate, the faster the investment will grow. This fact can be seen in Exhibit 5.5, which shows the growth in the future value of $1.00 at different interest rates and for different time periods into the future. First, notice that the growth in the future value over time is not linear, but exponential. In other words, the growth of the invested funds is accelerated by the compounding of interest. Second, the higher the interest rate, the more money accumulated for any time period. Looking at the right-hand side of the exhibit, you can

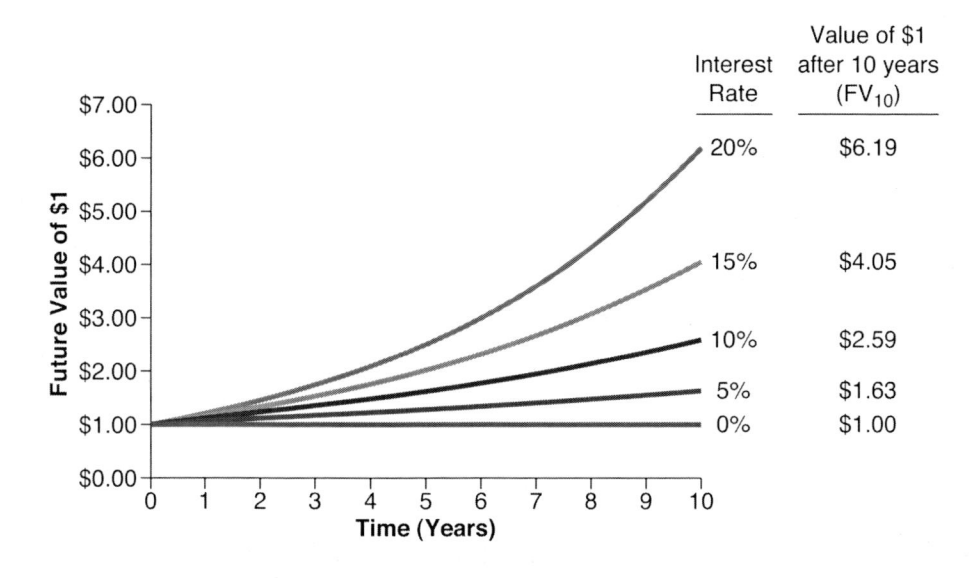

Exhibit 5.5
Future Value of $1 for Different Periods and Interest Rates

Interest Rate	Value of $1 after 10 years (FV$_{10}$)
20%	$6.19
15%	$4.05
10%	$2.59
5%	$1.63
0%	$1.00

The higher the interest rate, the faster the value of an investment will grow, and the larger the amount of money that will accumulate over time. Because of compounding, the growth over time is not linear but exponential—the dollar increase in the future value is greater in each subsequent period.

see the difference in total dollars accumulated if you invest a dollar for 10 years: At 5 percent, you will have $1.63; at 10 percent, you will have $2.59; at 15 percent, you will have $4.05; and at 20 percent, you will have $6.19. Finally, as you should expect, if you invest a dollar at 0 percent for 10 years, you will only have a dollar at the end of the period.

The Future Value Factor

To solve a future value problem, we need to know the future value factor, $(1 + i)^n$. Fortunately, almost any calculator suitable for college-level work has a power key (the y^x key) that we can use to make this computation. For example, to compute $(1.08)^{10}$, we enter 1.08, press the y^x key and enter 10, and press the "=" key. The number 2.159 should emerge.[4] Give it a try with your calculator.

Alternatively, we can use future value tables to find the future value factor at different interest rates and maturity periods. Exhibit 5.6 is an example of a future value table. For example, to find the future value factor $(1.08)^{10}$, we first go to the row corresponding to 10 years and then move along the row until we reach the 8 percent interest column. The entry is 2.159, which is identical to what we found when we used a calculator. This comes as no surprise, but we sometimes find small differences between calculator solutions and future value tables due to rounding differences. Exhibit A.1 at the end of the book provides a more comprehensive version of Exhibit 5.6.

Future value tables (and the corresponding present value tables) are rarely used today, partly because they are tedious to work with. In addition, the tables show values for only a limited number of interest rates and time periods. For example, what if the interest rate on your $100 investment was not a nice round number such as 10 percent but was 10.236 percent? You would not find that number in the future value table. In spite of their shortcomings, tables were very commonly used in the days before financial calculators and spreadsheet programs were readily available. You can still use them—for example, to check the answers from your computations of future value factors.

Applying the Future Value Formula

Next, we will review a number of examples of future value problems to illustrate the typical types of problems you will encounter in business and in your personal life.

SmartMoney's personal finance Web site provides a lot of useful information for day-to-day finance dealings at www.smartmoney.com/pf/?nav=dropTab.

Exhibit 5.6 Future Value Factors

Number of Years	Interest Rate per Year							
	1%	5%	6%	7%	8%	9%	10%
1	$1.010	$1.050	$1.060	$1.070	$1.080	$1.090	$1.100
2	1.020	1.103	1.124	1.145	1.166	1.188	1.210
3	1.030	1.158	1.191	1.225	1.260	1.295	1.331
4	1.041	1.216	1.262	1.311	1.360	1.412	1.464
5	1.051	1.276	1.338	1.403	1.469	1.539	1.611
10	1.105	1.629	1.791	1.967	2.159	2.367	2.594
20	1.220	2.653	3.207	3.870	4.661	5.604	6.727
30	1.348	4.322	5.743	7.612	10.063	13.268	17.449

To find a future value factor, simply locate the row with the appropriate number of periods and the column with the desired interest rate. The future value factor for 10 years at 8 percent is 2.159.

---

[4] An alternative way to perform the calculation is to multiply 1.08 by itself 10 times. However, we do not recommend this procedure.

THE POWER OF COMPOUNDING

Our first example illustrates the effects of compounding. Suppose you have an opportunity to make a $5,000 investment that pays 15 percent per year. How much money will you have at the end of 10 years? The time line for the investment opportunity is:

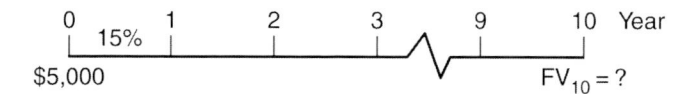

```
0        1     2     3      9     10   Year
|  15%   |     |     |      |     |
$5,000                           FV₁₀ = ?
```

We can apply Equation 5.1 to find the future value of $5,000 invested for 10 years at 15 percent interest. We want to multiply the principal amount (PV) times the appropriate future value factor for 10 years at 15 percent, which is $(1 + 0.15)^{10}$; thus:

$$FV_n = PV \times (1 + i)^n$$
$$FV_{10} = \$5,000 \times (1 + 0.15)^{10}$$
$$= \$5,000 \times 4.045558$$
$$= \$20,227.79$$

Now let's determine how much of the interest is from simple interest and how much is from interest on interest. The total compound interest earned is $15,227.79 ($20,227.79 − $5,000.00). The simple interest is the amount of interest paid on the original principal amount: $SI = P_0 \times i = \$5,000 \times 0.15 = \$750$ per year, which over 10 years is $750 × 10 = $7,500. The interest on interest must be the difference between the total compound interest earned and the simple interest: $15,227.79 − $7,500 = $7,727.79. Notice how quickly the value of an investment increases and how the reinvestment of interest earned—interest on interest—impacts that total compound interest when the interest rates are high.

You can find a compound interest calculator at SmartMoney.com: www.smartmoney.com/compoundcalc.

LEARNING BY DOING APPLICATION 5.1

The Power of Compounding

Problem: Your wealthy uncle passed away, and one of the assets he left to you was a savings account that your great-grandfather had set up 100 years ago. The account had a single deposit of $1,000 and paid 10 percent interest. How much money have you inherited, what is the total compound interest, and how much of the interest earned came from interest on interest?

Approach: We first need to determine the value of the inheritance, which is the future value of $1,000 retained in a savings account for 100 years at 10 percent interest. Our time line for the problem is:

```
0        1     2     3      99    100   Year
|  10%   |     |     |      |     |
$1,000                           FV₁₀₀ = ?
```

To calculate FV_{100}, we begin by computing the future value factor. We then plug this number into the future value formula (Equation 5.1) and solve for the total inheritance. Finally, we calculate the total compound interest and the total simple interest and find the difference between these two numbers, which will give us the interest earned on interest.

Solution:

First, we find the future value factor:

$$(1 + i)^n = (1 + 0.10)^{100} = (1.10)^{100} = 13,780.612$$

(continued)

Then we find the future value:

$$FV_n = PV \times (1 + i)^n$$
$$FV_{100} = \$1,000 \times (1.10)^{100}$$
$$= \$1,000 \times 13,780.612$$
$$= \$13,780,612$$

Your total inheritance is $13,780,612. The total compound interest earned is this amount less the original $1,000 investment, or $13,779,612:

$$\$13,780,612 - \$1,000 = \$13,779,612$$

The total simple interest earned is calculated as follows:

$$P_0 \times i = \$1,000 \times 0.10 = \$100 \text{ per year}$$
$$\$100 \times 100 \text{ years} = \$10,000$$

The interest earned on interest is the difference between the total compound interest earned and the simple interest:

$$\$13,779,612 - \$10,000 = \$13,769,612$$

That's quite a difference!

The following table shows the exponential growth of interest on interest in the savings account described in Learning by Doing Application 5.1. In the first year, simple interest equals compound interest. By year 10, total interest on interest, at $594, is still less than total simple interest, at $1,000. But after 20 years, interest on interest is $3,727—almost double the simple interest of $2,000. After 60 years, interest on interest is nearly 50 times the size of the simple interest—$297,482 versus $6,000. After 80 years, the difference is 255 times ($2,039,400 versus $8,000); and after 100 years, the difference is staggering ($13.78 million versus a mere $10,000). This example illustrates the power of compounding and explains why the future value curves in Exhibit 5.5 increase so sharply for longer time periods at higher interest rates.

Investment Period (years)	Total Compound Interest	Total Simple Interest	Total Interest on Interest
1	$100	$100	$0
10	$1,594	$1,000	$594
20	$5,727	$2,000	$3,727
40	$44,259	$4,000	$40,259
60	$303,482	$6,000	$297,482
80	$2,047,400	$8,000	$2,039,400
100	$13,779,612	$10,000	$13,769,612

> **BUILDING INTUITION**
>
> ### Compounding Drives Much of the Earnings on Long-Term Investments
>
> The earnings from compounding drive much of the return earned on a long-term investment. The reason is that the longer the investment period, the greater the proportion of total earnings from interest earned on interest. Interest earned on interest grows exponentially as the investment period increases.

COMPOUNDING MORE FREQUENTLY THAN ONCE A YEAR

Interest can, of course, be compounded more frequently than once a year. In Equation 5.1, the term n represents the number of periods and can describe annual, semiannual, quarterly, monthly, or daily payments. The more frequently interest payments are compounded, the larger the future value of $1 for a given time period. Equation 5.1 can be rewritten to explicitly recognize different compounding periods:

$$FV_n = PV \times (1 + i/m)^{m \times n} \tag{5.2}$$

where m is the number of times per year that interest is compounded and n is the number of periods specified in years.

Let's say you invest $100 in a bank account that pays a 5 percent interest rate semiannually (2.5 percent twice a year) for two years. In that case, the amount of interest you would have at the end of the period would be:

$$\begin{aligned} FV_2 &= \$100 \times (1 + 0.05/2)^{2 \times 2} \\ &= \$100 \times (1 + 0.025)^4 \\ &= \$100 \times 1.1038 \\ &= \$110.38 \end{aligned}$$

It is not necessary to "memorize" Equation 5.2; using Equation 5.1 will do fine. All you have to do is determine the interest paid per compounding period (i/m) and calculate the total number of compounding periods ($m \times n$) as the exponent for the future value factor. For example, if the bank compounds interest quarterly, then both the interest rate and compounding periods must be expressed in quarterly terms: ($i/4$) and ($4 \times n$).

During the late 1960s, the effects of compounding periods became an issue in banking. At that time, the interest rates that banks and thrift institutions could pay on consumer savings accounts were limited by regulation. However, financial institutions discovered they could keep their rates within the legal limit and pay their customers additional interest by increasing the compounding frequency. Prior to this, banks and thrifts had paid interest on savings accounts quarterly. You can see the difference between quarterly and daily compounding in Learning by Doing Application 5.2.

Moneychimp.com provides a compound interest calculator at www.moneychimp.com/calculator/compound_interest_calculator.htm.

LEARNING BY DOING APPLICATION 5.2

Changing the Compounding Period

Problem: Your grandmother has $10,000 she wants to put into a bank savings account for five years. The bank she is considering is within walking distance, pays 5 percent annual interest compounded quarterly (5/4 = 1.25 percent each quarter), and provides free coffee and doughnuts in the morning. Another bank in town pays 5 percent interest compounded daily. Getting to this bank requires a bus trip, but your grandmother can ride free as a senior citizen. More important, though, this bank does not serve coffee and doughnuts. Which bank should your grandmother select?

Approach: We need to calculate the difference between the two banks' interest payments. Bank A, which compounds quarterly, will pay one-fourth of the annual interest per quarter (0.05/4) = 0.0125, and there will be 20 compounding periods over the five-year investment horizon (5 years $\times$ 4). The time line for quarterly compounding is as follows:

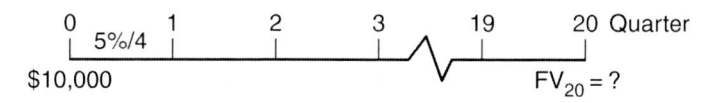

```
    0        1       2       3       19      20   Quarter
    | 5%/4   |       |       |       |       |
 $10,000                                  FV_20 = ?
```

(continued)

Bank B, which compounds daily, has 365 compounding periods per year. Thus, the daily interest rate is 0.000137 (0.05/365), and there are 1,825 (5 years × 365) compounding periods. The time line for daily compounding is:

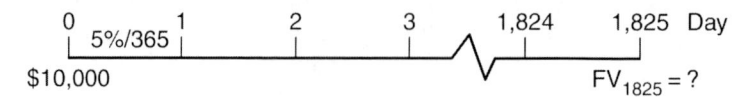

```
0         1         2         3        1,824   1,825  Day
|  5%/365 |         |         |   ⋯⋯   |       |
$10,000                                        FV₁₈₂₅ = ?
```

We use Equation 5.2 to solve for the future values the investment would generate at each bank. We then compare the two.

Solution:

Bank A:
$$FV_n = PV \times (1 + i/m)^{m \times n}$$
$$FV_{qtrly} = \$10{,}000 \times (1 + 0.05/4)^{4 \times 5}$$
$$= \$10{,}000 \times (1 + 0.0125)^{20}$$
$$= \$12{,}820.37$$

Bank B:
$$FV_n = PV \times (1 + i/m)^{m \times n}$$
$$FV_{daily} = \$10{,}000 \times (1 + 0.05/365)^{365 \times 5}$$
$$= \$10{,}000 \times (1 + 0.000137)^{1{,}825}$$
$$= \$12{,}840.03$$

With daily compounding, the additional interest earned by your grandmother is $19.66:

$$\$12{,}840.03 - \$12{,}820.37 = \$19.66$$

Given that the interest gained by daily compounding is less than $20, your grandmother should probably select her local bank and enjoy the daily coffee and doughnuts. (If she is on a diet, of course, she should take the higher interest payment and walk to the other bank).

CONTINUOUS COMPOUNDING

We can continue to divide the compounding interval into smaller and smaller time periods, such as minutes and seconds, until, at the extreme, we would compound continuously. In this case, m in Equation 5.2 would approach infinity (∞). The formula to compute the future value for continuous compounding (FV_∞) is stated as follows:

$$FV_\infty = PV \times e^{i \times n} \tag{5.3}$$

where e is the exponential function, which has a known mathematical value of about 2.71828, n is the number of periods specified in years, and i is the annual interest rate. Although the formula may look a little intimidating, it is really quite easy to apply. Look for a key on your calculator labeled e^x. If you don't have the key, you still can work the problem.

Let's go back to the example in Learning by Doing Application 5.2, in which your grandmother wants to put $10,000 in a savings account at a bank. How much money would she have at the end of five years if the bank paid 5 percent annual interest compounded continuously? To find out, we enter these values into Equation 5.3:

$$FV_\infty = PV \times e^{i \times n}$$
$$= \$10{,}000 \times e^{0.05 \times 5}$$
$$= \$10{,}000 \times e^{0.25}$$
$$= \$10{,}000 \times 2.71828^{0.25}$$
$$= \$10{,}000 \times 1.284025$$
$$= \$12{,}840.25$$

If your calculator has an exponent key, all you have to do to calculate $e^{0.25}$ is enter the number 0.25, then hit the e^x key, and the number 1.28403 should appear (depending on your calculator, you may have to press the equal [=] key for the answer to appear). Then multiply 1.284025 by $10,000, and you're done! If your calculator does not have an exponent key, then you can calculate $e^{0.25}$ by inputting the value of e (2.71828) and raising it to the 0.25 power using the y^x key, as described earlier in the chapter.

Let's look at your grandmother's $10,000 bank balance at the end of five years with several different compounding periods: yearly, quarterly, daily, and continuous:[5]

(1) Compounding Period	(2) Total Earnings	(3) Compound Interest	(4) Additional Interest
Yearly	$12,762.82	$2,762.82	—
Quarterly	$12,820.37	$2,820.37	$57.55 more than yearly compounding
Daily	$12,840.03	$2,840.03	$19.66 more than quarterly compounding
Continuous	$12,840.25	$2,840.25	$0.22 more than daily compounding

Notice that your grandmother's total earnings get larger as the frequency of compounding increases, as shown in column 2, but the earnings increase at a decreasing rate, as shown in column 4. The biggest gain comes when the compounding period goes from an annual interest payment to quarterly interest payments. The gain from daily compounding to continuous compounding is small on a modest savings balance such as your grandmother's. Twenty-two cents over five years will not buy grandmother a cup of coffee, let alone a doughnut. However, for businesses and governments with mega-dollar balances at financial institutions, the difference in compounding periods can be substantial.

Which Bank Offers Depositors the Best Deal?

DECISION-MAKING EXAMPLE 5.1

Situation: You have just received a bonus of $10,000 and are looking to deposit the money in a bank account for five years. You investigate the annual deposit rates of several banks and collect the following information:

Bank	Compounding Frequency	Annual Rate
A	Annually	5.00%
B	Quarterly	5.00%
C	Monthly	4.80%
D	Daily	4.85%

You understand that the more frequently interest is earned in each year, the more you will have at the end of your investment horizon. To determine which bank you should deposit your money in, you calculate how much money you will earn at the end of five years at each bank. You apply Equation 5.2 and come up with these results. Which bank should you choose?

Bank	Investment Amount	Compounding Frequency	Rate	Value after 5 Years
A	$10,000	Annually	5.00%	$12,762.82
B	$10,000	Quarterly	5.00%	$12,820.37
C	$10,000	Monthly	4.80%	$12,706.41
D	$10,000	Daily	4.85%	$12,744.11

(continued)

---

[5]The future value calculation for annual compounding is: $FV_{yearly} = \$10{,}000 \times (1.05)^5 = \$12{,}762.82$.

Decision: Even though you might expect Bank D's daily compounding to result in the highest value, the calculations reveal that Bank B provides the highest value at the end of five years. Thus, you should deposit the amount in Bank B because its higher rate offsets the more frequent compounding at Banks C and D.

USING EXCEL

Time Value of Money

Spreadsheet computer programs are a popular method for setting up and solving finance and accounting problems. Throughout this book, we will show you how to structure and calculate some problems using Microsoft Excel, a widely used spreadsheet program. Spreadsheet programs are like your financial calculator but are especially efficient at doing repetitive calculations. For example, once the spreadsheet program is set up, it will allow you to make computations using preprogrammed formulas. Thus, you can simply change any of the input cells, and the preset formula will automatically recalculate the answer based on the new input values. For this reason, we recommend that you use formulas whenever possible.

We begin our spreadsheet applications with time value of money calculations. As with the financial calculator approach, there are five variables used in these calculations, and knowing any four of them will let you calculate the fifth one. Excel has already preset formulas for you to use. These are as follows:

Solving for	Formula
PV	= PV(RATE, NPER, PMT, FV)
FV	= FV(RATE, NPER, PMT, PV)
Discount Rate	= RATE(NPER, PMT, PV, FV)
Payment	= PMT(RATE, NPER, PV, FV)
Number of Periods	= NPER(RATE, PMT, PV, FV)

To enter a formula, all you have to do is type in the equal sign, the abbreviated name of the variable you want to compute, and an open parenthesis, and Excel will automatically prompt you to enter the rest of the variables. Here is an example of what you would type to compute the future value:

1. =
2. FV
3. (

	A	B	C	D	E	F
1						
2			Time Value of Money Calculations			
3						
4	Your grandmother wants to put $10,000 into a bank savings account for five years. Bank A pays 5 percent					
5	interest compounded quarterly, while Bank B offers 5 percent compounded daily. Which bank should your					
6	grandmother choose?					
7						
8	To answer the question, we need to solve for the future value.					
9						
10	Problem set-up and solution:					
11						
12		Bank A	Bank B		Comment	
13	Present value	($10,000)	($10,000)		Value given	
14	Interest rate	0.01250	0.00014		Interest rate/# compounding periods per year	
15	Number of periods	20	1825		# years × # compounding periods per year	
16	Future value	$12,820.37	$12,840.03		See note below	
17						
18	The formula entered to calculate the future value for Bank A in cell B16 is =FV(B14, B15, 0, B13). Similarly, the					
19	formula to calculate the future value for Bank B in cell C16 is =FV(C14, C15, 0, C13). Since there are no					
20	payments, we enter PMT as zero. Also, notice that to be consistent with what we have said about cash inflows					
21	and outflows so far, the present value is entered as a negative number.					
22						
23						

Here are a few important things to note when entering the formulas: (1) be consistent with signs for cash inflows and outflows; (2) enter the rate of return as a decimal number, not a percentage; and (3) enter the amount of an unknown payment as zero.

To see how a problem is set up and how the calculations are made using a spreadsheet, return to Learning by Doing Application 5.2.

Calculator Tips for Future Value Problems

As we have mentioned, all types of future value calculations can be done easily on a financial calculator. Here we discuss how to solve these problems, and we identify some potential problem areas to avoid.

A financial calculator includes the following five basic keys for solving future value and present value problems:

5.2 Future Value and Compounding

| N | i | PV | PMT | FV |

The keys represent the following inputs:

- **N** is the number of periods. The periods can be days, months, quarters, or years.
- **i** is the interest rate per period, expressed as a percentage.
- **PV** is the present value or the original principal (P_0).
- **PMT** is the amount of any recurring payment.
- **FV** is the future value.

Given any four of these inputs, the financial calculator will solve for the fifth. Note that the interest rate key i differs with different calculator brands: Texas Instruments uses the I/Y key, Hewlett-Packard an i, %i or I/Y key, and Sharp the i key.

For future value problems, we need to use only four of the five keys: N for the number of periods, i for the interest rate (or growth rate), PV for the present value (at time zero), and FV for the future value in n periods. The PMT key is not used at this time, but, when doing a problem, always enter a zero to effectively clear the register.[6]

To solve a future value problem, enter the known data into your calculator. For example, if you know that the number of periods is five, key in 5 and press the N key. Repeat the process for the remaining known values. Once you have entered *all* of the values you know, then press the key for the unknown quantity, and you have your answer. Note that with some calculators, including the TI BAII Plus, you get the answer by first pressing the key labeled CPT (compute).

Let's try a problem to see how this works. Suppose we invest $5,000 at 15 percent for 10 years. How much money will we have in 10 years? To solve the problem, we enter data on the keys as displayed in the following calculation and solve for FV. Note that the initial investment of $5,000 is a negative number because it represents a cash outflow. Use the +/− key to make a number negative.

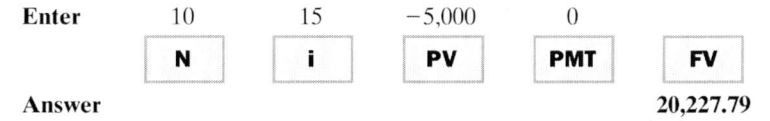

Enter	10	15	−5,000	0	
	N	i	PV	PMT	FV
Answer					20,227.79

If you did not get the correct answer of $20,227.79, you may need to consult the instruction manual that came with your financial calculator. However, before you do that, you may want to look through Exhibit 5.7, which lists the most common problems with using financial calculators. Also, note again that the PMT is entered as zero, which effectively clears the register.

One advantage of using a financial calculator is that if you have values for any three of the four variables in Equation 5.1, you can solve for the remaining variable at the press of a button. Suppose that you have an opportunity to invest $5,000 in a bank and that the bank will pay you $20,227.79 at the end of 10 years. What interest rate does the bank pay? The time line for our situation is as follows:

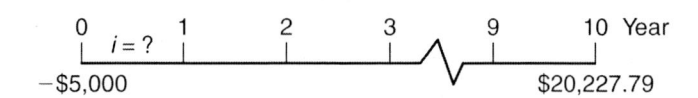

```
     0        1        2        3        9       10 Year
     | i = ?  |        |        |        |        |
  −$5,000                                      $20,227.79
```

We know the values for N (10 years), PV ($5,000), and FV ($20,227.79), so we can enter these values into our financial calculator:

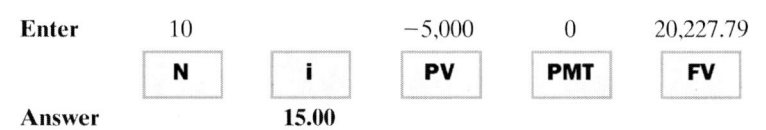

Enter	10		−5,000	0	20,227.79
	N	i	PV	PMT	FV
Answer		15.00			

---

[6]The PMT key is used for annuity calculations, which we will discuss in Chapter 6.

Exhibit 5.7 Tips for Using Financial Calculators

Use the Correct Compounding Period. Make sure that your calculator is set to compound one payment per period or per year. Because financial calculators are often used to compute monthly payments, some will default to monthly payments unless you indicate otherwise. You will need to consult your calculator's instruction manual because procedures for changing settings vary by manufacturer. Most of the problems you will work in other chapters of the book will compound annually.

Clear the Calculator Before Starting. Be sure you clear the data out of the financial register before starting to work a problem because most calculators retain information between calculations. Since the information may be retained even when the calculator is turned off, turning the calculator off and on will not solve this problem. Check your instruction manual for the correct procedure for clearing the financial register of your calculator.

Negative Signs on Cash Outflows. For certain types of calculations, it is critical that you input a negative sign for all cash outflows and a positive sign for all cash inflows. Otherwise, the calculator cannot make the computation, and the answer screen will display some type of error message.

Putting a Negative Sign on a Number. To create a number with a negative sign, enter the number first and then press the "change of sign key." These keys are typically labeled "CHS" or "+/−".

Interest Rate as a Percentage. Most financial calculators require that interest rate data be entered in percentage form, not in decimal form. For example, enter 7.125 percent as 7.125 and not 0.07125. Unlike nonfinancial calculators, financial calculators assume that rates are stated as percentages.

Rounding off Numbers. Never round off any numbers until all your calculations are complete. If you round off numbers along the way, you can generate significant rounding errors.

Adjust Decimal Setting. Most calculators are set to display two decimal places. You will find it convenient at times to display four or more decimal places when making financial calculations, especially when working with interest rates or present value factors. Again, consult your instruction manual.

Have Correct BEG or END mode. In finance, most problems that you solve will involve cash payments that occur at the end of each time period, such as with the ordinary annuities discussed in Chapter 6. Most calculators normally operate in this mode, which is usually designated as "END" mode. However, for annuities due, which are also discussed in Chapter 6, the cash payments occur at the beginning of each period. This setting is designated as the "BEG" mode. Most leases and rent payments fall into this category. When you bought your financial calculator, it was set in the END mode. Financial calculators allow you to switch between the END and BEG modes.

Following these tips will help you avoid problems that sometimes arise in solving time value of money problems with a financial calculator.

Press the interest rate (i) key, and 15.00 percent appears as the answer. Notice that the cash outflow ($5,000) was entered as a negative value and the cash inflow ($20,227.79) as a positive value. If both values were entered with the same sign, your financial calculator algorithm could not compute the equation, yielding an error message. Go ahead and try it.

> **Before You Go On**
> 1. What is compounding, and how does it affect the future value of an investment?
> 2. What is the difference between simple interest and compound interest?
> 3. How does changing the compounding period affect the amount of interest earned on an investment?

5.3 PRESENT VALUE AND DISCOUNTING

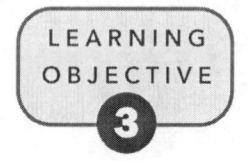

LEARNING OBJECTIVE 3

In our discussion of future value, we asked the question "If you put $100 in a bank savings account that paid 10 percent annual interest, how much money would accumulate in one year?" Another type of question that arises frequently in finance concerns present value. This question asks, "What is the value today of a cash flow promised in the future?" We'll illustrate the present value concept with a simple example.

Single-Period Investment

Suppose that a rich uncle gives you a bank certificate of deposit (CD) that matures in one year and pays $110. The CD pays 10 percent interest annually and cannot be redeemed until maturity. Being a student, you need the money and would like to sell the asset. What would be a fair price if you sold the CD today?

From our earlier discussion, we know that if we invest $100 in a bank at 10 percent for one year, it will grow to a future value of $110 = $100 × (1 + 0.10). It seems reasonable to conclude that if a CD has an interest rate of 10 percent and will have a value of $110 a year from now, it is worth $100 today.

More formally, to find the present value of a future cash flow, or its value today, we "reverse" the compounding process and divide the future value ($110) by the future value factor (1 + 0.10). The result is $100 = $110/(1 + 0.10), which is the same answer we derived from our intuitive calculation. If we write the calculations above as a formula, we have a one-period model for calculating the present value of a future cash flow:

$$PV = \frac{FV_1}{1+i}$$

The numerical calculation for the present value (PV) from our one-period model follows:

$$PV = \frac{FV_1}{1+i}$$
$$= \frac{\$110}{1+0.10}$$
$$= \frac{\$110}{1.10}$$
$$= \$100$$

We have noted that while future value calculations involve *compounding* an amount forward into the future, *present value* calculations involve the reverse. That is, present value calculations involve determining the current value (or present value) of a future cash flow. The process of calculating the present value is called **discounting**, and the interest rate i is known as the **discount rate**. Accordingly, the **present value (PV)** can be thought of as the *discounted value of a future amount*. The present value is simply the current value of a future cash flow that has been discounted at the appropriate discount rate.

Just as we have a future value factor, (1 + i), we also have a *present value factor*, which is more commonly called the *discount factor*. The discount factor, which is 1/(1 + i), is the reciprocal of the future value factor. This expression may not be obvious in the equation above, but note that we can write that equation in two ways:

1. $PV = \dfrac{FV}{1+i}$
2. $PV = FV_1 \times \dfrac{1}{1+i}$

discounting
the process by which the present value of future cash flows is obtained

discount rate
the interest rate used in the discounting process to find the present value of future cash flows

present value (PV)
the current value of future cash flows discounted at the appropriate discount rate

These equations amount to the same thing; the discount factor is explicit in the second one.

Multiple-Period Investment

Now suppose your uncle gives you another 10 percent CD, but this CD matures in two years and pays $121 at maturity. Like the other CD, it cannot be redeemed until maturity. From the previous section, we know that if we invest $100 in a bank at 10 percent for two years, it will grow to a future value of $121 = \$100 \times (1 + 0.10)^2$. To calculate the present value, or today's price, we divide the future value ($121) by the future value factor $(1 + 0.10)^2$. The result is $100 = \$121/(1 + 0.10)^2$.

If we capture the calculations we made as an equation, the result is a two-period model for computing the present value of a future cash flow:

$$PV = \frac{FV_2}{(1+i)^2}$$

Plugging the data from our example into the equation yields no surprises:

$$\begin{aligned} PV &= \frac{FV_2}{(1+i)^2} \\ &= \frac{\$121}{(1+0.10)^2} \\ &= \frac{\$121}{1.21} \\ &= \$100 \end{aligned}$$

By now, you know the drill. We can extend the equation to a third year, a fourth year, and so on until we reach n years:

Year	Equation
1	$PV = \dfrac{FV_1}{1+i}$
2	$PV = \dfrac{FV_2}{(1+i)^2}$
3	$PV = \dfrac{FV_3}{(1+i)^3}$
4	$PV = \dfrac{FV_4}{(1+i)^4}$
...	
n	$PV = \dfrac{FV_n}{(1+i)^n}$

The Present Value Equation

Given the pattern shown in the foregoing, we can see that the general formula for the present value is:[7]

$$PV = \frac{FV_n}{(1+i)^n} \qquad (5.4)$$

where:
PV = the value today ($t = 0$) of a cash flow or series of cash flows
FV_n = the future value at the end of period n
i = the discount rate, which is the interest rate per period
n = the number of periods, which could be years, month, days, or some other unit of time

---

[7]Equation 5.4 can also be written as $PV = FV_n \times (1+i)^{-n}$.

Note that Equation 5.4 is sometimes written in a slightly different way, which we will use sometimes in the book. The first form, introduced earlier, separates out the discount factor, $1/(1 + i)$:

$$PV = FV_n \times \frac{1}{(1 + i)^n}$$

In the second form, DF_n is the discount factor for the nth period: $DF_n = 1/(1 + i)^n$:

$$PV = FV_n \times DF_n$$

Future and Present Value Equations Are the Same

By now, you may have recognized that the present value equation, Equation 5.4, is just a restatement of the future value equation, Equation 5.1. That is, to get the future value (FV_n) of funds invested for n years, we multiply the original investment by $(1 + i)^n$. To find the present value of a future payment (FV_n), we divide FV_n by $(1 + i)^n$. Stated another way, we can start with the future value equation (Equation 5.1), $FV_n = PV \times (1 + i)^n$ and then solve it for PV; the resulting equation is the present value equation (Equation 5.4), $PV = FV_n/(1 + i)^n$.

Exhibit 5.8 illustrates the relationship between the future value and present value calculations for $100 invested at 10 percent interest. You can see from the exhibit that present value and future value are just two sides of the same coin. The formula used to calculate the present value is really the same as the formula for future value, just rearranged.

Applying the Present Value Formula

Let's work through some examples to see how the present value equation is used. Suppose you are interested in buying a new BMW 330 Sports Coupe a year from now. You estimate that the car will cost $40,000. If your local bank pays 5 percent interest on savings deposits, how much money will you need to save in order to buy the car as planned? The time line for the car purchase problem is as follows:

```
0                    5%                    1 Year
|_____|
PV = ?                                    $40,000
```

The problem is a direct application of Equation 5.4. What we want to know is how much money you have to put in the bank today to have $40,000 a year from now to buy

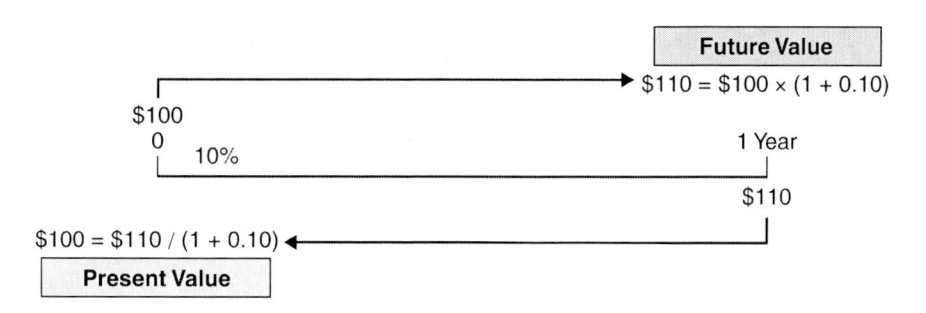

```
                                          Future Value
                                    → $110 = $100 × (1 + 0.10)
    $100
     0         10%                         1 Year
     |_____|
                                          $110
$100 = $110 / (1 + 0.10) ◄───────────────────┘
   Present Value
```

Exhibit 5.8
Comparing Future Value and Present Value Calculations
The future value and present value formulas are one and the same; the present value factor, $1/(1 + i)^n$, is just the reciprocal of the future value factor, $(1 + i)^n$.

your BMW. To find out, we compute the present value of $40,000 using a 5 percent discount rate:

$$PV = \frac{FV_1}{1+i}$$
$$= \frac{\$40,000}{1+0.05}$$
$$= \frac{\$40,000}{1.05}$$
$$= \$38,095.24$$

If you put $38,095.24 in a bank savings account at 5 percent today, you will have the $40,000 to buy the car in one year.

Since that's a lot of money to come up with, your mother suggests that you leave the money in the bank for two years instead of one year. If you follow her advice, how much money do you need to invest? The time line is as follows:

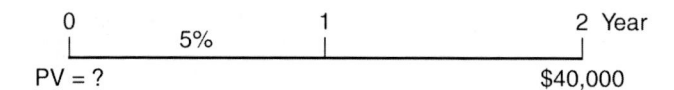

```
0                    1                    2 Year
|        5%          |                    |
PV = ?                                    $40,000
```

For a two-year waiting period, assuming the car price will stay the same, the calculation is:

$$PV = \frac{FV_2}{(1+i)^2}$$
$$= \frac{\$40,000}{(1+0.05)^2}$$
$$= \frac{\$40,000}{1.1025}$$
$$= \$36,281.18$$

Given the time value of money, the result is exactly what we would expect. The present value of $40,000 two years out is lower than the present value of $40,000 one year out—$36,281.18 compared with $38,095.24. Thus, if you are willing to leave your money in the bank for two years instead of one, you can make a smaller initial investment to reach your goal.

Now suppose your rich neighbor says that if you invest your money with him for one year, he will pay you 15 percent interest. The time line is:

```
0                                         1 Year
|        15%                              |
PV = ?                                    $40,000
```

The calculation for the initial investment at this new rate is as follows:

$$PV = \frac{FV_1}{1+i}$$
$$= \frac{\$40,000}{1+0.15}$$
$$= \frac{\$40,000}{1.15}$$
$$= \$34,782.61$$

Thus, when the interest rate, or discount rate, is 15 percent, the present value of $40,000 to be received in a year's time is $34,782.61, compared with $38,095.24 at a rate of

5 percent and a time of one year. Holding maturity constant, an increase in the discount rate decreases the present value of the future cash flow. This makes sense because when interest rates are higher, it is more valuable to have dollars in hand today to invest; thus, dollars in the future are worth less.

> **LEARNING BY DOING APPLICATION 5.3**
>
> ### European Graduation Fling
>
> **Problem:** Suppose you plan to take a "graduation vacation" to Europe when you finish college in two years. If your savings account at the bank pays 6 percent, how much money do you need to set aside today to have $8,000 when you leave for Europe?
>
> **Approach:** The money you need today is the present value of the amount you will need for your trip in two years. Thus, the value of FV_2 is $8,000. The interest rate is 6 percent. Using these values and the present value equation, we can calculate how much money you need to put in the bank at 6 percent to generate $8,000. The time line is:
>
> ```
> 0              1              2    Year
> |      6%      |              |
> PV = ?                      $8,000
> ```
>
> **Solution:**
>
> $$PV = FV_n \times \frac{1}{(1+i)^n}$$
> $$= FV_2 \times \frac{1}{(1+i)^2}$$
> $$= \$8{,}000 \times \frac{1}{(1.06)^2}$$
> $$= \$8{,}000 \times 0.889996$$
> $$= \$7{,}119.97$$
>
> Thus, if you invest $7,119.97 in your savings account today, at the end of two years you will have exactly $8,000.

The Relations among Time, the Discount Rate, and Present Value

From our discussion so far, we can see that (1) the farther in the future a dollar will be received, the less it is worth today, and (2) the higher the discount rate, the lower the present value of a dollar. Let's look a bit more closely at these relations.

Recall from Exhibit 5.5 that future value factors grow exponentially over time because of compounding. Similarly, present value factors become smaller the longer the time horizon. The reason is because the present value factor $1/(1 + i)^n$ is the reciprocal of the future value factor $(1 + i)^n$. Thus, the present value of $1 must become smaller as the time to payment becomes longer. You can see this relation in Exhibit 5.9, which shows the present value of $1 for various interest rates and time periods. For example, at 10 percent, the present value of $1 one year in the future is 90.9 cents ($1/1.10); at two years in the future, 82.6 cents [$1/(1.10)^2$]; at five years in the future, 62.1 cents [$1/(1.10)^5$]; and at thirty years in the future, 5.7 cents [$1/(1.10)^{30}$]. The relation is consistent with our view of the time value of money. That is, the longer you have to wait for money, the less it is worth today. Exhibit A.2, at the end of the book, provides present value factors for a wider range of years and interest rates.

154 CHAPTER 5 | The Time Value of Money

Exhibit 5.9 Present Value Factors

Number of Years	Interest Rate per Year						
	1%	5%	6%	7%	8%	9%	10%
1	$0.990	$0.952	$0.943	$0.935	$0.926	$0.917	$0.909
2	0.980	0.907	0.890	0.873	0.857	0.842	0.826
3	0.971	0.864	0.840	0.816	0.794	0.772	0.751
4	0.961	0.823	0.792	0.763	0.735	0.708	0.683
5	0.951	0.784	0.747	0.713	0.681	0.650	0.621
10	0.905	0.614	0.558	0.508	0.463	0.422	0.386
20	0.820	0.377	0.312	0.258	0.215	0.178	0.149
30	0.742	0.231	0.174	0.131	0.099	0.075	0.057

To locate a present value factor, find the row for the number of periods and the column for the proper discount rate. Notice that whereas future value factors grow larger over time and with increasing interest rates, present value factors become smaller. This pattern reflects the fact that the present value factor is the reciprocal of the future value factor.

Exhibit 5.10 shows the present values of $1 for different time periods and discount rates. For example, at 10 years, the present value of $1 discounted at 5 percent is 61 cents, at 10 percent it is 39 cents, and at 20 percent, 16 cents. Thus, the higher the discount rate, the lower the present value of $1 for a given time period. Exhibit 5.10 also shows that, just as with future value, the relation between the present value of $1 and time is not

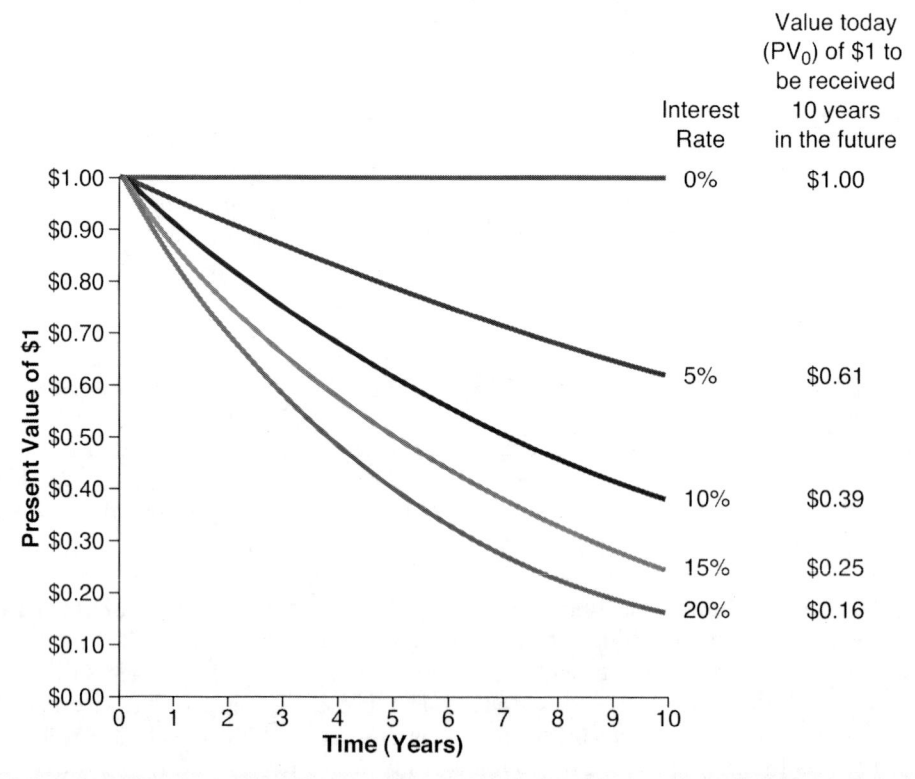

Interest Rate	Value today (PV$_0$) of $1 to be received 10 years in the future
0%	$1.00
5%	$0.61
10%	$0.39
15%	$0.25
20%	$0.16

Exhibit 5.10
Present Value of $1 for Different Time Periods and Discount Rates
The higher the discount rate, the lower the present value of $1 for a given time period. Just as with future value, the relation between the present value and time is not linear but exponential.

linear but exponential. Finally, it is interesting to note that if interest rates are zero, the present value of $1 is $1; that is, there is no time value of money. In this situation, $1,000 today has the same value as $1,000 a year from now or, for that matter, 10 years from now.

> **DECISION-MAKING EXAMPLE 5.2**
>
> ## Picking the Best Lottery Payoff Option
>
> **Situation:** Congratulations! You have won the $1 million lottery grand prize. You have been presented with several payout alternatives, and you have to decide which one to accept. The alternatives are as follows:
>
> - $1 million today
> - $1.2 million lump sum in two years
> - $1.5 million lump sum in five years
> - $2 million lump sum in eight years
>
> You are intrigued by the choice of collecting the prize money today or receiving double the amount of money in the future. Which payout option should you choose?
>
> Your cousin, a stockbroker, advises you that over the long term you should be able to earn 10 percent on an investment portfolio. Based on that rate of return, you make the following calculations:
>
> | Alternative | Nominal Value | Present Value |
> | --- | --- | --- |
> | Today | $1 million | $1 million |
> | 2 years | $1.2 million | $991,736 |
> | 5 years | $1.5 million | $931,382 |
> | 8 years | $2 million | $933,015 |
>
> **Decision:** As appealing as the higher amounts may sound, waiting for the big payout is not worthwhile in this case. Applying the present value formula has enabled you to convert future dollars into present, or current, dollars. Now the decision is simple—you can directly compare the present values. Given the above choices, you should take the $1 million today.

Calculator Tips for Present Value Problems

Calculating the discount factor (present value factor) on a calculator is similar to calculating the future value factor but requires an additional keystroke on most advanced-level calculators. The discount factor, $1/(1 + i)^n$, is the reciprocal of the future value factor, $(1 + i)^n$. The additional keystroke involves the use of the reciprocal key $(1/x)$ to find the discount factor. For example, to compute $1/(1.08)^{10}$, first enter 1.08, press the y^x key and enter 10, then press the equal (=) key. The number on the screen should be 2.159. This is the future value factor. It is a calculation you have made before. Now press the $1/x$ key, then the equal key, and you have the present value factor, 0.463!

Calculating present value (PV) on a financial calculator is the same as calculating the future value (FV_n) except that you solve for PV rather than FV_n. For example, what is the present value of $1,000 received 10 years from now at a 9 percent discount rate? To find the answer on your financial calculator, enter the following keystrokes:

Enter	10	9		0	1,000
	N	i	PV	PMT	FV
Answer			−422.41		

Then solve for the present value (PV), which is −$422.41. Notice that the answer has a negative sign. As we discussed previously, the $1,000 represents an inflow, and the $442.41 represents an outflow.

> **Before You Go On**
>
> 1. What is the present value and when is it used?
> 2. What is the discount rate? How does the discount rate differ from the interest rate in the future value equation?
> 3. What is the relation between the present value factor and the future value factor?
> 4. Explain why you would expect the discount factor to become smaller the longer the time to payment.

5.4 Additional Concepts and Applications

LEARNING OBJECTIVE 4

In this final section, we discuss several additional issues concerning present and future value, including how to find an unknown discount rate, how to estimate the length of time it will take to "double your money," and how to find the growth rates of various kinds of investments.

Finding the Interest Rate

In finance, some situations require you to determine the interest rate (or discount rate) for a given future cash flow. These situations typically arise when you want to determine the return on an investment. For example, an interesting Wall Street innovation is the *zero coupon bond*. These bonds pay no periodic interest; instead, at maturity the issuer (the firm that borrows the money) makes a payment that includes repayment of the amount borrowed plus interest. Needless to say, the issuer must prepare in advance to have the cash to pay off bondholders.

Suppose a firm is planning to issue $10 million worth of zero coupon bonds with 20 years to maturity. The bonds are issued in denominations of $1,000 and are sold for $90 each. In other words, you buy the bond today for $90, and 20 years from now, the firm pays you $1,000. If you bought one of these bonds, what would be your return on investment?

```
0        1      2       3       19      20  Year
| i = ?  |      |       |       |       |
-$90                                    $1,000
```

To find the return, we need to solve Equation 5.4, the present value equation, for i, the interest, or discount, rate. The $90 you pay today is the PV (present value), the $1,000 you get in 20 years is the FV (future value), and 20 years is n (the compounding period). The resulting calculation is as follows:

$$PV = \frac{FV_n}{(1+i)^n}$$

$$\$90 = \frac{\$1,000}{(1+i)^{20}}$$

$$(1+i)^{20} = \frac{\$1,000}{\$90}$$

$$1+i = \left(\frac{\$1,000}{\$90}\right)^{1/20}$$

$$i = (11.1111)^{1/20} - 1$$
$$= 1.1279 - 1$$
$$= 0.1279, \text{ or } 12.79\%$$

The rate of return on your investment, compounded annually, is 12.79 percent. Using a financial calculator, we arrive at the following solution:

Enter	20		−90	0	1,000
	N	i	PV	PMT	FV
Answer		12.79			

Interest Rate on a Loan

LEARNING BY DOING APPLICATION 5.4

Problem: Greg and Joan Hubbard are getting ready to buy their first house. To help make the down payment, Greg's aunt offers to loan them $15,000, which can be repaid in 10 years. If Greg and Joan borrow the money, they will have to repay Greg's aunt the amount of $23,750. What rate of interest would Greg and Joan be paying on the 10-year loan?

Approach: In this case, the present value is the value of the loan ($15,000), and the future value is the amount due at the end of 10 years ($23,750). To solve for the rate of interest on the loan, we can use the present value equation, Equation 5.4. Alternatively, we can use a financial calculator to compute the interest rate. The time line for the loan is as follows:

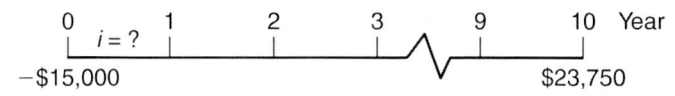

```
0       1    2    3       9    10  Year
 i = ?
−$15,000                       $23,750
```

Solution:

Using Equation 5.4:

$$PV = \frac{FV_n}{(1+i)^n}$$

$$\$15,000 = \frac{\$23,750}{(1+i)^{10}}$$

$$(1+i)^{10} = \frac{\$23,750}{\$15,000}$$

$$1+i = \left(\frac{\$23,750}{\$15,000}\right)^{1/10}$$

$$i = (1.58333)^{1/10} - 1$$
$$= 1.04703 - 1$$
$$= 0.04703, \text{ or } 4.703\%$$

Financial calculator steps:

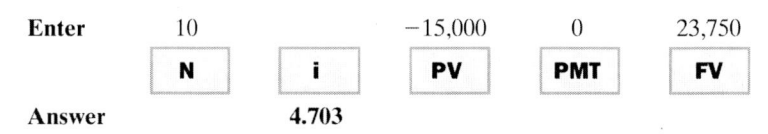

Enter	10		−15,000	0	23,750
	N	i	PV	PMT	FV
Answer		4.703			

The Rule of 72

People are fascinated by the possibility of doubling their money. Infomercials on television tout speculative land investments, claiming that "some investors have doubled their money in four years." Before there were financial calculators, people used rules of thumb to approximate difficult present value calculations. One such rule is the Rule of 72, which was used to determine the amount of time it takes to double an investment.

Rule of 72
a rule proposing that the time required to double money invested (TDM) approximately equals 72/i, where i is expressed as a percentage

The **Rule of 72** says that the time to double your money (TDM) approximately equals 72/i, where i is expressed as a percentage. Thus,

$$\text{TDM} = \frac{72}{i} \tag{5.5}$$

Applying the Rule of 72 to our land investment example suggests that if you double your money in four years, your annual rate of return will be 18 percent ($i = 72/4 = 18$).

Let's check the rule's accuracy by applying the present value formula to the land example. We are assuming that you will double our money in four years, so $n = 4$. We did not specify a present value or future value amount; however, doubling our money means that we will get back $2 (FV) for every $1 invested (PV). Using Equation 5.4 and solving for the interest rate (i), we find that $i = 0.1892$, or 18.92 percent.[8]

That's not bad for a simple rule of thumb: 18.92 percent versus 18 percent. Within limits, the Rule of 72 provides a quick "back of the envelope" method for determining the amount of time it will take to double an investment for a particular rate of return. The Rule of 72 is a linear approximation of a nonlinear function, and as such, the rule is fairly accurate for interest rates between 5 and 20 percent. Outside these limits, the rule is not very accurate.

Compound Growth Rates

The concept of compounding is not restricted to money. Any number that changes over time, such as the population of a city, changes at some compound growth rate. Compound growth occurs when the initial value of a number increases or decreases each period by the factor (1 + growth rate). As we go through the course, we will discuss many different types of interest rates, such as the discount rate on capital budgeting projects, the yield on a bond, and the internal rate of return on an investment. All of these "interest rates" can be thought of as growth rates (g) that relate future values to present values.

When we refer to the compounding effect, we are really talking about what happens when the value of a number increases or decreases by $(1 + \text{growth rate})^n$. That is, the future value of a number after n periods will equal the initial value times $(1 + \text{growth rate})^n$. Does this sound familiar? If we want, we can rewrite Equation 5.1 in a more general form as a compound growth rate formula, substituting g, the growth rate, for i, the interest rate:

$$\text{FV}_n = \text{PV} \times (1 + g)^n \tag{5.6}$$

where:

FV_n = future value of the economic factor, such as sales or population, at the end of period n
PV = original amount or present value of economic factor
g = growth rate per period
n = number of periods: a period may be a year but can also be a quarter, month, week, day, minute, or any other length of time

Suppose, for example, that because of an advertising campaign, a firm's sales increased from $20 million in 2007 to more than $35 million three years later. What has been the average annual growth rate in sales? Here, the future value is $35 million, the present value is $20 million, and n is 3 since we are interested in the annual growth rate over three years.

---

[8]Solve Equation 5.4 for i: $\text{PV} = \text{FV}_n/(1+i)^n$, where PV = $1, FV = $2, and $n = 4$.

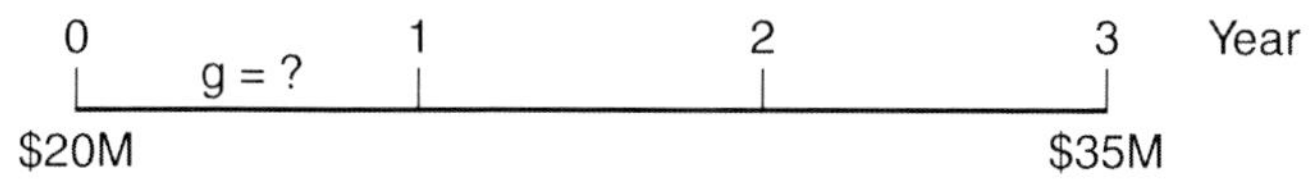

```
    0           1           2           3    Year
    |___g=?_____|_____|_____|
   $20M                                $35M
```

Applying Equation 5.6 and solving for the growth factor (g) yields:

$$FV_3 = PV \times (1 + g)^3$$
$$35 = 20 \times (1 + g)^3$$
$$1.75 = (1 + g)^3$$
$$g = (1.75)^{1/3} - 1$$
$$= 1.2051 - 1$$
$$= 0.2051, \text{ or } 20.51\%$$

Thus, sales grew nearly 21 percent per year. More precisely, we could say that sales grew at a **compound annual growth rate (CAGR)** of nearly 21 percent. If we use our financial calculator, we find the same answer:

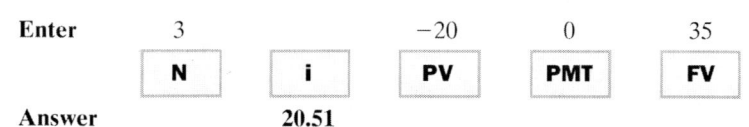

Enter	3		−20	0	35
	N	i	PV	PMT	FV
Answer		20.51			

compound annual growth rate (CAGR)

the average annual growth rate over a specified period of time

The Growth Rate of the World's Population

LEARNING BY DOING APPLICATION 5.5

Problem: Hannah, an industrial relations major, is writing a term paper and needs an estimate of how fast the world population is growing. In her almanac, she finds that the world's population was an estimated 6 billion people in 2000. The United Nations estimates that the population will reach 9 billion people in 2054. Calculate the annual population growth rate implied by these numbers. At that growth rate, what will be the world's population in 2010?

Approach: We first find the annual rate of growth through 2054 by applying Equation 5.6 for the 54-year period 2054–2000. For the purpose of this calculation, we can use the estimated population of 6 billion people in 2000 as the present value, the estimated future population of 9 million people as the future value, and 54 years as the number of compounding periods (n). We want to solve for g, which is the annual compound growth rate over the 54-year period. We can then plug the 54-year population growth rate in Equation 5.6 and solve for the world's population in 2010 (FV_{10}). Alternatively, we can get the answer by using a financial calculator.

Solution:

Using Equation 5.6, we find the growth rate as follows:

$$FV_n = PV \times (1 + g)^n$$
$$9 = 6 \times (1 + g)^{54}$$
$$1.5 = (1 + g)^{54}$$
$$(1.5)^{1/54} = 1 + g$$
$$g = (1.5)^{1/54} - 1$$
$$= 1.0075 - 1$$
$$= 0.0075, \text{ or } 0.75\%$$

The world's population in 2010 is therefore estimated to be:

$$FV_{10} = 6 \times (1 + 0.0075)^{10}$$
$$= 6 \times 1.0776$$
$$= 6.47 \text{ billion people}$$

(continued)

Using the financial calculator approach:

Enter	10	0.75	–6	0	
	N	i	PV	PMT	FV
Answer					6.47

LEARNING BY DOING APPLICATION 5.6

Calculating Projected Earnings

Problem: IBM's current earnings are $3.19 million. Wall Street analysts expect earnings to increase by 6 percent per year over the next three years. Using your financial calculator, determine what IBM's earnings should be in three years.

Approach: This problem involves the growth rate (g) of IBM's earnings. We already know the value of g, which is 6 percent, and we need to find the future value. Since the general compound growth rate formula, Equation 5.6, is the same as Equation 5.1, the future value formula, we can use the same calculator procedure we used earlier to find the future value. We enter the data on the calculator keys as shown below, using the growth rate value for the interest rate. Then we solve for the future value:

Solution:

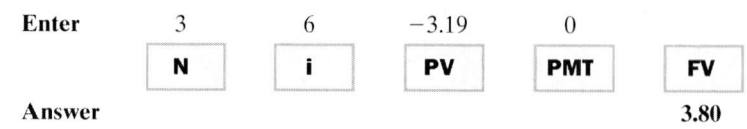

Enter	3	6	–3.19	0	
	N	i	PV	PMT	FV
Answer					3.80

Note that we enter $3.19 million as a negative number. This is because one cash flow must be negative—both cash flows cannot have the same sign. It makes no difference which cash flow number is negative and which is positive.

Concluding Comments

This chapter has introduced the basic principles of present value and future value. The table at the end of the chapter summarizes the key equations developed in the chapter. The basic equations for present value (Equation 5.4) and future value (Equation 5.1) are two of the most fundamental relations in finance and will be applied throughout the balance of the textbook.

> **Before You Go On**
>
> 1. What is the difference between the interest rate (i) and the growth rate (g) in the future value equation?

Summary of Learning Objectives

1. **Explain what the time value of money is and why it is so important in the field of finance.**

   The idea that money has a time value is one of the most fundamental concepts in the field of finance. The concept is based on the idea that most people prefer to have goods today rather than wait to have similar goods in the future. Since money buys goods, they would rather have money today than in the future. Thus, *a dollar today is worth more than a dollar received in the future.* Another way of viewing the time value of money is that your money is worth more today than at some point in the future because, if you had the money now, you could invest it and earn interest. Thus, the time value of money is the opportunity cost of forgoing consumption today.

Applications of the time value of money focus on the trade-off between current dollars and dollars received at some future date. This is an important element in financial decisions because most investment decisions require the comparison of cash invested today with the value of expected future cash inflows. Investment opportunities are undertaken only when the value of future cash inflows exceeds the cost of the investment (the initial cash outflow).

2. **Explain the concept of future value, including the meaning of *principal amount, simple interest,* and *compound interest,* and be able to use the future value formula to make business decisions.**

The future value is the sum to which an investment will grow after earning interest. The principal amount is the amount of the investment. Simple interest is the interest paid on the original investment; the amount of money earned on simple interest remains constant from period to period. Compound interest includes not only simple interest, but also interest earned on the reinvestment of previously earned interest, the so-called interest on interest. For future value calculations, the higher the interest rate, the faster the investment will grow. The application of the future value formula in business decisions is presented in Section 5.4.

3. **Explain the concept of present value and how it relates to future value, and be able to use the present value formula to make business decisions.**

The present value is the value today of a future cash flow. Computing the present value involves discounting future cash flows back to the present at an appropriate discount rate. The process of discounting cash flows adjusts the cash flows for the time value of money. Computationally, the present value factor is the reciprocal of the future value factor, or $1/(1 + i)$. The computation and application of the present value formula in business decisions is presented in Section 5.3.

4. **Discuss why the concept of compounding is not restricted to money, and be able to use the future value formula to calculate growth rates.**

Any number of changes that are observed over time in the physical and social sciences follow a compound growth rate pattern. The future value formula can be used in calculating these growth rates.

Summary of Key Equations

Equation	Description	Formula
5.1	Future value of an *n*-period investment with annual compounding	$FV_n = PV \times (1 + i)^n$
5.2	Future value with compounding more than annually	$FV_n = PV \times (1 + i/m)^{m \times n}$
5.3	Future value with continuous compounding	$FV_\infty = PV \times e^{i \times n}$
5.4	Present value	$PV = \dfrac{FV_n}{(1 + i)^n}$
5.5	Rule of 72	$TDM = \dfrac{72}{i}$
5.6	Future value with general growth rate	$FV_n = PV \times (1 + g)^n$

Self-Study Problems

5.1 Amit Patel is planning to invest $10,000 in a bank certificate of deposit (CD) for five years. The CD will pay interest of 9 percent. What is the future value of Amit's investment?

5.2 Megan Gaumer expects to need $50,000 as a down payment on a house in six years. How much does she need to invest today in an account paying 7.25 percent?

162　CHAPTER 5　The Time Value of Money

5.3 Kelly Martin has $10,000 that she can deposit into a savings account for five years. Bank A pays compounds interest annually, Bank B twice a year, and Bank C quarterly. Each bank has a stated interest rate of 4 percent. What amount would Kelly have at the end of the fifth year if she left all the interest paid on the deposit in each bank?

5.4 You have an opportunity to invest $2,500 today and receive $3,000 in three years. What will be the return on your investment?

5.5 Emily Smith deposits $1,200 in her bank today. If the bank pays 4 percent simple interest, how much money will she have at the end of five years? What if the bank pays compound interest? How much of the earnings will be interest on interest?

Solutions to Self-Study Problems

5.1 Present value of Amit's investment = PV = $10,000
Interest rate on CD = i = 9%
Number of years = n = 5

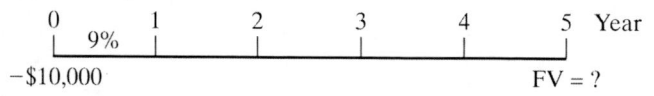

```
0       1       2       3       4       5  Year
  9%
-$10,000                                  FV = ?
```

$$FV_n = PV \times (1 + i)^n$$
$$= \$10,000 \times (1 + 0.09)^5$$
$$= \$15,386.24$$

5.2 Amount Megan will need in six years = FV_6 = $50,000
Number of years = n = 6
Interest rate on investment = i = 7.25%
Amount needed to be invested now = PV = ?

```
0       1       2       3       4       5       6  Year
  7.25%
PV = ?                                          FV = $50,000
```

$$PV = \frac{FV_n}{(1 + i)^n}$$
$$= \frac{\$50,000}{(1 + 0.0725)^6}$$
$$= \$32,853.84$$

5.3 Present value of Kelly's deposit = PV = $10,000
Number of years = n = 5
Interest rate = i = 4%
Compound period (m):

　　A = 1
　　B = 2
　　C = 4

Amount at the end of five years = FV_5 = ?

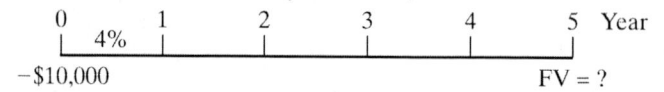

```
0       1       2       3       4       5  Year
  4%
-$10,000                                  FV = ?
```

Bank A:　$FV_n = PV \times (1 + i/m)^{m \times n}$
　　　　　$FV_5 = 10,000 \times (1 + 0.04/1)^{1 \times 5}$
　　　　　$FV_5 = \$12,166.53$

Bank B:　$FV_5 = 10,000 \times (1 + 0.04/2)^{2 \times 5}$
　　　　　$FV_5 = \$12,189.94$

Bank C:　$FV_5 = 10,000 \ (1 + 0.04/4)^{4 \times 5}$
　　　　　$FV_5 = \$12,201.90$

5.4 Your investment today = PV = $2,500
Amount to be received = FV_3 = $3,000
Time of investment = n = 3
Return on the investment = i = ?

$FV_n = PV \times (1 + i)^n$
$\$3{,}000 = \$2{,}500 \times (1 + i)^3$
$\dfrac{\$3{,}000}{\$2{,}500} = (1 + i)^3$
$i = 6.27\%$

5.5 Emily's deposit today = PV = $1,200
Interest rate = i = 4%
Number of years = n = 5
Amount to be received back = FV_5 = ?
  a. Future value with simple interest
    Simple interest per year = $1,200 × 0.04 = $48.00
    Simple interest for 5 years = $48 × 5 = $240.00
    FV_5 = $1,200 + $240 = $1,440.00
  b. Future value with compound interest
    $FV_5 = \$1{,}200 \times (1 + 0.04)^5$
    $FV_5 = \$1{,}459.98$
    Simple interest = ($1,440 − $1,200) = $240
    Interest on interest = $1,459.98 − $1,200 − $240 = $19.98

Critical Thinking Questions

5.1 Explain the phrase "a dollar today is worth more than a dollar tomorrow."

5.2 Explain the importance of a time line.

5.3 Differentiate future value from present value.

5.4 What are the two factors to be considered in time value of money?

5.5 Differentiate between compounding and discounting.

5.6 Explain how compound interest differs from simple interest.

5.7 If you were given a choice of investing in an account that paid quarterly interest and one that paid monthly interest, which one should you choose and why?

5.8 Growth rates are exponential over time. Explain.

5.9 What is the Rule of 72?

5.10 You are planning to take a spring break trip to Cancun your senior year. The trip is exactly two years away, but you want to be prepared and have enough money when the time comes. Explain how you would determine the amount of money you will have to save in order to pay for the trip.

Questions and Problems

5.1 Future value: Chuck Tomkovick is planning to invest $25,000 today in a mutual fund that will provide a return of 8 percent each year. What will be the value of the investment in 10 years?

BASIC

5.2 Future value: Ted Rogers is investing $7,500 in a bank CD that pays a 6 percent annual interest. How much will the CD be worth at the end of five years?

5.3 Future value: Your aunt is planning to invest in a bank deposit that will pay 7.5 percent interest semiannually. If she has $5,000 to invest, how much will she have at the end of four years?

5.4 Future value: Kate Eden received a graduation present of $2,000 that she is planning on investing in a mutual fund that earns 8.5 percent each year. How much money can she collect in three years?

5.5 Future value: Your bank pays 5 percent interest semiannually on your savings account. You don't expect the current balance of $2,700 to change over the next four years. How much money can you expect to have at the end of this period?

5.6 Future value: Your birthday is coming up and instead of any presents, your parents promised to give you $1,000 in cash. Since you have a part-time job and, thus, don't need the cash immediately, you decide to invest the money in a bank CD that pays 5.2 percent quarterly for the next two years. How much money can you expect to gain in this period of time?

5.7 Multiple compounding periods: Find the future value of an investment of $100,000 made today for five years and paying 8.75 percent for the following compounding periods:
a. Quarterly
b. Monthly
c. Daily
d. Continuous

5.8 Growth rates: Matt Murton, an outfielder for the Chicago Cubs, is expected to hit 25 home runs in 2008. If his home-run-hitting ability is expected to grow by 12 percent every year for the next five years, how many home runs is he expected to hit in 2013?

5.9 Present value: Roy Gross is considering an investment that pays 7.6 percent. How much will he have to invest today so that the investment will be worth $25,000 in six years?

5.10 Present value: Maria Addai has been offered a future payment of $750 two years from now. If her opportunity cost is 6.5 percent compounded annually, what should she pay for this investment today?

5.11 Present value: You brother has asked you for a loan and has promised to pay back $7,750 at the end of three years. If you normally invest to earn 6 percent, how much will you be willing to lend to your brother?

5.12 Present value: Tracy Chapman is saving to buy a house in five years. She plans to put 20 percent down at that time, and she believes that she will need $35,000 for the down payment. If Tracy can invest in a fund that pays 9.25 percent annually, how much will she need to invest today?

5.13 Present value: You want to buy some deep-discount bonds that have a value of $1,000 at the end of seven years. The bonds are said to pay 4.5 percent interest. How much should you pay for them today?

5.14 Present value: Elizabeth Sweeney wants to accumulate $12,000 by the end of 12 years. If the interest rate is 7 percent, how much will she have to invest today to achieve her goal?

5.15 Interest rate: You are in desperate need of cash and turn to your uncle, who has offered to lend you some money. You decide to borrow $1,300 and agree to pay back $1,500 in two years. Alternatively, you could borrow from your bank that is charging 6.5 percent interest. Should you go with your uncle or the bank?

5.16 Time to attain goal: You invest $150 in a mutual fund today that pays 9 percent interest. How long will it take to double your money?

INTERMEDIATE

5.17 Growth rate: Your finance textbook sold 53,250 copies in its first year. The publishing company expects the sales to grow at a rate of 20 percent for the next three years and by 10 percent in the fourth year. Calculate the total number of copies that the publisher expects to sell in years 3 and 4. Draw a time line to show the sales level for each of the next four years.

5.18 Growth rate: CelebNav, Inc., had sales last year of $700,000, and the analysts are predicting a good year for the start-up, with sales growing 20 percent a year for the next three years. After that, the sales should grow 11 percent per year for two years, at which time the owners are planning to sell the company. What are the projected sales for the last year of the company's operation?

5.19 Growth rate: You decide to take advantage of the current online dating craze and start your own Web site. You know that you have 450 people who will sign up immediately and, through a careful marketing research and analysis, determine that membership can grow by 27 percent in the first two years, 22 percent in year 3, and 18 percent in year 4. How many members do you expect to have at the end of four years?

5.20 Multiple compounding periods: Find the future value of an investment of $2,500 made today for the following rates and periods:
a. 6.25 percent compounded semiannually for 12 years
b. 7.63 percent compounded quarterly for 6 years
c. 8.9 percent compounded monthly for 10 years
d. 10 percent compounded daily for 3 years
e. 8 percent compounded continuously for 2 years

5.21 Growth rates: Xenix Corp had sales of $353,866 in 2008. If it expects its sales to be at $476,450 in three years, what is the rate at which the company's sales are expected to grow?

5.22 Growth rate: Infosys Technologies, Inc., an Indian technology company, reported a net income of $419 million this year. Analysts expect the company's earnings to be $1.468 billion in five years. What is the company's earnings expected growth rate?

5.23 Time to attain goal: Zephyr Sales Company has currently reported sales of $1.125 million. If the company expects its sales to grow at 6.5 percent annually, how long will it be before the company can double its sales? Use a financial calculator to solve this problem.

5.24 Time to attain goal: You are able to deposit $850 in a bank CD today, and you will withdraw the money only once the balance is $1,000. If the bank pays 5 percent interest, how long will it take you to attain your goal?

5.25 Time to attain goal: Neon Lights Company is a private company with sales of $1.3 million a year. They want to go public but have to wait until the sales reach $2 million. Providing that they are expected to grow at a steady 12 percent annually, when is the earliest that Neon Lights can start selling their shares?

5.26 Present value: Caroline Weslin needs to decide whether to accept a bonus of $1,900 today or wait two years and receive $2,100 then. She can invest at 6 percent. What should she do?

5.27 Multiple compounding periods: Find the present value of $3,500 under each of the following rates and periods:
  a. 8.9 percent compounded monthly for five years.
  b. 6.6 percent compounded quarterly for eight years.
  c. 4.3 percent compounded daily for four years.
  d. 5.7 percent compounded continuously for three years.

5.28 Multiple compounding periods: Samantha is looking to invest some money, so she can collect $5,500 at the end of three years. Which investment should she make given the following choices:
  a. 4.2 percent compounded daily
  b. 4.9 percent compounded monthly
  c. 5.2 percent compounded quarterly
  d. 5.4 percent compounded annually

5.29 You have $2,500 you want to invest in your classmate's start-up business. You believe the business idea to be great and hope to get $3,700 back at the end of three years. If all goes according to plan, what will be your return on investment? **ADVANCED**

5.30 Patrick Seeley has $2,400 that he is looking to invest. His brother approached him with an investment opportunity that could double his money in four years. What interest rate would the investment have to yield in order for Patrick's brother to deliver on his promise?

5.31 You have $12,000 in cash. You can deposit it today in a mutual fund earning 8.2 percent semiannually, or you can wait, enjoy some of it, and invest $11,000 in your brother's business in two years. Your brother is promising you a return of at least 10 percent on your investment. Whichever alternative you choose, you will need to cash in at the end of 10 years. Assume your brother is trustworthy and both investments carry the same risk. Which one will you choose? **EXCEL**

5.32 When you were born your parents set up a bank account in your name with an initial investment of $5,000. You are turning 21 in a few days and will have access to all your funds. The account was earning 7.3 percent for the first seven years, but then the rates went down to 5.5 percent for six years. The economy was doing well at the end of the 1990s, and your account was earning 8.2 percent for three years in a row. Unfortunately, the next two years you earned only 4.6 percent. Finally, as the economy recovered, your return jumped to 7.6 percent for the last three years. **EXCEL**
  a. How much money was in your account before the rates went down drastically (end of year 16)?
  b. How much money is in your account now (end of year 21)?
  c. What would be the balance now if your parents made another deposit of $1,200 at the end of year 7?

5.33 Cedric Benson, a top-five draft pick of the Chicago Bears, and his agent are evaluating three contract options. Each option offers a signing bonus and a series of payments over the **EXCEL**

life of the contract. Benson uses a 10.25 percent rate of return to evaluate the contracts. Given the cash flows for each option, which one should he choose?

Year	Cash Flow Type	Option A	Option B	Option C
0	Signing Bonus	$3,100,000	$4,000,000	$4,250,000
1	Annual Salary	$ 650,000	$ 825,000	$ 550,000
2	Annual Salary	$ 715,000	$ 850,000	$ 625,000
3	Annual Salary	$ 822,250	$ 925,000	$ 800,000
4	Annual Salary	$ 975,000	$1,250,000	$ 900,000
5	Annual Salary	$1,100,000		$1,000,000
6	Annual Salary	$1,250,000		

EXCEL **5.34** Surmec, Inc., reported earnings of $2.1 million last year. The company's primary business line is manufacturing of nuts and bolts. Since this is a mature industry, the analysts are certain that the sales will grow at a steady rate of 7 percent a year for as far as they can tell. The company reports net income that represents 23 percent of sales. The management would like to buy a new fleet of trucks but can only do so once the profit reaches $620,000 a year. At the end of what year will Surmec be able to buy the new fleet of trucks? What will the sales and profit be that year?

EXCEL **5.35** You are graduating in two years, and you start thinking about your future. You know that you will want to buy a house five years after you graduate and that you will want to put down $60,000. As of right now, you have $8,000 in your savings account. You are also fairly certain that once you graduate, you can work in the family business and earn $32,000 a year, with a 5 percent raise every year. You plan to live with your parents for the first two years after graduation, which will enable you to minimize your expenses and put away $10,000 each year. The next three years, you will have to live on your own as your younger sister will be graduating from college and has already announced her plan to move back into the family house. Thus, you will be able to save only 13 percent of your annual salary. Assume that you will be able to invest savings from your salary at 7.2 percent. At what interest rate will you need to invest the current savings account balance in order to achieve your goal? *Hint:* Draw a time line that shows all the cash flows for years 0 through 7. Remember, you want to buy a house seven years from now and your first salary will be in year 3.

Sample Test Problems

5.1 Santiago Hernandez is planning to invest $25,000 in a money market account for two years. The account pays interest of 5.75 percent compounded on a monthly basis. How much will Santiago Hernandez have at the end of two years?

5.2 Michael Carter is expecting an inheritance of $1.25 million in four years. If he had the money today, he could earn interest at an annual rate of 7.35 percent. What is the present value of this inheritance?

5.3 What is the future value of an investment of $3,000 for three years compounded at the following rates and frequencies:
a. 8.75 percent compounded monthly
b. 8.625 percent compounded daily
c. 8.5 percent compounded continuously

5.4 Twenty-five years ago, Amanda Cortez invested $10,000 in an account paying an annual interest rate of 5.75 percent. What is the value of the investment today? What is the interest on interest earned on this investment?

5.5 You just bought a corporate bond at $863.75 today. In five years the bond will mature and you will receive $1,000. What is the rate of return on this bond?

DISCOUNTED CASH FLOWS AND VALUATION

CHAPTER 6

LEARNING OBJECTIVES

1. Explain why cash flows occurring at different times must be adjusted to reflect their value as of a common date before they can be compared, and be able to compute the present value and future value for multiple cash flows.

2. Describe how to calculate the present value of an ordinary annuity and how an ordinary annuity differs from an annuity due.

3. Explain what a perpetuity is and how it is used in business, and be able to calculate the value of a perpetuity.

4. Discuss growing annuities and perpetuities, as well as their application in business, and be able to calculate their value.

5. Discuss why the effective annual interest rate (EAR) is the appropriate way to annualize interest rates, and be able to calculate EAR.

Landov LLC

Guidant Corporation ended one of the biggest takeover battles in the history of the medical-device industry when it announced that it had turned down a takeover bid from Johnson & Johnson (J & J) in favor of an offer from Boston Scientific. The acquisition price for Guidant, a top company in the market for implantable heart devices, was $27.2 billion. The deal was completed in April 2006.

Guidant's decision was remarkable in that it had agreed to merge with J & J as far back as December 2004 at an offer price of $25.4 billion. But then several costly product recalls and liability trials began to surface, which analysts believed could cost Guidant more than $2 billion in damages. As a result, J & J reduced its offer by nearly $4 billion. Soon after, Boston Scientific mounted a surprise takeover effort. After that, the two bidders made a series of offers interspersed with behind-the-scenes attacks on one another.

J & J appeared to be the winner when, in January 2006, its negotiators persuaded Guidant to back out of a previously announced merger with Boston Scientific at an offering price of $24.9 billion and to accept J & J's lower offer of $24.2 billion. Boston Scientific responded by raising its offer to $27.2 billion, and J & J withdrew.

In the excitement of a bidding war like this one, it is important not to lose sight of the central question: What is the firm really worth? A company invests in an asset—a business or a capital project—because it expects the asset to be worth more than it costs. That's how value is created. The value of a business is the sum of its discounted future cash flows. Thus, the task for both J & J and Boston Scientific was to estimate the value of the future cash flows that Guidant could generate under there ownership. This chapter, which discusses the discounting of future cash flows, provides the tools that help answer the key question in the Guidant bidding war: What is the firm worth?

CHAPTER PREVIEW

In the previous chapter, we introduced the concept of the time value of money: Dollars today are more valuable than dollars to be received in the future. Starting with that concept, we developed the basics of simple interest, compound interest, and future value calculations. We then went on to discuss present value and discounted cash flow analysis. This was all done in the context of a single cash flow.

In this chapter, we consider the value of multiple cash flows. Most business decisions, after all, involve cash flows over time. For example, if Mrs. Smith's, an Atlanta-based firm that makes frozen pies, wants to consider adding a production line, the decision will require an analysis of the project's expected cash flows over a number of periods. Initially, there will be large cash outlays to build and get the new line operational. Thereafter, the project should produce cash inflows for many years. Because the cash flows occur over time, the analysis must consider the time value of money, discounting each of the cash flows by using the present value formula.

We begin the chapter by describing calculations of future and present values for multiple cash flows. We then examine some situations in which future cash flows are level over time: These involve annuities, in which the cash flow stream goes on for a finite period, and perpetuities, in which the stream goes on forever. Next, we examine annuities and perpetuities in which the cash flows grow at a constant rate over time. These cash flows resemble common cash flow patterns encountered in business. Finally, we describe the effective annual interest rate and compare it with the annual percentage rate (APR), which is a rate that is used to describe the interest rate in consumer loans.

6.1 Multiple Cash Flows

LEARNING OBJECTIVE 1

We begin our discussion of the time value of multiple cash flows by calculating the future value and then the present value of multiple cash flows. These calculations, as you will see, are nothing more than applications of the techniques you learned in Chapter 5.

Future Value of Multiple Cash Flows

In Chapter 5, we worked through several examples that involved the future value of a lump sum of money invested in a savings account that paid 10 percent interest per year. But suppose you are investing more than one lump sum. Let's say you put $1,000 in your bank savings account today and another $1,000 a year from now. If the bank continues to pay 10 percent interest per year, how much money will you have at the end of two years?

To solve this future value problem, we can use Equation 5.1: $FV_n = PV \times (1 + i)^n$. First, however, we construct a time line so that we can see the magnitude and timing of the cash flows. As Exhibit 6.1 shows, there are two cash flows into the savings plan. The first cash flow is invested for two years and compounds to a value that is computed as follows:

$$FV_2 = PV \times (1 + i)^2$$
$$= \$1,000 \times (1 + 0.10)^2$$
$$= \$1,000 \times 1.21$$
$$= \$1,210$$

The second cash flow earns simple interest for a single period only and grows to:

$$FV_1 = PV \times (1 + i)$$
$$= \$1,000 \times (1 + 0.10)$$
$$= \$1,000 \times 1.10$$
$$= \$1,100$$

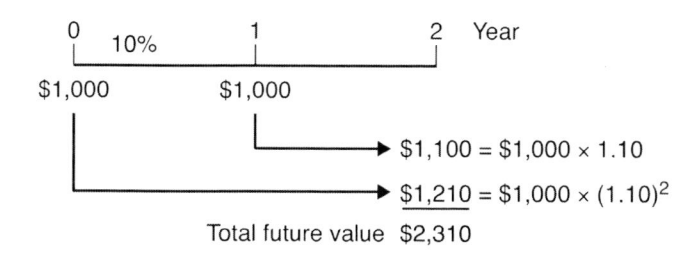

```
     0          1           2  Year
     |   10%    |           |
     $1,000    $1,000
                  |
                  └─→ $1,100 = $1,000 × 1.10
     └──────────────→ $1,210 = $1,000 × (1.10)²
                  Total future value  $2,310
```

Exhibit 6.1

Future Value of Two Cash Flows

This exhibit shows a time line for two cash flows invested in a savings account that pays 10 percent interest annually. The total amount in the savings account after two years is $2,310, which is the sum of the future values of the two cash flows.

As Exhibit 6.1 shows, the total amount of money in the savings account after two years is the sum of these two amounts, which is $2,310 ($1,100 + $1,210).

Now suppose that you expand your investment horizon to three years and invest $1,000 today, $1,000 a year from now, and $1,000 at the end of two years. How much money will you have at the end of three years? First, we draw a time line to be sure that we have correctly identified the time period for each cash flow. This is shown in Exhibit 6.2. Then we compute the future value of each of the individual cash flows using Equation 5.1. Finally, we add up the future values. The total future value is $3,641. The calculations are as follows:

$$FV_1 = PV \times (1 + i) = \$1,000 \times (1 + 0.10) = \$1,000 \times 1.100 = \$1,100$$
$$FV_2 = PV \times (1 + i)^2 = \$1,000 \times (1 + 0.10)^2 = \$1,000 \times 1.210 = \$1,210$$
$$FV_3 = PV \times (1 + i)^3 = \$1,000 \times (1 + 0.10)^3 = \$1,000 \times 1.331 = \underline{\$1,331}$$
$$\text{Total future value} \quad \$3,641$$

To summarize, solving future value problems with multiple cash flows involves a simple process. First, draw a time line to make sure that each cash flow is placed in the correct time period. Second, calculate the future value of each cash flow for its time period. Third, add up the future values. It's that simple!

Let's use this process to solve a practical problem. Suppose you want to buy a condominium in three years and estimate that you will need $20,000 for a down payment.

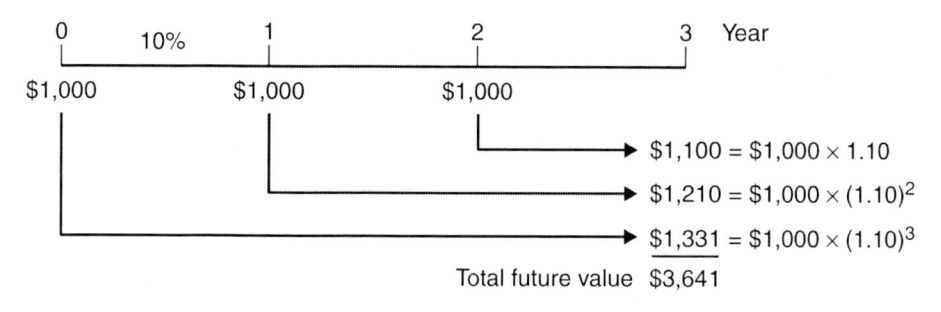

```
     0          1           2           3  Year
     |   10%    |           |           |
     $1,000    $1,000      $1,000
                              |
                              └─→ $1,100 = $1,000 × 1.10
                  └──────────────→ $1,210 = $1,000 × (1.10)²
     └──────────────────────────→ $1,331 = $1,000 × (1.10)³
                              Total future value  $3,641
```

Exhibit 6.2

Future Value of Three Cash Flows

The exhibit shows a time line for an investment program with a three-year horizon. The value of the investment at the end of three years is $3,641, the sum of the future values of the three separate cash flows.

If the interest rate you can earn at the bank is 8 percent and you can save $3,000 now, $4,000 at the end of the first year, and $5,000 at the end of the second year, how much money will you have to come up with at the end of the third year to have a $20,000 down payment?

The time line for the future value calculation in this problem looks like this:

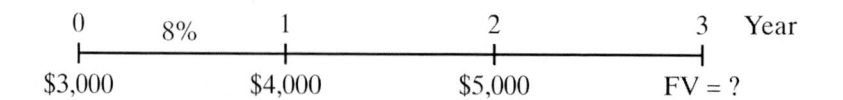

```
0         8%        1                 2                 3   Year
|───────────────────|─────────────────|─────────────────|
$3,000             $4,000            $5,000             FV = ?
```

To solve the problem, we need to calculate the future value for each of the expected cash flows, add up these values, and find the difference between this amount and the $20,000 needed for the down payment. Using Equation 5.1, we find that the future values of the cash flows at the end of the third year are:

$$FV_1 = PV \times (1 + i) = \$5,000 \times 1.08 = \$5,000 \times 1.0800 = \$ 5,400.00$$
$$FV_2 = PV \times (1 + i)^2 = \$4,000 \times (1.08)^2 = \$4,000 \times 1.1664 = \$ 4,665.60$$
$$FV_3 = PV \times (1 + i)^3 = \$3,000 \times (1.08)^3 = \$3,000 \times 1.2597 = \underline{\$ 3,779.14}$$
$$\text{Total future value} \quad \$13,844.74$$

At the end of the third year, you will have $13,844.74, so you will need an additional $6,155.26 ($20,000 − $13,844.74).

CALCULATOR TIP: CALCULATING THE FUTURE VALUE OF MULTIPLE CASH FLOWS

To calculate the future value of multiple cash flows with a financial calculator, we can use exactly the same process we used in Chapter 5. We simply calculate the future value of each of the individual cash flows, write down each computed future value, and add them up.

Alternatively, we can generally use a shortcut. More than likely, your financial calculator has a memory where you can store numbers; refer to your calculator's instruction manual for the keys to use. For the preceding example, you would use your financial calculator's memory (M) as follows: Calculate the future value of the first number, then store the value in the memory (M1); compute the second value, and store it in the memory (M2); compute the third value, and store it in the memory (M3). Finally, retrieve the three numbers from the memory and add them up (M1 + M2 + M3). The advantage of using the calculator's memory is that you eliminate two potential sources of error: (1) writing down a number incorrectly and (2) making a mistake when adding up the numbers.

LEARNING BY DOING APPLICATION 6.1

NEED MORE HELP?
WILEY PLUS
www.wileyplus.com

Government Contract in New Orleans

Problem: The firm you work for is considering bidding on a government contract to rebuild a power station in New Orleans that was damaged during Hurricane Katrina in 2005. The two-year contract will pay the firm $9,000 at the end of the second year. The firm's estimator believes that the project will require an initial expenditure of $5,000 for equipment. The expenses for years 1 and 2 are estimated at $1,000 per year. Because the cash inflow of $9,000 at the end of the contract exceeds the total cash outflows of $7,000 ($5,000 + $1,000 + $1,000), the estimator believes that the firm should accept the job. Drawing on your knowledge of finance from college, you point out that the estimator's decision process ignores the time value of money. Not fully understanding what you mean, the estimator asks you how the time value of money should be incorporated into the decision process. Assume that the appropriate interest rate is 18 percent.

Approach: First, construct the time line for the costs in this problem, as shown here:

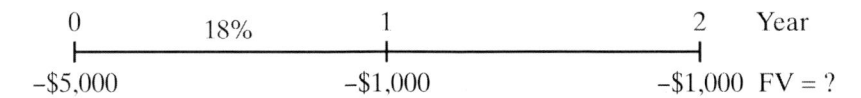

```
0           18%         1                    2        Year
├────────────────────────┼────────────────────┤
-$5,000                -$1,000              -$1,000   FV = ?
```

Second, use Equation 5.1 to convert all of the cash outflows into period-two dollars. This will make all the cash flows comparable because they will represent the same amount of purchasing power—period-two dollars. Finally, compare the sum of the cash outflows, stated in period-two dollars, to the $9,000 that you would receive under the contract.

Solution:

$FV_2 = PV \times (1 + i)^2 = -\$5,000 \times (1.18)^2 = -\$5,000 \times 1.3924 = -\$6,962$
$FV_1 = PV \times (1 + i) = -\$1,000 \times 1.18 = -\$1,000 \times 1.1800 = -\$1,180$
$FV_0 = PV \times (1 + i)^0 = -\$1,000 \times (1.18)^0 = -\$1,000 \times 1.0000 = -\$1,000$
Total net future value $\quad -\$9,142$

Once the future value calculations have been made, the decision is self-evident. With all the dollars stated as period-two dollars, the cash inflow (benefits) is $9,000 and the cash outflow (costs) is $9,142. Thus, the costs exceed the benefits, and the firm's management should reject the contract. If management accepts the contract, the value of the firm will be decreased.

Present Value of Multiple Cash Flows

In business situations, we often need to compute the present value of a series of future cash flows. We do this, for example, to determine the market price of a bond, to decide whether to purchase a new machine, or to determine the value of a business. Solving present value problems involving multiple cash flows is similar to solving future value problems involving multiple cash flows. First, we prepare a time line to identify the magnitude and timing of the cash flows. Second, we calculate the present value of each individual cash flow using Equation 5.4: $PV = FV_n/(1 + i)^n$. Finally, we add up the present values. The sum of the present values of a stream of future cash flows is their current market price, or value. There is nothing new here!

You can find plenty of problems to work out at StudyFinance.com, www.studyfinance.com/lectures/timevalue/index.mv.

USING THE PRESENT VALUE EQUATION

Next, we will work through some examples to see how we can use Equation 5.4 to find the present value of multiple cash flows. Suppose that your best friend needs cash and offers to pay you $1,000 at the end of each of the next three years if you will give him $3,000 cash today. You realize, of course, that because of the time value of money, the cash flows he has promised to pay are worth less than $3,000. If the interest rate on similar loans is 7 percent, how much should you pay for the cash flows your friend is offering?

To solve the problem, we first construct a time line, as shown in Exhibit 6.3. Then, using Equation 5.4, we calculate the present value for each of the three cash flows, as follows:

$PV = FV_1 \times 1/(1 + i) = FV_1 \times 1/1.07 = \$1,000 \times 0.9346 = \$934.58$
$PV = FV_2 \times 1/(1 + i)^2 = FV_2 \times 1/(1.07)^2 = \$1,000 \times 0.8734 = \$873.44$
$PV = FV_3 \times 1/(1 + i)^3 = FV_3 \times 1/(1.07)^3 = \$1,000 \times 0.8163 = \$816.30$
Total present value $\quad \$2,624.32$

If you view this transaction from a purely business perspective, you should not give your friend more than $2,624.32, which is the sum of the individual discounted cash flows.

```
 0           1         2         3   Year
 |---7%------|---------|---------|
 PV = ?    $1,000    $1,000    $1,000
```

$1,000 × 1/1.07 = $934.58
$1,000 × 1/(1.07)² = $873.44
$1,000 × 1/(1.07)³ = $816.30
$2,624.32 Total present value

Exhibit 6.3

Present Value of Three Cash Flows

The exhibit shows the time line for a three-year loan with a payment of $1,000 at the end of each year and an annual interest rate of 7 percent. To calculate the value of the loan today, we compute the present value of each of the three cash flows and then add them up. The present value of the loan is $2,624.32.

LEARNING BY DOING APPLICATION 6.2

The Value of a Gift to the University

Problem: Suppose that you made a gift to your university, pledging $1,000 per year for four years and $3,000 for the fifth year, for a total of $7,000. After making the first three payments, you decide to pay off the final two payments of your pledge because your financial situation has improved. How much should you pay to the university if the interest rate is 6 percent?

Approach: The key to understanding this problem, of course, is recognizing the need for a present value calculation. Because your pledge to the university is for future cash payments, the value of the amount you will pay for the remaining two years is worth less than the $4,000 ($1,000 + $3,000) you promised. If the appropriate discount rate is 6 percent, the time line for the cash payments for the remaining two years of the pledge is as follows:

```
 0         1         2   Year
 |---6%----|---------|
 PV = ?  $1,000    $3,000
```

We now need only calculate the present value of the last two payments.

Solution: The present value calculation for the last two payments is:

$PV = FV_1 \times 1/(1 + i) = \$1,000 \times 1/1.06 = \$943.40$
$PV = FV_2 \times 1/(1 + i)^2 = \$3,000 \times 1/(1.06)^2 = \$2,669.99$
Total present value $\$3,613.39$

The payment of $3,613.39 to the university today (the end of year 3) is a fair payment because at a 6 percent interest rate, it has precisely the same value as paying the university $1,000 at the end of year 4 and $3,000 at the end of year 5.

Now let's consider another example. Suppose you have the opportunity to buy a small business while you are in school. The business involves selling sandwiches, soft drinks, and snack foods to students from a truck that you drive around campus. The annual cash flows from the business have been predictable. You believe you can expand the business, and you estimate that cash flows will be as follows: $2,000 the first year, $3,000 the second and third years, and $4,000 the fourth year. At the end of the fourth year, the business will be closed down because the truck and other equipment will need to be replaced. The total of the estimated cash flows is $12,000. You did some research at school and found that a 10 percent discount rate would be appropriate. How much should you pay for the business?

To value the business, we compute the present value of the expected cash flows, discounted at 10 percent. The time line for the investment is:

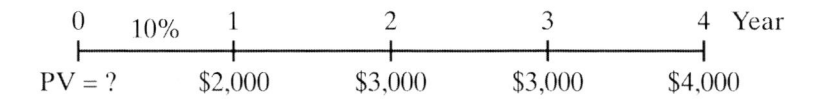

```
0      10%     1           2           3           4   Year
├───────────────┼───────────┼───────────┼───────────┤
PV = ?       $2,000      $3,000      $3,000      $4,000
```

We compute the present value of each cash flow and then add them up:

$$PV = FV_1 \times 1/(1+i) = \$2{,}000 \times 1/1.10 = \$2{,}000 \times 0.9091 = \$1{,}818.18$$
$$PV = FV_2 \times 1/(1+i)^2 = \$3{,}000 \times 1/(1.10)^2 = \$3{,}000 \times 0.8264 = \$2{,}479.34$$
$$PV = FV_3 \times 1/(1+i)^3 = \$3{,}000 \times 1/(1.10)^3 = \$3{,}000 \times 0.7513 = \$2{,}253.94$$
$$PV = FV_4 \times 1/(1+i)^4 = \$4{,}000 \times 1/(1.10)^4 = \$4{,}000 \times 0.6830 = \$2{,}732.05$$
$$\text{Total present value} \quad \$9{,}283.51$$

This computation tells us that the value of the business is $9,283.51. Of course, you should buy the business for the lowest price possible. If the price goes above $9,283.51, however, you should walk away from the deal. You should never pay more for an investment than it is worth.

CALCULATOR TIP: CALCULATING THE PRESENT VALUE OF MULTIPLE CASH FLOWS

To calculate the present value of future cash flows with a financial calculator, we use exactly the same process we used in finding the future value, except that we solve for the present value instead of the future value. We can compute the present values of the individual cash flows, save them in the calculator's memory, and then add them up to obtain the total present value.

LEARNING BY DOING APPLICATION 6.3

Buying a Used Car—Help!

Problem: For a student—or anyone else—buying a used car can be a harrowing experience. Once you find the car you want, the next difficult decision is how to pay for it—cash or a loan. Suppose the cash price you have negotiated for the car is $5,600, but that amount will stretch your budget for the year. The dealer says, "No problem. The car is yours for $4,000 down and payments of $1,000 per year for the next two years. Or you can put $2,000 down and pay $2,000 per year for two years. The choice is yours." Which offer is the best deal? The interest rate you can earn on your money is 8 percent.

Approach: In this problem, we have three alternative cash flows. We need to convert all of the cash flows (CF_n) into today's dollars (present value) and select the alternative with the lowest present value or price.[1] The time line for the three alternatives, along with the cash flows for each alternative, is as follows. (The cash flows at time zero represent the cash price of the car in the case of alternative A and the down payment in the case of alternatives B and C.)

```
                        0           8%          1                       2   Year
                        ├───────────────────────┼───────────────────────┤
Cash price or down payment                    CF₁                      CF₂
```

	Cash Price or Down Payment	CF_1	CF_2	Total
Alternative A	$5,600	-	-	$5,600
Alternative B	$4,000	$1,000	$1,000	$6,000
Alternative C	$2,000	$2,000	$2,000	$6,000

Now we use Equation 5.4 to find the present value of each alternative.

(continued)

---

[1] Up to this point, we have used the notation FV_n to represent a cash flow in period n. We have done this to stress that, for $n > 0$, we were referring to a future value. From this point on, we will use the notation CF_n, instead of FV_n, because the CF_n notation is more commonly used by financial analysts.

Solution:

Alternative A:

$$\$5{,}600 \times 1/(1.08)^0 = \$5{,}600.00$$

Alternative B:

$$\$4{,}000 \times 1/(1.08)^0 = \$4{,}000.00$$
$$\$1{,}000 \times 1/1.08 = \phantom{\$0{,}}925.93$$
$$\$1{,}000 \times 1/(1.08)^2 = \phantom{\$0{,}}857.34$$
$$\text{Total} \$5{,}783.27$$

Alternative C:

$$\$2{,}000 \times 1/(1.08)^0 = \$2{,}000.00$$
$$\$2{,}000 \times 1/1.08 = \$1{,}851.85$$
$$\$2{,}000 \times 1/(1.08)^2 = \$1{,}714.68$$
$$\text{Total} \$5{,}566.53$$

Once we have converted the three cash flow streams to present dollars, the answer is clear. Alternative C has the lowest present value, so it has the lowest price and is the alternative you should choose.

DECISION-MAKING EXAMPLE 6.1

The Investment Decision

Problem: You are thinking of buying a business, and your investment adviser presents you with two possibilities. Both businesses are priced at $60,000, and you have only $60,000 to invest. She has provided you with the cash flows for each business, along with the present value of the cash flows discounted at 10 percent, as follows:

	Cash flow per year ($ thousands)				
Business	1	2	3	Total	PV at 10%
A	$50	$30	$ 20	$100	$85.27
B	$ 5	$ 5	$100	$110	$83.81

Which business should you acquire?

Decision: At first glance, business B may look to be the best choice because its undiscounted cash flows for the three years total $110,000, versus $100,000 for A. However, to make the decision on the basis of the undiscounted cash flows ignores the time value of money. By discounting the cash flows, we eliminate the time value of money effect by converting all cash flows to current dollars. The present value of business A is $85,270 and that of B is $83,810. Thus, you should acquire business A.

Before You Go On

1. Explain how to calculate the future value of a stream of cash flows.
2. Explain how to calculate the present value of a stream of cash flows.
3. Why is it important to adjust all cash flows to a common date?

6.2 Level Cash Flows: Annuities and Perpetuities

In finance we commonly encounter contracts that call for the payment of equal amounts of cash over several time periods. For example, most business term loans and insurance policies require the holder to make a series of equal payments, usually monthly. Similarly, nearly all consumer loans, such as auto, personal, and home mortgage loans, call for equal monthly payments. Any financial contract that calls for equally spaced and level cash flows over a finite number of periods is called an **annuity**. If the cash flow payments continue forever, the contract is called a **perpetuity**. Most annuities are structured so that cash payments are received at the end of each period. Because this is the most common structure, these annuities are often called **ordinary annuities**.

Visit New York Life Insurance Company's Web site to learn more about investment products that pay out annuities: https://www.newyorklife.com/cda/0,3254,10468,00.html.

Present Value of an Annuity

LEARNING OBJECTIVE 2

We frequently need to find the **present value of an annuity (PVA)**. Suppose, for example, that a financial contract pays $2,000 at the end of each year for three years and the appropriate discount rate is 8 percent. The time line for the situation is:

```
0        8%       1           2           3    Year
|-----------------|-----------|-----------|
PV = ?          $2,000      $2,000      $2,000
```

annuity
a series of equally spaced and level cash flows extending over a finite number of periods

perpetuity
a series of level cash flows that continue forever

What is the most we should pay for this annuity? Of course, we have worked problems like this one before. All we need to do is calculate the present value of each individual cash flow (CF_n) and add them up. Using Equation 5.4, we find that the present value of the three year annuity (PVA_3) at 8 percent interest is:

$$PVA_3 = CF_1 \times \frac{1}{1+i} + CF_2 \times \frac{1}{(1+i)^2} + CF_3 \times \frac{1}{(1+i)^3}$$

$$= \$2,000 \times \frac{1}{1.08} + \$2,000 \times \frac{1}{(1.08)^2} + \$2,000 \times \frac{1}{(1.08)^3}$$

$$= \$1,851.85 + \$1,714.68 + \$1,587.66$$

$$= \$5,154.19$$

ordinary annuity
an annuity in which payments are made at the ends of the periods

This approach to computing the present value of an annuity works as long as the number of cash flows is relatively small. In many situations that involve annuities, however, the number of cash flows is large, and doing the calculations by hand would be tedious. For example, a typical 30-year home mortgage has 360 (12 months × 30 years) monthly payments.

present value of an annuity (PVA)
the present value of the cash flows from an annuity, discounted at the appropriate discount rate

Fortunately, our problem can be simplified because the cash flows (CF) for an annuity are all the same ($CF_1 = CF_2 = \ldots CF_n = CF$). Thus, the present value of an annuity (PVA_n) with n equal cash flows (CF) at interest rate i is the sum of the individual present value calculations:

$$PVA_n = CF \times \frac{1}{1+i} + CF \times \frac{1}{(1+i)^2} + \cdots + CF \times \frac{1}{(1+i)^n}$$

With some mathematical manipulations that are beyond the scope of this discussion, we can simplify this equation to yield a useful formula for the present value of an annuity:

$$PVA_n = \frac{CF}{i} \times \left[1 - \frac{1}{(1+i)^n}\right]$$

$$= CF \times \frac{1 - 1/(1+i)^n}{i}$$

(6.1)

where:

PVA_n = present value of an n period annuity
CF = level and equally spaced cash flow
i = discount rate, or interest rate
n = number of periods (often called the annuity's maturity)

Notice in Equation 6.1 that $1/(1 + i)^n$ is a term you have already encountered: It is the present value factor. Thus, we can also write Equation 6.1 as follows:

$$PVA_n = CF \times \frac{1 - \text{Present value factor}}{i}$$

where the term on the right is what we call the PV annuity factor:

$$\text{PV annuity factor} = \frac{1 - \text{Present value factor}}{i}$$

It follows that yet another way to state Equation 6.1 is:

$$PVA_n = CF \times \text{PV annuity factor}$$

Let's apply Equation 6.1 to the example involving a three-year annuity with a $2,000 annual cash flow. To solve for PVA_n, we first compute the PV annuity factor for three years at 8 percent. The calculation is made in two steps:

1. Calculate the present value factor for three years at 8 percent:

$$\begin{aligned}\text{Present value factor} &= \frac{1}{(1 + i)^n} \\ &= \frac{1}{(1 + 0.08)^3} \\ &= \frac{1}{(1.08)^3} \\ &= \frac{1}{1.2597} \\ &= 0.7938\end{aligned}$$

2. Calculate the PV annuity factor for three years at 8 percent, using the present value factor calculated in step 1:

$$\begin{aligned}\text{PV annuity factor} &= \frac{1 - \text{Present value factor}}{i} \\ &= \frac{1 - 0.7938}{0.08} \\ &= \frac{0.2062}{0.08} \\ &= 2.577\end{aligned}$$

We now can calculate PVA_3 by plugging our values into the equation:

$$\begin{aligned}PVA_3 &= CF \times \text{PV annuity factor} \\ &= \$2{,}000 \times 2.577 \\ &= \$5{,}154.00\end{aligned}$$

The calculation nearly agrees with our earlier hand calculation. The difference is due to rounding.

Investopedia is a great Web site for a variety of finance topics. For example, you can find a discussion of annuities at www.investopedia.com/articles/03/101503.asp.

ANNUITY TABLES: PRESENT VALUE FACTORS

Instead of calculating the PV annuity factor by hand, we can use tables that list selected annuity factors. Exhibit 6.4 contains some entries from such a table, and a more complete set of tables can be found in Appendix A. The annuity table shows the present value of a stream of cash flows that equals $1 a year for n years at different interest rates. Looking at the exhibit, we find that the value for a three-year annuity factor at 8 percent is 2.577, which agrees with our previous calculations.

Exhibit 6.4 Present Value Annuity Factors

Number of Years	1%	5%	6%	7%	8%	9%	10%
1	$0.990	$0.952	$0.943	$0.935	$0.926	$0.917	$0.909
2	1.970	1.859	1.833	1.808	1.783	1.759	1.736
3	2.941	2.723	2.673	2.624	2.577	2.531	2.487
4	3.902	3.546	3.465	3.387	3.312	3.240	3.170
5	4.853	4.329	4.212	4.100	3.993	3.890	3.791
10	9.471	7.722	7.360	7.024	6.710	6.418	6.145
20	18.046	12.462	11.470	10.594	9.818	9.129	8.514
30	25.808	15.372	13.765	12.409	11.258	10.274	9.427

The table of present value annuity factors shows the present value of $1 for different numbers of years and different interest rates. To locate the desired PV annuity factor, find the row for the appropriate number of years and the column for the proper interest rate.

LEARNING BY DOING APPLICATION 6.4

Computing a PV Annuity Factor

Problem: Compute the PV annuity factor for 30 years at a 10 percent interest rate.

Approach: First, we calculate the present value factor at 10 percent for 30 years. Then, using this value, we calculate the PV annuity factor.

Solution:

$$\text{Present value factor} = \frac{1}{(1+i)^n}$$
$$= \frac{1}{(1.10)^{30}}$$
$$= \frac{1}{17.4494}$$
$$= 0.0573$$

Then, using this value, we calculate the PV annuity factor:

$$\text{PV annuity factor} = \frac{1 - \text{Present value factor}}{i}$$
$$= \frac{1 - 0.0573}{0.10}$$
$$= \frac{0.9427}{0.10}$$
$$= 9.427$$

The answer matches the number in Exhibit 6.4.

(continued)

CALCULATOR TIP: FINDING THE PRESENT VALUE OF AN ANNUITY

There are four variables in a present value of an annuity equation (PVA_n, CF, n, and i), and if you know three of them, you can solve for the fourth in a few seconds with a financial calculator. The calculator key that you have not used so far is the PMT (payment) key, which is the key for level cash flows over the life of an annuity.

To illustrate problem solving with a financial calculator, we will revisit the financial contract that paid $2,000 per year for three years, discounted at 8 percent. To find the present value of the contract, we enter 8 percent for the interest rate (i), $2,000 for the payment (PMT), and 3 for the number of periods (N). The key for FV is not relevant for this calculation, so we enter zero into this register to clear it. The key entries and the answer are as follows:

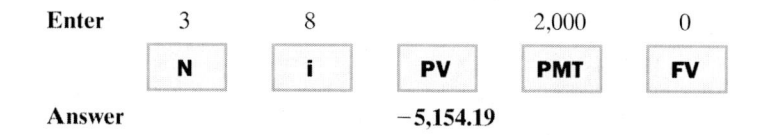

Enter	3	8		2,000	0
	N	i	PV	PMT	FV
Answer			−5,154.19		

The price of the contract is $5,154.19, which agrees with our other calculations. As discussed in Chapter 5, the negative sign on the financial calculator box indicates that $5,154.19 is a cash outflow.[2]

FINDING MONTHLY OR YEARLY PAYMENTS

A very common problem in finance is determining the payment schedule for a loan on a consumer asset, such as a car or a home that was purchased on credit. Nearly all consumer credit loans call for equal monthly payments. Suppose, for example, that you have just purchased a $450,000 condominium in Miami's South Beach district. You were able to put $50,000 down and obtain a 30-year fixed rate mortgage at 6.125 percent for the balance. What are your monthly payments?

In this problem we know the present value of the annuity. It is $400,000, the price of the condominium less the down payment ($450,000 − $50,000). We also know the number of payments; since the payments will be made monthly for 30 years, you will make 360 payments (12 months × 30 years). Because the payments are monthly, both the interest rate and maturity must be expressed in monthly terms. For consumer loans, to get the monthly interest rate, we divide the annual interest rate by 12. Thus, the monthly interest rate equals 0.51042 percent (6.125 percent/12 months). What we need to calculate is the monthly cash payments (CF) over the loan period. The time line looks like the following:

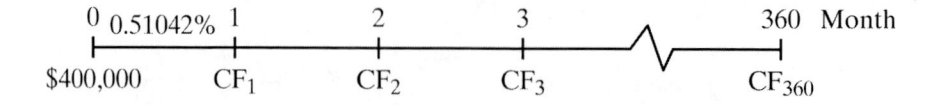

```
  0   0.51042%   1        2        3              360  Month
  ├──────────────┼────────┼────────┼──────⁄\──────┤
$400,000        CF₁      CF₂      CF₃            CF₃₆₀
```

To find CF (remember that $CF_1 = CF_2 = \ldots CF_{360} = CF$), we use Equation 6.1. We need to make two preliminary calculations:

---

[2] Recall that, when using a financial calculator, it is common practice to enter cash outflows as negative numbers and cash inflows as positive numbers. See Chapter 5 for a complete discussion the importance of assigning the proper sign (+ or −) to cash flows when using a financial calculator.

1. First, we calculate the present value factor for 360 months at 0.51042 percent per month (or, in decimal form, 0.0051042):

$$\text{Present value factor} = \frac{1}{(1+i)^n}$$
$$= \frac{1}{(1.0051042)^{360}}$$
$$= \frac{1}{6.25160595}$$
$$= 0.1599589$$

2. Next, we solve for the PV annuity factor:

$$\text{PV annuity factor} = \frac{1 - \text{Present value factor}}{i}$$
$$= \frac{1 - 0.1599589}{0.0051042}$$
$$= \frac{0.8400411}{0.0051042}$$
$$= 164.578406$$

We can now plug all the data into Equation 6.1 and solve it for CF:

$$PVA_n = CF \times \text{PV annuity factor}$$
$$\$400{,}000 = CF \times 164.578406$$
$$CF = \frac{\$400{,}000}{164.578406}$$
$$CF = \$2{,}430.45$$

Your mortgage payments will be about $2,430.45 per month.

To solve the problem on a financial calculator takes only a few seconds once the time line is prepared. The most common error students make when using financial calculators is failing to convert all contract variables to be consistent with the compounding period. Thus, if the contract calls for monthly payments, the interest rate and contract duration must be stated in monthly terms.

Having converted our data to monthly terms, we enter into the calculator: N = 360 (30 years × 12 months/year) months, i = 0.51042 (6.125 percent/12 months), PV = $400,000, and FV = 0 (to clear the register). Then, pressing the payment button (PMT), we find the answer, which is −$2,430.44. The necessary keystrokes are:

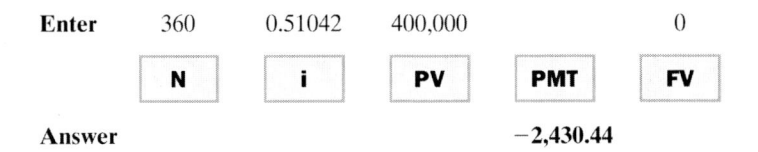

Enter	360	0.51042	400,000		0
	N	i	PV	PMT	FV
Answer				−2,430.44	

Notice that the hand and financial calculator answers differ by only 1 cent ($2,430.45 − $2,430.44). The answers are so close because when doing the hand calculation, we carried six to eight decimal places through the entire set of calculations. Had we rounded off each number as the calculations were made, the errors between the two calculation methods would have been about $2.00. The moral of the story is to round as few numbers as possible when making a series of hand calculations. The more numbers that are rounded during the calculations, the greater the possible rounding error.

> **LEARNING BY DOING**
> **APPLICATION 6.5**
>
> ## What Are Your Monthly Car Payments?
>
> **Problem:** You have decided to buy a new car, and the dealer's best price is $16,000. The dealer agrees to provide financing with a five-year auto loan at 12 percent interest. Using a financial calculator, calculate your monthly payments.
>
> **Approach:** All the problem data must be converted to monthly terms. The number of periods is 60 months (5 years × 12 months per year), and the monthly interest charge is 1 percent (12 percent/12 months). The time line for the car purchase is as follows: 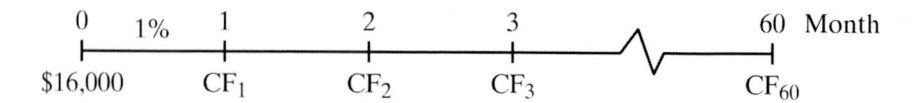
>
> ```
> 0      1%     1       2       3              60   Month
> |-------------|-------|-------|----~~~-------|
> $16,000     CF_1    CF_2    CF_3           CF_60
> ```
>
> Having converted our data to monthly terms, we enter the following values into the calculator: N = 60 months, i = 1, PV = $16,000, and FV = 0 (to clear the register). Pressing the payment key (PMT) will give us the answer.
>
> **Solution:**
>
> | Enter | 60 | 1 | 16,000 | | 0 |
> |---|---|---|---|---|---|
> | | N | i | PV | PMT | FV |
> | Answer | | | | −355.91 | |
>
> Note that since we entered $16,000 as a positive number, the monthly payment of $355.91 is a negative number.

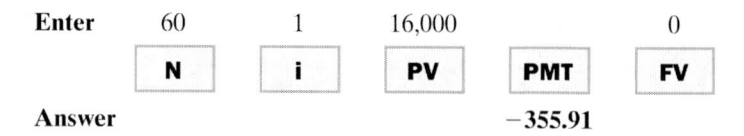

PREPARING A LOAN AMORTIZATION SCHEDULE

Once you understand how to calculate a monthly or yearly loan payment, you have all of the tools that you need to prepare a loan amortization schedule. The term *amortization* describes the way in which the principal (the amount borrowed) is repaid over the life of a loan. With an amortizing loan, some portion of each month's loan payment goes to paying down the principal. When the final loan payment is made, the unpaid principal is reduced to zero and the loan is paid off. The other portion of each loan payment is interest, which is payment for the use of outstanding principal (the amount of money still owed). Thus, with an **amortizing loan**, each loan payment contains some repayment of principal and an interest payment. Nearly all loans to consumers are amortizing loans.

A loan **amortization schedule** is just a table that shows the loan balance at the beginning and end of each period, the payment made during that period, and how much of that payment represents interest and how much represents repayment of principal. To see how an amortization schedule is prepared, consider an example. Suppose that you have just borrowed $10,000 at a 5 percent interest rate from a bank to purchase a car. Typically, you would make monthly payments on such a loan. For simplicity, however, we will assume that the bank allows you to make annual payments and that the loan will be repaid over five years. Exhibit 6.5 shows the amortization schedule for this loan.

To prepare a loan amortization schedule, we must first compute the loan payment. Since, for consumer loans, the amount of the loan payment is fixed, all the payments are identical in amount. Applying Equation 6.1 and noting from Exhibit

amortizing loan
a loan for which each loan payment contains repayment of some principal and a payment of interest that is based on the remaining principal to be repaid

amortization schedule
with regard to a loan, a table that shows the loan balance at the beginning and end of each period, the payment made during that period, and how much of that payment represents interest and how much represents repayment of principal

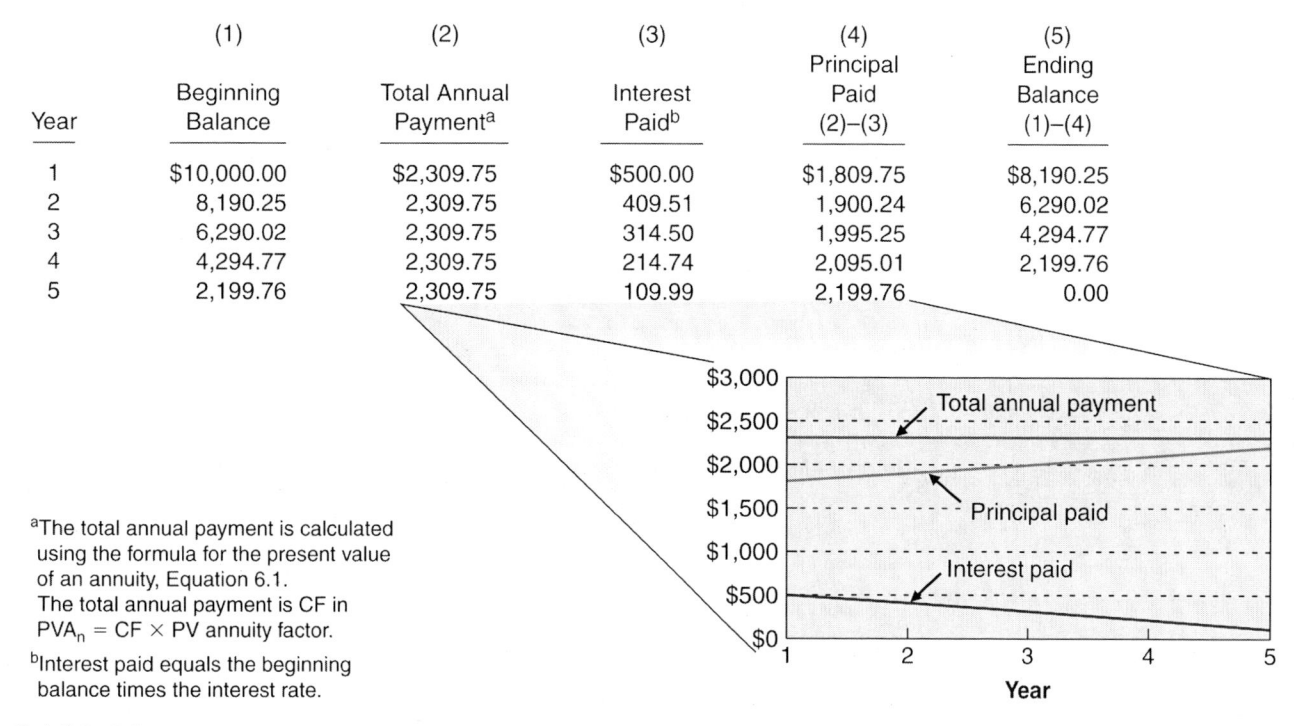

Year	(1) Beginning Balance	(2) Total Annual Payment[a]	(3) Interest Paid[b]	(4) Principal Paid (2)−(3)	(5) Ending Balance (1)−(4)
1	$10,000.00	$2,309.75	$500.00	$1,809.75	$8,190.25
2	8,190.25	2,309.75	409.51	1,900.24	6,290.02
3	6,290.02	2,309.75	314.50	1,995.25	4,294.77
4	4,294.77	2,309.75	214.74	2,095.01	2,199.76
5	2,199.76	2,309.75	109.99	2,199.76	0.00

[a] The total annual payment is calculated using the formula for the present value of an annuity, Equation 6.1. The total annual payment is CF in $PVA_n = CF \times PV$ annuity factor.

[b] Interest paid equals the beginning balance times the interest rate.

Exhibit 6.5
Amortization Table for a Five-Year, $10,000 Loan at 5 Percent Interest

A loan amortization table shows how regular payments of principal and interest are applied to repay a loan. The exhibit is an amortization table for a five-year, $10,000 loan with an interest rate of 5 percent and annual payments of $2,309.75. Notice that the interest paid declines with each payment, while the principal paid increases. These relations are illustrated in the pullout graphic in the exhibit.

6.4 that the PV annuity factor for five years at 5 percent is 4.329, we calculate as follows:

$$PVA_n = CF \times PV \text{ annuity factor}$$
$$\$10,000 = CF \times 4.329$$
$$CF = \frac{\$10,000}{4.329}$$
$$CF = \$2,310.00 \text{ per year}$$

Alternatively, we enter the values N = 5 years, i = 5 percent, and PV = $10,000 in a financial calculator and then press the PMT key to solve for the loan payment amount. The answer is −$2,309.75 per year. The difference between the two answers results from rounding. For the amortization table calculation, we will use the more precise answer from the financial calculator.

Turning to Exhibit 6.5, we can work through the amortization schedule to see how the table is prepared. For the first year, the values are determined as follows:

1. The amount borrowed, or the beginning principal balance, is $10,000.
2. The annual loan payment, as calculated earlier, is $2,309.75.
3. The interest payment for the first year is $500 and is calculated as follows:

$$\text{Interest payment} = i \times P_0$$
$$= 0.05 \times \$10,000$$
$$= \$500$$

4. The principal paid for the year is $1,809.75, calculated as follows:

$$\text{Principal paid} = \text{Loan payment} - \text{Interest payment}$$
$$= \$2{,}309.75 - \$500$$
$$= \$1{,}809.75$$

5. The ending principal balance is $8,190.25, computed as follows:

$$\text{Ending principal balance} = \text{Beginning principal balance} - \text{Principal paid}$$
$$= \$10{,}000 - \$1{,}809.75$$
$$= 8{,}190.25$$

Note that the ending principal balance for the first year ($8,190.25) becomes the beginning principal balance for the second year ($8,190.25), which in turn is used in calculating the interest payment for the second year:

$$\text{Interest payment} = i \times P_0$$
$$= 0.05 \times \$8{,}190.25$$
$$= \$409.51$$

This calculation makes sense because each loan payment includes some principal repayment. This is why the interest in column 3 declines each year. We repeat the calculations until the loan is fully amortized, at which point the principal balance goes to zero and the loan is paid off.

If you are preparing an amortization table for monthly payments, of course, all of your principal balances, loan payments, and interest rates must be adjusted to a monthly basis. For example, to calculate monthly payments for our auto loan, we would make the following adjustments: $n = 60$ payments (12 months per year $\times$ 5 years), $i = 0.4167$ percent (5 percent/12 months per year), and monthly payment = $188.71.

An interesting characteristic of amortized loans is the breakdown between the payment of interest and the repayment of principal in each loan payment. In the early years of a loan, interest payments are at their peak because very little principal has been repaid (see column 1). Near the end of the loan contract, when most of the principal has been paid off, payments to principal are at their peak, and interest payments have become smaller. Thus, as a loan is gradually paid off, the proportion of a monthly payment devoted to interest steadily declines, while the proportion used to reduce the principal steadily increases. The final loan payment repays just enough principal to pay off the loan in full.

Finally, the separation between interest and principal payments is also important for tax purposes. Individual taxpayers can deduct interest on a home mortgage for their principal residence and, within limits, on a second residence. For corporations, interest expense is tax deductible.

USING EXCEL

Loan Amortization Table

Loan amortization tables are most easily constructed using a spreadsheet program. Here, we have reconstructed the loan amortization table shown in Exhibit 6.5 using Excel.

Notice that all the values in the amortization table are obtained by using formulas. Once you have built an amortization table like this one, you can change any of the input variables, such as the loan amount, and all of the other numbers will automatically be updated.

6.2 Level Cash Flows: Annuities and Perpetuities

	A	B	C	D	E	F	G	H	I	J	K	L	M
1													
2							Loan Amortization Table						
3													
4			Loan amount		$10,000								
5			Interest rate		0.05								
6			Loan period		5								
7			PMT		$2,309.75								
8													
9			Year		Beginning Balance		Total Annual Payment		Simple Interest Paid		Principal Paid		Ending Balance
10			1		$10,000.00		$2,309.75		$500.00		$1,809.75		$8,190.25
11			2		8,190.25		2,309.75		409.51		1,900.24		6,290.02
12			3		6,290.02		2,309.75		314.50		1,995.25		4,294.77
13			4		4,294.77		2,309.75		214.74		2,095.01		2,199.76
14			5		2,199.76		2,309.75		109.99		2,199.76		0.00
15													
16	Corresponding formulas:												
17													
18			Payment:		=PMT(D5, D6, -D4)								
19													
20			Year		Beginning Balance		Total Annual Payment		Simple Interest Paid		Principal Paid		Ending Balance
21			1		=D4		=$D$7		=D10*$D$5		=F10-H10		=D10-J10
22			2		=L10		=$D$7		=D11*$D$5		=F11-H11		=D11-J11
23			3		=L11		=$D$7		=D12*$D$5		=F12-H12		=D12-J12
24			4		=L12		=$D$7		=D13*$D$5		=F13-H13		=D13-J13
25			5		=L13		=$D$7		=D14*$D$5		=F14-H14		=D14-J14
26													

FINDING THE INTEREST RATE

Another important calculation in finance is determining the interest, or discount, rate for an annuity. The interest rate tells us the rate of return on an annuity contract. For example, suppose your parents are getting ready to retire and decide to convert some of their retirement portfolio, which is invested in the stock market, into an annuity that guarantees them a fixed annual income. Their insurance agent asks for $350,000 for an annuity that guarantees to pay them $50,000 a year for 10 years. What is the rate of return on the annuity?

As we did when we found the payment amount, we can insert these values into Equation 6.1:

$$\text{PVA}_n = \text{CF} \times \frac{1 - 1/(1+i)^n}{i}$$

$$\$350{,}000 = \$50{,}000 \times \frac{1 - 1/(1+i)^{10}}{i}$$

To determine the rate of return for the annuity, we need to solve the equation for the unknown value i. Unfortunately, it is not possible to solve the resulting equation for i algebraically. The only way to solve the problem is by trial and error. We normally solve this kind of problem using a financial calculator or computer spreadsheet program that finds the solution for us. However, it is important to understand how the solution is arrived at by trial and error, so let's work this problem without such aids.

To start the process, we must select an initial value for i, plug it into the right-hand side of the equation, and solve the equation to see if the present value of the annuity stream equals $350,000, which is the left-hand side of the equation. If the present value of the annuity is too large (PVA > $350,000), we need to select a higher value for i. If the present value of the annuity stream is too small (PVA < $350,000), we need to select a smaller value. We continue the trial-and-error process until we find the value for i at which PVA = $350,000.

The key to getting started is to make the best guess we can as to the possible value of the interest rate given the information and data available to us. We will assume that the current bank savings rate is 4 percent. Since the annuity rate of return should exceed the bank rate, we will start our calculations with a 5 percent discount rate. The present value of the annuity is:

$$PVA_{5\%} = \$50,000 \times \frac{1 - 1/(1 + 0.05)^{10}}{0.05}$$
$$= \$50,000 \times 7.722$$
$$= \$386,100$$

That's a pretty good first guess, but our present value is greater than $350,000, so we need to try a higher discount rate.[4] Let's try 7 percent:

$$PVA_{7\%} = \$50,000 \times \frac{1 - 1/(1 + 0.07)^{10}}{0.07}$$
$$= \$50,000 \times 7.024$$
$$= \$351,200$$

The present value of the annuity is still slightly higher than $350,000, so we still need a larger value of i. How about 7.10 percent:

$$PVA_{7.1\%} = \$50,000 \times \frac{1 - 1/(1 + 0.071)^{10}}{0.071}$$
$$= \$50,000 \times 6.991$$
$$= \$349,550$$

The value is too small, but we now know that i is between 7.00 and 7.10 percent. On the next try, we need to use a slightly smaller value of i—say, 7.07 percent:

$$PVA_{7.07\%} = \$50,000 \times \frac{1 - 1/(1 + 0.0707)^{10}}{0.0707}$$
$$= \$50,000 \times 7.001$$
$$= \$350,050$$

Since this value is slightly too high, we should try a number for i that is only slightly greater than 7.07 percent. We'll try 7.073 percent:

$$PVA_{7.073\%} = \$50,000 \times \frac{1 - 1/(1 + 0.07073)^{10}}{0.07073}$$
$$= \$50,000 \times 7.000$$
$$= \$350,000$$

The cost of the annuity, $350,000, is now exactly the same as the present value of the annuity stream ($350,000); thus, 7.073 percent is the rate of return earned by the annuity.

It typically takes many more guesses to solve for the interest rate than it did in this example. Our "guesses" were good because we knew the answer before we started guessing! Clearly, solving for i by trial and error can be a long and tedious process. Fortunately, as mentioned, these types of problems are easily solved with a financial calculator or computer spreadsheet program. Next, we describe how to compute the interest rate or rate of return on an annuity on a financial calculator.

CALCULATOR TIP: FINDING THE INTEREST RATE

To illustrate how to find the interest rate for an annuity on a financial calculator, we will enter the information from the previous example. We know the number of periods

---

[4]Notice that we have rounded the PV annuity factor to three decimal places (7.722). If we use a financial calculator and do not round, we get a more precise answer of $386,086.75.

($N = 10$), the payment amount (PMT = $50,000), and the present value (PV = −$350,000), and we want to solve for the interest rate (i):

Enter	10		−350,000	50,000	0
	N	i	PV	PMT	FV
Answer		7.073			

The interest rate is 7.073 percent. Notice that we have used a negative sign for the present value of the annuity contract, representing a cash outflow, and a positive sign for the annuity payments, representing cash inflows. Using the present value formula, you must always have at least one inflow and one outflow. If we had entered both the PV and PMT amounts as positive values (or both as negative values), the calculator would have reported an error since the equation cannot be solved. As we have mentioned before, we could have reversed *all* of the signs—that is, made cash outflows positive and cash inflows negative—and still gotten the correct answer. Finally, the FV was entered as zero to make sure that the register was cleared.

Return on Investments: Good Deal or Bad?

LEARNING BY DOING APPLICATION 6.6

Problem: With some business opportunities you know the price of a financial contract and the promised cash flows, and you want to calculate the interest rate or rate of return on the investment. For example, suppose you have a chance to invest in a small business. The owner wants to borrow $200,000 from you for five years and will make yearly payments of $60,000 at the end of each year. Similar types of investment opportunities will pay 5 percent. Is this a good investment opportunity?

Approach: First, we draw a time line for this situation:

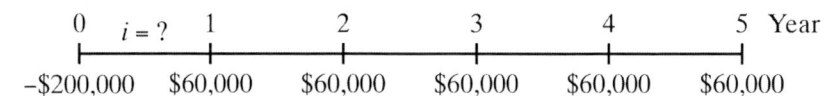

```
 0      i = ?   1         2         3         4         5 Year
 |--------------|---------|---------|---------|---------|
−$200,000     $60,000  $60,000   $60,000   $60,000   $60,000
```

To compute the rate of return on the investment, we need to compute the interest rate that equates the initial investment of $200,000 to the present value of the promised cash flows of $60,000 per year. We can use the trial-and-error approach with Equation 6.1, a financial calculator, or a spreadsheet program to solve this problem. Here we will use a financial calculator.

Solution: The financial calculator steps are:

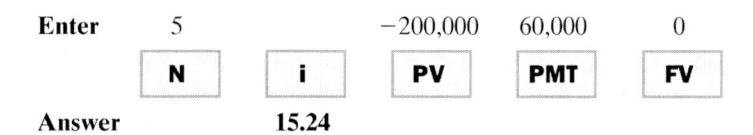

Enter	5		−200,000	60,000	0
	N	i	PV	PMT	FV
Answer		15.24			

The return on this investment is 15.24 percent, well above the market interest rate of 5 percent. It is a good investment opportunity.

The Pizza Dough Machine

DECISION-MAKING EXAMPLE 6.2

Problem: As the owner of a pizza parlor, you are considering whether to buy a fully automated pizza dough preparation machine. Your staff is wildly supportive of

(continued)

the purchase because it would eliminate a tedious part of their work. Your accountant provides you with the following information:

- The cost, including shipping, for the Italian Pizza Dough Machine is $25,000.
- Cash savings, including labor, raw materials, and tax savings due to depreciation, are $3,500 per year for 10 years.
- Present value of cash savings is $21,506 at a 10 percent discount rate.[5]

Given the above data, what should you do?

Decision: As you arrive at the pizza parlor in the morning, the staff is in a festive mood because word has leaked out that the new machine will save the shop $35,000 and only cost $25,000.

With a heavy heart, you explain that the analysis done at the water cooler by some of the staff is incorrect. To make economic decisions involving cash flows, even for a small business such as your pizza parlor, you cannot compare cash values from different time periods unless they are adjusted for the time value of money. The present value formula takes into account the time value of money and converts the future cash flows into current or present dollars. The cost of the machine is already in current dollars.

The correct analysis is as follows: the machine costs $25,000, and the present value of the cost savings is $21,506. Thus, the cost of the machine exceeds the benefits; the correct decision is not to buy the new dough preparation machine.

Future Value of an Annuity

Generally, when we are working with annuities, we are interested in computing their present value. On occasion, though, we need to compute the **future value of an annuity (FVA)**. Such computations typically involve some type of saving activity, such as a monthly savings plan. Another application is computing terminal values for retirement or pension plans with constant contributions.

future value of an annuity (FVA)
the value of an annuity at some point in the future

We will start with a simple example. Suppose that you plan to save $1,000 at the end of every year for four years with the goal of buying a racing bicycle. The bike you want is an Orbea Orca, a top-of-the-line Spanish racing bike that costs around $4,500. The bike has a carbon frame and forks, is fitted with Shimano Dura Ace components, and weighs 15 pounds, 7 ounces. If your bank pays 8 percent interest a year, will you have enough money to buy the bike at the end of four years?

To solve this problem, we can first lay out the cash flows on a time line, as we discussed earlier in this chapter. We can then calculate the future value for each cash flow using Equation 5.1, which is $FV_n = PV \times (1 + i)^n$. Finally, we can add up all the cash flows. The time line and calculations are shown in Exhibit 6.6. Given that the total future value of the four payments is $4,506.11, as shown in the exhibit, you should have enough money to buy the bike.

FUTURE VALUE OF ANNUITY EQUATIONS

Of course, most business applications involve longer periods of time than the Orbea bike example. One way to solve more complex problems involving the future value of an annuity is first to calculate the present value of the annuity, PVA, using Equation 6.1 and then to use Equation 5.1 to calculate the future value of the PVA. In practice, many

---
[5]The annuity present value factor for 10 years at 10 percent is 6.1446. Thus, PV_{10} = CF × Annuity factor = $3,500 × 6.1446 = $21,506.10. Using a financial calculator, PV_{10} = $21,505.98. The difference is due to rounding errors.

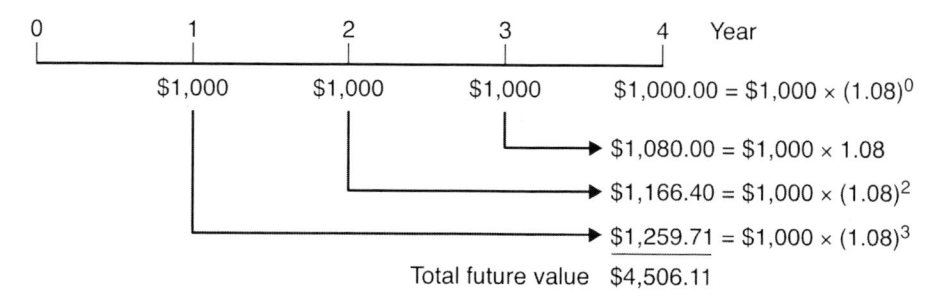

```
0         1         2         3         4    Year
|         |         |         |         |
       $1,000    $1,000    $1,000    $1,000.00 = $1,000 × (1.08)⁰
                                     $1,080.00 = $1,000 × 1.08
                                     $1,166.40 = $1,000 × (1.08)²
                                     $1,259.71 = $1,000 × (1.08)³
                          Total future value  $4,506.11
```

Exhibit 6.6

Future Value of a Four-Year Annuity: Orbea Orca Bicycle

The exhibit shows a time line for a savings plan to buy an Orbea bicycle. Under this savings plan, $1,000 is invested at the end of each year for four years at an annual interest rate of 8 percent. We find the value at the end of the four-year period by adding the future values of the separate cash flows, just as in Exhibits 6.1 and 6.2.

---

analyses condense this calculation into a single step by using the future value of annuity (FVA) formula, which we obtain by substituting PVA for PV in Equation 5.1.

$$\begin{aligned} FVA_n &= PVA_n \times (1+i)^n \quad (6.2) \\ &= \frac{CF}{i} \times \left[1 - \frac{1}{(1+i)^n}\right] \times (1+i)^n \\ &= \frac{CF}{i} \times \left[(1+i)^n - 1\right] \\ &= CF \times \frac{(1+i)^n - 1}{i} \end{aligned}$$

where:

FVA_n = future value of an annuity at the end of n periods
PVA_n = present value of an n period annuity
CF = level and equally spaced cash flow
i = discount rate, or interest rate
n = number of periods

We can rearrange Equation 6.2 to write it in terms of the Future value factor and the FV annuity factor:

$$\begin{aligned} FVA_n &= CF \times \frac{(1+i)^n - 1}{i} \\ &= CF \times \frac{\text{Future value factor} - 1}{i} \\ &= CF \times \text{FV annuity factor} \end{aligned}$$

As you would expect, there are tables listing FV annuity factors. Appendix A includes a table that shows the value of a $1 annuity for various interest rates and maturities.

Using Equation 6.2 to compute FVA for the Orbea bike problem is straightforward. The calculation and process are similar to those we developed for PVA problems. That is, we first calculate the FV annuity factor for four years at 8 percent:

$$\text{Future value factor} = (1+i)^n = (1.08)^4 = 1.36049$$

$$\text{FV annuity factor} = \frac{\text{Future value factor} - 1}{i} = \frac{1.36049 - 1}{0.08} = 4.5061$$

188 CHAPTER 6 | Discounted Cash Flows and Valuation

Now we can compute the future value of the annuity by multiplying the constant cash flow (CF) by the FV annuity factor. We plug our computed values into the equation:

$$FVA_n = CF \times FV\ annuity\ factor = \$1,000 \times 4.5061 = \$4,506.10$$

This value differs slightly from the one we calculated in Exhibit 6.6 because of rounding.

CALCULATOR TIP: FINDING THE FUTURE VALUE OF AN ANNUITY

The procedure for calculating the future value of an annuity on a financial calculator is precisely the same as the procedure for calculating the present value of an annuity discussed earlier. The only difference is that we use the FV (future value) key instead of the PV (present value) key. The PV key is entered as a zero to clear the register.

Let's work the Orbea bicycle problem on a calculator. Recall that we decided to put $1,000 in the bank at the end of each year for four years. The bank pays 8 percent interest. Clear the financial register and make the following entries:

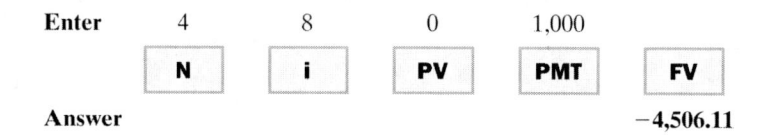

Enter	4	8	0	1,000	
	N	i	PV	PMT	FV
Answer					−4,506.11

The calculated value of $4,506.11 is the same as in Exhibit 6.6.

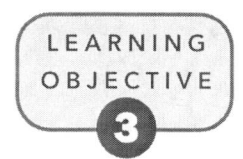

Perpetuities

LEARNING OBJECTIVE 3

A perpetuity is a constant stream of cash flows that goes on forever. Perpetuities in the form of bonds were used by the British Treasury Department to pay off the debt incurred by the government to finance the Napoleonic wars. These perpetual bonds, called *consols,* have no maturity date and are still traded in the international bond markets today.

The most important perpetuities in the securities markets today are preferred stock issues. The issuer of preferred stock promises to pay investors a fixed dividend forever unless a retirement date for the perferred stock has been set. If preferred stock dividends are not paid, all previous unpaid dividends must be repaid before any dividends are paid to common stockholders. This preferential treatment is one source of the term *preferred* stock.

From Equation 6.1, we can calculate the present value of a perpetuity by setting n, which is the number of periods, equal to infinity (∞).[6] When that is done, the value of the term $1/(1 + i)^\infty$ approaches 0, and thus:

$$\begin{aligned} PVA_\infty &= \frac{CF}{i} \times \left[1 - \frac{1}{(1+i)^\infty}\right] \\ &= \frac{CF}{i} \times [1 - 0] \\ &= \frac{CF}{i} \end{aligned} \quad (6.3)$$

As you can see, the present value of a perpetuity is the promised constant cash payment (CF) divided by the interest rate (i). A nice feature of the final equation ($PVA_\infty = CF/i$) is that it is algebraically very simple to work with, since it allows us to solve for i directly rather than by trial and error, as is required with Equations 6.1 and 6.2.

---

[6]Conversely, we can derive the formula for the present value of an ordinary annuity, Equation 6.1, from the formula for a perpetuity, as explained in the appendix at the end of this chapter.

For example, suppose you had a great experience during college at the school of business and decided to endow a chair in finance. Endowed chairs provide salary and research support for top faculty.[7] The goal of the chair is to provide the chair holder with $100,000 of additional financial support per year forever. If the rate of interest is 8 percent, how much money will you have to give the university foundation to provide the desired level of support? Using Equation 6.3, we find that the present value of the perpetuity is:

$$\text{PVA}_\infty = \frac{\text{CF}}{i} = \frac{\$100{,}000}{0.08} = \$1{,}250{,}000$$

Thus, a gift of $1.25 million will provide a constant annual payment of $100,000 to the chair holder forever.

There are two subtleties here that you should note. First, as mentioned earlier, the present value formula assumes that cash flows are paid at the end of the year. If our worthy chair holder needs to be paid when the chair is awarded, the donor would have to provide the university with an additional $100,000. Thus, the total gift would be $1.35 million. Note that the $100,000 is already in present value terms, so it can be added to the $1.25 million, which has been converted into present value terms. Second, in our problem, no adjustment was made for inflation. If the economy is expected to experience inflation, which is generally the case, the chair holder's purchasing power will decline each year.

LEARNING BY DOING APPLICATION 6.7

Preferred Stock Dividends

Problem: Suppose that you are the CEO of a public company and your investment banker recommends that you issue some preferred stock at $50 per share. Similar preferred stock issues are yielding 6 percent. What annual cash dividend does the firm need to offer to be competitive in the marketplace? In other words, what cash dividend paid annually forever would be worth $50 with a 6 percent discount rate?

Approach: As we have already mentioned, preferred stock is a type of perpetuity; thus, we can solve this problem by applying Equation 6.3. As usual, we begin by laying out the time line for the cash flows:

```
0  6%   1     2     3     4     5     6              ∞  Year
├──────┼─────┼─────┼─────┼─────┼─────┼──────/\/──────┤
PVA∞   CF    CF    CF    CF    CF    CF              CF
```

For preferred stock, PVA_∞ is the value of a share of stock, which is $50 per share. The discount rate is 6 percent. CF is the fixed-rate cash dividend, which is the unknown value. Knowing all this information, we can use Equation 6.3 and solve for CF.

Solution:

$$\text{PVA}_\infty = \frac{\text{CF}}{i}$$
$$\text{CF} = \text{PVA}_\infty \times i$$
$$= \$50 \times 0.06$$
$$= \$3$$

The annual dividend on the preferred stock would be $3 per share.

---

[7] The market for top research and teaching faculty is very competitive. Endowed chairs are a means that universities use to attract and retain their best faculty. The typical chair is endowed for $1 million or more and is usually named after the donor.

Annuities Due

annuity due
an annuity in which payments are made at the beginning of each period

More examples concerning topics discussed in this chapter can be found at Modlin.org: www.modlin.org/L1ModVidDemo.htm.

So far we have discussed only annuities whose cash flow payments occur at the end of the period, so-called ordinary annuities. Another type of annuity that is fairly common in business is known as an **annuity due.** Here, cash payments start immediately, at the beginning of the first period. For example, when you rent an apartment, the first rent payment is typically due immediately. The second rent payment is due the first of the second month, and so on. In this kind of payment pattern, you are effectively prepaying for the service.

Exhibit 6.7 compares the cash flows for an ordinary annuity and an annuity due. Note that both annuities are made up of four $1,000 cash flows and carry an 8 percent interest rate. Part A shows an ordinary annuity, in which the cash flows take place at the end of the period, and part B shows an annuity due, in which the cash flows take place at the beginning of the period. There are several ways to calculate the present and future values of an annuity due, and we discuss them next.

A. Ordinary Annuity (present value: four years at 8 percent)

With an ordinary annuity, the first cash flow occurs at the end of the first year.

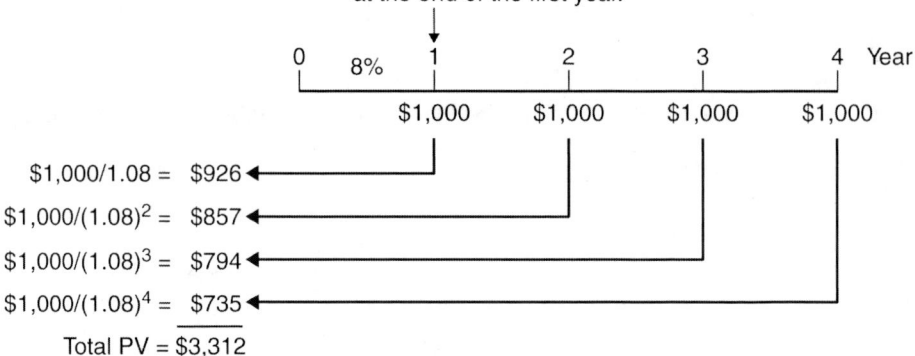

```
0    8%    1        2        3        4    Year
              $1,000   $1,000   $1,000   $1,000
```

$1,000/1.08 = $926
$1,000/(1.08)² = $857
$1,000/(1.08)³ = $794
$1,000/(1.08)⁴ = $735
Total PV = $3,312

B. Annuity Due (present value: four years at 8 percent)

With an annuity due, the first cash flow occurs at the beginning of the first year.

```
0    8%    1        2        3        4    Year
   $1,000   $1,000   $1,000   $1,000
```

$1,000/(1.08)⁰ = $1,000
$1,000/1.08 = $926
$1,000/(1.08)² = $857
$1,000/(1.08)³ = $794
Total PV = $3,577

Exhibit 6.7
Ordinary Annuity versus Annuity Due
The difference between an ordinary annuity (part A) and an annuity due (part B) is that with an ordinary annuity, the cash flows take place at the end of each period, while with an annuity due, the cash flows take place at the beginning of each period. As you can see in this example, the PV of the annuity due is larger than the PV of the ordinary annuity. The reason is that the cash flows of the annuity due are shifted forward one year and thus are discounted less.

PRESENT VALUE METHOD

One way to compute the present value of an annuity due is to discount each individual cash flow to the present, as shown in Exhibit 6.7B. Note that since the first $1,000 cash flow takes place at the current time ($t = 0$), the cash flow is already in present value terms. The present value of the cash flows is $3,577.

Compare this present value with the present value of the ordinary annuity, $3,312, as calculated in Exhibit 6.7A. It should be no surprise that the present value of the annuity due is larger than the present value of the ordinary annuity ($3,577 > $3,312), even though both annuities have four $1,000 cash flows. The reason is that the cash flows of the annuity due are shifted forward one year and, thus, are discounted less.

ANNUITY TRANSFORMATION METHOD

An easier way to work annuity due problems is to transform our formula for the present value of an annuity (Equation 6.1) so that it will work for annuity due problems. To do this, we pretend that each cash flow occurs at the end of the period (although it actually occurs at the beginning of the period) and use Equation 6.1. Since Equation 6.1 discounts each cash flow by one period too many, we then correct for the extra discounting by multiplying our answer by $(1 + i)$, where i is the discount rate or interest rate.

The relation between an ordinary annuity and an annuity due can be formally expressed as:

$$\text{Annuity due value} = \text{Ordinary annuity value} \times (1 + i) \qquad (6.4)$$

This relation is especially helpful because it works for both present value and future value calculations. Calculating the value of an annuity due using Equation 6.4 involves three steps:

1. Adjust the problem time line as if the cash flows were an ordinary annuity.
2. Calculate the present or future value as though the cash flows were an ordinary annuity.
3. Finally, multiply the answer by $(1 + i)$.

Let's calculate the value of the annuity due shown in Exhibit 6.7B using Equation 6.4, the transformation technique. First, we restate the time line as if the problem were an ordinary annuity; the revised time line looks like the one in Exhibit 6.7A. Second, we calculate the present value of the annuity as if the problem involved an ordinary annuity. The value of the ordinary annuity is $3,312, as shown in part A of the exhibit. Finally, we use Equation 6.4 to make the adjustment to an annuity due:

$$\begin{aligned} \text{Annuity due value} &= \text{Ordinary annuity value} \times (1 + i) \\ &= \$3,312 \times 1.08 \\ &= \$3,577 \end{aligned}$$

As they should, the answers for the two methods of calculation agree.[8]

Before You Go On

1. How do an ordinary annuity, an annuity due, and a perpetuity differ?
2. Give two examples of perpetuities.
3. What is the annuity transformation method?

---

[8]The easy way to calculate the present value or future value of an annuity due is by using the BEG/END switch in your financial calculator. All financial calculators have a key that switches the cash flow from the end of each period to the beginning of each period. The keys are typically labeled "BEG" for cash flows at the beginning of the period and "END" for the cash flows at the end of the period. To calculate the PV of an annuity due: (1) switch the calculator to the BEG mode, (2) enter the data, and (3) press the PV key for the answer. As an example, work the problem from Exhibit 6.7B using your financial calculator.

6.3 Cash Flows That Grow at a Constant Rate

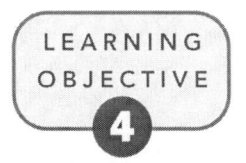

LEARNING OBJECTIVE 4

So far, we have been examining level cash flow streams. Often, though, management needs to value a cash flow stream that increases at a constant rate over time. These cash flow streams are called growing annuities or growing perpetuities.

Growing Annuity

growing annuity
an annuity in which the cash flows increase at a constant rate

Financial managers often need to compute the value of multiyear product or service contracts with cash flows that increase each year at a constant rate. These are called **growing annuities.** For example, you may want to value the cost of a 25-year lease that adjusts annually for the expected rate of inflation over the life of the contract. Equation 6.5 can be used to compute the present value of an annuity growing at a constant rate for a finite time period:

$$\text{PVA}_n = \frac{\text{CF}_1}{i - g} \times \left[1 - \left(\frac{1 + g}{1 + i}\right)^n \right] \qquad (6.5)$$

where:
PVA_n = present value of a growing annuity with n periods
CF_1 = cash flow one period in the future ($t = 1$)
i = interest rate, or discount rate
g = constant growth rate per period

You should be aware of several important points when applying Equation 6.5. First, the cash flow (CF_1) used is not the cash flow for the current period (CF_0), but is the cash flow to be received in the next period ($t = 1$). The relation between these two cash flows is $\text{CF}_1 = \text{CF}_0 \times (1 + g)$. Second, a necessary condition for using Equation 6.5 is that $i > g$. If this condition is not met ($i \leq g$), the calculations from the equation will be meaningless, as you will get a negative value for positive cash flows. A negative value essentially says that someone would have to pay you money to get you to accept a positive cash flow.

As an example of how Equation 6.5 is applied, suppose you work for a company that owns a number of coffee shops in the New York City area. One coffee shop is located in the Empire State Building, and your boss wants to know how much it is worth. The coffee shop has a 50-year lease, so we will assume that it will be in business for 50 years.[9] It produced cash flows of $300,000 after all expenses this year, and the discount rate used by similar businesses is 15 percent. You estimate that, over the long term, cash flows will grow at 2.5 percent per year because of inflation. Thus, you calculate that the coffee shop's cash flow next year (CF_1) will be $307,500, or $300,000 × (1 + 0.025).

Plugging the values from the coffee shop example into Equation 6.5 yields the following result:

$$\text{PVA}_n = \frac{\$307,500}{0.15 - 0.025} \times \left[1 - \left(\frac{1.025}{1.15}\right)^{50} \right]$$
$$= \$2,460,000 \times 0.9968$$
$$= \$2,452,128$$

The estimated value of the coffee shop is $2,452,128.

---

[9]For those interested, the Empire State Building has three coffee shops.

Growing Perpetuity

Sometimes cash flows are expected to grow at a constant rate indefinitely. In this case the cash flow stream is called a **growing perpetuity**. The formula to compute the present value for a growing perpetuity (PVA_∞) is as follows:

$$PVA_\infty = \frac{CF_1}{i - g} \tag{6.6}$$

> **growing perpetuity**
> a cash flow stream that grows at a constant rate forever

As before, CF_1 is the cash flow occurring at the end of the first period, i is the discount rate, and g is the constant rate of growth of the cash flow (CF). Equation 6.6 is an easy equation to work with, and it is used widely in the valuation of common stock for firms that have a policy and history of paying dividends that grow at a constant rate. It is also widely used in the valuation of entire companies, as we will discuss in Chapter 18.

Notice that we can easily derive Equation 6.6 from Equation 6.5 by setting n equal to ∞. If i is greater than g, as we said it must be, the term $[(1 + g)/(1 + i)]^\infty$ is equal to 0, leading to the following result:

$$\begin{aligned} PVA_\infty &= \frac{CF_1}{i - g} \times \left[1 - \left(\frac{1 + g}{1 + i}\right)^\infty\right] \\ &= \frac{CF_1}{i - g} \times [1 - 0] \\ &= \frac{CF_1}{i - g} \end{aligned}$$

This makes sense, of course, since Equation 6.5 describes a growing annuity and Equation 6.6 describes a growing cash flow stream that goes on forever. Notice that Equations 6.5 and 6.6 are exactly the same as Equations 6.1 and 6.3 when g equals zero.

To illustrate a growing perpetuity, we will consider an example. Suppose that you and a partner, after graduating from college, started a health and athletic club. Your concept included not only providing workout facilities, such as weights, treadmills, and elliptical trainers, but also promoting a healthy lifestyle through a focus on cooking and nutrition. The concept has proved popular, and after only five years, you have seven clubs in operation. Your accountant reports that the firm's cash flow last year was $450,000, and the appropriate discount rate for the club is 18 percent. You expect the firm's cash flows to increase by 5 percent per year, which includes 2 percent for expected inflation. The business has no fixed life, so you can assume it will continue operating indefinitely into the future. What is the value of the firm?

We can use Equation 6.6 to solve this problem. Although the equation is very easy to use, a common mistake is using the current period's cash flow (CF_0) and not the *next* period's cash flow (CF_1). Since the cash flow is growing at a constant growth rate, g, we simply multiply CF_0 by $(1 + g)$ to get the value of CF_1. Thus,

$$CF_1 = CF_0 \times (1 + g)$$

We can then substitute the result into Equation 6.6, which yields a helpful variant of this equation:

$$PVA_\infty = \frac{CF_1}{i - g} = \frac{CF_0 \times (1 + g)}{i - g}$$

Now we can insert the values for the health club into the equation and solve for PVA_∞:

$$\begin{aligned} PVA_\infty &= \frac{CF_0 \times (1 + g)}{i - g} \\ &= \frac{\$450{,}000 \times (1 + 0.05)}{0.18 - 0.05} \\ &= \$3{,}634{,}615 \end{aligned}$$

194 CHAPTER 6 | Discounted Cash Flows and Valuation

The business is worth $3,634,615.

The growing annuity and perpetuity formulas are useful, and we will be applying them later on in the book. Unfortunately, even though advanced financial calculators have special programs for annuities and perpetuities with constant cash flows, typical financial calculators do not include programs for growing annuities and perpetuities.

> **Before You Go On**
>
> 1. What is the difference between a growing annuity and a growing perpetuity?

6.4 The Effective Annual Interest Rate

LEARNING OBJECTIVE 5

In this chapter and the preceding one, there has been little question about which interest rate to use in a particular computation. In most cases, a single interest rate was supplied. When working with real market data, however, the situation is not so clear-cut. We often encounter interest rates that can be computed in different ways. In this final section, we try to untangle some of the issues that can cause problems.

Why the Confusion?

> **annual percentage rate (APR)**
> the simple interest rate charged per period multiplied by the number of periods per year

To better understand why interest rates can be so confusing, consider a familiar situation. Suppose you borrow $100 on your bank credit card and plan to keep the balance outstanding for one year. The credit card's stated interest rate is 1 percent per month. The federal Truth-in-Lending Act requires the bank and other financial institutions to disclose to consumers the **annual percentage rate (APR)** charged on a loan. The APR is the annualized interest rate using *simple interest*. Thus, the APR is defined as the simple interest charged per period multiplied by the number of periods per year. For the bank credit card loan, the APR is 12 percent (1 percent per month × 12 months).

At the end of the year, you go to pay off the credit card balance as planned. It seems reasonable to assume that with an APR of 12 percent, your credit card balance at the end of one year would be $112 (1.12 × $100). Wrong! The bank's *actual* interest rate is 1 percent per month, meaning that the bank will compound your credit card balance monthly, 12 times over the year. The bank's calculation for the balance due is $112.68 [$100 × $(1.01)^{12}$].[10] The bank is actually charging you 12.68 percent per year, and the total interest paid for the one-year loan is $12.68 rather than $12.00. This example raises a question: What is the correct way to annualize an interest rate?

Calculating the Effective Annual Interest Rate

> **effective annual interest rate (EAR)**
> the annual interest rate that reflects compounding within a year

In making financial decisions, the correct way to annualize an interest rate is to compute the effective annual interest rate. The **effective annual interest rate (EAR)** is defined as

---

[10] If you have any doubt about the total credit card debt at the end of one year, make the calculation 12 times on your calculator: the first month is $100 × 1.01 = 101.00; the second month is $101.00 × 1.01 = $102.01; the third month is $102.01 × 1.01 = $103.03; and so on for 12 months.

the annual growth rate that takes compounding into account. Mathematically, the EAR can be stated as follows:

$$1 + \text{EAR} = \left(1 + \frac{\text{Quoted interest rate}}{m}\right)^m \quad (6.7)$$

$$\text{EAR} = \left(1 + \frac{\text{Quoted interest rate}}{m}\right)^m - 1$$

where m is the number of compounding periods during a year. The **quoted interest rate** is by definition a *simple* annual interest rate, like the APR. That means that the quoted interest rate has been annualized by multiplying the rate per period by the number of periods per year. The EAR conversion formula accounts for the number of compounding periods and, thus, effectively adjusts the annualized quoted interest rate for the time value of money. Because the EAR is the true cost of borrowing and lending, it is the rate that should be used for making all finance decisions.

We will use our bank credit card example to illustrate the use of Equation 6.7. Recall that the credit card has an APR of 12 percent (1 percent per month). The APR is the quoted interest rate, and the number of compounding periods (m) is 12. Applying Equation 6.7, we find that the effective annual interest rate is:

$$\begin{aligned}\text{EAR} &= \left(1 + \frac{\text{Quoted interest rate}}{m}\right)^m - 1 \\ &= \left(1 + \frac{0.12}{12}\right)^{12} - 1 \\ &= (1.01)^{12} - 1 \\ &= 1.1268 - 1 \\ &= 0.1286, \text{ or } 12.68\%\end{aligned}$$

> **quoted interest rate**
> a simple annual interest rate, such as the APR

> Many useful financial calculators, including an APR calculator, can be found at Efunda.com. Go to www.efunda.com/formulae/finance/apr_calculator.cfm.

The EAR value of 12.68 percent is the true cost of borrowing the $100 on the bank credit card for one year. The EAR calculation adjusts for the effects of compounding and, hence, the time value of money.

Finally, notice that interest rates are quoted in the marketplace in three ways:

1. *The quoted interest rate.* This is an interest rate that has been annualized by multiplying the rate per period by the number of compounding periods. The APR is an example. All consumer borrowing and lending rates are annualized in this manner.

2. *The interest rate per period.* The bank credit card rate of 1 percent per month is an example of this kind of rate. You can find the interest rate per period by dividing the quoted interest rate by the number of compounding periods.

3. *The effective annual interest rate (EAR).* This is the interest rate actually paid (or earned), which takes compounding into account. Sometimes it is difficult to distinguish a quoted rate from an EAR. Generally, however, an annualized consumer rate is an APR rather than an EAR.

Comparing Interest Rates

When borrowing or lending money, it is sometimes necessary to compare and select among interest rate alternatives. Quoted interest rates are comparable when they cover the same overall time period, such as one year, and have the same number of compounding periods. If quoted interest rates are *not* comparable, we must adjust them to a common time period. The easiest way, and the correct way, to make interest rates comparable for making finance decisions is to convert them to effective annual interest rates. Consider an example.

Suppose you are the chief financial officer of a manufacturing company. The company is planning a $1 billion plant expansion and will finance it by borrowing money for five years. Three financial institutions have submitted interest rate quotes; all are APRs:

Lender A: 10.40 percent compound monthly

Lender B: 10.90 percent compounded annually

Lender C: 10.50 percent compounded quarterly

Although all the loans have the same maturity, the loans are not comparable because the APRs have different compounding periods. To make the adjustments for the different time periods, we apply Equation 6.7 to convert each of the APR quotes into an EAR:

$$\text{Lender A: EAR} = \left(1 + \frac{0.1040}{12}\right)^{12} - 1$$
$$= (1.0087)^{12} - 1$$
$$= 1.1091 - 1$$
$$= 0.1091, \text{ or } 10.91\%$$

$$\text{Lender B: EAR} = \left(1 + \frac{0.1090}{1}\right)^{1} - 1$$
$$= 1.1090 - 1$$
$$= 0.1090, \text{ or } 10.90\%$$

$$\text{Lender C: EAR} = \left(1 + \frac{0.1050}{4}\right)^{4} - 1$$
$$= (1.0263)^{4} - 1$$
$$= 1.1092 - 1$$
$$= 0.1092, \text{ or } 10.92\%$$

As shown, Lender B offers the lowest interest cost at 10.90 percent.

Notice the shift in rankings that takes place as a result of the EAR calculations. When we initially looked at the APR quotes, it appeared that Lender A offered the lowest rate and Lender B had the highest. After computing the EAR, we find that when we account for the effect of compounding, Lender B actually offers the lowest interest rate.

Another important point is that if all the interest rates are quoted as APRs with the same annualizing period, such as monthly, the interest rates are comparable and you can select the correct rate by simply comparing the quotes. That is, the lowest APR corresponds with the lowest cost of funds. Thus, it is correct for borrowers or lenders to make economic decisions with APR data as long as interest rates have the same maturity and the same compounding period. To find the true cost of the loan, however, it is still necessary to compute the EAR.

LEARNING BY DOING
APPLICATION 6.8

What Is the True Cost of a Loan?

Problem: During a period of economic expansion, Frank Smith became financially overextended and was forced to consolidate his debt with a loan from a consumer finance company. The consolidated debt provided Frank with a single loan and lower monthly payments than he had previously been making. The loan agreement quotes an APR of 20 percent, and Frank must make monthly payments. What is the true cost of the loan?

Approach: The true cost of the loan is the EAR, not the APR. Thus, we must convert the quoted rate into the EAR, using Equation 6.7, to get the true cost of the loan.

Solution:

$$\text{EAR} = \left(1 + \frac{\text{Quoted interest rate}}{m}\right)^m - 1$$
$$= \left(1 + \frac{0.20}{12}\right)^{12} - 1$$
$$= (1 + 0.0167)^{12} - 1$$
$$= (1.0167)^{12} - 1$$
$$= 1.2194 - 1$$
$$= 0.2194, \text{ or } 21.94\%$$

The true cost of the loan is 21.94 percent, not the 20 percent APR.

Consumer Protection Acts and Interest Rate Disclosure

In 1968 Congress passed the **Truth-in-Lending Act** to ensure that all borrowers receive meaningful information about the cost of credit so that they can make intelligent economic decisions.[11] The act applies to all lenders that extend credit to consumers, and it covers credit card loans, auto loans, home mortgage loans, home equity loans, home improvement loans, and some small-business loans. Similar legislation, the so-called **Truth-in-Savings Act,** applies to consumer savings vehicles such as certificates of deposit (CDs). These two pieces of legislation require by law that the APR be disclosed on all consumer loans and savings plans and that it be prominently displayed on advertising and contractual documents.

We know that the EAR, not the APR, represents the true economic interest rate. So why did the Truth-in-Lending and Truth-in-Savings Acts specify that the APR must be the disclosed rate? The APR was selected because it's easy to calculate and easy to understand. When the legislation was passed in 1969, computers were still using punch cards, and PCs and handheld calculators did not exist.[12] Down at the auto showroom, salespeople needed an easy way to explain and annualize the monthly interest charge, and the APR provided just such a method. And most important, if all the auto lenders quoted monthly APR, consumers could select the loan with the lowest economic interest cost.

Today, although lenders and borrowers are legally required to quote the APR, they run their businesses using interest rate calculations based on the present value and future value formulas. Consumers are bombarded with both APR and EAR rates, and confusion reigns. At the car dealership, for example, you may find that your auto loan's APR is 5 percent but the "actual borrowing rate" is 5.12 percent. And at the bank where your grandmother gets free coffee and doughnuts, she may be told that the bank's one-year CD has an APR of 3 percent, but it really pays 3.04 percent. Because of confusion arising from conflicting interest rates in the marketplace, some observers believe that the APR calculation has outlived its usefulness and should be abandoned by regulators and replaced by the EAR.

Truth-in-Lending Act
a federal law requiring lenders to fully inform borrowers of important information related to loans, including the annual percentage rate charged

Truth-in-Savings Act
a federal law requiring institutions offering consumer savings vehicles, such as certificates of deposit (CDs), to fully inform consumers of important information about the savings vehicles, including the annual percentage rate paid

The Appropriate Interest Rate Factor

Here is a final question to consider: What is the appropriate interest rate to use when making future or present value calculations? The answer is simple: use the EAR. Under no circumstance should the APR or any other quoted rate be used as the interest rate

---

[11] The Truth-in-Lending Act is Title I of the Consumer Credit Protection Act.

[12] The first handheld calculator was the Bomar Brain, which was first sold in 1971.

in present or future value calculations. Consider an example of using the EAR in such a calculation.

Petra, an MBA student at Georgetown University, has purchased a $100 savings note with a two-year maturity from a small consumer finance company. The contract states that the note has a 20 percent APR and pays interest quarterly. The quarterly interest rate is thus 5 percent (20 percent/4). Petra has several questions about the note: (1) What is the note's actual interest rate (EAR)? (2) How much money will she have at the end of two years? (3) When making the future value calculation, should she use the quarterly interest rate or the annual EAR?

To answer Petra's questions, we first compute the EAR, which is the actual interest earned on the note:

$$\begin{aligned} \text{EAR} &= \left(1 + \frac{\text{APR}}{m}\right)^m - 1 \\ &= \left(1 + \frac{0.20}{4}\right)^4 - 1 \\ &= (1 + 0.05)^4 - 1 \\ &= 1.21551 - 1 \\ &= 0.21551, \text{ or } 21.551\% \end{aligned}$$

Next, we calculate the future value of the note using the EAR. Because the EAR is an annual rate, for this problem we use a total of two compounding periods. The calculation is as follows:

$$\begin{aligned} \text{FV}_2 &= \text{PV} \times (1 + i)^n \\ &= \$100 \times (1 + 0.21551)^2 \\ &= \$100 \times 1.4775 \\ &= \$147.75 \end{aligned}$$

We can also calculate the future value using the quarterly rate of interest of 5 percent with a total of eight compounding periods. In this case, the calculation is as follows:

$$\begin{aligned} \text{FV}_2 &= \$100 \times (1 + 0.050)^8 \\ &= \$100 \times 1.4775 \\ &= \$147.75 \end{aligned}$$

The two calculation methods yield the same answer, $147.75.

In sum, any time you do a future value or present value calculation, you must use either the interest rate per period (quoted rate/m) or the EAR as the interest rate factor. It does not matter which of these you use. Both will properly account for the impact of compounding on the value of cash flows. Interest rate proxies such as the APR should never be used as interest rate factors for calculating future or present values. Because they do not properly account for the number of compounding periods, their use can lead to answers that are economically incorrect.

> **Before You Go On**
>
> 1. What is the APR, and why are lending institutions required to disclose this rate?
> 2. What is the correct way to annualize an interest rate in financial decision making?
> 3. Distinguish between quoted interest rate, interest rate per period, and effective annual interest rate.

Summary of Learning Objectives

1. **Explain why cash flows occurring at different times must be adjusted to reflect their value as of a common date before they can be compared, and be able to compute the present value and future value for multiple cash flows.**

   When making decisions involving cash flows over time, we should first identify the magnitude and timing of the cash flows and then adjust each individual cash flow to reflect its value as of a common date. For example, the process of discounting (compounding) the cash flows adjusts them for the time value of money because today's dollars are not equal in value to dollars in the future. Once all of the cash flows are in present (future) value terms, they can be compared to make decisions. Section 6.1 discusses the computation of present values and future values of multiple cash flows.

2. **Describe how to calculate the present value of an ordinary annuity and how an ordinary annuity differs from an annuity due.**

   An ordinary annuity is a series of equally spaced, level cash flows over time. The cash flows for an ordinary annuity are assumed to take place at the end of each period. To find the present value of an ordinary annuity, we multiply the present value of an annuity factor, which is equal to (1 − present value factor)/i, by the amount of the constant cash flow. An annuity due is an annuity in which the cash flows occur at the beginning of each period. A lease is an example of an annuity due. In this case, we are effectively prepaying for the service. To calculate the value of an annuity due, we calculate the present value (or future value) as though the cash flows were an ordinary annuity. We then multiply the ordinary annuity value times (1 + i). Section 6.2 discusses the calculation of the present value of an ordinary annuity and annuity due.

3. **Explain what a perpetuity is and how it is used in business, and be able to calculate the value of a perpetuity.**

   A perpetuity is like an annuity except that the cash flows are perpetual—they never end. British Treasury Department bonds, called consols, were the first widely used securities of this kind. The most common example of a perpetuity today is preferred stock. The issuer of preferred stock promises to pay fixed-rate dividends forever. To calculate the present value of a perpetuity, we simply divide the promised constant payment (CF) by the interest rate (i).

4. **Discuss growing annuities and perpetuities, as well as their application in business, and be able to calculate their value.**

   Financial managers often need to value cash flow streams that increase at a constant rate over time. These cash flow streams are called growing annuities or growing perpetuities. An example of a growing annuity is a 10-year lease contract with an annual adjustment for the expected rate of inflation over the life of the contract. If the cash flows continue to grow at a constant rate indefinitely, this cash flow stream is called a growing perpetuity. Application and calculation of cash flows that grow at a constant rate are discussed in Section 6.3.

5. **Discuss why the effective annual interest rate (EAR) is the appropriate way to annualize interest rates, and be able to calculate EAR.**

   The EAR is the annual growth rate that takes compounding into account. Thus, the EAR is the true cost of borrowing or lending money. When we need to compare interest rates, we must make sure that the rates to be compared have the same time and compounding periods. If interest rates are not comparable, they must be converted into common terms. The easiest way to convert rates to common terms is to calculate the EAR for each interest rate. The use and calculations of EAR are discussed in Section 6.4.

Summary of Key Equations

Equation	Description	Formula
6.1	Present value of an ordinary annuity	$PVA_n = \dfrac{CF}{i} \times \left[1 - \dfrac{1}{(1+i)^n}\right]$ $= CF \times \dfrac{1 - 1/(1+i)^n}{i}$ $= CF \times \dfrac{1 - \text{Present value factor}}{i}$ $= CF \times \text{PV annuity factor}$
6.2	Future value of an ordinary annuity	$FVA_n = \dfrac{CF}{i} \times \left[(1+i)^n - 1\right]$ $= CF \times \dfrac{(1+i)^n - 1}{i}$

200 CHAPTER 6 | Discounted Cash Flows and Valuation

$$= CF \times \frac{\text{Future value factor} - 1}{i}$$
$$= CF \times \text{FV annuity factor}$$

6.3	Present value of a perpetuity	$PVA_\infty = \dfrac{CF}{i}$
6.4	Value of an annuity due	Annuity due value = Ordinary annuity value $\times (1 + i)$
6.5	Present value of a growing annuity	$PVA_n = \dfrac{CF_1}{i - g} \times \left[1 - \left(\dfrac{1 + g}{1 + i}\right)^n\right]$
6.6	Present value of a growing perpetuity	$PVA_\infty = \dfrac{CF_1}{i - g}$
6.7	Effective annual interest rate	$EAR = \left(1 + \dfrac{\text{Quoted interest rate}}{m}\right)^m - 1$

Self-Study Problems

6.1 Kronka, Inc., is expecting cash flows of $13,000, $11,500, $12,750, and $9,635 over the next four years. What is the present value of these cash flows if the appropriate discount rate is 8 percent?

6.2 Your grandfather has agreed to deposit a certain amount of money each year into an account paying 7.25 percent annually to help you go to graduate school. Starting next year, and for the following four years, he plans to deposit $2,250, $8,150, $7,675, $6,125, and $12,345 into the account. How much will you have at the end of the five years?

6.3 Mike White is planning to save up for a trip to Europe in three years. He will need $7,500 when he is ready to make the trip. He plans to invest the same amount at the end of each of the next three years in an account paying 6 percent. What is the amount that he will have to save every year to reach his goal of $7,500 in three years?

6.4 Becky Scholes has $150,000 to invest. She wants to be able to withdraw $12,500 every year forever without using up any of her principal. What interest rate would her investment have to earn in order for her to be able to so?

6.5 Dynamo Corp. is expecting annual payments of $34,225 for the next seven years from a customer. What is the present value of this annuity if the discount rate is 8.5 percent?

Solutions to Self-Study Problems

6.1 The time line for Kronka's cash flows and their present value is as follows:

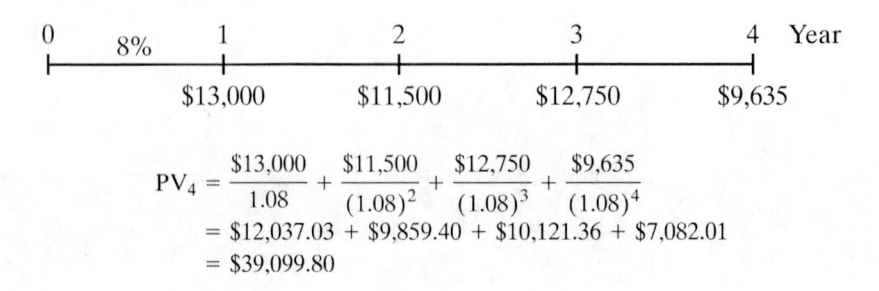

```
0        1         2         3         4    Year
   8%
         $13,000  $11,500   $12,750   $9,635
```

$$PV_4 = \frac{\$13{,}000}{1.08} + \frac{\$11{,}500}{(1.08)^2} + \frac{\$12{,}750}{(1.08)^3} + \frac{\$9{,}635}{(1.08)^4}$$
$$= \$12{,}037.03 + \$9{,}859.40 + \$10{,}121.36 + \$7{,}082.01$$
$$= \$39{,}099.80$$

6.2 The time line for your cash flows and their future value is as follows:

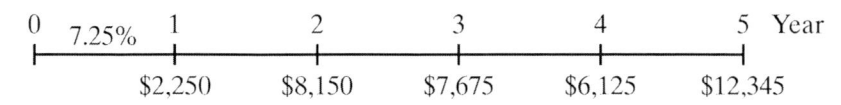

```
0    7.25%   1         2         3         4         5 Year
|------------|---------|---------|---------|---------|
           $2,250    $8,150    $7,675    $6,125   $12,345
```

$FV_5 = \$2{,}250 \times (1.0725)^4 + \$8{,}150 \times (1.0725)^3 + \$7{,}675 \times (1.0725)^2 + \$6{,}125 \times 1.0725 + \$12{,}345$
$= \$2{,}976.95 + \$10{,}054.25 + \$8{,}828.22 + \$6{,}569.06 + \$12{,}345.00$
$= \$40{,}773.48$

6.3 Amount Mike White will need in three years = FVA_3 = $7,500
Number of years = $n = 3$
Interest rate on investment = $i = 6.0\%$
Amount that Mike needs to invest every year = PMT = ?

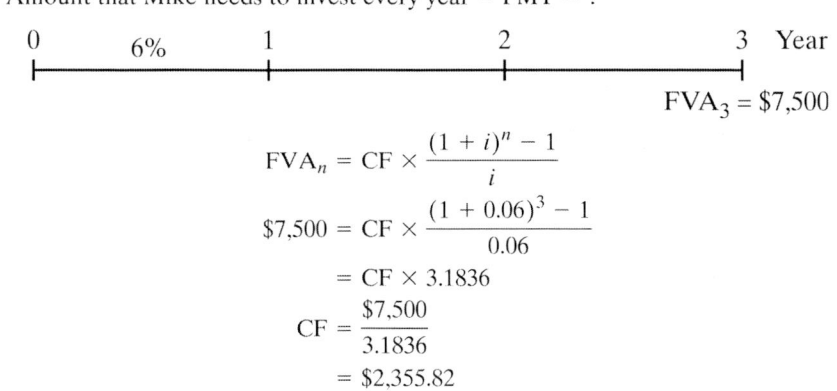

```
0      6%      1         2         3 Year
|--------------|---------|---------|
                              FVA₃ = $7,500
```

$$FVA_n = CF \times \frac{(1+i)^n - 1}{i}$$

$$\$7{,}500 = CF \times \frac{(1+0.06)^3 - 1}{0.06}$$

$$= CF \times 3.1836$$

$$CF = \frac{\$7{,}500}{3.1836}$$

$$= \$2{,}355.82$$

Mike will have to invest $2,355.82 every year for the next three years.

6.4 Present value of Becky Scholes's investment = $150,000
Amount needed annually = $12,500
This is a perpetuity!

$$PVA_\infty = \frac{CF}{i}$$

$$i = \frac{CF}{PVA_\infty} = \frac{\$12{,}500}{\$150{,}000}$$

$$i = 8.33\%$$

6.5 The time line for Dynamo's cash flows and their present value is as follows:

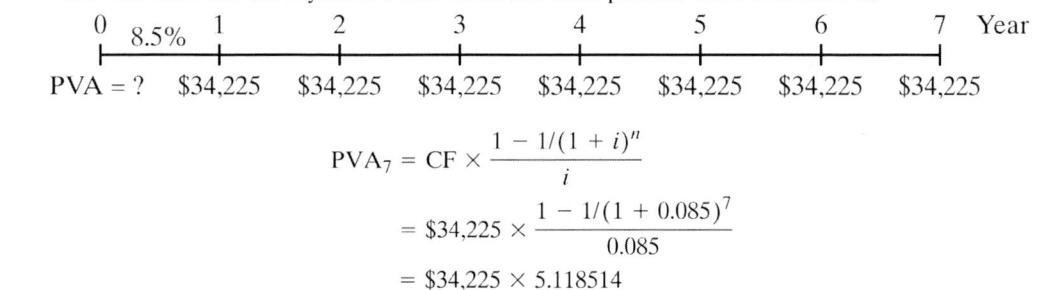

```
0    8.5%   1         2         3         4         5         6         7 Year
|-----------|---------|---------|---------|---------|---------|---------|
PVA=?    $34,225   $34,225   $34,225   $34,225   $34,225   $34,225   $34,225
```

$$PVA_7 = CF \times \frac{1 - 1/(1+i)^n}{i}$$

$$= \$34{,}225 \times \frac{1 - 1/(1+0.085)^7}{0.085}$$

$$= \$34{,}225 \times 5.118514$$

$$= \$175{,}181.14$$

Critical Thinking Questions

6.1 Identify the steps involved in computing the future value when you have multiple cash flows.

6.2 What is the key economic principle involved in calculating the present value and future value of multiple cash flows?

6.3 What is the difference between a perpetuity and an annuity?

6.4 Define *annuity due*. Would an investment be worth more if it were an ordinary annuity or an annuity due? Explain.

6.5 Raymond Bartz is trying to choose between two equally risky annuities, each paying $5,000 per year for five years. One is an ordinary annuity, the other is an annuity due. Which of the following statements is most correct?
  a. The present value of the ordinary annuity must exceed the present value of the annuity due, but the future value of an ordinary annuity may be less than the future value of the annuity due.
  b. The present value of the annuity due exceeds the present value of the ordinary annuity, while the future value of the annuity due is less than the future value of the ordinary annuity.
  c. The present value of the annuity due exceeds the present value of the ordinary annuity, and the future value of the annuity due also exceeds the future value of the ordinary annuity.
  d. If interest rates increase, the difference between the present value of the ordinary annuity and the present value of the annuity due remains the same.

6.6 Which of the following investments will have the highest future value at the end of three years? Assume that the effective annual rate for all investments is the same.
  a. You earn $3,000 at the end of three years (a total of one payment).
  b. You earn $1,000 at the end of every year for the next three years (a total of three payments).
  c. You earn $1,000 at the beginning of every year for the next three years (a total of three payments).

6.7 Explain whether or not each of the following statements is correct.
  a. A 15-year mortgage will have larger monthly payments than a 30-year mortgage of the same amount and same interest rate.
  b. If an investment pays 10 percent interest compounded annually, its effective rate will also be 10 percent.

6.8 When will the annual percentage rate (APR) be the same as the effective annual rate (EAR)?

6.9 Why is the EAR superior to the APR in measuring the true economic cost or return?

6.10 Suppose two investments have equal lives and multiple cash flows. A high discount rate tends to favor
  a. the investment with large cash flows early.
  b. the investment with large cash flows late.
  c. the investment with even cash flows.
  d. neither investment since they have equal lives.

Questions and Problems

BASIC

6.1 Future value with multiple cash flows: Konerko, Inc., expects to earn cash flows of $13,227, $15,611, $18,970, and $19,114 over the next four years. If the company uses an 8 percent discount rate, what is the future value of these cash flows at the end of year 4?

6.2 Future value with multiple cash flows: Ben Woolmer has an investment that will pay him the following cash flows over the next five years: $2,350, $2,725, $3,128, $3,366, and $3,695. If his investments typically earn 7.65 percent, what is the future value of the investment's cash flows at the end of five years?

6.3 Future value with multiple cash flows: You are a freshman in college and are planning a trip to Europe when you graduate from college at the end of four years. You plan to save the following amounts annually, starting today: $625, $700, $700, and $750. If the account pays 5.75 percent annually, how much will you have at the end of four years?

6.4 Present value with multiple cash flows: Saul Cervantes has just purchased some equipment for his landscaping business. He plans to pay the following amounts at the end of each of the next five years: $10,450, $8,500, $9,675, $12,500, and $11,635. If he uses a discount rate of 10.875 percent, what is the cost of the equipment he purchased today?

6.5 Present value with multiple cash flows: Jeremy Fenloch borrowed a certain amount from his friend and promised to repay him the amounts of $1,225, $1,350, $1,500, $1,600, and

$1,600 over the next five years. If the friend normally discounts investments at 8 percent annually, how much did Jeremy borrow?

6.6 Present value with multiple cash flows: Biogenesis Inc. expects the following cash flow stream over the next five years. The company discounts all cash flows at a 23 percent discount rate. What is the present value of this cash flow stream?

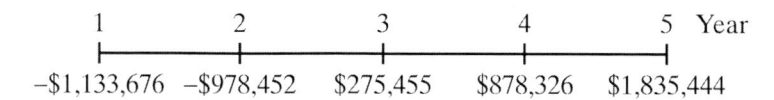

1	2	3	4	5 Year
−$1,133,676	−$978,452	$275,455	$878,326	$1,835,444

6.7 Present value of an ordinary annuity: An investment opportunity requires a payment of $750 for 12 years, starting a year from today. If your required rate of return is 8 percent, what is the value of the investment today?

6.8 Present value of an ordinary annuity: Dynamics Telecommunications Corp. has made an investment in another company that will guarantee it a cash flow of $22,500 each year for the next five years. If the company uses a discount rate of 15 percent on its investments, what is the present value of this investment?

6.9 Future value of an ordinary annuity: Robert Hobbes plans to invest $25,000 a year at the end of each year for the next seven years in an investment that will pay him a rate of return of 11.4 percent. How much money will Hobbes have at the end of seven years?

6.10 Future value of an ordinary annuity: Cecelia Thomas is a sales executive at a Baltimore firm. She is 25 years old and plans to invest $3,000 every year in an IRA account, beginning at the end of this year until she turns 65 years old. If the IRA investment will earn 9.75 percent annually, how much will she have in 40 years, when she turns 65 years old?

6.11 Future value of an annuity due: Refer to Problem 6.10. If Cecelia Thomas invests at the beginning of each year, how much will she have at age 65?

6.12 Computing annuity payment: Kevin Winthrop is saving for an Australian vacation in three years. He estimates that he will need $5,000 to cover his airfare and all other expenses for a week-long holiday in Australia. If he can invest his money in an S&P 500 equity index fund that is expected to earn an average return of 10.3 percent over the next three years, how much will he have to save every year if he starts saving at the end of this year?

6.13 Computing annuity payment: The Elkridge Bar & Grill has a seven-year loan of $23,500 with Bank of America. It plans to repay the loan in seven equal installments starting today. If the rate of interest is 8.4 percent, how much will each payment be worth?

6.14 Perpetuity: Your grandfather is retiring at the end of next year. He would like to ensure that he, and after he dies, his heirs receive payments of $10,000 a year forever, starting when he retires. If he can invest at 6.5 percent, how much does your grandfather need to invest to receive the desired cash flow?

6.15 Perpetuity: Calculate the perpetuity payments for each of the following cases:
a. $250,000 invested at 6 percent.
b. $50,000 invested at 12 percent.
c. $100,000 invested at 10 percent.

6.16 Effective annual interest rate: Raj Krishnan bought a Honda Accord for a price of $17,345. He put down $6,000 and financed the rest through the dealer at an APR of 4.9 percent for four years. What is the effective annual interest rate (EAR) if payments are made monthly?

6.17 Effective annual interest rate: Cyclone Rentals borrowed $15,550 from a bank for three years. If the quoted rate (APR) is 6.75 percent, and the compounding is daily, what is the effective annual interest rate (EAR)?

6.18 Growing perpetuity: You are evaluating a growing perpetuity product from a large financial services firm. The product promises an initial payment of $20,000 at the end of this year and subsequent payments will thereafter grow at a rate of 3.4 percent annually. If you use a 9 percent discount rate for investment products, what is the present value of this growing perpetuity?

6.19 Future value with multiple cash flows: Trigen Corp. is expecting to invest cash flows of $331,000, $616,450, $212,775, $818,400, $1,239,644, and $1,617,848 in research and development over the next six years. If the appropriate interest rate is 6.75 percent, what is the future value of these investment cash flows?

INTERMEDIATE

6.20 Future value with multiple cash flows: Stephanie Watson plans to adopt the following investment pattern beginning next year. She will invest $3,125 in each of the next three years and will then make investments of $3,650, $3,725, $3,875, and $4,000 over the following four years. If the investments are expected to earn 11.5 percent annually, how much will she have at the end of the seven years?

6.21 Present value with multiple cash flows: Carol Jenkins, a lottery winner, will receive the following payments over the next seven years. If she can invest her cash flows in a fund that will earn 10.5 percent annually, what is the present value of her winnings?

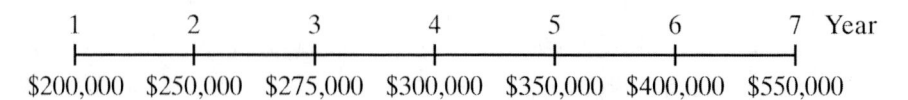

```
   1         2         3         4         5         6         7    Year
   |         |         |         |         |         |         |
$200,000  $250,000  $275,000  $300,000  $350,000  $400,000  $550,000
```

6.22 Computing annuity payment: Gary Whitmore is a high school sophomore. He currently has $7,500 in a savings account that pays 5.65 percent annually. Gary plans to use his current savings plus what he can save over the next four years to buy a car. He estimates that the car will cost $12,000 in four years. How much money should Gary save each year if he wants to buy the car?

6.23 Growing annuity: Modern Energy Company owns several gas stations. Management is looking to open a new station in the western suburbs of Baltimore. One possibility they are evaluating is to take over a station located at a site that has been leased from the county. The lease, originally for 99 years, currently has 73 years before expiration. The gas station generated a net cash flow of $92,500 last year, and the current owners expect an annual growth rate of 6.3 percent. If Modern Energy uses a discount rate of 14.5 percent to evaluate such businesses, what is the present value of this growing annuity?

6.24 Future value of annuity due: Jeremy Denham plans to save $5,000 every year for the next eight years, starting today. At the end of eight years, Jeremy will turn 30 years old and plans to use his savings toward the down payment on a house. If his investment in a mutual fund will earn him 10.3 percent annually, how much will he have saved in eight years when he will need the money to buy a house?

6.25 Present value of an annuity due: Grant Productions has borrowed a huge sum from the California Finance Company at a rate of 17.5 percent for a seven-year period. The loan calls for a payment of $1,540,862.19 each year beginning today. What is the amount borrowed by this company? Round to the nearest dollar.

6.26 Present value of an annuity due: Sharon Kabana has won a state lottery and will receive a payment of $89,729.45 every year, starting today, for the next 20 years. If she invests the proceeds at a rate of 7.25 percent, what is the present value of the cash flows that she will receive? Round to the nearest dollar.

6.27 Perpetuity: Calculate the present value of the following perpetuities:
 a. $1,250 discounted to the present at 7 percent.
 b. $7,250 discounted to the present at 6.33 percent.
 c. $850 discounted to the present at 20 percent.

6.28 Effective annual interest rate: Find the effective annual interest rate (EAR) on each of the following:
 a. 6 percent compounded quarterly.   c. 7.25 percent compounded semiannually.
 b. 4.99 percent compounded monthly.   d. 5.6 percent compounded daily.

6.29 Effective annual interest rate: Which of the following investments has the highest effective annual interest rate (EAR)?
 a. A bank CD that pays 8.25 percent compounded quarterly.
 b. A bank CD that pays 8.25 percent compounded monthly.
 c. A bank CD that pays 8.45 percent compounded annually.
 d. A bank CD that pays 8.25 percent compounded semiannually.
 e. A bank CD that pays 8 percent compounded daily (on a 365-day basis).

6.30 Effective annual interest rate: You are considering three alternative investments: (1) a three-year bank CD paying 7.5 percent compounded quarterly; (2) a three-year bank CD paying 7.3 percent compounded monthly; and (3) a three-year bank CD paying 7.75 percent compounded annually. Which investment has the highest effective annual interest rate?

ADVANCED

EXCEL®

6.31 Tirade Owens, a professional athlete, currently has a contract that will pay him a large amount in the first year of his contract and smaller amounts thereafter. He and his agent have asked the team to restructure the contract. The team, though reluctant, obliged. Tirade and his agent came up with a counter offer. What are the present values of each of the contracts using a 14 percent discount rate? Which of the three contacts has the highest present value?

Year	Current Contract	Team's Offer	Counter Offer
1	$8,125,000	$4,000,000	$5,250,000
2	$3,650,000	$3,825,000	$7,550,000
3	$2,715,000	$3,850,000	$3,625,000
4	$1,822,250	$3,925,000	$2,800,000

6.32 Gary Kornig will be 30 years old next year and wants to retire when he is 65. So far he has saved (1) $6,950 in an IRA account in which his money is earning 8.3 percent annually and (2) $5,000 in a money market account in which he is earning 5.25 percent annually. Gary wants to have $1 million when he retires. Starting next year, he plans to invest a fixed amount of money every year until he retires in a mutual fund in which he expects to earn 9 percent annually. How much will Gary have to invest every year to achieve his savings goal?

6.33 Babu Baradwaj is saving for his son's college tuition. His son is currently 11 years old and will begin college in seven years. Babu has an index fund investment worth $7,500 that is earning 9.5 percent annually. Total expenses at the University of Maryland, where his son says he plans to go, currently total $15,000 per year, but are expected to grow at roughly 6 percent each year. Babu plans to invest in a mutual fund that will earn 11 percent annually to make up the difference between the college expenses and his current savings. In total, Babu will make seven equal investments with the first starting today and with the last being made a year before his son begins college.
   a. What will be the present value of the four years of college expenses at the time that Babu's son starts college? Assume a discount rate of 5.5 percent.
   b. What will be the value of the index mutual fund when his son just starts college?
   c. What is the amount that Babu will have to have saved when his son turns 18 if Babu plans to cover all of his son's college expenses?
   d. How much will Babu have to invest every year in order to have enough funds to cover all his son's expenses?

6.34 You are now 50 years old and plan to retire at age 65. You currently have a stock portfolio worth $150,000, a 401(k) retirement plan worth $250,000, and a money market account worth $50,000. Your stock portfolio is expected to provide you annual returns of 12 percent, your 401(k) investment will earn you 9.5 percent annually, and the money market account earns 5.25 percent, compounded monthly.
   a. If you do not save another penny, what will be the total value of your investments when you retire at age 65?
   b. Assume you plan to invest $12,000 every year in your 401(k) plan for the next 15 years (starting one year from now). How much will your investments be worth when you retire at 65?
   c. Assume that you expect to live 25 years after you retire (until age 90). Today, at age 50, you take all of your investments and place them in an account that pays 8 percent (use the scenario from part b in which you continue saving). If you start withdrawing funds starting at age 66, how much can you withdraw every year (e.g., an ordinary annuity) and leave nothing in your account after a 25th and final withdrawal at age 90?
   d. You want your current investments, which are described in the problem statement, to support a perpetuity that starts a year from now. How much can you withdraw each year without touching your principal?

6.35 Trevor Diaz is looking to purchase a Mercedes Benz SL600 Roadster, which has an invoice price of $121,737 and a total cost of $129,482. Trevor plans to put down $20,000 and will pay the rest by taking on a 5.75 percent five-year bank loan. What is the monthly payment on this auto loan? Prepare an amortization table using Excel.

6.36 The Sundarams are buying a new 3,500-square-foot house in Muncie, Indiana, and will borrow $237,000 from Bank One at a rate of 6.375 percent for 15 years. What is their monthly loan payment? Prepare an amortization schedule using Excel.

6.37 Assume you will start on a job as soon as you graduate. You plan to start saving for your retirement when you turn 25 years old. Assume you are 21 years of age at the time of graduation. Everybody needs a break! Currently, you plan to retire when you turn 65 years old. After retirement, you expect to live at least until you are 85. You wish to be able to withdraw $40,000 (in today's dollars) every year from the time of your retirement until you are 85 years old (i.e., for 20 years). You can invest, starting when you turn 25 years old, in a portfolio fund. The average inflation rate is likely to be 5 percent.

a. Calculate the lump sum you need to have accumulated at age 65 to be able to draw the desired income. Assume that your return on the portfolio investment is likely to be 10 percent.

b. What is the dollar amount you need to invest every year, starting at age 26 and ending at age 65 (i.e., for 40 years) to reach the target lump sum at age 65?

c. Now answer questions a and b assuming your rate of return to be 8 percent per year, then again at 15 percent per year.

d. Now assume you start investing for your retirement when you turn 30 years old and analyze the situation under rate of return assumptions of (i) 8 percent, (ii) 10 percent, and (iii) 15 percent.

e. Repeat the analysis by assuming that you start investing when you are 35 years old.

Sample Test Problems

6.1 Groves Corp. is expecting annual cash flows of $225,000, $278,000, $312,500, and $410,000 over the next four years. If it uses a discount rate of 6.25 percent, what will be the present value of this cash flow stream?

6.2 Freisinger, Inc., is expecting a new project to start paying off, beginning at the end of next year. It expects cash flows to be as follows:

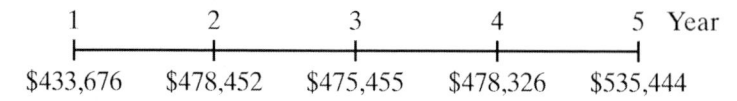

```
     1         2         3         4         5    Year
     |         |         |         |         |
  $433,676  $478,452  $475,455  $478,326  $535,444
```

If Freisinger can reinvest these cash flows to earn a return of 7.8 percent, what is the future value of this cash flow stream at the end of five years?

6.3 Vancouver, Canada is the site of the next Winter Olympics in 2010. City officials plan to build a new multipurpose stadium. The projected cost of the stadium in 2010 dollars is $7.5 million. Assume that it is 2007 and city officials intend to put away a certain amount at the end of each of the next three years in an account that will pay 8.75 percent. What is the annual payment necessary to meet the projected cost of the stadium?

6.4 You have just won a lottery that promises an annual payment of $118,312 beginning immediately. You will receive a total of 10 payments. If you can invest the cash flows in an investment paying 7.65 percent annually, what is the present value of this annuity?

6.5 Which of the following investments has the highest effective annual interest rate (EAR)?
a. A bank CD that pays 5.50 percent compounded quarterly.
b. A bank CD that pays 5.45 percent compounded monthly.
c. A bank CD that pays 5.65 percent compounded annually.
d. A bank CD that pays 5.55 percent compounded semiannually.
e. A bank CD that pays 5.35 percent compounded daily (on a 365-day basis).

Appendix: Deriving the Formula for the Present Value of an Ordinary Annuity

In this chapter we showed that the formula for a perpetuity can be obtained from the formula for the present value of an ordinary annuity if n is set equal to ∞. It is also possible to go the other way. In other words, the present value of an ordinary annuity formula can be derived from the formula for a perpetuity. In fact, this is how the annuity formula was originally obtained. To see how this was done, assume that someone has offered to pay you $1 per year forever, beginning next year, but that, in return, you will have to pay that person $1 per year forever, beginning in year $n + 1$.

The cash flows you will receive and the cash flows you will pay are represented in the following time line:

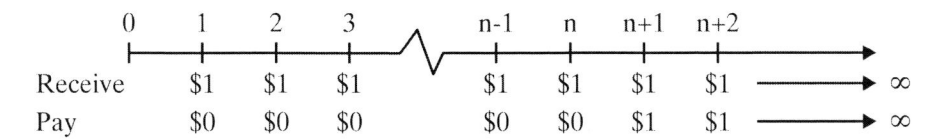

```
        0     1     2     3        n-1    n    n+1   n+2
        |-----|-----|-----|--/\----|-----|-----|-----|-----------> ∞
Receive      $1    $1    $1       $1    $1    $1    $1  --------> ∞
Pay          $0    $0    $0       $0    $0    $1    $1  --------> ∞
```

The first row of dollar values shows the cash flows for the perpetuity that you will receive. This perpetuity is worth:

$$PVA_{\infty,Receive} = \frac{\$1}{i} = \frac{CF}{i}$$

The second row shows the cash flows for the perpetuity that you will pay. The present value of what you owe is the value of a $1 perpetuity that is discounted for n years.

$$PVA_{\infty,Pay} = \frac{\$1/i}{(1+i)^n} = \frac{CF/i}{(1+i)^n}$$

Notice that if you subtract, year by year, the cash flows you would pay from the cash flows you would receive, you get the cash flows for an n-year annuity.

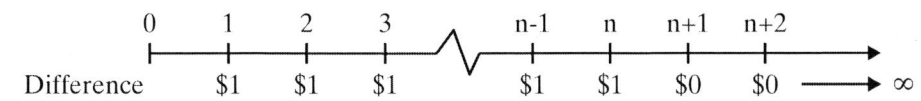

```
            0     1     2     3        n-1    n    n+1   n+2
            |-----|-----|-----|--/\----|-----|-----|-----|-----------> ∞
Difference       $1    $1    $1       $1    $1    $0    $0  --------> ∞
```

Therefore, the value of the offer equals the value of an n-year annuity. Solving for the difference between $PVA_{\infty,Receive}$ from $PVA_{\infty,Pay}$ we see that this is the same as Equation 6.1.

$$PVA_n = PVA_{\infty,Receive} - PVA_{\infty,Pay}$$

$$= \frac{CF}{i} - \frac{CF/i}{(1+i)^n}$$

$$= \frac{CF}{i} \times \left[1 - \frac{1}{(1+i)^n}\right]$$

Problem

6A.1 In the chapter text, you saw that the formula for a growing perpetuity can be obtained from the formula for the present value of a growing annuity if n is set equal to ∞. It is also possible to go the other way. In other words, the present value of a growing annuity formula can be derived from the formula for a growing perpetuity. In fact, this is how Equation 6.5 was actually derived. Show how Equation 6.5 can be derived from Equation 6.6.

Buy It on Credit and Be True to Your School[13]

ETHICS CASE

At the start of every school year, representatives from major banks come to campus to give students "free" credit cards. There are good reasons for banks to solicit students' business even though most students have neither steady jobs nor credit histories. First, students have a better record of paying their bills than the general public, because if they can't pay, usually their parents will. Second, students turn into loyal customers. Studies have shown that students keep their first credit card for an average of

---

[13] Sources: "Big Cards on Campus," *Business Week*, September 20, 1999, pp. 136–137; Marilyn Gardner, "A Generation Weighed Down by Debt," *Christian Science Monitor*, November 24, 2004; "Survey Reveals Aggressive Marketing of Credit Cards Continues on Many Maryland College Campuses," U.S. PIRG press release, February 19, 2004; and "Golden Eggs," *Boston Globe*, June 25, 2006.

15 years. That enables banks to sell them services over time, such as car loans, first mortgages, and (somewhat ironically) debt consolidation loans. Third and perhaps most importantly, students are ideal customers because they do not tend to pay off their credit balances each month, instead paying just the interest charges. One study in the 1990s revealed that 70 percent of students at four-year colleges had $2,000 or more of revolving debt. A more recent study in 2004 showed that 56 percent of college seniors have four or more cards and an average outstanding debt of $2,864.

Concern over Growing Student Debt

Concern has been growing that students cannot handle the debt they are taking on. According to a Consumer Federation study, college student debt almost tripled just in the 10 years between 1990 and 1999. This trend continues today. Many students fail to realize that when they apply for a car loan or a mortgage, the total ratio of debt to income is usually the most important factor determining whether they get the loan. Student educational loans are added to credit card debt, and that, in turn, is added to the requested loan amount to determine eligibility. When all the debt is summed up, many do not qualify for the loan they want. In many cases, people are forced to postpone marriage or purchase of a house because of their outstanding student loans and credit card debt.

To understand how students get into this kind of situation, consider the following hypothetical case. Suppose a student has a balance of $2,000 on a credit card. She makes the minimum payment every month but does not make any other purchases. Assuming a typical rate of interest, it would take six and one half years to pay off the credit card debt, and the student would have incurred interest charges of $2,500. As one observer noted, students like this one "will still be paying for all that pizza they bought in college when they are 30 years old."

A book published in 2000, *Credit Card Nation: The Consequences of America's Addiction to Credit*, was particularly critical of marketing credit cards to college students. The author, Robert Manning, identified a wide range of concerns, such as lowering of the age at which students can obtain credit cards, increasing credit limits on credit cards, students financing their education with credit card debt, and students using credit cards to conceal activities their parents might not approve of. Critics also point out that some of the advertising and marketing practices of the credit card companies are deceptive. In one case, for example, a credit card was touted as having no interest. That was true for the first month, but the annual percentage rate (APR) soared to 21 percent in the second month. Finally, many—including the students themselves—say that students do not receive sufficient education about how to manage credit card debt.

Supporters of credit card programs counter that most students do not "max out" their credit limits and that the three most common reasons for taking out a credit card are the establishment of a credit history, convenience, and emergency protection—all laudable goals.

Affinity Credit Cards

The marketing of credit cards to students has taken a new twist in relatively recent years. Banks compete fiercely to sign up students for their credit cards, and some banks are entering into exclusive arrangements with universities for the right to issue an affinity card—a credit card that features the university's name and logo. The card issuer may be willing to support the university to the tune of several million dollars in order to gain the exclusive right to issue the affinity card and to keep other banks off campus.

Georgetown University, for example, received $2 million from MBNA for a career counseling center; Michigan State received $5.5 million from MBNA for athletic and academic scholarship programs; and the University of Tennessee received $16 million from First USA primarily for athletics and scholarships. Universities gain other perks as well: They usually receive a half percent of the purchase value when the card is used. Often, they receive a fee for each new account, and sometimes they receive a small percentage of the loans outstanding. Every time a student uses the credit card, the university benefits.

Universities have been facing difficult financial times, and it is easy to understand why they enter into these arrangements. However, the price the university pays is that it becomes ensnared in the ethical issue of contributing to the rising level of student credit card debt. Moreover, universities with affinity credit cards cannot escape a conflict of interest: the higher student credit card debt climbs, the greater the revenues the university earns from the bank. As a result of these issues, some universities have increased the amount of information they provide to students about handling credit card debt, both through counseling and formal courses.

Certainly, learning to responsibly manage credit card purchases and any resulting debt is a necessary part of the passage to adulthood. We can applaud the fact that universities educate students about the dangers of excessive credit card debt. However, if universities make money on that debt, we must question whether they have less incentive to educate students about the associated problems.

Discussion Questions

1. Should universities enter into agreements to offer affinity credit cards to students?

2. Whether or not a university has an affinity credit card, does it have an obligation to educate students about credit card misuse and debt management?

3. Does the existence of an affinity credit card create a conflict of interest for a university if and when it adopts an education program on credit card misuse and debt management?

4. To what extent are students themselves responsible for their predicament?

RISK AND RETURN

CHAPTER

7

LEARNING OBJECTIVES

1. Explain the relation between risk and return.

2. Describe the two components of a total holding period return, and calculate this return for an asset.

3. Explain what an expected return is, and calculate the expected return for an asset.

4. Explain what the standard deviation of returns is, explain why it is especially useful in finance, and be able to calculate it.

5. Explain the concept of diversification.

6. Discuss which type of risk matters to investors and why.

7. Describe what the Capital Asset Pricing Model (CAPM) tells us and how to use it to evaluate whether the expected return of an asset is sufficient to compensate an investor for the risks associated with that asset.

Zuma Press

As the home mortgage market went into a tailspin in mid-2007, Countrywide Financial Corporation's stock price plummeted 63.7 percent, from a high of $41.91 per share on May 8 to $15.23 on October 19. Countrywide was one of the most prominent participants in the home mortgage market. Its stock price dropped in response to a rapid increase in defaults by mortgage borrowers as interest rates on adjustable-rate mortgages began to increase in response to an overall rise in interest rates.

The decline in the value of Countrywide's shares was compounded by the fact that it occurred at a time when the stock market as a whole was rising. Countrywide stockholders who did not hold diversified investment portfolios were much worse off after the 2007 stock price decline than they would have been if they had held diversified portfolios. They suffered large losses because they had not diversified their risk by investing in a variety of stocks and other types of assets. They bet on one company, and when that company's share price collapsed, so did the value of their investment portfolios.

Diversified Countrywide stockholders were better off in 2007, but they did not benefit as much when the home mortgage market took off and Countrywide's stock price rose 129 percent between July 2003 and July 2004. The accompanying exhibit shows how Countrywide's stock price and the S&P 500 index changed between the beginning of 2003 and October 2007.

The undiversified Countrywide stockholders took a lot of risk in anticipation of earning high returns. They did well when business was booming and paid a steep price when it was not. The concepts discussed in this chapter would have helped them better understand whether the expected returns on their stock justified the risks.

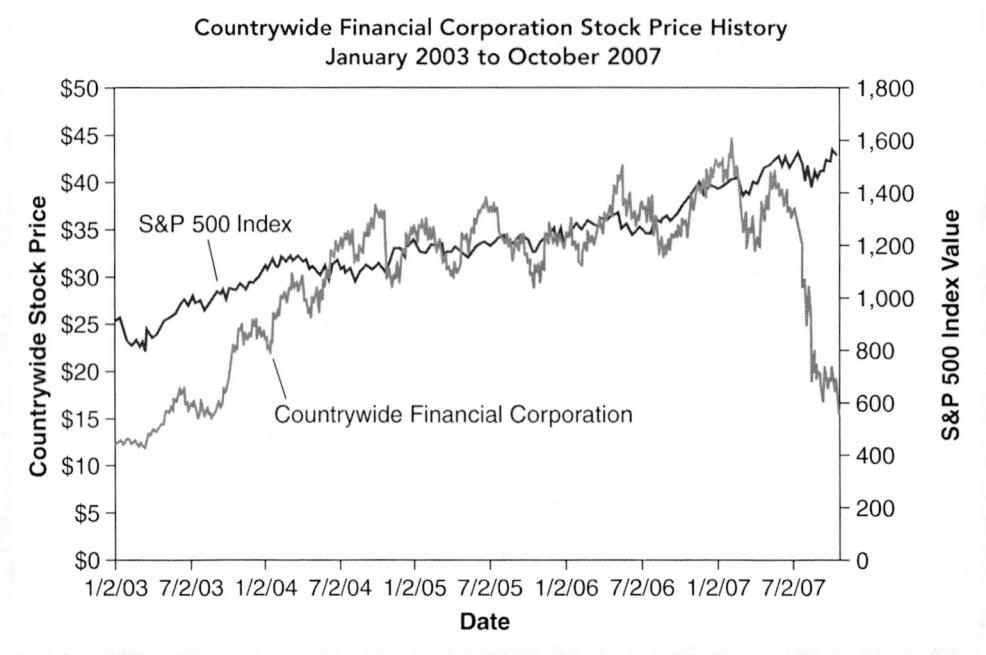

**Countrywide Financial Corporation Stock Price History
January 2003 to October 2007**

Countrywide's stock price increased rapidly from July 2003 to July 2004, but declined even faster in mid-2007. In contrast, the S&P 500 Index increased steadily during this period.

CHAPTER PREVIEW

Up to this point, we have often mentioned the rate of return that we use to discount cash flows, but we have not explained how that rate is determined. We have now reached the point where it is time to examine key concepts underlying the discount rate. This chapter introduces a quantitative framework for measuring risk and return. This framework will help you develop an intuitive understanding of how risk and return are related and what risks matter to investors. The relation between risk and return has implications for the rate we use to discount cash flows because the time value of money that we discussed in Chapters 5 and 6 is directly related to the returns that investors require. We must understand these concepts in order to determine the correct present value for a series of cash flows and to be able to make investment decisions that create value for stockholders.

We begin this chapter with a discussion of the general relation between risk and return to introduce the idea that investors require a higher rate of return from riskier assets. This is one of the most fundamental relations in finance. We next develop the statistical concepts required to quantify holding period returns, expected returns, and risk. We then apply these concepts to port-folios with a single asset, two assets, and more than two assets to illustrate the benefit of diversification. From this discussion, you will see how investing in more than one asset enables an investor to reduce the total risk associated with his or her investment portfolio, and you will learn how to quantify this benefit.

Once we have discussed the concept of diversification, we examine what it means for the relation between risk and return. We find that the total risk associated with an investment consists of two components: (1) unsystematic risk and (2) systematic risk. Diversification enables investors to eliminate the *unsystematic risk*, or unique risk, associated with an individual asset. Investors do not require higher returns for the *unsystematic risk* that they can eliminate through diversification. Only *systematic risk*—risk that cannot be diversified away—affects expected returns on an investment. The distinction between unsystematic and systematic risk and the recognition that unsystematic risk can be diversified away are extremely important in finance. After reading this chapter, you will understand precisely what the term *risk* means in finance and how it is related to the rates of return that investors require.

7.1 Risk and Return

The rate of return that investors require for an investment depends on the risk associated with that investment. The greater the risk, the larger the return investors require as compensation for bearing that risk. This is one of the most fundamental relations in finance. The *rate of return* is what you earn on an investment, stated in percentage terms. We will be more specific later, but for now you might think of *risk* as a measure of how certain you are that you will receive a particular return. Higher risk means you are less certain.

To get a better understanding of how risk and return are related, consider an example. You are trying to select the best investment from among the following three stocks:

Stock	Expected Return (%)	Risk Level (%)
A	12	12
B	12	16
C	16	16

Which would you choose? If you were comparing only Stocks A and B, you should choose Stock A. Both stocks have the same expected return, but Stock A has less risk. It does not make sense to invest in the riskier stock if the expected return is the same. Similarly, you can see that Stock C is clearly superior to Stock B. Stocks B and C have the same level of risk, but Stock C has a higher expected return. It would not make sense to accept a lower return for taking on the same level of risk.

But what about the choice between Stocks A and C? This choice is less obvious. Making it requires understanding the concepts that we discuss in the rest of this chapter.

> **BUILDING INTUITION**
>
> ### More Risk Means a Higher Expected Return
>
> The greater the risk associated with an investment, the greater the return investors expect from it. A corollary to this idea is that investors want the highest return for a given level of risk or the lowest risk for a given level of return. When choosing between two investments that have the same level of risk, investors prefer the investment with the higher return. Alternatively, if two investments have the same expected return, investors prefer the less risky alternative.

7.2 Quantitative Measures of Return

Before we begin a detailed discussion of the relation between risk and return, we should define more precisely what these terms mean. We begin with measures of return.

Holding Period Returns

When people refer to the return from an investment, they are generally referring to the total return over some *investment period,* or *holding period.* The **total holding period return** consists of two components: (1) capital appreciation and (2) income. The capital appreciation component of a return, R_{CA}, arises from a change in the price of the asset over the investment or holding period and is calculated as follows:

$$R_{CA} = \frac{\text{Capital appreciation}}{\text{Initial price}} = \frac{P_1 - P_0}{P_0} = \frac{\Delta P}{P_0}$$

where P_0 is the price paid for the asset at time zero and P_1 is the price at a later point in time.

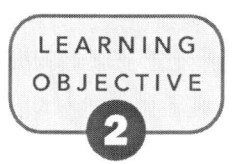

total holding period return
the total return on an asset over a specific period of time or holding period

The income component of a return arises from income that an investor receives from the asset while he or she owns it. For example, when a firm pays a cash dividend on its stock, the income component of the return on that stock, R_I, is calculated as follows:

$$R_I = \frac{\text{Cash flow}}{\text{Initial price}} = \frac{CF_1}{P_0}$$

where CF_1 is the cash flow from the dividend.

The total holding period return is simply the sum of the capital appreciation and income components of return:

$$R_T = R_{CA} + R_I = \frac{\Delta P}{P_0} + \frac{CF_1}{P_0} = \frac{\Delta P + CF_1}{P_0} \quad (7.1)$$

Let's consider an example of calculating the total holding period return on an investment. One year ago today, you purchased a share of Dell Inc. stock for $26.50. Today it is worth $29.00. Dell paid no dividend on its stock. What total return did you earn on this stock over the past year?

If Dell paid no dividend and you received no other income from holding the stock, the total return for the year equals the return from the capital appreciation, calculated as follows:

$$R_T = R_{CA} + R_I = \frac{P_1 - P_0 + CF_1}{P_0}$$
$$= \frac{\$29.00 - \$26.50 + \$0.00}{\$26.50}$$
$$= 0.0943, \text{ or } 9.43\%$$

What return would you have earned if Dell had paid a $1 dividend and today's price was $28.00? With the $1 dividend and a correspondingly lower price, the total return is the same:

$$R_T = R_{CA} + R_I = \frac{P_1 - P_0 + CF_1}{P_0} = \frac{\$28.00 - \$26.50 + \$1.00}{\$26.50} = 0.0943, \text{ or } 9.43\%$$

You can see from this example that a dollar of capital appreciation is worth the same as a dollar of income.

> You can download actual realized investment returns for a large number of stock market indexes at the Callan Associates Web site, www.callan.com/resource/periodic_table/pertbl.pdf.

LEARNING BY DOING APPLICATION 7.1

Calculating the Return on an Investment

Problem: You purchased a beat-up 1974 Datsun 240Z sports car a year ago for $1,500. Datsun is what Nissan, the Japanese car company, was called in the 1970s. The 240Z was the first in a series of cars that led to the Nissan 350Z that is being sold today. Recognizing that a mint-condition 240Z is a much sought-after car, you invested $7,000 and a lot of your time fixing up the car. Last week, you sold it to a collector for $18,000. Not counting the value of the time you spent restoring the car, what is the total return you earned on this investment over the one-year holding period?

Approach: Use Equation 7.1 to calculate the total holding period return. To calculate R_T using Equation 7.1, you must know P_0, P_1, and CF_1. In this problem, you can assume that the $7,000 was spent at the time you bought the car to purchase parts and materials. Therefore, your initial investment, P_0, was $1,500 + $7,000 = $8,500. Since there were no other cash inflows or outflows between the time that you bought the car and the time that you sold it, CF_1 equals $0.

Solution: The total holding period return is:

$$R_T = R_{CA} + R_I = \frac{P_1 - P_0 + CF_1}{P_0} = \frac{\$18,000 - \$8,500 + \$0}{\$8,500} = 1.118, \text{ or } 111.8\%$$

Expected Returns

LEARNING OBJECTIVE 3

Suppose that you are a senior who plays college baseball and that your team is in the College World Series. Furthermore, suppose that you have been drafted by the Washington Nationals and are coming up for what you expect to be your last at-bat as a college player. The fact that you expect this to be your last at-bat is important because you just signed a very unusual contract with the Nationals. Your signing bonus will be determined solely by whether you get a hit in your final collegiate at-bat. If you get a hit, then your signing bonus will be $800,000. Otherwise, it will be $400,000. This past season, you got a hit 32.5 percent of the times you were at bat (you did not get a hit 67.5 percent of the time), and you believe this reflects the likelihood that you will get a hit in your last collegiate at-bat.[1]

What is the expected value of your bonus? If you have taken a statistics course, you might recall that an expected value represents the sum of the products of the possible outcomes and the probabilities that those outcomes will be realized. In our example the expected value of the bonus can be calculated using the following formula:

$$E(\text{Bonus}) = (p_H \times B_H) + (p_{NH} \times B_{NH})$$

where E(Bonus) is your expected bonus, p_H is the probability of a hit, p_{NH} is the probability of no hit, B_H is the bonus you receive if you get a hit, and B_{NH} is the bonus you receive if you get no hit. Since p_H equals 0.325, p_{NH} equals 0.675, B_H equals $800,000, and B_{NH} equals $400,000, the expected value of your bonus is:

$$\begin{aligned} E(\text{Bonus}) &= (p_H \times B_H) + (p_{NH} \times B_{NH}) \\ &= (0.325 \times \$800{,}000) + (0.675 \times \$400{,}000) = \$530{,}000 \end{aligned}$$

Notice that the expected bonus of $530,000 is not equal to either of the two possible payoffs. Neither is it equal to the simple average of the two possible payoffs. This is because the expected bonus takes into account the probability of each event occurring. If the probability of each event had been 50 percent, then the expected bonus would have equaled the simple average of the two payoffs:

$$E(\text{Bonus}) = (0.5 \times \$800{,}000) + (0.5 \times \$400{,}000) = \$600{,}000$$

However, since it is more likely that you will not get a hit (a 67.5 percent chance) than that you will get a hit (a 32.5 percent chance), and the payoff is lower if you do not get a hit, the expected bonus is less than the simple average.

What would your expected payoff be if you got a hit 99 percent of the time? We intuitively know that the expected bonus should be much closer to $800,000 in this case. In fact, it is:

$$E(\text{Bonus}) = (0.99 \times \$800{,}000) + (0.01 \times \$400{,}000) = \$796{,}000$$

The key point here is that the expected value reflects the relative likelihoods of the possible outcomes.

We calculate an **expected return** in finance in the same way that we calculate any expected value. The expected return is a weighted average of the possible returns from an investment, where each of these returns is weighted by the probability that it will occur. In general terms, the expected return on an asset, $E(R_{Asset})$, is calculated as follows:

$$E(R_{Asset}) = \sum_{i=1}^{n} (p_i \times R_i) = (p_1 \times R_1) + (p_2 \times R_2) + \cdots + (p_n \times R_n) \quad (7.2)$$

where R_i is possible return i and p_i is the probability that you will actually earn return R_i. The summation symbol in this equation

$$\sum_{i=1}^{n}$$

expected return
an average of the possible returns from an investment, where each return is weighted by the probability that it will occur

---
[1] For simplicity, let's ignore the possibility of your hitting a sacrifice fly and other such outcomes.

is mathematical shorthand indicating that n values are added together. In Equation 7.2, each of the n possible returns is multiplied by the probability that it will be realized, and these products are then added together to calculate the expected return.

It is important to make sure that the sum of the n individual probabilities, the p_i's, always equals 1, or 100 percent, when you calculate an expected value. The sum of the probabilities cannot be less than 100 percent because you must account for all possible outcomes in the calculation. On the other hand, as you may recall from statistics, the sum of the probabilities of all possible outcomes cannot exceed 100 percent. For example, notice that the sum of the p_i's equals 1 in each of the expected bonus calculations that we discussed earlier (0.325 + 0.625 in the first calculation, 0.5 + 0.5 in the second, and 0.99 + 0.01 in the third).

The expected return on an asset reflects the return that you can expect to receive from investing in that asset over the period that you plan to own it. It is your best estimate of this return, given the possible outcomes and their associated probabilities.

Note that if each of the possible outcomes is equally likely (that is, $p_1 = p_2 = p_3 = \ldots = p_n = p = 1/n$), this formula reduces to the formula for a simple (equally weighted) average of the possible returns:

$$E(R_{Asset}) = \frac{\sum_{i=1}^{n}(R_i)}{n} = \frac{R_1 + R_2 + \cdots + R_n}{n}$$

To see how we calculate the expected return on an asset, suppose you are considering purchasing Dell, Inc., stock for $29.00 per share. You plan to sell the stock in one year. You estimate that there is a 30 percent chance that Dell stock will sell for $28.00 at the end of one year, a 30 percent chance that it will sell for $30.50, a 30 percent that it will sell for $32.50, and a 10 percent chance that it will sell for $36.00. If Dell pays no dividends on its shares, what is the return that you expect from this stock in the next year?

Since Dell pays no dividends, the total return on its stock equals the return from capital appreciation:

$$R_T = R_{CA} = \frac{P_1 - P_0}{P_0}$$

Therefore, we can calculate the return from owning Dell stock under each of the four possible outcomes using the approach we used for the similar Dell problem we solved earlier in the chapter. These returns are calculated as follows:

Dell Stock Price in One Year	Total Return
(1) $28.00	$\frac{\$28.00 - \$29.00}{\$29.00} = -0.0345$
(2) $30.50	$\frac{\$30.50 - \$29.00}{\$29.00} = 0.0517$
(3) $32.50	$\frac{\$32.50 - \$29.00}{\$29.00} = 0.1207$
(4) $36.00	$\frac{\$36.00 - \$29.00}{\$29.00} = 0.2414$

Applying Equation 7.2, the expected return on Dell stock over the next year is therefore 6.55 percent, calculated as follows:

$$E(R_{Dell}) = \sum_{i=1}^{n}(p_i \times R_i) = (p_1 \times R_1) + (p_2 \times R_2) + \cdots + (p_n \times R_n)$$

$$E(R_{Dell}) = (0.3 \times -0.0345) + (0.3 \times 0.0517) + (0.3 \times 0.1207) + (0.1 \times 0.2414)$$
$$= -0.01035 + 0.01551 + 0.03621 + 0.02414 = 0.0655, \text{ or } 6.55\%$$

Notice that the negative return is entered into the formula just like any other. Also notice that the sum of the p_i's equals 1.

LEARNING BY DOING APPLICATION 7.2

Calculating Expected Returns

Problem: You have just purchased 100 railroad cars that you plan to lease to a large railroad company. Demand for shipping goods by rail has recently increased dramatically due to the rising price of oil. You expect oil prices, which are currently at $115.00 per barrel, to reach $130.00 per barrel in the next year. If this happens, railroad shipping prices will increase, thereby driving up the value of your railroad cars as increases in demand outpace the rate at which new cars are being produced.

Given your oil price prediction, you estimate that there is a 30 percent chance that the value of your railroad cars will increase by 15 percent, a 40 percent chance that their value will increase by 25 percent, and a 30 percent chance that their value will increase by 30 percent in the next year. In addition to appreciation in the value of your cars, you expect to earn 10 percent on your investment over the next year (after expenses) from leasing the railroad cars. What total return do you expect to earn on your railroad car investment over the next year?

Approach: Use Equation 7.1 first to calculate the total return that you would earn under each of the three possible outcomes. Next use these total return values, along with the associated probabilities, in Equation 7.2 to calculate the expected total return.

Solution: To calculate the total returns using Equation 7.1,

$$R_T = R_{CA} + R_I = \frac{\Delta P}{P_0} + \frac{CF_1}{P_0}$$

you must recognize that $\Delta P/P_0$ is the capital appreciation under each outcome and that CF_1/P_0 equals the 10 percent that you expect to receive from leasing the rail cars. The expected returns for the three outcomes are:

Increase in Value of Rail Cars in One Year	Return from Leases	Total Return
15%	10%	$R_T = \frac{\Delta P}{P_0} + \frac{CF_1}{P_0} = 0.15 + 0.10 = 0.25$, or 25%
25%	10%	$R_T = \frac{\Delta P}{P_0} + \frac{CF_1}{P_0} = 0.25 + 0.10 = 0.35$, or 35%
30%	10%	$R_T = \frac{\Delta P}{P_0} + \frac{CF_1}{P_0} = 0.30 + 0.10 = 0.40$, or 40%

You can then use Equation 7.2 to calculate the expected return for your rail car investment:

$$E(R_{\text{Rail cars}}) = \sum_{i=1}^{3}(p_i \times R_i) = (p_1 \times R_1) + (p_2 \times R_2) + (p_3 \times R_3)$$
$$E(R_{\text{Rail cars}}) = (0.3 \times 0.25) + (0.4 \times 0.35) + (0.3 \times 0.40)$$
$$= 0.335, \text{ or } 33.5\%$$

Alternatively, since there is a 100 percent probability that the return from leasing the railroad cars is 10 percent, you could have simply calculated the expected increase in value of the railroad cars:

$$E\left(\frac{\Delta P}{P_0}\right) = (0.3 \times 0.15) + (0.4 \times 0.25) + (0.3 \times 0.30)$$
$$= 0.235, \text{ or } 23.5\%$$

and added the 10 percent to arrive at the answer of 33.5 percent. Of course, this simpler approach only works if the return from leasing is known with certainty.

216 CHAPTER 7 Risk and Return

DECISION-MAKING EXAMPLE 7.1

Using Expected Values in Decision Making

Situation: You are deciding whether you should advertise your pizza business on the radio or on billboards placed on local taxicabs. For $1,000 per month, you can either buy 20 one-minute ads on the radio or place your ad on 40 taxicabs.

There is some uncertainty regarding how many new customers will visit your restaurant after hearing one of your radio ads. You estimate that there is a 30 percent chance that 35 people will visit, a 45 percent chance that 50 people will visit, and a 25 percent chance that 60 people will visit. Therefore, you expect the following number of new customers to visit your restaurant in a month in response to each radio ad:

$$E(\text{New customers per ad}_{Radio}) = (0.30 \times 35) + (0.45 \times 50) + (0.25 \times 60) = 48$$

This means that you expect 20 one-minute ads to bring in $20 \times 48 = 960$ new customers.

Similarly, you estimate that there is a 20 percent chance you will get 20 new customers in response to an ad placed on a taxi, a 30 percent chance you will get 30 new customers, a 30 percent chance that you will get 40 new customers, and a 20 percent chance that you will get 50 new customers. Therefore, you expect the following number of new customers in response to each ad that you place on a taxi:

$$E(\text{New customers per ad}_{Taxi}) = (0.2 \times 20) + (0.3 \times 30) + (0.3 \times 40) + (0.2 \times 50) = 35$$

Placing ads on 40 taxicabs is therefore expected to bring in $40 \times 35 = 1,400$ new customers.

Which of these two advertising options is more attractive? Is it cost effective?

Decision: You should advertise on taxicabs. For a monthly cost of $1,000, you expect to attract 1,400 new customers with taxicab advertisements but only 960 new customers if you advertise on the radio.

The answer to the question of whether advertising on taxicabs is cost effective depends on how much gross profits (profits after variable costs) are increased by those 1,400 customers. Gross profits will have to increase by $1,000, or average 72 cents per new customer ($1,000/1,400) to cover the cost of the advertising campaign.

Before You Go On

1. What are the two components of a total holding period return?
2. How is the expected return on an investment calculated?

7.3 The Variance and Standard Deviation as Measures of Risk

We turn next to a discussion of the two most basic measures of risk used in finance—the variance and the standard deviation. These are the same variance and standard deviation measures that you have studied if you have taken a course in statistics.

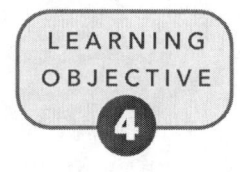

LEARNING OBJECTIVE 4

Calculating the Variance and Standard Deviation

Let's begin by returning to our College World Series example. Recall that you will receive a bonus of $800,000 if you get a hit in your final collegiate at-bat and a bonus of $400,000 if you do not. The expected value of your bonus is $530,000. Suppose you want to measure the risk, or uncertainty, associated with the payoff. How can you do this? One approach would be to compute a measure of how much, on average, the bonus payoffs deviate from the expected value. The underlying intuition here is that the greater the difference between the actual payoff and the expected value, the greater the risk. For example, you might calculate the difference between each individual bonus payment and the expected value and sum these differences. If you do this, you will get the following result:

$$\begin{aligned}\text{Risk} &= (\$800{,}000 - \$530{,}000) + (\$400{,}000 - \$530{,}000) \\ &= \$270{,}000 + (-130{,}000) \\ &= \$140{,}000\end{aligned}$$

Unfortunately, using this calculation to obtain a measure of risk presents two problems. First, since one difference is positive and the other difference is negative, one difference partially cancels the other. As a result, you are not getting an accurate measure of total risk. Second, this calculation does not take into account the number of potential outcomes or the probability of each outcome.

A better approach would be to square the differences (squaring the differences makes all the numbers positive) and multiply each difference by its associated probability before summing them up. This calculation yields the **variance (σ^2)** of the possible outcomes. The variance does not suffer from the two problems mentioned earlier and provides a measure of risk that has a consistent interpretation across different situations or assets. For the original bonus arrangement, the variance is:

variance (σ^2)
a measure of the uncertainty surrounding an outcome

$$\begin{aligned}\text{Var(Bonus)} = \sigma^2_{(\text{Bonus})} &= \{p_\text{H} \times [B_\text{H} - E(\text{Bonus})]^2\} \\ &\quad + \{p_\text{NH} \times [B_\text{NH} - E(\text{Bonus})]^2\} \\ &= [0.325 \times (\$800{,}000 - \$530{,}000)^2] \\ &\quad + [0.675 \times (\$400{,}000 - \$530{,}000)^2] \\ &= 35{,}100{,}000{,}000 \text{ dollars}^2\end{aligned}$$

Note that the square of the Greek symbol sigma, σ^2, is generally used to represent the variance.

Because it is somewhat awkward to work with units of squared dollars, in a calculation such as this we would typically take the square root of the variance. The square root gives us the **standard deviation (σ)** of the possible outcomes. For our example, the standard deviation is:

standard deviation (σ)
the square root of the variance

$$\sigma_{(\text{Bonus})} = (\sigma^2_{(\text{Bonus})})^{1/2} = (35{,}100{,}000{,}000 \text{ dollars}^2)^{1/2} = \$187{,}349.94$$

As you will see when we discuss the normal distribution, the standard deviation has a natural interpretation that is very useful for assessing investment risks.

The general formula for calculating the variance of returns can be written as follows:

$$\text{Var}(R) = \sigma^2_R = \sum_{i=1}^{n} \{p_i \times [R_i - E(R)]^2\} \tag{7.3}$$

Equation 7.3 simply extends the calculation illustrated above to the situation where there are n possible outcomes. Like the expected return calculation (Equation 7.2), Equation 7.3 can be simplified if all of the possible outcomes are equally likely. In this case it becomes:

$$\sigma^2_R = \frac{\sum_{i=1}^{n} [R_i - E(R)]^2}{n}$$

In both the general case and the case where all possible outcomes are equally likely, the standard deviation is simply the square root of the variance $\sigma_R = (\sigma^2_R)^{\frac{1}{2}}$.

Interpreting the Variance and Standard Deviation

normal distribution
a symmetric frequency distribution that is completely described by its mean and standard deviation; also known as a bell curve due to its shape

The variance and standard deviation are especially useful measures of risk for variables that are normally distributed—those that can be represented by a normal distribution. The **normal distribution** is a symmetric frequency distribution that is completely described by its mean (average) and standard deviation. Exhibit 7.1 illustrates what this distribution looks like. Even if you have never taken a statistics course, you have already encountered the normal distribution. It is the "bell curve" on which instructors often base their grade distributions. SAT scores and IQ scores are also based on normal distributions.

This distribution is very useful in finance because the returns for many assets tend to be approximately normally distributed. This makes the variance and standard deviation practical measures of the uncertainty associated with investment returns. Since the standard deviation is more easily interpreted than the variance, we will focus on the standard deviation as we discuss the normal distribution and its application in finance.

In Exhibit 7.1, you can see that the normal distribution is symmetric: the left and right sides are mirror images of each other. The mean falls directly in the center of the distribution, and the probability that an outcome is less than or greater than a particular distance from the mean is the same whether the outcome is on the left or the right side of the distribution. For example, if the mean is 0, the probability that a particular outcome is −3 or less is the same as the probability that it is +3 or more (both are 3 or more units from the mean). This enables us to use a single measure of risk for the normal distribution. That measure is the standard deviation.

The standard deviation tells us everything we need to know about the width of the normal distribution or, in other words, the variation in the individual values. This variation is what we mean when we talk about risk in finance. In general terms, risk is a measure of the range of potential outcomes. The standard deviation is an especially useful measure of risk because it tells us the probability that an outcome will fall a particular distance from the mean, or within a particular range. You

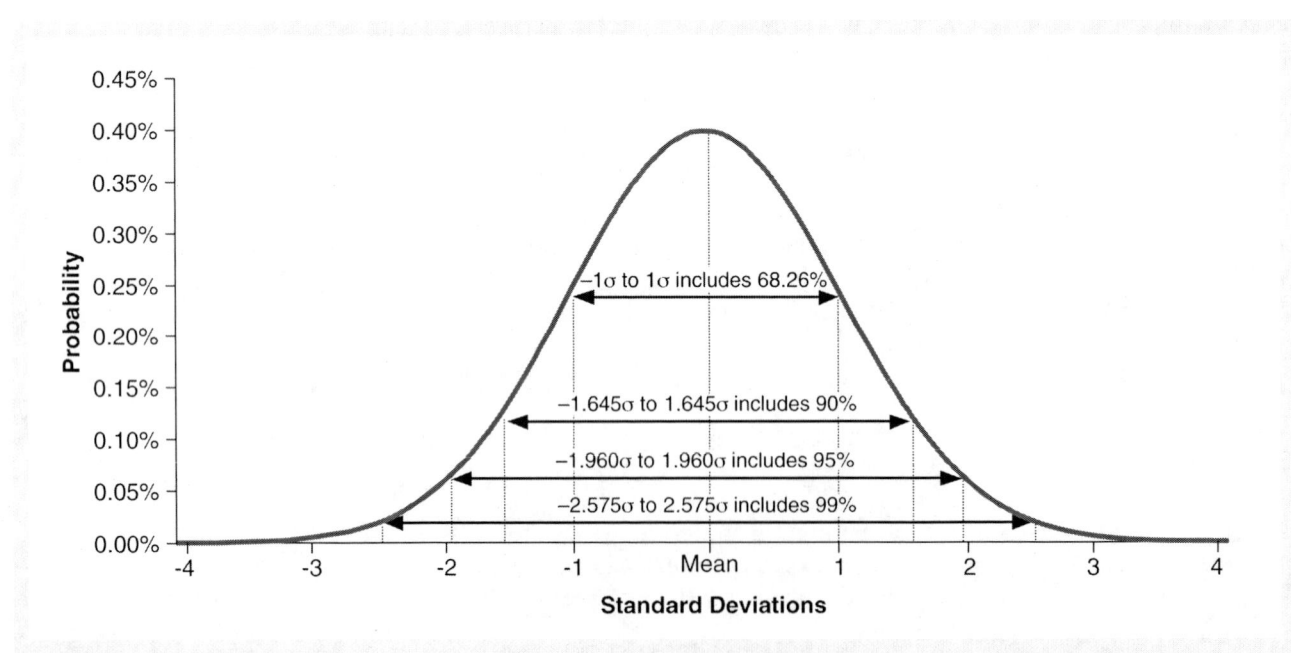

Exhibit 7.1
Normal Distribution
The normal distribution is a symmetric distribution that is described by its mean and standard deviation. The mean is the value that defines the center of the distribution, and the standard deviation, σ, describes the dispersion of the values centered around the mean.

can see this in the following table, which shows the fraction of all observations in a normal distribution that are within the indicated number of standard deviations from the mean.

Number of Standard Deviations from the Mean	Fraction of Total Observations
1.000	68.26%
1.645	90%
1.960	95%
2.575	99%

Since the returns on many assets are approximately normally distributed, the standard deviation provides a convenient way of computing the probability that the return on an asset will fall within a particular range. In these applications, the expected return on an asset equals the mean of the distribution, and the standard deviation is a measure of the uncertainty associated with the return.

For example, if the expected return for a real estate investment in Reno, Nevada, is 10 percent with a standard deviation of 2 percent, there is a 90 percent chance that the actual return will be within 3.29 percent of 10 percent. How do we know this? As shown in the table, 90 percent of all outcomes in a normal distribution have a value that is within 1.645 standard deviations of the mean value, and 1.645 × 2 percent = 3.29 percent. This tells us that there is a 90 percent chance that the realized return on the investment in Reno will be between 6.71 percent (10 percent − 3.29 percent) and 13.29 percent (10 percent + 3.29 percent), a range of 6.58 percent (13.29 percent − 6.71 percent).

You may be wondering what is *standard* about the standard deviation. The answer is that this statistic is standard in the sense that it can be used to directly compare the uncertainties (risks) associated with the returns on different investments. For instance, suppose you are comparing the real estate investment in Reno with a real estate investment in Las Cruces, New Mexico. Assume that the expected return on the Las Cruces investment is also 10 percent. If the standard deviation for the returns on the Las Cruces investment is 3 percent, there is a 90 percent chance that the actual return is within 4.935 percent (1.645 × 3 percent = 4.935 percent) of 10 percent. In other words, 90 percent of the time, the return will be between 5.065 percent (10 percent − 4.935 percent) and 14.935 percent (10 percent + 4.935 percent), a range of 9.87 percent (14.935 percent − 5.065 percent).

This range is exactly 9.87 percent/6.58 percent = 1.5 times as large as the range for the Reno investment opportunity. Notice that the ratio of the two standard deviations also equals 1.5 (3 percent/2 percent = 1.5). This is not a coincidence. We could have used the standard deviations to directly compute the relative uncertainty associated with the Las Cruces and Reno investment returns. The relation between the standard deviation of returns and the width of a normal distribution (the uncertainty) is illustrated in Exhibit 7.2.

Let's consider another example of how the standard deviation is interpreted. Suppose customers at your pizza restaurant have complained that there is no consistency in the number of slices of pepperoni that your cooks are putting on large pepperoni pizzas. One night you decide to work in the area where the pizzas are made so that you can count the number of pepperoni slices on the large pizzas to get a better idea of just how much variation there is. After counting the slices of pepperoni on 50 pizzas, you estimate that, on average, your pies have 18 slices of pepperoni and that the standard deviation is 3 slices.

With this information, you estimate that 95 percent of the large pepperoni pizzas sold in your restaurant have between 12.12 and 23.88 slices. You are able to estimate this range because you know that 95 percent of the observations in a normal distribution fall within 1.96 standard deviations of the mean. With a standard deviation of three slices, this implies that the number of pepperoni slices on 95 percent of your pizzas is within 5.88 slices of the mean (3 slices × 1.96). This, in turn, indicates a range of 12.12 (18 − 5.88) to 23.88 (18 + 5.88) slices.

220 CHAPTER 7 | Risk and Return

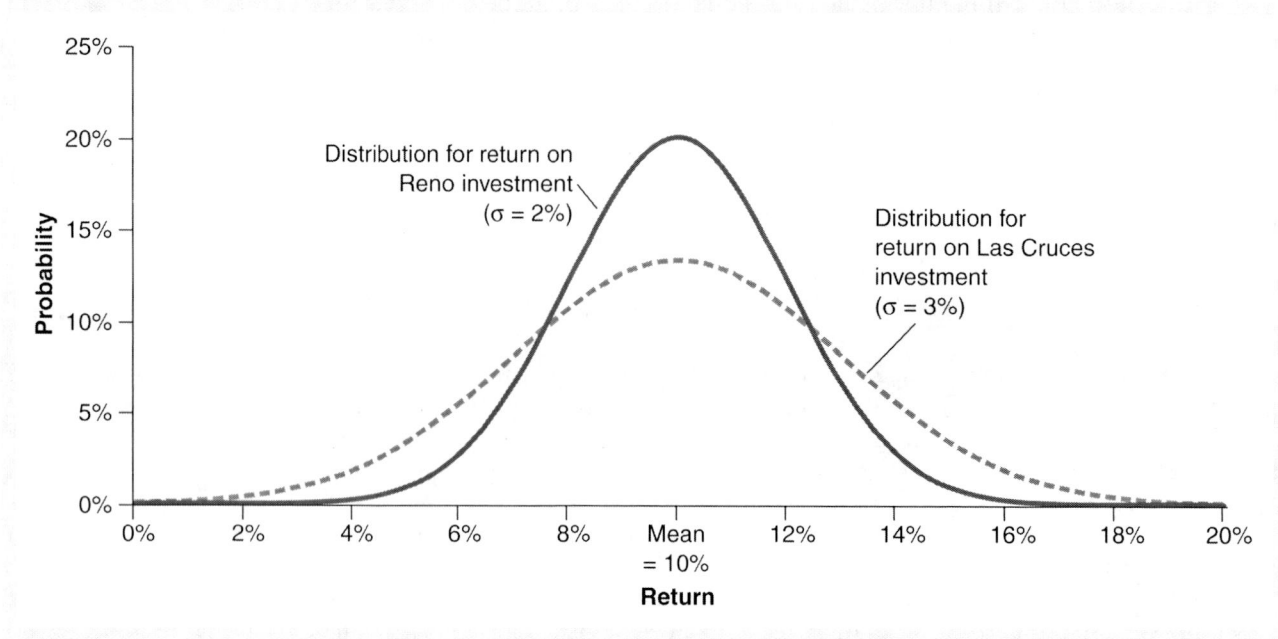

Exhibit 7.2
Standard Deviation and Width of the Normal Distribution
The larger standard deviation for the return on the Las Cruces investment means that the Las Cruces investment is riskier than the Reno investment. The actual return for the Las Cruces investment is more likely to be further from its expected return.

Since you put only whole slices of pepperoni on your pizzas, 95 percent of the time the number of slices is somewhere between 12 and 24. No wonder your customers are up in arms! In response to this information, you decide to implement a standard policy regarding the number of pepperoni slices that go on each type of pizza.

LEARNING BY DOING
APPLICATION 7.3

Understanding the Standard Deviation

Problem: You are considering investing in a share of Dell, Inc., stock and want to evaluate how risky this potential investment is. You know that stock returns tend to be normally distributed, and you have calculated the expected return on Dell stock to be 4.67 percent and the standard deviation of the annual return to be 23 percent. Based on these statistics, within what range would you expect the return on this stock to fall during the next year? Calculate this range for a 90 percent level of confidence (that is, 90 percent of the time, the returns will fall within the specified range).

Approach: Use the values in the previous table or Exhibit 7.1 to compute the range within which Dell's stock return will fall 90 percent of the time. First, find the number of standard deviations associated with a 90 percent level of confidence in the table or Exhibit 7.1 and then multiply this number by the standard deviation of the annual return for Dell's stock. Then subtract the resulting value from the expected return (mean) to obtain the lower end of the range and add it to the expected return to obtain the upper end.

Solution: From the table, you can see that we would expect the return over the next year to be within 1.645 standard deviations of the mean 90 percent of the time. Multiplying this value by the standard deviation of Dell's stock (23 percent) yields 23 percent × 1.645 = 37.835 percent. This means that there is a 90 percent chance that the return will be between −33.165 percent (4.67 percent − 37.835 percent) and 42.505 percent (4.67 percent + 37.835 percent).

While the expected return of 4.67 percent is relatively low, the returns on Dell stock vary considerably, and there is a reasonable chance that the stock return in the next year could be quite high or quite low (even negative). As you will see shortly, this wide range of possible returns is similar to the range we observe for typical shares in the U.S. stock market.

Historical Market Performance

Now that we have discussed how returns and risks can be measured, we are ready to examine the characteristics of the historical returns earned by securities such as stocks and bonds. Exhibit 7.3 illustrates the distributions of historical returns for some securities in the United States and shows the average and standard deviations of these annual returns for the period from 1926 to 2006.

Note that the statistics reported in Exhibit 7.3 are for indexes that represent total *average* returns for the indicated types of securities, not total returns on individual securities. We generally use indexes to represent the performance of the stock or bond markets. For instance, when news services report on the performance of the stock market, they often report that the Dow Jones Industrial Average (DJIA), or the S&P 500 Index, or the NASDAQ Composite Index went up or down on a particular day. These and other indexes were discussed in Chapter 2.

The plots in Exhibit 7.3 are arranged in order of decreasing risk, which is indicated by the decreasing standard deviation of the annual returns. The top plot shows returns for a small-stock index that represents the 10 percent of U.S. firms that have the lowest total equity value (number of shares multiplied by price per share). The second plot shows returns for the S&P 500 Index, representing large U.S. stocks. The remaining plots show three different types of government debt. Long-term government bonds are bonds sold by the U.S. government that mature in 20 years, intermediate-term government bonds are bonds that mature in five years, and U.S. Treasury bills are short-term debts of the U.S. government that mature in from 30 days to one year.

The key point to note in Exhibit 7.3 is that, on average, annual returns have been higher for riskier securities. Small stocks, which have the largest standard deviation of total returns, at 32.74 percent, also have the largest average return, 17.36 percent. On the other end of the spectrum, Treasury bills have the smallest standard deviation, 3.10 percent, and the smallest average annual return, 3.77 percent. Returns for small stocks in any particular year may have been higher or lower than returns for the other types of securities, but on average, they were higher. This is evidence that investors require higher returns for investments with greater risks.

The statistics in Exhibit 7.3 describe actual investment returns, as opposed to expected returns. In other words, they represent what has happened in the past. Financial analysts often use historical numbers such as these to estimate the returns that might be expected in the future. That is exactly what we did in the baseball example earlier in this chapter. We used the percentage of at-bats in which you got a hit this past season to estimate the likelihood that you would get a hit in your last collegiate at-bat. We assumed that your past performance was a reasonable indicator of your future performance.

To see how historical numbers are used in finance, let's suppose that you are considering investing in a fund that mimics the S&P 500 Index (this is what we call an *index fund*) and that you want to estimate what the returns on the S&P 500 Index are likely to be in the future. If you believe that the 1926 to 2006 period provides a reasonable indication of what we can expect in the future, then the average historical return on the S&P 500 Index of 12.30 percent provides a perfectly reasonable estimate of the return you can expect from your investment in the S&P 500 Index fund. In Chapter 13 we will explore in detail how historical data can be used in this way to estimate the discount rate used to evaluate projects in the capital budgeting process.

222 CHAPTER 7 | Risk and Return

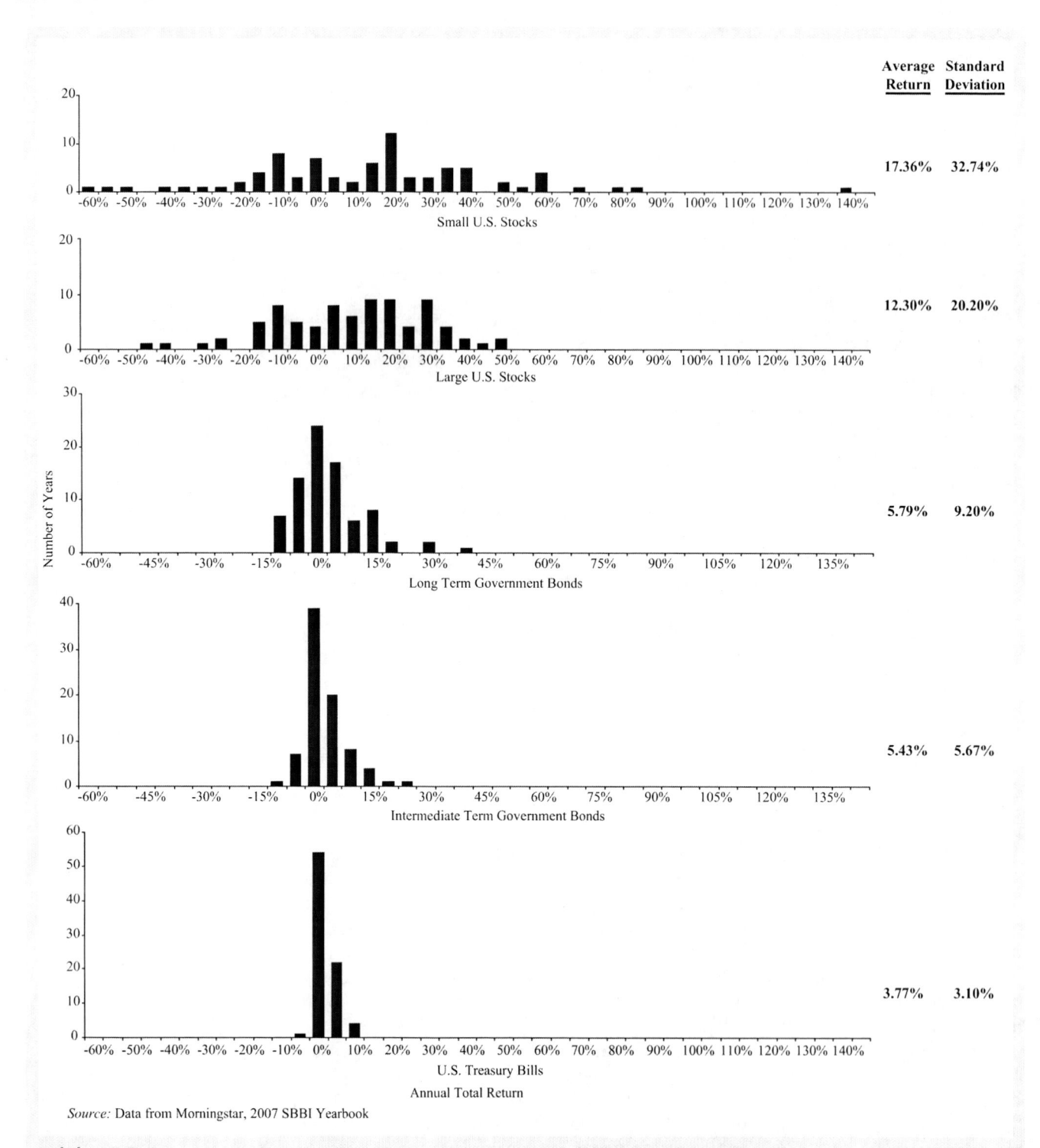

	Average Return	Standard Deviation
Small U.S. Stocks	17.36%	32.74%
Large U.S. Stocks	12.30%	20.20%
Long Term Government Bonds	5.79%	9.20%
Intermediate Term Government Bonds	5.43%	5.67%
U.S. Treasury Bills	3.77%	3.10%

Source: Data from Morningstar, 2007 SBBI Yearbook

Exhibit 7.3
Distributions of Annual Total Returns for U.S. Stocks and Bonds from 1926 to 2006

Higher standard deviations of return have historically been associated with higher returns. For example, between 1926 and 2006, the standard deviation of the annual returns for small stocks was higher than the standard deviations of the returns earned by other types of securities, and the average return that investors earned from small stocks was also higher. At the other end of the spectrum, the returns on Treasury bills had the smallest standard deviation, and Treasury bills earned the smallest average return.

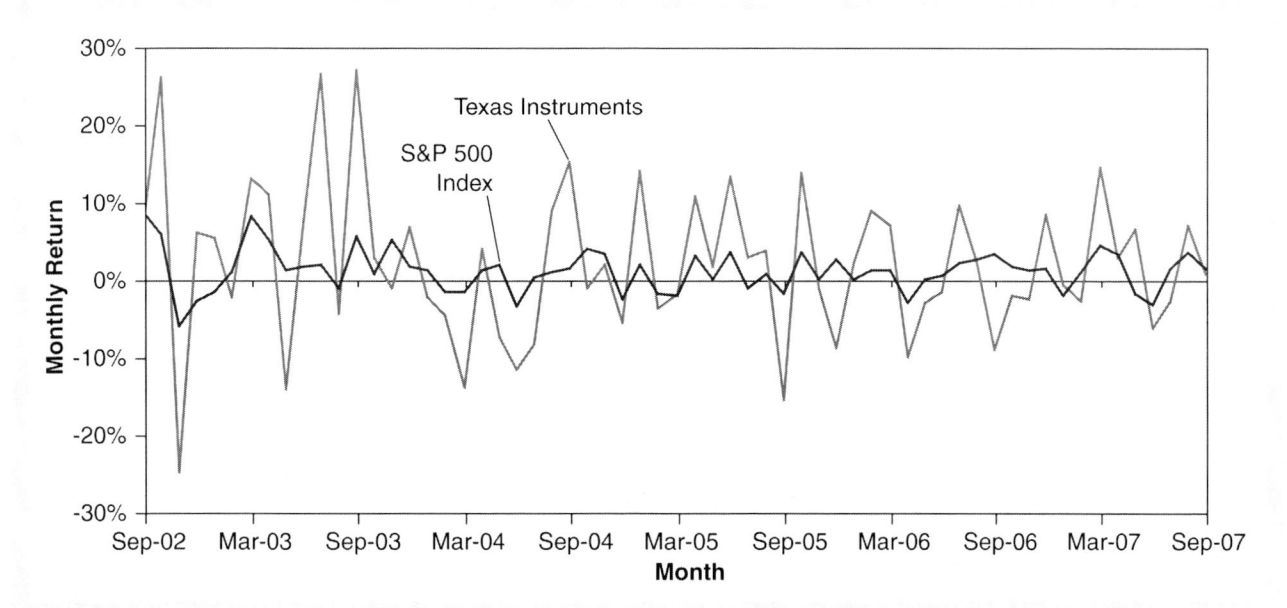

Exhibit 7.4
Monthly Returns for Texas Instruments and the S&P 500 Index from September 2002 through September 2007
The returns on shares of individual stocks tend to be much more volatile than the returns on portfolios of stocks, such as the S&P 500.

Comparing the historical returns for an individual stock with the historical returns for an index can also be instructive. Exhibit 7.4 shows such a comparison for Texas Instruments and the S&P 500 Index using monthly returns for the period from September 2002 to September 2007. Notice in the exhibit that the returns on Texas Instruments stock are much more volatile than the average returns on the firms represented in the S&P 500 Index. In other words, the standard deviation of returns for Texas Instruments stock is higher than that for the S&P 500 Index. This is not a coincidence; we will discuss shortly why returns on individual stocks tend to be riskier than returns on indexes.

One last point is worth noting while we are examining historical returns: the value of a $1.00 investment in 1926 would have varied greatly by 2006, depending on where that dollar was invested. Exhibit 7.5 shows that $1.00 invested in U.S. Treasury bills in 1926 would have been worth $19.29 by 2006. In contrast, that same $1.00 invested in small stocks would have been worth $15,922.43 by 2006![2] Over a long period of time, earning higher rates of return can have a dramatic impact on the value of an investment. This huge difference reflects the impact of compounding of returns (returns earned on returns), much like the compounding of interest we discussed in Chapter 5.

> **Before You Go On**
>
> 1. What is the relation between the variance and the standard deviation?
> 2. What relation do we generally observe between risk and return when we examine historical returns?
> 3. How would we expect the standard deviation of the return on an individual stock to compare with the standard deviation of the return on a stock index?

---

[2]From a practical standpoint, it would not really have been possible to grow $1.00 to $15,922.43 by investing in small U.S. stocks because this increase assumes that an investor is able to rebalance the stock portfolio by buying and selling shares as necessary at no cost. Since buying and selling shares is costly, the final wealth would have been lower. Nevertheless, even after transaction costs, it would have been much more profitable to invest in small stocks than in U.S. Treasury bills.

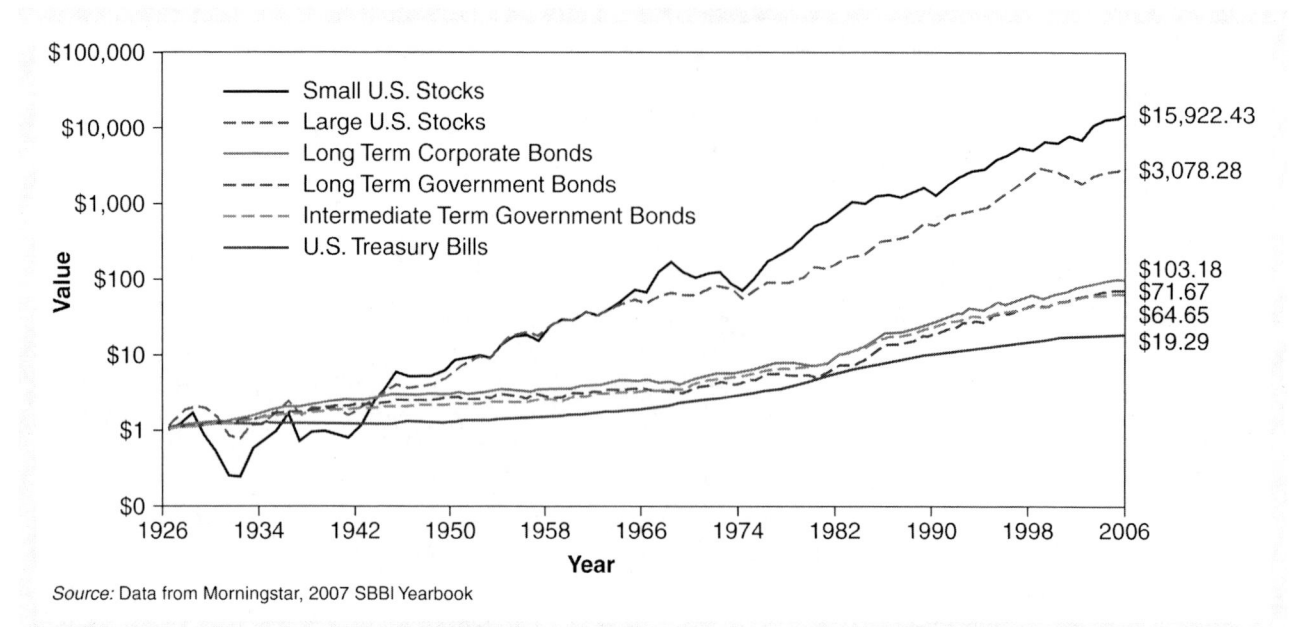

Exhibit 7.5
Cumulative Value of $1 Invested in 1926
The value of a $1 investment in stocks, small or large, grew much more rapidly than the value of a $1 investment in bonds or Treasury bills over the 1926 to 2006 period. This graph illustrates how earning a higher rate of return over a long period of time can affect the value of an investment portfolio. Although annual stock returns were less certain between 1926 and 2006, the returns on stock investments were much greater.

7.4 Risk and Diversification

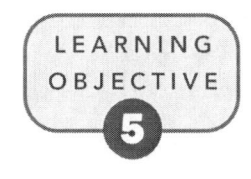

LEARNING OBJECTIVE 5

portfolio
the collection of assets an investor owns

diversification
a strategy of reducing risk by investing in two or more assets whose values do not always move in the same direction at the same time

It does not generally make sense to invest all of your money in a single asset. The reason is directly related to the fact that returns on individual stocks tend to be riskier than returns on indexes. By investing in two or more assets whose values do not always move in the same direction at the same time, an investor can reduce the risk of his or her collection of investments, or **portfolio**. This is the idea behind the concept of **diversification**.

This section develops the tools necessary to evaluate the benefits of diversification. We begin with a discussion of how to quantify risk and return for a single-asset portfolio, and then we discuss more realistic and complicated portfolios that have two or more assets. Although our discussion focuses on stock portfolios, it is important to recognize that the concepts discussed apply equally well to portfolios that include a range of assets, including stocks, bonds, and real estate, among others.

Single-Asset Portfolios

Returns for individual stocks from one day to the next have been found to be largely independent of each other and approximately normally distributed. In other words, the return for a stock on one day is largely independent of the return on that same stock the next day, two days later, three days later, and so on. Each daily return can be viewed as having been randomly drawn from a normal distribution where the probability associated with the return depends on how far it is from the expected value. If we know what the expected value and standard deviation are for the distribution of returns for a stock, it is possible to quantify the risks and expected returns that an investment in the stock might yield in the future.

To see how we might do this, assume that you are considering investing in one of two stocks for the next year: AMD or Intel. Also, to keep things simple, assume that there are only three possible economic conditions (outcomes) a year from now and that the returns on AMD and Intel under each of these outcomes are as follows:

Economic Outcome	Probability	AMD Return	Intel Return
Poor	0.2	−0.13	−0.10
Neutral	0.5	0.10	0.07
Good	0.3	0.25	0.22

With this information, we can calculate the expected returns for AMD and Intel by using Equation 7.2:

$$\begin{aligned} E(R_{AMD}) &= (p_{Poor} \times R_{Poor}) + (p_{Neutral} \times R_{Neutral}) + (p_{Good} \times R_{Good}) \\ &= (0.2 \times -0.13) + (0.5 \times 0.10) + (0.3 \times 0.25) \\ &= 0.099, \text{ or } 9.9\% \end{aligned}$$

and

$$\begin{aligned} E(R_{Intel}) &= (p_{Poor} \times R_{Poor}) + (p_{Neutral} \times R_{Neutral}) + (p_{Good} \times R_{Good}) \\ &= (0.2 \times -0.10) + (0.5 \times 0.07) + (0.3 \times 0.22) \\ &= 0.081, \text{ or } 8.1\% \end{aligned}$$

Similarly, we can calculate the standard deviations of the returns for AMD and Intel in the same way that we calculated the standard deviation for our baseball bonus example in Section 7.2:

$$\begin{aligned} \sigma^2_{R_{AMD}} &= \{p_{Poor} \times [R_{Poor} - E(R_{AMD})]^2\} + \{p_{Neutral} \times [R_{Neutral} - E(R_{AMD})]^2\} \\ &\quad + \{p_{Good} \times [R_{Good} - E(R_{AMD})]^2\} \\ &= [0.2 \times (-0.13 - 0.099)^2] + [0.5 \times (0.10 - 0.099)^2] + [0.3 \times (0.25 - 0.099)^2] \\ &= 0.01733 \\ \sigma_{R_{AMD}} &= (\sigma^2_{R_{AMD}})^{1/2} = (0.01733)^{1/2} = 0.13164, \text{ or } 13.164\% \end{aligned}$$

and

$$\begin{aligned} \sigma^2_{R_{Intel}} &= \{p_{Poor} \times [R_{Poor} - E(R_{Intel})]^2\} + \{p_{Neutral} \times [R_{Neutral} - E(R_{Intel})]^2\} \\ &\quad + \{p_{Good} \times [R_{Good} - E(R_{Intel})]^2\} \\ &= [0.2 \times (-0.10 - 0.081)^2] + [0.5 \times (0.07 - 0.081)^2] + [0.3 \times (0.22 - 0.081)^2] \\ &= 0.01241 \\ \sigma_{R_{Intel}} &= (\sigma^2_{R_{Intel}})^{1/2} = (0.01241)^{1/2} = 0.11140, \text{ or } 11.140\% \end{aligned}$$

Having calculated the expected returns and standard deviations for the expected returns on AMD and Intel stock, the natural question to ask is which provides the highest risk-adjusted return. Before we answer this question, let's return to the example at the beginning of Section 7.1. Recall that, in this example, we proposed choosing among three stocks: A, B, and C. We stated that investors would prefer the investment that provides the highest expected return for a given level of risk or the lowest risk for a given expected return. This made it fairly easy to choose between Stocks A and B, which had the same return but different risk levels, and between Stocks B and C, which had the same risk but different returns. We were stuck when trying to choose between Stocks A and C, however, because they differed in both risk and return. Now, armed with tools for quantifying expected returns and risk, we can at least take a first pass at comparing stocks such as these.

The **coefficient of variation (CV)** is a measure that can help us in making comparisons such as that between Stocks A and C. The coefficient of variation for stock i is calculated as follows:

$$CV_i = \frac{\sigma_{R_i}}{E(R_i)} \quad (7.4)$$

coefficient of variation (CV)
a measure of the risk associated with an investment for each one percent of expected return

In this equation, CV is a measure of the risk associated with an investment for each one percent of expected return.

Recall that Stock A has an expected return of 12 percent and a risk level of 12 percent, while Stock C has an expected return of 16 percent and a risk level of 16 percent. If we assume that the risk level given for each stock is equal to the standard deviation of its return, we can find the coefficients of variation for the stocks as follows:

$$\text{CV}(R_A) = \frac{0.12}{0.12} = 1.00 \quad \text{and} \quad \text{CV}(R_C) = \frac{0.16}{0.16} = 1.00$$

Since these values are equal, the coefficient of variation measure suggests that these two investments are equally attractive on a risk-adjusted basis.

Now returning to our AMD and Intel example, we find that the coefficients of variation for those shares are:

$$\text{CV}_{AMD} = \frac{\sigma_{R_{AMD}}}{E(R_{AMD})} = \frac{0.13164}{0.099} = 1.330$$

and

$$\text{CV}_{Intel} = \frac{\sigma_{R_{Intel}}}{E(R_{Intel})} = \frac{0.11140}{0.081} = 1.375$$

We can see that while AMD stock has a higher expected return (9.9 percent versus 8.1 percent) and a higher standard deviation of returns (13.154 percent versus 11.140 percent), it has a lower coefficient of variation than Intel stock. This tells us that the amount of risk for each one percent of expected return is lower for AMD shares than for Intel shares. On a risk-adjusted basis, then, the expected returns from AMD stock are more attractive.

LEARNING BY DOING APPLICATION 7.4

Calculating and Using the Coefficient of Variation

Problem: You are trying to choose between two investments. The first investment, a painting by Picasso, has an expected return of 14 percent with a standard deviation of 30 percent over the next year. The second investment, a pair of blue suede shoes once worn by Elvis, has an expected return of 20 percent with a standard deviation of return of 40 percent. What is the coefficient of variation for each of these investments, and what do these coefficients tell us?

Approach: Use Equation 7.4 to compute the coefficients of variation for the two investments.

Solution: The coefficients of variation are:

$$\text{CV}(R_{Painting}) = \frac{0.3}{0.14} = 2.14 \quad \text{and} \quad \text{CV}(R_{Shoes}) = \frac{0.4}{0.2} = 2.00$$

The coefficient of variation for the painting is slightly higher than that for Elvis's blue suede shoes. This indicates that the risk for each one percent of expected return is higher for the painting than for Elvis's shoes.

You can read about other ratios that are used to measure risk-adjusted returns for investments at the following Web site: www.andreassteiner.net/ performanceanalysis/ ?External_Analysis: Risk-Adjusted_ Performance_Measures.

Portfolios with More Than One Asset

It may seem like a good idea to evaluate investments by calculating a measure of risk for each one percent of expected return. However, the coefficient of variation has a critical shortcoming that is not quite evident when we are considering only a single asset. In order to explain this shortcoming, we must discuss the more realistic setting in which an investor has constructed a two-asset portfolio.

EXPECTED RETURN ON A PORTFOLIO WITH MORE THAN ONE ASSET

Suppose that you own a portfolio that consists of $500 of AMD stock and $500 of Intel stock and that over the next year you expect to earn returns on the AMD and Intel shares of 9.9 percent and 8.1 percent, respectively. How would you calculate the expected return for the overall portfolio?

Let's try to answer this question using our intuition. If half of your funds are invested in each stock, it would seem reasonable that the expected return for this portfolio should be a 50-50 mixture of the expected returns from the two stocks, or:

$$E(R_{Portfolio}) = (0.5 \times 0.099) + (0.5 \times 0.081) = 0.09, \text{ or } 9.0\%$$

Notice that this formula is just like the expected return formula for an individual stock. However, in this case, instead of multiplying outcomes by their associated probabilities, we are multiplying expected returns for individual stocks by the fraction of the total portfolio value that each of these stocks represents. In other words, the formula for the expected return for a two-stock portfolio is:

$$E(R_{Portfolio}) = x_1 E(R_1) + x_2 E(R_2)$$

where x_i represents the fraction of the portfolio invested in asset i. The corresponding equation for a portfolio with n assets is:

$$E(R_{Portfolio}) = \sum_{i=1}^{n} [x_i \times E(R_i)] \tag{7.5}$$
$$= [x_1 \times E(R_1)] + [x_2 \times E(R_2)] + \cdots + [x_n \times E(R_n)]$$

This equation is just like Equation 7.2, except that (1) the returns are expected returns for individual assets and (2) instead of multiplying by the probability of an outcome, we are multiplying by the fraction of the portfolio invested in each asset. Note that this equation can be used only if you have already calculated the expected return for each stock.

To see how Equation 7.5 is used to calculate the expected return on a portfolio with more than two assets, consider an example. Suppose that you were recently awarded a $500,000 grant from a national foundation to pursue your interest in advancing the art of noodling—a popular pastime in some parts of the country in which people catch 40- to 50-pound catfish by putting their hands into catfish holes and wiggling their fingers like noodles to attract the fish.[3] Since your grant is intended to support your activities for five years, you kept $100,000 to cover your expenses for the next year and invested the remaining $400,000 in U.S. Treasury bills and stocks. Specifically, you invested $100,000 in Treasury bills (TB) that yield 4.5 percent; $150,000 in Procter & Gamble stock (P&G), which has an expected return of 7.5 percent; and $150,000 in Exxon Mobil Corporation stock (EMC), which has an expected return of 9.0 percent. What is the expected return on this $400,000 portfolio?

In order to use Equation 7.5, we must first calculate x_i, the fraction of the portfolio invested in asset i, for each investment. These fractions are as follows:

$$x_{TB} = \frac{\$100,000}{\$400,000} = 0.25$$

$$x_{P\&G} = x_{EMC} = \frac{\$150,000}{\$400,000} = 0.375$$

Therefore, the expected return on the portfolio is:

$$E(R_{Portfolio}) = [x_{TB} \times E(R_{TB})] + [x_{P\&G} \times E(R_{P\&G})] + [x_{EMC} \times E(R_{EMC})]$$
$$= (0.25 \times 0.045) + (0.375 \times 0.075) + (0.375 \times 0.090)$$
$$= 0.0731, \text{ or } 7.31\%$$

---

[3] For more information on noodling, see the April 21, 2006, *New York Times* article titled "In the Jaws of a Catfish," by Ethan Todras-Whitehill.

LEARNING BY DOING APPLICATION 7.5

Calculating the Expected Return on a Portfolio

Problem: You have become concerned that you have too much of your money invested in your pizza restaurant and have decided to diversify your personal portfolio. Right now the pizza restaurant is your only investment. To diversify, you plan to sell 45 percent of your restaurant and invest the proceeds from the sale, in equal proportions, into a stock market index fund and a bond market index fund. Over the next year, you expect to earn a return of 15 percent on your remaining investment in the pizza restaurant, 12 percent on your investment in the stock market index fund, and 8 percent on your investment in the bond market index fund. What return will you expect from your diversified portfolio over the next year?

Approach: First, calculate the fraction of your portfolio that will be invested in each type of asset after you have diversified. Then use Equation 7.5 to calculate the expected return on the portfolio.

Solution: After you have diversified, 55 percent (100 percent − 45 percent) of your portfolio will be invested in your restaurant, 22.5 percent (45 percent × 0.50) will be invested in the stock market index fund, and 22.5 percent (45 percent × 0.50) will be invested in the bond market index fund. Therefore, from Equation 7.5, we know that the expected return for your portfolio is:

$$E(R_{Portfolio}) = [x_{Rest} \times E(R_{Rest})] + [x_{Stock} \times E(R_{Stock})] + [x_{Bond} \times E(R_{Bond})]$$
$$= (0.550 \times 0.15) + (0.225 \times 0.12) + (0.225 \times 0.08)$$
$$= 0.1275, \text{ or } 12.75\%$$

At 12.75 percent, the expected return is an average of the returns on the individual assets in your portfolio, weighted by the fraction of your portfolio that is invested in each.

RISK OF A PORTFOLIO WITH MORE THAN ONE ASSET

Now that we have calculated the expected return on a portfolio with more than one asset, the next question is how to quantify the risk of such a portfolio. Before we discuss the mechanics of how to do this, it is important to have some intuitive understanding of how volatility in the returns for different assets interact to determine the volatility of the overall portfolio.

The prices of two stocks in a portfolio will rarely, if ever, change by the same amount and in the same direction at the same time. Normally, the price of one stock will change by more than the price of the other. In fact, the prices of two stocks will frequently move in different directions. These differences in price movements affect the total volatility in the returns for a portfolio.

Exhibit 7.6 shows monthly returns for the stock of CSX (a railroad company) and Wal-Mart (the big retailer) over the period from September 2002 through September 2007. Notice that the returns on these shares are generally different and that the prices of the shares can move in different directions in a given month (one stock has a positive return when the other has a negative return). When the stock prices move in opposite directions, the change in the price of one stock offsets at least some of the change in the price of the other stock. As a result, the level of risk for a portfolio of the two stocks is less than the average of the risks associated with the individual shares.

This means that we *cannot* calculate the variance of a portfolio containing two assets simply by calculating the average of the variances of the individual stocks using a formula such as:

$$\sigma^2_{R_{\text{2 Asset portfolio}}} = x_1^2 \sigma^2_{R_1} + x_2^2 \sigma^2_{R_2}$$

where x_i represents the fraction of the portfolio invested in stock i and $\sigma^2_{R_i}$ is the variance of the return on stock i. We have to account for the fact that the returns on

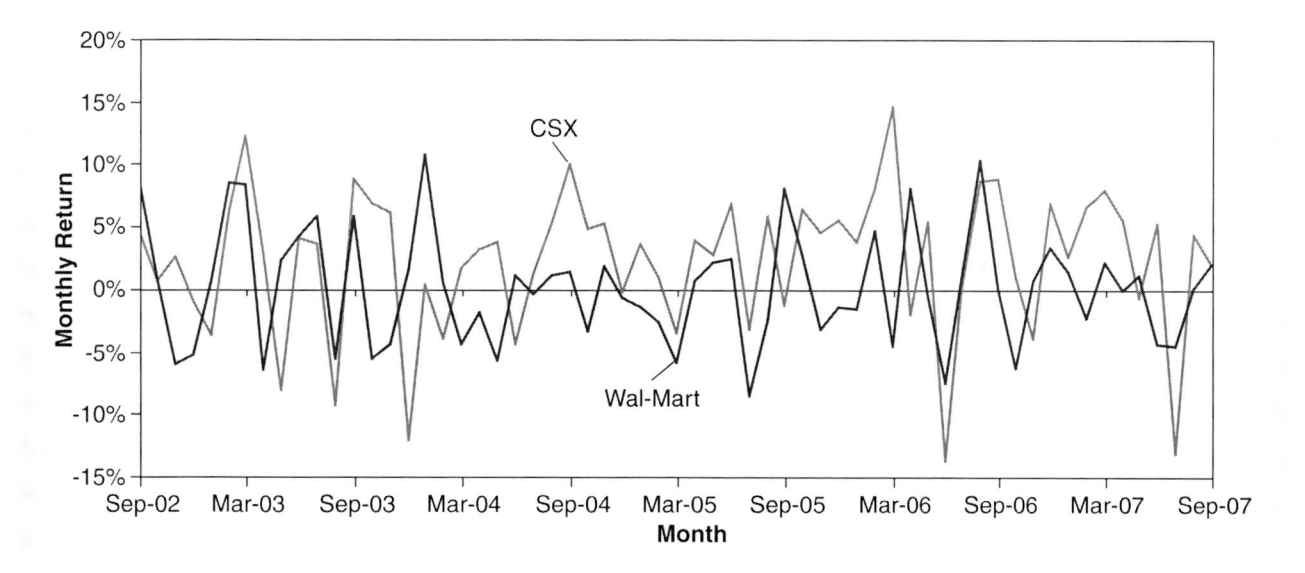

Exhibit 7.6
Monthly Returns for CSX and Wal-Mart Stock from September 2002 through September 2007
The returns on two stocks are generally different. In some periods, the return on one stock is positive, while the return on the other is negative. Even when the returns on both are positive or negative, they are rarely exactly the same.

different shares in a portfolio tend to partially offset each other. We do this by adding a third term to the formula. For a two-asset portfolio, we calculate the variance of the returns using the following formula:

$$\sigma^2_{R_{\text{2 Asset portfolio}}} = x_1^2 \sigma^2_{R_1} + x_2^2 \sigma^2_{R_2} + 2x_1 x_2 \sigma_{R_{1,2}} \quad (7.6)$$

where $\sigma_{R_{1,2}}$ is the **covariance** between stocks 1 and 2. The covariance is a measure of how the returns on two assets covary, or move together. The third term in Equation 7.6 accounts for the fact that returns from the two assets will offset each other to some extent. The covariance is calculated using the following formula:

covariance
a measure of how the returns on two assets covary, or move together

$$\text{Cov}(R_1, R_2) = \sigma_{R_{1,2}} = \sum_{i=1}^{n} \{p_i \times [(R_{1,i} - E(R_1)] \times [(R_{2,i} - E(R_2)]\} \quad (7.7)$$

where i represents outcomes rather than assets. Compare this equation with Equation 7.3, reproduced here:

$$\text{Var}(R) = \sigma^2_R = \sum_{i=1}^{n} \{p_i \times [R_i - E(R)]^2\}$$

You can see that the covariance calculation is very similar to the variance calculation. The difference is that, instead of squaring the difference between the value from each outcome and the expected value for an individual asset, we calculate the product of this difference for two different assets.

Just as it is difficult to directly interpret the variance of the returns for an asset—recall that the variance is in units of squared dollars—it is difficult to directly interpret the covariance of returns between two assets. We get around this problem by dividing the covariance by the product of the standard deviations of the returns for the two assets. This gives us the correlation, ρ, between the returns on those assets:

$$\rho = \frac{\sigma_{R_{1,2}}}{\sigma_{R_1} \sigma_{R_2}} \quad (7.8)$$

The correlation between the returns on two assets will always have a value between −1 and +1. This makes the interpretation of this variable straightforward. A *negative correlation* means that the returns tend to have opposite signs. For example, when the return on one asset is positive, the return on the other asset tends to be negative. If the correlation is exactly −1, the returns on the two assets are perfectly negatively correlated. In other words, when the return on one asset is positive, the return on the other asset will always be negative. A *positive correlation* means that when the return on one asset is positive, the return on the other asset also tends to be positive. If the correlation is exactly equal to +1, then the returns of the two assets are said to be perfectly positively correlated. The return on one asset will always be positive when the return on the other asset is positive. Finally, a *correlation of 0* means that the returns on the assets are not correlated. In this case, the fact that the return on one asset is positive or negative tells you nothing about how likely it is that the return on the other asset will be positive or negative.

Let's work an example to see how Equation 7.6 is used to calculate the variance of a portfolio that consists of 50 percent CSX and 50 percent Wal-Mart stock. Using the data plotted in Exhibit 7.6, we can calculate the variance of the annual returns for CSX and Wal-Mart stock, σ_R^2, to be 0.03949 and 0.02584, respectively. The covariance between the annual returns on these two stocks is 0.00782. We do not show the calculations for the variances and the covariance because each of these numbers was calculated using 60 different monthly returns. These calculations are too cumbersome to illustrate. Rest assured, however, that they were calculated using Equations 7.3 and 7.7.[4] With these values, we can calculate the variance of a portfolio that consists of 50 percent CSX stock and 50 percent Wal-Mart stock as:

$$\begin{aligned}\sigma^2_{R_{\text{Portfolio of CSX and Wal-Mart}}} &= x^2_{\text{CSX}}\sigma^2_{R_{\text{CSX}}} + x^2_{\text{Wal-Mart}}\sigma^2_{R_{\text{Wal-Mart}}} + 2x_{\text{CSX}}x_{\text{Wal-Mart}}\sigma_{R_{\text{CSX, Wal-Mart}}} \\ &= (0.5)^2(0.03949) + (0.5)^2(0.02584) + 2(0.5)(0.5)(0.00782) \\ &= 0.02024\end{aligned}$$

You can see that this portfolio variance is smaller than the variance of either CSX or Wal-Mart stock on its own.

If we calculate the standard deviations by taking the square roots of the variances, we find that the standard deviations for CSX, Wal-Mart, and the portfolio consisting of those two stocks are 0.199 (19.9 percent), 0.161 (16.1 percent), and 0.142 (14.2 percent), respectively.

Exhibit 7.7 illustrates the monthly returns for the portfolio of CSX and Wal-Mart stock, along with the monthly returns for the individual stocks. You can see in this exhibit that, while the returns on the portfolio vary quite a bit, this variation is slightly less than that for the individual company shares.

Using Equation 7.8, we can calculate the correlation of the returns between CSX and Wal-Mart stock as:

$$\rho = \frac{\sigma_{R_{1,2}}}{\sigma_{R_1}\sigma_{R_2}} = \frac{0.00782}{0.199 \times 0.161} = 0.244$$

The positive correlation tells us that the prices on CSX and Wal-Mart stock tend to move in the same direction. However, the correlation of less than one tells us that they do not always do so. The fact that the prices of these two shares do not always move together is the reason that the returns on a portfolio of the two stocks have less variation than the returns on the individual company shares. This example illustrates the benefit of *diversification*—how holding more than one asset with different risk characteristics can reduce the risk of a portfolio. Note that if the correlation of the returns between CSX and Wal-Mart stock equaled one, holding these two stocks would not reduce risk because their prices would always move up or down together.

As we add more and more stocks to a portfolio, calculating the variance using the approach illustrated in Equation 7.6 becomes increasingly complex. The reason for this is that we have to account for the covariance between each pair of assets. These more

---

[4]The only adjustment that we had to make was to account for the fact that our calculations used monthly returns rather than annual returns. This adjustment simply required us to multiply each number we calculated by 12 because there are 12 months in a year.

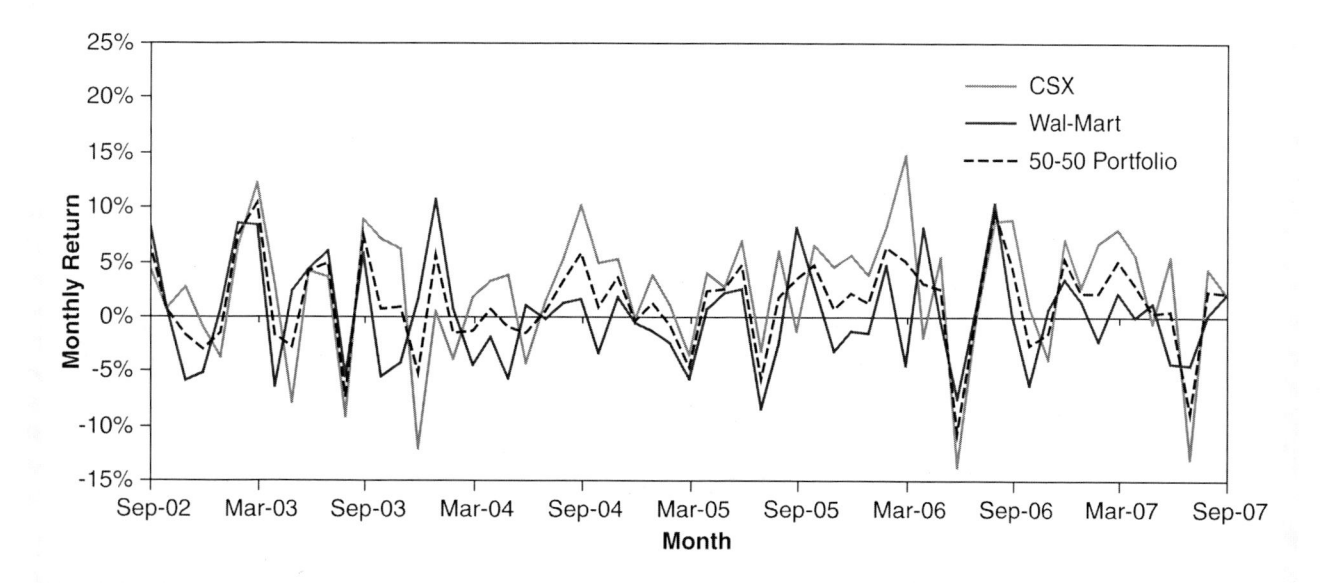

Exhibit 7.7
Monthly Returns for CSX and Wal-Mart Stock and for a Portfolio with 50 Percent of the Value in Each of these Two Stocks from September 2002 through September 2007
The variation in the returns from a portfolio that consists of CSX and Wal-Mart stock in equal proportions is less than the variation in the returns from either of those stocks alone.

extensive calculations are beyond the scope of this book, but they are conceptually the same as those for a portfolio with two assets.

Calculating the Variance of a Two-Asset Portfolio

LEARNING BY DOING APPLICATION 7.6

Problem: You are still planning to sell 45 percent of your pizza restaurant in order to diversify your personal portfolio. However, you have now decided to invest all of the proceeds in the stock market index fund. After you diversify, you will have 55 percent of your wealth invested in the restaurant and 45 percent invested in the stock market index fund. You have estimated the variances of the returns for these two investments and the covariance between their returns to be as follows:

$\sigma^2_{R_{Restaurant}}$	0.0625
$\sigma^2_{R_{Stock\ market\ index}}$	0.0400
$\sigma_{R_{Restaurant},\ Stock\ market\ index}$	0.0250

What will be the variance and standard deviation of your portfolio after you have sold the ownership interest in your restaurant and invested in the stock market index fund?

Approach: Use Equation 7.6 to calculate the variance of the portfolio and then take the square root of this value to obtain the standard deviation.

Solution:

The variance of the portfolio is:

$$\sigma^2_{R_{Portfolio}} = x^2_{R_{Restaurant}} \sigma^2_{R_{Restaurant}} + x^2_{R_{Stock\ market\ index}} \sigma^2_{R_{Stock\ market\ index}}$$
$$+ 2x_{Restaurant} x_{Stock\ market\ index} \sigma_{R_{Restaurant},\ Stock\ market\ index}$$
$$= [(0.55)^2 \times 0.0625] + [(0.45)^2 \times 0.0400] + (2 \times 0.55 \times 0.45 \times 0.0250)$$
$$= 0.0394$$

and the standard deviation is $(0.0394)^{1/2} = 0.1985$, or 19.85 percent.

(continued)

> Comparing the portfolio variance of 0.0394 with the variances of the restaurant, 0.0625, and the stock market index fund, 0.0400, shows once again that a portfolio with two or more assets can have a smaller variance (and thus a smaller standard deviation) than any of the individual assets in the portfolio.

> **BUILDING INTUITION**
>
> **Diversified Portfolios are Less Risky**
>
> Diversified portfolios generally have less risk for a given level of return than the individual risky assets in the portfolio. This is because the prices of individual assets rarely change by the same amount and in the same direction at the same time. As a result, some of the variation in an asset's price can be diversified away by owning another asset at the same time. This is important because it tells us that investors can eliminate some of the risk associated with individual investments by holding them in a diversified portfolio.

The Limits of Diversification

In the sample calculations for the portfolio containing CSX and Wal-Mart stock, we saw that the standard deviation of the returns for a portfolio consisting of equal investments in those two stocks was 14.2 percent from September 2002 through September 2007 and that this figure was lower than the standard deviation for either of the individual stocks (19.9 percent and 16.1 percent). You might wonder how the standard deviation for the portfolio is likely to change if we increase the number of assets in the portfolio. The answer is simple. If the returns on the individual stocks added to our portfolio do not all change in the same way, then increasing the number of stocks in the portfolio will reduce the standard deviation of the portfolio returns even further.

Let's consider a simple example to illustrate this point. Suppose that all assets have a standard deviation of returns that is equal to 40 percent and that the covariance between the returns for each pair of assets is 0.048. If we form a portfolio in which we have an equal investment in two assets, the standard deviation of returns for the portfolio will be 32.25 percent. If we add a third asset, the portfolio standard deviation of returns will decrease to 29.21 percent. It will be even lower, at 27.57 percent, for a four-asset portfolio. Exhibit 7.8 illustrates how the standard deviation for the portfolio declines as more stocks are added.

In addition to showing how increasing the number of assets decreases the overall risk of a portfolio, Exhibit 7.8 illustrates three other very important points. First, the decrease in the standard deviation for the portfolio gets smaller and smaller as more assets are added. You can see this effect by looking at the distance between the straight horizontal line and the plot of the standard deviation of the portfolio returns.

The second important point is that, as the number of assets becomes very large, the portfolio standard deviation does not approach zero. It decreases only so far. In the example in Exhibit 7.8, it approaches 21.9 percent. The standard deviation does not approach zero because we are assuming that the variations in the asset returns do not completely cancel each other out. This is a realistic assumption because in practice investors can rarely diversify away all risk. They can diversify away risk that is unique to the individual assets, but they cannot diversify away risk that is common to all assets. The risk that can be diversified away is called **diversifiable**, **unsystematic**, or **unique risk**, and the risk that cannot be diversified away is called **nondiversifiable** or **systematic risk**. In the next section, we will discuss systematic risk in detail.

The third key point illustrated in Exhibit 7.8 is that most of the risk-reduction benefits from diversification can be achieved in a portfolio with 15 to 20 assets. Of course, the number of assets required to achieve a high level of diversification depends on the covariances between the assets in the portfolio. However, in general, it is not necessary to invest in a very large number of different assets.

diversifiable, unsystematic, or unique risk
risk that can be eliminated through diversification

nondiversifiable or systematic risk
risk that cannot be eliminated through diversification

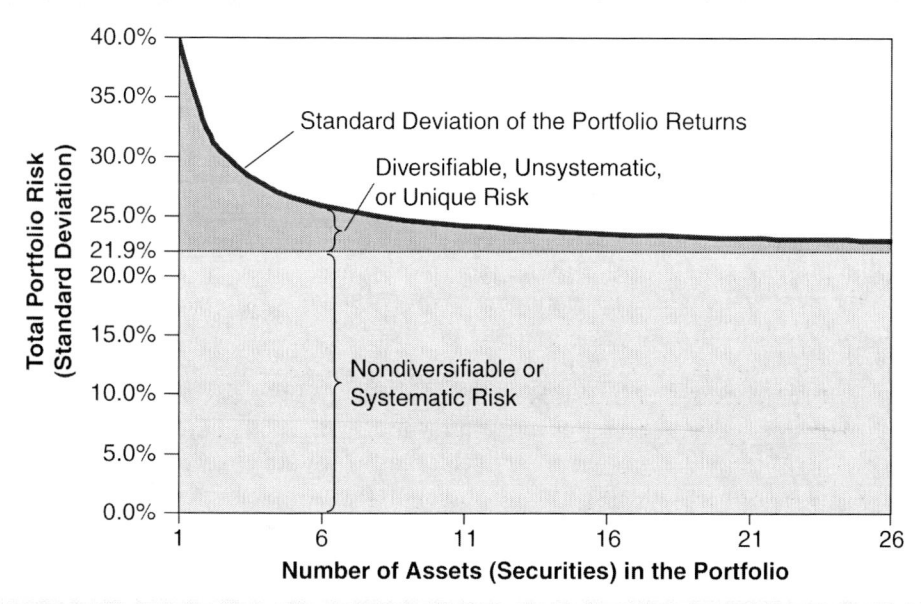

Exhibit 7.8
Unique and Systematic Risk in a Portfolio as the Number of Assets Increases
The total risk of a portfolio decreases as the number of assets increases. This is because the amount of unsystematic or unique risk in the portfolio decreases. The diversification benefit from adding another asset declines as the total number of assets in the portfolio increases and the unsystematic or unique risk approaches zero. Most of the diversification benefit can often be achieved with as few as 15 or 20 assets.

> **Before You Go On**
>
> 1. What does the coefficient of variation tell us?
> 2. What are the two components of total risk?
> 3. Why does the total risk of a portfolio not approach zero as the number of assets in a portfolio becomes very large?

7.5 Systematic Risk

The objective of diversification is to eliminate variations in returns that are unique to individual assets. We diversify our investments across a number of different assets in the hope that these unique variations will cancel each other out. With complete diversification, all of the unique risk is eliminated from the portfolio. An investor with a diversified portfolio still faces systematic risk, however, and we now turn our attention to that form of risk.

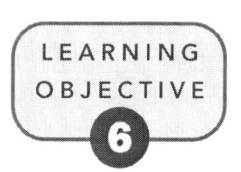

LEARNING OBJECTIVE 6

Why Systematic Risk Is All That Matters

The idea that unique, or unsystematic, risk can be diversified away has direct implications for the relation between risk and return. If the transaction costs associated with constructing a diversified portfolio are relatively low, then rational, informed investors, such as the students who are taking this class, will prefer to hold diversified portfolios.

Diversified investors face only systematic risk, whereas investors whose portfolios are not well diversified face systematic risk plus unsystematic risk. Because they face less risk, the diversified investors will be willing to pay higher prices for individual assets than the other investors. Therefore, expected returns on individual assets will be lower than the total risk (systematic plus unsystematic risk) of those assets suggests they should be.

To illustrate, consider two individual investors, Emily and Jane. Each of them is trying to decide if she should purchase stock in your pizza restaurant. Emily holds a diversified portfolio and Jane does not. Assume your restaurant's stock has five units of systematic risk and nine units of total risk. You can see that Emily faces less risk than Jane and will require a lower expected rate of return. Consequently, Emily will be willing to pay a higher price than Jane.

If the market includes a large number of diversified investors such as Emily, competition among these investors will drive the price of your shares up further. Competition among these investors will ultimately drive the price up to the point where the expected return just compensates all investors for the systematic risk associated with your stock. The bottom line is that because of competition among diversified investors only systematic risk is rewarded in asset markets. For this reason, we are concerned only about systematic risk when we think about the relation between risk and return in finance.

> **BUILDING INTUITION**
>
> **Systematic Risk Is the Risk That Matters**
>
> The required rate of return on an asset depends only on the systematic risk associated with that asset. Because unique (unsystematic) risk can be diversified away, investors can and will eliminate their exposure to this risk. Competition among diversified investors will drive the prices of assets to the point where the expected returns will compensate investors for only the systematic risk that they bear.

Measuring Systematic Risk

If systematic risk is all that matters when we think about expected returns, then we cannot use the standard deviation as a measure of risk.[5] The standard deviation is a measure of total risk. We need a way of quantifying the systematic risk of individual assets.

A natural starting point for doing this is to recognize that the most diversified portfolio possible will come closest to eliminating all unique risk. Such a portfolio provides a natural benchmark against which we can measure the systematic risk of an individual asset. What is the most diversified portfolio possible? The answer is simple. It is the portfolio that consists of all assets, including stocks, bonds, real estate, precious metals, commodities, art, baseball cards, and so forth from all over the world. In finance, we call this the **market portfolio**.

market portfolio
the portfolio of all assets

Unfortunately, we do not have very good data for most of these assets for most of the world, so we use the next best thing: the U.S. public stock market. A large number of stocks from a broad range of industries trade in this market. The companies that issue these stocks own a wide range of assets all over the world. These characteristics, combined with the facts that the U.S. market has been operating for a very long time and that we have very reliable and detailed information on prices for U.S. stocks, make the U.S. stock market a natural benchmark for estimating systematic risk.

market risk
a term commonly used to refer to nondiversifiable, or systematic, risk

Since systematic risk is, by definition, risk that cannot be diversified away, the systematic risk of an individual asset is really just a measure of the relation between the returns on the individual asset and the returns on the market. In fact, systematic risk is often referred to as **market risk**. To see how we might use data from the U.S. public

---

[5]This statement is true in the context of how expected returns are determined. However, the standard deviation is still a very useful measure of the risk faced by an individual investor who does not hold a diversified portfolio. For example, the owners of most small businesses have much of their personal wealth tied up in their businesses. They are certainly concerned about the total risk because it is directly related to the probability that they will go out of business and lose much of their wealth.

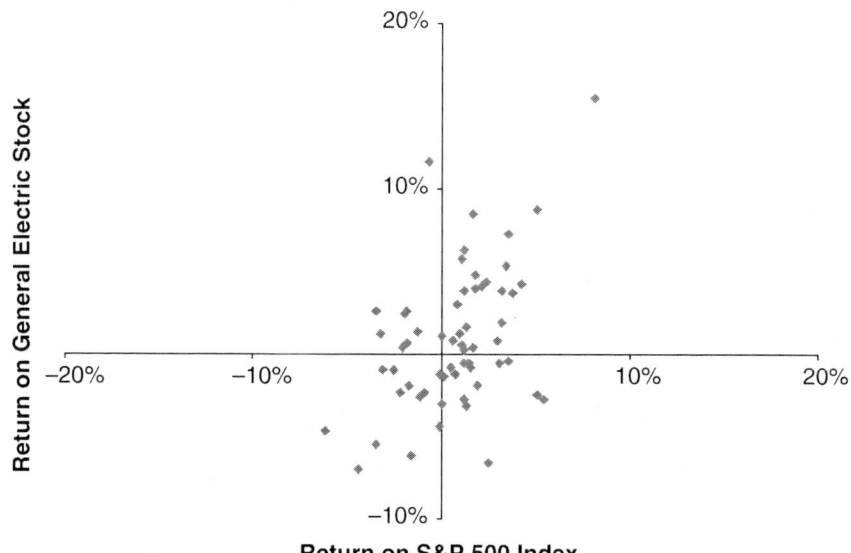

Exhibit 7.9
Plot of Monthly General Electric Company Stock and S&P 500 Index Returns: April 2003 to March 2008

The monthly returns on General Electric stock are positively related to the returns on the S&P 500 index. In other words, the return on General Electric's stock tends to be higher when the return on the S&P 500 index is higher and lower when the return on the S&P 500 index is lower.

---

stock market to estimate the systematic risk of an individual asset, look at Exhibit 7.9, which plots 60 historical monthly returns for General Electric Company (GE) against the corresponding monthly returns for the S&P 500 index (A proxy for the U.S. stock market). In this plot, you can see that returns on GE stock tend to be higher when returns on the S&P 500 tend to be higher. The measure of systematic risk that we use in finance is a statistical measure of this relation.

We quantify the relation between the returns on GE stock and the general market by finding the slope of the line that best represents the relation illustrated in Exhibit 7.9. Specifically, we estimate the slope of the *line of best fit*. We do this using the statistical technique called regression analysis. If you are not familiar with regression analysis, don't worry; the details are beyond the scope of this course. All you have to know is that this technique gives us the line that fits the data best.

Exhibit 7.10 illustrates the line that was estimated for the data in Exhibit 7.9 using regression analysis. Note that the slope of this line is 0.76. Recall from your math classes that the slope of a line equals the ratio of the rise (vertical distance) divided by the corresponding run (horizontal distance). In this case, the slope is the change in the return on GE stock divided by the change in the return on the U.S. stock market. A slope of 0.76 therefore means that, on average, the change in the return on GE stock was 0.76 times as large as the change in the return on the S&P 500 index. Thus, if the S&P 500 index goes up 1 percent, the average increase in GE's stock is 0.76 percent. This is a measure of systematic risk because it tells us that the volatility of the returns on GE stock is 0.76 times as large as that for the S&P 500 as a whole.

To explore this idea more completely, let's consider another, simpler example. Suppose that you have data for Nike stock and for the U.S. stock market for each of the past two years. In the first year, the return on the market was 10 percent, and the return on Nike stock was 15 percent. In the second year, the return on the market was 12 percent, and the return on Nike stock was 19 percent. From this information, we know that the return on Nike stock increased by 4 percent while the return on the market increased 2 percent. If we plotted the returns for Nike stock and for the market for each of the last two periods, as we did for GE stock and the market in Exhibits 7.9 and 7.10, and estimated

236 CHAPTER 7 Risk and Return

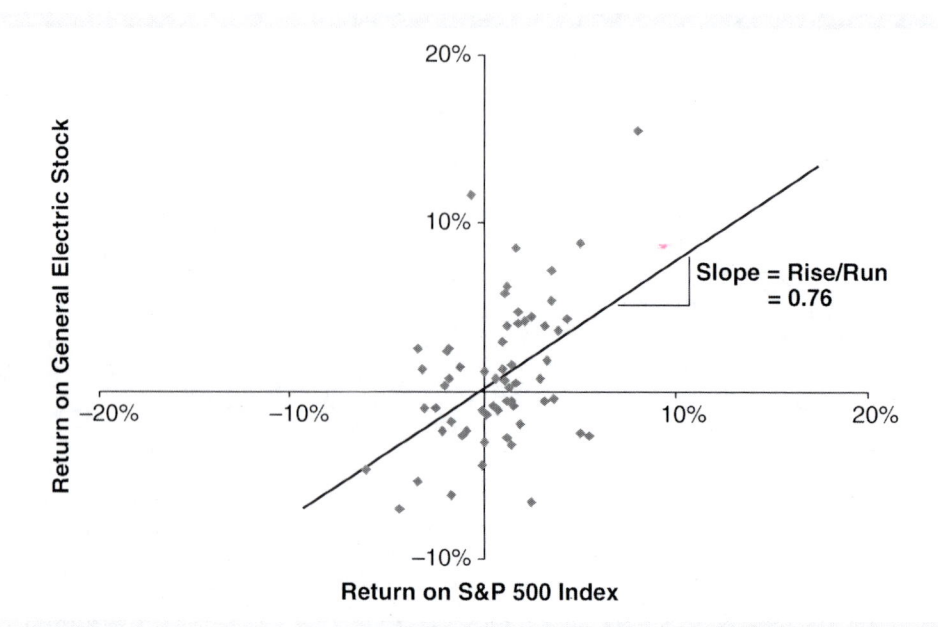

Exhibit 7.10

Slope of Relation Between General Electric Company Monthly Stock Returns and S&P 500 Index Returns: April 2003 to March 2008

The line shown in the exhibit best represents the relation between the monthly returns on General Electric stock and the returns on the S&P 500 index. The slope of this line, which equals 0.76, indicates that the return on General Electric stock tends to equal about 0.76 times the return on the S&P 500 index.

---

the line that best fit the data, it would be a line that connected the dots for the two periods. The slope of this line would equal 2, calculated as follows:

$$\text{Slope} = \frac{\text{Rise}}{\text{Run}} = \frac{\text{Change in Nike return}}{\text{Change in market return}} = \frac{19\% - 15\%}{12\% - 10\%} = \frac{4\%}{2\%} = 2$$

Although we have to be careful about drawing conclusions when we have only two data points, we might interpret the slope of 2 to indicate that new information that causes the market return to increase by 1 percent will tend to cause the return on Nike stock to increase by 2 percent. Of course, the reverse might also be true. That is, new information that causes the market return to decrease by 1 percent may also cause the return on Nike stock to go down by 2 percent. To the extent that the same information is driving the changes in returns on Nike stock and on the market, it would not be possible for an investor in Nike stock to diversify this risk away. It is nondiversifiable, or systematic, risk.

In finance, we call the slope of the line of best fit **beta**. Often we simply use the corresponding Greek letter, β, to refer to this measure of systematic risk. As shown below, a beta of 1 tells us that an asset has just as much systematic risk as the market. A beta higher than or lower than 1 tells us that the asset has more or less systematic risk than the market, respectively. A beta of 0 indicates a risk-free security, such as a U.S. Treasury bill.

> **beta (β)**
> a measure of nondiversifiable, systematic, or market, risk

A convenient place to find betas for individual companies is MSN Money Central at moneycentral.msn.com/home.asp. Just enter the stock symbol at the top of the page and hit "Enter" on your computer (try CSX, for example). You will get prices, an estimate of the beta, and other financial information.

$\beta = 1$	Same systematic risk as market
$\beta > 1$	More systematic risk than market
$\beta < 1$	Less systematic risk than market
$\beta = 0$	No systematic risk

Now you might ask yourself what happened to the unique risk of GE or Nike stock. This is best illustrated by the GE example, where we have more than two observations. As you can see in Exhibit 7.10, the line of best fit does not go through each data point. That is because some of the change in GE's stock price each month reflected information that did not affect the S&P 500 as a whole. That information is the unsystematic, or unique, component of the risk of GE's stock. The distance between each data point and the line of best fit represents variation in GE's stock return that can be attributed to this unique risk.

The positive slope (β) of the regression line in Exhibit 7.10 tells us that returns for the S&P 500 and for GE stock will tend to move in the same direction. The return on the S&P 500 and the return on GE's stock will not always change in the same direction, however, because the unique risk associated with GE stock can more than offset the effect of the market in any particular period. In the next section, we will discuss the implications of beta for the level (as opposed to the change) in the expected return for a stock such as GE.

> **Before You Go On**
>
> 1. Why are returns on the stock market used as a benchmark in measuring systematic risk?
> 2. How is beta estimated?
> 3. How would you interpret a beta of 1.5 for an asset? A beta of 0.75?

7.6 Compensation for Bearing Systematic Risk

Now that we have identified the measure of the risk that diversified investors care about—systematic risk—we are in a position to examine how this measure relates to expected returns. Let's begin by thinking about the rate of return that you would require for an investment. First, you would want to make sure that you were compensated for inflation. It would not make sense to invest if you expected the investment to return an amount that did not at least allow you to have the same purchasing power that the money you invested had when you made the investment. Second, you would want some compensation for the fact that you are giving up the use of your money for a period of time. This compensation may be very small if you are forgoing the use of your money for only a short time, such as when you invest in a 30-day Treasury bill, but it might be relatively large if you are investing for several years. Finally, you are also going to require compensation for the systematic risk associated with the investment.

When you invest in a U.S. government security such as a Treasury bill, note, or bond, you are investing in a security that has no risk of default. After all, the U.S. government can always increase taxes or print more money to pay you back. Changes in economic conditions and other factors that affect the returns on other assets do not affect the default risk of U.S. government securities. As a result, these securities do not have systematic risk, and their returns can be viewed as risk free. In other words, returns on government bonds reflect the compensation required by investors to account for the impact of inflation on purchasing power and for their inability to use the money during the life of the investment.

It follows that the difference between required returns on government securities and required returns for risky investments represents the compensation investors require for taking risk. Recognizing this allows us to write the expected return for an asset i as:

$$E(R_i) = R_{rf} + \text{Compensation for taking risk}_i$$

where R_{rf} is the return on a security with a risk-free rate of return, which analysts typically estimate by looking at returns on government securities. The compensation for taking risk, which varies with the risk of the asset, is added to the risk-free rate of return to get an estimate of the expected rate of return for an asset. If we recognize that the compensation for taking risk varies with asset risk and that systematic risk is what matters, we can write the preceding equation as follows:

$$E(R_i) = R_{rf} + (\text{Units of systematic risk}_i \times \text{Compensation per unit of systematic risk})$$

where units of systematic risk$_i$ is the number of units of systematic risk associated with asset i. Finally, if beta, β, is the appropriate measure for the number of units of systematic risk, we can also define compensation for taking risk as follows:

$$\text{Compensation for taking risk}_i = \beta_i \times \text{Compensation per unit of systematic risk}$$

where β_i is the beta for asset i.

Remember that beta is a measure of systematic risk that is directly related to the risk of the market as a whole. If the beta for an asset is 2, that asset has twice as much systematic risk as the market. If the beta for an asset is 0.5, then the asset has half as much systematic risk as the market. Recognizing this natural interpretation of beta suggests that the appropriate "unit of systematic risk" is the level of risk in the market as a whole and that the appropriate "compensation per unit of systematic risk" is the expected return required for the level of systematic risk in the market as a whole. The required rate of return on the market, over and above that of the risk-free return, represents compensation required by investors for bearing a market (systematic) risk. This suggests that:

$$\text{Compensation per unit of systematic risk} = E(R_m) - R_{rf}$$

where $E(R_m)$ is the expected return on the market. The term $E(R_m) - R_{rf}$ is called the *market risk premium*. Consequently, we can now write the equation for expected return as:

$$E(R_i) = R_{rf} + \beta_i[E(R_m) - R_{rf}] \tag{7.9}$$

7.7 The Capital Asset Pricing Model

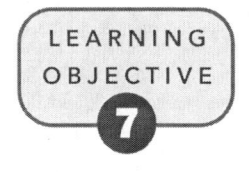

LEARNING OBJECTIVE 7

In deriving Equation 7.9, we intuitively arrived at the **Capital Asset Pricing Model (CAPM)**. Equation 7.9 is the CAPM, a model that describes the relation between risk and expected return. We will discuss the predictions of the CAPM in more detail shortly, but first let's look more closely at how it works.

Suppose that you want to estimate the expected return for a stock that has a beta of 1.5 and that the expected return on the market and risk-free rate are 10 percent and 4 percent, respectively. We can use Equation 7.9 (the CAPM) to find the expected return for this stock:

Capital Asset Pricing Model (CAPM)
a model that describes the relation between risk and expected return

$$E(R_i) = R_{rf} + \beta_i[E(R_m) - R_{rf}]$$
$$= 0.04 + [1.5 \times (0.10 - 0.04)] = 0.13, \text{ or } 13\%$$

Note that we must have three pieces of information in order to use Equation 7.9: (1) the risk-free rate, (2) beta, and (3) either the market risk premium or the expected return on the market. Recall that the market risk premium is the difference between the expected return on the market and the risk-free rate [$E(R_m) - R_{rf}$], which is 6 percent in the above example.

LEARNING BY DOING APPLICATION 7.7

Expected Returns and Systematic Risk

Problem: You are considering buying 100 shares of General Electric stock. Value Line (a financial reporting service) reports that the beta for General Electric is 0.76. The risk-free rate is 4 percent, and the market risk premium is 6 percent. What is the expected rate of return on General Electric stock according to the CAPM?

Approach: Use Equation 7.9 to calculate the expected return on General Electric stock.

Solution: The expected return is

$$E(R_{GE}) = R_{rf} + \beta_{GE}[E(R_m) - R_{rf}]$$
$$= 0.04 + (0.76 \times 0.06) = 0.0856, \text{ or } 8.56\%$$

The Security Market Line

Exhibit 7.11 displays a plot of Equation 7.9 to illustrate how the expected return on an asset varies with systematic risk. This plot shows that the relation between the expected return on an asset and beta is positive and linear. In other words, it is a straight line with a positive slope. The line in Exhibit 7.11 is known as the **Security Market Line (SML)**.

In Exhibit 7.11 you can see that the expected rate of return equals the risk-free rate when beta equals 0. This makes sense because when investors do not face systematic risk,

Security Market Line (SML)
a plot of the relation between expected return and systematic risk

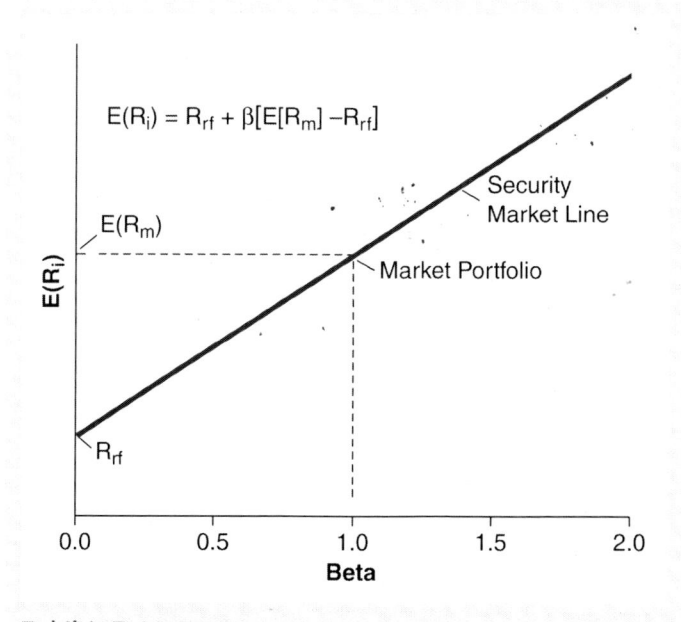

Exhibit 7.11
The Security Market Line
The Security Market Line (SML) is the line that shows the relation between expected returns and systematic risk, as measured by beta. When beta equals zero and there is no systematic risk, the expected return equals the risk free rate. As systematic risk (beta) increases, the expected return increases. This is an illustration of the positive relation between risk and return. The SML shows that it is systematic risk that matters to investors.

they will only require a return that reflects the expected rate of inflation and the fact that they are giving up the use of their money for a period of time. Exhibit 7.11 also shows that the expected return on an asset equals the expected return on the market when beta equals 1. This is not surprising given that both the asset and the market would have the same level of systematic risk if this were the case.

It is important to recognize that the SML illustrates what the CAPM predicts the expected total return should be for various values of beta. The actual expected total return depends on the price of the asset. You can see this from Equation 7.1:

$$R_T = \frac{\Delta P + CF_1}{P_0}$$

where P_0 is the price that the asset is currently selling for. If an asset's price implies that the expected return is greater than that predicted by the CAPM, that asset will plot above the SML in Exhibit 7.11. This means that the asset's price is lower than the CAPM suggests it should be. Conversely, if the expected return on an asset plots below the SML, this implies that the asset's price is higher than the CAPM suggests it should be. The point at which a particular asset plots relative to the SML, then, tells us something about whether the price of that asset might be low or high. Recognizing this fact can be helpful in evaluating the attractiveness of an investment such as the General Electric stock in Learning by Doing Application 7.7.

The Capital Asset Pricing Model and Portfolio Returns

The expected return for a portfolio can also be predicted using the CAPM. The expected return on a portfolio with n assets is calculated using the relation:

$$E(R_{n \text{ Asset portfolio}}) = R_{rf} + \beta_{n \text{ Asset portfolio}}[E(R_m) - R_{rf}]$$

Of course, this should not be surprising since investing in a portfolio is simply an alternative to investing in a single asset.

The fact that the SML is a straight line turns out to be rather convenient if we want to estimate the beta for a portfolio. Recall that the equation for the expected return for a portfolio with n assets was given by Equation 7.5:

$$\begin{aligned} E(R_{\text{Portfolio}}) &= \sum_{i=1}^{n} [x_i \times E(R_i)] \\ &= [x_1 \times E(R_1)] + [x_2 \times E(R_2)] + \cdots + [x_n \times E(R_n)] \end{aligned}$$

If we substitute Equation 7.9 into Equation 7.5 for each of the n assets and rearrange the equation, we find that the beta for a portfolio is simply a weighted average of the betas for the individual assets in the portfolio. In other words:

$$\beta_{n \text{ Asset portfolio}} = \sum_{i=1}^{n} x_i \beta_i = x_1 \beta_1 + x_2 \beta_2 + x_3 \beta_3 + \cdots + x_n \beta_n \quad (7.10)$$

where x_i is the proportion of the portfolio value that is invested in asset i, β_i is the beta of asset i, and n is the number of assets in the portfolio. This formula makes it simple to calculate the beta of any portfolio of assets once you know the betas of the individual assets. As an exercise, you might prove this to yourself by using Equations 7.5 and 7.9 to derive Equation 7.10.

Let's consider an example to see how Equation 7.10 is used. Suppose that you invested 25 percent of your wealth in a fully diversified market fund, 25 percent in risk-free Treasury bills, and 50 percent in a house with twice as much systematic risk as the market. What is the beta of your overall portfolio? What rate of return would you expect to earn from this portfolio if the risk-free rate is 4 percent and the market risk premium is 6 percent?

We know that the beta for the market must equal 1 by definition and that the beta for a risk-free asset equals 0. The beta for your home must be 2 since it has twice the systematic risk of the market. Therefore, the beta of your portfolio is:

$$\beta_{Portfolio} = x_{Fund}\beta_{Fund} + x_{TB}\beta_{TB} + x_{House}\beta_{House}$$
$$= (0.25 \times 1.0) + (0.25 \times 0.0) + (0.50 \times 2.0)$$
$$= 1.25$$

Your portfolio has 1.25 times as much systematic risk as the market. Based on Equation 7.9, you would, therefore, expect to earn a return of 11.5 percent, calculated as follows:

$$E(R_{Portfolio}) = R_{rf} + \beta_{Portfolio}[E(R_m) - R_{rf}]$$
$$= 0.04 + (1.25 \times 0.06) = 0.115, \text{ or } 11.5\%$$

LEARNING BY DOING APPLICATION 7.8

Portfolio Risk and Expected Return

Problem: You have recently become very interested in real estate. To gain some experience as a real estate investor, you have decided to get together with nine of your friends to buy three small cottages near campus. If you and your friends pool your money, you will have just enough to buy the three properties. Since each investment requires the same amount of money and you will have a 10 percent interest in each, you will effectively have one-third of your portfolio invested in each cottage.

While the cottages cost the same, they are different distances from campus and in different neighborhoods. You believe that this causes them to have different levels of systematic risk, and you estimate that the betas for the individual cottages are 1.2, 1.3, and 1.5. If the risk-free rate is 4 percent and the market risk premium is 6 percent, what will be the expected return on your real estate portfolio after you make all three investments?

Approach: There are two approaches that you can use to solve this problem. First, you can estimate the expected return for each cottage using Equation 7.9 and then calculate the expected return on the portfolio using Equation 7.5. Alternatively, you can calculate the beta for the portfolio using Equation 7.10 and then use Equation 7.9 to calculate the expected return.

Solution: Using the first approach, we find that Equation 7.9 gives us the following expected returns:

$$E(R_i) = R_{rf} + \beta_i[E(R_m) - R_{rf}]$$
$$= 0.04 + (1.2 \times 0.06) = 0.112, \text{ or } 11.2\%, \text{ for cottage 1}$$
$$= 0.04 + (1.3 \times 0.06) = 0.118, \text{ or } 11.8\%, \text{ for cottage 2}$$
$$= 0.04 + (1.5 \times 0.06) = 0.130, \text{ or } 13.0\%, \text{ for cottage 3}$$

Therefore, from Equation 7.5, the expected return on the portfolio is:

$$E(R_{Portfolio}) = [x_1 \times E(R_1)] + [x_2 \times E(R_2)] + [x_3 \times E(R_3)]$$
$$= (1/3 \times 0.112) + (1/3 \times 0.118) + (1/3 \times 0.13) = 0.12, \text{ or } 12.0\%$$

Using the second approach, from Equation 7.10, the beta of the portfolio is:

$$\beta_{Portfolio} = x_1\beta_1 + x_2\beta_2 + x_3\beta_3 = (1/3)(1.2) + (1/3)(1.3) + (1/3)(1.5) = 1.33333$$

and from Equation 7.9, the expected return is:

$$E(R_{Portfolio}) = R_{rf} + \beta_{Portfolio}[E(R_m) - R_{rf}]$$
$$= 0.04 + (1.33333 \times 0.06) = 0.120, \text{ or } 12.0\%$$

DECISION-MAKING EXAMPLE 7.2

Choosing between Two Investments

Situation: You are trying to decide whether to invest in one or both of two different stocks. Stock 1 has a beta of 0.8 and an expected return of 7.0 percent. Stock 2 has a beta of 1.2 and an expected return of 9.5 percent. You remember learning about the CAPM in school and believe that it does a good job of telling you what the appropriate expected return should be for a given level of risk. Since the risk-free rate is 4 percent and the market risk premium is 6 percent, the CAPM tells you that the appropriate expected rate of return for an asset with a beta of 0.8 is 8.8 percent. The corresponding value for an asset with a beta of 1.2 is 11.2 percent. Should you invest in either or both of these stocks?

Decision: You should not invest in either stock. The expected returns for both of them are below the values predicted by the CAPM for investments with the same level of risk. In other words, both would plot below the line in Exhibit 7.11. This implies that they are both overpriced.

Up to this point, we have focused on calculating the expected rate of return for an investment in any asset from the perspective of an investor, such as a stockholder. A natural question that might arise is how these concepts relate to the rate of return that should be used within a firm to evaluate a project. The short answer is that they are the same. The rate of return used to discount the cash flows for a project with a particular level of systematic risk is exactly the same as the rate of return that an investor would expect to receive from an investment in any asset having the same level of systematic risk. In Chapter 13 we will explore the relation between the expected return and the rate used to discount project cash flows in much more detail. By the time we finish that discussion, you will understand thoroughly how businesses determine the rate that they use to discount the cash flows from their investments.

> **Before You Go On**
>
> 1. How is the expected return on an asset related to its systematic risk?
> 2. What name is given to the relation between risk and expected return implied by the CAPM?
> 3. If an asset's expected return does not plot on the line in question 2 above, what does that imply about its price?

Summary of Learning Objectives

1. **Explain the relation between risk and return.**

   Investors require greater returns for taking greater risk. They prefer the investment with the highest possible return for a given level of risk or the investment with the lowest risk for a given level of return.

2. **Describe the two components of a total holding period return, and calculate this return for an asset.**

   The total holding period return on an investment consists of a capital appreciation component and an income component. This return is calculated using Equation 7.1. It is important to recognize that investors do not care whether they receive a dollar of return through capital appreciation or as a cash dividend. Investors value both sources of return equally.

3. **Explain what an expected return is, and calculate the expected return for an asset.**

   The expected return is a weighted average of the possible returns from an investment, where each of these returns is weighted by the probability that it will occur. It is calculated using Equation 7.2.

4. **Explain what the standard deviation of returns is, explain why it is especially useful in finance, and be able to calculate it.**

   The standard deviation of returns is a measure of the total risk associated with the returns from an asset. It is useful in evaluating returns in finance because the returns on many assets tend to be normally distributed. The standard deviation of returns provides a convenient measure of the dispersion of returns. In other words, it tells us about the probability that a return will fall within a particular distance from the expected value or within a particular range. To calculate the standard deviation, the variance is first calculated using Equation 7.3. The standard deviation of returns is then calculated by taking the square root of the variance.

5. **Explain the concept of diversification.**

   Diversification is a strategy of investing in two or more assets whose values do not always move in the same direction at the same time in order to reduce risk. Investing in a portfolio containing assets whose prices do not always move together reduces risk because some of the changes in the prices of individual assets offset each other. This can cause the overall volatility in the value of the portfolio to be lower than if it were invested in a single asset.

6. **Discuss which type of risk matters to investors and why.**

   Investors care about only systematic risk. This is because they can eliminate unique risk by holding a diversified portfolio. Diversified investors will bid up prices for assets to the point at which they are just being compensated for the systematic risks they must bear.

7. **Describe what the Capital Asset Pricing Model (CAPM) tells us and how to use it to evaluate whether the expected return of an asset is sufficient to compensate an investor for the risks associated with that asset.**

   The CAPM tells us that the relation between systematic risk and return is linear and that the risk-free rate of return is the appropriate return for an asset with no systematic risk. From the CAPM we know what rate of return investors will require for an investment with a particular amount of systematic risk (beta). This means that we can use the expected return predicted by the CAPM as a benchmark for evaluating whether expected returns for individual assets are sufficient. If the expected return for an asset is less than that predicted by the CAPM, then the asset is an unattractive investment because its return is lower than the CAPM indicates it should be. By the same token, if the expected return for an asset is greater than that predicted by the CAPM, then the asset is an attractive investment because its return is higher than it should be.

Summary of Key Equations

Equation	Description	Formula
7.1	Total holding period return	$R_T = R_{CA} + R_I = \dfrac{P_1 - P_0}{P_0} + \dfrac{CF_1}{P_0}$
7.2	Expected return on an asset	$E(R_{Asset}) = \sum\limits_{i=1}^{n} (p_i \times R_i)$
7.3	Variance of return on an asset	$Var(R) = \sigma_R^2 = \sum\limits_{i=1}^{n} \{p_i \times [R_i - E(R)]^2\}$
7.4	Coefficient of variation	$CV_i = \dfrac{\sigma R_i}{E(R_i)}$
7.5	Expected return for a portfolio	$E(R_{Portfolio}) = \sum\limits_{i=1}^{n} [x_i \times E(R_i)]$
7.6	Variance for a two-asset portfolio	$\sigma_{R_{2Asset\ portfolio}}^2 = x_1^2 \sigma_{R_1}^2 + x_2^2 \sigma_{R_2}^2 + 2x_1 x_2 \sigma_{R_{1,2}}$
7.7	Covariance between two assets	$\sigma_{R_{1,2}} = \sum\limits_{i=1}^{n} \{p_i \times [R_{1,i} - E(R_1)] \times [R_{2,i} - E(R_2)]\}$
7.8	Correlation between two assets	$\rho = \dfrac{\sigma_{R_{1,2}}}{\sigma_{R_1} \sigma_{R_2}}$
7.9	Expected return and systematic risk	$E(R_i) = R_{rf} + \beta_i [E(R_m) - R_{rf}]$
7.10	Portfolio beta	$\beta_{n\ Asset\ portfolio} = \sum\limits_{i=1}^{n} x_i \beta_i$

Self-Study Problems

7.1 Kaaran made a friendly wager with a colleague that involves the result from flipping a coin. If heads comes up, Kaaran must pay her colleague $15; otherwise, her colleague will pay Kaaran $15. What is Kaaran's expected cash flow, and what is the variance of that cash flow if the coin has an equal probability of coming up heads or tails? Suppose Kaaran's colleague is willing to handicap the bet by paying her $20 if the coin toss results in tails. If everything else remains the same, what are Kaaran's expected cash flow and the variance of that cash flow?

7.2 You know that the price of CFI, Inc., stock will be $12 exactly one year from today. Today the price of the stock is $11. Describe what must happen to the price of CFI, Inc., today in order for an investor to generate a 20 percent return over the next year. Assume that CFI does not pay dividends.

7.3 Two men are making a bet according to the outcome of a coin toss. You know that the expected outcome of the bet is that one man will lose $20. Suppose you know that if that same man wins the coin toss, he will receive $80. How much will he pay out if he loses the coin toss?

7.4 The expected value of a normal distribution of prices for a stock is $50. If you are 90 percent sure that the price of the stock will be between $40 and $60, then what is the variance of the stock price?

7.5 The JCHart Co. common shares have an expected return of 25 percent and a coefficient of variation of 2.0. What is the variance of JCHart Co. common share returns?

Solutions to Self-Study Problems

7.1 Part 1: E(cash flow) = (0.5 × −$15) + (0.5 × $15) = 0
$\sigma^2_{\text{Cash flow}}$ = [0.5 × (−$15 − $0)^2] + [0.5 × ($15 − $0)^2] = $225

Part 2: E(cash flow) = (0.5 × −$15) + (0.5 × $20) = $2.50
$\sigma^2_{\text{Cash flow}}$ = [0.5 × (−$15 − $2.50)^2] + [0.5 × ($20 − $2.50)^2] = $306.25

7.2 The expected return for CFI based on today's stock price is ($12 − $11)/$11 = 9.09 percent, which is lower than 20 percent. Since the stock price one year from today is fixed, the only way that you will generate a 20 percent return is if the price of the stock drops today. Consequently, the price of the stock today must drop to $10. It is found by solving the following: 0.2 = ($12 − x)/x, or x = $10.

7.3 Since you know that the probability of any coin toss outcome is equal to 0.5, you can solve the problem by setting up the following equation:

−$20 = (0.5 × $80) + (0.5 × x)

and solving for x:

0.5 × x = −$20 − (0.5 × $80)
x = [−$20 − (0.5 × $80)]/0.5 = −$120

which means that he pays $120 if he loses the bet.

7.4 Since you know that 1.645 standard deviations around the expected return captures 90 percent of the distribution, you can set up either of the following equations:

$40 = $50 − 1.645$\sigma$ or $60 = $50 + 1.645$\sigma$

and solve for σ. Doing this with either equation yields:

σ = $6.079 and σ^2 = 36.954

7.5 Since the coefficient of variation is $CV_i = \dfrac{\sigma_{R_i}}{E(R_i)}$, substituting in the coefficient of variation and E(R_i) allows us to solve for σ^2_{return} as follows:

$$2.0 = \dfrac{\sigma_{R_i}}{0.25}$$
$$\sigma_{R_i} = 0.5$$
$$\sigma^2_{R_i} = (0.5)^2 = 0.25$$

Critical Thinking Questions

7.1 Given that you know the risk as well as the expected return for two stocks, discuss what process you might utilize to determine which of the two stocks is a better buy. You may assume that the two stocks will be the only assets held in your portfolio.

7.2 What is the difference between the expected rate of return and the required rate of return? What does it mean if they are different for a particular asset at a particular point in time?

7.3 Suppose that the standard deviation of the returns on the shares of stock at two different companies is exactly the same. Does this mean that the required rate of return will be the same for these two stocks? How might the required rate of return on the stock of a third company be greater than the required rates of return on the stocks of the first two companies even if the standard deviation of the returns of the third company's stock is lower?

7.4 The correlation between stocks A and B is 0.50, while the correlation between stocks A and C is −0.5. You already own stock A and are thinking of buying either stock B or stock C. If you want your portfolio to have the lowest possible risk, would you buy stock B or C? Would you expect the stock you choose to affect the return that you earn on your portfolio?

7.5 The idea that we can know the return on a security for each possible outcome is overly simplistic. However, even though we cannot possibly predict all possible outcomes, this fact has little bearing on the risk-free return. Explain why.

7.6 Which investment category has shown the greatest degree of risk in the United States since 1926? Explain why that makes sense in a world where the price of a small stock is likely to be more adversely affected by a particular negative event than the price of a corporate bond. Use the same type of explanation to help explain other investment choices since 1926.

7.7 You are concerned about one of the investments in your fully diversified portfolio. You just have an uneasy feeling about the CFO, Iam Shifty, of that particular firm. You do believe, however, that the firm makes a good product and that it is appropriately priced by the market. Should you be concerned about the effect on your portfolio if Shifty embezzles a portion of the firm's cash?

7.8 The CAPM is used to price the risk in any asset. Our examples have focused on stocks, but we could also price the expected rate of return for bonds. Explain how debt securities are also subject to systematic risk.

7.9 In recent years, investors have correctly agreed that the market portfolio consists of more than just a group of U.S. stocks and bonds. If you are an investor who invests in only U.S. stocks, describe the effects on the risk in your portfolio.

7.10 You may have heard the statement that you should not include your home as an asset in your investment portfolio. Assume that your house will comprise up to 75 percent of your assets in the early part of your investment life. Evaluate the implications of omitting it from your portfolio when calculating the risk of your overall investment portfolio.

Questions and Problems

7.1 **Returns:** Describe the difference between a total holding period return and an expected return. **BASIC**

7.2 **Expected returns:** John is watching an old game show rerun on television called *Let's Make a Deal* in which the contestant chooses a prize behind one of two curtains. One of the curtains will yield a gag prize worth $150, and the other will give a car worth $7,200. The game show has placed a subliminal message on the curtain containing the gag prize, which makes the probability of choosing the gag prize equal to 75 percent. What is the expected value of the selection, and what is the standard deviation of that selection?

7.3 **Expected returns:** You have chosen biology as your college major because you would like to be a medical doctor. However, you find that the probability of being accepted to medical school is about 10 percent. If you are accepted to medical school, then your starting salary when you graduate will be $300,000 per year. However, if you are not accepted, then you would choose to work in a zoo, where you will earn $40,000 per year. Without considering the additional educational years or the time value of money, what is your expected starting salary as well as the standard deviation of that starting salary?

7.4 Historical market: Describe the general relation between risk and return that we observe in the historical bond and stock market data.

7.5 Single-asset portfolios: Stocks A, B, and C have expected returns of 15 percent, 15 percent, and 12 percent, respectively, while their standard deviations are 45 percent, 30 percent, and 30 percent, respectively. If you were considering the purchase of each of these stocks as the only holding in your portfolio, which stock should you choose?

7.6 Diversification: Describe how investing in more than one asset can reduce risk through diversification.

7.7 Systematic risk: Define systematic risk.

7.8 Measuring systematic risk: Susan is expecting the returns on the market portfolio to be negative in the near term. Since she is managing a stock mutual fund, she must remain invested in a portfolio of stocks. However, she is allowed to adjust the beta of her portfolio. What kind of beta would you recommend for Susan's portfolio?

7.9 Measuring systematic risk: Describe and justify what the value of the beta of a U.S. Treasury bill should be.

7.10 Measuring systematic risk: If the expected rate of return for the market is not much greater than the risk-free rate of return, what is the general level of compensation for bearing systematic risk?

7.11 CAPM: Describe the Capital Asset Pricing Model (CAPM) and what it tells us.

7.12 The Security market line: If the expected return on the market is 10 percent and the risk-free rate is 4 percent, what is the expected return for a stock with a beta equal to 1.5? What is the market risk premium for the set of circumstances described?

INTERMEDIATE

7.13 Expected returns: Jose is thinking about purchasing a soft drink machine and placing it in a business office. He knows that there is a 5 percent probability that someone who walks by the machine will make a purchase from the machine, and he knows that the profit on each soft drink sold is $0.10. If Jose expects a thousand people per day to pass by the machine and requires a complete return of his investment in one year, then what is the maximum price that he should be willing to pay for the soft drink machine? Assume 250 working days in a year and ignore taxes and the time value of money.

7.14 Interpreting the variance and standard deviation: The distribution of grades in an introductory finance class is normally distributed, with an expected grade of 75. If the standard deviation of grades is 7, in what range would you expect 95 percent of the grades to fall?

7.15 Calculating the variance and standard deviation: Kate recently invested in real estate with the intention of selling the property one year from today. She has modeled the returns on that investment based on three economic scenarios. She believes that if the economy stays healthy, then her investment will generate a 30 percent return. However, if the economy softens, as predicted, the return will be 10 percent, while the return will be −25 percent if the economy slips into a recession. If the probabilities of the healthy, soft, and recessionary states are 0.4, 0.5, and 0.1, respectively, then what are the expected return and the standard deviation of the return on Kate's investment?

7.16 Calculating the variance and standard deviation: Barbara is considering investing in a stock and is aware that the return on that investment is particularly sensitive to how the economy is performing. Her analysis suggests that four states of the economy can affect the return on the investment. Using the table of returns and probabilities below, find the expected return and the standard deviation of the return on Barbara's investment.

	Probability	Return
Boom	0.1	25.00%
Good	0.4	15.00%
Level	0.3	10.00%
Slump	0.2	−5.00%

7.17 Calculating the variance and standard deviation: Ben would like to invest in gold and is aware that the returns on such an investment can be quite volatile. Use the following table of states, probabilities, and returns to determine the expected return and the standard deviation of the return on Ben's gold investment.

	Probability	Return
Boom	0.1	40.00%
Good	0.2	30.00%
OK	0.3	15.00%
Level	0.2	2.00%
Slump	0.2	−12.00%

7.18 Single-asset portfolios: Using the information from Problems 7.15, 7.16, and 7.17, calculate each coefficient of variation.

7.19 Portfolios with more than one asset: Emmy is analyzing a two-stock portfolio that consists of a Utility stock and a Commodity stock. She knows that the return on the Utility stock has a standard deviation of 40 percent and the return on the Commodity stock has a standard deviation of 30 percent. However, she does not know the exact covariance in the returns of the two stocks. Emmy would like to plot the variance of the portfolio for each of three cases—covariance of 0.12, 0, and −0.12—in order to understand how the variance of such a portfolio would react. Do the calculation for each of the extreme cases (0.12 and −0.12), assuming an equal proportion of each stock in your portfolio.

7.20 Portfolios with more than one asset: Given the returns and probabilities for the three possible states listed here, calculate the covariance between the returns of Stock A and Stock B. For convenience, assume that the expected returns of Stock A and Stock B are 11.75 percent and 18 percent, respectively.

	Probability	Return(A)	Return(B)
Good	0.35	0.30	0.50
OK	0.50	0.10	0.10
Poor	0.15	−0.25	−0.30

7.21 Compensation for bearing systematic risk: You have constructed a diversified portfolio of stocks such that there is no unsystematic risk. Explain why the expected return of that portfolio should be greater than the expected return of a risk-free security.

7.22 Compensation for bearing systematic risk: Write out the equation for the covariance in the returns of two assets, Asset 1 and Asset 2. Using that equation, explain the easiest way for the two asset returns to have a covariance of zero.

7.23 Compensation for bearing systematic risk: Evaluate the following statement: By fully diversifying a portfolio, such as by buying every asset in the market, we can completely eliminate all types of risk, thereby creating a synthetic Treasury bill.

7.24 CAPM: Damien knows that the beta of his portfolio is equal to 1, but he does not know the risk-free rate of return or the market risk premium. He also knows that the expected return on the market is 8 percent. What is the expected return on Damien's portfolio?

7.25 David is going to purchase two stocks to form the initial holdings in his portfolio. Iron stock has an expected return of 15 percent, while Copper stock has an expected return of 20 percent. If David plans to invest 30 percent of his funds in Iron and the remainder in Copper, what will be the expected return from his portfolio? What if David invests 70 percent of his funds in Iron stock?

ADVANCED

7.26 Sumeet knows that the covariance in the return on two assets is −0.0025. Without knowing the expected return of the two assets, explain what that covariance means.

7.27 In order to fund her retirement, Glenda requires a portfolio with an expected return of 12 percent per year over the next 30 years. She has decided to invest in Stocks 1, 2, and 3, with 25 percent in Stock 1, 50 percent in Stock 2, and 25 percent in Stock 3. If Stocks 1 and 2 have expected returns of 9 percent and 10 percent per year, respectively, then what is the minimum expected annual return for Stock 3 that will enable Glenda to achieve her investment requirement?

7.28 Tonalli is putting together a portfolio of 10 stocks in equal proportions. What is the relative importance of the variance for each stock versus the covariance for the pairs of stocks in her portfolio? For this exercise, ignore the actual values of the variance and covariance terms and explain their importance conceptually.

7.29 Explain why investors who have diversified their portfolios will determine the price and, consequently, the expected return on an asset.

7.30 Brad is about to purchase an additional asset for his well-diversified portfolio. He notices that when he plots the historical returns of the asset against those of the market portfolio, the line of best fit tends to have a large amount of prediction error for each data point (the scatter plot is not very tight around the line of best fit). Do you think that this will have a large or a small impact on the beta of the asset? Explain your opinion.

7.31 The beta of an asset is equal to 0. Discuss what the asset must be.

7.32 The expected return on the market portfolio is 15 percent, and the return on the risk-free security is 5 percent. What is the expected return on a portfolio with a beta equal to 0.5?

7.33 Draw the Security Market Line (SML) for the case where the market risk premium is 5 percent and the risk-free rate is 7 percent. Now suppose an asset has a beta of −1.0 and an expected return of 4 percent. Plot it on your graph. Is the security properly priced? If not, explain what we might expect to happen to the price of this security in the market. Next, suppose another asset has a beta of 3.0 and an expected return of 20 percent. Plot it on your graph. Is this security properly priced? If not, explain what we might expect to happen to the price of this security in the market.

Sample Test Problems

7.1 Friendly Airlines stock is selling at a current price of $37.50 per share. If the stock does not pay a dividend and has a 12 percent expected return, what is the expected price of the stock one year from today?

7.2 Stefan's parents are about to invest their nest egg in a stock that he has estimated to have an expected return of 9 percent over the next year. If the stock is normally distributed with a 3 percent standard deviation, in what range will the stock return fall 95 percent of the time?

7.3 Elaine has narrowed her investment alternatives to two stocks (at this time she is not worried about diversifying): Stock M, which has a 23 percent expected return, and Stock Y, which has an 8 percent expected return. If Elaine requires a 16 percent return on her total investment, then what proportion of her portfolio will she invest in each stock?

7.4 You have just prepared a graph similar to Exhibit 7.9, comparing historical data for Pear Computer Corp. and the general market. When you plot the line of best fit for these data, you find that the slope of that line is 2.5. If you know that the market generated a return of 12 percent and that the risk-free rate is 5 percent, then what would your best estimate be for the return of Pear Computer during that same time period?

7.5 The CAPM predicts that the return of MoonBucks Tea Corp. is 23.6 percent. If the risk-free rate of return is 8 percent and the expected return on the market is 20 percent, then what is MoonBucks's beta?

BOND VALUATION AND THE STRUCTURE OF INTEREST RATES

CHAPTER 8

LEARNING OBJECTIVES

1. Explain what an efficient capital market is and why "market efficiency" is important to financial managers.

2. Describe the market for corporate bonds and three types of corporate bonds.

3. Explain how to calculate the value of a bond and why bond prices vary negatively with interest rate movements.

4. Distinguish between a bond's coupon rate, yield to maturity, and effective annual yield, and be able to calculate their values.

5. Explain why investors in bonds are subject to interest rate risk and why it is important to understand the bond theorems.

6. Discuss the concept of default risk and know how to compute a default risk premium.

7. Describe the factors that determine the level and shape of the yield curve.

NewsCom

Weil Gotshal is a New York-based law firm that specializes in corporate bankruptcies. On the night of December 1, 2001, about a dozen lawyers worked through the night in the firm's Houston office, struggling to pull together the materials necessary to file for a corporate bankruptcy: a list of all creditors, the dollar amounts of their claims, and the priority of the claims. When it was all done, Steve Vacek, a paralegal, logged onto the Web site for the Federal Bankruptcy Court in New York City. The blank form provided there was filled in, and the appropriate boxes were checked. At 4:28 A.M. on December 2, Vacek carefully moved the cursor to the box titled "submit" and clicked. In a matter of seconds, Enron—the nation's seventh largest company—had filed for bankruptcy, and a firm once called "America's greatest business" lay in shambles.

Enron's bankruptcy filing was just the beginning of an odyssey of financial destruction and human suffering that will play out over a 10- to 15-year period in the judicial system. For starters, Enron's collapse wiped out thousands of jobs, more than $60 billion in market value, and more than $2 billion in pension plans. As of August 2007, the Enron Creditor Recovery Corp., which exists to sell assets, pay debts, and conduct litigation, had distributed more than $11.7 billion to creditors. At the same time, fees to lawyers, financial advisers, and turnaround experts had exceeded $1 billion.

Among investors hurt by Enron's failure were bondholders. One of the major risks faced by bondholders is the risk of default—the risk that a firm that has issued bonds will not meet the terms of the bond contract. In Enron's case, the firm failed to make interest payments as promised. When bond defaults occur, bondholders can be lucky to get 60 cents on the dollar. Often they recover much less. In this chapter, we explore default risk, along with other topics related to the valuation of bonds.

CHAPTER PREVIEW

This chapter is all about bonds and how they are valued, or priced, in the marketplace. As you might suspect, the bond valuation models presented in this chapter are derived from the present value concepts discussed in Chapters 5 and 6. The market price of a bond is simply the present value of the promised cash flows (coupon and principal payments), discounted at the current market rate of interest for bonds of similar risk.

In the first part of the chapter, we discuss the concept of *efficient capital markets*. A capital market is efficient if current market prices reflect all relevant information about an asset's value. Economists care whether markets are efficient because the more efficient the markets, the more likely securities are to be priced at their true value. Not all financial markets are equally efficient.

Next, we discuss the corporate bond market, bond price information that is available, and the types of bonds found in the market. Then we develop the basic equation used to calculate bond prices and show how to compute the following characteristics of a bond: (1) yield to maturity and (2) effective annual yield. We next discuss interest rate risk and identify three bond theorems that describe how bond prices respond to changes in interest rates.

Finally, we explain why firms have different borrowing costs. We find that four factors affect a firm's cost of borrowing: (1) the debt's marketability, (2) default risk, (3) call risk, and (4) term to maturity.

8.1 Capital Market Efficiency

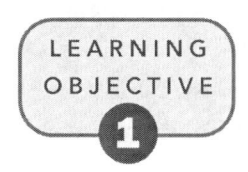

LEARNING OBJECTIVE 1

Security markets, such as the bond and stock markets, help bring buyers and sellers of securities together. They reduce the cost of buying and selling securities by providing a physical location or computer trading system where investors can trade securities. The supply and demand for securities are better reflected in organized markets because much of the total supply and demand for securities flows through these centralized locations or trading systems. Any price that balances the overall supply and demand for a security is a market equilibrium price.

Ideally, economists would like financial markets to price securities at their **true (intrinsic) value**. A security's true value is the present value of the cash flows an investor who owns that security can expect to receive in the future. This present value, in turn, reflects all available information about the size, timing, and riskiness of the cash flows at the time the price was set. As new information becomes available, investors adjust their cash flow estimates through buying and selling, and the price of a security adjusts to reflect this information.

Markets such as those just described are called "efficient" capital markets. More formally, in an **efficient capital market**, security prices fully reflect the knowledge and expectations of all investors at a particular point in time. If markets are efficient, investors and financial managers have no reason to believe the securities are not priced at or near their true value. The more efficient a security market, the more likely securities are to be priced at or near their true value.

The overall efficiency of a capital market depends on its *operational efficiency* and its *informational efficiency*. **Market operational efficiency** focuses on bringing buyers and sellers together at the lowest possible cost. The costs of bringing buyers and sellers together are called *transaction costs* and include such things as broker commissions and other fees and expenses. The lower these costs, the more operationally efficient

true (intrinsic) value
for a security, the value of the cash flows an investor who owns that security can expect to receive in the future

efficient capital market
market where prices reflect the knowledge and expectations of all investors

market operational efficiency
the degree to which the transaction costs of bringing buyers and sellers together are minimized

markets are. Why is operational efficiency important? If transaction costs are high, market prices will be more volatile, fewer financial transactions will take place, and prices will not reflect the knowledge and expectations of investors as accurately.

Markets exhibit **informational efficiency** if market prices reflect all relevant information about securities at a particular point in time. As suggested above, informational efficiency is influenced by operational efficiency, but it also depends on the availability of information and the ability of investors to buy and sell securities based on that information. In an informationally efficient market, market prices adjust quickly to new information as it becomes available. Prices adjust quickly because many security analysts and investors are gathering and trading on information about securities in a quest to make a profit. Note that competition among investors is an important driver of informational efficiency.

market informational efficiency
the degree to which current market prices reflect relevant information and, therefore, the true value of the security

The concept of market efficiency originated with the Ph.D. dissertation that Eugene Fama wrote at the University of Chicago. You can read an interview with Dr. Fama that relates to market efficiency and other concepts discussed in this chapter at library.dfaus.com/reprints/interview_fama_tanous.

Efficient Market Hypotheses

Public financial markets are efficient in part because regulators such as the SEC require issuers of publicly traded securities to disclose a great deal of information about those securities to investors. Investors are constantly evaluating the prospects for these securities and acting on the conclusions from their analyses by trading them. If the price of a security is out of line with what investors think it should be, then they will buy or sell that security, causing its price to adjust to reflect their assessment of its value. The ability of investors to easily observe transaction prices and trade volumes and to inexpensively trade securities in public markets contributes to the efficiency of this process. This buying and selling by investors is the mechanism through which prices adjust to reflect the market's consensus. The theory about how well this mechanism works is known as the **efficient market hypothesis**.

efficient market hypothesis
a theory concerning the extent to which information is reflected in security prices and how information is incorporated into security prices

Strong-Form Efficiency. The market for a security is perfectly informationally efficient if the security's price always reflects all available information. The idea that all information about a security is reflected in its price is known as the **strong-form** of the efficient market hypothesis. Few people really believe that market prices of public securities reflect all available information, however. It is widely accepted that insiders have information that is not reflected in the security prices. Thus, the concept of strong-form market efficiency represents the ideal case rather than the real world.

If a security market were strong-form efficient, then it would not be possible to earn abnormally high returns (returns greater than those justified by the risks) by trading on **private information**—information unavailable to other investors—because there would be no such information. In addition, since all available information would already be reflected in security prices, the price of a share of a particular security would change only when new information about its prospects became available.

strong-form (of the efficient market hypothesis)
the theory that security prices reflect all available information

private information
information that is not available to all investors

Semistrong-Form Efficiency. A weaker form of the efficient market hypothesis, known as the **semistrong-form**, holds only that all **public information**—information that is available to all investors—is reflected in security prices. Investors who have private information are able to profit by trading on this information before it becomes public. As a result of this trading, prices adjust to reflect the private information. For example, suppose that conversations with the customers of a firm indicate to an investor that the firm's sales, and thereby its cash flows, are increasing more rapidly than other investors expect. To profit from this information, the investor buys the firm's stock. By buying the stock, the investor helps drive up the price to the point where it accurately reflects the higher level of cash flows.

semistrong-form (of the efficient market hypothesis)
the theory that security prices reflect all public information but not all private information

public information
information that is available to all investors

The concept of semistrong-form efficiency is a reasonable representation of the public stock markets in developed countries such as the United States. In a market characterized by this sort of efficiency, as soon as information becomes public, it is quickly reflected in stock prices through trading activity. Studies of the speed at which new information is reflected in stock prices indicate that by the time you read a hot tip in the *Wall Street Journal* or a business magazine, it is too late to benefit by trading on it.

weak-form (of the efficient market hypothesis)
the theory that security prices reflect all information in past prices but do not reflect all private or all public information

Weak-Form Efficiency. The weakest form of the efficient market hypothesis is known, aptly enough, as the **weak-form.** This hypothesis holds that all information contained in past prices of a security is reflected in current prices but that there is both public and private information that is not. In a weak-form efficient market, it would not be possible to earn abnormally high returns by looking for patterns in security prices, but it would be possible to do so by trading on public or private information.

An important conclusion from efficient market theory is that at any point in time, all securities of the same risk class should be priced to offer the same expected return. The more efficient the market, the more likely this is to happen. Since both the bond and stock markets are relatively efficient, this means that securities of similar risk will offer the same expected return. This conclusion is important because it provides the basis for identifying the proper discount rate to use in applying the bond and stock valuation models developed in this chapter and Chapter 9.

> **Before You Go On**
> 1. How does information about a firm's prospects get reflected in its share price?
> 2. What is strong-form market efficiency? semistrong-form market efficiency? weak-form market efficiency?

8.2 Corporate Bonds

LEARNING OBJECTIVE 2

Now that we have discussed the concept of market efficiency, we are ready to discuss the market for corporate bonds and some of the types of bonds that firms issue.

Market for Corporate Bonds

The market for corporate bonds is enormous. At the end of 2007, for example, the value of corporate and foreign bonds outstanding in the U.S. was $10.1 trillion, making it the second largest portion of the U.S. capital market. The largest was the market for corporate equity, with a value of $20.8 trillion. The state and local government debt market was a distant third at $2.1 trillion. The most important investors in corporate bonds are big institutional investors such as life insurance companies, pension funds, and mutual funds. Because the primary investors are so big, trades in this market tend to involve very large blocks of securities.

Except for a small number of corporate bonds traded on the New York Stock Exchange, most secondary market transactions for corporate bonds take place through dealers in the over-the-counter (OTC) market. An interesting characteristic of the corporate bond market is that there are a large number of different bond issues that trade in the market. The reason is that while a corporation typically has a single issue of common stock outstanding, it may have a dozen or more different notes and bonds outstanding. Therefore, despite the large overall trading volume of corporate bonds, the bonds in any particular issue will not necessarily trade on a given day. As a result, the market for corporate bonds is thin compared to the market for money market securities or corporate stocks. On Wall Street, the term *thin* means that secondary market trades of individual securities are relatively infrequent. Thus, corporate bonds are less marketable than the securities that have higher daily trading volumes.

Prices in the corporate bond market also tend to be more volatile than prices of securities sold in markets with greater trading volumes. This is because a few large trades can have a larger impact on a security's price than numerous trades of various sizes. As a result, information is not reflected in prices as efficiently and the market for corporate bonds is not as efficient as those for highly marketable stocks or money market instruments, such as U.S. Treasury securities.

A primer on bonds can be found at the Yahoo! Finance Web site at finance.yahoo.com/bonds/bonds_101.

Bond Price Information

The corporate bond market has little *transparency* because it is almost entirely an OTC market. A financial market is transparent if it is easy to view prices and trading volume. An example of a transparent market is the New York Stock Exchange (NYSE), where price information on every trade and trade size are available for every transaction during the day. In contrast, corporate bond market transactions are widely dispersed, with dealers located all over the country, and there are an enormous number of different securities. Furthermore, many corporate bond transactions are negotiated directly between the buyer and the seller and there is little centralized reporting of these deals. As a result, information on individual corporate bond transactions is not widely published as the transactions occur, supporting our earlier statement that the corporate bond market is not as efficient as the stock or money markets.

> Investinginbonds.com is another Web site providing educational information about bonds and their markets. Go to www.investinginbonds.com/learnmore.asp?catid=5&subcatid=18.

Types of Corporate Bonds

Corporate bonds are long-term IOUs that represent claims against a firm's assets. Unlike stockholders' returns, most bondholders' returns are *fixed*; they receive only the interest payments that are promised plus the repayment of the loan amount at the end of the contract. Debt instruments where the interest paid to investors is fixed for the life of the contract are called **fixed-income securities**. We examine three types of fixed-income securities in this section.

> **fixed-income securities**
> debt instruments that pay interest in amounts that are fixed for the life of the contract

VANILLA BONDS

The most common bonds issued by corporations are called vanilla bonds on Wall Street. These bonds have coupon payments that are fixed for the life of the bond, and at maturity, the entire original principal is paid and the bonds are retired. Vanilla bonds have no special provisions, and the provisions they do have follow convention.

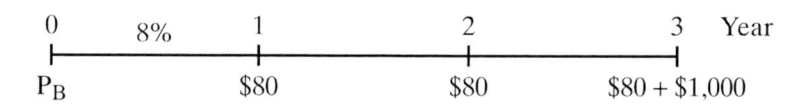

```
0         8%      1           2           3    Year
|-----------------|-----------|-----------|
P_B              $80         $80     $80 + $1,000
```

This time line shows the cash payments for a three-year vanilla bond with a $1,000 face value and an 8 percent coupon rate. P_B is the price (value) of the bond, which will be discussed in the next section. The $80 cash payments ($1,000 × 8 percent) made each year are called the coupon payments. **Coupon payments** are the interest payments made to bondholders. These payments are usually made annually or semiannually, and the payment amount (or rate) remains fixed for the life of the bond contract, which for our example is three years. The **face value**, or **par value**, for most corporate bonds is $1,000, and it is the principal amount owed to the bondholder at maturity. Finally, the bond's **coupon rate** is the annual coupon payment (C) divided by the bond's face value (F). Our vanilla bond pays $80 coupon interest annually, and the face value is $1,000. The coupon rate is thus:

> **coupon payments**
> the interest payments made to bondholders

> **face value, or par value**
> the amount on which interest is calculated and that is owed to the bondholder when a bond reaches maturity

> **coupon rate**
> the annual coupon payment of a bond divided by the bond's face value

$$\text{Coupon rate} = \frac{C}{F}$$
$$= \frac{\$80}{\$1,000}$$
$$= 8\%$$

ZERO COUPON BONDS

At times, corporations issue bonds that have no coupon payments but promise a single payment at maturity. The interest paid to a bondholder is the difference between the price paid for the bond and the face amount received at maturity. These bonds are sold at a price well below their face value because all of the interest is "paid" when the bonds are retired at maturity rather than in semiannual or yearly coupon payments.

The most frequent and regular issuer of zero coupon securities is the U.S. Department of Treasury, and perhaps the best-known zero coupon bond is a United States Saving Bond. Corporations also issue zero coupon bonds from time to time. Firms that are expanding operations but have little cash on hand are especially likely to use zero coupon bonds for funding. In the 1990s, the bond market was "flooded" with zero coupon bonds issued by telecommunications firms. These firms were spending huge amounts to build fiber-optic networks, which generated few cash inflows until they were completed.

> You can find information about zero coupon bonds at beginnersinvest.about.com/od/zerocouponbonds.

CONVERTIBLE BONDS

Corporate convertible bonds can be converted into shares of common stock at some predetermined ratio at the discretion of the bondholder. For example, a $1,000 face value bond may be convertible into 100 shares of common stock. The convertible feature allows the bondholders to share in the good fortunes of the firm if the firm's stock rises above a certain level. Specifically, it is to the bondholders' advantage to exchange their bonds for stock if the market value of the stock they receive exceeds the market value of the bonds.

Clearly, convertibility is an attractive feature for investors. Typically, the conversion ratio is set so that the firm's stock price must appreciate at least 15 to 20 percent before it is profitable to convert bonds into equity. As you would expect from our discussion, bondholders pay a premium (a higher price) for bonds with a conversion feature, which means the issuing firm is able to issue the bonds with a lower interest rate.

> **Before You Go On**
>
> 1. What are the main differences between the bond markets and stock markets?
> 2. A bond has a 7 percent coupon rate, a face value of $1,000, and a maturity of four years. On a time line, lay out the cash flows for the bond.
> 3. Explain what a convertible bond is.

8.3 Bond Valuation

LEARNING OBJECTIVE 3

We turn now to the topic of bond valuation—how bonds are priced. Throughout the book, we have stressed that the value, or price, of any asset is the present value of its future cash flows. The steps necessary to value an asset are as follows:

1. Estimate the expected future cash flows.
2. Determine the required rate of return, or discount rate. This rate depends on the riskiness of the cash flow stream.
3. Compute the discounted present value of the future cash flows. This present value is what the asset is worth at a particular point in time.

For bonds, the valuation procedure is relatively easy. The cash flows (coupon and principal payments) are contractual obligations of the firm and are known by market participants, since they are stated in the bond contract. Thus, market participants know the magnitude and timing of the expected cash flows as promised by the borrower (the bond issuer). The required rate of return, or discount rate, for a bond is the market interest rate, called the bond's *yield to maturity* (or more commonly, simply its *yield*). This rate is determined from the market prices of bonds that have features similar to those of the bond being valued; by "similar," we mean bonds that have the same term to maturity, the same bond rating (default risk class), and are similar in other ways.

Notice that the required rate of return is really investors' **opportunity cost**, which is the highest alternative return that is given up if a certain investment is made. For example, if bonds identical to the bond being valued—having the same risk—yield 9 percent, the threshold yield or required return on the bond being valued is 9 percent. Why? An investor would not buy a bond with an 8 percent yield when an identical bond yielding 9 percent was available.

Given the above information, we can compute the current value, or price, of a bond (P_B) by calculating the present value of the bond's expected cash flows:

$$P_B = PV \text{ (Coupon payments)} + PV \text{ (Principal payment)}$$

Next, we examine this calculation in detail.

> **opportunity cost**
> the return from the best alternative investment with similar risk that an investor gives up when he or she makes a certain investment

The Bond Valuation Formula

To begin, refer to Exhibit 8.1, which shows the cash flows for a three-year corporate bond with an 8 percent coupon rate and a $1,000 face value. If the market rate of interest on similar bonds is 10 percent and interest payments are made annually, what is the market price of the bond? In other words, how much should you be willing to pay for the promised cash flow stream?

There are a number of ways to solve this problem. Probably the simplest is to write the bond valuation formula in terms of the individual cash flows. Thus, the price of the bond (P_B) is the sum of the present value calculations for the coupon payments (C) and the principal amount (F) discounted at the required rate (*i*). That calculation follows:

$$P_B = PV \text{ (Each coupon payment)} + PV \text{ (Principal payment)}$$
$$= \left(C_1 \times \frac{1}{1+i}\right) + \left(C_2 \times \frac{1}{(1+i)^2}\right) + \left(C_3 \times \frac{1}{(1+i)^3}\right) + \left(F_3 \times \frac{1}{(1+i)^3}\right)$$
$$= \left(\$80 \times \frac{1}{1.10}\right) + \left(\$80 \times \frac{1}{(1.10)^2}\right) + \left(\$80 \times \frac{1}{(1.10)^3}\right) + \left(\$1,000 \times \frac{1}{(1.10)^3}\right)$$
$$= (\$80 \times 0.9091) + (\$80 \times 0.8264) + (\$80 \times 0.7513) + (\$1,000 \times 0.7513)$$
$$= \$72.73 + \$66.11 + \$60.10 + \$751.30$$
$$= \$950.24$$

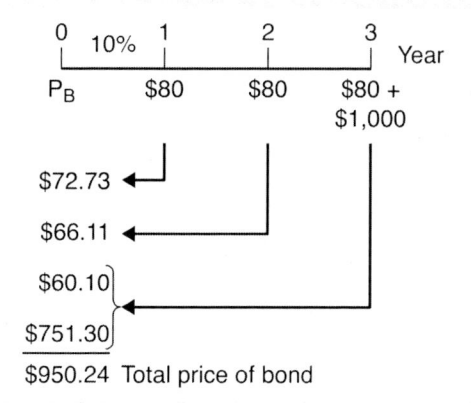

Exhibit 8.1
Cash Flows for a Three-Year Bond

The exhibit shows a time line for a three-year bond that pays an 8 percent coupon rate and has a face value of $1,000. How much should we pay for such a bond if the market rate of interest is 10 percent? To solve this problem, we discount the expected cash flows to the present and then add them up.

Notice that you could have simplified the calculation by combining the final coupon payment and the principal payment ($C_3 + F_3$), since both cash flows occur at time $t = 3$.

To develop the general bond pricing formula, we can write the equations for the price of a four-year, five-year, and six-year maturity bond, as follows:

$$P_B = \left(C_1 \times \frac{1}{1+i}\right) + \left(C_2 \times \frac{1}{(1+i)^2}\right) + \cdots + \left((C_4 + F_4) \times \frac{1}{(1+i)^4}\right)$$
$$= \left(C_1 \times \frac{1}{1+i}\right) + \left(C_2 \times \frac{1}{(1+i)^2}\right) + \cdots + \left((C_5 + F_5) \times \frac{1}{(1+i)^5}\right)$$
$$= \left(C_1 \times \frac{1}{1+i}\right) + \left(C_2 \times \frac{1}{(1+i)^2}\right) + \cdots + \left((C_6 + F_6) \times \frac{1}{(1+i)^6}\right)$$

If we continue the process for n periods, we arrive at the general equation for the price of the bond:

$$P_B = \left(C_1 \times \frac{1}{1+i}\right) + \left(C_2 \times \frac{1}{(1+i)^2}\right) + \cdots + \left((C_n + F_n) \times \frac{1}{(1+i)^n}\right)$$

In practice, the bond pricing equation is usually written with the discount factor shown as the denominator rather than being multiplied by $1/(1+i)$. Thus, the general equation for the price of a bond can be written as follows:

$$P_B = \frac{C_1}{1+i} + \frac{C_2}{(1+i)^2} + \cdots + \frac{C_n + F_n}{(1+i)^n} \tag{8.1}$$

where:

P_B = the price of the bond, or present value of the stream of cash payments
C_t = the coupon payment in period t, where $t = 1, 2, 3, \ldots, n$
F_n = par value or face value (principal amount) to be paid at maturity
i = market interest rate (discount rate or market yield)
n = number of periods to maturity

Note that there are five variables in the bond pricing equation. If we know any four of them, we can solve for the fifth.

Calculator Tip: Bond Valuation Problems

We can easily calculate bond prices using a financial calculator or a spreadsheet program. We solve for bond prices and bond yield in exactly the same way we solved for the present value (bond price) and discount rate (bond yield) in Chapter 6. There is nothing new to learn! We solve our example problem on a financial calculator as follows:

Enter	3	10		80	1,000
	N	i	PV	PMT	FV
Answer			−950.26		

Several points are worth noting:

1. Always draw a time line for the cash flows. This simple step will significantly reduce mistakes.

2. The PMT key enters the dollar amount of an ordinary annuity for n periods. In our example, keying in 3 with the N key and $80 with the PMT key enters an $80 annuity with the final payment made at the end of year 3.

3. Be sure that you enter the coupon and the principal payments separately. Do not enter the final coupon payment ($80) and principal amount ($1,000) as a single

entry of $1,080 on the FV key. The reason is that the PMT key is the annuity key, and when you enter N = 3, the $80 is entered in the calculator as a three-year ordinary annuity with a final payment of $80 in period $t = 3$. If you then enter $1,080 on the FV key, you will have an extra $80 in the final period ($t = 3$). For the example problem, we correctly entered the $80 coupon payments with the PMT key and the $1,000 principal payment with the FV key.

4. Finally, as we have mentioned in earlier chapters, you must be consistent throughout a problem in how you enter the signs (positive or negative) for cash inflows and cash outflows. For example, if you are a bond investor and decide to enter all cash inflows with a positive sign, then you must enter all coupon and principal payments with a positive sign. The price you paid for the bond, which is a cash outflow, must be entered as a negative number. This is the convention we will follow.

Par, Premium, and Discount Bonds

One of the mathematical properties of the bond formula is that whenever a bond's coupon rate is equal to the market rate of interest on similar bonds (the bond's yield), the bond will sell at par. We call such bonds **par-value bonds**. For example, say that you own a three-year bond with a face value of $1,000 and an annual coupon rate of 5 percent, when the yield or market rate of interest on similar bonds is 5 percent. The price of the bond, based on Equation 8.1, is:

par-value bonds
bonds that sell at par value, or face value; whenever a bond's coupon rate is equal to the market rate of interest on similar bonds, the bond will sell at par

$$P_B = \frac{\$50}{1.05} + \frac{\$50}{(1.05)^2} + \frac{\$1,050}{(1.05)^3}$$
$$= \$47.62 + \$45.35 + \$907.03$$
$$= \$1,000$$

As predicted, the bond's price equals its par value.

Now assume that the market rate of interest rises overnight to 8 percent. What happens to the price of the bond? Will the bond's price be below, above, or at par?

$$P_B = \frac{\$50}{1.08} + \frac{\$50}{(1.08)^2} + \frac{\$1,050}{(1.08)^3}$$
$$= \$46.30 + \$42.87 + \$833.52$$
$$= \$922.69$$

When i is equal to 8 percent, the price of the bond declines to $922.69. The bond sells below par; such bonds are called **discount bonds**.

discount bonds
bonds that sell at below par (face) value

Whenever a bond's coupon rate is lower than the market rate of interest on similar bonds, the bond will sell at a discount. This is true because of the fixed nature of a bond's coupon payments. Let's return to our 5 percent coupon bond. If the market rate of interest is 8 percent and our bond pays only 5 percent, no economically rational person would buy the bond at its par value. This would be like choosing a bond with a 5 percent yield over one with an 8 percent yield. We cannot change the coupon rate to 8 percent because it is fixed for the life of the bond. That is why bonds are called fixed-income securities! The only way to increase our bond's yield to 8 percent is to reduce the price of the bond to $922.69. At this price, the bond's yield will be precisely 8 percent, which is the current market rate for similar bonds. Through the price reduction of $77.31 ($1,000 - $922.69), the seller provides the new owner with additional "interest" in the form of a capital gain.

What would happen to the price of the bond if interest rates on similar bonds declined to 2 percent and the coupon rate remained at 5 percent? The price of our bond would rise to $1,086.52. At this price, the bond's yield would be precisely 2 percent, which is the current market yield. The $86.52 ($1,086.52 − $1,000) premium that the investor paid adjusts the bond's yield to 2 percent, which is the current market yield for similar bonds. Bonds that sell above par are called **premium bonds**. Whenever a bond's coupon rate is higher than the market rate of interest, the bond will sell at a premium.

premium bonds
bonds that sell at above par (face) value

Our discussion of bond pricing can be summarized as follows, where i is the market rate of interest:

1. $i >$ coupon rate—the bond sells for a discount
2. $i <$ coupon rate—the bond sells for a premium
3. $i =$ coupon rate—the bond sells at par value

This negative relation between changes in the level of interest rates and changes in the price of a bond (or any fixed-income security) is one of the most fundamental relations in corporate finance. The relation exists because the coupon payments on most bonds are fixed and the only way bonds can pay the current market rate of interest to investors is through adjustment of the price of the bond.

LEARNING BY DOING APPLICATION 8.1

Pricing a Bond

Problem: Your stockbroker is trying to sell you a 15-year bond with a 7 percent coupon, and the interest, or yield, on similar bonds is 10 percent. Is the bond selling for a premium, at par, or at a discount? Answer the question without making any calculations, and then prove that your answer is correct. The time line is as follows:

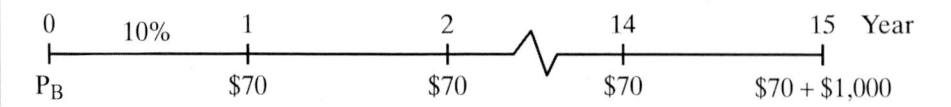

```
0        10%    1           2          14         15   Year
|---------------|-----------|----~~----|----------|
P_B             $70         $70        $70        $70 + $1,000
```

Approach: Since the market rate of interest is greater than the coupon rate ($i >$ coupon rate), the bond must sell at a discount.

Solution: To prove the answer is correct (or wrong), we can compute the bond's price with a financial calculator.

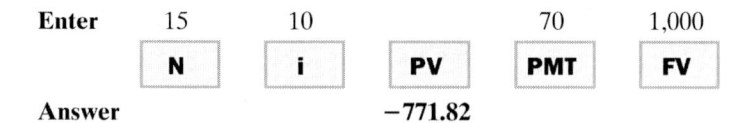

Enter	15	10		70	1,000
	N	i	PV	PMT	FV
Answer			−771.82		

The bond is selling at a discount, and it should. Why? The market rate of interest is 10 percent, and our bond is paying only 7 percent. Since the bond's coupon rate is fixed, the only way we can bring the bond's yield up to the current market rate of 10 percent is to reduce the price of the bond.

USING EXCEL

Bond Prices and Yields

Calculating bond prices and yields using a spreadsheet may seem daunting at first. However, understanding the terminology used in the formulas will make the calculations a matter of common sense:

Settlement date—the date a buyer purchases the bond.

Maturity date—the date the bond expires. If you know only the "*n*" (number of years remaining) of the bond, use a date that is *n* years in the future in this field.

Redemption—the security's redemption value per $10 face value. In other words, if the bond has a par of $1,000, you enter 100 in this field.

Frequency—the number of coupon payments per year.

Here is a spreadsheet showing the setup for calculating the price of the discount bond described in Learning by Doing Application 8.1.

We first use the =PRICE(settlement, maturity, rate, yield, redemption, frequency) formula in Excel to calculate the bond price as a percentage of par. We then multiply this percentage (77.18 in the above example) by $1,000 to obtain the bond price in dollars. A bond yield, which is discussed in the next section, is calculated in a similar manner, using the "=YIELD (settlement, maturity, rate, price, redemption, frequency)" formula.

	A	B	C	D
1				
2		Bond Price Calculations		
3	Inputs			
4	Settlement date	1/1/00		
5	Maturity date	1/1/15		
6	Rate	0.07		
7	Yield	0.10		
8	Redemption (% of par)	100		
9	Frequency	1		
10				
11	Bond Price			Formulas Used
12	Bond price as % of par	77.18		=PRICE(B4,B5,B6,B7,B8,B9)
13	Par value	$1,000.00		
14	Bond price	$771.82		=B12%*B13
15				

Semiannual Compounding

In Europe, bonds generally pay coupon interest on an annual basis. In contrast, in the United States, most bonds pay coupon interest semiannually—that is, twice a year. Thus, if a bond has an 8 percent coupon rate (paid semiannually), the bondholder will in one year receive two coupon payments of $40 each, totaling $80 ($40 × 2). We can modify Equation 8.1 as follows to adjust for coupon payments made more than once a year:

$$P_B = \frac{C/m}{1 + i/m} + \frac{C/m}{(1 + i/m)^2} + \frac{C/m}{(1 + i/m)^3} + \cdots + \frac{C/m + F_{mn}}{(1 + i/m)^{mn}} \quad (8.2)$$

where C is the annual coupon payment, m is the number of times coupon payments are made each year, n is the number of years to maturity, and i is the annual interest rate. In the case of a bond with semiannual coupon payments, m equals 2.

Whether we are computing bond prices annually, semiannually, quarterly, or for some other period, the computation is the same. We need only be sure that the bond's yield, coupon payment, and maturity are adjusted to be consistent with the bond's stated compounding period. Once that information is converted to the correct compounding period, it can simply be entered into Equation 8.1. Thus, there is really no need to memorize or use Equation 8.2 unless you find it helpful. Let's work an example to demonstrate.

Earlier we determined that a three-year, 5 percent coupon bond will sell for $922.69 when the market rate of interest is 8 percent. Our computation assumed that coupon payments were made annually. What is the price of the bond if the coupon payments are made semiannually? The time line for the semiannual bond situation follows:

```
0   8%/2   1         2         3         4         5         6   Semiannual period
├─────────┼─────────┼─────────┼─────────┼─────────┼─────────┤
P_B       $50/2     $50/2     $50/2     $50/2     $50/2     $50/2 + $1,000
```

We convert the bond data to semiannual compounding as follows: (1) the market yield is 4 percent semiannually (8 percent per year/2), (2) the coupon payment is

$25 semiannually ($50 per year/2), and (3) the total number of coupon payments is 6 (2 per year × 3 years). Plug the data into Equation 8.1, and the bond price is:

$$P_B = \frac{\$25}{1.04} + \frac{\$25}{(1.04)^2} + \frac{\$25}{(1.04)^3} + \frac{\$25}{(1.04)^4} + \frac{\$25}{(1.04)^5} + \frac{\$1,025}{(1.04)^6}$$
$$= \$921.37$$

Notice that the price of the bond is slightly less with semiannual compounding than with annual compounding ($921.37 < $922.69). The slight difference in price reflects the change in the timing of the cash flows and the interest rate adjustment.[1]

LEARNING BY DOING APPLICATION 8.2

Bond Pricing with Semiannual Coupon Payments

Problem: A corporate treasurer decides to purchase a 20-year Treasury bond with a 4 percent coupon rate. If the current market rate of interest for similar Treasury securities is 4.5 percent, what is the price of the bond?

Approach: Treasury securities pay interest semiannually, so this problem is best worked on a financial calculator because of the large number of compounding periods. We can convert the bond data to semiannual compounding as follows: (1) the bond's semiannual yield is 2.25 percent (4.5 percent per year/2), (2) the semiannual coupon payment is $20 [($1,000 × 4 percent)/2 = $40/2], and (3) the total number of compounding periods is 40 (2 per year × 20 years). Note that at maturity, the bond pays its principal, or face value, of $1,000 to the investor. Thus, the bond's time line for the cash payments is as follows:

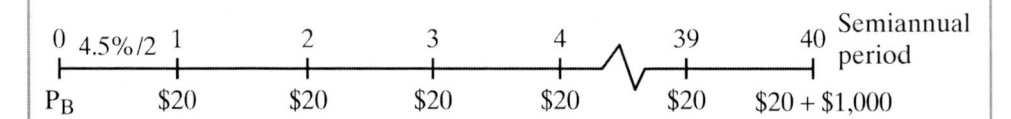

```
 0  4.5%/2   1       2       3       4            39      40     Semiannual
 ├──────────┼───────┼───────┼───────┼──── /\ ─────┼───────┤      period
 P_B        $20    $20     $20     $20           $20    $20+$1,000
```

Solution: We can enter the appropriate values on the financial calculator and solve for the present value:

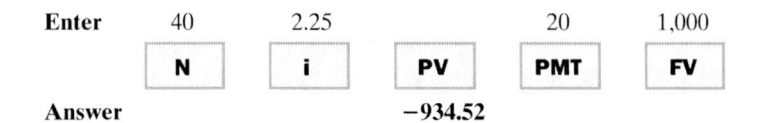

Enter	40	2.25		20	1,000
	N	i	PV	PMT	FV
Answer			−934.52		

The bond sells for a discount, and its price is $934.52.

Zero Coupon Bonds

As previously mentioned, zero coupon bonds have no coupon payments but promise a single payment at maturity. The price (or yield) of a zero coupon bond is simply a special case of Equation 8.2 in which all the coupon payments are equal to zero. Hence, the pricing equation is:

$$P_B = \frac{F_{mn}}{(1 + i/m)^{mn}} \qquad (8.3)$$

---

[1] If the bond sold at a premium, the reverse would be true; that is, the price with semiannual compounding would be slightly more than the price with annual compounding.

where:

P_B = the price of the bond
F_{mn} = the amount of the cash payment at maturity (face value)
i = the interest rate (yield) for n periods
n = number of periods until the payment is due
m = number of times interest is compounded each year

Notice that if a zero coupon bond compounds annually, $m = 1$ and Equation 8.3 becomes:

$$P_B = \frac{F_n}{(1 + i)^n}$$

This is similar to the annual bond pricing equation, Equation 8.1.

Now let's work an example. What is the price of a zero coupon bond with a $1,000 face value, 10-year maturity, and semiannual compounding when the market interest rate is 12 percent? Since the bond compounds interest semiannually, the number of compounding periods is 20 ($m \times n = 2 \times 10 = 20$). The semiannual interest is 6 percent (12 percent/2). The time line for the cash flows is as follows:

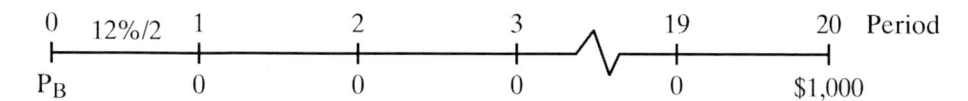

```
0    12%/2   1        2        3        19       20  Period
|------------|--------|--------|---//---|--------|
P_B           0        0        0        0       $1,000
```

Plugging the data into Equation 8.3, we find that the price of the bond is $311.80:

$$P_B = \frac{\$1,000}{(1.06)^{20}}$$
$$= \$1,000 \times 0.3118 = \$311.80$$

Notice that the zero coupon bond is selling at a deep discount. This should come as no surprise, since the bond has no coupon payment and all the dollars paid to investors are paid at maturity. Why are zero coupon bonds so heavily discounted compared with similar bonds that do have coupon payments? From Chapter 5, we know that because of the time value of money, dollars to be received in the future have less value than current dollars. Thus, zero coupon bonds, for which all the cash payments are made at maturity, must sell for less than similar bonds that make coupon payments before maturity.

LEARNING BY DOING APPLICATION 8.3

The Price of a Bond

Problem: An investor is considering buying a U.S. corporate bond with an eight-year maturity and a coupon rate of 6 percent. Similar bonds in the marketplace yield 14 percent. How much should the investor be willing to pay for the bond? Using Equation 8.1 (or 8.2), set up the equation to be solved, and then solve the problem using your financial calculator. Note that the discount rate used in the problem is the 14 percent market yield on similar bonds (bonds of similar risk), which is the investor's opportunity cost.

Approach: Since U.S. corporate bonds pay coupon interest semiannually, we first need to convert all of the bond data to reflect semiannual compounding: (1) the annual coupon payment is $60 per year (6 percent × $1,000) and the semiannual payment is $30 per period ($60/2); (2) the appropriate semiannual yield is 7 percent (14 percent/2); and (3) the total number of compounding periods is 16 (2 per year × 8 years). The time line for the semiannual cash flows is as follows:

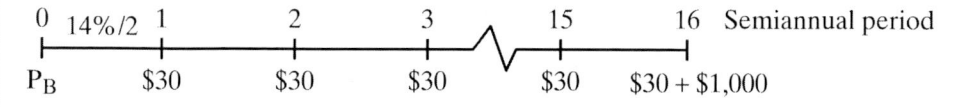

```
0   14%/2   1        2        3        15       16  Semiannual period
|-----------|--------|--------|---//---|--------|
P_B         $30      $30      $30      $30    $30 + $1,000
```

(continued)

Solution: Using Equation 8.1 (or 8.2), the setup is as follows:

$$P_B = \frac{\$30}{1.07} + \frac{\$30}{(1.07)^2} + \cdots + \frac{\$1,030}{(1.07)^{16}}$$

To solve the problem using a financial calculator, we enter the appropriate values and solve for PV:

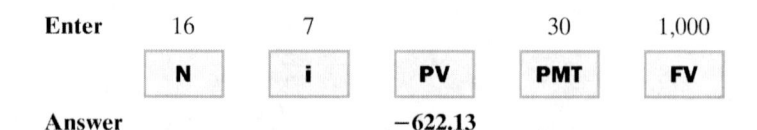

Enter	16	7		30	1,000
	N	i	PV	PMT	FV
Answer			−622.13		

The investor should be willing to pay $622.13 because the bond's yield at this price would be exactly 14 percent, which is the current market yield on similar bonds. If the investor paid more than $622.13, the investment would yield a return of less than 14 percent. In this situation the investor would be better off buying the similar bonds in the market that yield 14 percent. Of course, if the investor can buy the bond for less than $622.13, the price is a bargain, and the return on investment will be greater than the market yield.

> **Before You Go On**
> 1. Explain conceptually how bonds are priced.
> 2. What is the compounding period for most bonds sold in the United States?
> 3. What are zero coupon bonds, and how are they priced?

8.4 Bond Yields

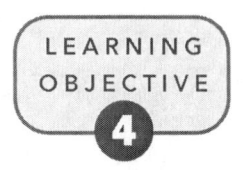

LEARNING OBJECTIVE 4

In dealing with bonds, we frequently know the bond's price but not its yield—or, more formally, the bond's yield to maturity. In this section, we discuss how to compute the yield to maturity and some other important bond yields.

Yield to Maturity

yield to maturity
for a bond, the discount rate that makes the present value of the coupon and principal payments equal to the price of the bond

The **yield to maturity** of a bond is the discount rate that makes the present value of the coupon and principal payments equal to the price of the bond. The yield to maturity can be viewed as a "promised yield" because it is the yield that the investor earns if the bond is held to maturity and all the coupon and principal payments are made as promised. A bond's yield to maturity changes daily as interest rates increase or decrease, but its calculation is always based on the issuer's promise to make interest and principal payments as stipulated in the bond contract.

Let's work through an example to see how a bond's yield to maturity is calculated. Suppose you decide to buy a three-year bond with a 6 percent coupon rate for $960.99. For simplicity, we will assume that the coupon payments are made annually. The time line for the cash flows is as follows:

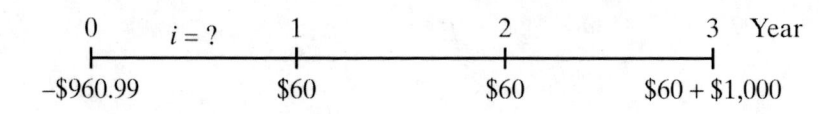

```
      0      i = ?    1           2           3     Year
      ├───────────────┼───────────┼───────────┤
   −$960.99         $60         $60      $60 + $1,000
```

To compute the yield to maturity, we apply Equation 8.1 and solve for i. We can set up the problem using Equation 8.1 as follows:

$$\$960.99 = \frac{\$60}{1+i} + \frac{\$60}{(1+i)^2} + \frac{\$1,060}{(1+i)^3}$$

As we discussed in Chapter 6, we cannot solve for i mathematically; we must find it by trial and error. We know that the bond is selling for a discount because its price is below par, so the yield must be higher than the 6 percent coupon rate. Let's try 7 percent.

$$\frac{\$60}{1.07} + \frac{\$60}{(1.07)^2} + \frac{\$1,060}{(1.07)^3} = \$973.76$$

The computed price of $973.76 is still greater than our market price of $960.99; thus, we need to use a slightly larger discount rate. Let's try 7.7 percent

$$\frac{\$60}{1.077} + \frac{\$60}{(1.077)^2} + \frac{\$1,060}{(1.077)^3} = \$955.95$$

Our computed value of $955.95 is now less than the market price of $960.99, so we need a lower discount rate. We'll try 7.5 percent.

$$\frac{\$60}{1.075} + \frac{\$60}{(1.075)^2} + \frac{\$1,060}{(1.075)^3} = \$960.99$$

At a discount rate of 7.5 percent, the price of the bond is exactly equal to the market price, and thus, the bond's yield to maturity is 7.5 percent.

We can, of course, also compute the bond's yield to maturity using a financial calculator. Computing the yield in this way is no different from computing the price, except that the unknown is the bond's yield. As with calculating the price of a bond, the major source of computational errors is failing to make sure that all the bond data are consistent with the bond's compounding period. The three variables that may require adjustment are: (1) the coupon payment, (2) the yield, and (3) the bond maturity.

For the three-year corporate bond discussed earlier, the bond data are already in a form that is consistent with the annual compounding period, so we enter it into the calculator and solve for i, which is the yield to maturity:

Enter	3		−960.99	60	1,000
	N	i	PV	PMT	FV
Answer		7.5			

The bond's yield to maturity is 7.5 percent, which is identical to the answer from our hand calculation.

Effective Annual Yield

Up to now, when pricing a bond with a semiannual compounding period, we assumed the bond's annual yield to be twice the semiannual yield. This is the convention used on Wall Street and by other practitioners who deal in bonds. However, notice that bond yields quoted in this manner are just like the bank credit card APR calculations discussed in Chapter 6. To get a credit card's APR, we multiplied the monthly interest rate of 1 percent by 12, for an APR of 12 percent. As you recall, interest rates (or yields) annualized in this manner do not take compounding into account. Hence, the values calculated are not the true cost of funds, and their use can lead to decisions that are economically incorrect.

effective annual yield (EAY) the annual yield that takes compounding into account; another name for the *effective annual interest rate (EAR)*

As a result, annualized yields calculated by multiplying a period yield by the number of compounding periods is only acceptable for decision-making purposes when comparing bonds that have the same compounding frequencies. Thus, for example, an investor must be careful when evaluating yields between European and U.S. bonds, since the European is compounded annually while the U.S. bond compounds interest twice a year.

The correct way to annualize an interest rate is to compute the effective annual interest rate (EAR). On Wall Street, the EAR is called the **effective annual yield (EAY);** thus, EAR = EAY. Drawing on Equation 6.7 (see Chapter 6), we find that the correct way to annualize the yield on a bond is as follows:

$$\text{EAY} = \left(1 + \frac{\text{Quoted interest rate}}{m}\right)^m - 1$$

where: Quoted interest rate = simple annual yield (semiannual yield × 2)
         m = the number of compounding periods per year

We can work through an example to clarify how the EAY differs from the yield to maturity. Suppose an investor buys a 30-year bond with a $1,000 face value for $800. The bond's coupon rate is 8 percent, and interest payments are made semiannually. What is the bond's yield to maturity, and what is its effective annual yield? To find out, we first need to convert the bond's annual data into semiannual data: (1) the 30-year bond has 60 compounding periods (30 years × 2 periods per year) and (2) the bond's semiannual coupon payment is $40 [($1,000 × 0.08)/2 = $80/2]. The time line for this bond is:

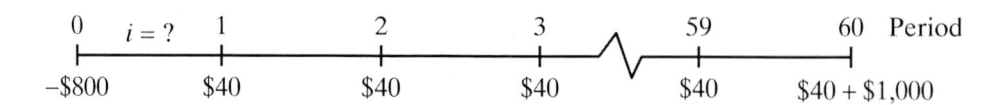

```
 0      i = ?   1       2       3              59        60    Period
 |--------------|-------|-------|---/\/\---|---------|
-$800          $40     $40     $40          $40      $40 + $1,000
```

We can set up the problem using Equation 8.1 as:

$$\$800 = \frac{\$40}{1 + i/2} + \frac{\$40}{(1 + i/2)^2} + \frac{\$40}{(1 + i/2)^3} + \cdots + \frac{\$40}{(1 + i/2)^{59}} + \frac{\$1,040}{(1 + i/2)^{60}}$$

However, solving an equation with so many terms can be time consuming. Therefore, we will solve for the yield to maturity using the yield function in a financial calculator as follows:

Enter	60		−800	40	1,000
	N	i	PV	PMT	FV
Answer		5.07			

The answer is 5.07 percent. We then multiply the semiannual yield by 2 to convert it to an annual yield: 2 × 5.07 = 10.14 percent. This is the bond's yield to maturity.

Now we will enter the appropriate values into the formula given earlier and calculate the EAY for the bond:

$$\text{EAY} = \left(1 + \frac{\text{Quoted interest rate}}{m}\right)^m - 1$$

$$= \left(1 + \frac{0.1014}{2}\right)^2 - 1$$

$$= (1.0507)^2 - 1 = 0.1040, \text{ or } 10.40\%$$

The EAY is 10.40 percent, compared with the annual yield to maturity of 10.14 percent. The EAY is greater because it takes into account the effects of compounding—earning interest on interest. As mentioned earlier, calculating the EAY is the proper way to annualize the bond's yield because it takes compounding into account.

A Bond's Yield to Maturity

LEARNING BY DOING APPLICATION 8.4

Problem: You can purchase a U.S. corporate bond from your broker for $1,099.50. The bond has a maturity of six years and an annual coupon rate of 5 percent. Another broker offers you a dollar Eurobond (a dollar-denominated bond sold overseas) with a yield of 3.17 percent, which is denominated in U.S. dollars and has the same maturity and credit rating as the U.S. corporate bond. Which bond should you buy?

Approach: Solving this problem involves two steps. First, we must compute the U.S. bond's yield to maturity. The bond pays coupon interest semiannually, so we have to convert the bond data to semiannual periods: (1) the number of compounding periods is 12 (6 years × 2 periods per year) and (2) the semiannual coupon payment is $25 [($1,000 × 0.05)/2 = $50/2]. Second, we must annualize the yield for the U.S. bond so that we can compare its yield with that of the Eurobond.

Solution: We can solve for the yield to maturity using a financial calculator:

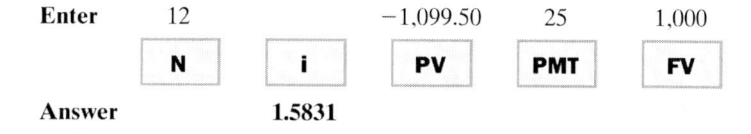

Enter	12		−1,099.50	25	1,000
	N	i	PV	PMT	FV
Answer		1.5831			

The answer, 1.5831 percent, is the semiannual yield. Since the Eurobond's yield, 3.17 percent, is an annualized yield because of that bond's yearly compounding, we must annualize the yield on the U.S. bond in order to compare the two.[2] We annualize the yield on the U.S. bond by computing its effective annual yield:

$$EAY = \left(1 + \frac{\text{Quoted interest rate}}{m}\right)^m - 1$$
$$= \left(1 + \frac{0.031661}{2}\right)^2 - 1$$
$$= (1.015831)^2 - 1 = 0.03191, \text{ or } 3.191\%$$

The U.S. corporate bond is a better deal because of its higher EAY (3.191 percent > 3.170 percent). Notice that if we had just annualized the yield on the U.S. bond by multiplying the semiannual yield by 2 (1.5831 percent × 2 = 3.1661 percent) and compared the simple yields for the Eurobond and the U.S. bond (3.170 percent > 3.1661 percent), we would have selected the Eurobond. This would have been the wrong economic decision.

Realized Yield

The yield to maturity tells the investor the return on a bond if the bond is held to maturity and all the coupon and principal payments are made as promised. More than likely, however, the investor will sell the bond before maturity. The **realized yield** is the return earned on a bond given the cash flows *actually received* by the investor. More formally, it is the interest rate at which the present value of the actual cash flows generated by the investment equals the bond's price. The realized yield allows investors to see the return they actually earned on their investment. It is the same as the holding period return discussed in Chapter 7.

Let's return to the situation involving a three-year bond with a 6 percent coupon that was purchased for $960.99 and had a promised yield of 7.5 percent. Suppose that

realized yield
for a bond, the interest rate at which the present value of the actual cash flows generated by a bond equals the bond's price

---

[2]Notice that, for annual compounding, the yield to maturity equals the EAY; for the Eurobond, the yield to maturity = 3.17 percent and EAY = (1 + Quoted interest rate/m)^m − 1 = (1 + 0.0317/1)^1 − 1 = (1 + 0.0317) − 1 = 0.0317, or 3.17 percent.

interest rates increased sharply and the price of the bond plummeted. Disgruntled, you sold the bond for $750.79 after having owned it for two years. The time line for the realized cash flows looks like this:

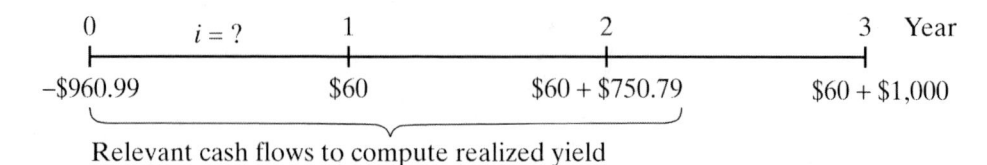

```
0           i = ?        1                2                3   Year
|------------------------|----------------|----------------|
-$960.99                $60         $60 + $750.79       $60 + $1,000
```

Relevant cash flows to compute realized yield

Substituting the cash flows into Equation 8.1 yields the following:

$$P_B = \$960.99 = \frac{\$60}{1+i} + \frac{\$60}{(1+i)^2} + \frac{\$750.79}{(1+i)^2}$$

We can solve this equation for i either by trial and error or with a financial calculator, as described earlier. Using a financial calculator, the solution is as follows:

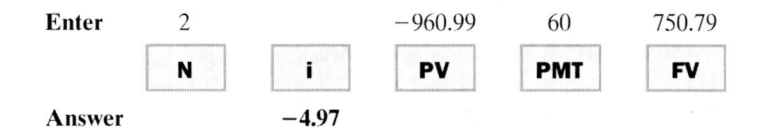

Enter	2		−960.99	60	750.79
	N	i	PV	PMT	FV
Answer		−4.97			

The result is a realized yield of negative 4.97 percent. The difference between the promised yield of 7.50 percent and the realized yield of negative 4.97 percent is 12.47 percent [7.50 − (−4.97)], which can be accounted for by the capital loss of $210.20 ($960.99 − $750.79) from the decline in the bond price.

> **Before You Go On**
>
> 1. Explain how bond yields are calculated.

8.5 Interest Rate Risk

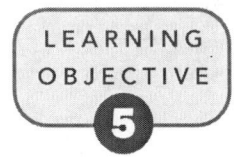

LEARNING OBJECTIVE 5

As discussed previously, the prices of bonds fluctuate with changes in interest rates, giving rise to **interest rate risk**. Anyone who owns bonds is subject to interest rate risk because interest rates are always changing in financial markets. A number of relations exist between bond prices and changes in interest rates. These relations are often called the bond theorems, but they apply to all fixed-income securities. It is important that investors and financial managers understand these relations.

interest rate risk
uncertainty about future bond values that is caused by the unpredictability of interest rates

Bond Theorems

1. **Bond prices are negatively related to interest rate movements.** As interest rates decline, the prices of bonds rise; and as interest rates rise, the prices of bonds decline. As mentioned earlier, this negative relation exists because the coupon rate on most bonds is fixed at the time the bonds are issued. Note that the negative relation is observed not only for bonds but also for all other financial claims that pay a fixed rate of interest to investors.

2. **For a given change in interest rates, the prices of long-term bonds will change more than the prices of short-term bonds.** In other words, long-term bonds have greater

Exhibit 8.2
Relation between Bond Price Volatility and Maturity

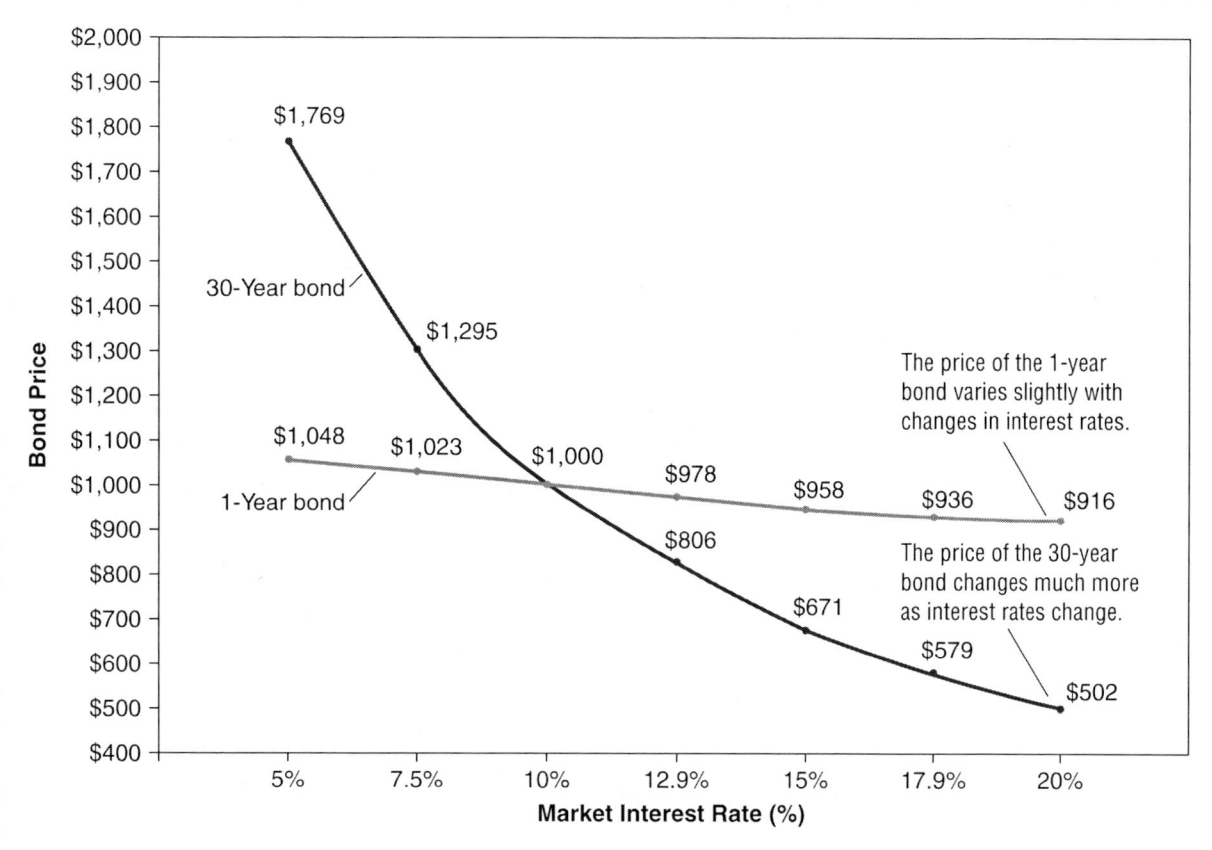

Note: Plots are for a 1-year bond and a 30-year bond with a 10 percent coupon rate and annual payment

The prices of a 1-year and a 30-year bond respond differently to changes in interest. The long-term bond has much wider price swings than the short-term bond, as predicted by the second bond theorem.

The price of the 1-year bond varies slightly with changes in interest rates.

The price of the 30-year bond changes much more as interest rates change.

30-Year bond values at various market interest rates: $1,769 (5%), $1,295 (7.5%), $1,000 (10%), $806 (12.9%), $671 (15%), $579 (17.9%), $502 (20%).

1-Year bond values: $1,048 (5%), $1,023 (7.5%), $1,000 (10%), $978 (12.9%), $958 (15%), $936 (17.9%), $916 (20%).

price volatility than short-term bonds. Thus, all other things being equal, long-term bonds are more risky than short-term bonds. Exhibit 8.2 illustrates the fact that bond values are not equally affected by changes in interest rates. The exhibit shows how the prices of a 1-year bond and a 30-year bond change with changing interest rates. As you can see, the long-term bond has much wider price swings than the short-term bond. Why? The answer is that long-term bonds receive much of their cash flows far into the future, and because of the time value of money, these cash flows are heavily discounted.

3. **For a given change in interest rates, the prices of lower-coupon bonds change more than the prices of higher-coupon bonds.** Exhibit 8.3 illustrates the relation between bond price volatility and coupon rates. The exhibit shows the prices of three 10-year bonds: a zero coupon bond, a 5 percent coupon bond, and a 10 percent coupon bond. Initially, the bonds are priced to yield 5 percent (see column 2). The bonds are then priced at yields of 6 and 4 percent (see columns 3 and 6). The dollar price changes for each bond given the appropriate interest rate change are recorded in columns 4 and 7, and percentage price changes (price volatilities) are shown in columns 5 and 8.

As shown in column 5, when interest rates increase from 5 to 6 percent, the zero coupon bond experiences the greatest percentage price decline, and the 10 percent bond experiences the smallest percentage price decline. Similar results

Exhibit 8.3 Relationship between Bond Price Volatility and the Coupon Rate

		Price Change If Yield Increases from 5% to 6%			Price Change If Yield Decreases from 5% to 4%		
(1)	(2)	(3)	(4)	(5)	(6)	(7)	(8)
Coupon Rate	Bond Price at 5% Yield	Bond Price at 6%	Loss from Increase in Yield	% Price Change	Bond Price at 4%	Gain from Decrease in Yield	% Price Change
0%	$613.91	$588.39	$25.52	−9.04%	$675.56	$61.65	10.04%
5%	$1,000.00	$926.40	$73.60	−7.36%	$1,081.11	$81.11	8.11%
10%	$1,386.09	$1,294.40	$91.69	−6.62%	$1,486.65	$100.56	7.25%

Note: Calculations are based on a bond with a $1,000 face value and a 10-year maturity and assume annual compounding.

The exhibit shows the prices of three 10-year bonds: a zero coupon bond, a 5 percent coupon bond, and a 10 percent coupon bond. Initially, the bonds are priced at a 5 percent yield (column 2). The bonds are then priced at yields of 6 and 4 percent (columns 3 and 6). The price changes shown are consistent with the third bond theorem: the smaller the coupon rate, the greater the percentage price change for a given change in interest rates.

are shown in column 8 for interest rate decreases. In sum, the lower a bond's coupon rate, the greater its price volatility, and hence, lower-coupon bonds have greater interest rate risk.

The reason for the higher interest rate risk for low-coupon bonds is essentially the same as the reason for the higher interest rate risk for long-term bonds. The lower the bond's coupon rate, the greater the amount of the bond's cash flow investors will receive at maturity. This is clearly seen with a zero coupon bond, where all of the bond's cash flows are received at maturity. The further into the future the cash flows will be received, the greater the impact of a change in the discount rate on their present value. Thus, all other things being equal, a given change in interest rates will have a greater impact on the price of a low-coupon bond than a higher-coupon bond with the same maturity.

Bond Theorem Applications

The bond theorems provide important information about bond price behavior for financial managers. For example, if you are the treasurer of a firm and are investing cash temporarily—say, for a few days—the last security you want to purchase is a long-term zero coupon bond. In contrast, if you are an investor and you expect interest rates to decline, you may well want to invest in long-term zero coupon bonds. This is because as interest rates decline, the price of long-term zero coupon bonds will increase more than that of any other type of bond.

Make no mistake, forecasting interest rate movements and investing in long-term bonds is a very high-risk strategy. In 1990, for example, executives at Shearson Lehman Hutton made a huge bet on interest rate movements and lost. Specifically, over a number of months, the firm made investments in long-term bonds that totaled $480 million. The bet was that interest rates would decline. When interest rates failed to decline and losses mounted, the Shearson team sold the bonds at a loss totaling $115 million. The executives responsible were fired for "lack of judgment."

The moral of the story is simple. Long-term bonds carry substantially more interest rate risk than short-term bonds, and investors in long-term bonds need to fully understand the magnitude of the risk involved. Furthermore, no one can predict interest rate movements consistently, including the Federal Reserve Bank (Fed)—and it controls the money supply.

DECISION-MAKING CHECKPOINT 8.1

Risk Taking

Situation: You work for the treasurer of a large manufacturing corporation where earnings are down substantially for the year. The treasurer's staff is convinced that interest rates are going to decline over the next three months, and they want to invest in fixed-income securities to make as much money as possible for the firm. The staff recommends investing in one of the following securities:

- Three-month T-bill
- Twenty-year corporate bond
- Twenty-year zero coupon Treasury bond

The treasurer asks you to answer the following questions about the staff's plan: (1) What is the underlying strategy of the proposed plan? (2) Which investment should be selected if the plan were to be executed? (3) What should the treasurer do?

Decision: First, the staff's strategy is based on the negative relation between interest rates and bond prices. Thus, if interest rates decline, bond prices will rise, and the firm will earn a capital gain. Second, to maximize earnings, the treasurer should select bonds that will have the largest price swing for a given change in interest rates. Bond theorems 2 and 3 suggest that for a given change in interest rates, low-coupon, long-term bonds will have the largest price swing. Thus, the treasurer should invest in the 20-year zero coupon Treasury bond. With respect to the plan's merits, the intentions are good, but the investment plan is pure folly. Generating "earnings" from risky financial investments is not the firm's line of business or one of its core competencies. As was discussed in Chapter 1, the treasurer's primary investment function is to invest idle cash in safe investments such as money market instruments that have very low default and interest rate risk.

Before You Go On

1. What is interest rate risk?
2. Explain why long-term bonds with zero coupons are riskier than short-term bonds that pay coupon interest.

8.6 The Structure of Interest Rates

In Chapter 2 we discussed the economic forces that determine the level of interest rates, and so far in this chapter, we have discussed how to price various types of debt securities. Armed with this knowledge, we now explore why, on the same day, different business firms have different borrowing costs. As you will see, market analysts have identified four risk characteristics of debt instruments that are responsible for most of the differences in corporate borrowing costs: the security's marketability, call provision, default risk, and term to maturity.

Marketability

The interest rate, or yield, on a security varies with its degree of marketability. Recall from Chapter 2 that marketability refers to the ease with which an investor can sell a security quickly at a low transaction cost. The transaction costs include all fees and the cost of searching for information. The lower the costs, the greater a security's marketability. Because investors prefer marketable securities, they must be paid a premium to purchase similar securities that are less marketable. The difference in interest rates or yields between a marketable security ($i_{\text{high mkt}}$) and a less marketable security ($i_{\text{low mkt}}$) is known as the *marketability risk premium* (MRP).

$$\text{MRP} = i_{\text{low mkt}} - i_{\text{high mkt}} > 0$$

U.S. Treasury bills have the largest and most active secondary market and are considered to be the most marketable of all securities. Investors can sell virtually any dollar amount of Treasury securities quickly without disrupting the market. Similarly, the securities of many well-known businesses enjoy a high degree of marketability, especially firms whose securities are traded on the major exchanges. For thousands of other firms whose securities are not traded actively, marketability can pose a problem and can raise borrowing costs substantially.

Call Provision

Most corporate bonds contain a call provision in their contract. A call provision gives the firm issuing the bonds the option to purchase the bond from an investor at a predetermined price (the call price), and the investor must sell the bond at that price. Bonds with a call provision sell at higher market yields than comparable noncallable bonds. Investors require the higher yield because call provisions work to the benefit of the borrower and the detriment of the investor. For example, if interest rates decline after the bond is issued, the issuer can call (retire) the bonds at the call price and refinance with a new bond issued at the lower prevailing market rate of interest. The issuing firm is delighted because the refinancing has lowered its interest expense. However, investors are less gleeful. When bonds are called, investors suffer a financial loss because they are forced to surrender their high-yielding bonds and reinvest their funds at the lower prevailing market rate of interest.

The difference in interest rates between a callable bond and a comparable noncallable bond is called the *call interest premium (CIP)* and can be defined as follows:

$$\text{CIP} = i_{\text{call}} - i_{\text{ncall}} > 0$$

where CIP is the call interest premium, i_{call} is the yield on a callable bond, and i_{ncall} is the yield on a noncallable bond of the same maturity and default risk. Thus, the more likely a bond is to be called, the higher the CIP and the higher the bond's market yield. Bonds issued during periods when interest rates are high are likely to be called when interest rates decline, and as a result, these bonds have a high CIP. Conversely, bonds sold when interest rates are relatively low are less likely to be called and have a smaller CIP.

Default Risk

LEARNING OBJECTIVE 6

Recall that any debt, such as a bond or a bank loan, is a formal promise by the borrower to make periodic interest payments and pay the principal as specified in the debt contract. Failure on the borrower's part to meet any condition of the debt or loan contract constitutes default. Recall from Chapter 4 that default risk refers to the possibility that the lender may not receive payments as promised.

THE DEFAULT RISK PREMIUM

Because investors are risk averse, they must be paid a premium to purchase a security that exposes them to default risk. The size of the premium has two components: (1) compensation for the expected loss if a default occurs and (2) compensation for bearing the risk that a default could occur. The degree of default risk a security possesses can be measured as the difference between the interest rate on a risky security and the interest rate on a default-free security—all other factors, such as maturity and marketability, held constant. The *default risk premium* (DRP) can thus be defined as follows:

$$DRP = i_{dr} - i_{rf}$$

where i_{dr} is the interest rate (yield) on a security that has default risk and i_{rf} is the interest rate (yield) on a risk-free security. U.S. Treasury securities are the best proxy measure for the risk-free rate. The larger the default risk premium, the higher the probability of default, and the higher the security's market yield.

BOND RATINGS

Many investors, especially individuals and smaller businesses, do not have the expertise to formulate the probabilities of default themselves, so they must rely on credit rating agencies to provide this information. The two most prominent credit rating agencies are Moody's Investors Service (Moody's) and Standard & Poor's (S&P). Both credit rating services rank bonds in order of their expected probability of default and publish the ratings as letter grades. The rating schemes used are shown in Exhibit 8.4. The highest-grade bonds, those with the lowest default risk, are rated Aaa (or AAA). The default risk premium on corporate bonds increases as the bond rating becomes lower.

Exhibit 8.4 also shows that bonds in the top four rating categories are called **investment-grade bonds**. Moody's calls bonds rated below Baa (or BBB) **noninvestment-grade bonds**, but most Wall Street practitioners refer to them as *speculative-grade bonds, high-yield bonds,* or *junk bonds*. The distinction between investment-grade and noninvestment-grade bonds is important because state and federal laws typically require commercial banks, insurance companies, pension funds, other financial institutions, and government agencies to purchase securities rated only as investment grade.

Exhibit 8.5 shows default risk premiums associated with selected bonds with investment-grade bond ratings in August 2007. The premiums measure the difference between yields on Treasury securities—which, as mentioned, are the proxy for the

> Fidelity Investment Company's Web site provides information on bond ratings at personal.fidelity.com/products/fixedincome/bondratings.shtml.

> **investment-grade bonds**
> bonds with low risk of default that are rated Baa (BBB) or above

> **noninvestment-grade bonds**
> bonds rated below Baa (or BBB) by rating agencies; often called *speculative-grade bonds, high-yield bonds,* or *junk bonds*

Exhibit 8.4 Corporate Bond Rating Systems

Explanation	Moody's	Standard & Poor's	Default Risk Premium	Regulatory Designation
Best quality, smallest degree of risk	Aaa	AAA	Lowest	Investment Grade
High quality, slightly more long-term risk than top rating	Aa	AA		
Upper-medium grade, possible impairment in the future	A	A		
Medium grade, lacks outstanding investment characteristics	Baa	BBB		
Speculative, protection may be very moderate	Ba	BB		Noninvestment Grade
Very speculative, may have small assurance of interest and principal payments	B	B		
Issues in poor standing, may be in default	Caa	CCC		
Speculative in a high degree, with marked shortcomings	Ca	CC		
Lowest quality, poor prospects of attaining real investment standing	C	C	Highest	

Moody's and Standard & Poor's use slightly different notation in their ratings of corporate bonds, but the interpretation is the same. Bonds with the highest credit standing are rated Aaa (or AAA) and have the lowest default risk. The credit rating declines as the default risk of the bonds increases.

Exhibit 8.5 Default Risk Premiums for Selected Bond Ratings

Security: Moody's Credit Rating	Security Yield (%) (1)	Risk-Free Rate[a] (%) (2)	Default Risk Premium (%) (1)−(2)
Aaa	5.27	4.63	0.64
Aa	5.54	4.63	0.91
A	6.00	4.63	1.37
Baa	6.12	4.63	1.49

[a]Ten-year Treasury bond yield as of August 24, 2007.

Sources: Federal Reserve Statistical Release H.15 (www.federalreserve.gov) and Moody's (www.moodys.com).

The default risk premium (DRP) measures the yield difference between the yield on Treasury securities (the risk-free rate) and the yields on riskier securities of the same maturity.

risk-free rate—and yields on riskier securities of similar maturity.[3] The 64-basis-point (0.64 percent) default risk premium on Aaa-rated corporate bonds represents the market consensus of the amount investors must be compensated to induce them to purchase typical Aaa-rated bonds instead of a risk-free security. As credit quality declines from Aaa to Baa, the default risk premiums increase from 64 basis points to 149 basis points.

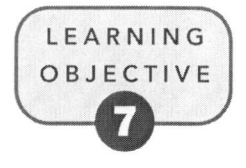

The Term Structure of Interest Rates

The term to maturity of a loan is the length of time until the principal amount is payable. The relation between yield to maturity and term to maturity is known as the **term structure of interest rates**. We can view the term structure visually by plotting the **yield curve**, a graph with term to maturity on the horizontal axis and yield to maturity on the vertical axis. Yield curves show graphically how market yields vary as term to maturity changes.

For yield curves to be meaningful, the securities used to plot the curves should be similar in all features (for example, default risk and marketability) except for maturity. We do not want to confound the relation of yield and term to maturity with other factors that also affect interest rates. We can best see the term structure relation by examining yields on U.S. Treasury securities because they have similar default risk (none) and marketability.

Exhibit 8.6 shows data and yield curve plots for Treasury securities in the 2000s. As you can see, the shape of the yield curve is not constant over time. As the general level of interest rises and falls, the yield curve shifts up and down and has different slopes. We can observe three basic shapes (slopes) of yield curves in the marketplace. First is the ascending, or upward-sloping, yield curve (May 2003 and February 2005), which is the yield curve most commonly observed. Descending, or downward-sloping, yield curves (September 2006) appear periodically and are earmarked by short-term rates (for example, six-month yield) exceeding long-term rates (for example, 10- or 20-year rates). Downward-sloping yield curves often appear before the beginning of a recession. Flat yield curves (not shown in the exhibit) are not common but do occur from time to time. Three factors affect the level and the shape (the slope) of the yield curve over time: the real rate of interest, the expected rate of inflation, and interest rate risk.

The real rate of interest is the base interest rate in the economy and is determined by individuals' time preference for consumption; that is, it tells us how much individuals

term structure of interest rates
the relation between yield and term to maturity

yield curve
a graph representing the term structure of interest rates, with the term to maturity on the horizontal axis and the yield on the vertical axis

Smart Money's Web site gives a good overview of yield curves. Go to www.smartmoney.com/onebond/index.cfm?story=yieldcurve.

---
[3]Default risk premiums are typically quoted in terms of basis points. A basis point is simply 1/100 of a percent. Therefore, 50 basis points equals 0.5 percent, 100 basis points equals 1.0 percent, and so on.

8.6 The Structure of Interest Rates

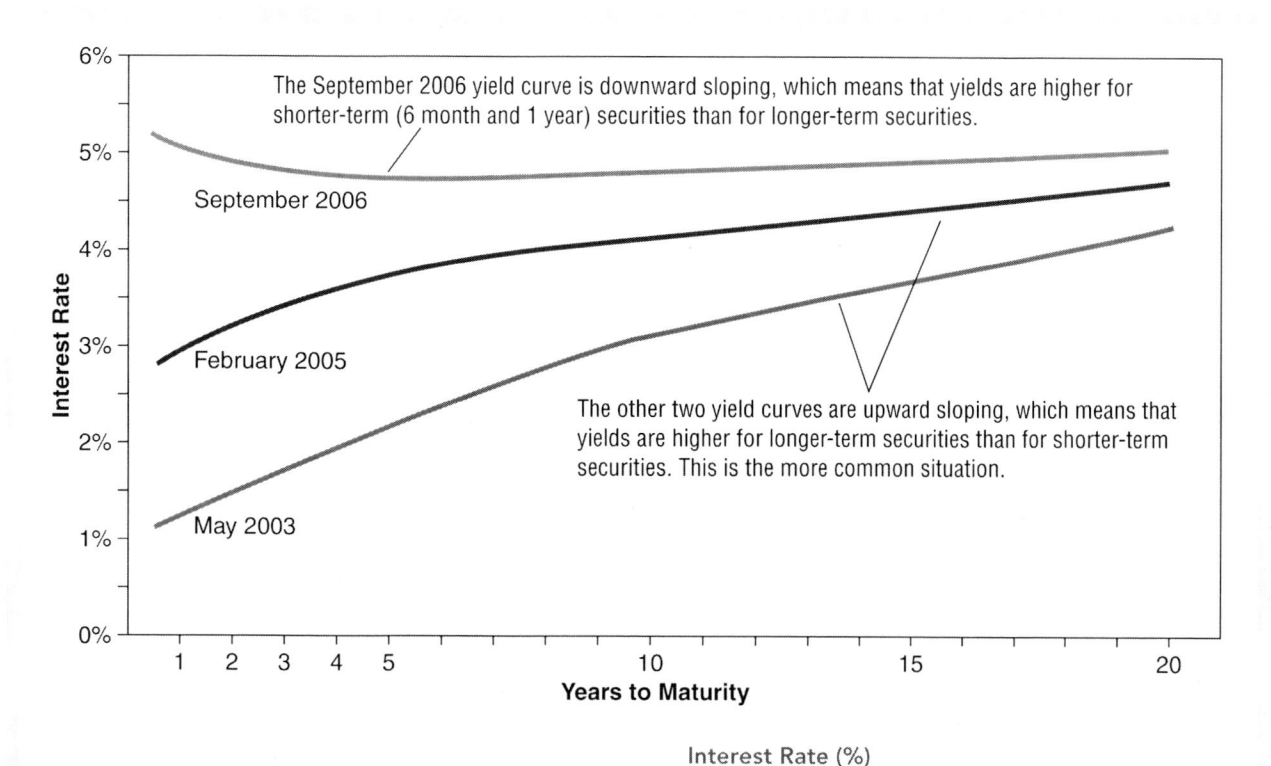

Terms to Maturity	Interest Rate (%) September 2006	February 2005	May 2003
6 months	5.10	2.86	1.08
1 year	4.99	3.05	1.14
5 year	4.68	3.78	2.33
10 years	4.73	4.16	3.34
20 years	4.95	4.60	4.28

Exhibit 8.6

Yield Curves for Treasury Securities at Three Different Points in Time

The shape, or slope, of the yield curve is not constant over time. The exhibit shows two shapes: (1) the curves for May 2003 and February 2005 are upward sloping, which is the shape most commonly observed, and (2) the curve for September 2006 is downward sloping for maturities out to 5 years.

The September 2006 yield curve is downward sloping, which means that yields are higher for shorter-term (6 month and 1 year) securities than for longer-term securities.

The other two yield curves are upward sloping, which means that yields are higher for longer-term securities than for shorter-term securities. This is the more common situation.

must be paid to forgo spending their money today. The real rate of interest varies with the business cycle, with the highest rates seen at the end of a period of business expansion and the lowest at the bottom of a recession. The real rate is not affected by the term to maturity. Thus, the real rate of interest affects the level of interest rates but not the shape of the yield curve.

The expected rate of inflation can influence the shape of the yield curve. If investors believe that inflation will be increasing in the future, the yield curve will be upward sloping because long-term interest rates will contain a larger inflation premium than short-term interest rates. The inflation premium is the market's best estimate of future inflation. Conversely, if investors believe inflation will be subsiding in the future, the prevailing yield will be downward sloping.

Finally, the presence of interest rate risk affects the shape of the yield curve. As discussed earlier, long-term bonds have greater price volatility than short-term bonds. Because investors are aware of this risk, they demand compensation in the form of an interest rate premium. It follows that the longer the maturity of a security, the greater its interest rate risk, and the higher the interest rate. It is important to note that the interest rate risk premium always adds an upward bias to the slope of the yield curve.

In sum, the cumulative effect of three economic factors determines the level and shape of the yield curve: (1) the cyclical movements of the real rate of interest affect the level of the yield curve, (2) the expected rate of inflation can bias the slope of the yield curve either positively or negatively, depending on market expectations of inflation, and (3) interest rate risk always provides an upward bias to the slope of the yield curve.

> **Before You Go On**
>
> 1. What are default risk premiums, and what do they measure?
> 2. Describe the two most prominent bond rating systems.
> 3. What are the key factors that most affect the level and shape of the yield curve?

Summary of Learning Objectives

1. **Explain what an efficient capital market is and why "market efficiency" is important to financial managers.**

   An efficient capital market is a market where security prices reflect the knowledge and expectations of all investors. Public markets, for example, are more efficient than private markets because issuers of public securities are required to disclose a great deal of information about these securities to investors and investors are constantly evaluating the prospects for these securities and acting on the conclusions from their analyses by trading them. Market efficiency is important to investors because it assures them that the securities they buy are priced close to their true value.

2. **Describe the market for corporate bonds and three types of corporate bonds.**

   The market for corporate bonds is a very large market in which the most important investors are large institutions. Most trades in this market take place through dealers in the OTC market, and the corporate bond market is relatively thin. Prices of corporate bonds tend to be more volatile than prices of securities that trade more frequently, such as stock and money markets, and the corporate bond market tends to be less efficient than markets for these other securities.

   A vanilla bond has fixed regular coupon payments over the life of the bond, and the entire principal is repaid at maturity. A zero coupon bond pays all interest and all principal at maturity. Since there are no payments before maturity, zero coupon bonds are issued at prices well below their face value. Convertible bonds can be exchanged for common stock at a predetermined ratio.

3. **Explain how to calculate the value of a bond and why bond prices vary negatively with interest rate movements.**

   The value of a bond is equal to the present value of the future cash flows (coupons and principal repayment) discounted at the market rate of interest for bonds with similar characteristics. Bond prices vary negatively with interest rates because the coupon rate on most bonds is fixed at the time the bond is issued. Therefore, as interest rates go up, investors seek other forms of investment that will allow them to take advantage of the higher returns. Because the bond's coupon payments are fixed, the only way the yields can be adjusted to the current market rate of interest is to reduce the bond's price. Similarly, when interest rates are declining, the yield on fixed-income securities will be higher relative to yield on similar securities price to market; the favorable yield will increase the demand for these securities, increasing their price and lowering their yield to the market yield.

4. **Distinguish between a bond's coupon rate, yield to maturity, and effective annual yield, and be able to calculate their values.**

   A bond's coupon rate is the stated interest rate on the bond when it is issued. U.S. bonds typically pay interest semiannually, whereas European bonds pay once a year. The yield to maturity is the expected return on a bond if it is held to its maturity date. The effective annual yield is the yield an investor actually earns in one year, adjusting for the effects of compounding. If the bond pays coupon payments more often than annually, the effective annual yield will be higher than the simple annual yield because of compounding. Work through Learning by Doing Applications 8.2, 8.3, and 8.4 to master these calculations.

5. **Explain why investors in bonds are subject to interest rate risk and why it is important to understand the bond theorems.**

   Because interest rates are always changing in the market, all investors who hold bonds are subject to interest rate risk. Interest rate risk is uncertainty about future bond values caused by fluctuations in interest rates. Three of the most important bond theorems can be summarized as follows:
   1. Bond prices are negatively related to interest rate movements.
   2. For a given change in interest rates, the prices of long-term bonds will change more than the prices of short-term bonds.
   3. For a given change in interest rates, the prices of lower-coupon bonds will change more than the prices of higher-coupon bonds.

   Understanding these relations is important because it helps investors to better understand why bond prices change and, thus, to make better decisions regarding the purchase or sale of bonds and other fixed-income securities.

6. **Discuss the concept of default risk and know-how to compute a default risk premium.**

   Default risk is the risk that the issuer will be unable to pay its debt obligation. Since investors are risk averse, they must be paid a premium to purchase a security that exposes them to default risk. The default risk premium has two components: (1) compensation for the expected loss if a default occurs and (2) compensation for bearing the risk that a default could occur. All factors held constant, the degree of default risk a security possesses can be measured as the difference between the interest rate on a risky security and the interest rate on a default-free security. The default risk is also reflected in the company's bond rating. The highest-grade bonds, those with the lowest default risk, are rated Aaa (or AAA). The default risk premium on corporate bonds increases as the bond rating becomes lower.

7. Describe the factors that determine the level and shape of the yield curve.

The level and shape of the yield curve are determined by three factors: (1) the real rate of interest, (2) the expected rate of inflation, and (3) interest rate risk. The real rate of interest is the base interest rate in the economy and varies with the business cycle. The real rate of interest affects only the level of the yield curve and not its shape. The expected rate of inflation does affect the shape of the yield curve. If investors believe inflation will be increasing in the future, for example, the curve will be upward sloping, as long-term rates will contain a larger inflation premium than short-term rates. Finally, interest rate risk, which increases with a security's maturity, adds an upward bias to the slope of the yield curve.

Summary of Key Equations

Equation	Description	Formula
8.1	Price of a bond	$P_B = \dfrac{C_1}{1+i} + \dfrac{C_2}{(1+i)^2} + \cdots + \dfrac{C_n + F_n}{(1+i)^n}$
8.2	Price of a bond making multiple payments each year	$P_B = \dfrac{C/m}{1+i/m} + \dfrac{C/m}{(1+i/m)^2} + \dfrac{C/m}{(1+i/m)^3} + \cdots + \dfrac{C/m + F_{mn}}{(1+i/m)^{mn}}$
8.3	Price of zero coupon bond	$P_B = \dfrac{F_{mn}}{(1+i/m)^{mn}}$

Self-Study Problems

8.1 Calculate the price of a five-year bond that has a coupon of 6.5 percent and pays annual interest. The current market rate is 5.75 percent.

8.2 Bigbie Corp. issued a five-year bond one year ago with a coupon of 8 percent. The bond pays interest semiannually. If the yield to maturity on this bond is 9 percent, what is the price of the bond?

8.3 Rockwell Industries has a three-year bond outstanding that pays a 7.25 percent coupon and is currently priced at $913.88. What is the yield to maturity of this bond? Assume annual coupon payments.

8.4 Hindenberg, Inc., has a 10-year bond that is priced at $1,100.00. It has a coupon of 8 percent paid semiannually. What is the yield to maturity on this bond?

8.5 Highland Corp., a U.S. company, has a five-year bond whose yield to maturity is 6.5 percent. The bond has no coupon payments. What is the price of this zero coupon bond?

Solutions to Self-Study Problems

8.1 The time line and calculations for the five-year bond are as follows:

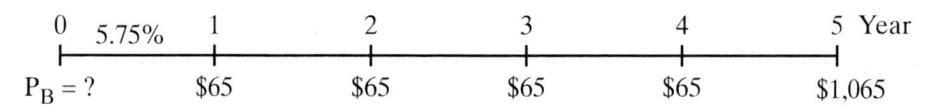

```
  0    5.75%   1       2       3       4       5 Year
  |------------|-------|-------|-------|-------|
P_B = ?       $65     $65     $65     $65    $1,065
```

$$P_B = \frac{C_1}{1+i} + \frac{C_2}{(1+i)^2} + \frac{C_3}{(1+i)^3} + \frac{C_4}{(1+i)^4} + \frac{C_5 + F_5}{(1+i)^5}$$

$$= \frac{\$65}{1.0575} + \frac{\$65}{(1.0575)^2} + \frac{\$65}{(1.0575)^3} + \frac{\$65}{(1.0575)^4} + \frac{\$65 + \$1,000}{(1.0575)^5}$$

$$= \$61.47 + \$58.12 + \$54.96 + \$51.95 + \$805.28$$

$$= \$1,031.81$$

8.2 We can find the price of Bigbie Corp.'s bond as follows:

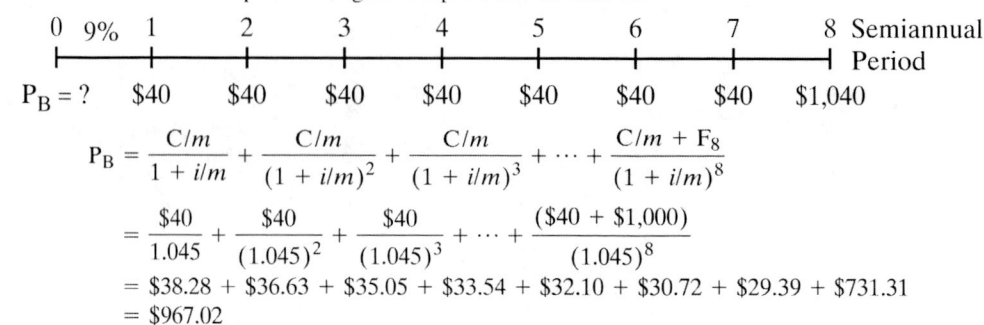

```
 0    9%   1      2      3      4      5      6      7      8  Semiannual
 |─────────|──────|──────|──────|──────|──────|──────|──────|  Period
P_B = ?   $40    $40    $40    $40    $40    $40    $40   $1,040
```

$$P_B = \frac{C/m}{1+i/m} + \frac{C/m}{(1+i/m)^2} + \frac{C/m}{(1+i/m)^3} + \cdots + \frac{C/m + F_8}{(1+i/m)^8}$$

$$= \frac{\$40}{1.045} + \frac{\$40}{(1.045)^2} + \frac{\$40}{(1.045)^3} + \cdots + \frac{(\$40 + \$1,000)}{(1.045)^8}$$

$$= \$38.28 + \$36.63 + \$35.05 + \$33.54 + \$32.10 + \$30.72 + \$29.39 + \$731.31$$

$$= \$967.02$$

Alternatively, we can use the present value annuity factor from chapter 6 and the present value equation from chapter 5 to solve for the price of the bond.

$$P_B = C \times \left[\frac{1 - \frac{1}{(1+i/m)^{mn}}}{i/m} \right] + \frac{F_n}{(1+i/m)^{mn}} = \$40 \times \left[\frac{1 - \frac{1}{(1+0.045)^8}}{0.045} \right] + \frac{\$1,000}{(1.045)^8}$$

$$= \$263.84 + \$703.19 = \$967.03$$

8.3 We start with a time line for Rockwell's bond:

```
     0         i = ?     1              2              3   Year
     |──────────────────|──────────────|──────────────|
P_B = -$913.88        $72.50          $72.50        $1,072.50
```

Use trial and error to solve for the yield to maturity (YTM). Since the bond is selling at a discount, we know that the yield to maturity is higher than the coupon rate.

Try YTM = 10%.

$$P_B = \frac{C_1}{1+i} + \frac{C_2}{(1+i)^2} + \frac{C_3 + F_3}{(1+i)^5}$$

$$\$913.88 = \frac{\$72.50}{1.10} + \frac{\$72.50}{(1.10)^2} + \frac{\$72.50 + \$1,000}{(1.10)^3}$$

$$= \$65.91 + \$59.92 + \$805.79$$

$$\neq \$931.61$$

Try a higher rate, say YTM = 11%.

$$P_B = \frac{C_1}{1+i} + \frac{C_2}{(1+i)^2} + \frac{C_3 + F_3}{(1+i)^5}$$

$$\$913.88 = \frac{\$72.50}{1.11} + \frac{\$72.50}{(1.11)^2} + \frac{\$72.50 + \$1,000}{(1.11)^3}$$

$$= \$65.32 + \$58.84 + \$784.20$$

$$\neq \$908.36$$

Since this is less than the price of the bond, we know that the YTM is between 10 and 11 percent and closer to 11 percent.

Try YTM = 10.75%.

$$P_B = \frac{C_1}{1+i} + \frac{C_2}{(1+i)^2} + \frac{C_3 + F_3}{(1+i)^5}$$

$$\$913.88 = \frac{\$72.50}{1.1075} + \frac{\$72.50}{(1.1075)^2} + \frac{\$72.50 + \$1,000}{(1.1075)^3}$$

$$= \$65.46 + \$59.11 + \$789.53$$
$$\cong \$914.09$$

Alternatively, we can use Equation 6.1 and the present value equation from Chapter 5 to solve for the price of the bond.

$$P_B = C \times \left[\frac{1 - \frac{1}{(1+i)^n}}{i}\right] + \frac{F_n}{(1+i)^n}$$

$$\$913.88 = \$72.50 \times \left[\frac{1 - \frac{1}{(1+0.1075)^3}}{0.1075}\right] + \frac{\$1,000}{(1.1075)^3}$$

$$= \$177.94 + \$736.15$$
$$\cong \$914.09$$

Thus, the YTM is approximately 10.75 percent. Using a financial calculator provides an exact YTM of 10.7594%.

8.4 The time line for Hindenberg's 10-year bond looks like this:

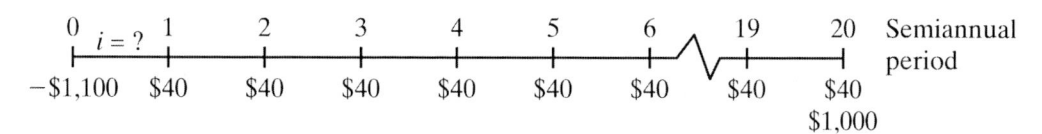

```
0  i=?  1    2    3    4    5    6    19   20   Semiannual
               period
-$1,100 $40  $40  $40  $40  $40  $40  $40  $40
                                              $1,000
```

The easiest way to calculate the yield to maturity is with a financial calculator. The inputs are as follows:

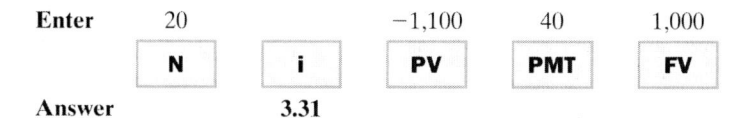

Enter	20		−1,100	40	1,000
	N	i	PV	PMT	FV
Answer		3.31			

The answer we get is 3.31 percent, which is the semiannual interest rate. To obtain an annualized yield to maturity, we multiply this by two:

$$\text{YTM} = 3.31\% \times 2$$
$$\text{YTM} = 6.62\%$$

8.5 You have the following information about Highland's bonds:

$$\text{YTM} = 6.5\%; m = 1$$
$$\text{No coupon payments}$$

Most U.S. bonds pay interest semiannually. Thus $m \times n = 2 \times 5 = 10$ and $i/2 = 0.065/2 = 0.0325$. Using Equation 8.3, we obtain the following calculation:

$$P_B = \frac{F_{mn}}{(1 + i/m)^{mn}}$$
$$= \frac{\$1,000}{(1 + 0.0325)^{10}}$$
$$= \$726.27$$

Critical Thinking Questions

8.1 You believe that you can make abnormally profitable trades by observing that the CFO of a certain company always wears his green suit on days that the firm is about to release positive information about his company. Describe which form of market efficiency is consistent with your belief.

8.2 Describe the informational differences that separate the three forms of market efficiency.

8.3 What economic conditions would prompt investors to take advantage of a bond's convertibility feature?

8.4 Define *yield to maturity*. Why is it important?

8.5 Define *interest rate risk*. How can CFOs manage this risk?

8.6 Explain why bond prices and interest rates are negatively related. What is the role of the coupon rate and term to maturity in this relation?

8.7 If rates are expected to increase, should investors look to long-term bonds or short-term securities? Explain.

8.8 Explain what you would assume the yield curve would look like during economic expansion and why.

8.9 An investor holds a 10-year bond paying a coupon of 9 percent. The yield to maturity of the bond is 7.8 percent. Would you expect the investor to be holding a par-value, premium, or discount bond? What if the yield to maturity were 10.2 percent? Explain.

8.10 a. Investor A holds a 10-year bond, while investor B holds an 8-year bond. If the interest rate increases by 1 percent, which investor will have the higher interest rate risk? Explain.
b. Investor A holds a 10-year bond paying 8 percent a year, while investor B also has a 10-year bond that pays a 6 percent coupon. Which investor will have the higher interest rate risk? Explain.

Questions and Problems

BASIC

8.1 Bond price: BA Corp is issuing a 10-year bond with a coupon rate of 8 percent. The interest rate for similar bonds is currently 6 percent. Assuming annual payments, what is the present value of the bond?

8.2 Bond price: Pierre Dupont just received a gift from his grandfather. He plans to invest in a five-year bond issued by Venice Corp that pays annual coupons of 5.5 percent. If the current market rate is 7.25 percent, what is the maximum amount Pierre should be willing to pay for this bond?

8.3 Bond price: Knight, Inc., has issued a three-year bond that pays a coupon of 6.10 percent. Coupon payments are made semiannually. Given the market rate of interest of 5.80 percent, what is the market value of the bond?

8.4 Bond price: Regatta Inc. has seven-year bonds outstanding that pay a 12 percent coupon rate. Investors buying the bond today can expect to earn a yield to maturity of 8.875 percent. What is the current value of these bonds? Assume annual coupon payments.

8.5 Bond price: You are interested in investing in a five-year bond that pays 7.8 percent coupon with interest to be received semiannually. Your required rate of return is 8.4 percent. What is the most you would be willing to pay for this bond?

8.6 Zero coupon bonds: Diane Carter is interested in buying a five-year zero coupon bond whose face value is $1,000. She understands that the market interest rate for similar investments is 9 percent. Assume annual coupon payments. What is the current price of this bond?

8.7 Zero coupon bonds: Ten-year zero coupon bonds issued by the U.S. Treasury have a face value of $1,000 and interest is compounded semiannually. If similar bonds in the market yield 10.5 percent, what is the value of these bonds?

8.8 Zero coupon bonds: Northrop Real Estate Company is planning to fund a development project by issuing 10-year zero coupon bonds with a face value of $1,000. Assuming semiannual compounding, what will be the price of these bonds if the appropriate discount rate is 14 percent?

8.9 Yield to maturity: Ruth Hornsby is looking to invest in a three-year bond that pays semiannual coupons at a coupon rate of 5.875 percent. If these bonds have a market price of $981.13, what yield to maturity and effective annual yield can she expect to earn?

8.10 Yield to maturity: Rudy Sandberg wants to invest in four-year bonds that are currently priced at $868.43. These bonds have a coupon rate of 6 percent and pay semiannual coupons. What is the current market yield on this bond?

8.11 Realized yield: Josh Kavern bought 10-year, 12 percent coupon bonds issued by the U.S. Treasury three years ago at $913.44. If he sells these bonds, which have a face value of $1,000, at the current price of $804.59, what is the realized yield on the bonds? Assume annual coupons on similar coupon-paying bonds.

8.12 Realized yield: Four years ago, Lisa Stills bought six-year, 5.5 percent coupon bonds issued by the Fairways Corp. for $947.68. If she sells these bonds at the current price of $894.52, what will be the realized yield on the bonds? Assume annual coupons on similar coupon-paying bonds.

8.13 Bond price: The International Publishing Group is raising $10 million by issuing 15-year bonds with a coupon rate of 8.5 percent. Coupon payments will be annual. Investors buying the bond currently will earn a yield to maturity of 8.5 percent. At what price will the bonds sell in the marketplace? Explain.

INTERMEDIATE

8.14 Bond price: Pullman Corp issued 10-year bonds four years ago with a coupon rate of 9.375 percent. At the time of issue, the bonds sold at par. Today bonds of similar risk and maturity will pay annual coupons of 6.25 percent. Assuming semiannual coupon payments, what will be the current market price of the firm's bonds?

8.15 Bond price: Marshall Company is issuing eight-year bonds with a coupon rate of 6.5 percent and semiannual coupon payments. If the current market rate for similar bonds is 8 percent, what will be the bond price? If the company wants to raise $1.25 million, how many bonds does the firm have to sell?

8.16 Bond price: Rockne, Inc., has outstanding bonds that will mature in six years and pay an 8 percent coupon, interest being paid semiannually. If you paid $1,036.65 today and your required rate of return was 6.6 percent, did you pay the right price for the bond?

8.17 Bond price: Nanotech, Inc., has a bond issue maturing in seven years and paying a coupon rate of 9.5 percent (semiannual payments). The company wants to retire a portion of the issue by buying the securities in the open market. If it can refinance at 8 percent, how much will Nanotech pay to buy back its current outstanding bonds?

8.18 Zero coupon bonds: Kintel, Inc., wants to raise $1 million by issuing six-year zero coupon bonds with a face value of $1,000. Its investment banker states that investors would use an 11.4 percent discount rate on such bonds. At what price would these bonds sell in the marketplace? How many bonds would the firm have to issue to raise $1 million? Assume semiannual coupon payments.

8.19 Zero coupon bonds: Rockinghouse Corp. plans to issue seven-year zero coupon bonds. It has learned that these bonds will sell today at a price of $439.76. Assuming annual coupon payments, what is the yield to maturity on these bonds?

8.20 Yield to maturity: Electrolex, Inc., has four-year bonds outstanding that pay a coupon rate of 6.6 percent semiannually. If these bonds are currently selling at $914.89, what is the yield to maturity that an investor can expect to earn on these bonds? What is the effective annual yield?

8.21 Yield to maturity: Serengeti Corp. has five-year bonds outstanding that pay a coupon of 8.8 percent. If these bonds are priced at $1,064.86, what is the yield to maturity on these bonds? Assume semiannual coupon payments. What is the effective annual yield?

8.22 Yield to maturity: Adrienne Dawson is planning to buy 10-year zero coupon bonds issued by the U.S. Treasury. If these bonds with a face value of $1,000 are currently selling at $404.59, what is the expected return on these bonds? Assume that interest compounds semiannually on similar coupon paying bonds.

8.23 Realized yield: Brown & Co. issued seven-year bonds two years ago that can be called after five years. The bond makes semiannual coupon payments at a coupon rate of 7.875 percent. The bond has a market value of $1,053.40, and the call price is $1,078.75. If the bonds are called by the firm, what is the investor's realized yield?

8.24 Realized yield: Trevor Price bought 10-year bonds issued by Harvest Foods five years ago for $936.05. The bonds make semiannual coupon payments at a rate of 8.4 percent. If the current price of the bond is $1,048.77, what is the yield that Trevor would earn by selling the bonds today?

8.25 Realized yield: You bought a six-year bond issued by Runaway Corp. four years ago. At that time, you paid $974.33 for the bond. The bond pays a coupon rate of 7.375 percent, and interest is paid semiannually. Currently, the bond is priced at $1,023.56. What yield can you expect to earn on this bond if you sell it today?

8.26 Lopez Information Systems is planning to issue 10-year bonds. The going market rate for such bonds is 8.125 percent. Assume that coupon payments will be semiannual. The firm

ADVANCED

is trying to decide between issuing an 8 percent coupon bond or a zero coupon bond. The company needs to raise $1 million.
   a. What will be the price of the 8 percent coupon bonds?
   b. How many coupon bonds would have to be issued?
   c. What will be the price of the zero coupon bonds?
   d. How many zero coupon bonds will have to be issued?

8.27 Showbiz, Inc., has issued eight-year bonds with a coupon of 6.375 percent and semiannual coupon payments. The market's required rate of return on such bonds is 7.65 percent.
   a. What is the market price of these bonds?
   b. Now assume that the above bond is callable after five years at an 8.5 percent premium on the face value. What is the expected return on this bond?

8.28 Peabody Corp. has seven-year bonds outstanding. The bonds pay a coupon of 8.375 percent semiannually and are currently worth $1,063.49. The bonds can be called in three years at a price of $1,075.
   a. What is the yield to maturity on the bond?
   b. What is the effective annual yield?
   c. What is the realized yield on the bonds if they are called?
   d. If you plan to invest in this bond today, what is the expected yield on the investment? Explain.

8.29 Maryland Department of Transportation has issued 25-year bonds that pay semiannual coupons at a rate of 9.875 percent. The current market rate for similar securities is 11 percent.
   a. What is the bond's current market value?
   b. What will be the bond's price if rates in the market (i) decrease to 9 percent or (ii) increase to 12 percent?
   c. Refer to your answers in part b. How do the interest rate changes affect premium bonds and discount bonds?
   d. Suppose the bond were to mature in 12 years. How do the interest rate changes in part b affect the bond prices?

8.30 Rachette Corp. has 18-year bonds outstanding. These bonds, which pay semiannual coupons, have a coupon rate of 9.735 percent and a yield to maturity of 7.95 percent.
   a. Compute the bond's current price.
   b. If the bonds can be called after five more years at a premium of 13.5 percent over par value, what is the investor's realized yield?
   c. If you bought the bond today, what is your expected rate of return? Explain.

Sample Test Problems

8.1 Torino Foods issued 10-year bonds three years ago with a coupon of 6 percent. If the current market rate is 8.5 percent and the bonds pay annual coupons, what is the current market price of this bond?

8.2 Kim Sundaram recently bought a 20-year zero coupon bond which compounds interest semiannually. If the current market rate is 7.75 percent, what is the maximum price he should have paid for this bond?

8.3 Five-year bonds of Infotech Corporation are currently priced at $1,065.23. They pay semiannual coupons of 8.5 percent. If you bought these bonds today, what would be the yield to maturity and effective annual yield that you would earn?

8.4 The Gold Company wants to borrow on a five-year term from its bank. The lender determines that the firm should pay a default risk premium of 1.75 percent over the treasury rate. The five-year treasury rate is currently 5.65 percent. The firm also faces a marketability risk premium of 0.80 percent. What is the total borrowing cost to the firm?

8.5 Trojan Corp. has issued seven-year bonds that are paying 7 percent semiannual coupons. If the opportunity cost for Brianna Lindner is 8.25 percent, what is the maximum price that she would be willing to pay for this bond?

STOCK VALUATION

CHAPTER 9

LEARNING OBJECTIVES

1. List and describe the four types of secondary markets.

2. Explain why many financial analysts treat preferred stock as a special type of bond rather than as an equity security.

3. Describe how the general dividend-valuation model values a share of stock.

4. Discuss the assumptions that are necessary to make the general dividend-valuation model easier to use, and be able to use the model to compute the value of a firm's stock.

5. Explain why g must be less than R in the constant-growth dividend model.

6. Explain how valuing preferred stock with a stated maturity differs from valuing preferred stock with no maturity date, and be able to calculate the price of a share of preferred stock under both conditions.

NewsCom

Finding the actual market price of a share of publicly traded stock is easy. You can just look it up in the *Wall Street Journal*. But don't expect the market price to stay the same; stock prices change all the time—sometimes dramatically.

Take Wednesday, February 28, 2007, when the Dow Jones Industrial Average declined by 546 points. This was the biggest point drop since the first day of trading following the September 11 terrorist attack in 2001. In percentage terms, the 3.29 percent decline was the worst since March 2003. On that day, a wave of selling was set off by a sharp decline in the Chinese stock market, followed by falling prices in other Asian stock markets. Once the sell-off was under way in Asia, it spread to Europe and the United States.

In the United States, analysts attributed the plunge in stock prices to various causes: investors' concerns over consumers' declining confidence in the economy, falling housing prices, shrinking profits on Wall Street, and the high percentage of substandard loans held by banks and other lenders. Not helping matters, a few days before the plunge, Alan Greenspan, the former chairman of the Federal Reserve, had delivered a speech in which he did not rule out the possibility of a recession in the United States during the current year.

When stock prices rise or fall, how do investors or financial managers know when it is time to sell or buy? In other words, how can they tell if the market price of a stock reflects its value? One approach is to develop a stock-valuation model and compare the estimate from the model with the market price. If the market price is below the estimate, the stock may be undervalued, in which case an investor might buy the stock. (Of course, other factors may also weigh into the final decision to buy.) In this chapter, we develop and apply stock-valuation models that enable us to estimate a stock's value. The models are very similar to those used by Wall Street firms.

CHAPTER PREVIEW

This chapter focuses on equity securities and how they are valued. We first examine the fundamental factors that determine a stock's value; then we discuss several valuation models. These models tell us what a stock's price *should* be. We can compare our estimates from such models with *actual* market prices.

Why are stock-valuation formulas important for you to study in a corporate finance course? First, management may want to know if the firm's stock is undervalued or overvalued. For example, if the stock is undervalued, management may want to repurchase shares of stock to reissue in the future or postpone an equity offering until the stock price increases. Second, as we mentioned in Chapter 1, the overarching goal of financial management is to maximize the current value of the firm's stock. To make investment or financing decisions that increase stockholder value, you must understand the fundamental factors that determine the market value of the firm's stock.

We begin this chapter with a discussion of the secondary markets for equity securities and their efficiency, explain how to read stock market price listings in the newspaper, and introduce the types of equity securities that firms typically issue. Then we develop a general valuation model and demonstrate that the value of a share of stock is the present value of *all* expected future cash dividends. We use some simplifying assumptions about dividend payments to implement this valuation model. These assumptions correspond to actual practice and allow us to develop several specific valuation models that are theoretically sound.

9.1 The Market for Stocks

Equity securities are certificates of ownership of a corporation. Equities are the most visible securities on the financial landscape. At the end of 2007, more than $20.8 trillion worth of public equity securities were outstanding in the United States alone. Every day Americans eagerly track the ups and downs of the stock market. Most people instinctively believe that the performance of the stock market is an important barometer of the country's economic health. Also fueling interest is the large number of people who actually own equity securities through their pension or retirement plans. Households own more than 36 percent of outstanding corporate equity.

Secondary Markets

Recall from Chapter 2 that the stock market consists of primary and secondary markets. In the primary market, firms sell new shares of stock to investors to raise money. In secondary markets, outstanding shares of stock are bought and sold among investors. We will discuss the primary markets for bonds and equity securities further in Chapter 15. Our focus here is on secondary markets.

Any trade of a security after its primary offering is said to be a secondary market transaction. Most secondary market transactions do not directly affect the firm that issues the securities. For example, when an investor buys 100 shares of AT&T stock on the NYSE, the exchange of money is only between the investors buying and selling the securities; AT&T's cash position is not affected.

The presence of a secondary market does, however, affect the issuer indirectly. Simply put, investors will pay a higher price for primary securities that have an active secondary market because of the marketability the secondary market provides. As a result, firms whose securities trade on a secondary market can sell their new debt or equity issues at a lower funding cost than firms selling similar securities that have no secondary market.

Secondary Markets and Their Efficiency

In the United States, most secondary market transactions take place on one of the many stock exchanges, the two most important being the NYSE and NASDAQ. Measured in terms of total volume of activity and total equity value of the firms listed, the NYSE is the largest in the world and NASDAQ is the second largest. However, in terms of the number of companies listed and shares traded on a daily basis, NASDAQ is larger than the NYSE. In general, firms listed on the NYSE tend to be larger in size, and their shares trade more frequently than firms whose securities trade on NASDAQ.

The role of these and other secondary markets is to bring buyers and sellers together. As we discussed in Chapter 8, ideally we would like security markets to be as efficient as possible. Markets are efficient when current market prices of securities traded reflect all available information relevant to the security. If this is the case, security prices will be near or at their true value. The more efficient the market, the more likely this is to happen.

There are four types of secondary markets, and each type differs according to the amount of price information available to investors, which in turn, affects the efficiency of the market. We discuss the four types of secondary markets—direct search, brokered, dealer, and auction—in the order of their increasing market efficiency.

For an in-depth discussion of market efficiency, visit www.investorhome.com/emh.htm.

LEARNING OBJECTIVE 1

Direct Search. The secondary markets furthest from the ideal of complete availability of price information are those in which buyers and sellers must seek each other out directly. In these markets, individuals bear the full cost of locating and negotiating, and it is typically too costly for them to conduct a thorough search to locate the best price. Securities that sell in direct search markets are usually bought and sold so infrequently that few third parties, such as a brokers or dealers, find it profitable enough to serve the market. In these markets, sellers often rely on word-of-mouth communication to find interested buyers. The common stock of small private companies is a good example of a security that trades in this manner.

Broker. When trading in a security issue becomes sufficiently heavy, brokers find it profitable to offer specialized search services to market participants. Brokers bring buyers and sellers together to earn a fee, called a commission. To provide investors with an incentive to hire them, brokers may charge a commission that is less than the cost of a direct search. Brokers are not passive agents but aggressively seek out buyers or sellers and try to negotiate an acceptable transaction price for their clients. The presence of active brokers increases market efficiency because brokers are in frequent contact with market participants and are likely to know what constitutes a "fair" price for a security.

Dealer. If the trading in a given security has sufficient volume, market efficiency is improved if there is someone in the marketplace to provide continuous bidding (selling or buying) for the security. Dealers provide this service by holding inventories of securities, which they own, and then buying and selling from the inventory to earn a profit. Unlike brokers, dealers have capital at risk. Dealers earn their profits from the *spread* on the securities they trade—the difference between their **bid price** (the price at which they buy) and their **offer (ask) price** (the price at which they sell). NASDAQ is the best-known example of a dealer market.

The advantage of a dealer over a brokered market is that brokers cannot guarantee that an order to buy or sell will be executed promptly. This uncertainty about the speed of execution creates price risk. During the time a broker is trying to sell a security, its price may change and the client could suffer a loss. A dealer market eliminates the need for time-consuming searches for a fair deal because buying and selling take place immediately from the dealer's inventory of securities.

Dealers make markets in securities using electronic computer networks to quote prices at which they are willing to buy or sell a particular security. These networks

bid price
the price a securities dealer will pay for a given stock

offer (ask) price
the price at which a securities dealer seeks to sell a given stock

Exhibit 9.1 NYSE Stock Listings from the *Wall Street Journal*

(1)	(2)	(3)	(4)	(5)	(6)
Company Name	Symbol	High	Low	Close	Net Change
AAR Corp.	AIR	30.28	29.51	29.62	−0.60
ABM Industries, Inc.	ABM	23.15	22.14	22.23	−0.99
ABM AMRO Holding N.V. Ads	ABN	46.25	45.33	45.41	−1.36
ACA Capital Holdings, Inc.	ACA	7.15	6.63	6.66	−0.43
ACCO Brands Corp.	ABD	23.44	22.74	22.80	−0.54
ACE Ltd.	ACE	58.56	56.65	56.73	−2.09
AES Corp.	AES	18.37	17.68	17.76	−0.63
AFLAC, Inc.	AFL	53.36	52.10	52.10	−1.37
AGCO Corp.	AG	41.45	40.13	40.23	−1.57
AGL Resources Inc.	ATG	39.19	38.27	38.30	−0.75
AK Steel Holding Corp.	AKS	36.59	35.54	36.05	−0.78
AMB Property Corp.	AMB	53.14	52.14	52.14	−1.01
AMCOL International Corp.	ACO	30.92	29.71	29.81	−1.15
AMR Corp.	AMR	23.90	23.24	23.36	−0.63
APT Satellite Holdings Ltd.	ATS	1.81	1.77	1.77	...

Source: Wall Street Journal Online, August 28, 2007.

enable dealers to electronically survey the prices quoted by different dealers to help establish their sense of a fair price and to trade. A major development in the 1990s was the opening of the so-called electronic communications network (ECN). ECN is a Web site that allows individual investors to trade securities directly with one another, much like dealers.

Auction. In an auction market, buyers and sellers confront each other directly and bargain over price. The participants can communicate orally if they are located in the same place, or the information can be transmitted electronically. The New York Stock Exchange is the best-known example of an auction market. In the NYSE, the auction for a security takes place at a specific location on the floor of the exchange, called a **post**. The auctioneer in this case is the **specialist**, who is designated by the exchange to represent orders placed by public customers. Specialists, as the name implies, handle a small set of securities and are also allowed to act as dealers. Thus, in reality, the NYSE is an auction market that also has some features of a dealer market. In recent years, the NYSE has been moving toward electronic trading with the SuperDOT system (DOT stands for "designated order turnaround"), which allows orders to be transmitted electronically to specialists.

post
a specific location on the floor of a stock exchange at which auctions for a particular security take place

specialist
the trader designated by an exchange to represent orders placed by public customers at auctions of securities; specialists handle a small set of securities and are also allowed to act as dealers

Reading the Stock Market Listings

The *Wall Street Journal*, the *Financial Times*, and other newspapers provide stock listings for the major stock exchanges, such as the NYSE, NASDAQ, and the relevant regional exchanges. Exhibit 9.1 shows a small section of a listing from the *Wall Street Journal* for the NYSE.

Exhibit 9.1 (continued)

(7)	(8)	(9)	(10)	(11)	(12)
	52-Week				
Volume	High	Low	Dividend	Yield	PE	YTD % Change
234,500	34.95	20.08	...	...	21	1.5
195,000	31.20	17.50	0.48	2.2	11	−2.1
705,700	52.03	27.15	1.60e	3.5	...	41.7
106,100	16.55	4.79	...	...	dd	−56.09
284,000	27.45	19.72	...	...	56	−13.9
1,495,20	64.32	52.00	1.08	1.9	7	−6.3
4,972,70	24.24	16.69	...	...	dd	−19.4
1,552,70	57.44	42.50	0.82	1.6	17	13.3
708,400	46.47	22.47	...	...	dd	30.0
400,900	44.67	34.76	1.64	4.3	14	−1.6
2,703,10	41.87	11.57	...	...	27	113.3
734,500	65.38	48.10	2.00	3.8	23	−11.0
91,800	35.68	21.85	0.64f	2.1	19	7.5
3,068,50	41.00	19.23	...	...	15	−22.7
3,500	2.60	1.20	...	...	...	14.2

In the exhibit, go to the entry for ABM Industries, which is highlighted. ABM is a San Francisco-based facility service contractor that provides janitorial, parking, engineering, security, lighting, and mechanical services for commercial, industrial, institutional, and retail facilities. Look at column 2, which provides the trading (ticker) symbol of the company—ABM. The trading symbol is used in requesting price quotes or company information and in placing a trade. Columns 3 and 4 show the high price ($23.15 per share) and low price ($22.14 per share) for the day, and column 5 shows that ABM's closing price at the end of the day was $22.23 per share. The closing price, which is the price at which the last trade took place, was a $0.99 decrease from the close on the previous day (column 6). The trading volume of shares for the day, which for ABM is 195,000 shares of stock, is listed in column 7. Column 8 shows the firm's highest price ($31.20 per share) and lowest price ($17.50 per share) over the past 52 weeks.

Column 9 shows ABM's annual cash dividend per share, which is $0.48. Although the annual dividend is shown here, most firms, including ABM, pay dividends quarterly, or four times a year. Column 10 shows ABM's **dividend yield**, which is 2.2 percent. The dividend yield is calculated by dividing the annual dividend payout by the current market price. For ABM, that calculation is $0.48/$22.23 = 0.0215, or 2.2 percent. If you scan the dividend yields, you will see that a number of firms pay no dividend at all; for those that pay dividends, the dividend yields range from 1.6 percent to 4.3 percent. Investors are willing to accept low dividend payouts, or none at all, as long as they expect higher cash dividends and/or a higher stock price in the future.

Column 11 shows ABM's price-earnings (P/E) ratio, which—as you may recall from Chapter 4—is the stock's current price per share divided by its earnings per share. For ABM, the P/E ratio is 11 times. This tells us that investors are currently willing to pay a price per share 11 times the earnings per share for ABM stock. A P/E ratio of 11 is fairly low. To justify a higher P/E ratio, investors must believe that the firm has good prospects for earnings growth in the future. We will have more to say about the P/E ratio in later chapters. Finally, Column 12 shows the percentage change in price for the stock for the calendar year. In ABM's case the price has gone down by 2.1 percent.

> To monitor stocks trading on the New York Stock Exchange, visit the NYSE Web site at marketrac.nyse.com/mt/index.html.

> **dividend yield**
> a stock's dividend payout divided by its current price

Common and Preferred Stock

common stock
an equity share that represents the basic ownership claim in a corporation; the most common type of equity security

Equity securities take several forms. The most prevalent type of equity security, as its name implies, is **common stock**. Common stock represents the basic ownership claim in a corporation. One of the basic rights of the owners is to vote on all important matters that affect the life of the company, such as the election of the board of directors or a proposed merger or acquisition. Owners of common stock are not guaranteed any dividend payments and have the lowest-priority claim on the firm's assets in the event of bankruptcy. Legally, common stockholders enjoy limited liability; that is, their losses are limited to the original amount of their investment in the firm, and their personal assets cannot be taken to satisfy the obligations of the corporation. Finally, common stocks are perpetuities in the sense that they have no maturity. Common stock can be retired only if management buys it in the open market from investors or if the firm is liquidated, in which case its assets are sold, as described in the next section.

preferred stock
an equity share in a corporation that entitles the owner to preferred treatment over owners of common stock with respect to dividend payments and claims against the firm's assets in the event of bankruptcy or liquidation but that typically has no voting rights

Like common stock, **preferred stock** represents an ownership interest in the corporation, but as the name implies, preferred stock receives preferential treatment over common stock. Specifically, preferred stockholders take precedence over common stockholders in the payment of dividends and in the distribution of corporate assets in the event of liquidation. Unlike the interest payments on bonds, which are contractual obligations, preferred stock dividends are declared by the board of directors, and if a dividend is not paid, the lack of payment is not legally viewed as a default.

Preferred stock is legally a form of equity. Thus, preferred stock dividends are paid by the issuer with after-tax dollars. Even though preferred stock is an equity security, the owners have no voting privileges unless the preferred stock is convertible into common stock. Preferred stocks are generally viewed as perpetuities because they have no maturity. However, most preferred stocks are not true perpetuities because their share contracts often contain call provisions and can even include *sinking fund* provisions, which require management to retire a certain percentage of the stock issue annually until the entire issue is retired.

Preferred Stock: Debt or Equity?

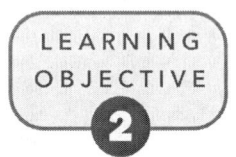

LEARNING OBJECTIVE 2

One of the ongoing debates in finance is whether preferred stock is debt or equity. A strong case can be made that preferred stock is a special type of bond. The argument behind this case is as follows. First, regular (nonconvertible) preferred stock confers no voting rights. Second, preferred stockholders receive a fixed dividend, regardless of the firm's earnings, and if the firm is liquidated, they receive a stated value (usually par) and not a residual value. Third, preferred stocks often have "credit" ratings that are similar in nature to those issued to bonds. Fourth, preferred stock is sometimes convertible into common stock. Finally, most preferred stock issues are not true perpetuities. For these reasons, many investors consider preferred stock to be a special type of debt rather than equity.

> Before You Go On
>
> 1. How do dealers differ from brokers?
> 2. What does the price-earnings ratio tell us?
> 3. Why is preferred stock often viewed as a special type of a bond rather than a stock?

9.2 Common Stock Valuation

In earlier chapters we emphasized that the value of any asset is the present value of its future cash flows. The steps in valuing an asset are as follows:

1. Estimate the future cash flows.

2. Determine the required rate of return, or discount rate, which depends on the riskiness of the future cash flows.

3. Compute the present value of the future cash flows to determine what the asset is worth.

It is relatively straightforward to apply these steps in valuing a bond because the cash flows are stated as part of the bond contract and the required rate of return or discount rate is just the yield to maturity on bonds with comparable risk characteristics. However, common stock valuation is more difficult for several reasons. First, while the expected cash flows for bonds are well documented and easy to determine, common stock dividends are much less certain. Dividends are declared by the board of directors, and a board may or may not decide to pay a cash dividend at a particular time. Thus, the size and the timing of dividend cash flows are less certain. Second, common stocks are true perpetuities in that they have no final maturity date. Thus, firms never have to redeem them. In contrast, bonds have a finite maturity. Finally, unlike the rate of return, or yield, on bonds, the rate of return on common stock is not directly observable. Thus, grouping common stocks into risk classes is more difficult than grouping bonds. Keeping these complexities in mind, we now turn to a discussion of common stock valuation.

> You can read about stock-valuation models at the Motley Fool: www.fool.com/research/2000/features000406.htm.

A One-Period Model

Let's assume that you have a genie that can tell the future with perfect certainty. Suppose you are thinking about buying a share of stock and selling it after a year. The genie volunteers that in one year you will be able to sell the stock for $100 ($P_1$) and it will pay an $8 dividend ($D_1$) at the end of the year. The time line for the transaction is:

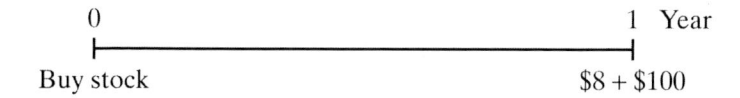

```
0                                    1  Year
|————————————————————————————————————|
Buy stock                            $8 + $100
```

If you and the other investors require a 20 percent return on investments in securities in this risk class, what price would you be willing to pay for the stock today?

The value of the stock is the present value of the future cash flows you can expect to receive from it. The cash flows you will receive are as follows: (1) the $8 dividend and (2) the $100 sale price. Using a 20 percent rate of return, we see that the value of the stock equals the present value (PV) of the dividend plus the present value of the cash received from the sale of the stock:

$$\begin{aligned} PV(stock) &= PV(dividend) + PV(sale\ price) \\ &= \frac{\$8}{1 + 0.2} + \frac{\$100}{1 + 0.2} \\ &= \frac{\$8 + \$100}{1.2} = \frac{\$108}{1.2} \\ &= \$90 \end{aligned}$$

Thus, the value of the stock today is $90. If you pay $90 for the stock, you will have a one-year holding period return of exactly 20 percent. More formally, the time line and the current value of the stock for our one-period model can be as shown:

```
0                                               1  Year
├───────────────────────────────────────────────┤
P₀                                              D₁ + P₁
```

$$P_0 = \frac{D_1 + P_1}{1 + R}$$

where:

P_0 = the current value, or price, of the stock
D_1 = dividend paid at the end of the period
P_1 = price of the stock at the end of the period
R = required return on common stock, or discount rate, in a particular risk class

Note that P_0 denotes time zero, which is today; P_1 is the price one period later; P_2 is two periods in the future; and so on. Note also that when we speak of the price (P) in this context, we mean the value—what we have determined is what the price *should* be, given our model—not the actual market price. Our one-period model provides an estimate of what the market price should be.

Now what if at the beginning of year 2, we are again asked to determine the price of a share of common stock with the same dividend pattern and a one-year holding period. As in our first calculation, the current price (P_1) of the stock is the present value of the dividend and the stock's sale price, both received at the end of the year (P_2). Specifically, our time line and the stock pricing formula are as follows:

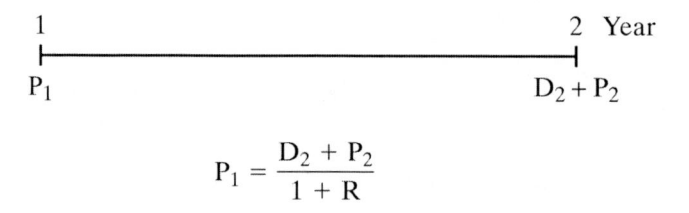

```
1                                               2  Year
├───────────────────────────────────────────────┤
P₁                                              D₂ + P₂
```

$$P_1 = \frac{D_2 + P_2}{1 + R}$$

If we repeat the process again at the beginning of year 3, the result is similar:

$$P_2 = \frac{D_3 + P_3}{1 + R}$$

and at the beginning of year 4:

$$P_3 = \frac{D_4 + P_4}{1 + R}$$

Each single-period model discounts the dividend and sale price at the end of the period by the required return.

A Perpetuity Model

Unfortunately, although our one-period model is correct, it is not very realistic. We need a stock-valuation formula for perpetuity, not for one or two periods. However, we can string together a series of one-period stock pricing models to arrive at a stock perpetuity model. Here is how we are going to do it.

First, we will construct a two-period stock-valuation model. The time line for the two-period model follows:

```
0                    1                    2   Period
├────────────────────┼────────────────────┤
P₀ ◄──────(D₁+ P₁)
           P₁ ◄──────(D₂+ P₂)
```

To construct our two-period model, we start with our initial single-period valuation formula:

$$P_0 = \frac{D_1 + P_1}{1 + R}$$

Now we substitute into this equation the expression derived earlier for $P_1 = (D_2 + P_2)/(1 + R)$, which is as follows:

$$P_0 = \frac{D_1 + [(D_2 + P_2)/(1 + R)]}{1 + R}$$

Solving this equation results in a stock-valuation model for two periods:

$$P_0 = \frac{D_1}{1 + R} + \frac{D_2}{(1 + R)^2} + \frac{P_2}{(1 + R)^2}$$

Finally, we combine the second-period terms, resulting in this two-period stock valuation equation:

$$P_0 = \frac{D_1}{1 + R} + \frac{D_2 + P_2}{(1 + R)^2}$$

This equation shows that the price of a share of stock for two periods is the present value of the dividend in period 1 (D_1) plus the present value of the dividend and sale price in period 2 (D_2 and P_2).

Now let's construct a three-period model. The time line for the three-period model is:

```
0              1              2              3   Period
├──────────────┼──────────────┼──────────────┤
P₀ ◄────(D₁+ P₁)
        P₁ ◄────(D₂ + P₂)
                P₂ ◄────(D₃ + P₃)
```

If we substitute the equation for P_2 into the two-period valuation model shown above, we have a three-period model, which is shown in the following equations. Recall that $P_2 = (D_3 + P_3)/(1 + R)$. This model was developed in precisely the same way as our two-period model:

$$P_0 = \frac{D_1}{1 + R} + \frac{D_2}{(1 + R)^2} + \frac{P_2}{(1 + R)^2}$$

$$= \frac{D_1}{1 + R} + \frac{D_2}{(1 + R)^2} + \frac{(D_3 + P_3)/(1 + R)}{(1 + R)^2}$$

$$= \frac{D_1}{1 + R} + \frac{D_2}{(1 + R)^2} + \frac{D_3}{(1 + R)^3} + \frac{P_3}{(1 + R)^3}$$

$$= \frac{D_1}{1 + R} + \frac{D_2}{(1 + R)^2} + \frac{D_3 + P_3}{(1 + R)^3}$$

By now, it should be clear that we could go on to develop a four-period model, a five-period model, a six-period model, and so on, ad infinitum. The ultimate result is the following equation:

$$P_0 = \frac{D_1}{1+R} + \frac{D_2}{(1+R)^2} + \frac{D_3}{(1+R)^3} + \cdots + \frac{D_t}{(1+R)^t} + \frac{P_t}{(1+R)^t}$$

Here, t is the number of time periods, which can be any number from one to infinity (∞).

In summary, we have developed a model showing that the value, or price, of a share of stock today (P_0) is the present value of all future dividends and the stock's sale price in the future. Although theoretically sound, this model is not practical to apply because the number of dividends could be infinite. It is unlikely that we can successfully forecast an infinite number of dividend payments or a stock's sale price far into the future. What we need are some realistic simplifing assumptions.

The General Dividend Valuation Model

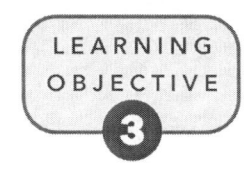

LEARNING OBJECTIVE 3

In the preceding equation, notice that the final term, as in the earlier valuation models, is always the sale price of the stock in period t (P_t) and that t can be any number, including infinity. The model assumes that we can forecast the sale price of the stock far into the future, which does not seem very likely in real life. However, as a practical matter, as P_t moves further out in time toward infinity, the value of the P_t approaches zero. Why? No matter how large the sale price of the stock, the present value of P_t will approach zero because the discount factor approaches zero. Therefore, if we go out to infinity, we can ignore the $P_t/(1+R)^t$ term and write our final equation as:

$$P_0 = \frac{D_1}{1+R} + \frac{D_2}{(1+R)^2} + \frac{D_3}{(1+R)^3} + \frac{D_4}{(1+R)^4} + \frac{D_5}{(1+R)^5} + \cdots + \frac{D_\infty}{(1+R)^\infty}$$

$$= \sum_{t=1}^{\infty} \frac{D_t}{(1+R)^t} \qquad (9.1)$$

where:

P_0 = the current value, or price, of the stock
D_t = the dividend received in period t, where $t = 1, 2, 3, \ldots, \infty$
R = the required return on common stock or discount rate

Equation 9.1 is a general expression for the value of a share of stock. It says that the price of a share of stock is the present value of *all* expected future dividends:

$$\text{Stock price} = \text{PV(All future dividends)}$$

The formula does not assume any specific pattern for future dividends, such as a constant growth rate. Nor does it make any assumption about when the share of stock is going to be sold in the future. Furthermore, the model says that to compute a stock's current value, we need to forecast an infinite number of dividends, which is a daunting task at best.

Equation 9.1 provides some insights into why stock prices are changing all the time and why, at certain times, price changes can be dramatic. Equation 9.1 implies that the underlying value of a share of stock is determined by the market's expectations of the future cash flows (from dividends) that the firm can generate. In efficient markets, stock prices change constantly as new information becomes available and is incorporated into the firm's market price. For publicly traded companies, the market is inundated with facts and rumors, such as when a firm fails to meet sales projections, the CEO resigns or is fired, or a class-action suit is filed against one of its products. Some events may have little or no impact on the firm's cash flows and, hence, its stock price. Others can have very large effects on cash flows. Examples include Hurricane Katrina's impact on businesses in the Gulf Coast region in 2005 or the effects of the subprime mortgage market collapse in 2007, which led to a sharp slowdown in the economy in 2008.

The Growth Stock Pricing Paradox

An interesting issue concerning growth stocks arises out of the fact that the stock-valuation equation is based on dividend payments. *Growth stocks* are typically defined as the stocks of companies whose earnings are growing at above-average rates and are expected to continue to do so for some time. A company of this type typically pays little or no dividends on its stock because management believes that the company has a number of high-return investment opportunities and that both the company and its investors will be better off if earnings are reinvested rather than paid out as dividends.

To illustrate the problem with valuing growth stocks, let's suppose that the earnings of Acme Corporation are growing at an exceptionally high rate. The company's stock pays no dividends, and management states that there are no plans to pay any dividends. Based on our stock-valuation equation, what is the value of Acme's stock?

Obviously, since all the dividend values are zero, the value of our growth stock is zero!

$$P_0 = \frac{0}{1+R} + \frac{0}{(1+R)^2} + \frac{0}{(1+R)^3} + \cdots = 0$$

How can the value of a growth stock be zero? What is going on here?

The problem is that our definition of growth stocks was less than precise. Our application of Equation 9.1 assumes that Acme will never pay a dividend. If Acme had a charter that stated it would *never* pay dividends and would *never* liquidate itself (unless it went bankrupt), the value of its stock would indeed be zero. Equation 9.1 predicts and common sense says that if you own stock in a company that will *never* pay you any cash, the market value of those shares of stock are worth absolutely nothing. As you may recall, this is a point we emphasized in Chapter 1.

What we should have said is that a growth stock is stock in a company that *currently* has exceptional investment opportunities and thus is not *currently* paying dividends because it is reinvesting earnings. At some time in the future, growth stock companies will pay dividends or will liquidate themselves (for example, by selling out to other companies) and pay a single large "cash dividend." People who buy growth stocks expect rapid price appreciation because management reinvests the cash flows from earnings internally in investment projects believed to have high rates of return. If the internal investments succeed, the stock's price should go up significantly, and investors can sell their stock at a price that is higher than the price they paid.

> **Before You Go On**
> 1. What is the general formula used to calculate the price of a share of a stock? What does it mean?
> 2. What are growth stocks and why do they typically pay little or no dividends?

9.3 Stock Valuation: Some Simplifying Assumptions

LEARNING OBJECTIVE 4

Conceptually, our dividend model (Equation 9.1) is consistent with the notion that the value of an asset is the discounted value of future cash flows. Unfortunately, at a practical level, the model is not easy to use because of the difficulty of estimating future dividends over a long period of time. We can, however, make some simplifying assumptions about the pattern of dividends that will make the model more manageable. Fortunately, these assumptions closely resemble the way many firms manage their dividend payments. We have a choice among three different assumptions: (1) Dividend payments remain constant over time; that is, they have a growth rate of zero. (2) Dividends have a constant growth rate; for example, they grow at 3 percent per year. (3) Dividends have a mixed growth rate pattern; that is, dividends have one payment pattern and then switch to another. Next, we discuss each assumption in turn.

Zero-Growth Dividend Model

The simplest assumption is that dividends will have a growth rate of zero. Thus, the dividend payment pattern remains constant over time:

$$D_1 = D_2 = D_3 = \cdots = D_\infty$$

In this case the dividend-discount model (Equation 9.1) becomes:

$$P_0 = \frac{D}{1+R} + \frac{D}{(1+R)^2} + \frac{D}{(1+R)^3} + \frac{D}{(1+R)^4} + \frac{D}{(1+R)^5} + \cdots + \frac{D}{(1+R)^\infty}$$

This cash flow pattern essentially describes a perpetuity with a constant cash flow. You may recall that we developed an equation for such a perpetuity in Chapter 6. Equation 6.3 said that the present value of a perpetuity with a constant cash flow is CF/i, where CF is the constant cash flow and i is the interest rate. In terms of our stock-valuation model, we can present the same relationship as follows:

$$P_0 = \frac{D}{R} \tag{9.2}$$

where:

P_0 = the current value, or price, of the stock
D = the constant cash dividend received in each time period
R = the required return on common stock or discount rate

This model fits the dividend pattern for common stock of a company that is not growing and has little growth potential or for preferred stock, which we discuss in the next section.

For example, the Del Mar Corporation is a small printing company that serves a rural three-county area near San Diego, California. The county's economic base has remained constant over the years, and Del Mar's sales and earnings reflect this trend. The firm pays a $5 dividend per year, and the board of directors has no plans to change the dividend. The firm's investors are mostly local businesspeople who expect a 20 percent return on their investment. What should be the price of the firm's stock?

Since the cash dividend payments are constant, we can use Equation 9.2 to find the price of the stock:

$$P_0 = \frac{D}{R} = \frac{\$5}{0.20} = \$25 \text{ per share}$$

LEARNING BY DOING
APPLICATION 9.1

The Value of a Small Business

Problem: For the past 15 years, a family has operated the gift shop in a luxury hotel near Rodeo Drive in Los Angeles. The hotel management wants to sell the gift shop to the family members rather than paying them to operate it. The family's accountant will incorporate the new business and estimates that it will generate an annual cash dividend of $150,000 for the stockholders. The hotel will provide the family with an infinite guarantee for the space and a generous buyout plan in the event that the hotel closes its doors. The accountant estimates that a 20 percent discount rate is appropriate. What is the value of the stock?

Approach: Assuming that the business will operate indefinitely and that its growth is constrained by its circumstances, the zero-growth discount model can be used to value the stock. Thus, we can use Equation 9.2. Since the number of shares outstanding is not known, we can simply interpret P_0 as being the total value of the outstanding stock.

Solution:

$$P_0 = \frac{D}{R} = \frac{\$150{,}000}{0.20} = \$750{,}000$$

Constant-Growth Dividend Model

Under the next dividend assumption, cash dividends do not remain constant but instead grow at some average rate g from one period to the next forever. The rate of growth can be positive or negative. And, as it turns out, a constant-growth rate is not a bad approximation of the actual dividend pattern for some firms. Constant dividend growth is an appropriate assumption for mature companies with a history of stable growth.

You may have concerns about the assumption of an infinite time horizon. In practice, though, it does not present a problem. It is true that most companies do not live on forever. We know, however, that the further in the future a cash flow will occur, the smaller its present value. Thus, far-distant dividends have a small present value and contribute very little to the price of the stock. For example, as shown in Exhibit 9.2, with constant dividends and a 15 percent discount rate, dividends paid during the first 10 years account for more than 75 percent of the value of a share of stock, while dividends paid after the twentieth year contribute less than 6 percent of the value.

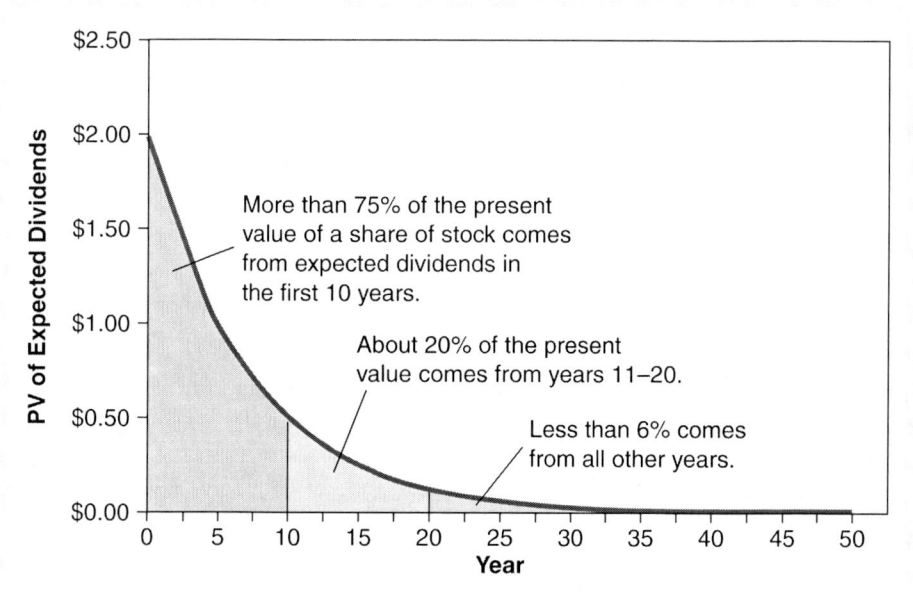

Note: Calculations based on discount rate of 15% and constant dividends.

Exhibit 9.2
Impact on Stock Prices of Near and Distant Future Dividends
Dividends expected far in the future have a smaller present value than dividends expected in the next few years, and so they have less effect on the price of the stock. As you can see in the exhibit, with constant dividends more than 75 percent of the current price of a share of stock comes from expected dividends in the first 10 years.

Identifying and applying the constant-growth dividend model is fairly straightforward. First, we need a model to compute the value of dividend payments for any time period. We will assume that the cash dividends grow at a constant rate g from one period to the next forever. This situation is an application of the compound growth rate formula, Equation 5.6, developed in Chapter 5:

$$FV_n = PV \times (1 + g)^n$$

where g is the compound growth rate and n is the number of compounding periods. We can apply this formula to our dividend payments. We note that D_0 is the current dividend, paid at time $t = 0$, and it grows at a constant growth rate g. The next dividend, paid at time $t = 1$, is D_1, which is just the current dividend (D_0) multiplied by the growth factor, $(1 + g)$. Thus, $D_1 = D_0 \times (1 + g)$. The general formula for dividend values over time is stated as follows:

$$D_t = D_0 \times (1 \times g)^t \tag{9.3}$$

where:

D_t = dividend payment in period t, where $t = 1, 2, 3, \ldots, \infty$
D_0 = dividend paid in the current period, $t = 0$
g = the constant-growth rate for dividends

Equation 9.3 allows us to compute the dividend payment for any time period.

Notice that to compute the dividend for any period, we multiply D_0 by the growth rate factor to some power, but we *always* start with D_0.

We can now develop the constant-growth dividend model, which is easy to do because it is just an application of Equation 6.6 from Chapter 6. Equation 6.6 says that the present value of a growing perpetuity (PVA_∞) is the growing cash flow value (CF_1) from period 1, divided by the difference between the discount rate (i) and the rate of growth (g) of the cash flow (CF_1):

$$PVA_\infty = \frac{CF_1}{i - g}$$

We can represent this same relationship as follows:

$$P_0 = \frac{D_1}{R - g} \tag{9.4}$$

where:

P_0 = the current value, or price, of the stock
D_1 = the dividend paid in the next period ($t = 1$)
g = the constant-growth rate for dividends
R = the required return on common stock or discount rate

In other words, the constant-growth dividend model tells us that the current price of a share of stock is the next period dividend divided by the difference between the discount rate and the dividend growth rate. Note that PVA_∞ is the current value or price of the stock (P_0), which is the present value of the dividend cash flows.

As discussed in Chapter 6, the growing-perpetuity model is valid only as long as the growth rate is less than the discount rate, or required rate of return. In terms of Equation 9.4, then, the value of g must be less than the value of R ($g < R$). If the equation is used in situations where R is equal to or less than g ($R \leq g$), the computed results will be meaningless.

Finally, notice that if $g = 0$, there is no dividend growth, the dividend payment pattern becomes a constant no-growth dividend stream, and Equation 9.4 becomes $P_0 = D/R$. This equation is precisely the same as Equation 9.2, which is our zero-growth dividend model. Thus, Equation 9.2 is just a special case of Equation 9.4 where $g = 0$.

Let's work through an example using the constant-growth dividend model. Big Red Automotive is a regional auto parts supplier based in Oklahoma City. At the firm's year-end stockholders' meeting, the CFO announces that this year's dividend will be $4.81. The announcement conforms to Big Red's dividend policy, which sets dividend growth at a 4 percent annual rate. Investors who own stock in similar types of firms expect to earn a return of 18 percent. What is the value of the firm's stock?

First, we need to compute the cash dividend payment for next year (D_1). Applying Equation 9.3 for $t = 1$ yields the following:

$$D_1 = D_0 \times (1 + g) = \$4.81 \times (1 + 0.04) = \$4.81 \times 1.04 = \$5.00$$

Next, we apply Equation 9.4 to find the value of the firm's stock, which is $35.71 per share:

$$P_0 = \frac{D_1}{R - g} = \frac{\$5.00}{0.18 - 0.04} = \frac{\$5.00}{0.14} = \$35.71$$

LEARNING BY DOING APPLICATION 9.2

Big Red Grows Faster

Problem: Using the information given in the text, compute the value of Big Red's stock if dividends grow at 12 percent rather than 4 percent. Explain why the answer makes sense.

Approach: First compute the cash dividend payment for next year (D_1) using the 12 percent growth rate. Then apply Equation 9.4 to solve for the firm's stock price.

Solution:

$$D_1 = \$4.81 \times 1.12 = \$5.39$$

$$P_0 = \frac{\$5.39}{0.18 - 0.12} = \frac{\$5.39}{0.06} = \$89.83$$

The higher stock value of $89.93 is no surprise because dividends are now growing at a rate of 12 percent rather than 4 percent. Hence, value from cash payments to investors (dividends) is expected to be larger.

Computing Future Stock Prices

The constant-growth dividend model (Equation 9.4) can be modified to determine the value, or price, of a share of stock at any point in time. In general, the price of a share of stock, P_t, can be expressed in terms of the dividend in the next period (D_{t+1}), g, and R, when the dividends from D_{t+1} forward are expected to grow at a constant rate. Thus, the price of a share of stock at time t is as follows:

$$P_t = \frac{D_{t+1}}{R - g} \quad (9.5)$$

Notice that Equation 9.4 is just a special case of Equation 9.5 in which $t = 0$. To be sure that you understand this, set up Equation 9.5 to compute a stock's current price at $t = 0$. When you are done, the resulting equation should look exactly like Equation 9.4.

An example will illustrate how Equation 9.5 is used. Suppose that a firm has a current dividend (D_0) of $2.50, R is 15 percent, and g is 5 percent. What is the price of the stock today (P_0), and what will it be in five years (P_5)? To help visualize the problem, we will lay out a time line and identify some of the important variables necessary to solve the problem:

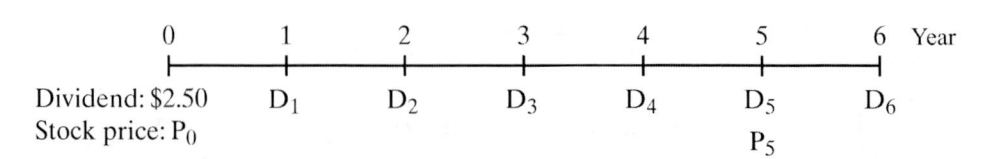

```
           0      1      2      3      4      5      6   Year
           ├──────┼──────┼──────┼──────┼──────┼──────┤
Dividend: $2.50  D₁     D₂     D₃     D₄     D₅     D₆
Stock price: P₀                                P₅
```

To find the current stock price, we can apply Equation 9.4, but we must first compute the dividend for the next period (D_1), which is at $t = 1$. Using Equation 9.3, we compute the firm's dividend for next year:

$$D_1 = D_0 \times (1 + g) = \$2.50 \times 1.05 = \$2.625$$

Now we can use Equation 9.4 to find the price of the stock today:

$$P_0 = \frac{D_1}{R - g} = \frac{\$2.625}{0.15 - 0.05} = \frac{\$2.625}{0.10} = \$26.25$$

Now we will find the value of the stock in five years. In this situation Equation 9.5 is expressed as:

$$P_5 = \frac{D_6}{R - g}$$

We need to compute D_6, and we do so by using Equation 9.3:

$$D_6 = D_0 \times (1 + g)^6 = 2.50 \times (1.05)^6 = 2.50 \times 1.34 = \$3.35$$

The price of the stock in five years is therefore:

$$P_5 = \frac{\$3.35}{0.15 - 0.05} = \frac{\$3.35}{0.10} = \$33.50$$

Finally, note that $\$33.50/(1.05)^5 = \$26.25$, which is the value today.

LEARNING BY DOING
APPLICATION 9.3

Procter & Gamble's Current Stock Price

NEED MORE HELP?
WILEY PLUS
www.wileyplus.com

Problem: Suppose that the current cash dividend on Procter & Gamble's common stock is $4.72. Financial analysts expect the dividends to grow at a constant rate of 6 percent per year, and investors require a 10 percent return on this class of stock. What should be the current price of a share of Procter & Gamble stock?

Approach: In this scenario, $D_0 = \$4.72$, $R = 0.10$, and $g = 0.06$. We first find D_1 using Equation 9.3, and we then calculate the value of a share using Equation 9.4.

Solution:

$$\text{Dividend: } D_1 = D_0 \times (1 + g) = \$4.72 \times 1.06 = \$5.00$$

$$\text{Value of a share: } P_0 = \frac{D_1}{R - g} = \frac{\$5.00}{0.10 - 0.06} = \frac{\$5.00}{0.04} = \$125.00$$

LEARNING BY DOING APPLICATION 9.4

Procter & Gamble's Future Stock Price

Problem: Continuing the example in Learning by Doing Application 9.3, what should Procter & Gamble's stock price be seven years from now (P_7)?

Approach: This is an application of Equation 9.5. We first need to calculate Procter & Gamble's dividend in period 8, using Equation 9.3. Then we can apply Equation 9.5 to compute the estimated price of the stock seven years in the future.

Solution:

Dividend in period 8: $D_8 = D_0 \times (1 + g)^8 = \$4.72 \times (1.06)^8 = \$4.72 \times 1.594 = \$7.52$

Price of a share in 7 years: $P_7 = \dfrac{D_8}{R - g} = \dfrac{\$7.52}{0.10 - 0.06} = \dfrac{\$7.52}{0.04} = \$188.00$

The Relationship between R and g

We previously mentioned that the divided growth model provides valid solutions only when $g < R$. Students frequently ask what happens to Equation 9.4 or 9.5 if this condition does not hold (if $g \geq R$). Mathematically, as g approaches R, the stock price becomes larger and larger, and when $g = R$, the value of the stock is infinite, which is, of course, nonsense. When the growth rate (g) is larger than the discount rate (R), the constant-growth dividend model tells us that the value of the stock is negative. You will see in Chapter 20 that this is not possible. The value of a share of stock can never be negative.

From a practical perspective, the growth rate in the constant-growth dividend model cannot be greater than the sum of the long-term rate of inflation and the long-term real growth rate of the economy. Since this model assumes that the firm will grow at a constant rate forever, any growth rate that is greater than this sum would imply that the firm will eventually take over the entire economy. Of course, we know this is not possible. Since the sum of the long-term rate of inflation and the long-term real growth rate has historically been less than 6 to 7 percent, the growth rate (g) is virtually always less than the discount rate (R) for the stocks that we would want to use the constant-growth dividend model to value.

It is possible for firms to grow faster than the long-term rate of inflation plus the real growth rate of the economy—just not forever. A firm that is growing at such a high rate is said to be growing at a supernormal growth rate. We must use a different model to value the stock of a firm like this. We discuss one such model next.

Mixed (Supernormal) Growth Dividend Model

For many firms, it is not appropriate to assume that dividends will grow at a constant rate. Firms typically go through *life cycles* and, as a result, exhibit different dividend patterns over time.

During the early part of their lives, successful firms experience a supernormal rate of growth in earnings. These firms tend to pay lower dividends or no dividends at all because many good investment projects are available to them and management wants to reinvest earnings in the firm to take advantage of these opportunities. If a growth firm does not pay regular dividends, investors receive their returns from capital appreciation of the firm's stock (which reflects increases in expected future dividends), from a cash or stock payout if the firm is acquired, or possibly from a large special cash dividend. As a firm matures, it will settle into a growth rate at or below the long-term rate of inflation plus the long-term real growth rate of the economy. When a firm reaches this stage, it will typically be paying a fairly predictable regular dividend.

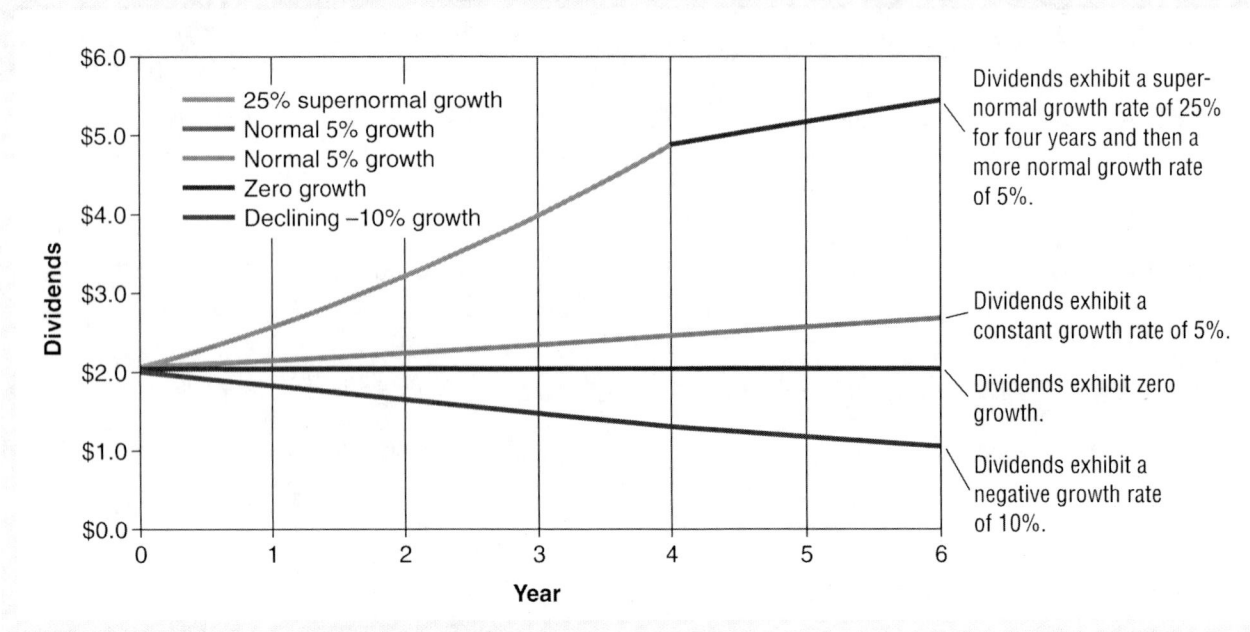

Exhibit 9.3
Dividend Growth Rate Patterns

Exhibit 9.3 shows several dividend growth curves. In the top curve, dividends exhibit a supernormal growth rate of 25 percent for four years, then a more sustainable nominal growth rate of 5 percent (this might, for example, be made up of 2.5 percent growth from inflation plus a 2.5 percent real growth rate). By comparison, the remaining curves show dividends with a constant nominal growth rate of 5 percent, a zero-growth rate, and a negative 10 percent growth rate.

As mentioned earlier, successful companies often experience supernormal growth early in their life cycles. During the 1990s, for example, firms such as Microsoft, Cisco, and Intel experienced supernormal growth. Older companies that reinvent themselves with new products or strategies may also experience periods of supernormal growth. In the 1990s, Lou Gerstner is credited with strategically repositioning IBM from primarily a manufacturer of computers to a provider of software and consulting services. Under Gerstner's leadership, IBM stock generated huge returns for investors.

To value a share of stock for a firm with supernormal dividend growth patterns, we do not need to develop any new equations. Instead, we can apply Equation 9.1, our general dividend model, and Equation 9.5, which gives us the price of a share of stock with constant dividend growth at any point in time.

We will illustrate with an example. Suppose a company's expected dividend pattern for three years is as follows: $D_1 = \$1, D_2 = \$2, D_3 = \$3$. After three years, the dividends are expected to grow at a constant rate of 6 percent a year. What should the current price (P_0) of the firm's stock be if the required rate of return demanded by investors is 15 percent?

We begin by drawing a time line, as shown in Exhibit 9.4. We recommend that you prepare a time line whenever you solve a problem with a complex dividend pattern so that you can be sure the cash flows are placed in the proper time periods. The critical element in working these problems is to correctly identify when the constant growth starts and to value it properly.

Looking at Exhibit 9.4, it is easy to see that we have two different dividend patterns: (1) D_1 through D_3 represent a mixed dividend pattern, which can be valued using Equation 9.1, the general dividend-valuation model. (2) After the third year, dividends

9.3 Stock Valuation: Some Simplifying Assumptions

```
              Nonconstant Growth          Constant growth at 6%
          |—————————————————————▶|————————————————————————▶
Time    0        1        2        3        4        5       Year
        |        |        |        |        |        |
Dividends     $1.00    $2.00    $3.00    $3.18    $3.37
Key Variables P₀  D₁       D₂       D₃       D₄
```

Exhibit 9.4
Time Line for Nonconstant-Dividend Pattern
The exhibit shows a time line for a nonconstant-growth dividend pattern. The time line makes it easy to see that we have two different dividend patterns. For three years, the dividends are expected to grow at a nonconstant rate; after that, they are expected to grow at a constant rate of 6 percent.

show a constant-growth rate of 6 percent, and this pattern can be valued using Equation 9.5, the constant-growth dividend-valuation model. Thus, our valuation model is:

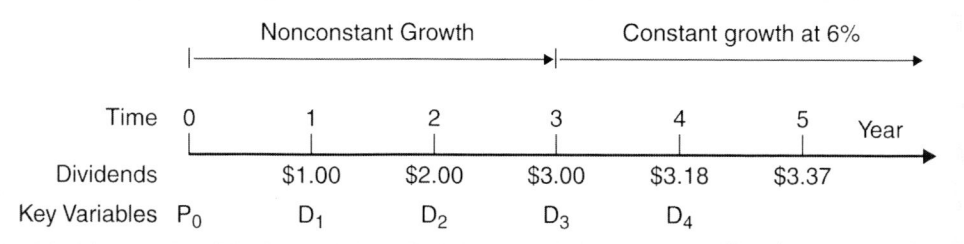

$$P_0 = PV\,(\text{Mixed dividend growth}) + PV\,(\text{Constant dividend growth})$$

Combining these present values yields the following result:

$$P_0 = \underbrace{\frac{D_1}{(1+R)} + \frac{D_2}{(1+R)^2} + \frac{D_3}{(1+R)^3}}_{\text{PV of mixed-growth dividend payments}} + \underbrace{\frac{P_3}{(1+R)^3}}_{\text{Value of constant-growth dividend payments}}$$

The value of the constant-growth dividend stream is P_3, which is the value, or price, at time $t = 3$. More specifically, P_3 is the value of the future cash dividends discounted to time period $t = 3$. With a required rate of return of 15%, the value of these dividends is calculated as follows:

$$D_4 = D_3 \times (1 + g) = \$3.00 \times 1.06 = \$3.18$$

$$P_3 = \frac{D_4}{R - g} = \frac{\$3.18}{0.15 - 0.06}$$

$$= \frac{\$3.18}{0.09}$$

$$= \$35.33$$

We find the value of P_3 using Equation 9.5, which allows us to compute stock prices in the future for stocks with constant dividend growth. Note that the equation gives us the value, as of year 3, of a constant-growth perpetuity that begins in year 4. This formula always gives us the value as of one period before the first cash flow.

Now, since P_3 is at time period $t = 3$, we must discount it back to the present ($t = 0$). This is accomplished by dividing P_3 by the appropriate discount factor—$(1 + R)^3$.

Plugging the values for the dividends, P_3, and R into the above mixed-growth equation results in the following:

$$P_0 = \frac{\$1.00}{1.15} + \frac{\$2.00}{(1.15)^2} + \frac{\$3.00}{(1.15)^3} + \frac{\$35.33}{(1.15)^3}$$

$$= \$0.87 + \$1.51 + \$1.97 + \$23.23$$

$$= \$27.58$$

Thus, the value of the stock is $27.58.

We can write a general equation for the supernormal growth situation, where dividends grow first at a nonconstant rate until period t and then at a constant rate, as follows:

$$P_0 = \frac{D_1}{1+R} + \frac{D_2}{(1+R)^2} + \cdots + \frac{D_t}{(1+R)^t} + \frac{P_t}{(1+R)^t} \qquad (9.6)$$

If the supernormal growth period ends and dividends grow at a constant rate, g, then P_t is calculated from Equation 9.5 as follows:

$$P_t = \frac{D_{t+1}}{R-g}$$

The two preceding equations can also be applied when dividends are constant over time, since we know that $g = 0$ is just a special case of the constant-growth dividend model ($g > 0$).

Let's look at another example, this time using Equation 9.6. Suppose that Redteck is a high-tech medical device firm located in Lincoln, Nebraska. The company is three years old and has experienced spectacular growth since its inception. You are a financial analyst for a stock brokerage firm and have just returned from a two-day visit to the company. You learned that Redteck plans to pay no dividends for the next five years. In year 6, management plans to pay a large, special cash dividend, which you estimate to be $25 per share. Then, beginning in year 7, management plans to pay a constant annual dividend of $6 per share for the foreseeable future. The appropriate discount rate for the stock is 12 percent, and the current market price is $25 per share. Your boss doesn't think the stock is worth the price. You think that it's a bargain and that you should recommend it to the firm's clients. Who is right?

Our first step in answering this question is to lay out on a time line the expected dividend payments:

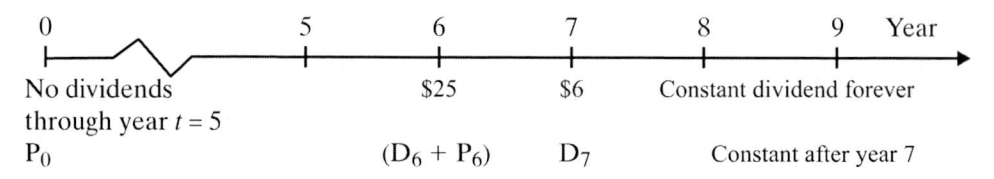

```
0                    5      6         7           8           9      Year
|--------/\---------|------|---------|-----------|-----------|
No dividends              $25        $6          Constant dividend forever
through year t = 5
P_0                       (D_6 + P_6) D_7         Constant after year 7
```

This situation is a direct application of Equation 9.6, which is the mixed dividend model. That is, there are two different dividend cash streams: (1) the mixed dividends, which in this case comprise a single dividend paid in year 6 (Equation 9.1) and (2) the constant dividend stream ($g = 0$) of $6 per year forever (Equation 9.5). The value of the common stock can be computed as follows:

P_0 = PV (Mixed dividend growth) + PV (Constant dividends with no growth)

Applying Equation 9.6 to the cash flows presented in the problem yields:

$$\begin{aligned} P_0 &= \frac{D_1}{1+R} + \frac{D_2}{(1+R)^2} + \cdots + \frac{D_t}{(1+R)^t} + \frac{P_t}{(1+R)^t} \\ &= \frac{D_6}{(1+R)^6} + \frac{P_6}{(1+R)^6} \\ &= \frac{D_6 + P_6}{(1+R)^6} \end{aligned}$$

Note that the first term in the second line computes the present value of the large $25 dividend paid in year 6. In the second term, P_6 is the discounted value of the constant $6 dividend payments made in perpetuity, valued to period $t = 6$. To compute the present value of P_6, we divide it by the appropriate discount factor, which is $(1+R)^6$.

Next, we plug the data given earlier into the above equation:

$$P_0 = \frac{\$25 + P_6}{(1.12)^6}$$

We can see that we still need to compute the value of P_6 using Equation 9.5:

$$P_t = \frac{D_{t+1}}{R - g}$$

Equation 9.5 is easy to apply since the dividend payments remain constant over time. Thus, $D_{t+1} = \$6$ and $g = 0$. P_6 is calculated as follows:

$$P_6 = \frac{D_7}{R - g} = \frac{\$6}{0.12 - 0} = \frac{\$6}{0.12}$$
$$= \$50$$

The calculation for P_0 is, therefore:

$$P_0 = \frac{\$25 + \$50}{(1.12)^6}$$
$$= \frac{\$75}{1.9738}$$
$$= \$38.00$$

The stock's current market price is $25, and if your estimates of dividend payments are correct, the stock's value is $38 per share. This suggests that the stock is a bargain and that your boss is incorrect.

> **Before You Go On**
>
> 1. What three different models are used to value stocks based on different dividend patterns?
> 2. Explain why the growth rate *g* must always be less than the rate of return *R*.

9.4 Valuing Preferred Stock

LEARNING OBJECTIVE 6

As mentioned earlier in the chapter, preferred stocks are hybrid securities, falling someplace between bonds and common stock. For example, preferred stock has a higher-priority claim on the firm's assets than common stock but a lower-priority claim than the firm's creditors in the event of default. In computing the value of preferred stock, however, the critical issue is whether the preferred stock has an effective "maturity." If the preferred stock contract has a sinking fund that calls for the mandatory retirement of the stock over a scheduled period of time, financial analysts will tend to treat the stock as if it were a bond with a fixed maturity.

The most significant difference between preferred stock with a fixed maturity and a bond is the risk of default. Bond coupon payments are a legal obligation of the firm, and failure to pay them results in default, whereas preferred stock dividends are declared by the board of directors, and failure to pay dividends does not result in default. Even though it is not a legal default, the failure to pay a preferred stock dividend as promised is not a trivial event. It is a serious financial breach that can signal to

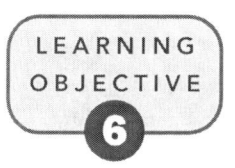

Riskglossary.com offers a good discussion of preferred stock, including its valuation. Go to www.riskglossary.com/link/preferred_stock.htm.

the market that the firm is in serious financial difficulty. As a result, managers make every effort to pay preferred stock dividends as promised.

Preferred Stock with a Fixed Maturity

Because preferred stock with an effective maturity is considered similar to a bond, we can use the bond valuation model developed in Chapter 8 to determine its price, or value. Applying Equation 8.2 requires only that we recognize that the coupon payments (C) are now dividend payments (D) and the preferred stock dividends are paid quarterly. Thus, Equation 8.2 can be restated as the price of a share of preferred stock (PS_0):

$$\text{Preferred stock price} = \text{PV (Dividend payments)} + \text{PV (Par value)} \quad (9.7)$$

$$PS_0 = \frac{D/m}{1 + i/m} + \frac{D/m}{(1 + i/m)^2} + \frac{D/m}{(1 + i/m)^3} + \cdots + \frac{D/m + P_{mn}}{(1 + i/m)^{mn}}$$

where:

- D = the annual preferred stock dividend payment
- P = the stated (par) value of the preferred stock
- i = the yield to maturity of the preferred stock
- m = the number of times dividend payments are made each year
- n = the number of years to maturity

For preferred stock with quarterly dividend payments, m equals 4.

Consider an example of how this equation is used. Suppose that a utility company's preferred stock has an annual dividend payment of $10 (paid quarterly), a stated (par) value of $100, and an effective maturity of 20 years owing to a sinking fund requirement. If similar preferred stock issues have market yields of 8 percent, what is the value of the preferred stock?

First, we convert the data to quarterly compounding as follows: (1) the market yield is 2 percent quarterly (8 percent per year/4), (2) the dividend payment is $2.50 quarterly ($10 per year/4), and (3) the total number of dividend payments is 80 (4 per year × 20 years). Plugging the data into Equation 8.1, we find that the value of the preferred stock is:

$$PS_0 = \frac{\$2.50}{1.02} + \frac{\$2.50}{(1.02)^2} + \cdots + \frac{\$102.50}{(1.02)^{80}}$$
$$= \$119.87$$

We can, of course, also solve this problem on a financial calculator. The keystrokes are as follows:

Enter	80	2		2.50	100
	N	i	PV	PMT	FV
Answer			−119.87		

LEARNING BY DOING APPLICATION 9.5

Computing the Yield on Preferred Stock

Problem: San Diego Gas and Electric (SDG&E) has a preferred stock issue outstanding that has a stated value of $100 that will be retired by the company in 15 years and that pays a $2 dividend each quarter. If the preferred stock is currently selling for $95, what is the stock's yield to maturity?

Approach: We compute the yield to maturity on this preferred stock in exactly the same way we compute the yield to maturity on a bond. We already know that the quarterly dividend rate is $2, but we must convert the number of periods to allow for quarterly compounding. The total number of compounding periods is 60 (4 per year × 15 years). Using Equation 8.2, we can enter the data and find i, the stock's yield to maturity through trial and error. Alternatively, we can solve the problem easily on a financial calculator.

Solution: Applying Equation 8.2:

$$PS_0 = \frac{\$2}{1+i} + \frac{\$2}{(1+i)^2} + \cdots + \frac{\$102}{(1+i)^{60}}$$

Financial calculator steps:

Enter	60		−95	2	100
	N	i	PV	PMT	FV
Answer		2.15			

The preferred stock's yield is 2.15 percent per quarter, and the annual yield is 8.60 percent (2.15 percent × 4).

Perpetuity Preferred Stock

Some preferred stock issues have no maturity. These securities have dividends that are constant over time ($g = 0$), and the fixed dividend payments go on forever. Thus, these preferred stocks can be valued as perpetuities, using Equation 9.2:

$$P_0 = \frac{D}{R}$$

where D is a constant cash dividend and R is the interest rate, or required rate of return.

Let's work an example. Suppose that Northwest Airlines has a perpetual preferred stock issue that pays a dividend of $5 per year. Investors require an 18 percent return on such an investment. What should be the value of the preferred stock? Applying Equation 9.2, we find that the value is:

$$P_0 = \frac{D}{R} = \frac{\$5.00}{0.18} = \$27.78$$

Before You Go On

1. Why can skipping payment of a preferred dividend be a bad signal?
2. How is a preferred stock with a fixed maturity valued?

Summary of Learning Objectives

1. **List and describe the four types of secondary markets.**

   The four types of secondary markets are: (1) direct search, (2) broker, (3) dealer, and (4) auction. In direct search markets, buyers and sellers seek each other out directly. In broker markets, brokers bring buyers and sellers together for a fee. Trades in dealer markets go through dealers who buy securities at one price and sell at a higher price. The dealers face the risk that prices could decline while they own the securities. Auction markets have a fixed location where buyers and sellers confront each other directly and bargain over the transaction price.

2. **Explain why many financial analysts treat preferred stock as a special type of bond rather than as an equity security.**

   Preferred stock represents ownership in a corporation and entitles the owner to a dividend, which must be paid before dividends are paid to common stockholders. Similar to bonds, preferred stock issues have credit ratings, are sometimes convertible to common stock, and are often callable. Unlike owners of common stock, owners of nonconvertible preferred stock do not have voting rights and do not participate in the firm's profits beyond the fixed dividends they receive. Because of their strong similarity to bonds, many financial analysts treat preferred stock that are not true perpetuities as a form of debt rather than equity.

3. **Describe how the general dividend-valuation model values a share of stock.**

   The general dividend-valuation model values a share of stock as the present value of all future cash dividend payments, where the dividend payments are discounted using the rate of return required by investors for a particular risk class.

4. **Discuss the assumptions that are necessary to make the general dividend-valuation model easier to use, and be able to use the model to compute the value of a firm's stock.**

   The problems with the general dividend-valuation model are that the exact discount rate that should be used is unknown, dividends are often uncertain, and some companies do not pay dividends at all. To make the model easier to apply, we make assumptions about the dividend payment patterns of business firms. These simplifying assumptions allow the development of more manageable models, and they also conform with the actual dividend policies of many firms. Dividend patterns include the following: (1) dividends are constant (zero growth), as computed in Learning by Doing Application 9.1; (2) dividends have a constant-growth pattern (they grow forever at a constant rate g), as computed in Learning by Doing Application 9.2; and (3) dividends grow first at a nonconstant rate than at a constant rate, as computed in the Redteck example at the end of Section 9.3.

5. **Explain why g must be less than R in the constant-growth dividend model.**

   The constant-growth dividend model assumes that dividends will grow at a constant rate forever. With the constant-growth model, if $g = R$, the value of the denominator is zero and the value of the stock is infinite, which of course, is nonsense. If $g > R$, the value of the denominator is negative, as is the value of the stock, which also does not make economic sense. Thus, g must always be less than R ($g < R$).

6. **Explain how valuing preferred stock with a stated maturity differs from valuing preferred stock with no maturity date, and be able to calculate the price of a share of preferred stock under both conditions.**

   When preferred stock has a maturity date, financial analysts value it as they value any other fixed obligation—that is, like a bond. To value such preferred stock, we can use the bond valuation model from Chapter 8. Before using the model, we need to recognize that we will be using dividends in the place of coupon payments and that the par value of the stock will replace the par value of the bond. In addition, while bond coupons are paid semiannually, preferred dividends are paid quarterly. When a preferred stock has no stated maturity, it becomes a perpetuity, with the dividend becoming the constant payment that goes on forever. We use the perpetuity valuation model represented by Equation 9.2 to price such stocks. The calculations appear in Learning by Doing Application 9.5 and the Northwest Airlines example at the end of Section 9.4.

Summary of Key Equations

Equation	Description	Formula
9.1	The general dividend-valuation model	$P_0 = \dfrac{D_1}{1+R} + \dfrac{D_2}{(1+R)^2} + \dfrac{D_3}{(1+R)^3} + \dfrac{D_4}{(1+R)^4} + \dfrac{D_5}{(1+R)^5} + \cdots + \dfrac{D_\infty}{(1+R)^\infty}$ $= \sum_{t=1}^{\infty} \dfrac{D_t}{(1+R)^t}$
9.2	Zero-growth dividend model	$P_0 = \dfrac{D}{R}$
9.3	Value of a dividend at time t in a constant-growth scenario	$D_t = D_0 \times (1+g)^t$
9.4	Constant-growth dividend model	$P_0 = \dfrac{D_1}{R - g}$
9.5	Value of a stock at time t when dividends grow at a constant rate	$P_t = \dfrac{D_{t+1}}{R - g}$
9.6	Supernormal growth stock-valuation model	$P_0 = \dfrac{D_1}{1+R} + \dfrac{D_2}{(1+R)^2} + \cdots + \dfrac{D_t}{(1+R)^t} + \dfrac{P_t}{(1+R)^t}$
9.7	Value of preferred stock with a fixed maturity	$PS_0 = \dfrac{D/m}{1 + i/m} + \dfrac{D/m}{(1 + i/m)^2} + \dfrac{D/m}{(1 + i/m)^3} + \cdots + \dfrac{D/m + P_{mn}}{(1 + i/m)^{mn}}$

Self-Study Problems

9.1 Ted McKay has just bought the common stock of Ryland Corp. The company expects to grow at the following rates for the next three years: 30 percent, 25 percent, and 15 percent. Last year the company paid a dividend of $2.50. Assume a required rate of return of 10 percent. Compute the expected dividends for the next three years and also the present value of these dividends.

9.2 Merriweather Manufacturing Company has been growing at a rate of 6 percent for the past two years, and the company's CEO expects the company to continue to grow at this rate for the next several years. The company paid a dividend of $1.20 last year. If your required rate of return was 14 percent, what is the maximum price that you would be willing to pay for this company's stock?

9.3 Clarion Corp. has been selling electrical supplies for the past 20 years. The company's product line has seen very little change in the past five years, and the company does not expect to add any new items for the foreseeable future. Last year, the company paid a dividend of $4.45 to its common stockholders. The company is not expected to grow its revenues for the next several years. If your required rate of return for such firms is 13 percent, what is the current value of this company's stock?

9.4 Barrymore Infotech is a fast-growing communications company. The company did not pay a dividend last year and is not expected to do so for the next two years. Last year the company's growth accelerated, and they expect to grow at a rate of 35 percent for the next five years before slowing down to a more stable growth rate of 7 percent for the next several years. In the third year, the company has forecasted a dividend payment of $1.10. Calculate the price of the company's stock at the end of its rapid growth period (i.e., at the end of five years). Your required rate of return for such stocks is 17 percent. What is the current price of this stock?

9.5 You are interested in buying the preferred stock of a bank that pays a dividend of $1.80 every quarter. If you discount such cash flows at 8 percent, what is the price of this stock?

Solutions to Self-Study Problems

9.1 Expected dividends for Ryland Corp and their present value:

```
0        10%      1           2           3  Year
|─────────────────|───────────|───────────|
D₀ = $2.50       D₁          D₂          D₃
```

$g_1 = 30\%$ $\quad\quad\quad g_2 = 25\%$ $\quad\quad\quad g_3 = 15\%$

$D_1 = D_0 \times (1 + g_1) = \$2.50 \times (1 + 0.30) = \$3.25$
$D_2 = D_1 \times (1 + g_2) = \$3.25 \times (1 + 0.25) = \$4.06$
$D_3 = D_2 \times (1 + g_3) = \$4.06 \times (1 + 0.15) = \$4.67$
Present value of the dividends = $PV(D_1) + PV(D_2) + PV(D_3)$
$\quad\quad\quad\quad\quad\quad\quad\quad\quad\quad\quad\;\; = \$2.96 + \$3.36 + \$3.51$
$\quad\quad\quad\quad\quad\quad\quad\quad\quad\quad\quad\;\; = \$9.83$

9.2 Present value of Merriweather stock:

```
0        14%      1           2           3  Year
|─────────────────|───────────|───────────|
D₀ = $1.20       D₁          D₂          D₃
```

$g = 6\%$

$D_1 = D_0(1 + g)$
$\quad\; = \$1.20 \times (1 + 0.06)$
$\quad\; = \$1.27$

$$P_0 = \frac{D_1}{R - g}$$
$$= \frac{\$1.27}{0.14 - 0.06}$$
$$= \$15.88$$

The maximum price you should be willing to pay for this stock is $15.88.

9.3 Present value of Clarion Corp. stock:

```
0      13%    1           2           3   Year
|─────────────|───────────|───────────|────►
D₀ = $4.45    D₁          D₂          D₃
```

$g = 0\%$

Since the company's dividends are not expected to grow,

$D_0 = D_1 = D_2 = \ldots D_\infty = \$4.45 = D$

$$\text{Present value of the stock} = \frac{D}{R}$$
$$= \$4.45/0.13$$
$$= \$34.23$$

9.4 Present value of Barrymore Infotech stock:

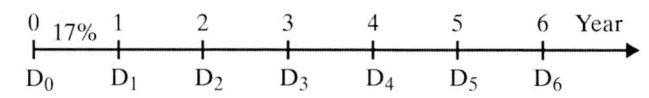

```
0   17%  1      2      3      4      5      6   Year
|────────|──────|──────|──────|──────|──────|────►
D₀       D₁     D₂     D₃     D₄     D₅     D₆
```

g_1 to $g_5 = 35\%$ $g_6 = 7\%$

$D_0 = D_1 = D_2 = 0$
$D_3 = \$1.100$
$D_4 = D_3 \times (1 + g_4) = \$1.10 \times (1 + 0.35) = \$1.485$
$D_5 = D_4 \times (1 + g_5) = \$1.485 \times (1 + 0.35) = \$2.005$
$D_6 = D_5 \times (1 + g_6) = \$2.005 \times (1 + 0.07) = \$2.145$

Price of stock at $t = 5$:

$$P_5 = \frac{D_6}{R - g}$$
$$= \frac{\$2.145}{0.17 - 0.07}$$
$$= \$21.45$$

Present value of the dividends = $PV(D_1) + PV(D_2) + PV(D_3) + PV(D_4) + PV(D_5)$
$$= \$0 + \$0 + \$0.69 + \$0.79 + \$0.91$$
$$= \$2.39$$

Present value of stock:

$$P_0 = PV(\text{Dividends}) + PV(P_5)$$
$$= \$2.39 + \frac{\$21.45}{(1.17)^5}$$
$$= \$2.39 + \$9.78$$
$$= \$12.17$$

9.5 Present value of preferred bank stock:

Quarterly dividend on preferred stock = $D = \$1.80$
Required rate of return = 8%
Current price of stock:

$$P_0 = \frac{D}{R}$$
$$= \frac{\$1.80 \times 4}{0.08}$$
$$= \$90.00$$

Critical Thinking Questions

9.1 Why can the market price of a security differ from its true value?

9.2 Why are investors and managers concerned about market efficiency?

9.3 Why are common stockholders considered to be more at risk than the holders of other types of securities?

9.4 How can individual stockholders avoid double taxation?

9.5 What does it mean when a company has a very high P/E ratio? Give examples of industries in which you believe high P/E ratios are justified.

9.6 Preferred stock is considered to be nonparticipating because:
   a. investors do not participate in the election of the firm's directors.
   b. investors do not participate in the determination of the dividend payout policy.
   c. investors do not participate in the firm's earnings growth.
   d. none of the above.

9.7 Explain why preferred stock is considered to be a hybrid of equity and debt securities.

9.8 Why is stock valuation more difficult than bond valuation?

9.9 You are currently thinking about investing in a stock valued at $25.00 per share. The stock recently paid a dividend of $2.25 and is expected to grow at a rate of 5 percent for the foreseeable future. You normally require a return of 14 percent on stocks of similar risk. Is the stock overpriced, underpriced, or correctly priced?

9.10 Stock A and Stock B are both priced at $50 per share. Stock A has a P/E ratio of 17, while Stock B has a P/E ratio of 24. Which is the more attractive investment, considering everything else to be the same, and why?

Questions and Problems

9.1 Present value of dividends: Fresno Corp. is a fast-growing company. The company expects to grow at a rate of 30 percent over the next two years and then slow down to a growth rate of 18 percent for the following three years. If the last dividend paid by the company was $2.15, estimate the dividends for the next five years. Compute the present value of these dividends if the required rate of return was 14 percent.

BASIC

9.2 Zero growth: Nynet, Inc., paid a dividend of $4.18 last year. The company does not expect to increase its dividend for the next several years. If the required rate of return is 18.5 percent, what is the current price of the stock?

9.3 Zero growth: Knight Supply Corp. has seen no growth for the past several years and expects the trend to continue. The firm last paid a dividend of $3.56. If you require a rate of return of 13 percent, what is the current stock price?

9.4 Zero growth: Ron Santana is interested in buying the stock of First National Bank. While the bank expects no growth in the near future, Ron is attracted by the dividend income. Last year the bank paid a dividend of $5.65. If Ron requires a return of 14 percent on such stocks, what is the maximum price he should be willing to pay?

9.5 Zero growth: The current stock price of Largent, Inc., is $44.72. If the required rate of return is 19 percent, what is the dividend paid by this firm, which is not expected to grow in the near future?

9.6 Constant growth: Moriband Corp. just declared a dividend of $2.15 yesterday. The company is expected to grow at a steady rate of 5 percent for the next several years. If stocks such as these require a rate of return of 15 percent, what should be the market value of this stock?

9.7 Constant growth: Nyeil, Inc., is a consumer products firm growing at a constant rate of 6.5 percent. The firm's last dividend was $3.36. If the required rate of return was 18 percent, what is the market value of this stock?

9.8 Constant growth: Reco Corp. is expected to pay a dividend of $2.25 next year. The forecast for the stock price a year from now is $37.50. If the required rate of return is 14 percent, what is the current stock price? Assume constant growth.

9.9 Constant growth: Proxicam, Inc., is expected to grow at a constant rate of 7 percent. If the company's next dividend is $1.15 and its current price is $22.35, what is the required rate of return on this stock?

9.10 Preferred stock valuation: X-Centric Energy Company has issued perpetual preferred stock with a par of $100 and a dividend of 4.5 percent. If the required rate of return is 8.25 percent, what is the stock's current market price?

9.11 Preferred stock valuation: The First Bank of Ellicott City has issued perpetual preferred stock with a $100 par value. The bank pays a quarterly dividend of $1.65 on this stock. What is the current price of this preferred stock given a required rate of return of 11.6 percent?

9.12 Preferred stock: The preferred stock of Axim Corp. is selling currently at $47.13. If the required rate of return is 12.2 percent, what is the dividend paid by this stock?

9.13 Preferred stock: Each quarter, Sirkota, Inc., pays a dividend on its perpetual preferred stock. Today the stock is selling at $63.37. If the required rate of return for such stocks is 15.5 percent, what is the quarterly dividend paid by this firm?

INTERMEDIATE

9.14 Constant growth: Kay Williams is interested in purchasing the common stock of Reckers, Inc., which is currently priced at $37.45. The company expects to pay a dividend of $2.58 next year and expects to grow at a constant rate of 7 percent.
a. What should the market value of the stock be if the required rate of return is 14 percent?
b. Is this a good buy? Why or why not?

9.15 Constant growth: The required rate of return is 23 percent. Ninex Corp. has just paid a dividend of $3.12 and expects to grow at a constant rate of 5 percent. What is the expected price of the stock three years from now?

9.16 Constant growth: Jenny Banks is interested in buying the stock of Fervan, Inc., which is growing at a constant rate of 6 percent. Last year the firm paid a dividend of $2.65. The required rate of return is 16 percent. What is the current price for this stock? What would be the price of the stock in year 5?

9.17 Nonconstant growth: Tre-Bien, Inc., is a fast-growing technology company. The firm projects a rapid growth of 30 percent for the next two years, then a growth rate of 17 percent for the following two years. After that, the firm expects a constant-growth rate of 8 percent. The firm expects to pay its first dividend of $2.45 a year from now. If the required rate of return on such stocks is 22 percent, what is the current price of the stock?

9.18 Nonconstant growth: ProCor, a biotech firm, forecasted the following growth rates for the next three years: 35 percent, 28 percent, and 22 percent. The company then expects to grow at a constant rate of 9 percent for the next several years. The company paid a dividend of $1.75 last week. If the required rate of return is 20 percent, what is the market value of this stock?

9.19 Nonconstant growth: Revarop, Inc., is a fast-growth stock and expects to grow at a rate of 23 percent for the next four years. It then will settle to a constant-growth rate of 6 percent. The first dividend will be paid in year 3 and be equal to $4.25. If the required rate of return is 17 percent, what is the current price of the stock?

9.20 Nonconstant growth: Quansi, Inc., expects to pay no dividends for the next six years. It has projected a growth rate of 25 percent for the next seven years. After seven years, the firm will grow at a constant rate of 5 percent. Its first dividend to be paid in year 7 will be worth $3.25. If your required rate of return is 24 percent, what is the stock worth today?

9.21 Nonconstant growth: Staggert Corp. will pay dividends of $5.00, $6.25, $4.75, and $3.00 for the next four years. Thereafter, the company expects its growth rate to be at a constant rate of 6 percent. If the required rate of return is 18.5 percent, what is the current market price of the stock?

9.22 Nonconstant growth: Diaz Corp. is growing rapidly at a rate of 35 percent for the next seven years. The first dividend, to be paid three years from now, will be worth $5. After seven years, the company will settle to a constant-growth rate of 8.5 percent. What is the market value for this stock given a required rate of return of 14 percent?

9.23 Nonconstant growth: Tin-Tin Waste Management, Inc., is growing rapidly. Dividends are expected to grow at rates of 30 percent, 35 percent, 25 percent, and 18 percent over the next four years. Thereafter the company expects to grow at a constant rate of 7 percent. The stock is currently selling at $47.85, and the required rate of return is 16 percent. Compute the dividend for the current year (D_0).

9.24 Riker Departmental Stores has forecasted a high growth rate of 40 percent for the next two years, followed by growth rates of 25 percent and 20 percent for the following two years. It then expects to stabilize its growth to a constant rate of 7.5 percent for the next several years. The firm paid a dividend of $3.50 recently. If the required rate of return is 18 percent, what is the current market price of the stock?   **ADVANCED**

9.25 Courtesy Bancorp issued perpetual preferred stock a few years ago. The bank pays an annual dividend of $4.27, and your required rate of return is 12.2 percent.
  a. What is the value of the stock given your required rate of return?
  b. Should you buy this stock if its current market price is $34.41? Explain.

9.26 Rhea Kirby owns shares in Ryoko Corp. Currently, the market price of the stock is $36.34. The company expects to grow at a constant rate of 6 percent for the foreseeable future. Its last dividend was worth $3.25. Rhea's required rate of return for such stocks is 16 percent. She wants to find out whether she should sell her shares or add to her holdings.
  a. What is the value of this stock?
  b. Based on your answer to part a, should Rhea buy additional shares in Ryoko Corp? Why or why not?

9.27 Perry, Inc., declared a dividend of $2.50 yesterday. You are interested in investing in this company, which has forecasted a constant-growth rate of 7 percent for the next several years. The required rate of return is 18 percent.
  a. Compute the expected dividends D_1, D_2, D_3, and D_4.
  b. Find the present value of these four dividends.
  c. What is the price of the stock four years from now (P_4)?
  d. Calculate the present value of P_4. Add the answer you got in part b. What is the price of the stock today?
  e. Use the equation for constant growth (Equation 9.4) to compute the price of the stock today.

9.28 Zweite Pharma is a fast-growing drug company. The company forecasts that in the next three years, its growth rates will be 30 percent, 28 percent, and 24 percent, respectively. Last week it declared a dividend of $1.67. After three years, the company expects a more stable growth rate of 8 percent for the next several years. The required rate of return is 14 percent.   **EXCEL**
  a. Compute the dividends for the next three years, and find its present value.
  b. Calculate the price of the stock at the end of year 3, when the firm settles to a constant-growth rate.
  c. What is the current price of the stock?

9.29 Triton Inc. expects to grow at a rate of 22 percent for the next five years and then settle to a constant-growth rate of 6 percent. The company's most recent dividend was $2.35. The required rate of return is 15 percent.   **EXCEL**
  a. Find the present value of the dividends during the rapid-growth period.
  b. What is the price of the stock at the end of year 5?
  c. What is the price of the stock today?

9.30 Ceebros Builders is expanding very fast and expects to grow at a rate of 25 percent for the next four years. The company recently declared a dividend of $3.60 but does not expect to pay any dividends for the next three years. In year 4, it intends to pay a $5 dividend and thereafter grow it at a constant-growth rate of 6 percent. The required rate of return on such stocks is 20 percent.   **EXCEL**
  a. Calculate the present value of the dividends during the fast-growth period.
  b. What is the price of the stock at the end of the fast-growth period (P_4)?
  c. What is the stock price today?
  d. Would today's stock price be driven by the length of time you intend to hold the stock?

Sample Test Problems

9.1 Mason Corp. is a manufacturer of consumer staples and has experienced no growth for the past five years while paying out a dividend of $3.50 every year. The CFO of the firm expects the firm to have no growth for the foreseeable future. If the required rate of return is 10 percent, what is the price of this stock today?

9.2 Bucknell, Inc., recently paid a dividend of $2.10. The firm forecasts a growth of 6 percent for the next several years. What is the price of the stock today with a discount rate of 13 percent?

9.3 Bradley Corp. is growing at a constant rate of 7.2 percent every year. Last week the company paid a dividend of $1.85. If the required rate of return is 15 percent, what will be the stock's price four years from now?

9.4 Wichita Technologies is expected to grow at a rate of 35 percent for the next three years and then settle to a constant-growth rate of 7 percent. The company will pay no dividend for the first two years and pay a dividend of $1.25 in year 3. What will be the company's price when the company's supernormal growth ends? What is the price of the stock today? The firm's required rate of return is 12 percent.

9.5 UNC Bancorp has issued preferred stock with no maturity date. It has a par value of $100 and pays a quarterly dividend of $2.25. If the required rate of return is 8 percent, what is the price of the stock today?

Insider Trading: Have I Got a Stock Tip for You!

ETHICS CASE

Everyone would like to get a stock tip that will yield a huge return on a small investment. That's human nature. But stock tips can be mixed blessings. Consider the following example: Dr. Sam Waksal developed a promising cancer drug called Erbitux. As the CEO of ImClone, Waksal was an entrepreneur as well as an immunologist. Waksal sold an interest in Erbitux to the pharmaceutical company Bristol Myers for $42 billion.

It was a Bristol Myers executive who informed Waksal that the Federal Drug Administration (FDA) was not going to approve the drug because there were insufficient data to determine its effectiveness; thus, new clinical trials were needed. Investors had expected approval, and once the FDA decision was made public, ImClone stock was certain to face a sharp decline in price. At least in the short term, some people were going to lose a lot of money.

One of those people was, of course, Waksal himself. He had millions of shares of ImClone. So did his family. Waksal told his daughter and father to sell their shares. In addition, Waksal transferred 79,000 of his own shares to his daughter to sell. Waksal knew that it was illegal under federal law for him or his family members to trade on inside information. And in the end, all three were indicted and later convicted of violating federal security laws.

Waksal was guilty of insider trading. As we pointed out in Chapter 1, insider trading results from information asymmetry, which arises when one party in a business transaction has information that is unavailable to the other parties in the transaction. To be legally actionable, insider trading must involve information that has not been publicly announced, as you might expect. In addition, the information must be material. *Material* means that the information will cause a significant change in the stock price—the price will go either up or down as a result of the event the information concerns. Examples of material corporate events include the introduction of a new product line, an acquisition, a divestiture, a key executive appointment, and the failure or success of a product under development.

Martha Stewart Enters the Picture

Waksal's conviction is not the only part of this story. Waksal was friends with the celebrity Martha Stewart, who also owned ImClone stock. On the day before the negative FDA announcement, Stewart sold 4,000 shares of ImClone worth $230,000. Did Stewart sell her shares on the basis of inside information regarding the FDA decision? Stewart's sale certainly looked suspicious, and the Securities and Exchange Commission (SEC) started an investigation and asked her to explain her sale. In her discussions with the SEC, Stewart did not admit to insider trading.

Stewart claimed that she had a prearranged order in place to sell her ImClone stock when it dipped below $60 per share. The stock did dip below $60 the day before the FDA announcement. Federal prosecutors, however, alleged that she and her broker, Peter Bacanovic, had doctored stock transaction records to support her story. In the SEC indictment, it was clear that they did not believe her explanation.

It is also interesting to note that Stewart is not alleged to have received a tip from Waksal himself. Indeed, she contacted Waksal only after the sale, when she called him to ask what was happening to the company. However, it is alleged that her broker, Bacanovic, received a tip that Waksal and his daughter had placed orders to sell shares of ImClone.

Martha Stewart was eventually convicted in a criminal trial, but convicted of what? The most serious charges, which involved securities fraud and insider trading, were thrown out of court. She was convicted only of lying to investigators. However, Stewart was also charged in a civil suit, and in that suit, the insider trading charge would have been allowed in court. After serving a jail term, Stewart eventually reached an agreement with the SEC to settle the insider trading accusations. Under the agreement, she must pay $195,000, covering her gains from the trading and penalties, although she does not admit to any wrongdoing.

Conclusions

What can we conclude about insider trading? The ethical issues can be analyzed at two levels: At the institutional level, we can ask whether the insider trading laws are ethical. At the individual level, we can ask why a person would engage in this illegal behavior.

Institutional Level. Fairness is the ethical basis of the insider trading laws. If the competitive system is to work, it must operate on an even playing field. If insiders have material financial information not available to the public, then the playing field is not level. Note what the SEC said in its press release: "It is fundamentally unfair for someone to have an edge on the market just because she has a stockbroker who is willing to break the rules and give her an illegal tip. It's worse still when the individual engaging in the insider trading is the Chairman and CEO of a public company." However, not everyone is convinced by this argument. Using a utilitarian framework, others argue that persons acting on insider information bring information to the market quicker and thus make the market more efficient for the benefit of all.

Both sides have a point. One of the keystone propositions of efficient financial markets is that no participant should possess a significant *unfair* advantage over others. If you believe that the deck of cards is stacked against you and that some people who trade have access to inside information, you will collect your money and invest it elsewhere. Conversely, without inside information, there would be little reason for trading securities. Unless you know some information that affects securities' prices that others do not know, why trade? Furthermore, how would information relevant to security prices be released to the market unless some traded on that information?

The bottom line is that too much or too little inside information trading seems to be detrimental to financial markets. The critical question is how much inside information is optimal. There is no consensus among economists on an answer.

Individual Level. At the individual level, we must evaluate the motivation of the inside traders. Waksal, for example, knew that insider trading was illegal. Why did he do it? In an interview on CBS's *60 Minutes*, Waksal admitted that he did not think that he would get caught. Investigation showed that Waksal had been guilty of a number of ethical lapses in his life. He had been dismissed from a number of academic and research positions for questionable conduct. Aristotle would say he had a weak character. If Stewart had not tried to obscure what she did and simply told the truth to investigators, most legal experts are convinced she would not have been convicted of anything.

Questions

1. Discuss whether it would be unethical to buy a stock based on some information you found in the trash that had been thrown away by mistake.

2. Suppose you are the printer who has been given the job of preparing the official announcement of the FDA report. Can you use that information for personal gain? Why or why not?

3. Some argue that insider trading brings information to the market more quickly and thus is morally acceptable on the grounds of efficiency. Do you agree with that argument? Why or why not?

Sources: Press release from Securities and Exchange Commission, June 4, 2003; *CBS News*, www.cbsnews.com/2005/19/02/60minutes/main576328.shtml; CNNMoney.com, money.cnn.com/2004/03/05/news/companies/martha_verdict; Landon Thomas, Jr., "The Return of Martha Stewart, the Civil Case." *New York Times*, May 25, 2006, Section C, p.1; and Landon Thomas, Jr., "Stewart Deal Resolves Stock Case," *New York Times*, August 8, 2006, www.nytimes.com/2006/08/08/business/.

CHAPTER 10

THE FUNDAMENTALS OF CAPITAL BUDGETING

LEARNING OBJECTIVES

1. Discuss why capital budgeting decisions are the most important investment decisions made by a firm's management.

2. Explain the benefits of using the net present value (NPV) method to analyze capital expenditure decisions, and be able to calculate the NPV for a capital project.

3. Describe the strengths and weaknesses of the payback period as a capital expenditure decision-making tool, and be able to compute the payback period for a capital project.

4. Explain why the accounting rate of return (ARR) is not recommended for use as a capital expenditure decision-making tool.

5. Be able to compute the internal rate of return (IRR) for a capital project, and discuss the conditions under which the IRR technique and the NPV technique produce different results.

6. Explain the benefits of a postaudit review of a capital project.

Getty Images

In March 2007, Intel Corporation announced plans to build a $2.5 billion facility in Dalian, China, to make computer chip wafers. The company expects the plant to be completed in the first half of 2010. The plant will be Intel's largest investment in Asia, and when completed, is expected to employ about five thousand people. To put the $2.5 billion project in perspective, in 2006 Intel's total revenues were $35.4 billion, and its capital expenditures totaled $5.8 billion, or 16.4 percent of sales.

Intel's announcement illustrates not only the large amount of cash involved in a major capital project but also the strategic importance such an investment can have. When he announced the project, Intel's president and CEO, Paul Otellini, pointed out that China was Intel's fastest-growing major market. It was imperative, said Otellini, that Intel invest in markets that will provide for future growth.

The Dalian project involves considerable downside risk for Intel. For example, if the demand for chip wafers proves to be less than expected, the project could be a significant drain on earnings. In addition, international transactions are subject to country risk. If China experiences political or economic instability, the financial consequences for Intel could be severe.

It is clear that investment decisions of this magnitude must be carefully scrutinized, and their costs and benefits carefully weighed. How do firms make capital budgeting decisions that involve billions of dollars? In this chapter, we examine this decision-making process and introduce some of the financial models that aid in the process.

CHAPTER PREVIEW

This chapter is about capital budgeting, a topic we first visited in Chapter 1. Capital budgeting is the process of deciding which capital investments the firm should make.

We begin the chapter with a discussion of the types of capital projects that firms undertake and how the capital budgeting process is managed within the firm. When making capital investment decisions, management's goal is to select projects that will increase the value of the firm.

Next we examine some of the techniques used to evaluate capital budgeting decisions. We first discuss the net present value (NPV) method, which is the capital budgeting approach recommended in this book. The NPV method takes into account the time value of money and provides a direct measure of how much a capital project will increase the value of the firm.

We then examine the payback method and the accounting rate of return. As methods of selecting capital projects, both methods have some serious deficiencies. Finally, we discuss the internal rate of return (IRR), which is the expected rate of return for a capital project. Like the NPV, the IRR involves discounting a project's future cash flows. It is a popular and important alternative to the NPV technique. However, in certain circumstances, the IRR can lead to incorrect decisions. We close by discussing evidence on techniques financial managers actually use when making capital budgeting decisions.

10.1 An Introduction to Capital Budgeting

We begin with an overview of capital budgeting, followed by a discussion of some important concepts you will need to understand in this and later chapters.

The Importance of Capital Budgeting

Capital budgeting decisions are the most important investment decisions made by management. The objective of these decisions is to select investments in real assets that will increase the value of the firm. These investments *create value* when they are worth more than they cost. Capital investments are important because they can involve substantial cash outlays and, once made, are not easily reversed. They also define what the company is all about—the firm's lines of business and its inherent business risk. For better or worse, capital investments produce most of a typical firm's revenues for years to come.

Capital budgeting *techniques* help management systematically analyze potential business opportunities in order to decide which are worth undertaking. As you will see, not all capital budgeting techniques are equal. The best techniques are those that determine the value of a capital project by discounting all of the cash flows generated by the project and thus account for the time value of money. We focus on these techniques in this chapter.

In the final analysis, capital budgeting is really about management's search for the best capital projects—those that add the greatest value to the firm. Over the long term, the most successful firms are those whose managements consistently search for and find capital investment opportunities that increase firm value.

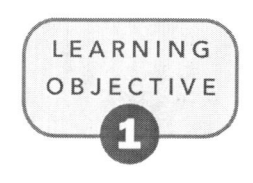

LEARNING OBJECTIVE 1

capital budgeting
the process of choosing the real assets in which the firm will invest

You can read about a real-world example of how capital budgeting techniques are used at www.acq.osd.mil/dpap/contractpricing/vol2chap9.htm.

The Capital Budgeting Process

The capital budgeting process starts with a firm's strategic plan, which spells out its strategy for the next three to five years. Division managers then convert the firm's strategic objectives into business plans. These plans have a one- to two-year time horizon, provide a detailed description of what each division should accomplish during the period covered by the plan, and have quantifiable targets that each division is expected to achieve. Behind each division's business plan is a capital budget that details the resources management believes it needs to get the job done.

The capital budget is generally prepared jointly by the CFO's staff and financial staffs at the divisional and lower levels and reflects, in large part, the activities outlined in the divisional business plans. Many of these proposed expenditures are routine in nature, such as the repair or purchase of new equipment at existing facilities. Less frequently, firms face broader strategic decisions, such as whether to launch a new product, build a new plant, enter a new market, or buy a business. Exhibit 10.1 identifies some reasons that firms initiate capital projects.

Exhibit 10.1 Key Reasons for Making Capital Expenditures

Reason	Description
Renewal:	Over time, equipment must be repaired, overhauled, rebuilt, or retrofitted with new technology to keep the firm's manufacturing or service operations going. For example, a company that has a fleet of delivery trucks may decide to overhaul the trucks and their engines rather than purchase new trucks. Renewal decisions typically do not require an elaborate analysis and are made on a routine basis.
Replacement:	At some point, an asset will have to be replaced rather than repaired or overhauled. This typically happens when the asset is worn out or damaged. The major decision is whether to replace the asset with a similar piece of equipment or purchase equipment that would require a change in the production process. Sometimes, replacement decisions involve equipment that is operating satisfactorily but has become obsolete. The new or retrofitted equipment may provide cost savings with respect to labor or material usage and/or may improve product quality. These decisions typically originate at the plant level.
Expansion:	Strategically, the most important motive for capital expenditures is to expand the level of operating output. One type of expansion decision involves increasing the output of existing products. This may mean new equipment to produce more products or expansion of the firm's distribution system. These types of decisions typically require a more complex analysis than a renewal or replacement decision. Another type of expansion decision involves producing a new product or entering a new market. This type of expansion often involves large dollar amounts and significant business risk and requires the approval of the firm's board of directors.
Regulatory:	Some capital expenditures are required by federal and state regulations. These mandatory expenditures usually involve meeting workplace safety standards and environmental standards.
Other:	This category includes items such as parking facilities, office buildings, and executive aircraft. Many of these capital expenditures are hard to analyze because it is difficult to estimate their cash inflows. Ultimately, the decisions can be more subjective than analytical.

Capital budgeting decisions are the most important investment decisions made by management. Many of these decisions are routine in nature, but from time to time, managers face broader strategic decisions that call for significant capital investments.

Sources of Information

Where does a firm get all of the information it needs to make capital budgeting decisions? Most of the information is generated within the firm, and, for expansion decisions, it often starts with sales representatives and marketing managers who are in the marketplace talking to potential and current customers on a day-to-day basis. For example, a sales manager with a new product idea might present the idea to management and the marketing research group. If the product looks promising, the marketing research group will estimate the size of the market and a market price. If the product requires new technology, the firm's research and development group must decide whether to develop the technology or to buy it. Next, cost accountants and production engineers determine the cost of producing the product and any capital expenditures necessary to manufacture it. Finally, the CFO's staff takes the data and estimates the cost of the project and the cash flows it will generate over time. The project is a viable candidate for the capital budget if the present value of the cash benefits exceeds the project's cost.

Classification of Investment Projects

Potential capital budgeting projects can be classified into three types: (1) **independent projects**, (2) **mutually exclusive projects**, and (3) **contingent projects**.

INDEPENDENT PROJECTS

Projects are independent when their cash flows are unrelated. With independent projects, accepting or rejecting one project does not eliminate the other projects from consideration (assuming the firm has unlimited funds to invest). For example, suppose a firm has unlimited funding and management wants to: (1) build a new parking ramp at its headquarters; (2) acquire a small competitor; and (3) add manufacturing capacity to one of its plants. Since the cash flows for each project are unrelated, accepting or rejecting one of the projects will have no effect on the others.

MUTUALLY EXCLUSIVE PROJECTS

When projects are mutually exclusive, acceptance of one project precludes acceptance of the others. Typically, mutually exclusive projects perform the same function, and thus, only one project needs to be accepted. For example, when BMW decided to manufacture automobiles in the United States, it considered three possible manufacturing sites (or capital projects). Once BMW management had selected the Spartanburg, South Carolina, site, the other two possible locations were out of the running.

CONTINGENT PROJECTS

With contingent projects, the acceptance of one project is contingent on the acceptance of another. There are two types of contingency situations. In the first type of situation, the contingent product is *mandatory*. For example, when a public utility company (such as your local electric company) builds a power plant, it must also invest in suitable pollution control equipment to meet federal environmental standards. The pollution control investment is a mandatory contingent project. When faced with mandatory contingent projects, it is best to treat all of the projects as a single investment for the purpose of evaluation. This provides management with the best measure of the value created by these projects.

In the second type of situation, the contingent project is *optional*. For example, suppose Dell invests in a new computer for the home market. This computer has a feature that allows Dell to bundle a proprietary gaming system. The gaming system is a contingent project but is an optional add-on to the new computer. In these situations, the optional contingent project should be evaluated *independently* and should be accepted or rejected on its own merits.

> **independent projects**
> projects whose cash flows are unrelated
>
> **mutually exclusive projects**
> projects for which acceptance of one precludes acceptance of the other
>
> **contingent project**
> a project whose acceptance depends on the acceptance of another project

Basic Capital Budgeting Terms

In this section we briefly introduce two terms that you will need to be familiar with—*cost of capital* and *capital rationing*.

COST OF CAPITAL

> **cost of capital**
> the required rate of return for a capital investment

The **cost of capital** is the rate of return that a capital project must earn to be accepted by management. The cost of capital can be thought of as an opportunity cost. Recall from Chapter 8 that an *opportunity cost* is the value of the most valuable alternative given up if a particular investment is made.

Let's consider the opportunity cost concept in the context of capital budgeting decisions. When investors buy shares of stock in a company or loan money to a company, they are giving management money to invest on their behalf. Thus, when a firm's management makes capital investments, they are really investing stockholders' and creditors' money in *real assets*—plant and equipment. Since stockholders and creditors could have invested their money in *financial assets*, the minimum rate of return they are willing to accept on an investment in a real asset is the rate they could have earned investing in financial assets that have similar risk. The rate of return that investors can earn on financial assets with similar risk is an *opportunity cost* because investors lose the opportunity to earn that rate if the money is invested in a real asset instead. It is therefore the rate of return that investors will require for an investment in a capital project. In other words, this rate is the cost of capital. It is also known as the **opportunity cost of capital**. Chapter 13 discusses how we estimate the opportunity cost of capital in practice.

> **opportunity cost of capital**
> the return an investor gives up when his or her money is invested in one asset rather than the best alternative asset

BUILDING INTUITION

Investment Decisions Have Opportunity Costs

When any investment is made, the opportunity to earn a return from an alternative investment is lost. The lost return can be viewed as a cost that arises from a lost opportunity. For this reason, it is called an *opportunity cost*. The opportunity cost of capital is the return an investor gives up when his or her money is invested in one asset rather than the best alternative asset. For example, suppose that a firm invests in a piece of equipment rather than returning money to stockholders. If stockholders could have earned an annual return of 12 percent on a stock with cash flows that are as risky as the cash flows the equipment will produce, this is the opportunity cost of capital associated with the investment in the piece of equipment.

CAPITAL RATIONING

> **capital rationing**
> a situation where a firm does not have enough capital to invest in all attractive projects and must therefore ration capital

When a firm has all the money it needs to invest in all the capital projects that meet its capital selection criteria, the firm is said to be operating without a *funding constraint*, or *resource constraint*. Firms are rarely in this position, especially growth firms. Typically, a firm has a fixed number of dollars available for capital expenditures, and the number of qualified projects that need funding exceeds the funds that are available. Therefore, the firm must allocate its funds to the subset of projects that will provide the largest overall increase in stockholder value. The process of limiting, or rationing, capital expenditures in this way is called **capital rationing**. Capital rationing and its implications for capital budgeting are discussed in Chapter 12.

> **Before You Go On**
>
> 1. Why are capital investments the most important decisions made by a firm's management?
> 2. What are the differences between capital projects that are independent, mutually exclusive, and contingent?

10.2 Net Present Value

In this section we discuss a capital budgeting method that is consistent with this goal of financial management—to maximize the wealth of the firm's owners. It is called the **net present value (NPV) method**, and it is one of the most basic concepts underlying corporate finance. The NPV method tells us the amount by which the benefits from a capital expenditure exceed its costs. It is the capital budgeting technique recommended in this book.

Valuation of Real Assets

Throughout the book, we have emphasized that the value of any asset is the present value of its future cash flows. In Chapters 8 and 9, we developed valuation models for financial assets, such as bonds, preferred stock, and common stock. We now extend our discussion of valuation models from financial to real assets. The steps used in valuing an asset are the same whether the asset is real or financial:

1. Estimate the future cash flows.

2. Determine the required rate of return, or discount rate, which depends on the riskiness of the future cash flows.

3. Compute the present value of the future cash flows to determine what the asset is worth.

The valuation of real assets, however, is less straightforward than the valuation of financial assets, for several reasons.

First, in many cases, cash flows for financial assets are well documented in a legal contract. If they are not, we are at least able to make some reasonable assumptions about what they are. For real assets, much less information exists. Specialists within the firm, usually from the finance, marketing, and production groups, often prepare estimates of future cash flows for capital projects with only limited information.

Second, many financial securities are traded in public markets, and these markets are reasonably efficient. Thus, market data on rates of return are accessible. For real assets, no such markets exist. As a result, we must estimate required rates of return on real assets (opportunity costs) from market data on financial assets; this can be difficult to do.

NPV—The Basic Concept

The NPV of a project is the difference between the present value of the project's future cash flows and the present value of its cost. The NPV can be expressed as follows:

$$\text{NPV} = \text{PV (Project's future cash flows)} - \text{PV(Cost of the project)}$$

If a capital project has a positive NPV, the value of the cash flows the project is expected to generate exceeds the project's cost. Thus, a positive NPV project increases the value of the firm and, hence, stockholders' wealth. If a capital project has a negative NPV, the value of the cash flows from the project is less than its cost. If accepted, a negative NPV project will decrease the value of the firm and stockholders' wealth.

To illustrate these important points, consider an example. Suppose a firm is considering building a new marina for pleasure boats. The firm has a genie that can tell the future with perfect certainty. The finance staff estimates that the marina will cost $3.50 million. The genie volunteers that the market value of the marina is $4.25 million.

CCH Business Owner's Toolkit is a valuable Web source for information about running a business, including capital budget analysis. Go to www.toolkit.cch.com/text/p06_6500.asp.

LEARNING OBJECTIVE 2

net present value (NPV) method
a method of evaluating a capital investment project which measures the difference between its cost and the present value of its expected cash flows

Assuming this information is correct, the NPV for the marina project is a positive $750,000 ($4.25 million − $3.50 million). Management should accept the project because the excess of market value over cost increases the value of the firm by $750,000. Why is a positive NPV a *direct* measure of how much a capital project will increase the value of the firm? If management wanted to, the firm could sell the marina for $4.25 million, pay the $3.50 million in expenses, and deposit $750,000 in the bank. The value of the firm would increase by the $750,000 deposited in the bank. In sum, the NPV method tells us which capital projects to select and how much value they add to the firm.

NPV and Value Creation

We have just said that any project with a positive NPV should be accepted because it will increase the value of the firm. Let's take a moment to think about this proposition. What makes a capital asset worth more than it costs? In other words, how does management create value with capital investments?

HOW VALUE IS CREATED

Suppose that when you were in college, you worked part time at a successful pizza parlor near campus. During this time, you learned a lot about the pizza business. After graduation, you purchased a pizza parlor for $100,000 that was in a good location but had been forced to close because of a lack of profits. The owners had let the restaurant and the quality of the pizzas deteriorate, and the wait staff had been rude, especially to college students. Once you purchased the restaurant, you immediately invested $40,000 to fix it up: you painted the building, spruced up the interior, replaced some of the dining room furniture, and added an eye-catching, 1950s-style neon sign to attract attention. You also spent $15,000 for a one-time advertising blitz to quickly build a customer base. More important, you improved the quality of the pizzas you sold, and you built a profitable takeout business. Finally, you hired your wait staff carefully and trained them to be customer friendly.

Almost immediately the restaurant was earning a substantial profit and generating substantial cash flows. The really good news was that several owners of local pizzerias wanted to buy your restaurant. After intense negotiations with several of the potential buyers, you accepted a cash offer of $475,000 for the business shortly after you purchased it.

What is the NPV for the pizza parlor? For this investment, the NPV is easy to calculate. We do not need to estimate future cash flows and discount them because we already have an estimate of the present value of the cash flows the pizza parlor is expected to produce—$475,000. Someone is willing to pay you $475,000 because he or she believes the future cash flows are worth that amount. The cost of your investment includes the purchase price of the restaurant, the cost to fix it up, and the cost of the initial advertising campaign, which totals $155,000 ($100,000 + $40,000 + $15,000). Thus, the NPV for the pizza parlor is:

$$\text{NPV} = \text{PV (Project's future cash flows)} - \text{PV(Cost of the project)}$$
$$= \$475,000 - \$155,000$$
$$= \$320,000$$

The $475,000 price paid for the pizza parlor exceeds the cost ($155,000) by $320,000. You have created $320,000 in value. How did you do this? You did it by improving the food, customer service, and dining ambiance while keeping prices competitive. Your management skills and knowledge of the pizza business resulted in significant growth in the current year's cash flows and the prospect of even larger cash flows in the future.

Where did the $320,000 in value you created go? The NPV of your investment is the amount that your personal net worth increased because of the investment. For an ongoing business, the result would have been a $320,000 increase in the value of the firm.

How about the original owners? Why would they sell a business worth $475,000 to you for $100,000? The answer is simple; if they could have transformed the business as you did, they would have done so. Instead, when they ran the business, it lost money! They sold it to you because you offered them a price reflecting its value to them.

MARKET DATA VERSUS DISCOUNTED CASH FLOWS

Our pizza parlor example is greatly simplified by the fact that we can observe the price that someone is willing to pay for the asset. In most capital project analyses, we have to estimate the market value of the asset by *forecasting* its future cash flows and discounting them by the cost of capital. The discounted value of a project's future cash flows is an estimate of its value, or the market price for which it can be sold.

Framework for Calculating NPV

We now describe a framework for analyzing capital budgeting decisions using the NPV method. As you will see, the NPV technique uses the discounted cash flow technique developed in Chapters 5 and 6 and applied in Chapters 8 and 9. The good news, then, is that the NPV method requires only the application of what you already know.

The five-step framework discussed in this section and the accompanying cash flow worksheet (Exhibit 10.2) can help you systematically organize a project's cash flow data and compute its NPV. Most mistakes people make when working capital budgeting problems result from problems with cash flows: not identifying a cash flow, getting a cash flow in the wrong time period, or assigning the wrong sign to a cash flow. What can make cash flow analysis difficult in capital budgeting is this: there are often multiple cash flows in a single time period, and some are cash inflows and others are cash outflows.

As always, we recommend that you prepare a time line when doing capital budgeting problems. A sample time line is shown in Exhibit 10.2, along with an identification of the cash flows for each period. Our goal is to compute the net cash flow (NCF) for each time period t, where $NCF_t = $ (Cash inflows $-$ Cash outflows) for the period t. For a capital project, the time periods (t) are usually in years, and t varies from the current

Exhibit 10.2
Sample Worksheet for Net Present Value Analysis

In addition to following the five-step framework for solving NPV analysis problems, we recommend that you use a worksheet with a time line like the one shown here to help you determine the proper cash flows for each period.

Time line	0	1	2	3	4	5 Year
Cash Flows:						
Initial cost	$-CF_0$					
Inflows (CIF)		CIF_1	CIF_2	CIF_3	CIF_4	CIF_5
Outflows (COF)		$-COF_1$	$-COF_2$	$-COF_3$	$-COF_4$	$-COF_5$
Salvage value						SV
Net cash flow	$-NCF_0$	NCF_1	NCF_2	NCF_3	NCF_4	NCF_5

$$NPV = -NCF_0 + \sum_{t=1}^{5} \frac{NCF_t}{(1+k)^t}$$

period ($t = 0$) to some finite time period that is the estimated life of the project ($t = n$). Recall that getting the correct sign on each cash flow is critical to getting the correct answer to a problem. As you have seen in earlier chapters, the convention in finance problem solving is that cash inflows carry a positive sign and cash outflows carry a negative sign. Finally, note that all cash flows in this chapter are on an after-tax basis. We will make adjustments for tax consequences on specific transactions such as the calculation of a project's salvage value.

Our five-step framework for analysis is as follows:

1. **Determine the cost of the project.** We first need to identify and add up all of the expense items related to the cost of the project. In most cases, the cost of a project is incurred during the first year; hence, this cash outflow is already in current dollars. However, some projects have negative cash flows for several years because it takes two or three years to get the projects up and running. If the cash payments for the project extend beyond one year, the dollars paid in the second year and beyond must be discounted for the appropriate time period. Negative cash flows can also occur when a project sustains an operating loss during the start-up years. Turning to Exhibit 10.2, we have incurred a single negative cash flow ($-CF_0$) for the total cost of the project, where $NCF_0 = -CF_0$; thus, NCF_0 has a negative value.

2. **Estimate the project's future cash flows over its expected life.** Capital projects typically generate some cash inflows from revenues (CIF_t) for each period, along with some cash outflows (COF_t) that represent expenses incurred to generate the revenues. In most cases revenues exceed expenses, and thus, NCF_t is positive where $t \geq 1$. However, this may not always be the case. For example, if the project is the purchase of a piece of equipment, it is possible for NCF_3 to have a negative value ($CIF_3 < COF_3$) if the equipment is projected to need a major overhaul or must be replaced during the third year. Finally, you also need to pay attention to a project's final cash flow, which is $t = 5$ in Exhibit 10.2. There may be a salvage value (SV) at the end of the project, which is a cash inflow. In that case $NCF = (CIF_5 - COF_5 + SV)$. The important point is that for each time period, we must identify all the cash flows that take place, assign each cash flow its proper sign, and algebraically add up all the cash flows; the total is the NCF for that time period with the correct sign.

3. **Determine the riskiness of the project and the appropriate cost of capital.** The third step is to identify for each project its risk-adjusted cost of capital, which takes into account the riskiness of the project's cash flows. The riskier the project, the higher its cost of capital. The cost of capital is the discount rate used in determining the present value of the future expected cash flows. In this chapter, the cost of capital and any risk adjustments will be supplied, and no calculations will be required for this step.

4. **Compute the project's NPV.** The NPV, as you know, is the present value of the net cash flows the project is expected to generate minus the cost of the project.

5. **Make a decision.** If the NPV is positive, the project should be accepted because all projects with a positive NPV will increase the value of the firm. If the NPV is negative, the project should be rejected; projects with negative NPVs will decrease the value of the firm.

You might be wondering about how to handle a capital project with an NPV of 0. Technically, management should be indifferent to accepting or rejecting projects such as this because they neither increase nor decrease the value of the firm. At a practical level, projects rarely have an NPV equal to 0, and most firms have more good capital projects (with NPV > 0) than they can fund. Thus, this is not an issue that generates much interest among practitioners.

Net Present Value Techniques

The NPV of a capital project can be stated in equation form as the present value of all net cash flows (inflows − outflows) connected with the project, whether in the current period or in the future. The NPV equation can be written as follows:

$$NPV = NCF_0 + \frac{NCF_1}{1+k} + \frac{NCF_2}{(1+k)^2} + \cdots + \frac{NCF_n}{(1+k)^n} \qquad (10.1)$$

$$= \sum_{t=0}^{n} \frac{NCF_t}{(1+k)^t}$$

where:

NCF_t = Net cash flow (cash inflows − cash outflows) in period t, where $t = 1, 2, 3, \ldots, n$
k = The cost of capital
n = The project's estimated life

Next, we will work an example to see how the NPV is calculated for a capital project. Suppose you are the president of a small regional firm located in Chicago that manufactures frozen pizzas, which are sold to grocery stores and to firms in the hospitality and food service industry. Your market research group has developed an idea for a "pocket" pizza that can be used as an entrée with a meal or as an "on the go" snack. The sales manager believes that, with an aggressive advertising campaign, sales of the product will be about $300,000 per year. The cost to modify the existing production line will also be $300,000, according to the plant manager. The marketing and plant managers estimate that the cost to produce the pocket pizzas, to market and advertise them, and to deliver them to customers will be about $220,000 per year. The product's life is estimated to be five years, and the specialized equipment necessary for the project has an estimated salvage value of $30,000. The appropriate cost of capital is 15 percent.

When analyzing capital budgeting problems, we typically have a lot of data to sort through. The worksheet approach introduced earlier is helpful in keeping track of the data in an organized format. Exhibit 10.3 shows the time line and relevant cash flows for the pocket pizza project. The steps in analyzing the project's cash flows and determining its NPV are as follows:

1. *Determine the cost of the capital project.* The cost of the project is the cost to modify the existing production line, which is $300,000. This is a cash outflow (negative sign).

2. *Estimate the capital project's future cash flows over its expected life.* The project's future cash inflows come from sales of the new product. Sales are estimated at $300,000 per year (positive sign). The cash outflows are the costs to manufacture and distribute the new product, which are $220,000 per year (negative sign). The life of the project is five years. The project has a salvage value of $30,000, which is a cash inflow (positive sign). The net cash flow (NCF) per time period is just the sum of the cash inflows and cash outflows for that period. For example, the NCF for period $t = 0$ is −$300,000 the NCF for period $t = 1$ is $80,000, and so on, as you can see in Exhibit 10.3.

3. *Determine the riskiness of the project and appropriate cost of capital.* The discount rate is the cost of capital, which is 15 percent.

4. *Compute the project's NPV.* To compute the project's NPV, we apply Equation 10.1 by plugging in the NCF values for each time period and using the cost of capital, 15 percent, as the discount rate. The equation looks like this (the figures are in thousands of dollars):

Time line	0	1	2	3	4	5 Year
Cash Flows:						
Initial cost	−$300					
Inflows		$300	$300	$300	$300	$300
Outflows		−$220	−$220	−$220	−$220	−$220
Salvage						30
Net cash flow	−$300	$80	$80	$80	$80	$110

Exhibit 10.3
Pocket Pizza Project Time Line and Cash Flows ($ thousands)
The worksheet approach introduced in Exhibit 10.2 is helpful in organizing the data given for the pocket pizza project.

$$NPV = \sum_{t=0}^{n} \frac{NCF_t}{(1+k)^t}$$

$$= -\$300 + \frac{80}{1.15} + \frac{80}{(1.15)^2} + \cdots + \frac{80}{(1.15)^4} + \frac{(80+30)}{(1.15)^5}$$

$$= -\$300 + \$69.57 + \$60.49 + \$52.60 + \$45.74 + \$54.69$$

$$= -\$300 + \$283.09$$

$$= -\$16.91$$

The NPV for the pocket pizza project is therefore −$16,910.

5. *Make a decision.* The pocket pizza project has a negative NPV, which indicates that the project is not a good investment and should be rejected. If management undertook this project, the value of the firm would decrease by $16,910; and, if the firm had one hundred thousand shares of stock outstanding, we can estimate that the project would decrease the value of each share by about 17 cents ($16,910/100,000 shares).

CALCULATING NPV WITH A FINANCIAL CALCULATOR

Using a financial calculator is an easier way to calculate the present value of the future cash flows. In this example you should recognize that the cash flow pattern is a five-year ordinary annuity with an additional cash inflow in the fifth year. This is exactly the cash pattern for a bond with annual coupon payments and payment of principal at maturity we saw in Chapter 8. We can find the present value using a financial calculator, with $80 being the annuity stream for five years and $30 the salvage value at year 5:

Enter	5	15		80	30
	N	i	PV	PMT	FV
Answer			−283.09		

The PV of the future cash flows is −$283.09. With that information, we can compute the NPV using Equation 10.1 as follows:

$$NPV = \sum_{t=1}^{n} \frac{NCF_t}{(1+k)^t} - NCF_0$$

$$= \$283.09 - \$300.00$$

$$= -\$16.91$$

LEARNING BY DOING APPLICATION 10.1

The Dough's Up: The Self-Rising Pizza Project

Problem: Let's continue our frozen pizza example. Suppose the head of the research and development (R&D) group announces that R&D engineers have developed a breakthrough technology—self-rising frozen pizza dough that, when baked, rises and tastes exactly like fresh-baked dough.

The cost is $300,000 to modify the production line. Sales of the new product are estimated at $200,000 for the first year, $300,000 for the next two years, and $500,000 for the final two years. It is estimated that production, sales, and advertising costs will be $250,000 for the first year and will then decline to a constant $200,000 per year. There is no salvage value at the end of the product's life, and the appropriate cost of capital is 15 percent. Is the project, as proposed, economically viable?

Approach: To solve the problem, work through the steps for NPV analysis given in the text.

Solution: Exhibit 10.4 shows the project's cash flows.

1. The cost to modify the production line is $300,000, which is a cash outflow and the cost of the project.

2. The future cash flows over the expected life of the project are laid out on the time line in Exhibit 10.4. The project's life is five years. The NCFs for the capital project are negative at the beginning of the project and in the first year (−$300,000 and −$50,000) and thereafter are positive.

Time line	0	1	2	3	4	5 Year
Cash Flows:						
Initial cost	−$300					
Inflows		$200	$300	$300	$500	$500
Outflows		−$250	−$200	−$200	−$200	−$200
Salvage						
Net cash flow	−$300	−$50	$100	$100	$300	$300

Exhibit 10.4
Self-Rising Pizza Dough Project Time Line and Cash Flows ($ thousands)
The worksheet shows the time line and cash flows for the self-rising pizza dough project in Learning by Doing Application 10.1. As always, it is important to assign each cash flow to the appropriate year and to give it the proper sign. Once you have computed the net cash flow for each time period, solving for NPV is just a matter of plugging the data into the NPV formula.

(continued)

3. The appropriate cost of capital is 15 percent.

4. The values are substituted into Equation 10.1 to calculate the NPV:

$$NPV = NCF_0 + \frac{NCF_1}{1+k} + \frac{NCF_2}{(1+k)^2} + \cdots + \frac{NCF_n}{(1+k)^n}$$

$$= -\$300{,}000 - \frac{\$50{,}000}{1.15} + \frac{\$100{,}000}{(1.15)^2} + \frac{\$100{,}000}{(1.15)^3} + \frac{\$300{,}000}{(1.15)^4} + \frac{\$300{,}000}{(1.15)^5}$$

$$= -\$300{,}000 - \$43{,}478 + \$75{,}614 + \$65{,}752 + \$171{,}526 + \$149{,}153$$

$$= \$118{,}567$$

5. The decision is based on the NPV. The NPV for the self-rising pizza dough project is $118,567. Because the NPV is positive, management should accept the project. The project is estimated to increase the value of the firm by $118,567.

USING EXCEL

Net Present Value

Net present value problems are most commonly solved using a spreadsheet program. The program's design is good for keeping track of all the cash flows and the periods in which they occur. The following spreadsheet setup for Learning by Doing Application 10.1 shows how to calculate the NPV for the self-rising pizza dough machine:

Notice that the NPV formula does not take into account the cash flow in year zero. Therefore, you only enter into the NPV formula the cash flows in years 1 through 5, along with the discount rate. You then add the cash flow in year zero to the total from the NPV formula calculation to get the NPV for the investment.

	A	B	C	D	E
1					
2		Net Present Value Calculations			
3					
4		Year		Cash Flow	
5		0		-$300,000	
6		1		-50,000	
7		2		100,000	
8		3		100,000	
9		4		300,000	
10		5		300,000	
11					
12		Cost of capital		0.15	
13					
14		**NPV**		**$118,567**	
15		Formula used		=NPV(D12, D6:D10)+D5	
16					

DECISION-MAKING EXAMPLE 10.1

The IS Department's Capital Projects

Situation: Suppose you are the manager of the information systems (IS) department of the frozen pizza manufacturer we have been discussing. Your department has identified four possible capital projects with the following NPVs: (1) $4,500, (2) $3,000, (3) $0.0, and (4) −$1,000. What should you decide about each project if the projects are independent? What should you decide if the projects are mutually exclusive?

> **Decision:** If the projects are independent, you should accept projects 1 and 2, both of which have a positive NPV, and reject project 4. Project 3, with an NPV of zero, could be either accepted or rejected. If the projects are mutually exclusive and you can accept only one of them, it should be project 1, which has the largest NPV.

Concluding Comments on NPV

Some concluding comments about the NPV method are in order. First, as you may have noticed, the NPV computations are rather mechanical once we have the cash flows and have determined the cost of capital. The real difficulty is estimating or forecasting the future cash flows. Although this may seem to be a daunting task, firms with experience in producing and selling a particular type of product can usually generate fairly accurate estimates of sales volumes, prices, and production costs. However, problems can arise with the cash flow estimates when a project team becomes "enamored" with a project. Wanting a project to succeed, a project team can be too optimistic about the cash flow projections.

Second, we must recognize that the calculated values for NPV are estimates based on management's informed judgment; they are not real market data. Like any estimate, they can be too high or too low. The only way to determine a project's "true" NPV is to put the asset up for sale and see what price market participants are willing to pay for it. An example of this approach was the sale of our pizza parlor; however, situations such as this are the exception, not the rule.

Finally, there is nothing wrong with using estimates to make business decisions as long as they are based on informed judgments and not guesses. Most business managers are routinely required to make decisions that involve expectations about future events. In fact, that is what business is really all about—dealing with uncertainty and making decisions that involve risk.

In conclusion, the NPV approach is the method we recommend for making capital investment decisions. The accompanying table summarizes NPV decision rules and the method's key advantages and disadvantages.

Summary of Net Present Value (NPV) Method

Decision Rule: NPV > 0 ⇨ Accept the project.
NPV < 0 ⇨ Reject the project.

Key Advantages	Key Disadvantages
1. Uses the discounted cash flow valuation technique to adjust for the time value of money.	1. Can be difficult to understand without an accounting and finance background.
2. Provides a direct (dollar) measure of how much a capital project will increase the value of the firm.	
3. Consistent with the goal of maximizing stockholder value.	

> **Before You Go On**
>
> 1. What is the NPV of a project?
> 2. If a firm accepts a project with a $10,000 NPV, what is the effect on the value of the firm?
> 3. What are the five steps used in NPV analysis?

10.3 The Payback Period

payback period
the length of time required to recover a project's initial cost

The payback period is one of the most widely used tools for evaluating capital projects. The **payback period** is defined as the number of years it takes for the cash flows from a project to recover the project's initial investment. With the payback method for evaluating projects, a project is accepted if its payback period is below some specified threshold. Although it has serious weaknesses, this method does provide some insight into a project's risk; the more quickly you recover the cash, the less risky is the project.

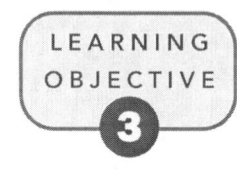

Computing the Payback Period

LEARNING OBJECTIVE 3

To compute the payback period, we need to know the project's cost and estimate its future net cash flows. The net cash flows and the project cost are the same values that we used to compute the NPV calculations. The payback (PB) equation can be expressed as follows:

$$PB = \text{Years before cost recovery} + \frac{\text{Remaining cost to recover}}{\text{Cash flow during the year}} \quad (10.2)$$

Exhibit 10.5 shows the net cash flows (row 1) and cumulative net cash flows (row 2) for a proposed capital project with an initial cost of $70,000. The payback period calculation for our example is:

$$PB = \text{Years before cost recovery} + \frac{\text{Remaining cost to recover}}{\text{Cash flow during the year}}$$

$$= 2 \text{ years} + \frac{\$70,000 - \$60,000}{\$20,000}$$

$$= 2 \text{ years} + \frac{\$10,000}{\$20,000}$$

$$= 2 \text{ years} + 0.5$$

$$= 2.5 \text{ years}$$

Let's look at this calculation in more detail. Note in Exhibit 10.5 that the firm recovers cash flows of $30,000 in the first year and $30,000 in the second year, for a total of $60,000 over the two years. During the third year, the firm needs to recover

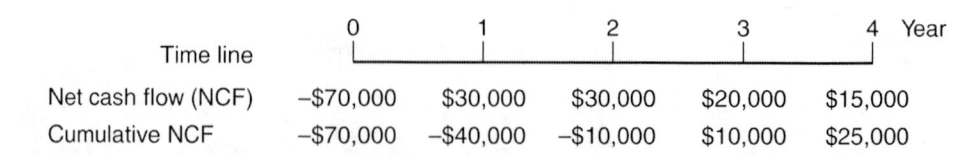

Time line	0	1	2	3	4 Year
Net cash flow (NCF)	−$70,000	$30,000	$30,000	$20,000	$15,000
Cumulative NCF	−$70,000	−$40,000	−$10,000	$10,000	$25,000

Exhibit 10.5
Payback Period Cash Flows and Calculations
The exhibit shows the net and cumulative net cash flows for a proposed capital project with an initial cost of $70,000. The cash flow data are used to compute the payback period, which is 2.5 years.

only $10,000 ($70,000 − $60,000) to pay back the full cost of the project. The third-year cash flow is $20,000, so we will have to wait 0.5 year ($10,000/$20,000) to recover the final amount. Thus, the payback period for this project is 2.5 years (2 + 0.5).

The idea behind the payback period method is simple: the shorter the payback period, the faster the firm gets its money back and the more desirable the project. However, there is no economic rationale that links the payback method to stockholder value maximization. Firms that use the payback method accept all projects having a payback period under some threshold and reject those with a payback period over this threshold. If a firm has a number of projects that are mutually exclusive, the projects are selected in order of their payback rank: projects with the shortest payback period are selected first.

LEARNING BY DOING APPLICATION 10.2

A Payback Calculation

Problem: A firm has two capital projects, A and B, which are under review for funding. Both projects cost $500, and the projects have the following cash flows:

Year	Project A	Project B
0	−$500	−$500
1	100	400
2	200	300
3	200	200
4	400	100

What is the payback period for each project? If the projects are independent, which project should management select? If the projects are mutually exclusive, which project should management accept? The firm's payback cutoff point is two years.

Approach: Use Equation 10.2 to calculate the number of years it takes for the cash flows from each project to recover the project's initial investment. If the two projects are independent, you should accept the projects that have a payback period that is less than or equal to two years. If the projects are mutually exclusive, you should accept the project with the shortest payback period if that payback period is also less than or equal to two years.

Solution: The payback for project A requires only that we calculate the first term in Equation 10.2—Years before recovery: the first year recovers $100, the second year $200, and the third year $200, for a total of $500 ($100 + $200 + $200). Thus, in three years, the $500 investment is fully recovered, so $PB_A = 3.00$.

For project B, the first year recovers $400 and the second year $300. Since we need only part of the second-year cash flow to recover the initial cost, we calculate both terms in Equation 10.2 to obtain the payback time.

$$PB = \text{Years before cost recovery} + \frac{\text{Remaining cost to recover}}{\text{Cash flow during the year}}$$

$$PB_A = 3 \text{ years}$$

$$PB_B = 1 \text{ year} + \frac{\$500 - \$400}{\$300}$$

$$= 1 \text{ year} + \frac{\$100}{\$300}$$

$$= 1.33 \text{ years}$$

Whether the projects are independent or mutually exclusive, management should accept only project B since project A's payback period exceeds the two-year cutoff point.

Exhibit 10.6 Payback Period with Various Cash Flow Patterns

Year	A	B	C	D	E
0	−$500	−$500	−$500	−$500	−$500
1	200	300	250	500	200
2	300	100	250	0	200
3	400	50	−250	0	200
4	500	0	250	−5,000	5,000
Payback (years)	2.0	∞	2.0/4.0	1.0/∞	2.5
NPV	$450	−$131	−$115	−$2,924	$2,815

Cost of capital = 15%

Each of the five capital budgeting projects shown in the exhibit calls for an initial investment of $500, but all have different cash flow patterns. The bottom part of the exhibit shows each project's payback period, along with its net present value for comparison.

How the Payback Period Performs

We have worked through some simple examples of how the payback period is computed. Now we will consider several more complex situations to see how well the payback period performs as a capital budgeting criterion. Exhibit 10.6 illustrates five different capital budgeting projects. The projects all have an initial investment of $500, but each one has a different cash flow pattern. The bottom part of the exhibit shows each project's payback period, along with its net present value for comparison. We will assume that management has set a payback period of two years as the cutoff point for an acceptable project.

Project A: The cash flows for project A are $200 in the first year and $300 in the second, for a total of $500; thus, the project's payback period is two years. Under our acceptance criterion, management should accept this project. Project A also has a positive NPV of $450, so the two capital budgeting decision rules agree.

Project B: Project B never generates enough cash flows to pay off the original investment of $500: $300 + $100 + $50 = $450. Thus, the project payback period is infinite. With an infinite payback period, the project should be rejected. Also, as you would expect, Project B's NPV is negative. So far, the payback period and NPV methods have agreed on which projects to accept.

Project C: Project C has a payback period of two years: $250 + $250 = $500. Thus, according to the payback criteria, it should be accepted. However, the project's NPV is a negative $115, which indicates that the project should be rejected. Why the conflict? Look at the cash flows after the payback period of two years. In year 3 the project requires an additional investment of $250 (a cash outflow) and now is in a deficit position; that is, the cash balance is now only $250 ($250 + $250 − $250). Then, in the final year, the project earns an additional $250, recovering the cost of the original investment. The project's payback is really four years. The payback period analysis can lead to erroneous decisions because the rule does not consider cash flows after the payback period.

Projects D and E: Projects D and E dramatically illustrate the problem when a capital budgeting evaluation tool fails to consider cash flows after the payback period. Project D has a payback period of one year, suggesting that it should be accepted, and project E has a payback period of 2.5 years, suggesting that it should be rejected. However, a simple look at the future cash flows suggests otherwise. It is clear that project D, with a negative $5,000 cash flow in year 4, is a disaster and should be rejected, while project E, with a positive $5,000 "windfall" in year 4, should be accepted. Indeed, the NPV analysis confirms these conclusions: project D has a negative NPV of $2,924, and project E has a positive NPV of $2,815. In both instances, the payback rule led to the wrong economic decision. These examples illustrate that a rapid payback does not necessarily mean a good investment.

Discounted Payback Period

One of the weaknesses of the ordinary payback period is that it does not take into account the time value of money. All dollars received before the cutoff period are given equal weight. To address this problem, some financial managers use a variant of the payback period called the **discounted payback period**. This payback calculation is similar to the ordinary payback calculation except that the future cash flows are discounted by the cost of capital.

discounted payback period
the length of time required to recover a project's initial cost, accounting for the time value of money

The major advantage of the discounted payback is that it tells management how long it takes a project to reach an NPV of zero. Thus, any capital project that meets a firm's decision rule must also have a positive NPV. This is an improvement over the standard payback calculation, which can accept projects with negative NPVs. Regardless of the improvement, the discounted payback method is not widely used by businesses, and it still ignores all cash flows after the arbitrary cutoff period, which is a major flaw.

To see how the discounted payback period is calculated, turn to Exhibit 10.7. The exhibit shows the net cash flows for a proposed capital project along with both the cumulative and discounted cumulative cash flows; thus, we can compute both the ordinary and the discounted payback periods for the project and then compare them. The cost of capital is 10 percent.

The first two rows show the nondiscounted cash flows, and we can see by inspection that the ordinary payback period is two years. We do not need to make any additional calculations because the cumulative cash flows equal zero at precisely two years. Now let's turn our attention to the lower two rows, which show the project's discounted and cumulative discounted cash flows. Note that the first year's cash flow is $20,000 and its discounted value is $18,182 ($20,000 × 0.9091), and the second year's cash flow is also $20,000 and its discounted value is $16,529 ($20,000 × 0.8264). Now, looking at the cumulative discounted cash flows row, notice that it turns positive between two and three years. This means that the discounted payback period is two years plus some

Time line	0	1	2	3 Year
Net cash flow (NCF)	−$40,000	$20,000	$20,000	$20,000
Cumulative NCF	−$40,000	−$20,000	$0	$20,000
Discounted NCF (at 10%)	−$40,000	$18,182	$16,529	$15,026
Cumulative discounted NCF	−$40,000	−$21,818	−$5,289	$9,737

Payback period = 2 years + $0/$20,000 = 2 years
Discounted payback period = 2 years + $5,289/$15,026 = 2.35 years
NPV = $49,737 −$40,000 = $9,737
Cost of capital = 10%

Exhibit 10.7
Discounted Payback Period Cash Flows and Calculations
The exhibit shows the net and cumulative net cash flows for a proposed capital project with an initial cost of $40,000. The cash flow data are used to compute the discounted payback period for a 10 percent cost of capital, which is 2.35 years.

fraction of the third year's discounted cash flow. The exact discounted payback period computed value is 2 + ($5,289/$15,026) = 2 + 0.35 = 2.35.

As expected, the discounted payback period is longer than the ordinary payback period (2 < 2.35), and in 2.35 years the project will reach a NPV = 0. The project NPV is positive ($9,737); therefore, we should accept the project. But notice that the payback decision criteria are ambiguous. If we use 2.0 years as the payback criterion, we reject the project and if we use 2.5 or 3.0 years as criterion, the project is accepted. The lack of a definitive decision rule remains a major problem with the payback period as a capital budgeting tool.

Evaluating the Payback Rule

In spite of its lack of sophistication, the standard payback period is widely used in business in part because it provides an intuitive and simple measure of a project's liquidity risk. This makes sense because projects that pay for themselves quickly are less risky than projects whose paybacks occur further in the future. There is a strong feeling in business that "getting your money back quickly" is an important standard when making capital investments. Probably the greatest advantage of the payback period is its simplicity; it is easy to calculate and easy to understand, making it especially attractive to business executives with little training in accounting and finance.

When compared with the NPV method, however, the payback method has some serious shortcomings. First, the standard payback method does not use discounting; hence, it ignores the time value of money. Second, it does not adjust or account for differences in the riskiness of projects. Another problem is that there is no economic rationale for establishing cutoff criteria. Who is to say that a particular cutoff, such as two years, is optimal with regard to maximizing stockholder value?

Finally, perhaps the greatest shortcoming of the payback method is its failure to consider cash flows after the payback period, as illustrated by projects D and E in Exhibit 10.6. This is true whether or not the cash flows are discounted. As a result of this feature, the payback method is biased toward shorter-term projects, which tend to free up cash more quickly. Consequently, projects for which cash inflows tend to occur further in the future, such as research and development investments, new product launches, and entry into new lines of business, are at a disadvantage when the payback method is used. The accompanying table summarizes major features of the payback period.

Summary of Payback Method

Decision Rule: Payback period ≤ Payback cutoff point ⇨ Accept the project.
Payback period > Payback cutoff point ⇨ Reject the project.

Key Advantages	Key Disadvantages
1. Easy to calculate and understand for people without a strong finance background.	1. Most common version does not account for time value of money.
2. A simple measure of a project's liquidity.	2. Does not consider cash flows past the payback period.
	3. Bias against long-term projects such as research and development and new product launches.
	4. Arbitrary cutoff point.

> **Before You Go On**
>
> 1. What is the payback period?
> 2. Why does the payback period provide a measure of a project's liquidity risk?
> 3. What are the main shortcomings of the payback method?

10.4 The Accounting Rate of Return

We turn next to a capital budgeting technique based on the **accounting rate of return (ARR)**, sometimes called the *book value rate of return*. This method computes the return on a capital project using accounting numbers—the project's net income (NI) and book value (BV)—rather than cash flow data. The ARR can be calculated in a number of ways, but the most common definition is:

$$\text{ARR} = \frac{\text{Average net income}}{\text{Average book value}} \quad (10.3)$$

where:

Average net income = $(NI_1 + NI_2 + \cdots + NI_n)/n$
Average book value = $(BV_1 + BV_2 + \cdots + BV_n)/n$
n = the project's estimated life

accounting rate of return (ARR)
a rate of return on a capital project based on average net income divided by average assets over the project's life; also called the *book value rate of return*

Although ARR is fairly easy to understand and calculate, as you probably guessed, it has a number of major flaws as a tool for evaluating capital expenditure decisions. Besides the fact that AAR is based on accounting numbers rather than cash flows, it is not really even an accounting-based rate of return. Instead of discounting a project's cash flows over time, it simply gives us a number based on average figures from the income statement and balance sheet. Thus, the ARR ignores the time value of money. Also, as with the payback method, there is no economic rationale that links a particular acceptance criterion to the goal of maximizing stockholder value.

Because of these major shortcomings, the ARR technique should not be used to evaluate the viability of capital projects under any circumstances. You may wonder why we even included the ARR technique in the book if it is a poor criterion for evaluating projects. The reason is simply that we want to be sure that if you run across the ARR method at work, you will recognize it and be aware of its shortcomings.

> **Before You Go On**
> 1. What are the major shortcomings of using the ARR method as a capital budgeting method?

10.5 Internal Rate of Return

The **internal rate of return**, known in practice as the **IRR**, is an important and legitimate alternative to the NPV method. The NPV and IRR techniques are closely related in that both involve discounting the cash flows from a project; thus, both account for the time value of money. When we use the NPV method to evaluate a capital project, the discount rate is the rate of return required by investors for investments with similar risk, which is the project's opportunity cost of capital. When we use the IRR, we are looking for the rate of return associated with a project so that we can determine whether this rate is higher or lower than the project's opportunity cost of capital.

We can define the IRR as the discount rate that equates the present value of a project's expected cash inflows to the present value of the project's outflows:

PV(Project's future cash flows) = PV(Cost of the project)

internal rate of return (IRR)
the discount rate at which the present value of a project's expected cash inflows equals the present value of the project's outflows

This means that we can also describe the IRR as the discount rate that causes the NPV to equal zero. This relation can be written in a general form as follows:

$$\text{NPV} = \text{NCF}_0 + \frac{\text{NCF}_1}{1 + \text{IRR}} + \frac{\text{NCF}_2}{(1 + \text{IRR})^2} + \cdots + \frac{\text{NCF}_n}{(1 + \text{IRR})^n} \quad (10.4)$$

$$= \sum_{t=0}^{n} \frac{\text{NCF}_t}{(1 + \text{IRR})^t} = 0$$

Because of their close relation, it may seem that the IRR and the NPV are interchangeable—that is, either should accept or reject the same capital projects. After all, both methods are based on whether the project's return exceeds the cost of capital and, hence, whether the project will add value to the firm. In many circumstances, the IRR and NPV methods do give us the same answer. As you will see later, however, some of the mathematical properties of the IRR equation can lead to incorrect decisions concerning whether to accept or reject a particular capital project.

Calculating the IRR

The IRR is an expected rate of return like the yield to maturity we calculated for bonds in Chapter 8. Thus, in calculating the IRR, we need to apply the same trial-and-error method we used in Chapter 8. We will begin by doing some IRR calculations by trial and error so that you understand the process, and then we will switch to the financial calculator, which provides an answer more quickly and is less prone to mistakes.

TRIAL-AND-ERROR METHOD

Suppose that Ford Motor Company has an investment opportunity with cash flows as shown in Exhibit 10.8 and that the cost of capital is 12 percent. We want to find the IRR for this project. Using Equation 10.4, we will substitute various values for IRR into the equation to compute the project's IRR by trial and error. We continue this process until we find the IRR value that makes Equation 10.4 equal zero.

A good starting point is to use the cost of capital as the discount rate. Note that when we discount the NCFs by the cost of capital, we are calculating the project's NPV:

$$\text{NPV} = \text{NCF}_0 + \frac{\text{NCF}_1}{1 + \text{IRR}} + \frac{\text{NCF}_2}{(1 + \text{IRR})^2} + \cdots + \frac{\text{NCF}_n}{(1 + \text{IRR})^n}$$

$$\text{NPV}_{12\%} = -\$560 + \frac{\$240}{1.12} + \frac{\$240}{(1.12)^2} + \frac{\$240}{(1.12)^3} = \$16.44$$

Exhibit 10.8
Time Line and Expected Net Cash Flows for the Ford Project ($ thousands)
The cash flow data in the exhibit are used to compute the project's IRR, which is 13.7 percent. Since the IRR is higher than Ford's cost of capital, the IRR criterion indicates the project should be accepted. The project's NPV is a positive $16,440, which also indicates that Ford should accept the project. Thus, the IRR and NPV methods have reached the same conclusion.

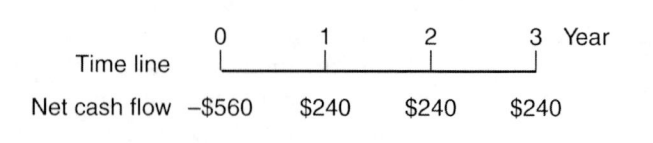

Time line	0	1	2	3 Year
Net cash flow	−$560	$240	$240	$240

IRR = 13.7%
Cost of capital = 12%
NPV = $576.44 − $560.00 = $16.44

Recall that the result we are looking for is zero. Because our result is $16.44, the discount rate of 12 percent is too low, and we must try a higher rate. Let's try 13 percent:

$$\text{NPV}_{13\%} = -\$560 + \frac{\$240}{1.13} + \frac{\$240}{(1.13)^2} + \frac{\$240}{(1.13)^3} = \$6.68$$

We are very close; let's try 14 percent:

$$\text{NPV}_{14\%} = -\$560 + \frac{\$240}{1.14} + \frac{\$240}{(1.14)^2} + \frac{\$240}{(1.14)^3} = -\$2.81$$

Because our result is now a negative number, we know the correct rate is between 13 and 14 percent, and looking at the magnitude of the numbers, we know that the answer is closer to 14 percent. Let's try 13.7 percent.

$$\text{NPV}_{13.7\%} = -\$560 + \frac{\$240}{1.137} + \frac{\$240}{(1.137)^2} + \frac{\$240}{(1.137)^3} = 0$$

Good guess! This means that the NPV of Ford's capital project is zero at a discount rate of 13.7 percent. Ford's required rate of return is the cost of capital, which is 12.0 percent. Since the project's IRR of 13.7 percent exceeds Ford's cost of capital, the IRR criterion indicates that the project should be accepted.

The project's NPV is a positive $16,440, which also indicates that Ford should go ahead with the project. Thus, both the IRR and NPV have reached the same conclusion.

LEARNING BY DOING APPLICATION 10.3

Calculating the IRR at Larry's

Problem: Larry's Ice Cream in the DuPont Circle area of Washington, D.C., is famous for its gourmet ice cream. However, some customers have asked for a health-oriented, low-cal, soft yogurt. The machine that makes this confection is manufactured in Italy and costs $5,000 plus $1,750 for installation. Larry estimates that the machine will generate a net cash flow of $2,000 a year (the shop closes November through March of each year). Larry also estimates the machine's life to be 10 years and that it will have a $400 salvage value. His cost of capital is 15 percent. Larry thinks the machine is overpriced and it's a bum deal. Is he right?

Approach: The IRR for an investment is the discount rate at which the NPV is zero. Thus, we can use Equation 10.4 to solve for the IRR and then compare this value with Larry's cost of capital. If the IRR is greater than the cost of capital, the project has a positive NPV and should be accepted.

Solution: The total cost of the machine is $6,750 ($5,000 + $1,750), and the final cash flow at year 10 is $2,400 ($2,000 + $400).

```
0      1       2       3        9       10  Year
  15%
-$6,750  $2,000  $2,000  $2,000  $2,000  $2,400
```

$$\text{NPV} = \text{NCF}_0 + \frac{\text{NCF}_1}{1 + \text{IRR}} + \frac{\text{NCF}_2}{(1 + \text{IRR})^2} + \cdots + \frac{\text{NCF}_n}{(1 + \text{IRR})^n} = 0$$

$$\text{NPV}_{15.00\%} = -\$6,750 + \frac{\$2,000}{1.15} + \frac{\$2,000}{(1.15)^2} + \cdots + \frac{\$2,400}{(1.15)^{10}} = \$3,386.41$$

$$\text{NPV}_{27.08\%} = -\$6,750 + \frac{\$2,000}{1.2708} + \frac{\$2,000}{(1.2708)^2} + \cdots + \frac{\$2,400}{(1.2708)^{10}} = \$0.00$$

The hand trial-and-error calculations are shown in these equations. The first calculation uses 15 percent, the cost of capital, our recommended starting point, and the answer is $3,386.41 (which is also the project's NPV). Because the value is a positive number, we need to use a larger discount rate than 15 percent. Our guess is 27.08 percent. At that value, NPV = 0; thus, the IRR for the yogurt machine is 27.08 percent.

(continued)

Because the project's future cash flow pattern resembles that for a bond, we can also solve for the IRR on a financial calculator, just as we would solve for the yield to maturity. Just enter the data directly into the corresponding keys on the calculator and press the interest key and we have our answer—27.08 percent.

Enter	10		−6,750	2,000	400
	N	i	PV	PMT	FV
Answer		27.08			

As with present value calculations, for projects with unequal cash flows, you should consult your financial calculator's manual.

Because the project's IRR exceeds Larry's cost of capital of 15 percent, the project should be accepted. Larry is wrong.

USING EXCEL

Internal Rate of Return

You know that calculating IRR by hand can be tedious. The trial-and-error method can take a long time and can be quite frustrating. Knowing all the cash flows and an approximate rate will allow you to use a spreadsheet formula to get an answer instantly.

The accompanying spreadsheet shows the setup for calculating the IRR for the low-cal yogurt machine at Larry's Ice Cream Parlor that is described in Learning by Doing Application 10.3.

Here are a couple of important points to note about IRR calculations using spreadsheet programs:

1. Unlike the NPV formula, the IRR formula accounts for all cash flows, including the initial investment in year 0, so there is no need to add this cash flow later.

2. In order to calculate the IRR, you will need to provide a "guess" value, or a number you estimate is close to the IRR. A good value to start with is the cost of capital. To learn more about why this value is needed, you should go to your spreadsheet's help manual and search for "IRR."

	A	B	C	D	E
1					
2		IRR Calculations			
3					
4			Year		Cash Flow
5			0		-$6,750
6			1		2,000
7			2		2,000
8			3		2,000
9			4		2,000
10			5		2,000
11			6		2,000
12			7		2,000
13			8		2,000
14			9		2,000
15			10		2,400
16					
17		Cost of capital			0.15
18					
19		IRR			27.08%
20		Formula used			=IRR(E5:E15, E17)
21					
22	Remember to keep track of signs - cash outflows are negative and cash inflows are positive.				
23					
24					

When the IRR and NPV Methods Agree

In the Ford example, the IRR and NPV methods agree. The two methods will *always* agree when you are evaluating *independent* projects and the projects' cash flows are *conventional*. As discussed earlier, an independent project is one that can be selected with no effect on any other project, assuming the firm faces no resource constraints. A project with **conventional cash flows** is one with an initial cash outflow followed by one or more future cash inflows. Put another way, after the initial investment is made (cash outflow), all the cash flows in each future year are positive (inflows). For example, the purchase of a bond involves a conventional cash flow. You purchase the bond for a price (cash outflow), and in the future you receive coupon payments and a principal payment at maturity (cash inflows).

conventional cash flow
a cash flow pattern made up of an initial cash outflow that is followed by one or more cash inflows

Let's look more closely at the kinds of situations in which the NPV and the IRR methods agree. A good way to visualize the relation between the IRR and NPV methods is to graph NPV as a function of the discount rate. The graph, called an **NPV profile**, shows the NPV of the project at various costs of capital.

NPV profile
a graph showing NPV as a function of the discount rate

Exhibit 10.9 shows the NPV profile for the Ford project. We have placed the NPVs on the vertical axis, or y-axis, and the discount rates on the horizontal axis, or x-axis. We used the calculations from our earlier example and made some additional NPV calculations at various discount rates, as follows:

Discount Rate	NPV ($ thousands)
0%	$160
5	94
10	37
15	−12
20	−54
25	−92
30	−124

As you can see, a discount rate of 0 percent corresponds with an NPV of $160,000; a discount rate of 5 percent with an NPV of $94,000; and so forth. As the discount rate increases, the NPV curve declines smoothly. Not surprisingly, the curve intersects the x-axis at precisely the point where the NPV is 0 and the IRR is 13.7 percent.

The NPV profile in Exhibit 10.9 illustrates why the NPV and IRR methods lead to identical accept-reject decisions for the Ford project. The IRR of 13.7 percent precisely marks the point at which the NPV changes from a positive to a negative value.

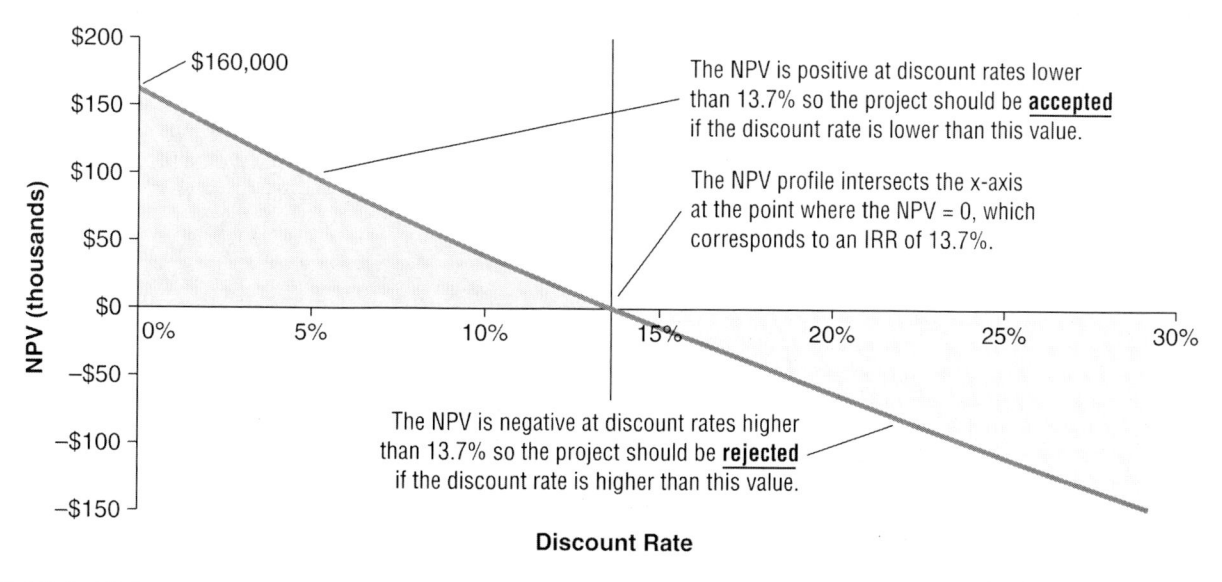

Exhibit 10.9
NPV Profile for the Ford Project

In the NPV profile for the Ford project, the NPV value is on the vertical (y) axis and the discount rate is on the horizontal (x) axis. You can see that as the discount rate increases, the NPV profile curve declines smoothly and intersects the x-axis at precisely the point where the NPV is 0 and the IRR is 13.7 percent—the point at which the NPV changes from a positive to a negative value. Thus, the NPV and IRR methods lead to identical accept-or-reject decisions for the Ford project.

Whenever a project is independent and has conventional cash flows, the result will be as shown in the exhibit. The NPV will decline as the discount rate increases, and the IRR and the NPV methods will result in the same capital expenditure decision.

When the NPV and IRR Methods Disagree

We have seen that the IRR and NPV methods lead to identical investment decisions for capital projects that are independent and that have conventional cash flows. However, if either of these conditions is not met, the IRR and NPV methods can produce different accept-reject decisions.

UNCONVENTIONAL CASH FLOWS

Unconventional cash flows can cause a conflict between the NPV and IRR decision rules. In some instances the cash flows for an unconventional project are just the reverse of those of a conventional project: the initial cash flow is positive, and all subsequent cash flows are negative. For example, consider a life insurance company that sells a lifetime annuity to a retired person. The company receives a single cash payment, which is the price of the annuity (cash inflow), and then makes monthly payments to the retiree for the rest of his or her life (cash outflows). In this case, we need only reverse the IRR decision rule and accept the project if the IRR is *less* than the cost of capital to make the IRR and NPV methods agree. The intuition in this example is that the life insurance company is effectively borrowing money from the retiree and the IRR is a measure of the cost of that money. The cost of capital is the rate at which the life insurance company can borrow elsewhere. An IRR less than the cost of capital means that the lifetime annuity provides the insurance company with money at a lower cost than alternative sources.

When a project's future cash flows include both positive and negative cash flows, the situation is more complicated. An example of such a project is an assembly line that will require one or more major renovations over its lifetime. Another common business situation is a project that has conventional cash flows except for the final cash flow, which is negative. The final cash flow might be negative because extensive environmental cleanup is required at the end of the project, such as the cost for decommissioning a nuclear power plant, or because the equipment originally purchased has little or no salvage value and is expensive to remove.

Consider an example. Suppose a firm invests in a gold-mining operation that costs $55 million and has an expected life of two years. In the first year, the project generates a cash inflow of $150 million. In the second year, extensive environmental and site restoration is required, so the expected cash flow is a negative $100 million. The time line for these cash flows follows.

```
                0                       1                      2  Year
                ├───────────────────────┼──────────────────────┤
Cash flow    -$55                    $150                   -$100
(millions)
```

Once again, the best way to understand the effect of these cash flows is to look at an NPV profile. Shown here are NPV calculations we made at various discount rates to generate the data necessary to plot the NPV profile shown in Exhibit 10.10:

Discount Rate	NPV ($ millions)
0%	−$5.00
10	−1.28
20	0.56
30	1.21
40	1.12
50	0.56
60	−0.31
70	−1.37

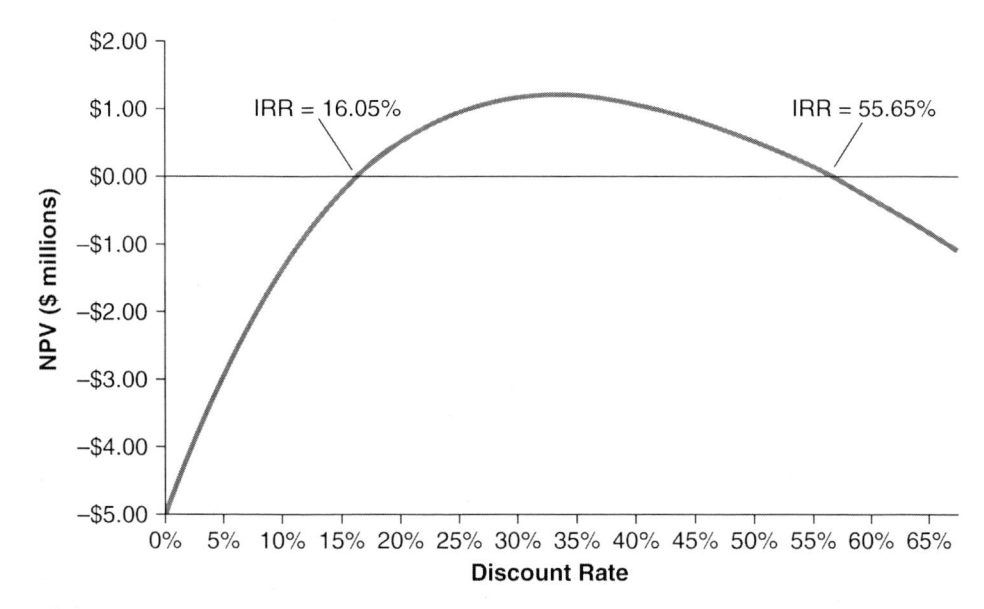

Exhibit 10.10
NPV Profile for Gold-Mining Operation Showing Multiple IRR Solutions

The gold-mining operation has unconventional cash flows. Because there are two cash flow sign reversals, we end up with two IRRs—16.05 percent and 55.65 percent—neither of them correct. In situations like this, the IRR provides a solution that is suspect, and therefore, the results should not be used for capital budgeting decisions.

Looking at the data in the table, you can probably spot a problem. The NPV is initially negative (−$5.00); then, at a discount rate of 20 percent, switches to positive ($0.56); and then, at a discount rate of 60 percent, switches back to negative (−$0.31).

The NPV profile in Exhibit 10.10 shows the results of this pattern: we have two IRRs, one at 16.05 percent and the other at 55.65 percent. Which is the correct IRR, or are both correct? Actually, there is no correct answer; the results are meaningless, and you should not try to interpret them. Thus, in this situation, the IRR technique provides information that is suspect and should not be used for decision making.

How many IRR solutions can there be for a given cash flow? The maximum number of IRR solutions is equal to the number of sign reversals in the cash flow stream. For a project with a conventional cash flow, there is only one cash flow sign reversal; thus, there is only one IRR solution. In our mining example, there are two cash flow sign reversals; thus, there are two IRR solutions.

Finally, for some cash flow patterns, it is impossible to compute an IRR. These situations can occur when the initial cash flow ($t = 0$) is either a cash inflow or outflow and is followed by cash flows with two or more sign reversals. An example of such a cash flow pattern is $NCF_0 = \$15$, $NCF_1 = -\$25$, and $NCF_2 = \$20$. This type of cash flow pattern might occur on a building project where the contractor is given a prepayment, usually the cost of materials and supplies ($15); then does the construction and pays the labor cost (−$25); and finally, upon completion of the work, receives the final payment ($20). Note that when it is not possible to compute an IRR, the project either has a positive NPV or a negative NPV for all possible discount rates. In this example, the NPV is always positive.

MUTUALLY EXCLUSIVE PROJECTS

The other situation in which the IRR can lead to incorrect decisions is when capital projects are mutually exclusive—that is, when accepting one project means rejecting the other. For example, suppose you own a small store in the business district of Seattle that is currently vacant. You are looking at two business opportunities: opening an upscale coffee house or opening a copy center. Clearly, you cannot pursue both projects at the same location; these two projects are mutually exclusive.

When you have mutually exclusive projects, how do you select the best alternative? If you are using the NPV method, the answer is easy. You select the project that has the highest NPV because it will increase the value of the firm by the largest amount. If you are using the IRR method, it would seem logical to select the project with the highest IRR. In this case, though, the logic is wrong! You cannot tell which mutually exclusive project to select just by looking at the projects' IRRs.

Let's consider another example to illustrate the problem. The cash flows for two projects, A and B, are as follows:

Year	Project A	Project B
0	−$100	−$100
1	50	20
2	40	30
3	30	50
4	30	65

The IRR is 20.7 percent for project A and 19.0 percent for project B. Because the two projects are mutually exclusive, only one project can be accepted. If you were following the IRR decision rule, you would accept project A. However, as you will see, it turns out that project B might be the better choice.

The following table shows the NPVs for the two projects at several discount rates:

Discount Rate	NPV of Project A	NPV of Project B
0%	$50.0	$65.0
5%	34.5	42.9
10%	21.5	24.9
13%	14.8	15.7
15%	10.6	10.1
20%	1.3	−2.2
25%	−6.8	−12.6
30%	−13.7	−21.3
IRR	20.7%	19.0%

Notice that the project with the higher NPV depends on what rate of return is used to discount the cash flows. Our example shows a conflict in ranking order between the IRR and NPV methods at discount rates between 0 and 13 percent. In this range, project B has the lower IRR, but it has the higher NPV and should be the project selected. If the discount rate is above 15 percent, however, project A has the higher NPV as well as the higher IRR. In this range there is no conflict between the two evaluation methods.

Now take a look at Exhibit 10.11, which shows the NPV profiles for projects A and B. As you can see, there is a point, called the **crossover point**, at which the NPV profiles for projects A and B intersect. The crossover point here is at a discount rate of 14.3 percent. For any cost of capital above 14.3 percent, the NPV for project A is higher than that for project B; thus, project A should be selected if its NPV is positive. For any cost of capital below the crossover point, project B should be selected.

Another conflict involving mutually exclusive projects concerns comparisons of projects that have significantly different costs. The IRR does not adjust for these differences in size. What the IRR gives us is a rate of return on each dollar invested. In contrast, the NPV method computes the total dollar value created by the project. The difference in results can be significant, as can be seen in Decision-Making Example 10.2.

crossover point

the discount rate at which the NPV profiles of two projects cross and, thus, at which the NPVs of the projects are equal

10.5 Internal Rate of Return

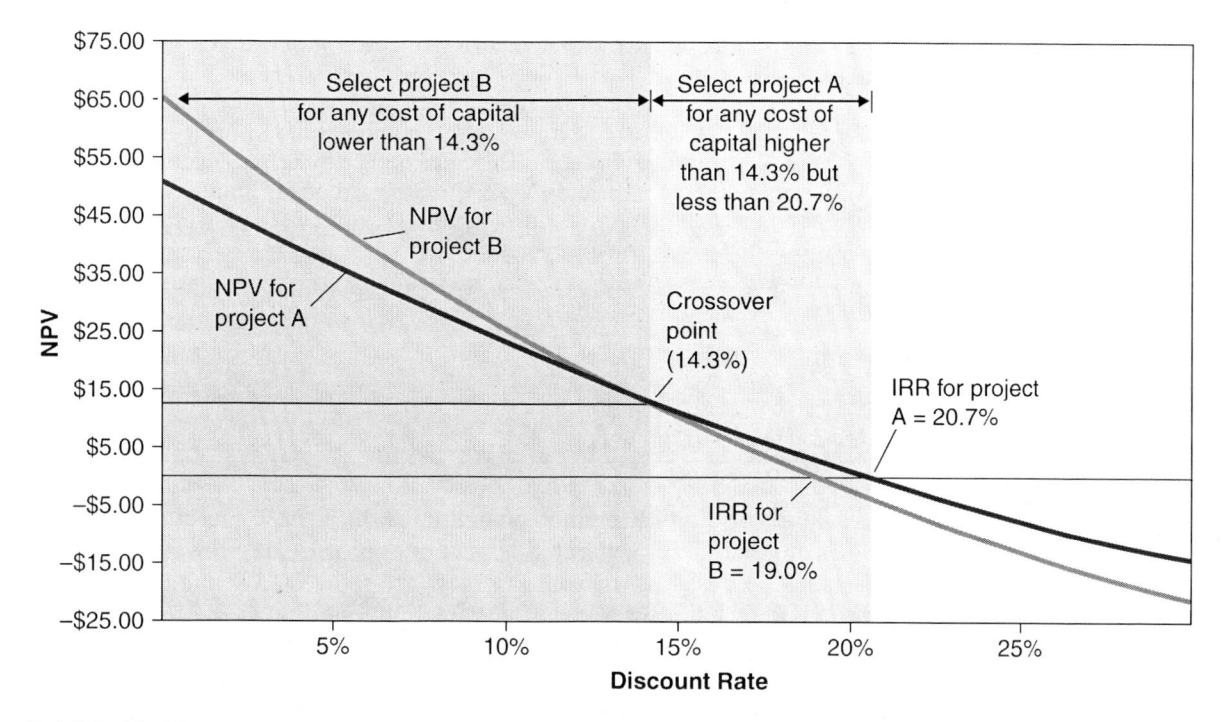

Exhibit 10.11

NPV Profiles for Two Mutually Exclusive Projects

The NPV profiles for two projects often cross over each other. When evaluating mutually exclusive projects, it is helpful to know where this crossover point is. For projects A and B in the exhibit, the crossover point is at 14.3 percent. For any cost of capital above 14.3 percent but below 20.7 percent the NPV for project A is higher than that for project B and is positive; thus, project A should be selected. For any cost of capital below the crossover point, the NPV of project B is higher, and project B should be selected.

The Lemonade Stand versus the Convenience Store

DECISION-MAKING EXAMPLE 10.2

Situation: Suppose you work for an entrepreneur who owns a number of small businesses in Fresno, California, as well as a small piece of property near California State University at Fresno, which he believes would be an ideal site for a student-oriented convenience store. His 12-year-old son, who happens to be in the office after school, says he has a better idea: his father should open a lemonade stand. Your boss tells you to find the NPV and IRR for both projects, assuming a 10 percent discount rate. After collecting data, you present the following analysis:

Year	Lemonade Stand	Convenience Store
0	−$1,000	−$1,000,000
1	850	372,000
2	850	372,000
3	850	372,000
4	850	372,000
IRR	76.2%	18.0%
NPV	$1,694	$179,190

Assuming the projects are mutually exclusive, which should be selected?

(continued)

> **Decision:** Your boss, who favors the IRR method, looks at the analysis and declares his son a genius. The IRR decision rule suggests that the lemonade stand, with its 76.2 percent rate of return, is the project to choose! You point out that the goal of capital budgeting is to select projects or combinations of projects that maximize the value of the firm, his business. The convenience store adds by far the greater value: $179,190 compared with only $1,694 for the lemonade stand. Although the lemonade stand has a high rate of return, its small size precludes it from being competitive against the larger project.[1]

Modified Internal Rate of Return (MIRR)

A major weakness of the IRR method compared with the NPV method concerns the rate at which the cash flows generated by a capital project are reinvested. The NPV method assumes that cash flows from a project are reinvested at the cost of capital, whereas the IRR technique assumes they are reinvested at the IRR. Determining which is the better assumption depends on which rate better represents the rate that firms can actually earn when they reinvest a project's cash flows over time. It is generally believed that the cost of capital, which is often lower than the IRR, better reflects the rate that firms are likely to earn. Using the IRR may thus involve overly optimistic assumptions regarding reinvestment rates.

To eliminate the reinvestment rate assumption of the IRR, some practitioners prefer to calculate the **modified internal rate of return (MIRR)**. In this approach, each operating cash flow is converted to a future value at the end of the project's life, compounded at the cost of capital. These values are then summed up to get the project's *terminal value (TV)*. The MIRR is the interest rate that equates the project's cost (PV_{Cost}), or cash outflows, with the future value of the project's cash inflows at the end of the project (PV_{TV}).[2] Because each future value is computed using the cost of capital as the interest rate, the reinvestment rate problem is eliminated.

We can set up the equation for the MIRR in the same way we set up Equation 10.4 for the IRR:

$$\text{PV(Cost of the project)} = \text{PV(Cash inflows)} \tag{10.5}$$
$$PV_{Cost} = PV_{TV}$$
$$PV_{Cost} = \frac{TV}{(1 + MIRR)^n}$$

> **modified internal rate of return (MIRR)**
>
> an internal rate of return (IRR) measure which assumes that cash inflows are reinvested at the opportunity cost of capital until the end of the project

To compute the MIRR, we have to make two preliminary calculations. First, we need to calculate the value of PV_{Cost}, which is the present value of the cash outflows that make up the investment cost of the project. Since for most capital projects, the investment cost cash flows are incurred at the beginning of the project, $t = 0$, there is often no need to calculate a present value. If investment costs are incurred over time ($t > 0$), then the cash flows must be discounted at the cost of capital for the appropriate time period.

Second, we need to compute the terminal value (TV). To do this, we find the future value of each operating cash flow at the end of the project's life, compounded at the

---

[1] The solution ignores the opportunity cost of the land. As we will discuss in Chapter 11, if your boss could sell the land or use it land in some other way that has value, then there is an opportunity cost associated with using it for the convenience store.

[2] As we pointed out in Chapter 5, financial decision-making problems can be solved either by discounting cash flows to the beginning of the project or by using compounding to find the future value of cash flows at the end of a project's life.

cost of capital. We then sum up these future values to get the project's TV. Mathematically, the TV can be expressed as:

$$TV = CF_1(1+k)^{n-1} + CF_2(1+k)^{n-2} + \cdots + CF_n(1+k)^{n-n}$$
$$= \sum_{t=1}^{n} CF_t(1+k)^{n-t}$$

where:

TV = the project's terminal value
CF_t = cash flow from operations in period t
k = the cost of capital
n = the project life

Once we have computed the values of PV_{Cost} and TV, we use Equation 10.5 to compute the MIRR.

To illustrate, let's return to the Ford Motor Company example shown in Exhibit 10.8. Recall that the cost of the project is $560, incurred at $t = 0$, and that the discount rate is 12 percent. To determine the MIRR for the project, we start by calculating the terminal value of the cash flows, as shown on the following time line:

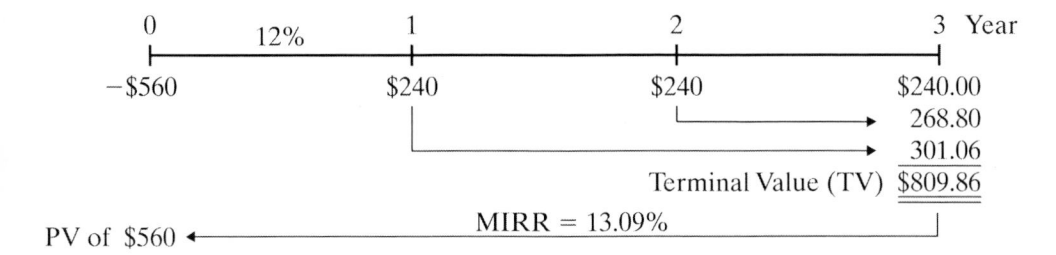

```
0           12%        1              2            3  Year
|----------------------|--------------|------------|
-$560                 $240          $240         $240.00
                                                  268.80
                                                  301.06
                                Terminal Value (TV) $809.86
PV of $560 ←            MIRR = 13.09%
```

The terminal value of $809.86 equals the sum of the $240 in year 1 compounded at 12 percent for two years plus the $240 in year 2 compounded at 12 percent for 1 year plus the $240 in year 3. Mathematically, this calculation is:

$$TV = CF_1(1+k)^{n-1} + CF_2(1+k)^{n-2} + \cdots + CF_n(1+k)^{n-n}$$
$$= \$240(1.12)^2 + \$240(1.12) + \$240 = \$809.86$$

With the information that the cost of the project is $560 and the TV is $809.86, we can calculate the MIRR using Equation 10.5:

$$PV_{Cost} = \frac{TV}{(1+MIRR)^n}$$
$$\$560 = \frac{\$809.86}{(1+MIRR)^3}$$
$$(1+MIRR)^3 = \frac{\$809.86}{\$560} = 1.4462$$
$$(1+MIRR) = (1.4462)^{1/3} = 1.1309$$
$$MIRR = 1.1309 - 1 = 0.1309$$
$$= 13.09\%$$

At 13.09 percent, the MIRR is higher than Ford's cost of capital of 12 percent, so the project should be accepted.

IRR versus NPV: A Final Comment

The IRR method, as noted, is an important alternative to the NPV method. As we have seen, it accounts for the time value of money, which is not true of methods such as the payback period and accounting rate of return. Furthermore, the IRR technique has

To read an article that warns finance managers using the IRR about the method's pitfalls, visit www.cfo.com/printable/article.cfm/3304945?f=options.

great intuitive appeal. Many business practitioners are in the habit of thinking in terms of rates of return, whether the rates relate to their common-stock portfolios or their firms' capital expenditures. To these practitioners, the IRR method just seems to make sense. Indeed, we suspect that the IRR's popularity with business managers results more from its simple intuitive appeal than from its merit.

On the downside, we have seen that the IRR method has several flaws. One of these can be eliminated by using the MIRR. Nevertheless, we believe that the NPV should be the primary method used to make capital budgeting decisions. Decisions made by the NPV method are consistent with the goal of maximizing the value of the firm's stock, and the NPV tells management the dollar amount by which each project is expected to increase the value of the firm.

Review of Internal Rate of Return (IRR)

Decision Rule: IRR > Cost of capital ⇨ Accept the project.
IRR < Cost of capital ⇨ Reject the project.

Key Advantages	Key Disadvantages
1. Intuitively easy to understand. 2. Based on discounted cash flow technique.	1. With nonconventional cash flows, IRR approach can yield no usable answer or multiple answers. 2. A lower IRR can be better if a cash inflow is followed by cash outflows. 3. With mutually exclusive projects, IRR can lead to incorrect investment decisions.

Before You Go On

1. What is the IRR method?
2. In capital budgeting, what is a conventional cash flow pattern?
3. Why should the NPV method be the primary decision tool used in making capital investment decisions?

10.6 Capital Budgeting in Practice

LEARNING OBJECTIVE 6

Capital expenditures are big-ticket items in the U.S. economy. According to the Department of Commerce, U.S. businesses invested $1.15 trillion in capital goods in 2005. The sectors with the largest capital expenditures were manufacturing, $165.2 billion; finance and insurance, $161.6 billion; and real estate and rental and leasing, $103.2 billion. Capital investments also represent large expenditures for individual firms, though the amount spent can vary widely from year to year. For example, over the last several years, Verizon has expanded rapidly to increase its market share in the wireless business. Its capital expenditures, at 20.4 percent of sales, were among the highest for Fortune 1000 firms in 2005. More typical are the capital expenditure figures for Exxon, Cisco, and Kellogg Company, shown in the accompanying table. Given the large dollar amounts and the strategic importance of capital expenditures, it is no surprise that corporate managers spend considerable time and energy analyzing them.

Company	2005 Capital Expenditures ($ billions)	2005 Sales ($ billions)	Capital Expenditures as a Percent of Sales
Verizon	$15.3	$75.1	20.4%
Exxon Mobil	13.8	370.7	3.7
Cisco	0.7	24.8	2.8
Kellogg Co.	0.4	10.2	3.9

Exhibit 10.12 Capital Budgeting Techniques Used by Business Firms

Capital Budgeting Tool	Percent of Surveyed Firms That Use the Technique Frequently	
	1981	1999
Payback period	5.0	56.7
Accounting rate of return (ARR)	10.7	20.3
Internal rate of return (IRR)	65.3	75.7
Net present value (NPV)	16.5	74.9

Sources: Stanley, Marjorie T. and Stanley B. Block, "A Survey of Multinational Capital Budgeting" *The Financial Review*, March 1984. Graham, John R. and Campbell R. Harvey, "The Theory and Practice of Corporate Finance," *Journal of Financial Economics*, May/June 2001.

The exhibit summarizes evidence from two studies that examined the use of capital budgeting techniques by businesses. As you can see, over time more firms have come to use the NPV and IRR techniques. Surprisingly, though, even in 1999, 20.3 percent still computed the accounting rate of return.

Practitioners' Methods of Choice

Because of the importance of capital budgeting, over the years a number of surveys have asked financial managers what techniques they actually use in making capital investment decisions. Exhibit 10.12, which summarizes the results from two such studies, reveals significant changes over time. As shown, in 1981 only 16.5 percent of the financial managers surveyed frequently used the NPV approach, and the payback period and accounting rate of return approaches were used even less frequently. Most firms, 65.3 percent, used the IRR method. However, practices changed in the 1980s and 1990s. By 1999, 74.9 percent of the firms surveyed were frequently using the NPV technique, 75.7 percent were using the IRR, and 56.7 percent were using the payback period method. As you can see, the most recent findings reflect a much better alignment between practitioners and the academic community. As you can also see, many financial managers use multiple capital budgeting tools.

An article that surveys the use of capital budgeting techniques by the CFOs of Fortune 500 companies can be found at faculty.fuqua.duke.edu/~jgraham/website/SurveyJACF.pdf.

Ongoing and Postaudit Reviews

Management should systematically review the status of all ongoing capital projects and perform postaudit reviews on all completed capital projects. In a **postaudit review**, management compares the actual performance of a project with what was projected in the capital budgeting proposal. For example, suppose a new microchip was expected to earn a 20 percent IRR, but the product's actual IRR turned out to be 9 percent. A postaudit examination would determine why the project failed to achieve its expected financial goals. Project reviews keep all people involved in the capital budgeting process honest because they know that the project and their performance will be reviewed and that they will be held accountable for the results.

postaudit review
an audit to compare actual project results with the results projected in the capital budgeting proposal

Managers should also conduct *ongoing reviews* of capital projects in progress. Such a review should challenge the business plan, including the cash flow projections and the operating cost assumptions. For example, Intel undoubtedly has periodically reviewed the viability of its $2.5 billion computer chip wafer plant in China and made adjustments to reflect changing business conditions. Business plans are management's best estimates of future events at the time they are prepared, but as new information becomes available, the decision to undertake a capital project and the nature of that project must be reassessed.

Management must also evaluate people responsible for implementing a capital project. They should monitor whether the project's revenues and expenses are meeting projections. If the project is not at plan, the difficult task for management is to determine whether the problem is a flawed plan or poor execution by the implementation team. Good plans can fail if they are poorly executed at the operating level.

> **Before You Go On**
>
> 1. What shifts have taken place in the capital budgeting techniques used by U.S. companies?

Summary of Learning Objectives

1. **Discuss why capital budgeting decisions are the most important investment decisions made by a firm's management.**

   Capital budgeting is the process by which management decides which productive assets the firm should invest in. Because capital expenditures involve large amounts of money, are critical to achieving the firm's strategic plan, define the firm's line of business over the long term, and determine the firm's profitability for years to come, they are considered the most important investment decisions made by management.

2. **Explain the benefits of using the net present value (NPV) method to analyze capital expenditure decisions, and be able to calculate the NPV for a capital project.**

   The net present value (NPV) method leads to better investment decisions than other techniques because the NPV method does the following: (1) it uses the discounted cash flow valuation approach, which accounts for the time value of money, and (2) provides a direct measure of how much a capital project is expected to increase the dollar value of the firm. Thus, NPV is consistent with the top management goal of maximizing stockholder value. NPV calculations are described in Section 10.2 and Learning by Doing Application 10.1.

3. **Describe the strengths and weaknesses of the payback period as a capital expenditure decision-making tool, and be able to compute the payback period for a capital project.**

   The payback period is the length of time it will take for the cash flows from a project to recover the cost of the project. The payback period is widely used, mainly because it is simple to apply and easy to understand. It also provides a simple measure of liquidity risk because it tells management how quickly the firm will get its money back. The payback period has a number of shortcomings, however. For one thing, the payback period, as most commonly computed, ignores the time value of money. We can overcome this objection by using discounted cash flows to calculate the payback period. Regardless of how the payback period is calculated, however, it fails to take account of cash flows recovered after the payback period. Thus, the payback period is biased in favor of short-lived projects. Also, the hurdle rate used to identify what payback period is acceptable is arbitrarily determined. Payback period calculations are described in Section 10.3 and Learning by Doing Application 10.2.

4. **Explain why the accounting rate of return (ARR) is not recommended as a capital expenditure decision-making tool.**

   The ARR is based on accounting numbers, such as book value and net income, rather than cash flow data. As such, it is not a true rate of return. Instead of discounting a project's cash flows over time, it simply gives us a number based on average figures from the income statement and balance sheet. Furthermore, as with the payback method, there is no economic rationale for establishing the hurdle rate. Finally, the ARR does not account for the size of the projects when a choice between two projects of different sizes must be made.

5. **Be able to compute the internal rate of return (IRR) for a capital project, and discuss the conditions under which the IRR technique and the NPV technique produce different results**

   The IRR is the expected rate of return for an investment project; it is calculated as the discount rate that equates the present value of a project's expected cash inflows to the present value of the project's outflows—in other words, as the discount rate at which the NPV is equal to zero. Calculations are shown in Section 10.5 and Learning by Doing Application 10.3. If a project's IRR is greater than the required rate of return, the cost of capital, the project is accepted. The IRR rule often gives the same investment decision for a project as the NPV rule. However, the IRR method does have operational pitfalls that can lead to incorrect decisions. Specifically, when a project's cash flows are unconventional, the IRR calculation may yield no solution or more than one IRR. In addition, the IRR technique cannot be used to rank projects that are mutually exclusive because the project with the highest IRR may not be the project that would add the greatest value to the firm if accepted—that is, the project with the highest NPV.

6. **Explain the benefits of a postaudit review of a capital project.**

   Postaudit reviews of capital projects allow management to determine whether the project's goals were met and to quantify the benefits or costs of the project. By conducting these reviews, managers can avoid similar mistakes and possibly better recognize opportunities.

Summary of Key Equations

Equation	Description	Formula
10.1	Net present value	$\text{NPV} = \text{NCF}_0 + \dfrac{\text{NCF}_1}{1+k} + \dfrac{\text{NCF}_2}{(1+k)^2} + \cdots + \dfrac{\text{NCF}_n}{(1+k)^n}$ $= \sum_{t=0}^{n} \dfrac{\text{NCF}_t}{(1+k)^t}$
10.2	Payback period	$\text{PB} = \text{Years before cost recovery} + \dfrac{\text{Remaining cost to recover}}{\text{Cash flow during the year}}$
10.3	Accounting rate of return	$\text{ARR} = \dfrac{\text{Average net income}}{\text{Average book value}}$
10.4	Internal rate of return	$\text{NPV} = \sum_{t=0}^{n} \dfrac{\text{NCF}_t}{(1+\text{IRR})^t} = 0$
10.5	Modified internal rate of return	$\text{PV}_{\text{Cost}} = \dfrac{\text{TV}}{(1+\text{MIRR})^n}$

Self-Study Problems

10.1 Premium Manufacturing Company is evaluating two forklift systems to use in its plant that produces the towers for a windmill power farm. The costs and the cash flows from these systems are shown here. If the company uses a 12 percent discount rate for all projects, determine which forklift system should be purchased using the net present value (NPV) approach.

	Year 0	Year 1	Year 2	Year 3
Otis Forklifts	−$3,123,450	$979,225	$1,358,886	$2,111,497
Craigmore Forklifts	−$4,137,410	$875,236	$1,765,225	$2,865,110

10.2 Rutledge, Inc., has invested $100,000 in a project that will produce cash flows of $45,000, $37,500, and $42,950 over the next three years. Find the payback period for the project.

10.3 Perryman Crafts Corp. is evaluating two independent capital projects that will each cost the company $250,000. The two projects will provide the following cash flows:

Year	Project A	Project B
1	$80,750	$32,450
2	93,450	76,125
3	40,235	153,250
4	145,655	96,110

Which project will be chosen if the company's payback criterion is three years? What if the company accepts all projects as long as the payback period is less than five years?

10.4 Terrell Corp. is looking into purchasing a machine for its business that will cost $117,250 and will be depreciated on a straight-line basis over a five-year period. The sales and expenses (excluding depreciation) for the next five years are shown in the following table. The company's tax rate is 34 percent.

	Year 1	Year 2	Year 3	Year 4	Year 5
Sales	$123,450	$176,875	$242,455	$255,440	$267,125
Expenses	$137,410	$126,488	$141,289	$143,112	$133,556

The company will accept all projects that provide an accounting rate of return (ARR) of at least 45 percent. Should the company accept this project?

10.5 Refer to Problem 10.1. Compute the IRR for each of the two systems. Is the choice different from the one determined by NPV?

Solutions to Self-Study Problems

10.1 NPVs for two forklift systems:
NPV for Otis Forklifts:

$$NPV = \sum_{t=0}^{n} \frac{NCF_t}{(1+k)^t}$$

$$= -\$3,123,450 + \frac{\$979,225}{1 + 0.12} + \frac{\$1,358,886}{(1.12)^2} + \frac{\$2,111,497}{(1.12)^3}$$

$$= -\$3,123,450 + \$874,308 + \$1,083,296 + \$1,502,922$$

$$= \$337,076$$

NPV for Craigmore Forklifts:

$$NPV = \sum_{t=0}^{n} \frac{NCF_t}{(1+k)^t}$$

$$= -\$4,137,410 + \frac{\$875,236}{1 + 0.12} + \frac{\$1,765,225}{(1.12)^2} + \frac{\$2,865,110}{(1.12)^3}$$

$$= -\$4,137,410 + \$781,461 + \$1,407,227 + \$2,039,329$$

$$= \$90,607$$

Premium should purchase the Otis forklift since it has a larger NPV.

10.2 Payback period for Rutledge project:

Year	CF	Cumulative Cash Flow
0	($100,000)	($100,000)
1	45,000	(55,000)
2	37,500	(17,500)
3	42,950	25,450

$$\text{Payback period} = \text{Years before cost recovery} + \frac{\text{Remaining cost to recover}}{\text{Cash flow during the year}}$$

$$= 2 + \frac{\$17,500}{\$42,950}$$

$$= 2.41 \text{ years}$$

10.3 Payback periods for Perryman projects A and B:

Project A

Year	Cash Flow	Cumulative Cash Flows
0	($250,000)	($250,000)
1	80,750	(169,250)
2	93,450	(75,800)
3	40,235	(35,565)
4	145,655	110,090

Project B

Year	Cash Flow	Cumulative Cash Flows
0	($250,000)	($250,000)
1	32,450	(217,550)
2	76,125	(141,425)
3	153,250	11,825
4	96,110	107,935

Payback period for project A:

$$\text{Payback period} = \text{Years before cost recovery} + \frac{\text{Remaining cost to recover}}{\text{Cash flow during the year}}$$

$$= 3 + \frac{\$35{,}565}{\$145{,}655}$$

$$= 3.24 \text{ years}$$

Payback period for Project B:

$$\text{Payback period} = \text{Years before cost recovery} + \frac{\text{Remaining cost to recover}}{\text{Cash flow during the year}}$$

$$= 2 + \frac{\$141{,}425}{\$153{,}250}$$

$$= 2.92 \text{ years}$$

If the payback period is three years, project B will be chosen. If the payback criterion is five years, both A and B will be chosen.

10.4 Evaluation of Terrell Corp. project:

	Year 1	Year 2	Year 3	Year 4	Year 5
Sales	$123,450	$176,875	$242,455	$255,440	$267,125
Expenses	137,410	126,488	141,289	143,112	133,556
Depreciation	23,450	23,450	23,450	23,450	23,450
EBIT	($37,410)	$26,937	$77,716	$88,878	$110,119
Taxes (34%)	12,719	9,159	26,423	30,219	37,440
Net Income	($24,691)	$17,778	$51,293	$58,659	$72,679
Beginning Book Value	117,250	93,800	70,350	46,900	23,450
Less: Depreciation	(23,450)	(23,450)	(23,450)	(23,450)	(23,450)
Ending Book Value	$93,800	$70,350	$46,900	$23,450	$0

$$\text{Average net income} = (-\$24{,}691 + \$17{,}778 + \$51{,}293 + \$58{,}659 + \$72{,}679)/5$$
$$= \$35{,}143.60$$
$$\text{Average book value} = (\$93{,}800 + \$70{,}350 + \$46{,}900 + \$23{,}450 + \$0)/5$$
$$= \$46{,}900.00$$
$$\text{Accounting rate of return} = \$35{,}143.60/\$46{,}900.00$$
$$= 74.93\%$$

The company should accept the project.

10.5 IRRs for two forklift systems:

Otis Forklifts:
First compute the IRR by the trial-and-error approach.

NPV (Otis) = $337,075 > 0
Use a higher discount rate to get NPV = 0!
At $k = 15$ percent:

$$\text{NPV} = -\$3{,}123{,}450 + \frac{\$979{,}225}{1 + 0.15} + \frac{\$1{,}358{,}886}{(1.15)^2} + \frac{\$2{,}111{,}497}{(1.15)^3}$$

$$= -\$3{,}123{,}450 + \$851{,}500 + \$1{,}027{,}513 + \$1{,}388{,}344$$

$$= \$143{,}907$$

Try a higher rate. At $k = 17$ percent:

NPV = −$3,123,450 + $836,944 + $992,685 + $1,318,357
    = $24,536

Try a higher rate. At $k = 17.5$ percent:

NPV = −$3,123,450 + $833,383 + $984,254 + $1,301,598
    = −$4,215

Thus, the IRR for Otis is less than 17.5 percent. Using a financial calculator, you can find the exact rate to be 17.43 percent.

Craigmore Forklifts:
First compute the IRR using the trial-and-error approach.

NPV (Craigmore) = $90,606 > 0

Use a higher discount rate to get NPV = 0!
At k = 15 percent:

$$\text{NPV} = -\$4,137,410 + \frac{\$875,236}{1.15} + \frac{\$1,765,225}{(1.12)^2} + \frac{\$2,865,110}{(1.12)^3}$$
$$= -\$4,137,410 + \$761,075 + \$1,334,764 + \$1,883,856$$
$$= -\$157,715$$

Try a lower rate. At k = 13 percent:

$$\text{NPV} = -\$4,137,410 + \$774,545 + \$1,382,430 + \$1,985,665$$
$$= \$5,230$$

Try a higher rate. At k = 13.1 percent:

$$\text{NPV} = -\$4,137,410 + \$773,860 + \$1,379,987 + \$1,980,403$$
$$= -\$3,161$$

Thus, the IRR for Craigmore is less than 13.1 percent. The exact rate is 13.06 percent. Based on the IRR, we would still pick Otis over Craigmore forklift systems.

Critical Thinking Questions

10.1 Explain why the cost of capital is referred to as the "hurdle" rate in capital budgeting.

10.2 **a.** A company is building a new plant on the outskirts of Smallesville. The town has offered to donate the land, and as part of the agreement, the company will have to build an access road from the main highway to the plant. How will the project of building of the road be classified in capital budgeting analysis?
b. Sykes, Inc., is considering two projects: a plant expansion and a new computer system for the firm's production department. Classify each of these projects as independent, mutually exclusive, or contingent projects and explain your reasoning.
c. Your firm is currently considering the upgrading of the operating systems of all the firm's computers. The firm can choose the Linux operating system that a local computer services firm has offered to install and maintain. Microsoft has also put in a bid to install the new Windows Vista operating system for businesses. What type of project is this?

10.3 In the context of capital budgeting, what is "capital rationing"?

10.4 Explain why we use discounted cash flows instead of actual market price data.

10.5 **a.** A firm takes on a project that would earn a return of 12 percent. If the appropriate cost of capital is also 12 percent, did the firm make the right decision? Explain.
b. What is the impact on the firm if it accepts a project with a negative NPV?

10.6 Identify the weaknesses of the payback period method.

10.7 What are the strengths and weaknesses of the accounting rate of return approach?

10.8 Under what circumstances might the IRR and NPV approaches have conflicting results?

10.9 A company estimates that an average-risk project has a cost of capital of 8 percent, a below-average risk project has a cost of capital of 6 percent, and an above-average risk project has a cost of capital of 10 percent. Which of the following independent projects should the company accept? Project A has below-average risk and a return of 6.5 percent. Project B has above-average risk and a return of 9 percent. Project C has average risk and a return of 7 percent.

10.10 Elkridge Construction Company has an overall (composite) cost of capital of 12 percent. This cost of capital reflects the cost of capital for an Elkridge Construction project with average risk. However, the firm takes on projects of various risk levels. The company experience suggests that low-risk projects have a cost of capital of 10 percent and high-risk projects have a cost of capital of 15 percent. Which of the following projects should the company select to maximize shareholder wealth?

Project	Expected Return	Risk
1. Single-family homes	13%	Low
2. Multifamily residential	12	Average
3. Commercial	18	High
4. Single-family homes	9	Low
5. Commercial	13	High

Questions and Problems

10.1 Net present value: Riggs Corp. is planning to spend $650,000 on a new marketing campaign. It believes that this action will result in additional cash flows of $325,000 over the next three years. If the discount rate is 17.5 percent, what is the NPV on this project?

BASIC

10.2 Net present value: Kingston, Inc., is looking to add a new machine at a cost of $4,133,250. The company expects this equipment will lead to cash flows of $814,322, $863,275, $937,250, $1,017,112, $1,212,960, and $1,225,000 over the next six years. If the appropriate discount rate is 15 percent, what is the NPV of this investment?

10.3 Net present value: Crescent Industries is planning to replace some existing machinery in its plant. The cost of the new equipment and the resulting cash flows are shown in the accompanying table. If the firm uses an 18 percent discount rate for projects like this, should the firm go ahead with the project?

Year	Cash Flow
0	−$3,300,000
1	875,123
2	966,222
3	1,145,000
4	1,250,399
5	1,504,445

10.4 Net present value: Franklin Mints, a confectioner, is looking to purchase a new jellybean-making machine at a cost of $312,500. The company projects that the cash flows from this investment will be $121,450 for the next seven years. If the appropriate discount rate is 14 percent, what is the NPV for the project?

10.5 Payback: Quebec, Inc., is purchasing machinery at a cost of $3,768,966. The company expects, as a result, cash flows of $979,225, $1,158,886, and $1,881,497 over the next three years. What is the payback period?

10.6 Payback: Northern Specialties just purchased inventory-management computer software at a cost of $1,645,276. Cost savings from the investment over the next six years will be reflected in the following cash flow stream: $212,455, $292,333, $387,479, $516,345, $645,766, and $618,325. What is the payback period on this investment?

10.7 Payback: Nakamichi Bancorp has made an investment in banking software at a cost of $1,875,000. The institution expects productivity gains and cost savings over the next several years. If the firm is expected to generate cash flows of $586,212, $713,277, $431,199, and $318,697 over the next four years, what is the investment's payback period?

10.8 Average accounting rate of return (ARR): Capitol Corp. is expecting to generate after-tax income of $63,435 over each of the next three years. The average book value of their equipment over that period will be $212,500. If the firm's acceptance decision on any project is based on an ARR of 37.5 percent, should this project be accepted?

10.9 Internal rate of return: Refer to Problem 10.4. What is the IRR that Franklin Mints can expect on this project?

10.10 Internal rate of return: Hathaway, Inc., a resort company, is refurbishing one of its hotels at a cost of $7.8 million. The firm expects that this will lead to additional cash flows of $1.8 million for the next six years. What is the IRR of this project? If the appropriate cost of capital is 12 percent, should it go ahead with this project?

10.11 Net present value: Champlain Corp. is investigating two computer systems. The Alpha 8300 costs $3,122,300 and will generate annual cost savings of $1,345,500 over the next

INTERMEDIATE

five years. The Beta 2100 system costs $3,750,000 and will produce cost savings of $1,125,000 in the first three years and then $2 million for the next two years. If the company's discount rate for similar projects is 14 percent, what is the NPV for the two systems? Which one should be chosen based on the NPV?

10.12 Net present value: Briarcrest Condiments is a spice-making firm. Recently, it developed a new process for producing spices. This calls for acquiring machinery that would cost $1,968,450. The machine will have a life of five years and will produce cash flows as shown in the table. What is the NPV if the discount rate is 15.9 percent?

Year	Cash Flow
1	$512,496
2	−242,637
3	814,558
4	887,225
5	712,642

10.13 Net present value: Cranjet Industries is expanding its product line and its production capacity. The costs and expected cash flows of the two independent projects are given in the following table. The firm uses a discount rate of 16.4 percent for such projects.
a. Are these projects independent or mutually exclusive?
b. What are the NPVs of the two projects?
c. Should both projects be accepted? or either? or neither? Explain your reasoning.

Year	Product Line Expansion	Production Capacity Expansion
0	−$2,575,000	−$8,137,250
1	600,000	2,500,000
2	875,000	2,500,000
3	875,000	2,500,000
4	875,000	3,250,000
5	875,000	3,250,000

10.14 Net present value: Emporia Mills is evaluating two heating systems. Costs and projected energy savings are given in the following table. The firm uses 11.5 percent to discount such project cash flows. Which system should be chosen?

Year	System 100	System 200
0	−$1,750,000	−$1,735,000
1	275,223	750,000
2	512,445	612,500
3	648,997	550,112
4	875,000	384,226

10.15 Payback: Creative Solutions, Inc., has invested $4,615,300 on equipment. The firm uses payback period criteria of not accepting any project that takes more than four years to recover costs. The company anticipates cash flows of $644,386, $812,178, $943,279, $1,364,997, $2,616,300, and $2,225,375 over the next six years. Does this investment meet the firm's payback criteria?

10.16 Discounted payback: Timeline Manufacturing Co. is evaluating two projects. The company uses payback criteria of three years or less. Project A has a cost of $912,855, and project B's cost will be $1,175,000. Cash flows from both projects are given in the following table. What are their discounted payback periods, and which will be accepted with a discount rate of 8 percent?

Year	Project A	Project B
1	$86,212	$586,212
2	313,562	413,277
3	427,594	231,199
4	285,552	

10.17 Payback: Regent Corp. is evaluating three competing pieces of equipment. Costs and cash flow projections for all three are given in the following table. Which would be the best choice based on payback period?

Year	Type 1	Type 2	Type 3
0	−$1,311,450	−$1,415,888	−$1,612,856
1	212,566	586,212	786,212
2	269,825	413,277	175,000
3	455,112	331,199	175,000
4	285,552	141,442	175,000
5	121,396		175,000
6			175,000

10.18 Discounted payback: Nugent Communication Corp. is investing $9,365,000 in new technologies. The company expects significant benefits in the first three years after installation (as can be seen by the cash flows), and a constant amount for four more years. What is the discounted payback period for the project assuming a discount rate of 10 percent?

Years	1	2	3	4–7
Cash Flows	$2,265,433	$4,558,721	$3,378,911	$1,250,000

10.19 Modified internal rate of return (MIRR): Morningside Bakeries has recently purchased equipment at a cost of $650,000. The firm expects to generate cash flows of $275,000 in each of the next four years. The cost of capital is 14 percent. What is the MIRR for this project?

10.20 Modified internal rate of return (MIRR): Sycamore Home Furnishings is looking to acquire a new machine that can create customized window treatments. The equipment will cost $263,400 and will generate cash flows of $85,000 over each of the next six years. If the cost of capital is 12 percent, what is the MIRR on this project?

10.21 Internal rate of return: Great Flights, Inc., an aviation firm, is exploring the purchase of three aircrafts at a total cost of $161 million. Cash flows from leasing these aircrafts is expected to build slowly as shown in the following table. What is the IRR on this project? The required rate of return is 15 percent.

Years	Cash Flow
1–4	$23,500,000
5–7	72,000,000
8–10	80,000,000

10.22 Internal rate of return: Compute the IRR on the following cash flow streams:
a. An initial investment of $25,000 followed by a single cash flow of $37,450 in year 6
b. An initial investment of $1 million followed by a single cash flow of $1,650,000 in year 4
c. An initial investment of $2 million followed by cash flows of $1,650,000 and $1,250,000 in years 2 and 4, respectively

10.23 Internal rate of return: Compute the IRR for the following project cash flows.
a. An initial outlay of $3,125,000 followed by annual cash flows of $565,325 for the next eight years
b. An initial investment of $33,750 followed by annual cash flows of $9,430 for the next five years
c. An initial outlay of $10,000 followed by annual cash flows of $2,500 for the next seven years

10.24 Draconian Measures, Inc., is evaluating two independent projects. The company uses a 13.8 percent discount rate for such projects. Cost and cash flows are shown in the table. What are the NPVs of the two projects? **ADVANCED**

Year	Project 1	Project 2
0	−$8,425,375	−$11,368,000
1	3,225,997	2,112,589
2	1,775,882	3,787,552
3	1,375,112	3,125,650
4	1,176,558	4,115,899
5	1,212,645	4,556,424
6	1,582,156	
7	1,365,882	

10.25 Refer to Problem 10.24.
 a. What are the IRRs for both projects?
 b. Does the IRR decision criterion differ from the earlier decisions?
 c. Explain how you would expect the management of Draconian Measures to decide.

10.26 Dravid, Inc., is currently evaluating three projects that are independent. The cost of funds can be either 13.6 percent or 14.8 percent depending on their financing plan. All three projects cost the same at $500,000. Expected cash flow streams are shown in the following table. Which projects would be accepted at a discount rate of 14.8 percent? What if the discount rate was 13.6 percent?

Year	Project 1	Project 2	Project 3
1	$ 0	$ 0	$245,125
2	125,000	0	212,336
3	150,000	500,000	112,500
4	375,000	500,000	74,000

10.27 Intrepid, Inc., is looking to invest in two or three independent projects. The costs and the cash flows are given in the following table. The appropriate cost of capital is 14.5 percent. Compute the IRRs and identify the projects that will be accepted.

Year	Project 1	Project 2	Project 3
0	−$275,000	−$312,500	−$500,000
1	63,000	153,250	212,000
2	85,000	167,500	212,000
3	85,000	112,000	212,000
4	100,000		212,000

10.28 Jekyll & Hyde Corp. is evaluating two mutually exclusive projects. Their cost of capital is 15 percent. Costs and cash flows are given in the following table. Which project should be accepted?

Year	Project 1	Project 2
0	−$1,250,000	−$1,250,000
1	250,000	350,000
2	350,000	350,000
3	450,000	350,000
4	500,000	350,000
5	750,000	350,000

10.29 Larsen Automotive, a manufacturer of auto parts, is planning to invest in two projects. The company typically compares project returns to a cost of funds of 17 percent. Compute the IRRs based on the given cash flows, and state which projects will be accepted.

Year	Project 1	Project 2
0	−$475,000	−$500,000
1	300,000	117,500
2	110,000	181,300
3	125,000	244,112
4	140,000	278,955

EXCEL **10.30** Compute the IRR for each of the following cash flow streams:

Year	Project 1	Project 2	Project 3
0	−$10,000	−$10,000	−$10,000
1	4,750	1,650	800
2	3,300	3,890	1,200
3	3,600	5,100	2,875
4	2,100	2,750	3,400
5		800	6,600

EXCEL **10.31** Primus Corp. is planning to convert an existing warehouse into a new plant that will increase its production capacity by 45 percent. The cost of this project will be $7,125,000.

It will result in additional cash flows of $1,875,000 for the next eight years. The discount rate is 12 percent.
  a. What is the payback period?
  b. What is the NPV for this project?
  c. What is the IRR?

10.32 Quasar Tech Co. is investing $6 million in new machinery that will produce the next-generation routers. Sales to its customers will amount to $1,750,000 for the next three years and then increase to $2.4 million for three more years. The project is expected to last six years and cost the firm annually $898,620 (excluding depreciation). The machinery will be depreciated to zero by year 6 using the straight-line method. The company's tax rate is 30 percent, and the cost of capital is 16 percent. **EXCEL®**
  a. What is the payback period?
  b. What is the average accounting return (ARR)?
  c. Calculate the project NPV.
  d. What is the IRR for the project?

10.33 Skywards, Inc., an airline caterer, is purchasing refrigerated trucks at a total cost of $3.25 million. After-tax net income from this investment is expected to be $750,000 for the next five years. Annual depreciation expense was $650,000. The cost of capital is 17 percent. **EXCEL®**
  a. What is the discounted payback period?
  b. Compute the ARR.
  c. What is the NPV on this investment?
  d. Calculate the IRR.

10.34 Trident Corp. is evaluating two independent projects. The costs and expected cash flows are given in the following table. The cost of capital is 10 percent. **EXCEL®**

Year	A	B
0	−$312,500	−$395,000
1	121,450	153,552
2	121,450	158,711
3	121,450	166,220
4	121,450	132,000
5	121,450	122,000

  a. Calculate the project's NPV.
  b. Calculate the project's IRR.
  c. What is the decision based on NPV? What is the decision based on IRR? Is there a conflict?
  d. If you are the decision maker for the firm, which project or projects will be accepted? Explain your reasoning.

10.35 Tyler, Inc., is looking to move to a new technology for its production. The cost of equipment will be $4 million. The discount rate is 12 percent. Cash flows that the firm expects to generate are as follows. **EXCEL®**

Years	CF
0	−$4,000,000
1–2	0
3–5	$845,000
6–9	$1,450,000

  a. Compute the payback and discounted payback period for the project.
  b. What is the NPV for the project? Should the firm go ahead with the project?
  c. What is the IRR, and what would be the decision under the IRR?

10.36 Given the following cash flows for a capital project, calculate the NPV and IRR. The required rate of return is 8 percent. **CFA PROBLEMS**

Year	0	1	2	3	4	5
Cash Flow	−$50,000	$15,000	$15,000	$20,000	$10,000	$5,000

	NPV	IRR
a.	$1,905	10.9%
b.	$1,905	26.0%
c.	$3,379	10.9%
d.	$3,379	26.0%

10.37 Given the following cash flows for a capital project, calculate its payback period and discounted payback period. The required rate of return is 8 percent.

Year	0	1	2	3	4	5
Cash Flow	−$50,000	$15,000	$15,000	$20,000	$10,000	$5,000

The discounted payback period is
a. 0.16 year longer than the payback period.
b. 0.80 year longer than the payback period.
c. 1.01 years longer than the payback period.
d. 1.85 years longer than the payback period.

10.38 An investment of $100 generates after-tax cash flows of $40 in Year 1, $80 in Year 2, and $120 in Year 3. The required rate of return is 20 percent. The net present value is closest to
a. $42.22
b. $58.33
c. $68.52
d. $98.95

10.39 An investment of $150,000 is expected to generate an after-tax cash flow of $100,000 in one year and another $120,000 in two years. The cost of capital is 10 percent. What is the internal rate of return?
a. 28.19 percent
b. 28.39 percent
c. 28.59 percent
d. 28.79 percent

10.40 An investment has an outlay of 100 and after-tax cash flows of 40 annually for four years. A project enhancement increases the outlay by 15 and the annual after-tax cash flows by 5. As a result, the vertical intercept of the NPV profile of the enhanced project shifts
a. up and the horizontal intercept shifts left.
b. up and the horizontal intercept shifts right.
c. down and the horizontal intercept shifts left.
d. down and the horizontal intercept shifts right.

Sample Test Problems

10.1 Net present value: Techno Corp. is considering developing new computer software. The cost of development will be $675,000, and the company expects the revenue from the sale of the software to be $195,000 for each of the next six years. If the discount rate is 14 percent, what is the net present value of this project?

10.2 Payback method: Parker Office Supplies is looking to replace its outdated inventory-management software. The cost of the new software will be $168,000. Cost savings is expected to be $43,500 for each of the first three years and then to drop off to $36,875 for the next two years. What is the payback period for this project?

10.3 Accounting rate of return: Fresno, Inc., is expecting to generate after-tax income of $156,435 over each of the next three years. The average book value of its equipment over that period will be $322,500. If the firm's acceptance decision on any project is based on an ARR of 40 percent, should this project be accepted?

10.4 Internal rate of return: Refer to Problem 10.1. What is the IRR on this project?

10.5 Net present value: Raycom, Inc., needs a new overhead crane, and two alternatives are available. Crane T costs $1.35 million and will produce cost savings of $765,000 for the next three years. Crane R will cost the firm $1.675 million and will lead to annual cost savings of $815,000 for the next three years. The required rate of return is 15 percent. Which of the two options should Raycom choose based on NPV calculations, and why?

CASH FLOWS AND CAPITAL BUDGETING

CHAPTER

11

LEARNING OBJECTIVES

1. Explain why incremental after-tax free cash flows are relevant in evaluating a project, and be able to calculate them for a project.

2. Discuss the five general rules for incremental after-tax free cash flow calculations, and explain why cash flows stated in nominal (real) dollars should be discounted using a nominal (real) discount rate.

3. Describe how distinguishing between variable and fixed costs can be useful in forecasting operating expenses.

4. Explain the concept of equivalent annual cost, and be able to use it to compare projects with unequal lives, decide when to replace an existing asset, and calculate the opportunity cost of using an existing asset.

5. Determine the appropriate time to harvest an asset.

Wang Hui/NewsCom

On the morning of February 1, 2008, Microsoft Corporation management announced an offer to acquire Yahoo! Inc. for a total of $44.6 billion in cash and stock. By the end of the day, Microsoft's stock price was down 6.6 percent while the S&P 500 stock market index was up 1.2 percent. The decline of 6.6 percent represented a drop of more than $20 billion in the total value of Microsoft's common stock. This drop, combined with the increase in the S&P 500 index, suggests that investors thought the acquisition of Yahoo! had a very large negative Net Present Value (NPV).

When the managers of Microsoft announced their interest in acquiring Yahoo!, they were really announcing a $44.6 billion investment. Despite its size, this investment was viewed by stock market investors from the same perspective as any capital project that a firm might pursue. Investors tried to estimate whether the NPV of the cash flows from the proposed Yahoo! acquisition was positive or negative. The financial model that they used to evaluate this investment is the same one that you saw in Chapter 10. The decrease in the value of Microsoft's stock on the day of the announcement reflected the market's estimate of the NPV from this investment proposal.

In Chapter 10, we stressed understanding the NPV concept and the mechanics of discounting cash flows. This chapter focuses on *what* cash flows are discounted and *how* they are calculated and used in practice. The topics covered in this chapter are central to the goal of value creation. It is necessary to understand them in order to determine which projects have positive NPVs and which projects have negative NPVs. Only if you can do this will you be able to choose the projects that create value.

CHAPTER PREVIEW

In Chapter 10 we saw that capital budgeting involves comparing the benefits and costs associated with a project to determine whether the project creates value for stockholders. These benefits and costs are reflected in the cash flows that the project is expected to produce. The NPV is a dollar measure of the amount by which the present value of the benefits exceeds the present value of the costs. Chapters 11 through 13 discuss how analysts actually apply the concepts introduced in Chapter 10 in capital budgeting. This chapter and Chapter 12 focus on cash flows, while Chapter 13 covers concepts related to the discount rate.

The major focus of this chapter is on the cash flows from a project. We begin with a discussion of how to calculate the cash flows used to compute the NPV of a project and how these cash flows differ from accounting earnings. We then present five rules to follow when you calculate free cash flows. We also address some concepts that will help you better understand cash flow calculations.

Next, we discuss how analysts actually forecast a project's cash flows. Since the cash flows generated by a project will almost certainly differ from the forecasts, it is important to have a framework that helps minimize errors and ensures that forecasts are internally consistent. We discuss such a framework in this part of the chapter.

In the last section, we examine some special cases that arise in capital budgeting problems. For example, we describe how to choose between two projects that have different lives, how to determine when an existing piece of equipment should be replaced, how to determine the cost of using excess capacity for a project, and when to harvest (or sell) an asset.

11.1 Calculating Project Cash Flows

We begin our discussion of cash flows in capital budgeting by describing the mechanics of cash flow calculations and the rules for estimating the cash flows for individual projects. You will see that the approach we use to calculate cash flows is similar to that used to prepare the accounting statement of cash flows discussed in Chapter 3. However, there are three very important differences:

1. Most important, the cash flows used in capital budgeting calculations are based on forecasts of *future* cash revenues, expenses, and investment outlays. In contrast, the accounting statement of cash flows is a record of *past* cash flows that might not reflect what can be expected in the future.

2. The accounting statement of cash flows reports a measure of the cash flows for the firm as a whole. In capital budgeting we generally forecast cash flows associated with an individual project.

3. The capital budgeting cash flow calculation is designed to estimate total cash flows, while the accounting statement of cash flows is intended to reconcile changes in the balance sheet cash accounts (for example, bank account balances). If there are any cash outflows or inflows to or from creditors or stockholders, total cash flows will differ from the changes in the cash balances because the total cash flow calculation does not include these inflows or outflows.

> **BUILDING INTUITION**
>
> **Capital Budgeting is Forward Looking**
>
> In capital budgeting, we estimate the NPV of the cash flows that a project is *expected to produce in the future*. In other words, all of the cash flow estimates are forward looking. This is very different from the accounting statement of cash flows, which provides a record of historical cash flows.

Incremental After-Tax Free Cash Flows

The cash flows we discount in an NPV analysis are the **incremental after-tax free cash flows** that are expected from the project. The term *incremental* refers to the fact that these cash flows reflect how much the firm's total after-tax free cash flows will change if the project is adopted. Thus, we define the incremental after-tax free cash flows (FCF) for a project as the total after-tax free cash flows the firm would produce with the project, less the total after-tax free cash flows the firm would produce without the project.

$$\text{FCF}_{\text{Project}} = \text{FCF}_{\text{Firm with project}} - \text{FCF}_{\text{Firm without project}} \quad (11.1)$$

In other words, $\text{FCF}_{\text{Project}}$ equals the net effect the project will have on the firm's cash revenues, costs, taxes, and investment outlays. This is what stockholders care about.

Throughout the rest of this chapter, we will refer to the total incremental after-tax free cash flows associated with a project simply as the FCF from the project. For convenience, we will drop the "Project" subscript from the FCF in Equation 11.1.

The FCF for a project is what we generically referred to as NCF in Chapter 10. The term *free cash flows*, which is commonly used in practice, refers to the fact that the firm is free to distribute these cash flows to creditors and stockholders because these are the cash flows that are left over after a firm has made necessary investments in working capital and long-term assets. The cash flows associated with financing a project (cash outflows or inflows to or from creditors or stockholders) are not included in the FCF calculation because, as we will discuss in Chapter 13, these are accounted for in the discount rate that is used in an NPV analysis. All of these points will become clearer as we discuss the FCF calculation next.

> **incremental after-tax free cash flows**
>
> the difference between the total after-tax free cash flows at a firm with a project and the total after-tax free cash flows at the same firm without that project; a measure of a project's total impact on the free cash flows at a firm

The FCF Calculation

The FCF calculation is illustrated in Exhibit 11.1. Let's begin with an overall review of how the calculation is done. After that, we will look more closely at details of the calculation.

Exhibit 11.1 — The Free Cash Flow Calculation

Explanation	Calculation	Formula
The change in the firm's cash income, excluding interest expense, resulting from the project.	Revenue	Revenue
	−Cash operating expenses	−Op Ex
	Earnings before interest, taxes, depreciation, and amortization	EBITDA
	−Depreciation and amortization	−D&A
	Operating profit	EBIT
	× (1 − Firm's marginal tax rate)	×(1 − t)
	Net operating profit after tax	NOPAT
Adjustments for the impact of depreciation and amortization and investments on FCF.	+ Depreciation and amortization	+D&A
	Cash flow from operations	CF Opns
	− Capital expenditures	−Cap Exp
	− Additions to working capital	−Add WC
	Free cash flow	FCF

This exhibit shows how the incremental after-tax free cash flow (FCF) for a project is calculated. The FCF equals the change in the firm's cash income, excluding interest expense, that the project is responsible for, plus depreciation and amortization for the project, minus all required capital expenditures and investments in working capital. FCF also equals the incremental after-tax cash flow from operations minus the capital expenditures and investments in working capital required for the project.

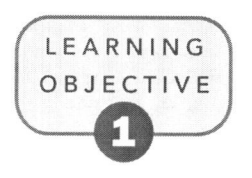

incremental cash flow from operations (CF Opns)
the cash flow that a project generates after all operating expenses and taxes have been paid but before any cash outflows for investments

incremental capital expenditures (Cap Exp)
the investments in property, plant, and equipment and other long-term assets that must be made if a project is pursued

incremental additions to working capital (Add WC)
the investments in working capital items, such as accounts receivable, inventory, and accounts payable, that must be made if the project is pursued

When we calculate the FCFs for a project, we first compute the **incremental cash flow from operations (CF Opns)** for each year during the project's life. This is the cash flow that the project is expected to generate after all operating expenses and taxes have been paid. To obtain the FCF, we then subtract the **incremental capital expenditures (Cap Exp)** and the **incremental additions to working capital (Add WC)** required for the project. Cap Exp and Add WC represent the investments in long-term assets, such as property, plant, and equipment, and in working capital items, such as accounts receivable, inventory, and accounts payable, which must be made if the project is pursued.

Since the FCF calculation gives us the after-tax cash flows from operations over and above what is necessary to make any required investments, the FCFs for a project are the cash flows that the security holders can expect to receive from the project. This is why we discount the FCFs when we compute the NPV.

The formula for the FCF calculation can also be written as:

$$FCF = [(\text{Revenue} - \text{Op Ex} - \text{D\&A}) \times (1 - t)] + \text{D\&A} - \text{Cap Exp} - \text{Add WC} \tag{11.2}$$

where Revenue is the incremental revenue (net sales) associated with the project, D&A is the **incremental depreciation and amortization** associated with the project, and t is the **firm's marginal tax rate**.

> ### BUILDING INTUITION
>
> ### Incremental After-Tax Free Cash Flows Are What Stockholders Care About
>
> When evaluating a project, managers focus on the FCF that the project is expected to produce because that is what stockholders care about. The FCFs reflect the impact of the project on the firm's overall cash flows. They also represent the additional cash flows that can be distributed to security holders if the project is accepted. Only after-tax cash flows matter because these are the cash flows that are actually available for distribution after taxes are paid to the government.

incremental depreciation and amortization (D&A)
the depreciation and amortization charges that are associated with a project

firm's marginal tax rate (t)
the tax rate that is applied to each additional dollar of earnings at a firm

stand-alone principle
the principle that allows us to treat each project as a stand-alone firm when we perform an NPV analysis

Let's use Equation 11.2 to work through an example. Suppose you are considering purchasing new truck for your plumbing business. This truck will increase revenues $50,000 and operating expenses $30,000 in the next year. Depreciation and amortization charges for the truck will equal $10,000 next year, and your firm's marginal tax rate will be 35 percent. Capital expenditures of $3,000 will be required to offset wear and tear on the truck, but no additions to working capital will be required. To calculate the FCF for the project in the next year, you can simply substitute the appropriate values into Equation 11.2:

$$\begin{aligned} FCF &= [(\text{Revenue} - \text{Op Ex} - \text{D\&A}) \times (1 - t)] + \text{D\&A} - \text{Cap Exp} - \text{Add WC} \\ &= [(\$50{,}000 - \$30{,}000 - \$10{,}000) \times (1 - 0.35)] + \$10{,}000 - \$3{,}000 - \$0 \\ &= \$13{,}500 \end{aligned}$$

The FCF calculated with Equation 11.2 equals the total cash flow the firm will produce with the project less the total cash flow the firm will produce without the project. Even so, it is important to note that it is not necessary to actually estimate the firm's total cash flows in an NPV analysis. We need only estimate the cash outflows and inflows that arise as a direct result of the project in order to value it. The idea that we can evaluate the cash flows from a project independently of the cash flows for the firm is known as the **stand-alone principle**. The stand-alone principle says that we can treat the project as if it were a stand-alone firm that has its own revenue, expenses, and investment requirements. NPV analysis compares the present value of the FCF from this stand-alone firm with the cost of the project.

To fully understand the stand-alone principle, it is helpful to consider an example. Suppose that you own shares of stock in Dell, Inc., and that Dell's stock is currently selling for $29.35. Now suppose that Dell's management announces it will immediately invest $2.3 billion in a new production and distribution center that is expected to produce after-tax cash flows of $0.6 billion per year forever. Since Dell has 2.3 billion shares outstanding and uses no debt, this means that the investment will equal $1.00 per share ($2.3/2.3) and that the annual increase in the cash flows is expected to be $0.26 per share ($0.6/2.3). How should this announcement affect the value of a share of Dell stock?

If the appropriate cost of capital for the project is 10 percent, then from Equation 9.2 and the discussion in Chapter 10, we know that the value of a share of Dell's stock should increase by D/R = $0.26/0.10 = $2.60 less the $1.00 invested, or $2.60 − $1.00 = $1.60, making each share of Dell stock worth $29.35 + $1.60 = $30.95 after the announcement. This example illustrates how the stand-alone principle allows us to simply add the value of a project's cash flows to the value of the firm's other cash flows to obtain the total value of the firm with the project.

Cash Flows from Operations

Let's examine Exhibit 11.1 in more detail to better understand why FCF is calculated as it is. First, note that the incremental cash flow from operations, CF Opns, equals the **incremental net operating profits after tax (NOPAT)** plus D&A.

If you refer back to the discussion of the income statement in Chapter 3, you will notice that NOPAT is essentially a cash measure of the incremental net income from the project without interest expenses. In other words, it is the impact of the project on the firm's cash net income, excluding the effects of any interest expenses associated with financing the project. We exclude interest expenses when calculating NOPAT because, as we mentioned earlier, the cost of financing a project is reflected in the discount rate.

We use the firm's marginal tax rate, t, to calculate NOPAT because the profits from a project are assumed to be incremental to the firm. Since the firm already pays taxes, the appropriate tax rate for FCF calculations is the tax rate that the firm will pay on any *additional* profits that are earned because the project is adopted. You may recall from Chapter 3 that this rate is the marginal tax rate. We will discuss taxes in more detail later in this chapter.

We add incremental depreciation and amortization, D&A, to NOPAT when calculating CF Opns because, as in the accounting statement of cash flows, D&A represents a noncash charge that reduces the firm's tax obligation. Note that we subtract D&A before computing the taxes that the firm would pay on the incremental earnings for the project. This accounts for the ability of the firm to deduct D&A when computing taxes. However, since D&A is a noncash charge, we have to add it back to NOPAT in order to get the cash flow from operations right.

The net effect of subtracting D&A, computing the taxes, and then adding D&A back is to reduce the taxes attributable to earnings from the project. For example, suppose that EBITDA for a project is $100.00, D&A is $50.00, and t is 35 percent. If we did not subtract D&A before computing taxes and add it back to compute CF Opns, the taxes owed for the project would be $100.00 × 0.35 = $35.00 and CF Opns would be $100.00 − $35.00 = $65.00. This would understate CF Opns from this project by $17.50 since deducting D&A reduces the firm's tax obligation by this amount. With this deduction, the correct tax obligation is ($100.00 − $50.00) × 0.35 = $17.50 and the correct CF Opns is $100.00 − $17.50 = $82.50. We get exactly this value when we compute CF Opns as shown in Exhibit 11.1 and Equation 11.2:

$$\text{CF Opns} = [(\text{Revenue} - \text{Op Ex} - \text{D\&A}) \times (1 - t)] + \text{D\&A}$$

since Revenue − Op Ex = EBITDA, as shown in Exhibit 11.1, we can write:

$$\begin{aligned}\text{CF Opns} &= [(\text{EBITDA} - \text{D\&A}) \times (1 - t)] + \text{D\&A} \\ &= [(\$100.00 - \$50.00) \times (1 - 0.35)] + \$50.00 \\ &= \$82.50\end{aligned}$$

> **incremental net operating profits after tax (NOPAT)**
> a measure of the impact of a project on the firm's cash net income, excluding the effects of any interest expenses associated with financing the project

Note also that the definition of CF Opns differs from that in the accounting statement of cash flows in that it ignores changes in working capital accounts and other accounting adjustments. In financial calculations, investments in working capital are treated separately, and there is no need for special accounting adjustments because CF Opns is based on cash flow estimates, not accounting numbers.

Cash Flows Associated with Investments

Once we have estimated CF Opns, we simply subtract cash flows associated with the required investments to obtain the FCF for a project in a particular period. Investments can be required to purchase long-term **tangible assets**, such as property, plant, and equipment, to purchase **intangible assets**, such as a patent, or to fund **current assets**, such as accounts receivables and inventories. Recall from Chapter 3 that net investments in property, plant and equipment, and working capital items are also deducted in the accounting statement of cash flows. You can see this in the long-term investing and operating activities sections of that statement.

It is important to recognize that all investments that are incremental to a project must be accounted for. The most obvious investments are those in the land, buildings, and machinery and equipment that are acquired for the project. However, investments in intangible assets can also be required. For example, a manufacturing firm may purchase the right to use a particular production technology. Incremental investments in long-term tangible assets and intangible assets are collectively referred to as incremental capital expenditures (Cap Exp).

In addition to tangible and intangible assets, such as those described earlier, it is also necessary to account for incremental additions to working capital (Add WC). For example, if the product being produced is going to be sold on credit, thereby generating additional accounts receivable, the cost of providing that credit must be accounted for. Similarly, if it will be necessary to hold product in inventory, the cost of financing that inventory must be considered.

> **tangible assets**
> physical assets such as property, plant, and equipment

> **intangible assets**
> nonphysical assets such as patents, mailing lists, or brand names

> **current assets**
> assets, such as accounts receivable and inventories, that are expected to be liquidated (collected or sold) within one year

The FCF Calculation: An Example

Let's work a more comprehensive example to see how FCF is calculated in practice. Suppose that you work at an outdoor performing arts center and are evaluating a project to increase the number of seats by building four new box seating areas and adding 5,000 seats for the general public. Each box seating area is expected to generate $400,000 in incremental annual revenue, while each of the new seats for the general public will generate $2,500 in incremental annual revenue. The incremental expenses associated with the new boxes and seating will amount to 60 percent of the revenues. These expenses include hiring additional personnel to handle concessions, ushering, and security. The new construction will cost $10 million and will be fully depreciated (to a value of zero dollars) on a straight-line basis over the 10-year life of the project. The center will have to invest $1 million in additional working capital immediately, but the project will not require any other working capital investments during its life. This working capital will be recovered in the last year of the project. The center's marginal tax rate is 30 percent. What are the incremental cash flows from this project?

When evaluating a project, it is generally helpful to first organize your calculations by setting up a worksheet such as the one illustrated in Exhibit 11.2. A worksheet like this helps ensure that the calculations are completed correctly. The left-hand column in Exhibit 11.2 shows the actual calculations that will be performed. Other columns are included for each of the years during the life of the project, from year 0 (today) through the last year in the life of the project (year 10). In this example the cash flows will be exactly the same for years 1 through 9; therefore, for illustration purposes, we will only include a single column to represent these years. If you were using a spreadsheet program, you would normally include one column for each year.

Unless there is information to the contrary, we can assume that the investment outlay for this project will be made today (year 0). We do this because in a typical project,

11.1 Calculating Project Cash Flows

Exhibit 11.2 FCF Calculation Worksheet for the Performing Arts Center Project

	Year 0	Years 1 to 9	Year 10
Revenue			
−Op Ex			
EBITDA			
−D&A			
EBIT			
×(1 − t)			
NOPAT			
+D&A			
CF Opns			
−Cap Exp			
−Add WC			
FCF			

A free cash flow (FCF) calculation table is useful in evaluating a project. It helps organize the calculations and ensure that they are completed correctly.

no revenue will be generated and no expenses will be incurred until after the investment has been made. Consequently, the only cash flows in year 0 are those for new construction (Cap Exp = $10,000,000) and additional working capital (Add WC = $1,000,000). The FCF in year 0 will therefore equal −$11,000,000.

In years 1 through 9, incremental revenue (Revenue) will equal:

Box seating ($400,000 × 4)	$ 1,600,000
Public seating ($2,500 × 5,000)	$12,500,000
Total incremental net revenue	$14,100,000

Incremental Op Ex will equal 0.60 × $14,100,000 = $8,460,000. Finally, depreciation (there is no amortization in this example) is computed as:

D&A = (Cap Exp − Salvage value of Cap Exp)/Depreciable life of the investment
   = ($10,000,000 − $0)/10 years
   = $1,000,000

Note that only the Cap Exp are depreciated and that these capital expenditures will be completely depreciated or written off over the 10-year life of the project because no salvage value is anticipated. Working capital is not depreciated because it is an investment that will be recovered at the end of the project.

The cash flows in year 10 will be the same as those in years 1 through 9 except that the $1 million invested in additional working capital will be recovered in the last year. The $1 million is added back to (or a negative number is subtracted from) the incremental cash flows from operations in the calculation of the year 10 cash flows.

The completed cash flow calculation worksheet for this example is presented in Exhibit 11.3. We could have completed the calculations without the worksheet. However, as mentioned, a cash flow calculation worksheet is a useful tool because it helps us make sure we don't forget anything. Once we have set the worksheet up, calculating the incremental cash flows is simply a matter of filling in the blanks. As you will see in the following discussion, correctly filling in some blanks can be difficult at times, but the worksheet keeps us organized by reminding us which blanks have yet to be filled in.

Notice that with a discount rate of 10 percent, the NPV of the cash flows in Exhibit 11.3 is $15,487,664. As in Chapter 10, the NPV is obtained by calculating the present values of all of the cash flows and adding them up. You might confirm this by doing this calculation yourself.

Exhibit 11.3 Completed FCF Calculation Worksheet for the Performing Arts Center Project

	Year 0	Years 1 to 9	Year 10
Revenue		$14,100,000	$14,100,000
−Op Ex		8,460,000	8,460,000
EBITDA		$ 5,640,000	$ 5,640,000
−D&A		1,000,000	1,000,000
EBIT		$ 4,640,000	$ 4,640,000
×(1 − t)		0.70	0.70
NOPAT		$ 3,248,000	$ 3,248,000
+D&A		1,000,000	1,000,000
CF Opns		$ 4,248,000	$ 4,248,000
−Cap Exp	$10,000,000	0	0
−Add WC	1,000,000	0	−1,000,000
FCF	−$11,000,000	$ 4,248,000	$ 5,248,000
NPV @ 10%	$15,487,664		

The completed calculation table shows how the incremental after-tax free cash flows (FCF) for the performing arts center project are computed, along with the NPV for that project when the cost of capital is 10 percent.

USING EXCEL

Performing Arts Center Project

Cash flow calculations for capital budgeting problems are best set up and solved using a spreadsheet application.

Here is the setup for the performing arts center project:

Key Assumptions:

Row	A	B
2	Life of the project (Years)	10
3	Number of new boxes	4
4	Annual incremental revenue per box	$400,000
5	Number of new seats	5,000
6	Annual incremental revenue per seat	$2,500
7	Incremental expense (% of revenue)	60%
8	Construction cost (Cap Exp)*	$10,000
9	Depreciation (per year)*	$1,000
10	Additional investment in Year 0 (Add WC)*	$1,000
11	WC to be recovered in Year 10*	($1,000)
12	Tax rate	30%
13	Cost of capital	10%
14	Note: * denotes figures in millions of dollars	

Cash Flow Calculations for Performing Arts Center Project ($ millions)

	Year 0	1	2	3	4	5	6	7	8	9	10
Revenue		$14,100	$14,100	$14,100	$14,100	$14,100	$14,100	$14,100	$14,100	$14,100	$14,100
Operating Expenses		8,460	8,460	8,460	8,460	8,460	8,460	8,460	8,460	8,460	8,460
EBITDA		5,640	5,640	5,640	5,640	5,640	5,640	5,640	5,640	5,640	5,640
Less: Depreciation & Amortization		1,000	1,000	1,000	1,000	1,000	1,000	1,000	1,000	1,000	1,000
EBIT		4,640	4,640	4,640	4,640	4,640	4,640	4,640	4,640	4,640	4,640
Less Taxes		1,392	1,392	1,392	1,392	1,392	1,392	1,392	1,392	1,392	1,392
NOPAT		3,248	3,248	3,248	3,248	3,248	3,248	3,248	3,248	3,248	3,248
Plus: Depreciation & Amortization		1,000	1,000	1,000	1,000	1,000	1,000	1,000	1,000	1,000	1,000
Cash Flows from Operations		4,248	4,248	4,248	4,248	4,248	4,248	4,248	4,248	4,248	4,248
Less: Capital Expenditures	$10,000	0	0	0	0	0	0	0	0	0	0
Less: Changes in Working Capital	$1,000	0	0	0	0	0	0	0	0	0	($1,000)
Free Cash Flow	($11,000)	$4,248	$4,248	$4,248	$4,248	$4,248	$4,248	$4,248	$4,248	$4,248	$5,248
NPV	$15,488										

The following is the formula setup for the performing arts center project. As we did in Exhibit 11.3, we have combined years 1 through 9 in a single column to save space. As mentioned in previous chapters, notice that none of the values in the actual worksheet are hard coded but instead use references from the key assumptions list, or specific formulas. This allows for an easy analysis of the impact of changes in the assumption.

	A	B	C	D	E	V
1	Key Assumptions:					
2	Life of the project (Years)	10				
3	Number of new boxes	4				
4	Annual incremental revenue per box	400000				
5	Number of new seats	5000				
6	Annual incremental revenue per seat	2500				
7	Incremental expense (% of revenue)	0.6				
8	Construction cost (Cap Exp)*	10000				
9	Depreciation (per year)*	=B8/B2				
10	Additional investment in Year 0 (Add WC)*	1000				
11	WC to be recovered in Year 10*	(1000)				
12	Tax rate	0.3				
13	Cost of capital	0.1				
14	Note: * denotes figures in millions of dollars					
15						
16	Cash Flow Calculations for Performing Arts Center Project ($ millions)					
17				Year		
18			0	1-9		10
19	Revenue			=($B$3*$B$4+$B$5*$B$6)/1000		=($B$3*$B$4+$B$5*$B$6)/1000
20	Operating Expenses			=$B$7*D19		=$B$7*V19
21	EBITDA			=D19-D20		=V19-V20
22	Less: Depreciation & Amortization			=$B$9		=$B$9
23	EBIT			=D21-D22		=V21-V22
24	Less Taxes			=D23*$B$12		=V23*$B$12
25	NOPAT			=D23-D24		=V23-V24
26						
27	Plus: Depreciation & Amortization			=$B$9		=$B$9
28	Cash Flows from Operations			=D25+D27		=V25+V27
29	Less: Capital Expenditures		=B8	0		0
30	Less: Changes in Working Capital		=B10	0		=B11
31						
32	Free Cash Flow		=B28-B29-B30	=D28-D29-D30		=V28-V29-V30
33						
34	NPV		=NPV(B13, D32:V32)+B32			
35						

FCF versus Accounting Earnings

It is worth stressing again that the FCF we have been discussing in this section is what matters to investors. The impact of a project on a firm's overall value or on its stock price does not depend on how the project affects the company's accounting earnings. It depends only on how the project affects the company's FCF.

Recall that accounting earnings can differ from cash flows for a number of reasons, making accounting earnings an unreliable measure of the costs and benefits of a project. For example, as soon as a firm sells a good or provides a service, its income statement will reflect the associated revenue and expenses, regardless of whether the customer has made any actual payments.

Accounting earnings also reflect noncash charges, such as depreciation and amortization, which are intended to account for the costs associated with deterioration of the assets in a business as those assets are used. Depreciation and amortization rules can cause substantial differences between cash flows and reported income because the assets acquired for a project are generally depreciated over several years, even though the actual cash outflow for their acquisition typically takes place at the beginning of the project.

DECISION-MAKING EXAMPLE 11.1

Free Cash Flows

Situation: You have saved $6,000 and plan to use $5,500 to buy a motorcycle. However, just before you go visit the motorcycle dealer, a friend of yours asks you to invest your $6,000 in a local pizza delivery business he is starting. Assuming he can raise the money, your friend has two alternatives regarding how to market the business. As illustrated below, both of these alternatives have an NPV of $2,614 with an opportunity cost of capital of 12 percent. You will receive all free cash flows from the business until you have recovered your $6,000 plus 12 percent interest. After that, you and your friend will split any additional cash proceeds. Which alternative would you prefer that your friend choose?

	Alternative 1			Alternative 2		
	Year 0	Year 1	Year 2	Year 0	Year 1	Year 2
Revenue		$12,000	$12,000		$16,000	$8,000
−Op Ex		4,000	6,000		8,000	4,240
EBITDA		$ 8,000	$ 6,000		$ 8,000	$3,760
−D&A		2,500	2,500		2,500	2,500
EBIT		$ 5,500	$ 3,500		$ 5,500	$1,260
×(1 − t)		0.75	0.75		0.75	0.75
NOPAT		$ 4,125	$ 2,625		$ 4,125	$ 945
+D&A		2,500	2,500		2,500	2,500
CF Opns		$ 6,625	$ 5,125		$ 6,625	$3,445
−Cap Exp	$5,000	2,000	500	$5,000	500	500
−Add WC	1,000		(1,000)	1,000		(1,000)
FCF	−$6,000	$ 4,625	$ 5,625	−$6,000	$ 6,125	$3,945
NPV at 12%	$2,614			$2,614		

Decision: If you expect no cash from other sources during the next year, you should insist that your friend choose alternative 2. This is the only alternative that will produce enough FCF next year to purchase the motorcycle. Alternative 1 will produce $6,625 in CF Opns but will require $2,000 in capital expenditures. You will not be able to take more than $4,625 from the business in year 1 under alternative 1 without leaving the business short of cash.

Before You Go On

1. Why do we care about incremental cash flows at the firm level when we evaluate a project?
2. Why is D&A first subtracted and then added back in FCF calculations?
3. What types of investments should be included in FCF calculations?

11.2 Estimating Cash Flows in Practice

LEARNING OBJECTIVE 2

Now that we have discussed what FCFs are and how they are calculated, we are ready to focus on some important issues that arise when we estimate FCFs in practice. The first of these issues is determining which cash flows are incremental to the project and which are not. In this section we begin with a discussion of five general rules that help us do this. We then discuss why it is important to distinguish between nominal and real cash flows and to use one or the other consistently in our calculations. Next, we discuss some concepts regarding tax rates and depreciation that are crucial to the calculation of FCF in practice. Finally, we describe and illustrate special factors that must be considered when calculating FCF for the final year of a project.

Five General Rules for Incremental After-Tax Free Cash Flow Calculations

As discussed earlier, we must determine how a project would change the after-tax free cash flows of the firm in order to calculate its NPV. This is not always simple to do, especially in a large firm that has a complex accounting system and many other projects that are not independent of the project being considered. Fortunately, there are five rules that can help us isolate the FCFs specific to an individual project even under the most complicated circumstances.

Rule 1: Include cash flows and only cash flows in your calculations. Do not include allocated costs unless they reflect cash flows. Examples of allocated costs are charges that accountants allocate to individual businesses to reflect their share of the corporate overhead (the costs associated with the senior managers of the firm, centralized accounting and finance functions, and so forth).

To see how allocated costs can differ from actual costs (and cash flows), consider a firm with $3 million of annual corporate overhead expenses and two identical manufacturing plants. Each of these plants would typically be allocated one-half, or $1.5 million, of the corporate overhead when their accounting profitability is estimated.

Suppose now that the firm is considering building a third plant that would be identical to the other two. If this plant is built, it will have no impact on the annual corporate overhead cash expense. Someone in accounting might argue that the new plant should be able to support its "fair share" of the $3 million overhead, or $1 million, and that this overhead should be included in the cash flow calculation. Of course, this person would be wrong. Since total corporate overhead costs will not change if the third plant is built, no overhead should be included when calculating the incremental FCFs for this plant.

Rule 2: Include the impact of the project on cash flows from other product lines. If the product associated with a project is expected to affect sales of one or more other products at the firm, you must include the expected impact of the new project on the cash flows from the other products when computing the FCFs. For example, consider the analysis that analysts at Apple Computer would have done before giving the go-ahead for the development of the iPhone. Since, like the iPod, the iPhone can store music, these analysts might have expected that the introduction of the iPhone would reduce annual iPod sales. If so, they would have had to account for the reduction in cash flows from lost iPod sales when they forecast the FCFs for the iPhone.

Similarly, if a new product is expected to boost sales of another, complementary, product, then the increase in cash flows associated with the new sales from that complementary product line should also be reflected in the FCFs. For example, suppose that the introduction of the iPhone will increase the total number of music playing devices (iPhones plus iPods) that Apple sells by 1 million units per year and that the average purchaser of a music playing device buys and downloads 100 digital songs from Apple. The digital music that Apple sells is a complementary product, and the cash flows from the sale of 100 million (1 million music playing devices × 100 songs) additional songs each year should be included in the analysis of the iPhone project. If Apple did not introduce the iPhone, it would not have those sales.

Rule 3: Include all opportunity costs. By opportunity costs, we mean the cost of giving up another opportunity.[1] Opportunity costs can arise in many different

---

[1] The concept of opportunity cost here is similar to that discussed in Chapter 10, in the context of the opportunity cost of capital.

ways. For example, a project may require the use of a building or a piece of equipment that could otherwise be sold or leased to someone else. To the extent that selling or leasing the building or piece of equipment would generate additional cash flow for the firm and the opportunity to realize that cash flow must be forgone if the project is adopted, it represents an opportunity cost.

To see why this is so, suppose that a project will require the use of a piece of equipment that the firm already has and that can be sold for $50,000 on the used-equipment market. If the project is accepted, the firm will lose the opportunity to sell the piece of equipment for $50,000. This is a $50,000 cost that must be included in the project analysis. Accepting the project reduces the amount of money that the firm can realize from selling excess equipment by this amount.

Rule 4: Forget sunk costs. Sunk costs are costs that have already been incurred. All that matters when you evaluate a project at a particular point in time is how much you have to invest in the future and what you can expect to receive in return for that investment. Past investments are irrelevant.

To see this, consider the situation in which your company has invested $10 million in a project that has not yet generated any cash inflows. Also assume that circumstances have changed so the project, which was originally expected to generate cash inflows with a present value of $20 million, is now expected to generate cash inflows with a value of only $2 million. To receive this $2 million, however, you will have to invest another $1 million. Should you do it? Of course you should!

If you stop investing now, you will have lost $10 million. If you make the investment, your total loss will be $9 million. Although neither is an attractive alternative, it should be clear that it is better to lose $9 million than it is to lose $10 million. The conclusion is the same if you ignore the previous investment and recognize that the choice is between never receiving anything and receiving an NPV of $1 million ($1 million investment and $2 million return). The point here is that, while it is often painful to do, you should ignore sunk costs when computing FCF.

Rule 5: Include only after-tax cash flows in the cash flow calculations. The incremental pretax earnings of a project matter only to the extent that they affect the after-tax cash flows that the firm's investors receive. For an individual project, as mentioned earlier, we compute the after-tax cash flows using the firm's marginal tax rate because this is the rate that will be applied against the incremental cash flows generated by the project.

Let's use the performing arts center project to illustrate how these rules are applied in practice. Suppose the following requirements and costs are associated with this project:

1. The chief financial officer requires that each project be assessed 5 percent of the initial investment to account for costs associated with the accounting, marketing, and information technology departments.
2. It is very likely that increasing the number of seats will reduce revenues next door at the cinema that your employer also owns. Attendance at the cinema is expected to be lower only when the performing arts center is staging a big event. The total impact is expected to be a reduction of $500,000 each year, before taxes, in the operating profits (EBIT) of the cinema. The depreciation of the cinema's assets will not be affected.
3. If the project is adopted, the new seating will be built in an area where exhibits have been placed in the past when the center has hosted guest lectures by well-known painters or sculptors. The performing arts center will no longer be able to host such events, and revenue will be reduced by $600,000 each year as a result.
4. The center has already spent $400,000 researching demand for new seating.
5. You have just discovered that a new salesperson will be hired if the center goes ahead with the expansion. This person will be responsible for sales and service of

the four new luxury boxes and will be paid $75,000 per year, including salary and benefits. The $75,000 is not included in the 60 percent figure for operating expenses that was previously mentioned.

What impact will these requirements and costs have on the FCFs for the project?

1. The 5 percent assessment sounds like an allocated overhead cost. To the extent that this assessment does not reflect an actual increase in cash costs, it should not be included. It is not relevant to the project. The analysis should include only cash flows.

2. The impact of the expansion on the operating profits of the cinema is an example of how a project can erode or cannibalize business in another part of a firm. The $500,000 reduction in EBIT is relevant and should be included in the analysis.

3. The loss of the ability to use the exhibits area represents a $600,000 opportunity cost. The center is giving up revenue from guest lecturers that require exhibit space in order to build the additional seating. This opportunity cost will be partially offset by elimination of the operating expenses associated with the guest lectures.

4. The $400,000 for research has already been spent. The decision of whether to accept or reject the project will not alter the amount spent for this research. This is a sunk cost that should not be included in the analysis.

5. The $75,000 annual salary for the new salesperson is an incremental cost that should be included in the analysis. Even though the marketing department is a corporate overhead department, in this case the salesperson must be hired specifically because of the new project.

Exhibit 11.4 shows the impact of the changes described earlier on the cash flows outlined in Exhibit 11.3. Note that Revenue and Op Ex after year 0 have been reduced from $14,100,000 and $8,460,000, respectively, in Exhibit 11.3 to $13,500,000 and $8,100,000, respectively, in Exhibit 11.4. These changes reflect the $600,000 loss of

Exhibit 11.4 Adjusted FCF Calculations and NPV for the Performing Arts Center Project

	Year 0	Years 1 to 9	Year 10
Revenue		$13,500,000	$13,500,000
−Op Ex		8,100,000	8,100,000
−New salesperson's salary		75,000	75,000
−Lost cinema EBIT		500,000	500,000
EBITDA		$ 4,825,000	$ 4,825,000
−D&A		1,000,000	1,000,000
EBIT		$ 3,825,000	$ 3,825,000
×(1 − t)		0.70	0.70
NOPAT		$ 2,677,500	$ 2,677,500
+D&A		1,000,000	1,000,000
CF Opns		$ 3,677,500	$ 3,677,500
−Cap Exp	$10,000,000	0	0
−Add WC	1,000,000	0	−1,000,000
FCF	−$11,000,000	$ 3,677,500	$ 4,677,500
NPV @ 10%	$11,982,189		

The adjustments described in the text result in changes in the FCF calculations and a different NPV for the performing arts center project.

revenues and the reduction in costs (60 percent of revenue) associated with the loss of the ability to host guest lectures. The $75,000 expense for the new salesperson's salary and the $500,000 reduction in the EBIT of the cinema are then subtracted from Revenue, along with Op Ex. These changes result in EBITDA of $4,825,000 in Exhibit 11.4, compared with EBITDA of $5,640,000 in Exhibit 11.3. The net result is a reduction in the project NPV from $15,487,664 (in Exhibit 11.3) to $11,982,189 (in Exhibit 11.4).

> **LEARNING BY DOING**
> **APPLICATION 11.1**
>
> ## Using the General Rules for FCF Calculations
>
> **Problem:** You have owned and operated a pizza parlor for several years. The space that you lease for your pizza parlor is considerably larger than the space you need. To more efficiently utilize this space, you are considering subdividing it and opening a hamburger joint. You know that your analysis should consider the overall impact of the hamburger project on the total cash flows of your business, but beyond estimating revenues and costs from hamburger-related sales and the investment required to get the hamburger business started, you are unsure what else you should consider. Based on the five general rules for incremental after-tax cash flow calculations, what other factors should you consider?
>
> **Approach:** Careful consideration of each of the five rules provides insights concerning the other factors that should be considered.
>
> **Solution:** Rule 1 suggests that you should consider the impact of the hamburger stand on actual overhead expenses, such as the cost of additional accounting support. Rule 2 indicates that you should consider the potential for the hamburger business to take sales away from (or cannibalize) the pizza business. Rule 3 suggests that you should carefully consider the opportunity cost associated with the excess space or any excess equipment that might be used for the hamburger business. If you could lease the extra space to someone else, for example, then the amount that you could receive by doing so is an opportunity cost and should be included in the analysis. Similarly, the price for which any excess equipment could be sold represents an opportunity cost. Rule 4 simply reminds you to consider cash flows from this point forward only. Forget sunk costs. Finally, Rule 5 tells you not to forget to account for the impact of taxes in your cash flow calculations.

You can learn more about incremental free cash flows at Investopedia.com, www.investopedia.com.

nominal dollars
dollar amounts that are not adjusted for inflation. The purchasing power of a nominal dollar amount depends on when that amount is received.

real dollars
inflation-adjusted dollars; the actual purchasing power of dollars stated in "real" terms is the same regardless of when those dollars are received

Nominal versus Real Cash Flows

In addition to following the five rules for incremental after-tax cash flow calculations, it is very important to make sure that all cash flows are stated in either nominal dollars or real dollars—not a mixture of the two. The concepts of nominal and real dollars are directly related to the discussion in Chapter 2 that distinguishes between (1) the nominal rate of interest and (2) the real rate of interest. **Nominal dollars** are the dollars that we typically think of. They represent the actual dollar amounts that we expect a project to generate in the future, without any adjustments. To the extent that there is inflation, the purchasing power of each nominal dollar will decline over time. When prices are going up, a given nominal dollar amount will buy less and less over time. **Real dollars** represent dollars stated in terms of constant purchasing power. When we forecast in real dollars, the purchasing power of the dollars in one period is equal to the purchasing power of the dollars in any other period.

To illustrate the difference between nominal and real dollars, let's consider an example. Suppose that the rate of inflation is expected to be 5 percent next year and that you just lent $100 to a friend for one year. If your friend is not paying any interest, the nominal dollar amount you expect to receive in one year is $100. At that time, though, the purchasing power, in today's terms, of this $100 is expected to be only

$95.24: \$100/(1 + \Delta P_e) = \$100/1.05 = \$95.24$, where ΔP_e is the expected rate of inflation, as discussed in Chapter 2. In other words, if inflation is as expected, when your friend repays the $100, it will buy only what $95.24 would buy today. You will have earned a real return of $(\$95.24 - \$100)/\$100 = -0.0476$, or -4.76 percent, on this loan. Another way of thinking about this loan is that your friend is expected to repay you with dollars having a real value of $95.24.

To understand the importance of making sure that all cash flows are stated in either nominal dollars or real dollars, it is useful to write the cost of capital (k) from Chapter 10 as:

$$1 + k = (1 + \Delta P_e) \times (1 + r) \qquad (11.3)$$

In Equation 11.3, k is the nominal cost of capital that is normally used to discount cash flows and r is the real cost of capital.[2] This equation tells us that the nominal cost of capital equals the real cost of capital, adjusted for the expected rate of inflation. This means that whenever we discount a cash flow using the nominal cost of capital, the discount rate we are using reflects both the expected rate of inflation (ΔP_e) and a real return (r). If, on the one hand, we discounted a *real cash flow* using the *nominal cost of capital*, we would be overcompensating for expected inflation in the discounting process. On the other hand, if we discounted a *nominal cash flow* using the *real cost of capital* (r), we would be undercompensating for expected inflation.

In capital budgeting, we normally forecast cash flows in nominal dollars and discount them using the nominal cost of capital.[3] As an alternative, we can state the cash flows in real terms and discount them using the real cost of capital. This alternative calculation will give us exactly the same NPV. To see this, consider a project that will require an investment of $50,000 in year 0 and will produce FCFs of $20,000 a year in years 1 through 4. With a 15 percent nominal cost of capital, the NPV for this project is:

$$\begin{aligned} NPV &= FCF_0 + \frac{FCF_1}{1+k} + \frac{FCF_2}{(1+k)^2} + \frac{FCF_3}{(1+k)^3} + \frac{FCF_4}{(1+k)^4} \\ &= -\$50{,}000 + \frac{\$20{,}000}{1.15} + \frac{\$20{,}000}{(1.15)^2} + \frac{\$20{,}000}{(1.15)^3} + \frac{\$20{,}000}{(1.15)^4} \\ &= -\$50{,}000 + \$17{,}391 + \$15{,}123 + \$13{,}150 + \$11{,}435 \\ &= \$7{,}099 \end{aligned}$$

Equation 11.3 can be used to calculate the real cost of capital if we recognize that it can be rearranged algebraically as:

$$r = \frac{1+k}{1+\Delta P_e} - 1$$

With a 5 percent expected rate of inflation, the real cost of capital is therefore:

$$r = \frac{1+k}{1+\Delta P_e} - 1 = \frac{1.15}{1.05} - 1 = 0.09524, \text{ or } 9.524\%$$

---

[2] As discussed in chapter 2, if we multiply the two terms on the right-hand side of Equation 11.3, we get $1 + k = 1 + \Delta P_e + r + \Delta P_e r$. Since the last term in this equation, $\Delta P_e r$, is the product of two fractions, it is a very small number and is often ignored in practice. Without this term, Equation 11.3 becomes $1 + k = 1 + \Delta P_e + r$ or $k = \Delta P_e + r$.

[3] Note that when we use the term *cost of capital* without distinguishing between the nominal or real cost of capital, we are referring to the *nominal* cost of capital. This is the convention that is used in practice. In this example, we use the terms *nominal* or *real* whenever we refer to the cost of capital for clarity. In the rest of this book, however, we follow convention by simply using the term *cost of capital* to refer to the nominal cost of capital.

Discounting the nominal cash flows by the rate of inflation tells us that the real cash flows are:

Year 0	Year 1	Year 2	Year 3	Year 4
−$50,000	$\dfrac{\$20{,}000}{1+0.05}$	$\dfrac{\$20{,}000}{(1+0.05)^2}$	$\dfrac{\$20{,}000}{(1+0.05)^3}$	$\dfrac{\$20{,}000}{(1+0.05)^4}$
= −$50,000	= $19,047.6	= $18,140.6	= 17,276.8	= $16,454.0

Therefore, when we discount the real cash flows using the real cost of capital, we see that the NPV is:

$$\begin{aligned}\text{NPV} &= -\$50{,}000 + \frac{\$19{,}047.6}{1.09524} + \frac{\$18{,}140.6}{(1.09524)^2} + \frac{\$17{,}276.8}{(1.09524)^3} + \frac{\$16{,}454.0}{(1.09524)^4} \\ &= -\$50{,}000 + \$17{,}391 + \$15{,}123 + \$13{,}150 + \$11{,}435 \\ &= \$7{,}099\end{aligned}$$

Notice that the present value of each of the annual cash flows is exactly the same when we use nominal cash flows and when we use real cash flows. This has to be the case because when we stated the NPV calculation in real dollars, we first divided the discount rate by 1.05. We then reduced the value of the future cash flows by discounting them by 5 percent. This is equivalent to reducing the numerator and the denominator in each present value calculation by the same fraction, which must result in the same answer.

LEARNING BY DOING APPLICATION 11.2

The Investment Decision and Nominal versus Real Dollars

Problem: You are trying to decide how to invest $25,000, which you just inherited from a distant relative. You do not want to take any risks with this money because you want to use it as a down payment on a home when you graduate in three years. Therefore, you have decided to invest the money in securities that are guaranteed by the U.S. government. You are considering two alternatives: a three-year Treasury note and an inflation-indexed Treasury security. If you invest in the three-year Treasury note, you will be paid 3 percent per year in interest and will get your $25,000 back at the end of three years. If you invest in the inflation-indexed security, you will be paid 1 percent per year plus an amount that reflects actual inflation in each of the next three years. For example, if inflation equals 2 percent per year for each of the next three years, you will receive 3 percent each year in total interest. This interest on the inflation-indexed security will compound, and you will receive a single payment at the end of three years. If you expect inflation to average 2.5 percent per year over the next three years, should you invest in the three-year Treasury note or in the inflation-indexed Treasury security?

Approach: Compare the 3 percent return on the three-year Treasury note, which is a nominal rate of return, with the nominal rate of return that you can expect to receive from the inflation-indexed security and invest in the security with the highest rate. The nominal rate on the inflation-indexed security in each year equals the real rate of 1 percent plus the rate of inflation.

Solution: Without doing any detailed calculations, it is apparent that you should invest in the inflation-indexed security. The reason is that if the rate of inflation turns out to be 2.5 percent, the inflation-indexed security will yield 3.5 percent (1 percent plus the 2.5 percent inflation adjustment) per year. With this investment, the real purchasing power of your money will increase by 1 percent per year. This will be true regardless of what inflation turns out to be during the three-year period. Assuming that you can reinvest the annual interest payments from the three-year Treasury note at 3 percent, if you buy this security, the real purchasing power of your money will increase by only 0.5 percent (3 percent interest rate less 2.5 percent inflation) per year.

Tax Rates and Depreciation

The United States has a very complicated corporate tax system. Corporations pay taxes at the federal, state, and local levels. Some governmental jurisdictions tax income, while others tax property or some other measure of value. Furthermore, a wide variety of deductions and adjustments are made to income or other measures of value when computing the actual taxes that a corporation owes. A detailed discussion of the different taxes that corporations pay and how they are computed is beyond the scope of this textbook. However, at this point, it is important that you are familiar with the progressive tax system that we have in the United States and with the depreciation methods used for computing corporate tax obligations. These concepts are especially important in capital budgeting.

> You can calculate the impact of inflation on purchasing power using the inflation calculator at www.westegg.com/inflation. This calculator tells you how much it would cost you, in nominal dollars, to buy the same goods in any two years, beginning in the year 1800.

MARGINAL AND AVERAGE TAX RATES

A **progressive tax system**, which we have in the United States, is one in which taxpayers pay a progressively larger share of their income in taxes as their income rises. This happens in a progressive tax system because the marginal tax rate at low levels of income is lower than the marginal tax rate at high levels of income. Recall from Chapter 3 that the marginal tax rate is the rate paid on the last dollar earned. The tax system in the United States is progressive for both individuals and corporations. For example, Exhibit 11.5 presents the 2007 federal tax rate schedule for single individuals. Notice that the percentage tax owed beyond the base amount in each row of Exhibit 11.5 increases as taxable income increases. In other words, the marginal tax rate, as well as the average tax rate, increases as an individual moves from one tax bracket to the next.

Exhibit 11.6 shows the 2007 tax rate schedule faced by a typical U.S. corporation (you may recall that a variation of this tax rate schedule is also presented in Exhibit 3.6). Notice that this schedule is also progressive. The U.S. corporate tax system in 2007 was structured so that the marginal rate exactly equaled the average tax rate for all levels of income above $18,333,333. If the corporation's taxable income is below $18,333,333, the marginal tax rate will not necessarily be the same as the average tax rate. These rates differ in all tax brackets below $18,333,333, except the $335,000 to $10 million bracket. Remember that since we use marginal tax rates in capital budgeting, you cannot simply divide the dollar taxes paid by the taxable income for a company to estimate the tax rate. This calculation gives you the average, not the marginal, tax rate.

> **progressive tax system**
> a tax system in which the marginal tax rate at low levels of income is lower than the marginal tax rate at high levels of income

Exhibit 11.5 U.S. Tax Rate Schedule for Single Individual in 2007

Taxable Income More Than	But Not More Than	Tax Owed
$0	$7,825	10% of amount beyond $0
$7,825	$31,850	$782.50 + 15% of amount beyond $7,825
$31,850	$77,100	$4,386.25 + 25% of amount beyond $31,850
$77,100	$160,850	$15,698.75 + 28% of amount beyond $77,100
$160,850	$349,700	$39,148.75 + 33% of amount beyond $160,850
$349,700	no limit	$101,469.25 + 35% of amount beyond $349,700

The income tax system for individuals in the United States is progressive in that the tax rate increases with income. For very low income levels—say, $20,000 per year—individuals pay only 15 percent on each additional dollar they earn. For individuals who earn more than $349,700, this rate is 35 percent.

Exhibit 11.6 U.S. Corporate Tax Rate Schedule in 2007

Taxable Income More Than	But Not More Than	Tax Owed
$0	$50,000	15% of amount beyond $0
$50,000	$75,000	$7,500 + 25% of amount beyond $50,000
$75,000	$100,000	$13,750 + 34% of amount beyond $75,000
$100,000	$335,000	$22,250 + 39% of amount beyond $100,000
$335,000	$10,000,000	$113,900 + 34% of amount beyond $335,000
$10,000,000	$15,000,000	$3,400,000 + 35% of amount beyond $10,000,000
$15,000,000	$18,333,333	$5,150,000 + 38% of amount beyond $15,000,000
$18,333,333	----------	35% on all income

Just like the tax system for individuals, the tax system for corporations in the United States is progressive, with marginal tax rates ranging from 15 percent to as high as 39 percent.

LEARNING BY DOING APPLICATION 11.3

Calculating Marginal and Average Tax Rates

Problem: Assume that you are operating the pizza parlor and hamburger joint described in Learning by Doing Application 11.1. Because the business has become complicated, you have incorporated. From now on, earnings are subject to the corporate tax rates presented in Exhibit 11.6. If your corporation's total taxable income is $200,000 in 2007, how much does it owe in federal taxes? What are the corporation's marginal and average federal tax rates? If you were considering buying a new oven, which tax rate would you use when computing the free cash flows?

Approach: Use the rates presented in Exhibit 11.6 to calculate the total amount that you owe. The marginal federal tax rate is the rate in the "Tax Owed" column in Exhibit 11.6 that corresponds to the row in which the total taxable income earned by your restaurant is found. The ratio of the total amount that you owe divided by your total taxable income equals the average federal tax rate. You would use the tax rate that would be applied to the incremental after-tax free cash flows associated with the new oven.

Solution: From Exhibit 11.6, you can see that with a taxable income of $200,000, your corporation will owe taxes of $22,250 + ($100,000 × 0.39) = $61,250. The marginal tax rate is 39 percent, and the average tax rate is $61,250/$200,000 = 0.306, or 30.6 percent. You will use the marginal rate of 39 percent when computing the free cash flows for the new oven.

TAX DEPRECIATION

Corporations keep two sets of books. One set is kept for preparing financial statements in accordance with generally accepted accounting principles (GAAP). These are the financial statements that appear in the annual report and other documents filed with the Securities and Exchange Commission (SEC). The other set is kept for computing the taxes that the corporation actually pays. Corporations must keep two sets of books because the GAAP rules for computing income are different from the rules that the IRS uses.

One especially important difference from a capital budgeting perspective is that the depreciation methods allowed by GAAP differ from those allowed by the IRS. The straight-line depreciation method illustrated earlier in this chapter in the performing arts center example is allowed by GAAP and is often used for financial reporting. In contrast, an "accelerated" method of depreciation, called the **Modified Accelerated Cost Recovery System (MACRS)**, has been in use for U.S. federal tax calculations since the Tax Reform Act of 1986 went into effect.[4] MACRS is an accelerated system in the sense that depreciation charges for all assets other than nonfarm real property (for example, buildings) are higher in the early years of an asset's life than with the straight-line method. MACRS thus enables a firm to deduct depreciation charges sooner, thereby realizing the tax savings sooner and increasing the present value of the tax savings. Since we want to estimate the actual incremental cash flows from a project in capital budgeting, we use the depreciation method allowed by the IRS in our calculations. This is the method that determines how much of a tax deduction a corporation actually receives for an investment.

Exhibit 11.7 lists the percentage of the cost of an asset that can be depreciated in each year for assets with 3-, 5-, 7-, 10-, 15-, and 20-year allowable recovery periods. The recovery periods for specific types of assets are specified in the tax law that is passed

Modified Accelerated Cost Recovery System (MACRS)
the accelerated depreciation method that has been in use for U.S. federal taxes since the Tax Reform Act of 1986 went into effect

Exhibit 11.7 MACRS Depreciation Schedules by Allowable Recovery Period

Year	3-Year	5-Year	7-Year	10-Year	15-Year	20-Year
1	33.33%	20.00%	14.29%	10.00%	5.00%	3.75%
2	44.45	32.00	24.49	18.00	9.50	7.22
3	14.81	19.20	17.49	14.40	8.55	6.68
4	7.41	11.52	12.49	11.52	7.70	6.18
5		11.52	8.93	9.22	6.93	5.71
6		5.76	8.92	7.37	6.23	5.29
7			8.93	6.55	5.90	4.89
8			4.46	6.55	5.90	4.52
9				6.56	5.91	4.46
10				6.55	5.90	4.46
11				3.28	5.91	4.46
12					5.90	4.46
13					5.91	4.46
14					5.90	4.46
15					5.91	4.46
16					2.95	4.46
17						4.46
18						4.46
19						4.46
20						4.46
21						2.24
Total	100.00%	100.00%	100.00%	100.00%	100.00%	100.00%

The MACRS schedule lists the tax depreciation rates that firms use for assets placed into service after the Tax Reform Act of 1986 went into effect. The table indicates the percentage of the cost of the asset that can be depreciated in each year during the period that it is being used. Year 1 is the year in which the asset is first placed into service.

---

[4]Although some assets that were acquired before 1986 are still being depreciated using earlier methods, the vast majority of depreciation for existing assets and all depreciation for new assets are based on MACRS.

by Congress and signed by the president. For instance, in 2007, the allowable recovery period was 5 years for computers and automobiles, 7 years for office furniture, 10 years for water transportation equipment such as barges, 15 years for telephone distribution facilities, 20 years for farm buildings, 27.5 years for residential rental property, and 39.5 years for nonresidential real property (such as manufacturing buildings). Residential rental and nonresidential real property are depreciated using the straight-line method. Depreciation charges are intended to represent the cost of wear and tear on assets in the course of business. However, since they are set through a political process, they may be greater than or less than the actual cost of this wear and tear.

Note that the percentages in each column of Exhibit 11.7 add up to 100 percent. This is because the tax law allows firms to depreciate 100 percent of the cost of an asset regardless of the expected salvage value of that asset. Consequently, when we use the MACRS schedule to determine the tax depreciation, we do not have to worry about the expected salvage value for the asset.[5]

Let's consider an example to show how MACRS is applied. Suppose you are evaluating a project that will require the purchase of an automobile for $25,000. Since an automobile is a five-year asset under MACRS, you can use the percentages for a five-year asset in Exhibit 11.7 to calculate the annual depreciation deductions:

Year 1:	$25,000 × 0.2000 =	$5,000
Year 2:	$25,000 × 0.3200 =	$8,000
Year 3:	$25,000 × 0.1920 =	$4,800
Year 4:	$25,000 × 0.1152 =	$2,880
Year 5:	$25,000 × 0.1152 =	$2,880
Year 6:	$25,000 × 0.0576 =	$1,440
Total		$25,000

Notice that even though the automobile is a five-year asset, there is a depreciation charge in the sixth year. This is because MACRS assumes that the asset is placed in service in the middle of the first year. As a result, the firm is allowed a deduction for half of a year in year 1, a full year in years 2 through 5, and half of a year in year 6.

Recall that the FCF calculation, Equation 11.1, included incremental depreciation along with incremental amortization (D&A). We put depreciation and amortization together in the calculation because amortization is a noncash charge (deduction) like depreciation. It is beyond the scope of this book to discuss amortization in detail because the rules that govern it are complex. However, you should know that amortization, like depreciation, is a deduction that is allowed under the tax law to compensate for the decline in value of certain, mainly intangible, assets used by a business.

> You can read more about tax rates and depreciation rules at the Internal Revenue Service Web site, www.irs.gov.

Computing the Terminal-Year FCF

The FCF in the last, or terminal, year of a project's life often includes cash flows that are not typically included in the calculations for other years. For instance, in the final year of a project, the assets acquired during the life of the project may be sold and the working capital that has been invested may be recovered. The cash flows that result from the sale of assets and recovery of working capital must be included in the calculation of the terminal-year FCF.

In the performing arts center example discussed earlier, the cash flows in year 0 are different from the cash flows in the other years (see Exhibit 11.3). The year 0 cash flows include only cash flows associated with incremental capital expenditures (Cap Exp) and additions to working capital (Add WC). They do not include incremental cash flows from operations (CF Opns). The principle behind including only these cash flows in year 0 is that the investments must be made before any cash flows from operations are realized. In some cases, such as large construction projects, up-front investments may be

---

[5]Under GAAP accounting rules, if the salvage value can be estimated with reasonable certainty, it should be used in computing depreciation. However, in practice the expected salvage value of new assets is so uncertain that it is typically assumed to equal $0 even for financial reporting purposes.

required over several years, but these investments typically also are made before the project begins to generate revenue.

The year 10, or terminal year, cash flows in the performing arts center example are also different from those in the other years. They include both CF Opns and investment cash flows that reflect recovery of net working capital investments. Net incremental additions to working capital (Add WC) that are due to the project are calculated as follows:

$$\text{Add WC} = \text{Change in cash and cash equivalents} + \text{Change in accounts receivable} + \text{Change in inventories} - \text{Change in accounts payable} \quad (11.4)$$

where the changes in cash and cash equivalents, accounts receivable, inventories, and accounts payable represent changes in the values of these accounts that result from the adoption of the project.

Looking at the components of Add WC, we can see that cash and cash equivalents, accounts receivable, and inventories require the investment of capital, while accounts payable represent capital provided by suppliers. When a project ends, the cash and cash equivalents are no longer needed, the accounts receivable are collected, the inventories are sold, and the accounts payable are paid. In other words, the firm recovers the net working capital that has been invested in the project. To reflect this in the FCF calculation, the cash flow in the last year of the project typically includes a *negative investment in working capital* that equals the cumulative investment in working capital over the life of the project. It is very important to make sure that the recovery of working capital is reflected in the cash flows in the last year of a project. In some businesses, working capital can account for 20 percent or more of revenue, and excluding working capital recovery from the calculations can cause you to substantially understate the NPV of a project.

In some projects, there will also be incremental capital expenditures (Cap Exp) in the terminal year. This is because the assets acquired for the project are being sold or there are disposal costs associated with them. In the performing arts center example, Cap Exp is $0 in year 10. This is because we were assuming that, other than the working capital, the investments at the beginning of the project would have no salvage value, there would be no disposal costs associated with the assets, and there would be no clean-up costs associated with the project in year 10. When an asset is expected to have a salvage value, we must include the salvage value realized from the sale of the asset and the impact of the sale on the firm's taxes in the terminal-year FCF calculations. Any costs that must be incurred to dispose of assets should also be included. Finally, clean-up costs, such as those associated with restoring the environment after a strip-mining project, also must be included in the terminal-year FCF.

The salvage value realized from the sale of the assets used in a project includes both the cash that is actually realized when they are sold and, if the salvage value of any asset differs from its depreciated value, the tax implications from the sale. To better understand how taxes affect the terminal-year cash flows for a project, let's make the performing arts center example more realistic. Recall that the initial Cap Exp in the performing arts center example was $10 million, that we used straight-line depreciation, and that we assumed that the salvage value would be $0 in year 10. Now that we know about MACRS, let's more realistically assume that the allowable recovery period for this investment under MACRS is 10 years.

Exhibit 11.8 presents the depreciation calculations for this investment under MACRS. Note that since the amount of depreciation now changes over time, we can no longer present years 1 through 9 together as we did in Exhibit 11.3. Also note that because MACRS allows only a half year of depreciation in year 1, the book value of the investment is greater than $0 at the end of year 10. In this case it is $328,000.

If we still assume a salvage value of $0 for this investment, the fact that the book value is positive means that the firm will have a tax loss when it writes off the remaining value of the investment at the end of the project. In other words, when the project ends, the firm will take a deduction when computing its taxes that equals the remaining $328,000 book value of the asset. With a 30 percent tax rate, this will result in a tax

Exhibit 11.8 MACRS Depreciation Calculations for the Performing Arts Center Project ($ thousands)

	Year 1	Year 2	Year 3	Year 4	Year 5	Year 6	Year 7	Year 8	Year 9	Year 10
Depreciation Calculations										
Beginning book value	$10,000	$9,000	$7,200	$5,760	$4,608	$3,686	$2,949	$2,294	$1,639	$983
MACRS percentage	10.00%	18.00%	14.40%	11.52%	9.22%	7.37%	6.55%	6.55%	6.56%	6.55%
MACRS depreciation	$1,000	$1,800	$1,440	$1,152	$922	$737	$655	$655	$656	$655
Ending book value	$9,000	$7,200	$5,760	$4,608	$3,686	$2,949	$2,294	$1,639	$983	$328

Using the percentages from the schedule in Exhibit 11.7, we can calculate the tax (MACRS) depreciation for each year during the life of the performing arts center project.

savings of $328,000 × 0.30 = $98,400. This tax savings must be reflected in the cash flow calculations in year 10. Exhibit 11.9 illustrates the cash flow and NPV calculations for the performing arts center example with these changes. The $98,400 tax savings is included as a negative capital expenditure in year 10 (as −98 since we are rounding to thousands).[6] Notice that the NPV has increased from $15,487,664 in Exhibit 11.3 to $15,610,135. The $122,471 difference reflects the present value of the tax savings from using MACRS depreciation instead of straight-line depreciation plus the tax savings from the disposal of the asset.

If the salvage value is greater than $0 but less than the book value of $328,000, the tax savings will be smaller than $98,400, and if the salvage value exceeds the book value, the firm will actually have a gain on the sale of the asset that will increase its tax liability. In either of these cases, you must include the proceeds from the sale of the assets and the tax effects in your cash flow calculations.

Exhibit 11.9 FCF Calculations and NPV for Performing Arts Center Project with MACRS Depreciation ($ thousands)

	Year 0	Year 1	Year 2	Year 3	Year 4	Year 5	Year 6	Year 7	Year 8	Year 9	Year 10
Revenue		$14,100	$14,100	$14,100	$14,100	$14,100	$14,100	$14,100	$14,100	$14,100	$14,100
−Op Ex		8,460	8,460	8,460	8,460	8,460	8,460	8,460	8,460	8,460	8,460
EBITDA		$5,640	$5,640	$5,640	$5,640	$5,640	$5,640	$5,640	$5,640	$5,640	$5,640
−D&A		1,000	1,800	1,440	1,152	922	737	655	655	656	655
EBIT		$4,640	$3,840	$4,200	$4,488	$4,718	$4,903	$4,985	$4,985	$4,984	$4,985
×(1−t)		0.70	0.70	0.70	0.70	0.70	0.70	0.70	0.70	0.70	0.70
NOPAT		$3,248	$2,688	$2,940	$3,142	$3,303	$3,432	$3,490	$3,490	$3,489	$3,490
+D&A		1,000	1,800	1,440	1,152	922	737	655	655	656	655
CF Opns		$4,248	$4,488	$4,380	$4,294	$4,225	$4,169	$4,145	$4,145	$4,145	$4,145
−Cap Exp	$10,000	0	0	0	0	0	0	0	0	0	−98
−Add WC	1,000	0	0	0	0	0	0	0	0	0	−1,000
FCF	−$11,000	$4,248	$4,488	$4,380	$4,294	$4,225	$4,169	$4,145	$4,145	$4,145	$5,243

NPV @ 10% $15,610.135

This exhibit shows the FCF calculations and the NPV for the performing arts center project when MACRS is used to compute depreciation. These calculations correspond to those in Exhibit 11.3, which reflect straight-line depreciation. Notice that the NPV is greater with the MACRS system because the tax shields from the depreciation are realized sooner.

---

[6]Including the tax savings as negative capital expenditure increases the FCF in year 10 since we subtract all capital expenditures.

Exhibit 11.10 FCF Calculations and NPV for the Performing Arts Center Project with a $1 Million Salvage Value in Year 10 ($ thousands)

	Year 0	Year 1	Year 2	Year 3	Year 4	Year 5	Year 6	Year 7	Year 8	Year 9	Year 10
CF Opns		$4,248	$4,488	$4,380	$4,294	$4,225	$4,169	$4,145	$4,145	$4,145	$4,145
−Cap Exp	$10,000	0	0	0	0	0	0	0	0	0	−798
−Add WC	1,000	0	0	0	0	0	0	0	0	0	−1,000
FCF	−$11,000	$4,248	$4,488	$4,380	$4,294	$4,225	$4,169	$4,145	$4,145	$4,145	$5,943
NPV @ 10%	$15,880.016										

This exhibit shows the FCF calculations and NPV for the performing arts center project assuming that the salvage value of the $10 million capital investment is $1 million in year 10. All other assumptions are the same as in Exhibit 11.9.

The general formula for calculating the tax on the salvage value for an asset is:

Tax on sale of an asset = (Selling price of asset − Book value of asset) × t

where t is the firm's marginal tax rate.

To make sure we know how we use this equation, suppose that the salvage value (selling price) in year 10 of the $10,000,000 investment in the performing arts center project is expected to be $1,000,000 and that the book value remains $328,000. In this case the firm will pay additional taxes of ($1,000,000 − $328,000) × 0.30 = $201,600 on the sale of the assets. Deducting this amount from the $1,000,000 that the firm receives from the sale of the assets yields after-tax proceeds of $798,400 and the cash flows illustrated in Exhibit 11.10.

Accounting for Taxes When Assets Are Sold

LEARNING BY DOING APPLICATION 11.4

Problem: You have decided to replace an oven in your pizza parlor. The old oven originally cost $20,000. Depreciation charges of $15,000 have been taken since you acquired it, resulting in a current book value of $5,000. The owner of a restaurant down the street has offered you $3,000 for the old oven. If you accept this offer, how will the sale affect the cash flows from your business? Assume the marginal tax rate for your business is 39 percent.

Approach: First use the general formula presented above to calculate the tax on the salvage value. Then subtract (add) any tax obligation (savings) from (to) the amount that you will receive for the oven to obtain the total impact of the sale on the cash flows to your business.

Solution: If you sell the old oven, you will receive a cash inflow of $3,000 from the purchaser in return for an asset with a book value of $5,000. With a 39 percent marginal tax rate, this will result in a tax of:

Tax on sale of an asset = (Selling price of asset − Book value of asset) × t
= ($3,000 − $5,000) × 0.39 = −$780

Since you are selling the oven for less than its book value, you will realize a tax savings of $780. Therefore, the total impact of the sale on the cash flows from your business will be $3,000 + $780 = $3,780. Of course, the purchase price of the new oven will probably more than offset this amount.

(continued)

> Note that if the sale price exceeded the book value of the oven by $2,000, you would have a taxable gain and would have to pay $780. In this case, the cash flows received from the purchaser would be reduced, rather than increased, by $780.

Expected Cash Flows

It is very important to realize that in an NPV analysis we use the *expected* FCF for each year of the life of the project. Similar to the expected values calculated in Chapter 7, the expected FCF for a particular year equals the sum of the products of the possible outcomes (FCFs) and the probabilities that those outcomes will be realized.

To better illustrate this point, suppose that you have just invented a new board game and are trying to decide whether you should produce and sell it. If you decide to go ahead with this project, you estimate that it will cost you $100,000 for the equipment necessary to produce and distribute the game. Also suppose you think there are three possible outcomes if you make this investment—the game is very successful, game sales are acceptable but not exceptional, and game sales are poor—and that the probabilities associated with these outcomes are 25 percent, 50 percent, and 25 percent, respectively. If the FCFs under each of these three outcomes are as illustrated in Exhibit 11.11, then the expected values that you would discount in your NPV analysis are −$100.00, $48.75, $53.75, and $35.00 for years 0, 1, 2, and 3, respectively.[7] You should confirm that each of these values is correct to make sure that you understand how to calculate an expected FCF.

With these FCF estimates, we can now calculate the NPV of the board game project. For instance, if your cost of capital is 10 percent, the NPV is:

$$\begin{aligned} \text{NPV} &= \text{FCF}_0 + \frac{\text{FCF}_1}{1+k} + \frac{\text{FCF}_2}{(1+k)^2} + \frac{\text{FCF}_3}{(1+k)^3} \\ &= -\$100 + \frac{\$48.75}{1.10} + \frac{\$53.75}{(1.10)^2} + \frac{\$35.00}{(1.10)^3} \\ &= -\$100 + \$44.32 + \$44.42 + \$26.30 \\ &= \$15.04 \end{aligned}$$

Since the project has a positive NPV, you should accept it.

We use *expected* FCFs in a NPV analysis because uncertainties regarding project cash flows that are unique to the project should be reflected in the cash flow forecasts. In Chapter 13 we will discuss why analysts who try to account for such uncertainties by adjusting the discount rate, rather than the cash flows, are wrong.

Exhibit 11.11 Expected FCFs for New Board Game ($ thousands)

| | | Year | | | |
Outcome	Probability	0	1	2	3
Game is very successful	0.25	−$100	$70	$90	$60
Game sales are acceptable	0.50	−100	50	55	40
Game sales are poor	0.25	−100	25	15	0
Expected FCF		−$100.00	$48.75	$53.75	$35.00

The expected FCF for each year during the life of the board game project equals the weighted average of the possible FCFs in that year.

---

[7] For simplicity, the dollar values in Exhibit 11.11 and the associated calculations on this page are reported in thousands.

> **BUILDING INTUITION**
>
> **We Discount *Expected* Cash Flows in an NPV Analysis**
>
> Not only are the FCFs that we discount forward looking, but they also reflect *expected* FCFs. Each FCF is a weighted average of the cash flows from each possible future outcome, where the cash flow from each outcome is weighted by the estimated probability that the outcome will be realized. The expected FCF represents the single best estimate of what the actual FCF will be.

> **Before You Go On**
>
> 1. What are the five general rules for calculating FCF?
> 2. What is the difference between nominal and real dollars? Why is it important not to mix them in an NPV analysis?
> 3. What is a progressive tax system? What is the difference between a firm's marginal and average tax rates?
> 4. How can FCF in the terminal year of a project's life differ from FCF in the other years?
> 5. Why is it important to understand that cash flow forecasts in an NPV analysis are expected values?

11.3 Forecasting Free Cash Flows

Earlier, we discussed how to calculate the incremental free cash flows (FCFs) for a project. Of course, when we evaluate a project, we do not know exactly what the cash flows will be, and so we must forecast them. As the performing arts center example suggests, analysts do this for each line item in the FCF calculation for each year during the life of a project. We are now ready to discuss how these forecasts are prepared.

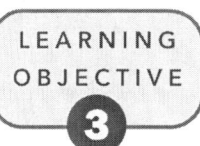

LEARNING OBJECTIVE 3

Cash Flows from Operations

To forecast the incremental cash flows from operations (CF Opns) for a project, we must forecast the incremental net revenue (Revenue), operating expenses (Op Ex), and depreciation and amortization (D&A) associated with the project, as well as the firm's marginal tax rate. To forecast Revenue, analysts typically estimate the number of units that will be sold and the per-unit sales price for each year during the life of the project. The product of the number of units sold and the per-unit sales price equals the Revenue (assuming that the project does not affect other product lines). Separating the Revenue forecast into incremental unit sales and price forces the analyst to think clearly about how well the project has to perform in terms of actual unit sales in order to achieve the forecasted Revenue.

When forecasting Op Ex, analysts often distinguish between **variable costs**, which vary directly with unit sales, and **fixed costs**, which do not. To illustrate the difference, consider a situation in which the managers of a firm plan to introduce a video game player that uses virtual reality technology. An overseas design and manufacturing company will produce the components and ship them to the company, which will assemble, package, and ship the finished product. The main variable costs will be those associated with purchasing the components; the labor required for assembling the players; packaging materials; shipping; and perhaps sales and marketing. These variable costs will rise in direct proportion to the number of units produced. If the number of units doubles, for example, we would expect these costs to approximately double. Fixed costs, such as the costs associated with assembly space (assuming output can be increased by

> You can find a number of free Excel spreadsheets that can be used to forecast free cash flows and use these cash flows to value projects and entire firms at Matt Evans's Web site, www.exinfm.com/free_spreadsheets.html. Follow the links to the Web sites of the individual contributors, and you will find even more free cash flow models and related information.

variable costs
costs that vary directly with the number of units sold

fixed costs
costs that do not vary directly with the number of units sold

adding shifts rather than obtaining additional space) and administrative expenses, will not increase directly with the number of units sold.[8]

Distinguishing between variable and fixed costs simplifies the forecasting problem. If company analysts estimate Revenue for a project from unit sales and price forecasts, as described earlier, then the analysts can forecast variable costs by multiplying the variable cost per unit by the number of units expected to be sold each year. Fixed cost forecasts, in contrast, will not typically vary as closely with unit sales. They tend to be based on explicit estimations of the cost of manufacturing (assembly) space, salaries and number of people required for administration of the project, and so forth.

Since D&A is determined by the amounts invested in depreciable assets and the lives over which these assets can be depreciated, this line item in the CF Opns calculation is computed based on the incremental capital expenditures (Cap Exp) associated with the project, the allowable recovery period, and the depreciation method used. Consequently, it is very important to carefully think through the size and timing of the Cap Exp and the nature of those assets to properly estimate the D&A deductions.

As discussed earlier, the tax rate that should be used when forecasting CF Opns is the marginal rate the firm expects to pay on the incremental cash flows generated by the project *in the future*. Past tax rates are relevant only to the extent that they tell us something about future tax rates. Federal, state, and local officials can change tax rates in the future, and to the extent that such changes can be predicted, they should be reflected in the cash flow forecasts. Unfortunately, such changes are difficult to predict. As a result, analysts normally use the firm's current marginal tax rate.

Investment Cash Flows

As discussed earlier, we must consider two general classes of investments when calculating FCF: incremental capital expenditures (Cap Exp) and incremental additions to working capital (Add WC). Each presents its own special challenges in the preparation of forecasts. In this section, we consider several issues related to forecasting Cap Exp and Add WC.

CAPITAL EXPENDITURES

Cap Exp forecasts in an NPV analysis reflect the expected level of investment during each year of the project's life, including any inflows from salvage values and any tax costs or benefits associated with asset sales. As illustrated in the performing arts center example, capital expenditures are typically required at the beginning of a project. Many projects require an initial investment for the assets necessary to produce a product and then little or no investment until the end of the project, when the assets are sold for their salvage value.

Some projects, however, require substantial periodic investments to replace or refurbish assets or to shut down operations (clean-up costs) at the end of the project's life. For example, a chemical plant project might require a substantial investment every few years to refurbish worn equipment. In addition, environmental regulations are likely to require that the property on which a chemical plant is built be restored to its previous condition when it is dismantled. These are like the clean-up costs for the strip mine that we mentioned earlier. Investments such as these should be included in cash flow forecasts wherever appropriate.

WORKING CAPITAL

As shown in Equation 11.4, cash flow forecasts in an NPV analysis include four working capital items: (1) cash and cash equivalents, (2) accounts receivable, (3) inventories, and (4) accounts payable.

---

[8] In some instances, costs are "fixed" in the short run but variable in the long run. For example, if a firm leases manufacturing space under a long-term contract, it may not be possible to reduce the lease expense immediately if demand for the firm's products falls. However, it will be possible to do so at the expiration of the lease.

Requirements for cash and cash equivalents and accounts receivable are typically forecast as constant percentages of revenue. The cash and cash-equivalent requirements represent the amount of cash needed to make timely payments to suppliers and employees, as well as for other ongoing expenses. This amount tends to vary with the nature of the project, but analysts can gain insights into the required level of cash, as a percentage of revenue, by examining the cash-to-revenue ratios for companies that operate comparable businesses. For example, if you are forecasting cash flows for a hotel project, you might look at the ratio of cash to revenue at public companies that are focused on the hotel business for an indication of how much cash is required per dollar of revenue.

Forecasting accounts receivable is relatively straightforward. If customers will be given 30 days to pay for purchases and, on average, are expected to take 30 days to pay, the average accounts receivable balance will equal 30 days worth of revenue or 30 days/365 days per year = 0.0822, or 8.22 percent of annual revenue. This represents the amount of money that must be set aside to finance purchases by customers. For example, a company with $100 million in annual revenue can expect to have $8.22 million invested in accounts receivable at any point in time if its customers take an average of 30 days to pay for their purchases.

Inventories and accounts payables are generally forecast as a percentage of the cost of goods sold. Inventories are forecast this way because the cost of goods sold represents a measure of the amount of money actually invested in inventories. Accounts payable are forecast this way because the cost of goods sold is a measure of the amount of money actually owed to suppliers.

> **Before You Go On**
>
> 1. What is the difference between variable and fixed costs, and what are examples of each?
> 2. How are working capital items forecast? Why are accounts receivable typically forecast as a percentage of revenue and accounts payable and inventories as percentages of the cost of goods sold?

11.4 Special Cases (Optional)

Now that we have discussed the fundamental concepts underlying NPV analysis (in Chapter 10) and how cash flows are calculated (in this chapter), we can turn our attention to some special cases that arise in capital budgeting. As you will see, dealing with these special cases generally involves the application of concepts that we have already discussed, along with a dose of common sense.

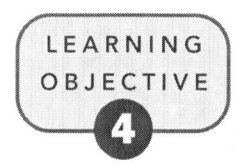

LEARNING OBJECTIVE 4

Projects with Different Lives

One problem that arises quite often in capital budgeting involves choosing between two mutually exclusive investments. Recall from Chapter 10 that if investments are mutually exclusive, the manager can choose one investment or the other but not both. This choice is simple if the expected lives of the two investments are the same. We choose the investment with the larger NPV. This type of problem was illustrated in Chapter 10.

The analysis becomes more complicated, however, if the investments have different lives. For example, suppose that you run a lawn-mowing service and have to replace one of your mowers. Further suppose that you have two options: mower A, which costs

$250 and is expected to last two years, and mower B, which costs $360 and is expected to last three years.

If the mowers are identical in every other way and you expect to be in the mowing business for a long time (in other words, you are going to continue to replace mowers as they wear out for the foreseeable future), then you cannot decide which mower to buy simply by comparing the $250 cost of mower A with the $360 cost of mower B. Mower A will provide two years of service, while mower B will provide three years of service.[9]

You might be tempted to choose the mower with the lowest initial investment per year of service. For example, you might choose mower B because the initial investment is $120 per year of service ($360 for three years) while mower A requires an initial investment of $125 per year of service ($250 for two years). As you will see, however, this reasoning can get you into trouble.

In this situation, we can effectively make the lives of the mowers the same by assuming repeated investments over some identical period and comparing the NPVs of their costs. In the mower example, we can do this by considering a six-year investment period. We determine the six-year period by multiplying the life of mower A by the life of mower B ($2 \times 3 = 6$). In six years you would buy mower A three times—in years 0, 2, and 4—or mower B twice—in years 0 and 3. If we assume that the cost of each mower will remain the same over the next six years, and if we use a 10 percent opportunity cost of capital, the NPVs of the *costs* of the two alternatives are:

$$\text{NPV} = \text{FCF}_0 + \frac{\text{FCF}_1}{1+k} + \frac{\text{FCF}_2}{(1+k)^2} + \cdots + \frac{\text{FCF}_n}{(1+k)^n}$$

$$\text{NPV}_A = -\$250 + \frac{-\$0}{1.10} + \frac{-\$250}{(1.10)^2} + \frac{-\$0}{(1.10)^3} + \frac{-\$250}{(1.10)^4} + \frac{-\$0}{(1.10)^5} + \frac{-\$0}{(1.10)^6}$$
$$= -\$627.36$$

$$\text{NPV}_B = -\$360 + \frac{-\$0}{1.10} + \frac{-\$0}{(1.10)^2} + \frac{-\$360}{(1.10)^3} + \frac{-\$0}{(1.10)^4} + \frac{-\$0}{(1.10)^5} + \frac{-\$0}{(1.10)^6}$$
$$= -\$630.47$$

Notice that mower A is actually cheaper over a six-year investment cycle. Over this period, it costs $627.36/6 = $104.56 per year in today's dollars, while mower B costs $630.47/6 = $105.08 per year.

Often, a much more efficient way of solving a problem of this nature is to compute the **equivalent annual cost (EAC)**. The EAC can be calculated as follows:

equivalent annual cost (EAC)

the annual dollar amount of an annuity that has a life equal to that of a project and that also has a present value equal to the present value of the cash flows from the project; the term comes from the fact that the EAC calculation is often used to calculate a constant annual cost associated with projects in order to make comparisons

$$\text{EAC}_i = k \, \text{NPV}_i \left[\frac{(1+k)^t}{(1+k)^t - 1} \right] \tag{11.5}$$

where k is the opportunity cost of capital, NPV_i is normal NPV of the investment i, and t is the life of the investment.

Using Equation 11.5, we find that the EACs for mowers A and B are:

$$\text{EAC}_A = (0.1)(-\$250) \left[\frac{(1+0.1)^2}{(1+0.1)^2 - 1} \right] = -\$144.05$$

and

$$\text{EAC}_B = (0.1)(-\$360) \left[\frac{(1+0.1)^3}{(1+0.1)^3 - 1} \right] = -\$144.76$$

We can see that the EAC gives us the same answer as equating the lives of the investments and calculating the NPVs over a six-year investment cycle. This is to be ex-

---

[9] If you don't expect to replace the machines as they wear out (for instance, if you plan to quit the mowing business in one year), then you can calculate the NPV of each mower, including the salvage values that you expect to realize for each at the end of the year, and choose the mower with the larger NPV.

pected, since the EAC simply reflects the annuity that has the same present value as the cost of an investment over the investment period we are considering. For instance, the NPV of the EAC for mower A over a six-year period is

$$NPV_A = \frac{-\$144.05}{1.1} + \frac{-\$144.05}{(1.1)^2} + \frac{-\$144.05}{(1.1)^3} + \frac{-\$144.05}{(1.1)^4} + \frac{-\$144.05}{(1.1)^5} + \frac{-\$144.05}{(1.1)^6}$$
$$= -\$627.38$$

This is the same NPV we obtained earlier (allowing for rounding differences).

The problem is similar but a bit more complicated if the revenues or operating costs associated with the two mowers differ. For simplicity, let's continue to assume that the mowers will generate the same revenue per year, but let's also assume that mower A will cost $50 per year to maintain and mower B will cost $55 per year to maintain. The NPVs of the two mowers in this case are

$$NPV_A = -\$250 + \frac{-\$50}{1.10} + \frac{-\$50}{(1.10)^2} = -\$336.78$$
$$NPV_B = -\$360 + \frac{-\$55}{1.10} + \frac{-\$55}{(1.10)^2} + \frac{-\$55}{(1.10)^3} = -\$496.78$$

The EACs are

$$EAC_A = (0.1)(-\$336.78)\left[\frac{(1+0.1)^2}{(1+0.1)^2 - 1}\right] = -\$194.05$$

and

$$EAC_B = (0.1)(-\$496.78)\left[\frac{(1+0.1)^3}{(1+0.1)^3 - 1}\right] = -\$199.76$$

Of course, we still want to choose mower A in this case since all that has really happened is that the EAC of mower A has gone up by $50 and the EAC of mower B has gone up by $55. In contrast, if the annual cost of maintaining mower A is $50 and the annual cost of maintaining mower B is $49, we would choose mower B. As confirmation, you should try the calculations for this example.

One other point should be made about the EAC concept. Despite its name, it does not apply only to costs. If we included revenues in the above analysis and both mowers had positive NPVs, we could still use the EAC formula to compare the two alternatives. The only difference in this case is that the decision criteria would be to choose the most positive EAC instead of the least negative.

LEARNING BY DOING APPLICATION 11.5

Using EAC to Compare Projects

Problem: You are looking at new ovens for your pizza parlor, and you see two models that would work equally well. Model A would cost $40,000 and last 10 years. Model B would cost $50,000 but would last 12 years and would require $500 less electricity per year than model A. Which model is less expensive? Assume a 10 percent opportunity cost of capital.

Approach: Use the EAC formula in Equation 11.5 to calculate the EAC of the initial investment for each model of oven. Add the annual electricity savings to the EAC of the initial investment for Model B. Choose the model with the smallest total EAC.

(continued)

Solution: The EACs for the initial investments in the two ovens are as follows:

$$EAC_A = (0.1)(-\$40{,}000)\left[\frac{(1+0.1)^{10}}{(1+0.1)^{10}-1}\right] = -\$6{,}509.82$$

$$EAC_B = (0.1)(-\$50{,}000)\left[\frac{(1+0.1)^{12}}{(1+0.1)^{12}-1}\right] = -\$7{,}338.17$$

Now since the electricity savings would be $500 per year in nominal dollars, we can simply add this amount to the EAC calculated for model B above to get the true $EAC_B = -\$7{,}338.16 + \$500 = -\$6{,}838.16$.[10] Since the EAC for model B is still more negative than that for model A, we would conclude that model A would be less expensive over its expected useful life.

When to Harvest an Asset

LEARNING OBJECTIVE 5

Another problem that arises from time to time involves deciding when to harvest an investment. A classic example occurs in the timber industry, where a decision must be made about when to harvest timber. The longer the harvest is delayed, the greater the number of board feet that can be obtained (since trees grow) and, assuming the price of lumber is constant, the greater the value of the harvested lumber. If the number of board feet that will be realized in the harvest and the price per board foot at any point in time is known, making the right decision involves a relatively straightforward application of concepts that we have already discussed.

For example, suppose that you own some land on which you planted pine trees 10 years ago. The trees can be harvested and sold to a pulp mill at any time now, but you want to make sure that you choose the point in time that maximizes the NPV of your investment in the trees. You have estimated the NPV (which equals the after-tax cash flow *at the time of the harvest*) of harvesting the trees today (year 10) and for each of the next four years to be as follows:

$$NPV_{10} = \$35{,}000$$
$$NPV_{11} = \$40{,}250$$
$$NPV_{12} = \$45{,}483$$
$$NPV_{13} = \$49{,}576$$
$$NPV_{14} = \$52{,}550$$

If each of these NPVs is stated in dollars as of the time when the harvest would take place, we cannot compare them directly. They must first be restated in dollars adjusted to the same point in time. If the opportunity cost of capital is 10 percent, we can make this adjustment simply by discounting each of the NPV values to year 10. The discounted values are as follows:

$$NPV_{10,10} = \$35{,}000$$
$$NPV_{10,11} = \$40{,}250/1.1 = \$36{,}591$$
$$NPV_{10,12} = \$45{,}483/(1.1)^2 = \$37{,}589$$
$$NPV_{10,13} = \$49{,}576/(1.1)^3 = \$37{,}247$$
$$NPV_{10,14} = \$52{,}550/(1.1)^4 = \$35{,}892$$

where $NPV_{x,y}$ refers to the NPV in year x dollars if the trees are harvested in year y. From these numbers, we can see that harvesting at the end of year 12 will produce the largest NPV in today's dollars.

---

[10] We could have also calculated the NPV for model B by discounting the $500 annual electricity savings by 10 percent and adding the present value of that savings stream to the $50,000 initial cost. Using this NPV in the EAC formula would also yield −$6,838.16.

If you calculate the percentage increase in the nominal NPV values above, you can see that they increase by 15 percent from year 10 to 11, by 13 percent from year 11 to 12, by 9 percent from year 12 to 13, and by 6 percent from year 13 to 14. The optimal time to harvest is at the end of the year before the first year in which the rate of increase is no longer greater than or equal to the cost of capital. At this time it becomes optimal to harvest the trees and invest the proceeds in alternative investments that yield the opportunity cost of capital because you can earn more from the alternative investments. An alternative way of thinking about this is that you do not want to harvest as long as the asset is earning a return that is greater than or equal to the opportunity cost of capital. This general principle applies to all problems of this kind.

In our example, we are ignoring the fact that the sooner we harvest the trees, the sooner we can plant the next crop. In this sense the solution is somewhat simplistic—we should really be considering the NPVs for a series of crops—but it illustrates the key points that (1) you must state all NPV values as of the same point in time and (2) the optimal time to harvest an asset is when it is no longer earning at least the opportunity cost of capital.

Outside of the timber industry, these ideas are widely used to decide when to exit investments. For example, leveraged-buyout specialists, who buy companies with the intention of improving and then selling them within a few years, perform a very similar type of analysis when choosing the appropriate time to sell a company.

When to Replace an Existing Asset

Occasionally, financial managers are asked to determine the appropriate time to replace an existing piece of equipment that is still operating. In these situations they must answer two fundamental questions: Do the benefits of replacing the existing machine exceed the costs, and if they do not now, when will they?

Let's examine how these questions can be answered for a situation that commonly arises in the lawn-mowing business. Suppose you have an old mower that is working perfectly well, but you are considering upgrading to a faster model. The old mower will run for another three years before it has to be replaced and will generate cash inflows, net of costs, of $6,500 for each of the next three years. The new mower costs $2,000 and would bring in net cash flows of $7,000 for four years. When should you replace the old mower?

Solving this problem is simply a matter of computing the EAC for the new mower and comparing it with the annual cash inflows from the old mower. With a 10 percent opportunity cost of capital, the NPV of the new mower is:

$$\text{NPV}_{\text{New mower}} = -\$2,000 + \frac{\$7,000}{1.1} + \frac{\$7,000}{(1.1)^2} + \frac{\$7,000}{(1.1)^3} + \frac{\$7,000}{(1.1)^4}$$
$$= -\$2,000 + \$6,364 + \$5,785 + \$5,259 + \$4,781$$
$$= \$20,189$$

Therefore, the EAC is:

$$\text{EAC}_{\text{New mower}} = (0.1)(\$20,189)\left[\frac{(1 + 0.1)^4}{(1 + 0.1)^4 - 1}\right] = \$6,369$$

In this example, the old mower should not be replaced until it wears out because it will generate net cash inflows of $6,500 for each of the next three years, while the EAC for the new mower is only $6,369.

Now suppose that, instead of remaining constant at $6,500, cash inflows from the old mower will decline from $6,500 in year 1, to $6,000 in year 2, and to $5,500 in year 3 as maintenance expenditures and downtime increase near the end of the old mower's useful life. If the EAC for the new mower is $6,369, the old machine should be replaced after the first year.

DECISION-MAKING EXAMPLE 11.2

Deciding When to Replace an Asset

Situation: You are trying to decide when to replace your car. It is already five years old, and maintenance costs keep increasing each year as more and more parts wear out and need to be replaced. You do not really care whether or not your car is new. You just want a car that gets you around at the lowest cost. You expect maintenance costs for your car over the next five years to increase by $500 per year from $500 this past year. Your car will be worthless in five years. As an alternative, you can buy a new car with a five-year warranty that will cover all maintenance costs. The new car will cost $15,000, and you expect to be able to sell it for $10,000 in five years. The gas mileage for both cars is the same. Remembering what you learned in corporate finance, you calculate the EAC for each option using a 10 percent opportunity cost of capital. The NPV for your old car is:

$$NPV_{Old\ car} = \frac{-\$1,000}{1.1} + \frac{-\$1,500}{(1.1)^2} + \frac{-\$2,000}{(1.1)^3} + \frac{-\$2,500}{(1.1)^4} + \frac{-\$3,000}{(1.1)^5}$$
$$= -\$7,221.69$$

and the EAC is −$1,905.06. The NPV for the new car is:

$$NPV_{New\ car} = -\$15,000 + \frac{\$10,000}{(1.1)^5}$$
$$= -\$8,790.79$$

and the EAC is −$2,318.99. When should you replace your old car?

Decision: The EAC for the new car is more negative than the EAC for your old car, suggesting that you should not replace your old car. However, if you compare the EAC for the new car with the annual maintenance costs you expect for your old car, you will see that the annual maintenance costs rise above the EAC of the new car in year 4. Assuming that the economics of the new car remain the same, you should replace your car after year 3.

The Cost of Using an Existing Asset

In Section 11.2 we discussed five general rules for calculating the incremental after-tax free cash flows associated with a project. The third rule is *to include all opportunity costs*. Unfortunately, opportunity costs are not always directly observable. Sometimes they have to be computed. This is particularly true when the opportunity cost relates to the use of excess capacity associated with an existing asset.

To see how we can evaluate opportunity costs of this kind, consider an example. Suppose you run a plant that mixes, bags, and ships potting soil—the soil often used for potted plants kept in people's homes. The bagging machine at your plant has sufficient excess capacity to handle forecasted increases in sales for the next five years if you stick to the potting-soil business. However, one of your managers has proposed that your plant diversify into the mulch business. If you began using the existing bagging machine to bag mulch, you would have to purchase a second bagging machine in three years instead of in five years. The cost of a second, identical machine would be $100,000, and this machine would have a five-year life. If the appropriate opportunity cost of capital is 10 percent, how should you account for the opportunity cost of using the bagging machine when computing the NPV of the mulch project?

The first step is to compute the EAC for the second bagging machine. It is:

$$EAC_{Bagging\ machine} = (0.1)(-\$100,000)\left[\frac{(1+0.1)^5}{(1+0.1)^5 - 1}\right] = -\$26,380$$

This tells us that the bagging machine costs $26,380 per year. If you decide to get into the mulch business, this cost, which would not otherwise be incurred until year 5, will also be incurred in years 3 and 4. Therefore, the opportunity cost of using the excess bagging capacity equals the present value of the additional cost incurred in years 3 and 4:

$$\text{NPV}_{\text{Bagging machine opportunity cost}} = \frac{-\$26,380}{(1.1)^3} + \frac{-\$26,380}{(1.1)^4} = -\$37,838$$

This cost should be included in the incremental cash flows for the mulch business. If the mulch project has a negative NPV with this cost, you might consider examining whether it has a positive NPV if you run the mulch business for only the next three years, while there is no constraint on the bagging capacity. A positive NPV in this latter analysis would indicate that the project should be pursued for three years and then abandoned.

> **Before You Go On**
>
> 1. When can we *not* simply compare the NPVs of two mutually exclusive projects?
> 2. How do we decide when to harvest an asset?
> 3. Under what circumstance would you replace an old machine that is still operating with a new one?

Summary of Learning Objectives

1. **Explain why incremental after-tax free cash flows are relevant in evaluating a project, and be able to calculate them for a project.**

   The incremental after-tax free cash flows, FCFs, for a project equal the expected change in the total after-tax cash flows of the firm if the project is adopted. The impact of a project on the firm's total cash flows is the appropriate measure of cash flows because these are the cash flows that reflect all of the costs and benefits from the project and only the costs and benefits from the project. The incremental after-tax free cash flows are calculated using Equation 11.2. This calculation is also illustrated in Exhibit 11.1.

2. **Discuss the five general rules for incremental after-tax free cash flow calculations, and explain why cash flows stated in nominal (real) dollars should be discounted using a nominal (real) discount rate.**

   The five general rules are as follows:

   Rule 1: *Include cash flows and only cash flows in your calculations.* Stockholders care about only the impact of a project on the firm's cash flows.

   Rule 2: *Include the impact of the project on cash flows from other product lines.* If a project affects the cash flows from other projects, we must take this fact into account in NPV analysis in order to fully capture the impact of the project on the firm's total cash flows.

   Rule 3: *Include all opportunity costs.* If an asset is used for a project, the relevant cost for that asset is the value that could be realized from its most valuable alternative use. By including this cost in the NPV analysis, we capture the change in the firm's cash flows that is attributable to the use of this asset for the project.

   Rule 4: *Forget sunk costs.* The only costs that matter are those to be incurred from this point on.

   Rule 5: *Include only after-tax cash flows in the cash flow calculations.* Since stockholders receive cash flows after taxes have been paid, they are concerned only about after-tax cash flows.

   Since a nominal discount rate reflects both the expected rate of inflation and a real return, we would be overadjusting for inflation if we discounted a real cash flow with a nominal rate. Similarly, if we discounted a nominal cash flow using a real discount rate, we would be undercompensating for expected inflation in the discounting process. This is why we discount nominal cash flows using only a nominal discount rate and we discount real cash flows using only a real discount rate.

3. **Describe how distinguishing between variable and fixed costs can be useful in forecasting operating expenses.**

   Variable costs vary directly with the number of units sold, while fixed costs do not. When forecasting operating expenses, it is often useful to treat variable and fixed costs separately. We can forecast variable costs by multiplying unit variable costs by the number of units sold. Fixed costs are more accurately based on the specific characteristics of those costs, rather than as a function of sales. Separating fixed costs from the variable also makes it easier to identify the factors that will cause them to change over time and therefore easier to forecast them.

4. **Explain the concept of equivalent annual cost, and be able to use it to compare projects with unequal lives, decide when to replace an existing asset, and**

calculate the opportunity cost of using an existing asset.

The equivalent annual cost (EAC) is the annualized cost of an investment that is stated in nominal dollars. In other words, it is the annual payment from an annuity that has the same NPV and the same life as the project. Since it is a measure of the annual cost or cash inflow from a project, the EAC for one project can be compared directly with the EAC from another project, regardless of the lives of those two projects. Applications of the EAC concept are presented in Section 11.4.

5. **Determine the appropriate time to harvest an asset.**

The appropriate time to harvest an asset is that point in time where harvesting the asset yields the largest present value, in today's dollars, of the project NPV.

Summary of Key Equations

Equation	Description	Formula
11.1	Incremental free cash flow definition	$FCF_{Project} = FCF_{Firm\ with\ project} - FCF_{Firm\ without\ project}$
11.2	Incremental free cash flow calculation	$FCF = [(Revenue - Op\ Ex - D\&A) \times (1-t)] + D\&A - Cap\ Exp - Add\ WC$
11.3	Inflation and real components of cost of capital	$1 + k = (1 + \Delta P_e) \times (1 + r)$
11.4	Incremental additions to working capital	Add WC = Change in cash and cash equivalents + Change in accounts receivable + Change in inventories − Change in accounts payable
11.5	Equivalent annual cost	$EAC_i = k\ NPV_i \left[\dfrac{(1+k)^t}{(1+k)^t - 1} \right]$

Self-Study Problems

11.1 Explain why the announcement of a new investment is usually accompanied by a change in the firm's stock price.

11.2 In calculating the NPV of a project, should we use all of the cash flows associated with the project or incremental free cash flows from the project? Why?

11.3 You are considering opening another restaurant in the TexasBurgers chain. The new restaurant will have annual revenue of $300,000 and operating expenses of $150,000. The annual depreciation and amortization for the assets used in the restaurant will equal $50,000. An annual capital expenditure of $10,000 will be required to offset wear and tear on the assets used in the restaurant, but no additions to working capital will be required. The marginal tax rate will be 40 percent. Calculate the incremental annual free cash flow for the project.

11.4 Sunglass Heaven, Inc., is launching a new store in a shopping mall in Houston. The annual revenue of the store depends on the weather conditions in the summer in Houston. The annual revenue will be $240,000 in a sizzling summer with a probability of 0.3, $80,000 in a cool summer with a probability of 0.2, and $150,000 in a normal summer with a probability of 0.5. What is the expected annual revenue for the store?

11.5 Sprigg Lane Manufacturing, Inc., needs to purchase a new central air-conditioning system for a plant. There are two choices. The first system costs $50,000 and is expected to last 10 years, and the second system costs $72,000 and is expected to last 15 years. Assume that the opportunity cost of capital is 10 percent. Which air-conditioning system should Sprigg Lane purchase?

Solutions to Self-Study Problems

11.1 A firm's investments cause changes in its future after-tax cash flows and stockholders are the residual claimants (owners) of those cash flows. Therefore, the stock price should increase when stockholders expect an investment to have a positive NPV, and decrease when it is expected to have a negative NPV.

11.2 We should use incremental free cash flows from the project. Incremental cash flows reflect the amount by which the firm's total cash flows will change if the project is adopted. In other words, incremental cash flows represent the net difference in cash revenues, costs, and investment outlays at the firm level with and without the project, which is precisely what the stockholders care about.

11.3 The incremental annual free cash flow is calculated as follows:

FCF = [($300,000 − $150,000 − $50,000) × (1 − 0.4)] + $50,000 − $10,000 = $100,000

11.4 The expected annual revenue is

(0.3 × $240,000) + (0.2 × $80,000) + (0.5 × $150,000) = $163,000

11.5 The equivalent annual cost for each system is as follows:

$$EAC_1 = (0.1)(\$50,000)\left[\frac{(1.1)^{10}}{(1.1)^{10} - 1}\right] = \$8,137.27$$

$$EAC_2 = (0.1)(\$72,000)\left[\frac{(1.1)^{15}}{(1.1)^{15} - 1}\right] = \$9,466.11$$

Therefore, Sprigg Lane should purchase the first one.

Critical Thinking Questions

11.1 Do you agree or disagree with the following statement given the techniques discussed in this chapter? We can calculate future cash flows precisely and obtain an exact value for the NPV of an investment.

11.2 What are the differences between forecasted cash flows used in capital budgeting calculations and past accounting earnings?

11.3 Suppose that FRA Corporation already has divisions in both Dallas and Houston. FRA is now considering setting up a third division in Austin. This expansion will require that one senior manager from Dallas and one from Houston relocate to Austin. Ignore relocation expenses. Is their annual compensation relevant to the decision to expand?

11.4 MusicHeaven, Inc., is a producer of MP3 players, which currently have either 20 gigabytes or 30 gigabytes of storage. Now the company is considering launching a new production line making mini MP3 players with 5 gigabytes of storage. Analysts forecast that MusicHeaven will be able to sell 1 million such mini MP3 players if the investment is taken. In making the investment decision, discuss what the company should consider other than the sales of the mini MP3 players.

11.5 QualityLiving Trust is a real estate investment company that builds and remodels apartment buildings in northern California. It is currently considering remodeling a few idle buildings that it owns into luxury apartment buildings in San Jose. The company bought those buildings eight months ago. How should the market value of the buildings be treated in the evaluating this project?

11.6 High-End Fashions, Inc., bought a production line of ankle-length skirts last year at a cost of $500,000. This year, however, miniskirts are hot in the market and ankle-length skirts are completely out of fashion. High-End has the option to rebuild the production line and use it to produce miniskirts with a cost of $300,000 and expected revenue of $700,000. How should the company treat the cost of $500,000 of the old production line in evaluating the rebuilding plan?

11.7 How is the MACRS depreciation method under IRS rules different from that under GAAP rules? What is the implication on incremental after-tax cash flows from firms' investments?

11.8 Explain the difference between marginal and average tax rates, and identify which of these rates is used in capital budgeting and why.

11.9 When two mutually exclusive projects have different lives, how can an analyst determine which is better? What is the underlying assumption in this method?

11.10 What is the opportunity cost of using an existing asset? Give an example of the opportunity cost of using the excess capacity of a machine.

11.11 You are providing financial advice to a shrimp farmer who will be harvesting his last crop of farm-raised shrimp. His current shrimp crop is very young and will, therefore, grow and become more valuable as their weight increases. Describe how you would determine the appropriate time to harvest the entire crop of shrimp.

Questions and Problems

BASIC

11.1 Calculating project cash flows: Why do we use forecasted free cash flows instead of forecasted accounting earnings in estimating the NPV of a project?

11.2 The FCF calculation: How do we calculate incremental after-tax free cash flows from forecasted earnings of a project? What are the common adjustment items?

11.3 The FCF calculation: How do we adjust for depreciation when we calculate incremental after-tax free cash flow from EBITDA? What is the intuition for the adjustment?

11.4 Nominal versus real cash flows: What is the difference between nominal and real cash flows? Which rate of return should we use to discount each type of cash flow?

11.5 Taxes and depreciation: What is the difference between average tax rate and marginal tax rate? Which one should we use in calculating incremental after-tax cash flows?

11.6 Computing terminal-year FCF: Healthy Potions, Inc., a pharmaceutical company, bought a machine that produces pain-reliever medicine at a cost of $2 million five years ago. The machine has been depreciated over the past five years, and the current book value is $800,000. The company decides to sell the machine now at its market price of $1 million. The marginal tax rate is 30 percent. What are the relevant cash flows? How do they change if the market price of the machine is $600,000 instead?

11.7 Cash flows from operations: What are variable costs and fixed costs? What are some examples of each? How are these costs estimated in forecasting operating expenses?

11.8 Investment cash flows: Six Twelve, Inc., is considering opening up a new convenience store in downtown New York City. The expected annual revenue is $800,000. To estimate the increase in working capital, analysts estimate the ratio of cash and cash-equivalents to revenue to be 0.03 and the ratios of receivables, inventories, and payables to revenue to be 0.05, 0.10, and 0.04, respectively, in the same industry. What is the incremental cash flow related to working capital when the store is opened?

11.9 Investment cash flows: Keswick Supply Company wants to set up a division that provides copy and fax services to businesses. Customers will be given 20 days to pay for such services. The annual revenue of the division is estimated to be $25,000. Assuming that the customers take the full 20 days to pay, what is the incremental cash flow associated with accounts receivable?

11.10 Expected cash flows: Define *expected cash flows*, and explain why this concept is important in evaluating projects.

11.11 Projects with different lives: Explain the concept of equivalent annual cost and how it is used to compare projects with different lives.

11.12 Replace an existing asset: Explain how we decide the optimal time to replace an existing asset with a new one.

INTERMEDIATE

11.13 Nominal versus real cash flows: You are buying a sofa. You will pay $200 today and make three consecutive annual payments of $300 in the future. The real rate of return is 10 percent, and the expected inflation rate is 4 percent. What is the actual price of the sofa?

11.14 Nominal versus real cash flows: You are graduating in two years. You want to invest your current savings of $5,000 in bonds and use the proceeds to purchase a new car when you graduate and start to work. You can invest the money in either bond A, a two-year bond with a 3 percent annual interest rate, or bond B, an inflation-indexed two-year bond paying 1 percent real interest above the inflation rate (assume this bond makes annual interest payments). The inflation rate over the next two years is expected to be 1.5 percent. Assume that both bonds are default free and have the same market price. Which bond should you invest in?

11.15 Marginal and average tax rates: Given the U.S. Corporate Tax Rate Schedule in Exhibit 11.6, what is the marginal tax rate and average tax rate of a corporation that generates a taxable income of $12 million in 2007?

11.16 Investment cash flows: Healthy Potions, Inc., is considering investing in a new production line for eye drops. Other than investing in the equipment, the company needs to increase its cash and cash equivalents by $10,000, increase the level of inventory by $30,000, increase accounts receivable by $25,000, and increase accounts payable by $5,000 at the beginning of the project. Healthy Potions will recover these changes in working capital at the end of the project 10 years later. Assume the appropriate discount rate is 12 percent. What are the present values of the relevant cash flows?

11.17 Cash flows from operations: Given the soaring price of gasoline, Ford is considering introducing a new production line of gas-electric hybrid sedans. The expected annual unit sales of the hybrid cars is 30,000; the price is $22,000 per car. Variable costs of production are $10,000 per car. The fixed overhead including salary of top executives is $80 million per year. However, the introduction of the hybrid sedan will decrease Ford's sales of regular sedans by 10,000 cars per year; the regular sedans have a unit price of $20,000, a unit variable cost of $12,000, and fixed costs of $250,000 per year. Depreciation costs of the production plant are $50,000 per year. The marginal tax rate is 40 percent. What is the incremental annual cash flow from operations?

11.18 FCF and NPV for a project: Archer Daniels Midland Company is considering buying a new farm that it plans to operate for 10 years. The farm will require an initial investment of $12 million. This investment will consist of $2 million for land and $10 million for trucks and other equipment. The land, all trucks, and all other equipment is expected to be sold at the end of 10 years for a price of $5 million, $2 million above book value. The farm is expected to produce revenue of $2 million each year, and annual cash flow from operations equals $1.8 million. The marginal tax rate is 35 percent, and the appropriate discount rate is 10 percent. Calculate the NPV of this investment.

11.19 Projects with different lives: You are starting a family pizza parlor and need to buy a motorcycle for delivery orders. You have two models in mind. Model A costs $9,000 and is expected to run for six years; model B is more expensive, with a price of $14,000, and has an expected life of 10 years. The annual maintenance costs are $800 for model A and $700 for model B. Assume that the opportunity cost of capital is 10 percent. Which one should you buy?

11.20 When to harvest an asset: Predator LLC, a leveraged-buyout specialist, recently bought a company and wants to determine the optimal time to sell it. The partner in charge of this investment has estimated the after-tax cash flows at different times as follows: $700,000 if sold one year later; $1,000,000 if sold two years later; $1,200,000 if sold three years later; and $1,300,000 if sold four years later. The opportunity cost of capital is 12 percent. When should Predator sell the company? Why?

11.21 Replace an existing asset: Bell Mountain Vineyards is considering updating its current manual accounting system with a high-end electronic system. While the new accounting system would save the company money, the cost of the system continues to decline. The Bell Mountain's opportunity cost of capital is 10 percent, and the costs and values of investments made at different times in the future are as follows:

Year	Cost	Value of Future Savings (at time of purchase)
0	$5,000	$7,000
1	4,500	7,000
2	4,000	7,000
3	3,600	7,000
4	3,300	7,000
5	3,100	7,000

When should Bell Mountain buy the new accounting system?

11.22 Replace an existing asset: You have a 1993 Nissan that is expected to run for another three years, but you are considering buying a new Hyundai before the Nissan wears out. You will donate the Nissan to Goodwill when you buy the new car. The annual maintenance cost is $1,500 per year for the Nissan and $200 for the Hyundai. The price of your favorite Hyundai model is $18,000, and it is expected to run for 15 years. Your opportunity cost of capital is 3 percent. Ignore taxes. When should you buy the new Hyundai?

11.23 Replace an existing asset: Assume that you are considering replacing your old Nissan with a new Hyundai, as in the previous problem. However, the annual maintenance cost of the old Nissan increases as time goes by. It is $1,200 in the first year, $1,500 in the second year, and $1,800 in the third year. When should you replace the Nissan with the new Hyundai in this case?

11.24 When to harvest an existing asset: Anaconda Manufacturing Company currently owns a mine that is known to contain a certain amount of gold. Since Anaconda does not have any gold-mining expertise, the company plans to sell the entire mine and base the selling price on a fixed multiple of the spot price for gold at the time of the sale. Analysts at Anaconda have forecast the spot price for gold and have determined that the price will increase by 14 percent, 12 percent, 9 percent, and 6 percent during the next one, two, three, and four years, respectively. If Anaconda's opportunity cost of capital is 10 percent, what is the optimal time for Anaconda to sell the mine?

11.25 Replace an existing asset: You are thinking about delivering pizzas in your spare time. Since you must use your own car to deliver the pizzas, you will wear out your current car one year earlier, which is one year from today, than if you did not take on the delivery job. You estimate that when you purchase a new car, regardless of when that occurs, you will pay $20,000 for the car and it will last you five years. If your opportunity cost of capital is 7 percent, what is the opportunity cost of using your car to deliver pizzas?

ADVANCED

11.26 You are the CFO of SlimBody, Inc., a retailer of the exercise machine Slimbody6® and related accessories. Your firm is considering opening up a new store in Los Angeles. The store will have a life of 20 years. It will generate annual sales of 5,000 exercise machines, and the price of each machine is $2,500. The annual sales of accessories will be $600,000, and the operating expenses of running the store, including labor and rent, will amount to 50 percent of the revenues from the exercise machines. The initial investment in the store will equal $30 million and will be fully depreciated on a straight-line basis over the 20-year life of the store. Your firm will need to invest $2 million in additional working capital immediately, and recover it at the end of the investment. Your firm's marginal tax rate is 30 percent. The opportunity cost of opening up the store is 10 percent. What are the incremental free cash flows from this project at the beginning of the project as well as in years 1–19 and 20? Should you approve it?

11.27 Rocky Mountain Lumber, Inc., is considering purchasing a new wood saw that costs $50,000. The saw will generate revenues of $100,000 per year for five years. The cost of materials and labor needed to generate these revenues will total $60,000 per year, and other cash expenses will be $10,000 per year. The machine is expected to sell for $1,000 at the end of its five-year life and will be depreciated on a straight-line basis over five years to zero. Rocky Mountain's tax rate is 34 percent, and its opportunity cost of capital is 10 percent. Should the company purchase the saw? Explain why or why not?

11.28 A beauty product company is developing a new fragrance named Happy Forever. There is a probability of 0.5 that consumers will love Happy Forever, and in this case, annual sales will be 1 million bottles; a probability of 0.4 that consumers will find the smell acceptable and annual sales will be 200,000 bottles; and a probability of 0.1 that consumers will find the smell weird and annual sales will be only 50,000 bottles. The selling price is $38, and the variable cost is $8 per bottle. Fixed production costs will be $1 million per year and depreciation will be $1.2 million. Assume that the marginal tax rate is 40 percent. What are the expected annual incremental cash flows from the new fragrance?

11.29 Great Fit, Inc., is a company that makes clothing. The company has a product line that produces women's tops of regular sizes. The same machine could be used to produce petite sizes as well. However, the remaining life of the machines will be reduced from four years to two years if the petite size production is added. The cost of identical machines with a life of eight years is $2 million. Assume the opportunity cost of capital is 8 percent. What is the opportunity cost of adding petite sizes?

11.30 Biotech Partners LLC has been farming a new strain of radioactive-material-eating bacteria that the electrical utility industry can use to help dispose of its nuclear waste. Two opposing factors affect Biotech's decision of when to harvest the bacteria. The bacteria are currently growing at a 22 percent annual rate, but due to known competition from other top firms, Biotech analysts estimate that the price for the bacteria will decline according to the schedule below. If the opportunity cost of capital is 10 percent, then when should Biotech harvest the entire bacteria colony at one time?

Year	Change in Price Due to Competition (%)
1	5%
2	−2
3	−8
4	−10
5	−15
6	−25

11.31 ACME Manufacturing is considering replacing an existing production line with a new line that has a greater output capacity and operates with less labor than the existing line. The new line would cost $1 million, have a five-year life, and be depreciated using MACRS over three years. At the end of five years, the new line could be sold as scrap for $200,000 (in year 5 dollars). Because the new line is more automated, it would require fewer operators, resulting in a savings of $40,000 per year before tax and unadjusted for inflation (in today's dollars). Additional sales with the new machine are expected to result in additional net cash inflows, before tax, of $60,000 per year (in today's dollars). If ACME invests in the new line, a one-time investment of $10,000 in additional working capital will be required. The tax rate is 35 percent, the opportunity cost of capital is 10 percent, and the annual rate of inflation is 3 percent. What is the NPV of the new production line?

11.32 The alternative to investing in the new production line in Problem 11.31 is to overhaul the existing line, which currently has both a book value and a salvage value of $0. It would cost $300,000 to overhaul the existing line, but this expenditure would extend its useful life to five years. The line would have a $0 salvage value at the end of five years. The overhaul outlay would be capitalized and depreciated using MACRS over three years. Should ACME replace or renovate the existing line?

CFA PROBLEMS

11.33 FITCO is considering the purchase of new equipment. The equipment costs $350,000, and an additional $110,000 is needed to install it. The equipment will be depreciated straight-line to zero over a five-year life. The equipment will generate additional annual revenues of $265,000, and it will have annual cash operating expenses of $83,000. The equipment will be sold for $85,000 after five years. An inventory investment of $73,000 is required during the life of the investment. FITCO is in the 40 percent tax bracket, and its cost of capital is 10 percent. What is the project NPV?
  a. $47,818
  b. $63,658
  c. $80,189
  d. $97,449

11.34 After estimating a project's NPV, the analyst is advised that the fixed capital outlay will be revised upward by $100,000. The fixed capital outlay is depreciated straight-line over an eight-year life. The tax rate is 40 percent, and the required rate of return is 10 percent. No changes in cash operating revenues, cash operating expenses, or salvage value are expected. What is the effect on the project NPV?
  a. $100,000 decrease
  b. $73,325 decrease
  c. $59,988 decrease
  d. No change

11.35 When assembling the cash flows to calculate an NPV or IRR, the project's after-tax interest expenses should be subtracted from the cash flows for
  a. the NPV calculation, but not the IRR calculation
  b. the IRR calculation, but not the NPV calculation
  c. both the NPV calculation and the IRR calculation
  d. neither the NPV calculation nor the IRR calculation

Sample Test Problems

11.1 You purchased 100 shares of stock in an oil company, Texas Energy, Inc., at $50 per share. The company has 1 million shares outstanding. Ten days later, Texas Energy announced an investment in an oil field in east Texas. The probability that the investment will be successful and generate an NPV of $10 million is 0.2; the probability that the investment will be a failure and generate an NPV of negative $1 million is 0.8. How would you expect the stock price to change upon the company's announcement of the investment?

11.2 A chemical company is considering buying a magic fan for its plant. The magic fan is expected to work forever and help cool the machines in the plant and, hence, reduce their maintenance costs by $4,000 per year. The cost of the fan is $30,000. The appropriate discount rate is 10 percent and the marginal tax rate is 40 percent. Should the company buy the magic fan?

11.3 Hogvertz Elvin Catering (HEC) is considering switching from its old food maker to a new Wonder Food Maker. Both food makers will remain useful for the next 10 years, but the new food maker will generate a depreciation expense of $5,000 per year, while the old food maker will generate a depreciation expense of $4,000 per year. What is the after-tax cash flow effect from depreciation of switching to the new food maker for HEC if the firm's marginal tax rate is 40 percent and the discount rate is 12 percent?

11.4 The Long-Term Financing Company has identified an alternative project that is similar to a project currently under consideration in all respects except one. That is, the new project will reduce the need for working capital by $10,000 during the 30-year life of the project. The cost of capital is 18 percent and the marginal corporate tax rate for the firm is 34 percent. What is the after-tax present value of this new alternative project?

11.5 Choice Masters must choose between two projects of unequal lives. Project 1 has a NPV of $50,000 and will be viable for five years. The discount rate for project 1 and project 2 is 10 percent. Project 2 will be viable for seven years. In order for Choice Master to be indifferent between the two projects, what must the NPV of project 2 be?

Doing the Right Thing: The Schwan Food Company

ETHICS CASE

In September 1994, an outbreak of salmonella struck southern and southeast Minnesota. The most common way to be afflicted with salmonella is through tainted food products. On October 7, 1994, the Minnesota Department of Health (MDH) contacted The Schwan Food Company about the MDH's plans to issue an advisory recommending that consumers not eat Schwan's ice cream. The MDH advisory was based on a preliminary study.

Obviously Schwan, which has a reputation for high quality, had a dilemma. How should the company respond, and when should it respond? Until further evidence was presented, Schwan could not even be sure that its ice cream was involved.

Nonetheless, Schwan acted immediately. On October 7, Schwan issued a press release announcing the voluntary recall of all its ice cream products. Schwan also announced the shutdown of its ice cream plant in Marshall, Minnesota. A 24-hour hotline was established. Schwan also offered to pay for tests that would help diagnose a customer's illness and determine whether it could be linked to salmonella.

Hundreds of subsequent tests at Schwan's ice cream plant in Marshall, Minnesota, tested negative for salmonella. Yet between October 8 and October 10, the MDH hotline reported that, based on calls received, it believed that over 1,200 people had become ill after eating Schwan's ice cream. Only later did tests determine that salmonella was present in some samples of Schwan's ice cream that had been taken from the homes of those who had become sick. How had the ice cream become contaminated? This was the mystery.

The Company's Ethical Foundation

In addition to its reputation for quality, Schwan also has a solid reputation as a highly ethical company. Marvin Schwan, the founder of Schwan, walked the talk when it came to ethics. He set an example with his own conduct and expected employees to walk the straight and narrow. In 1991, Marvin wrote a statement of values that Schwan would embody. These values included hard work, enthusiasm, integrity, growth, and helping one another. Clearly, some of these values are ethical in nature. Schwan also has a company Credo that has quality as its focal point. The Credo begins as follows:

We believe that to achieve the Vision of Our Heritage of Quality Policy, our family of businesses must operate under the following principles:

Total Quality Commitment

1. Quality is customer satisfaction and includes both internal and external customers.
2. Total quality includes quality service, quality products, quality relationships, and is EVERYONE's responsibility.

A key to understanding Schwan's quick and effective response to the salmonella crisis is a portion of the value statement made by Marvin Schwan: "The Schwan Food Company has a sacred trust with its customers, and integrity means doing what is right regardless of the consequences." Just as Johnson & Johnson had done years before when it based its response to the Tylenol crisis by involving its own Credo, Schwan embraced its Credo and Mr. Schwan's statement of values in determining how it would respond to the October 7 notification by the MDH.

Taking Action before Responsibility Had Been Established

As mentioned, Schwan acted immediately on October 7 to protect its customers without confirmation that its ice cream was involved in the salmonella outbreak. By October 9 a total recall plan was in place. Among the items in Schwan's recall plan were provisions for giving refunds to customers. Ads appeared that communicated the recall information. All of this occurred before it was absolutely certain that Schwan's ice cream was involved in the salmonella outbreak.

Schwan worked with its wholesale accounts in numerous states and personally delivered information letters regarding the recall to thousands of individual customers on scheduled individual delivery routes. Schwan also shut down its ice cream plant, and microbiological testing began in earnest. In addition to the testing at the plant, all Schwan's plant employees were tested for salmonella. Also tested were hundreds of finished ice cream products as well as the tankers that had carried the ice cream premix. Observers agree that both the recall and the overall Schwan's response went above and beyond what was normally done in this kind of situation.

Schwan's Plant Not the Cause of the Contamination

Finally the mystery was solved. The MDH ultimately determined that the Schwan's plant was not the cause of the ice cream contamination. The MDH determined that the contamination was caused when tanker trucks that had previously carried nonpasteurized liquid eggs were later used to transport pasteurized ice cream premix from vendors to the Schwan's plant. Schwan brought a lawsuit against the tanker truck company and the ice cream mix vendors alleging, among other things, that these shipments to Schwan of ice cream premix which contained salmonella were in violation of contractual agreements. As a result of the MDH's determination and the information obtained in the lawsuit, Schwan now uses only dedicated tankers to transport the ice cream premix. A dedicated tanker is one that is used exclusively by Schwan for shipping items used in Schwan's production of foodstuffs. Schwan also built and now uses a pasteurization unit that subjects the already pasteurized ice cream premix to an additional pasteurization process upon its arrival at the Schwan's plant.

Both before and after this incident, Schwan has continually proven to be a leader in food quality and safety. Schwan was the first company to distribute irradiated ground beef nationwide. Moreover, any ground beef it sells from the route trucks has been electronically pasteurized. And, with respect to food allergies, Schwan has initiated a corporate-wide practice of putting allergen labeling on its food products.

Litigation from Incident

As is usually the case in these situations, there was class action litigation even though the salmonella crisis may not have been as extensive as originally thought. However, thousands of Schwan's customers recognized that Schwan was not at fault and either accepted Schwan's offers of discount coupons and/or replacement product or simply refused to sue Schwan. Schwan also responded so well to customer complaints that the class-action lawsuits were resolved relatively quickly, and a three-judge panel of the Minnesota Court of Appeals said: "that so few plaintiffs objected to the settlement is a significant factor that supports the fairness and adequacy of the settlement terms." A front-page article in the November 1995 issue of *Corporate Legal Times* was titled "A Model to Follow—Schwan Beats Salmonella and Possible Disaster."

Many now argue that Schwan emerged from the crisis a stronger company than it had been before. It held on to most of its original customers and added new customers as well. Some of Schwan's route drivers found that some customers did not even want to return the ice cream products that had been labeled for recall!

Questions

1. Is Schwan's reputation for high quality and integrity a financial asset that should be recognized and counted as part of the financial value of the company?

2. Taking responsibility for a problem when one is not even sure one is the cause of the problem is costly. Was Schwan correct in moving so quickly to shut down its plant and conduct a voluntary recall of all its ice cream products?

3. Taking responsibility often implies liability. Sometimes lawyers argue against admitting anything that even resembles liability, given the possible legal consequences. Again, did Schwan overreact by moving so quickly to protect its customers and the public at large?

CHAPTER 12

EVALUATING PROJECT ECONOMICS AND CAPITAL RATIONING

LEARNING OBJECTIVES

1. Explain and be able to demonstrate how variable costs and fixed costs affect the volatility of pretax operating cash flows and accounting operating profits.

2. Calculate and distinguish between the degree of pretax cash flow operating leverage and the degree of accounting operating leverage.

3. Define and calculate the pretax operating cash flow and accounting operating profit break-even points and the crossover levels of unit sales for a project.

4. Define sensitivity analysis, scenario analysis, and simulation analysis, and describe how they are used to evaluate the risks associated with a project.

5. Explain how the profitability index can be used to rank projects when a firm faces capital rationing, and describe the limitations that apply to the profitability index.

Mel Longhurst/Capital Pictures/Digital Railroad, Inc.

Video Gaming Technologies (VGT) ranked number one on the *Inc.* 500 list of fastest-growing privately held companies in 2005. Revenue at VGT, which manufactures gaming machines for the casino industry, had increased 9,721 percent over the previous three years, to $99.8 million. The company continued to grow rapidly after 2005, with revenue reaching $180.1 million in 2006. But even for a slot machine manufacturer, success of this magnitude is not a sure thing.

As with any other capital investment, starting a business involves a great deal of uncertainty. If you put yourself in the shoes of Jon Yarbrough, the founder of VGT, you can imagine the concerns he had when he founded the company in 1991. How large would the market for gaming machines be in the future? How big a share of that market could his firm get? The size of the market would depend on many things that were out of his control, such as the demand for casino gambling and the number of new casinos that opened. VGT's share of the market and, ultimately, its profitability would depend on the firm's ability to design machines that were more appealing to casino customers than those of competing companies.

As Yarbrough contemplated starting VGT, he was no doubt asking himself a number of questions: What level of unit sales would be required to cover costs? What would happen if the business did not earn enough to cover its costs? What if the business was initially successful but competitors reacted by slashing their prices? What were the odds that the business would be successful? If it was not successful, how bad were things likely to get? If it was successful, how good would the upside be? Answering questions such as these is part of any thorough project analysis. This chapter discusses some of the tools and methods used to obtain the answers.

CHAPTER PREVIEW

Financial analysts who forecast the free cash flows used in an NPV analysis realize that actual cash flows will almost certainly differ from their forecasts. No one can predict the future! For this reason, it is important to understand the economic characteristics of a project and the implications of being wrong. This chapter discusses key tools and methods that analysts use to develop this understanding. It also discusses how managers choose from among available positive NPV projects when they do not have enough money to invest in all of them.

We first discuss how a project's cost structure affects its risk and how analysts measure this effect. We then describe break-even analysis, which is used to determine how many units must be sold in order for a project to break even. These concepts help analysts better understand the economic characteristics of projects and provide insights into how projects can be structured to maximize their value.

We next describe how financial analysts evaluate the uncertainties associated with cash flow forecasts. These techniques allow analysts to determine which characteristics of a project have the greatest impact on the level of the cash flows, how market or economic conditions affect the cash flows of the business, and the probability that certain levels of cash flows will be realized.

We end with a discussion of the tools and methods that help managers choose the bundle of projects that creates the greatest overall value for stockholders when there is not enough capital to invest in all of the positive NPV projects that managers have identified.

12.1 Variable Costs, Fixed Costs, and Project Risk

Two questions are always on the mind of a financial analyst evaluating a project: "How wrong can my free cash flow forecasts be?" and "What are the implications if my forecasts are wrong?" It is natural to ask these questions, since the actual free cash flows (FCF) for a project will almost certainly differ from the forecasted FCF. This section and Sections 12.2 to 12.4 discuss some important tools that help provide answers.

LEARNING OBJECTIVE 1

To fully understand how to evaluate project risk, you must first understand how variable costs and fixed costs affect the risk of a business. Recall from Chapter 11 that variable costs are costs that vary directly with the number of units sold. An example of a variable cost is the cost of the ingredients that a pizza parlor uses to make its pizzas. The total cost of these ingredients increases or decreases as the number of pizzas sold increases or decreases. Fixed costs, in contrast, do not vary with unit sales—at least in the short run. An example of a fixed cost in a pizza parlor is the salary of the manager. As pizza sales go up and down from month to month, the cost of the manager's salary remains constant.

The cash flows and accounting profits for a project are sensitive to the proportion of its costs that is variable and the proportion that is fixed. A project with a higher proportion of fixed costs will have cash flows and accounting profits that are more sensitive to changes in revenues than an otherwise identical project with a lower proportion of fixed costs. This is because the costs of a project with a higher proportion of fixed costs will not change as much when revenue changes.

To illustrate this point, we can represent the incremental cash operating expenses, Op Ex, from Equation 11.2 as

$$\text{Op Ex} = \text{VC} + \text{FC} \qquad (12.1)$$

where VC is the incremental variable costs associated with a project and FC is the incremental fixed costs. Equation 12.1 simply says that all cash operating expenses are either variable costs or fixed costs.

Let's carry this equation a bit further. We know from Exhibit 11.1 that

$$\text{EBITDA} = \text{Revenue} - \text{Op Ex}$$

Thus, Equation 12.1 suggests that we can write EBITDA as

$$\text{EBITDA} = \text{Revenue} - \text{VC} - \text{FC}$$

You might recall from Chapter 11 that EBITDA is the incremental earnings before interest, taxes, depreciation, and amortization and Revenue is the incremental revenue from a project. EBITDA is often called **pretax operating cash flow** because it equals the incremental pretax *cash* operating profits from a project. Strictly speaking, EBITDA is not a complete measure of operating cash flow because it does not include the effects of working capital requirements on cash flows. Nevertheless, it is a very commonly used measure.

pretax operating cash flow
earnings before interest, taxes, depreciation, and amortization, or EBITDA

Cost Structure and Sensitivity of EBITDA to Revenue Changes

To see how writing the calculation of EBITDA in terms of fixed and variable costs can be helpful, consider this situation: You have been trying to decide whether to buy a hammock-manufacturing business in which hammocks are currently made by hand.[1] Now you have become aware of the existence of an automated hammock-manufacturing system. This means that, in addition to deciding whether to go into the hammock business, you must choose between two manufacturing alternatives: (1) investing in manufacturing equipment that will largely automate the production process and (2) relying on the current manufacturing method in which hammocks are produced by hand. Assume that the per-unit variable costs (Unit VC) and the total FC and depreciation and amortization (D&A) for the two alternatives are as presented in Exhibit 12.1. How would you evaluate the relative advantages and disadvantages of the automated and the manual production alternatives?

One thing you might do is compare the sensitivity of EBITDA to changes in revenue for the two alternatives. This can help you better understand the risks and returns for the alternatives. To see why, assume that the sensitivity of EBITDA to changes in revenue is higher for one alternative than for the other. This means that EBITDA for the more sensitive alternative will decline more when revenue is lower than expected. A larger decline in EBITDA can cause problems not only because it reduces the value of the project more, but also because it has a greater impact on the amount of cash that the firm has available to fund other positive NPV projects. In an extreme case, a drop in EBITDA can unexpectedly force the firm to invest additional money into the project. On the positive side, EBITDA will increase more when revenue is greater than expected if the level of sensitivity is higher. Whether this potential benefit justifies the risks is a decision that you would have to make when choosing between the two alternatives. Comparing the sensitivity of EBITDA to changes in revenue for the two alternatives will at least help you better understand the trade-offs.

---

[1] A hammock is a hanging bed that is often made of rope and hung between two trees.

12.1 Variable Costs, Fixed Costs, and Project Risk

Exhibit 12.1 Unit and Annual Costs for Hammock Project

	Automated Production	Manual Production
Unit VC:		
Labor	$1	$5
Rope	5	5
Spacer bars	2	2
Hardware	2	2
Packaging	2	2
Shipping and other	4	4
Total	$16	$20
FC	$35,000	$4,000
D&A	$10,000	$1,000

To evaluate the automated and manual production alternatives in our hammock-manufacturing example, we start with information about the variable costs per unit (Unit VC), fixed costs (FC), and depreciation and amortization (D&A).

Distinguishing between fixed and variable costs enables us to calculate the sensitivity of EBITDA to changes in revenue. For example, suppose you expect to sell 10,000 hammocks next year at an average price of $25 each. Based on the costs in Exhibit 12.1, you would forecast EBITDA to be $55,000 under the automated production alternative and $46,000 under the manual production alternative.[2] These calculations are presented in Exhibit 12.2.

Although selling 10,000 units represents your best estimate of what you can expect, you might also envision a situation in which demand would be poor and sales would equal only 8,000 units, 20 percent less than your best estimate of 10,000 units.

Exhibit 12.2 EBITDA under Alternative Production Technologies

	Automated Production	Manual Production
Units sold	10,000	10,000
Unit price	$25	$25
Unit VC	$16	$20
Revenue	$250,000	$250,000
− VC	160,000	200,000
− FC	35,000	4,000
EBITDA	$ 55,000	$ 46,000

Here we calculate EBITDA for the automated and manual production alternatives in the hammock-manufacturing example. The calculations use the information provided in Exhibit 12.1 and assume that 10,000 units are sold at a price of $25 per unit.

---

[2] VC equals Unit VC (or cost per unit) times the number of units sold. If we know Unit VC, we can therefore calculate VC for different levels of unit sales.

Exhibit 12.3 Changes in EBITDA under Alternative Production Technologies

	Automated Production		Manual Production	
	Expected Demand (1)	Poor Demand (2)	Expected Demand (3)	Poor Demand (4)
Units sold	10,000	8,000	10,000	8,000
Unit price	$25	$25	$25	$25
Unit VC	$16	$16	$20	$20
Revenue	$250,000	$200,000	$250,000	$200,000
− VC	160,000	128,000	200,000	160,000
− FC	35,000	35,000	4,000	4,000
EBITDA	$ 55,000	$ 37,000	$ 46,000	$ 36,000
Percent change in revenue[a]		−20.0%		−20.0%
Percent change in EBITDA		−32.7%		−21.7%

[a]The percent change in revenue is calculated as:

Percent change = (Revenue$_{Poor}$ − Revenue$_{Expected}$)/Revenue$_{Expected}$
= ($200,000 − $250,000)/$250,000 = −0.20, or −20%

All other percent changes are calculated this way in the exhibits.

EBITDA for the automated and manual production alternatives in the hammock-manufacturing example decline by different amounts when the number of units sold declines 20 percent and the unit price remains the same.

Distinguishing between fixed and variable costs makes it relatively straightforward to determine how EBITDA would be affected if only 8,000 units were sold. This "Poor Demand" scenario is illustrated in columns 2 and 4 of Exhibit 12.3 for the automated production and manual production alternatives (assuming that Unit VC does not change with unit sales). Columns 1 and 3 are identical to the two columns in Exhibit 12.2.

Exhibit 12.3 shows that EBITDA is much more sensitive to changes in revenue with the automated production process than with the manual process. A 20 percent decline in revenue results in a 32.7 percent decline in EBITDA with the automated production process but only a 21.7 percent decline in EBITDA with the manual production process—an 11 percentage point difference. The reason for the difference is that more of the total costs are fixed with the automated process, making it more difficult to adjust costs when revenue changes. Because of this difference, the difference in EBITDA under the two production alternatives shrinks from $9,000 ($55,000 − $46,000) to only $1,000 ($37,000 − $36,000) when unit sales are 8,000 instead of 10,000.

You can see how the difference in EBITDA shrinks as the number of units sold decreases in Exhibit 12.4, which shows how EBITDA changes as the number of units sold changes for both the manual and the automated production process. Notice that the relation between EBITDA and the number of units sold is steeper with the automated production process, where there are more fixed costs. A steeper line indicates that EBITDA for the automated production process is more sensitive to changes in the number of units sold.

Note also that the effect of changes in the number of units sold is symmetrical because the relation between EBITDA and the number of units sold is linear. This means that the automated production process will produce larger declines in EBITDA when unit sales are lower than expected as well as larger increases in EBITDA when unit sales are higher than expected. This is exactly what we were referring to earlier when we said that when pretax operating cash flows are more sensitive to changes in revenue,

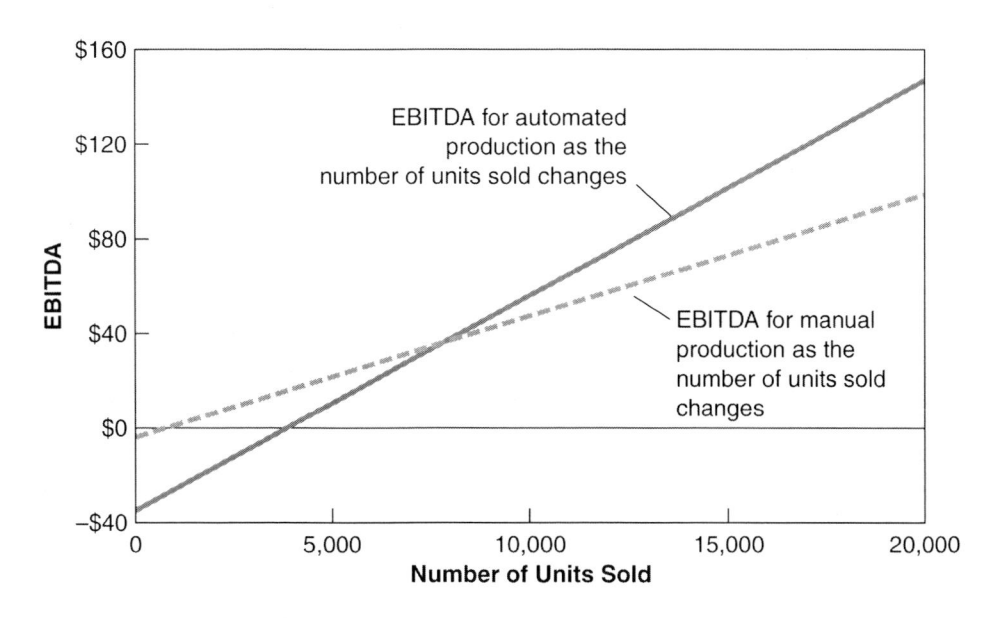

**Exhibit 12.4
EBITDA for Different Levels of Unit Sales**
The sensitivity of EBITDA to changes in unit sales differs for the automated and manual production alternatives in the hammock-manufacturing example. The steeper line for the automated production alternative means that EBITDA for this alternative is more sensitive to changes in the number of units sold.

they will decline more when revenue is lower than expected and increase more when revenue is greater than expected.

Cost Structure and Sensitivity of EBIT to Revenue Changes

Exhibit 12.5 expands the analysis in Exhibit 12.3 to illustrate how the sensitivity of accounting operating profits (EBIT) to changes in revenue differs under the two manufacturing alternatives. The sensitivity of EBIT to changes in revenue is of concern to managers because EBIT is a performance measure that is of interest to investors.

In Exhibit 12.5 you can see that the 20 percent decline in revenue results in a 40 percent decline in EBIT with the automated production process but only a 22.2 percent decline in EBIT with the manual production process. The difference in the decline in EBIT is 17.8 percentage points! This difference is larger than the 11 percentage point difference for EBITDA because the EBITDA calculation does not include D&A. Depreciation and amortization acts just like a fixed cost when we include it in the calculation because it is based on the amount that was invested in the project, rather than in unit sales. Therefore, when we include D&A in the EBIT calculation, we effectively increase the proportion of costs that are fixed. Since D&A is larger for the automated production alternative, this, in turn, makes EBIT more sensitive to changes in revenue.

If we re-created Exhibit 12.4 for EBIT, the lines would also be linear and the slope would be steeper for the automated production process than for the manual production process. As was the case with EBITDA, the linear relation between changes in revenue and EBIT indicates that there are benefits and costs associated with using the automated production process. When deciding whether to use the automated process, you must weigh the prospect of higher accounting operating profits if unit sales exceed expected levels against concerns about lower accounting operating profits if unit sales are below expectations. In other words, you must decide whether the potential for earning a higher return with the automated manufacturing process justifies the risks. In Chapter 16 we will discuss how greater volatility in operating profits increases the chances that a firm will be forced into bankruptcy.

Exhibit 12.5 Changes in EBITDA and EBIT under Alternative Production Technologies

	Automated Production		Manual Production	
	Expected Demand (1)	Poor Demand (2)	Expected Demand (3)	Poor Demand (4)
Units sold	10,000	8,000	10,000	8,000
Unit price	$25	$25	$25	$25
Unit VC	$16	$16	$20	$20
Revenue	$250,000	$200,000	$250,000	$200,000
− VC	160,000	128,000	200,000	160,000
− FC	35,000	35,000	4,000	4,000
EBITDA	$ 55,000	$ 37,000	$ 46,000	$ 36,000
− D&A	10,000	10,000	1,000	1,000
EBIT	$ 45,000	$ 27,000	$ 45,000	$ 35,000
Percent change in revenue		−20.0%		−20.0%
Percent change in EBITDA		−32.7%		−21.7%
Percent change in EBIT		−40.0%		−22.2%

The EBIT values for the automated and manual production alternatives in the hammock-manufacturing example decline more than the EBITDA values when the number of units sold declines 20 percent and the unit price remains the same. This occurs because the fixed nature of depreciation and amortization (D&A) charges has the same effect as other fixed costs. When D&A is greater than zero, the percentage change in EBIT is greater than the percentage change in EBITDA.

BUILDING INTUITION

High Fixed Costs Mean Larger Fluctuations in Cash Flows and Profits

The higher the proportion of fixed costs to variable costs in a project, the more pretax operating cash flows (EBITDA) and accounting operating profits (EBIT) will vary as revenue varies. This is true because it is more difficult to change fixed costs than to change variable costs when unit sales change. If unit sales decline, EBITDA and EBIT will drop more in a business where fixed costs represent a larger proportion of total costs. Conversely, if unit sales increase, EBITDA and EBIT will increase more in a business with higher fixed costs.

LEARNING BY DOING APPLICATION 12.1

Forecasting EBIT

Problem: You have decided to start a business that provides in-home technical computer support to people in the community near your university. You have seen national advertisements for a company that provides these services in other communities. You would run this business out of your dorm room, and you know plenty of students who have the necessary technical skills and would welcome the opportunity to earn more than the university pays under its work-study programs. To get up and running quickly, you would have to invest in a computer system, an advertising campaign, three vehicles, and tools. You would also want to have enough cash to keep the business going until it began to generate positive cash flows. All of this would require about $100,000, which is about all that you think you can borrow on your credit cards, against your car, and from friends and family.

You are now working on the financial forecasts for the business. You plan to charge $45 for house calls lasting up to 30 minutes and $25 for each additional 30 minutes. Since you expect that the typical house call will require 60 minutes, you expect it to result in revenue of $70. You also estimate that monthly fixed operating costs (FC) which include an advertising contract with a local radio station and a small salary for you, will total $3,000. Unit VC, including the technicians' pay, gas, and so forth, will total $20 for the typical house call. Monthly depreciation and amortization charges (D&A) will be $1,000. Finally, you expect that after six months the business will average 120 house calls per month. Given this information, what do you expect the monthly EBIT to be in six months?

Approach: Since EBIT = Revenue − VC − FC − D&A (see, for example, Exhibit 12.5), you can forecast the expected monthly EBIT in six months by using this equation and the values for Revenue, VC, FC, and D&A that you expect in six months.

Solution: The calculation is as follows:

Revenue	$70 per house call × 120 calls	$8,400
− VC	$20 per house call × 120 calls	2,400
− FC		3,000
− D&A		1,000
EBIT		$2,000

Fixed Costs and Fluctuations in EBIT

LEARNING BY DOING APPLICATION 12.2

Problem: As you prepare the financial forecast for your computer-support business, you worry about the impact of fluctuations in the number of house calls on EBIT. You decide to examine how converting some fixed costs to variable costs will affect the sensitivity of EBIT to changes in the number of house calls. In a conversation with the manager at the radio station where you would be advertising, you discover that instead of paying $1,500 per month under a long-term advertising contract, you can get the same level of advertising for $1,600, where $1,000 of the total cost is fixed and $600 is variable. That is, in a given month, if you used the full level of advertising, you would pay $1,600, but you would also have the ability to reduce advertising costs to $1,000 by cutting back on the number of advertisements. You wonder how this contract would affect the sensitivity of EBIT to a decrease in the monthly number of house calls—say, from 120 to 90.

Approach: To determine how the sensitivity of EBIT differs between the $1,500 per month long-term contract and the contract that has only $1,000 of fixed costs, you must calculate EBIT under each alternative contact for 120 house calls and for 90 house calls. Using these EBIT values, you must next calculate the percentage decrease in EBIT if the number of monthly house calls declines from 120 to 90 for each alternative. You can then compare the percentage decreases to see the difference in the sensitivity of EBIT to the decrease in the number of house calls.

Solution: For the $1,500 monthly fixed contract: As we determined in Learning by Doing Application 12.1, EBIT is $2,000 with 120 house calls per month. With 90 house calls per month instead of 120, revenue would be $6,300 ($70 per house call × 90) per month instead of $8,400 ($70 per house call × 120) and EBIT would decline to $500:

$$\text{EBIT} = \text{Revenue} - \text{VC} - \text{FC} - \text{D\&A}$$
$$= \$6,300 - (\$20 \times 90) - \$3,000 - \$1,000$$
$$= \$500$$

This represents a 75 percent decrease in EBIT ([$500 − $2,000]/$2,000 = −0.75, or −75 percent).

For the $1,600 monthly contract with $1,000 fixed: Switching to the alternative advertising arrangement would increase unit variable costs by $5 ($600/120 calls) but

(continued)

would decrease fixed costs by $500 (from $3,000 to $2,500). EBIT with 120 house calls per month would equal $1,900:

$$\begin{aligned} EBIT &= \text{Revenue} - VC - FC - D\&A \\ &= \$8,400 - (\$25 \times 120) - \$2,500 - \$1,000 \\ &= \$1,900 \end{aligned}$$

With 90 house calls, EBIT would decline to $550:

$$EBIT = \$6,300 - (\$25 \times 90) - \$2,500 - \$1,000 = \$550$$

This represents a 71 percent decrease in EBIT ([$550 − $1,900]/$1,900 = −0.71, or −71 percent).

If the business averaged 120 house calls per month, EBIT under the alternative advertising arrangement would be $100 lower than EBIT under the original advertising arrangement. However, it would actually be $50 higher if the business averaged only 90 house calls per month because you would be able to cut back on advertising expenses under the alternative agreement if demand was poor.[3]

USING EXCEL

Examining the Impact of Changes in Your Assumptions

One of the main advantages of using a spreadsheet program for financial analysis is that it enables us to perform a sensitivity analysis in a matter of seconds. Once the spreadsheet is carefully set up with all the relevant key assumptions and calculations, we can change any one of the assumptions and immediately see the effect on the bottom line.

Following is a setup for Learning by Doing Applications 12.1 and 12.2 that analyzes the impact of the alternative advertising schemes on the EBIT of the in-home technical computer-support business.

	A	B	C	D	E	F	G	H	I	J
1										
2	Key Assumptions:	Fixed Advertising Contract with More House Calls		Alternative Advertising Contract with Fewer House Calls						
3	House call up to 30 minutes	$45		$45						
4	Each additional 30 minutes	$25		$25						
5	Revenue from typical call - unit (60 min.)	$70		$70						
6	FC	$3,000		$2,500						
7	VC/unit (technician's pay, gas, etc.)	$20		$20						
8	Alternative advertising option VC			$600						
9	VC/unit of alternative advertising option			$5	=D8/B11					
10	Monthly D&A	$1,000		$1,000						
11	Volume of calls per month	120		90						
12										
13										
14	Fixed Advertising Contract:						Alternative Advertising Contract:			
15	Revenue	$8,400	=B11*B5				Revenue	$6,300	=D11*D5	
16	Less: Variable cost (VC)	$2,400	=B11*B7				Less: Variable cost (VC)	$2,250	=D11*D7+D11*D9	
17	Less: Fixed cost (FC)	$3,000	=B6				Less: Fixed cost (FC)	$2,500	=D6	
18	Less: Depreciation and Amortization	$1,000	=B10				Less: Depreciation and Amortization	$1,000	=D10	
19	EBIT	$2,000	=B15-B16-B17-B18				EBIT	$550	=H15-H16-H17-H18	
20										
21										

---

[3]We are assuming here that you will cut back on advertising expenditures if revenue declines and that a modest decrease in advertising will not adversely affect demand for your services. Of course, under certain circumstances, you might actually increase advertising expenditures if demand for your service declines.

Once again, notice that the actual EBIT calculation is entirely derived from formulas utilizing inputs from the key assumptions. To see how you can use the model for sensitivity analysis, change the volume number in the alternative advertising scenario back to 120. When you do this, EBIT will equal $1,900, just as it does in the text.

> **Before You Go On**
>
> 1. Why do analysts care about how sensitive EBITDA and EBIT are to changes in revenue?
> 2. How is the proportion of fixed costs in a project's cost structure related to the sensitivity of EBITDA and EBIT to changes in revenue?

12.2 Calculating Operating Leverage

> **LEARNING OBJECTIVE 2**

The examples in Section 12.1 illustrate the impact of **operating leverage** on pretax operating cash flows and on accounting operating profits when revenue changes. Operating leverage is a measure of the relative amounts of fixed and variable costs in a project's cost structure. It is the major factor that determines the sensitivity of EBITDA or EBIT to changes in revenue. The higher a project's operating leverage, the greater these sensitivities. Two measures of operating leverage often used by analysts are the degree of pretax cash flow operating leverage and the degree of accounting operating leverage.

operating leverage
a measure of the relative amounts of fixed and variable costs in a project's cost structure; operating leverage is higher with more fixed costs

Degree of Pretax Cash Flow Operating Leverage

The **degree of pretax cash flow operating leverage (Cash Flow DOL)** provides us with a measure of how sensitive pretax operating cash flows are to changes in revenue. It is calculated using the following formula:

$$\text{Cash Flow DOL} = 1 + \frac{\text{Fixed costs}}{\text{Pretax operating cash flows}} = 1 + \frac{\text{FC}}{\text{EBITDA}} \quad (12.2)$$

degree of pretax cash flow operating leverage (Cash Flow DOL)
a measure of the sensitivity of cash flows from operations (EBITDA) to changes in revenue

Using the FC and EBITDA values in Exhibit 12.2, we can calculate Cash Flow DOL for the automated production alternative in the hammock-manufacturing example as follows:

$$\text{Cash Flow DOL}_{\text{Automated}} = 1 + \frac{\text{FC}}{\text{EBITDA}} = 1 + \frac{\$35,000}{\$55,000} = 1.64$$

This indicates that a 1 percent change in revenue will change pretax operating cash flow, EBITDA, by 1.64 percent. A measure such as this provides analysts with a convenient way of summarizing how much pretax operating cash flow will differ from forecasts if revenue is below or above the expected level.

You should be aware of one limitation to this measure: Cash Flow DOL changes with the level of revenue. In other words, the sensitivity is not the same for all levels of revenue. As a result, a particular Cash Flow DOL measure is only useful for modest changes in revenue. To understand why this limitation exists, notice that the numerator in the fraction in Equation 12.2, FC, does not vary with revenue. In contrast, the denominator, EBITDA, varies directly with revenue if the pretax operating cash flow margin is positive. If revenue is larger, the denominator in Equation 12.2 will be larger for any project that has a positive pretax operating cash flow margin. This, in turn, will cause Cash Flow DOL to become smaller as revenue increases. In contrast, if revenue is lower, the denominator in the fraction will be smaller, and Cash Flow DOL will be larger.

Exhibit 12.6 EBITDA with Unit Sales of 10,000 and 20,000 for the Automated Production Alternative

Units sold	10,000	20,000
Unit price	$25	$25
Unit VC	$16	$16
Revenue	$250,000	$500,000
− VC	160,000	320,000
− FC	35,000	35,000
EBITDA	$ 55,000	$145,000

For the automated production alternative in the hammock-manufacturing example, EBITDA increases from $55,000 to $145,000 when unit sales increase from 10,000 to 20,000 units.

Consider, for example, how Cash Flow DOL changes for the automated production alternative if unit sales are 20,000 instead of 10,000. Exhibit 12.6 shows us that EBITDA will equal $145,000 with unit sales of 20,000. Therefore, Cash Flow DOL under the automated production alternative would be only 1.24:

$$\text{Cash Flow DOL}_{\text{Automated}} = 1 + \frac{\$35,000}{\$145,000} = 1.24$$

Degree of Accounting Operating Leverage

degree of accounting operating leverage (Accounting DOL)
a measure of the sensitivity of accounting operating profits (EBIT) to changes in revenue

While Cash Flow DOL is a measure of the sensitivity of pretax operating cash flows to changes in revenue, the **degree of accounting operating leverage (Accounting DOL)** is a measure of how sensitive accounting operating profits (EBIT) are to changes in revenue. The formula for Accounting DOL is as follows:

$$\text{Accounting DOL} = 1 + \frac{\text{Fixed charges}}{\text{Accounting operating profits}} \quad (12.3)$$

$$= 1 + \frac{FC + D\&A}{EBITDA - D\&A}$$

$$= 1 + \frac{FC + D\&A}{EBIT}$$

In this formula, D&A is treated as a fixed cost and is added to FC to obtain the total of the cash and noncash fixed costs that would be reflected in the income statement if the project were adopted. This total is then divided by total accounting operating profits (EBIT).[4]

The only difference between Accounting DOL and Cash Flow DOL is that Accounting DOL focuses on EBIT, whereas Cash Flow DOL focuses on EBITDA. This means that the calculations differ only in the way that D&A is treated, since EBIT = EBITDA − D&A. Note that Accounting DOL will always be larger than Cash Flow DOL if D&A is greater than zero. This is because, compared with the calculation

---

[4] The term *accounting operating profits* is used here to refer to EBIT, even though EBIT is not actually computed using accounting numbers when we forecast cash flows for a financial analysis. The term is used to refer to the fact that noncash charges, D&A, are subtracted when computing this measure of earnings, just as is done in the calculation of accounting operating profits.

in Equation 12.2, the calculation in Equation 12.3 will have a larger numerator and a smaller denominator when D&A is greater than zero.

Let's apply the Accounting DOL formula to the automated production alternative in the hammock example. Using the values of FC, D&A, and EBIT from column 1 in Exhibit 12.5, we get:

$$\text{Accounting DOL}_{\text{Automated}} = 1 + \frac{FC + D\&A}{EBIT}$$
$$= 1 + \frac{\$35,000 + \$10,000}{\$45,000}$$
$$= 2.00$$

This tells us that a 1 percent change in revenue will result in a 2 percent change in EBIT. In other words, EBIT will change by twice as much, in percentage terms, as revenue with the automated production alternative!

In comparison, the Accounting DOL for the manual production alternative (column 3 in Exhibit 12.5) is only 1.11:

$$\text{Accounting DOL}_{\text{Manual}} = 1 + \frac{\$4,000 + \$1,000}{\$45,000} = 1.11$$

A 1 percent change in revenue will result in only a 1.11 percent change in EBIT with the manual production alternative.

Calculating Cash Flow and Accounting DOL

LEARNING BY DOING APPLICATION 12.3

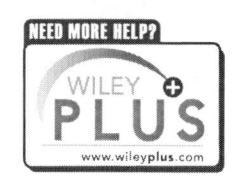

Problem: You have decided to calculate the operating leverage for the in-home computer-support business you are thinking about starting. What will Cash Flow DOL and Accounting DOL be in six months if EBIT is $2,000, FC is $3,000, and D&A is $1,000?

Approach: Use Equations 12.2 and 12.3 to calculate Cash Flow DOL and Accounting DOL, respectively.

Solution: From Equation 12.2, Cash Flow DOL is:

$$\text{Cash Flow DOL} = 1 + \frac{FC}{EBIT + D\&A} = 1 + \frac{\$3,000}{\$2,000 + \$1,000} = 2.00$$

From Equation 12.3, Accounting DOL is:

$$\text{Accounting DOL} = 1 + \frac{FC + D\&A}{EBIT} = 1 + \frac{\$3,000 + \$1,000}{\$2,000} = 3.00$$

One important insight that you should take away from this discussion is that the volatility of pretax operating cash flows (EBITDA) and accounting operating profits (EBIT) are strongly influenced by two factors: (1) volatility in revenue and (2) operating leverage. If there is no uncertainty regarding costs, these are the only two factors that determine volatility in EBITDA and EBIT. It is always a good idea to pay special attention to these two factors when you are evaluating the uncertainty associated with the cash flows or the accounting profits from a project.

BUILDING INTUITION

Revenue Changes Drive Profit Volatility Through Operating Leverage

If there is no uncertainty about costs, volatility in pretax operating cash flows (EBITDA) and accounting operating profits (EBIT) will be driven entirely by changes in revenue and operating leverage. If a project has any fixed costs associated with it, operating leverage will magnify changes in revenue. The degree of operating leverage is a direct measure of how much more volatile EBITDA and EBIT will be than revenue.

Before You Go On

1. How does operating leverage change when there is an increase in the proportion of a project's costs that are fixed?
2. What do the degree of pretax cash flow operating leverage (Cash Flow DOL) and the degree of accounting operating leverage (Accounting DOL) tell us?

12.3 Break-Even Analysis

LEARNING OBJECTIVE 3

A question that naturally comes to mind when we consider operating leverage is this: What level of unit sales or revenue is necessary for a project to break even? This is an important question because it helps us better understand how successful the project will have to be in order to succeed. In this section, we discuss **break-even analysis,** which tells us how many units must be sold in order for a project to break even on a cash flow or accounting profit basis. Break-even analysis also helps us understand how sensitive cash flows and accounting profits are to changes in the number of units that will be sold.

break-even analysis
an analysis that tells us how many units must be sold in order for a project to break even on a cash flow or accounting profit basis

See what the U.S. Small Business Administration has to say about break-even analysis at www.sba.gov/starting_business/financing/breakeven.html.

Pretax Operating Cash Flow Break-Even

When evaluating a project, we might want to know what level of unit sales is necessary for the project to break even on operations from a pretax operating cash flow perspective. In other words, how many units must be sold for pretax operating cash flow to equal $0? This is a very important question; if the project fails to break even from a pretax operating cash flow perspective, the firm will have to put more cash into the project to keep it going. The **pretax operating cash flow (EBITDA) break-even point** is calculated as follows:

$$\text{EBITDA Break-even} = \frac{\text{FC}}{\text{Price} - \text{Unit VC}} \quad (12.4)$$

For our hammock-manufacturing example, we can calculate the EBITDA break-even points for the automated and manual production alternatives as follows:

pretax operating cash flow (EBITDA) break-even point
the number of units that must be sold for pretax operating cash flow to equal $0

$$\text{EBITDA Break-even}_{\text{Automated}} = \frac{\$35,000}{\$25 - \$16} = 3,889 \text{ units}$$

$$\text{EBITDA Break-even}_{\text{Manual}} = \frac{\$4,000}{\$25 - \$20} = 800 \text{ units}$$

In each of these calculations, we are simply dividing the fixed costs, FC, by the **per-unit contribution** (Price − Unit VC). The per-unit contribution is how much is left from the sale of a single unit after all the variable costs associated with that unit have been paid. This is the amount that is available to help cover FC for the project.

In the hammock-manufacturing example, we see that if the automated production alternative is selected instead of the manual production alternative, almost five times as many units (3,889 versus 800 units) will have to be sold before the project breaks even on a pretax operating cash flow basis in a particular year. This is because the automated production alternative has much higher fixed costs ($35,000 versus $4,000) than the manual production alternative, but its per-unit contribution is not proportionately higher (only $9 versus $5).

Because the pretax operating cash flow break-even points are the unit sales levels at which EBITDA equals $0, they are the unit sales levels at which the lines in Exhibit 12.4 cross the $0 point. You can see this in Exhibit 12.7, which is the same as Exhibit 12.4, except that, for simplicity, it plots EBITDA only from 0 to 10,000 units.

In addition to illustrating the operating cash flow break-even points, Exhibit 12.7 shows that the automated production alternative has a larger EBITDA than the manual production alternative if sales exceed 7,750 units. This is because the larger per-unit contribution of the automated production alternative more than makes up for the higher fixed charges at this level of unit sales. We can compute the EBITDA **crossover level of unit sales (CO)**—the level above which the automated production alternative has higher pretax operating cash flows—as follows:

$$CO_{EBITDA} = \frac{FC_{Alternative\ 1} - FC_{Alternative\ 2}}{\text{Unit contribution}_{Alternative\ 1} - \text{Unit contribution}_{Alternative\ 2}} \quad (12.5)$$

where Unit contribution stands for the per-unit contribution. The calculation for our example is as follows:

$$CO_{EBITDA} = \frac{FC_{Automated} - FC_{Manual}}{\text{Unit contribution}_{Automated} - \text{Unit contribution}_{Manual}}$$

$$= \frac{\$35,000 - \$4,000}{\$9 - \$5}$$

$$= 7,750 \text{ units}$$

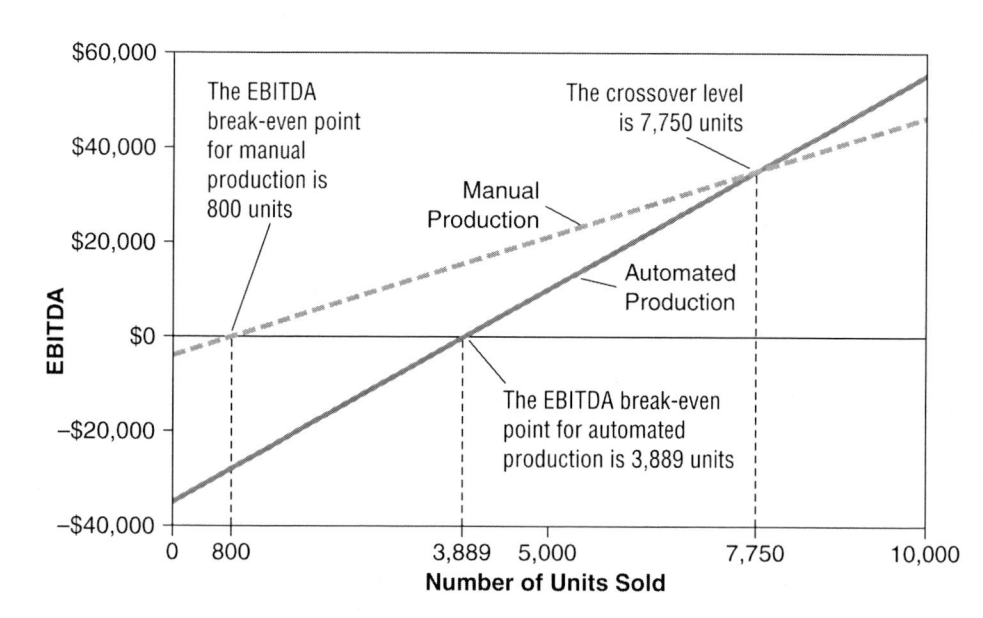

per-unit contribution
the amount that is left over from the sale of a single unit after all the variable costs associated with that unit have been paid; this is the amount that is available to help cover FC for the project

Learn more about fixed and variable costs and how they relate to break-even analysis from the CCH Business Owner's Toolkit at www.toolkit.cch.com/text/P06_7510.asp.

crossover level of unit sales (CO)
the level of unit sales at which cash flows or profitability for one project alternative switches from being lower than that of another alternative to being higher

Exhibit 12.7
EBITDA Break-Even Points and Crossover Level of Unit Sales
The EBITDA break-even points for the automated and manual production alternatives in the hammock-manufacturing example tell us the unit sales at which pretax operating cash flows equals $0. The crossover level of unit sales for EBITDA (CO_{EBITDA}) tells us the number of units at which the pretax operating cash flows become higher for the automated process than for the manual process.

Equation 12.5 can be used to calculate the crossover level of unit sales for any two alternatives that differ in the amount of operating leverage they employ.

> **LEARNING BY DOING APPLICATION 12.4**
>
> ### Calculating the EBITDA Break-Even Point
>
> **Problem:** Calculate the expected pretax operating cash flow (EBITDA) break-even number of house calls for the in-home computer-support business after six months.
>
> **Approach:** Use Equation 12.4 to calculate EBITDA break-even for a project.
>
> **Solution:** From Learning by Doing Application 12.1, we know that the monthly fixed costs are $3,000, the average revenue per house call (Price) is $70, and the variable cost per house call (Unit VC) is $20. Therefore, using Equation 12.4, we can calculate the EBITDA break-even as follows:
>
> $$\text{EBITDA break-even} = \frac{FC}{\text{Price} - \text{Unit VC}} = \frac{\$3{,}000}{\$70 - \$20} = 60 \text{ house calls}$$

Accounting Break-Even

accounting operating profit (EBIT) break-even point
the number of units that must be sold for accounting operating profit to equal $0

We might also be interested in determining what level of unit sales is necessary for the project to break even on operations from an accounting operating profit perspective. This is called the **accounting operating profit (EBIT) break-even point.** It is calculated using Equation 12.6:

$$\text{EBIT break-even} = \frac{FC + D\&A}{\text{Price} - \text{Unit VC}} \qquad (12.6)$$

When we calculate the accounting operating profit break-even point, we are calculating how many units must be sold to avoid an accounting operating loss. This is important to know because an accounting operating loss indicates that the project might not be able to cover its cash expenses and the wear and tear on physical assets as reflected in D&A.

For the automated production alternative in the hammock-manufacturing business, the break-even point is calculated as follows:

$$\begin{aligned}\text{EBIT break-even}_{\text{Automated}} &= \frac{FC_{\text{Automated}} + D\&A_{\text{Automated}}}{\text{Price} - \text{Unit VC}_{\text{Automated}}} \\ &= \frac{\$35{,}000 + \$10{,}000}{\$25 - \$16} \\ &= 5{,}000 \text{ units}\end{aligned}$$

Similarly, for the manual production alternative:

$$\text{EBIT break-even}_{\text{Manual}} = \frac{\$4{,}000 + \$1{,}000}{\$25 - \$20} = 1{,}000 \text{ units}$$

The accounting operating profit break-even points for the automated and manual production alternatives are 5,000 and 1,000 units, respectively.

The accounting operating profit break-even points are larger than the corresponding pretax operating cash flow break-even points because in Equation 12.6 we are including the noncash D&A charges in the numerator in the calculation. Since the denominator of the fraction is the same in Equations 12.4 and 12.6, the accounting operating profit break-even points will always be larger when D&A is positive.

In addition to the accounting operating profit break-even points, we can also calculate the crossover level of unit sales for EBIT. The equation that we use to do this is:

$$CO_{EBIT} = \frac{(FC + D\&A)_{Alternative\ 1} - (FC + D\&A)_{Alternative\ 2}}{Unit\ contribution_{Alternative\ 1} - Unit\ contribution_{Alternative\ 2}} \quad (12.7)$$

Notice that the only difference between Equations 12.5 and 12.7 is that D&A is included in the numerator in Equation 12.7.

The calculation for our hammock-manufacturing example is as follows:

$$CO_{EBIT} = \frac{(FC + D\&A)_{Automated} - (FC + D\&A)_{Manual}}{Unit\ contribution_{Automated} - Unit\ contribution_{Manual}}$$

$$= \frac{(\$35,000 + \$10,000) - (\$4,000 + \$1,000)}{\$9 - \$5}$$

$$= 10,000\ units$$

Calculating the EBIT Break-Even Point

LEARNING BY DOING APPLICATION 12.5

Problem: Calculate the expected accounting operating profit break-even number of house calls for the in-home computer-support business after six months of operation.

Approach: Use Equation 12.6 to calculate EBIT break-even for the business.

Solution: From Learning by Doing Application 12.1, we know that the monthly fixed cost is $3,000, the monthly D&A is $1,000, the average revenue per house call (Price) is $70, and the variable cost per house call (Unit VC) is $20. Therefore, using Equation 12.6, we find that the accounting operating profit break-even point after six months is:

$$EBIT\ break\text{-}even = \frac{FC + D\&A}{Price - Unit\ VC} = \frac{\$3,000 + \$1,000}{\$70 - \$20} = 80\ house\ calls$$

Your company must make 80 house calls to break even on an accounting operating profit basis.

By comparing this calculation and the calculation in Learning by Doing Application 12.4, you can see that the accounting operating profit break-even point (80 house calls) is higher than the pretax operating cash flow break-even point (60 house calls). As we explained in the text, this is so because D&A is included in the accounting operating profit break-even calculation.

Using Break-Even Numbers

DECISION-MAKING EXAMPLE 12.1

Situation: You have just finished calculating the pretax operating cash flow and accounting operating profit break-even numbers for the in-home computer-support business. These numbers are as follows:

- Pretax operating cash flow break-even point: 720 house calls per year (60 per month)

(continued)

- Accounting operating profit break-even point: 960 house calls per year (80 per month)

You have also just heard that the national company that provides these services is going to move to the town in which you are located. This has caused you to reduce your estimate of the annual number of house calls you can expect for your business in half, from 1,440 (120 per month) to 720. How will this affect your decision to enter this business?

Decision: With annual unit sales of 720, EBIT will be negative and EBITDA will equal $0. With EBITDA of $0, the business will not generate any cash flows that can be used to make necessary investments, let alone enable you to earn the opportunity cost of capital on the money you invest in this business. You can see this by referring back to the FCF calculation in Equation 11.2 or Exhibit 11.1. This is a case where you do not even need to calculate the NPV to know that it is negative.

The cash flow and accounting break-even calculations are useful in helping us understand how many units must be sold to break even in a particular period of time, such as a month or a year. Although these are valuable calculations, it is important to recognize that they do not tell us what it takes for a project to break even in an economic sense—in other words, how many units must be sold over the life of a project to achieve an NPV of $0. This sort of *economic* break-even analysis is typically performed in the context of an NPV analysis. We do not discuss this approach in this book; however, if you are interested in learning how to perform these calculations, you can see examples on the WileyPlus Web site for this text.

> **Before You Go On**
>
> 1. How is the per-unit contribution related to the accounting operating profit break-even point?
> 2. What is the difference between the pretax operating cash flow break-even point and the accounting operating profit break-even point?

12.4 Risk Analysis

LEARNING OBJECTIVE 4

In the preceding sections, we noted that two key factors—(1) the volatility of revenue and (2) operating leverage—determine the volatility of pretax operating cash flows (EBITDA) and operating profits (EBIT) when there is no uncertainty regarding costs. We also discussed how changes in unit sales influence the volatility of EBITDA and EBIT.

Unit sales is only one of many factors that an analyst must predict when forecasting the cash flows associated with a project. As with forecasts of unit sales, forecasting the values of these other factors involves a high degree of uncertainty. For example, the price of a product depends on the supply and demand for the product, which are often difficult to predict. Similarly, future values of operating expenses, capital expenditures, and additions to working capital can be very uncertain. Financial analysts often resort to sensitivity analysis, scenario analysis, and simulation analysis to obtain a better understanding of how errors in forecasting these factors affect the attractiveness of a project. In other words, these analyses help answer the questions "How wrong can I be?" and "What are the implications of being wrong?"

In this section we illustrate the application of sensitivity, scenario, and simulation analysis using the automated production alternative from our hammock-manufacturing example. With expected unit sales of 10,000 per year and the other indicated assumptions, the yearly free cash flows and NPV for this alternative are calculated in Exhibit 12.8.

Exhibit 12.8 Incremental Free Cash Flows and NPV for the Automated Hammock Production Alternative

Assumptions:

Opportunity cost of capital	10%		Initial investment	$40,000
Unit sales	10,000		D&A	$10,000
Unit price	$25		Annual Cap Exp	$8,000
Unit VC	$16		Add WC	$2,000
FC	$35,000		Tax Rate	35%

	\multicolumn{5}{c}{Year}
	0	1	2	3	4
Revenue		$250,000	$250,000	$250,000	$250,000
− VC		160,000	160,000	160,000	160,000
− FC		35,000	35,000	35,000	35,000
EBITDA		$55,000	$55,000	$55,000	$55,000
− D&A		10,000	10,000	10,000	10,000
EBIT		$45,000	$45,000	$45,000	$45,000
− Taxes		15,750	15,750	15,750	15,750
NOPAT		$29,250	$29,250	$29,250	$29,250
+ D&A		10,000	10,000	10,000	10,000
CF Opns		$39,250	$39,250	$39,250	$39,250
− Cap Exp	$40,000	8,000	8,000	8,000	8,000
− Add WC		2,000	2,000	2,000	2,000
FCF	($40,000)	$29,250	$29,250	$29,250	$29,250
NPV	$52,719				

This exhibit shows the calculation of the yearly incremental pretax free cash flows (FCF) and the NPV of the automated production alternative in the hammock-manufacturing example assuming the project has a four year life. The FCF calculation is illustrated in Exhibit 11.1.

Sensitivity Analysis

Sensitivity analysis involves examining the sensitivity of the output from an analysis, such as the NPV estimate in Exhibit 12.8, to changes in *individual* assumptions. In a sensitivity analysis, an analyst might examine how a project's NPV changes if there is a decrease in the value of individual cash inflow assumptions or an increase in the value of individual cash outflow assumptions. For example, if unit sales are 10 percent lower than expected, if FC is 10 percent higher than expected, or if annual Cap Exp is 10 percent higher than expected, then an analyst could calculate that the NPV of the automated production alternative in Exhibit 12.8 declines by 35.2 percent, 13.7 percent, and 4.8 percent, respectively, when these values are changed one at a time. These numbers would tell the analyst that the NPV for the automated alternative is much more sensitive to the unit sales assumption than to the assumptions regarding FC or Cap Exp.

This information is very useful because it helps the analyst identify the critical assumptions. These are the assumptions the analyst should pay special attention to when evaluating the project. It does not make sense to allocate substantial analytical resources to investigating assumptions that are of little importance. In our example, the numbers suggest that the analyst should be especially careful when developing the unit sales forecasts.

> **sensitivity analysis**
> examination of the sensitivity of the results from a financial analysis to changes in individual assumptions

Scenario Analysis

As we have just seen, sensitivity analysis is a form of "what if" analysis that is very useful in identifying key assumptions. However, the individual assumptions in a financial analysis are often related to each other; their values do not tend to change one at a time. As a result, sensitivity analysis is not very useful in examining how the attractiveness of a project might vary under different economic scenarios. An analyst who wants to examine how the results from a financial analysis will change under alternative scenarios will thus perform a **scenario analysis**.

Suppose, for example, that the forecasted cash flows in Exhibit 12.8 represent the performance of the automated hammock-manufacturing alternative under expected future economic conditions. Let's consider how these cash flows might change if economic conditions turn out to be weaker or stronger than expected. In a scenario in which economic conditions are weaker than in the most likely case, we would expect unit sales to be less than 10,000 because overall demand for hammocks will be lower. The price at which the firm sells its hammocks is also likely to be lower because the firm will probably reduce prices in an effort to boost sales. On the bright side, unit variable costs might also be lower because the demand for rope, spacer bars, hardware, and so forth will decline in a weak market and producers of those products may reduce the prices they charge the firm. In contrast to the weak economic scenario, stronger economic conditions might result in higher-than-expected unit sales, prices, and unit variable costs. Exhibit 12.9 illustrates how these assumptions and the resulting project NPV might vary under the alternative scenarios.

In Exhibit 12.9 we can see that the project will have a negative NPV if economic conditions are weak. Furthermore, the decline in NPV if economic conditions are weaker than expected ($70,054, the difference between $52,719 and negative $17,335) is less than the increase in NPV if economic conditions are stronger than expected ($86,537, the difference between $139,256 and $52,719). The range of NPV values under the three scenarios is $156,591 (the range between negative $17,335 and $139,256).

Although this analysis can help us better understand how much uncertainty is associated with an NPV estimate, it is important to remember that *there is only one NPV value for a project* and that the FCF values we use in an NPV analysis represent the expected incremental free cash flows. For instance, in our example, suppose there is a 50 percent chance that the most likely economic conditions will occur, a 25 percent chance that economic conditions will be weak, and a 25 percent chance that economic conditions will be strong. The NPV calculation would be based on the expected values for unit sales, the unit price, and unit variable costs.

Recall that an expected value represents the sum of the products of the possible outcomes and the probabilities that those outcomes will be realized. Therefore, the

> **scenario analysis**
> an analytical method concerned with how the results from a financial analysis will change under alternative scenarios

Exhibit 12.9 NPV Values for the Automated Hammock Production Alternative for Three Scenarios

Economic Conditions	Unit Sales	Unit Price	Unit Variable Costs	NPV
Strong	12,000	$28	$17	$139,256
Expected	10,000	$25	$16	$52,719
Weak	8,000	$22	$15	($17,335)

Different economic scenarios result in different NPV values for the automated production alternative in the hammock-manufacturing example. The expected unit sales, unit prices, and unit variable costs vary depending on economic conditions.

expected values for unit sales, the unit price, and unit variable costs in this example are calculated as follows:

$$\text{Expected unit sales} = (0.25 \times 12{,}000) + (0.50 \times 10{,}000) + (0.25 \times 8{,}000)$$
$$= 10{,}000 \text{ units}$$
$$\text{Expected unit price} = (0.25 \times \$28) + (0.50 \times \$25) + (0.25 \times \$22) = \$25$$
$$\text{Expected unit variable costs} = (0.25 \times \$17) + (0.50 \times \$16) + (0.25 \times \$15) = \$16$$

Therefore, the NPV of the project would equal $52,719, as illustrated in Exhibit 12.8.

Simulation Analysis

Simulation analysis is like scenario analysis except that in simulation analysis an analyst uses a computer to examine a large number of scenarios in a short period of time. Rather than selecting individual values for each of the assumptions—such as unit sales, unit price, and unit variable costs—the analyst assumes that those assumptions can be represented by statistical distributions. For instance, unit sales might be assumed to have a normal distribution with a mean value of 10,000 units and a standard deviation of 1,500 units, while prices might be assumed to follow a related normal distribution with a mean of $25 and a standard deviation of $5. A computer program then calculates the free cash flows associated with a large number of scenarios by repeatedly drawing numbers for the distributions for various assumptions, plugging them into the free cash flow model, and computing the yearly free cash flows. It is not uncommon to compute 10,000 alternative sets of free cash flows. The average of the annual free cash flows generated in this way is then computed to obtain the expected free cash flows for each year during the life of the project. These expected free cash flows can then be discounted using the opportunity cost of capital to obtain the NPV for the project.

In addition to providing an estimate of the expected free cash flows, simulation analysis provides information on the distribution of the free cash flows that the project is likely to produce in each year. For example, if simulation analysis is used to compute 10,000 alternative sets of free cash flows, there will be 10,000 cash flow estimates for each year. From these estimates, an analyst can estimate the probability that the free cash flows in a given year will be greater than $0, greater than $1,000, or greater than any other number. By summing up the free cash flows over time within each alternative set of cash flows, the analyst can also estimate the probability of recovering the initial investment in the project by any particular point in the project's life.

A discussion of the actual techniques used in simulation analysis is beyond the scope of this book. However, you should be aware that sophisticated financial analysts commonly use simulation analysis to evaluate the riskiness of projects. You are likely to see it in practice if you are ever involved with project analysis.

> **simulation analysis**
> an analytical method that uses a computer to quickly examine a large number of scenarios and obtain probability estimates for various values in a financial analysis

> You can download trial versions of Excel add-in programs for sensitivity analysis and simulation analysis from Treeplan.com at www.treeplan.com.

> **Before You Go On**
>
> 1. How is a sensitivity analysis used in project analysis?
> 2. How does a scenario analysis differ from a sensitivity analysis?
> 3. What is a simulation analysis, and what can it tell us?

12.5 Investment Decisions with Capital Rationing

LEARNING OBJECTIVE 5

Our discussion of capital budgeting so far has focused on tools that help us determine whether an individual project creates value for stockholders, as well as helping us better understand other economic characteristics of projects. Although these analyses are critical parts of the capital budgeting process, they get us only part way to where we want to be. They do not tell us what to do when, as is often the case, a firm does not have enough money to invest in all available positive NPV projects. In other words, they do not tell us how to identify the *bundle* or combination of positive NPV projects that creates the greatest total value for stockholders when there are capital constraints or, as we called it in Chapter 10, *capital rationing*.

In an ideal world, of course, we could accept all positive NPV projects because we would be able to finance them. If managers and investors agreed on which projects had positive NPVs, investors would provide capital to those projects because returns from them would be greater than the returns the investors could earn elsewhere in the capital markets. However, the world is not ideal, and, as noted in Chapter 10, firms often cannot invest in all of the available projects with positive NPVs. It can be difficult for outside investors to accurately assess the risks and returns associated with the firm's projects. Consequently, investors may require returns for their capital that are too high, and the firm may face capital constraints. Managers might be forced to reject positive NPV projects because investors are not providing enough capital to fund those projects at reasonable rates.

Capital Rationing in a Single Period

> **profitability index (PI)**
> a measure of the value a project generates for each dollar invested in that project

The basic principle that we follow in choosing the set of projects that creates the greatest value in a given period is to select the projects that yield the largest value *per dollar invested*. We can do this by computing the **profitability index (PI)** for each project and choosing the projects with the largest profitability indexes until we run out of money. The profitability index is computed as follows:

$$\text{PI} = \frac{\text{Benefits}}{\text{Costs}} = \frac{\text{Present value of future free cash flows}}{\text{Initial investment}} = \frac{\text{NPV} + \text{Initial investment}}{\text{Initial investment}} \quad (12.8)$$

where Initial investment is the up-front investment required to fund the project.

To illustrate, let's return to the example from Chapter 11 in which we were considering when to replace a lawn mower. Recall that the new mower would cost $2,000 and would bring in net cash flows of $7,000 for four years. With a discount rate of 10 percent, we saw that the NPV of this mower is $20,189. The PI for this investment is calculated as follows:

$$\text{PI} = (\$20{,}189 + \$2{,}000)/\$2{,}000 = 11.09$$

This means that an investment in the new mower is expected to generate $11.09 of value for every dollar invested.

Now consider the case in which we have several projects to choose from in a given year but do not have enough money to invest in all of them. For example, suppose that we have identified the four positive NPV projects listed in Exhibit 12.10 and have only $10,000 to invest. How do we choose from among the four projects when we cannot afford to invest in all of them?

Our objective in a case such as this is to identify the bundle or combination of positive NPV projects that creates the greatest total value for stockholders. The PI is helpful in such a situation because it helps us choose the projects that create the most value per dollar invested. We use the PI to do this by following a four-step procedure:

1. Calculate the PI for each project.
2. Rank the projects from highest PI to lowest PI.
3. Starting at the top of the list (the project with the highest PI) and working your way down (to the project with the lowest PI), select the projects that the firm can afford.
4. Repeat the third step by starting with the second project on the list, the third project on the list, and so on to make sure that a more valuable bundle cannot be identified.

12.5 Investment Decisions with Capital Rationing

Exhibit 12.10 Positive NPV Investments This Year

Project	Year 0	Year 1	Year 2	NPV @ 10%	PI
A	−$5,000	$5,500	$6,050	$5,000	2.000
B	−$3,000	$2,000	$3,850	$2,000	1.667
C	−$3,000	$4,400	$0	$1,000	1.333
D	−$2,000	$1,500	$1,375	$500	1.250

With only $10,000 to invest, how do we choose among these four positive-NPV projects? The exhibit shows the yearly free cash flows, NPV, and profitability index (PI) for the projects. The PI values indicate the value of the expected future free cash flows per dollar invested in each project.

Applying this process to the projects in Exhibit 12.10, we would choose to accept projects A, B, and D. We would begin by choosing projects A and B because they have the largest PIs and we have enough money to invest in both. Since choosing projects A and B means we would no longer have enough money to invest in project C, we would skip C and choose D, for which we do have enough money. Projects A, B, and D would generate a total of $7,500 in total value for stockholders. Following the fourth step reveals that no other combination of projects has a larger total NPV than projects A, B, and D, so we would select these projects.

Ranking Projects Using the PI

LEARNING BY DOING APPLICATION 12.6

Problem: You have identified the following seven positive NPV investments for your in-home computer-support business. If you have $50,000 to invest this year, which projects should you accept?

Project	Investment	NPV @10%
Buy new notebook computer	$ 3,000	$ 500
Buy employee training program	8,000	4,000
Buy new tool set	500	1,000
Buy office condo	40,000	5,000
Buy used car	12,000	4,000
Paint existing cars	4,000	2,000
Buy new test equipment	10,000	2,000

Approach: Use the four-step procedure presented in the text to determine which projects you should accept.

Solution: Calculating the PI and ranking the projects from highest to lowest PI yields the following:

Project	Investment	NPV @10%	PI
Buy new tool set	$ 500	$1,000	$1,500/$500 = 3.000
Buy employee training program	8,000	4,000	$12,000/$8,000 = 1.500
Paint existing cars	4,000	2,000	$6,000/$4,000 = 1.500
Buy used car	12,000	4,000	$16,000/$12,000 = 1.333
Buy new test equipment	10,000	2,000	$12,000/$10,000 = 1.200
Buy new notebook computer	3,000	500	$3,500/$3,000 = 1.167
Buy office condo	40,000	5,000	$45,000/$40,000 = 1.125

With $50,000 to invest, you should invest in all projects except the office condo. This strategy will require $37,500 and is expected to result in a total NPV of $13,500. The $12,500 that you have left over can be held in the business until an appropriate use for the money is identified, or it can be distributed to the stockholder (you).

DECISION-MAKING EXAMPLE 12.2

Ranking Investment Alternatives

Situation: The profitability index concept does not apply only to a firm's investments in projects. It can also apply to your personal investments. For example, suppose that you have just inherited $50,000 and want to invest it in ways that create as much value as possible. After researching investment alternatives, you have identified five investments that you believe will have positive NPVs. You estimate that the NPVs and PIs for these investments are as follows:

Project	Investment	NPV	PI
But a new car for your business	$20,000	$10,000	1.500
Buy a duplex apartment near campus	50,000	22,500	1.450
Start a small moving business	25,000	10,000	1.400
Invest in your roommate's Internet business	15,000	5,000	1.333
Buy a collection of old comic books	5,000	1,000	1.200

Which investment(s) should you choose?

Decision: You should invest in the duplex apartment. If you begin the selection process by choosing the new car because it has the largest PI and then work your way down the list until you reach a total investment of $50,000, you will see that you can invest in the car, the moving business, and the comic books. These three investments have a total NPV of $21,000. However, the investment in the duplex apartment alone has an NPV of $22,500. Investing in the duplex apartment will create more total value.

This problem illustrates why the procedure for using PI to choose projects has four steps. Without the fourth step, which tells us to repeat the third step beginning with the second project, the third project, and so on, we would not have identified the duplex apartment as the best alternative.

Capital Rationing across Multiple Periods

The PI concept is relatively straightforward and easy to apply if you are choosing among projects in a single period. However, if you are faced with capital rationing over several years, the investments you choose this year can affect your ability to make investments in future years. This can happen if you plan on reinvesting some or all of the cash flows generated by the projects you invest in this year. In such a situation, you cannot rely solely on the PI to identify the projects you should invest in this year. You must maximize the total NPV across all of the years in which you will be investing.

Let's look more closely at how multiperiod concerns can cause you to deviate from PI-based investment choices in a given year. Suppose you operate a business that will generate $10,000 per year for new investments. Furthermore, suppose that today (year 0) you are choosing among projects A, B, C, and D in Exhibit 12.11 and that, based on the PIs of the individual projects, you choose to invest in projects A, B, and D. The total NPV from these projects will be $7,500, and the total year 1 cash flow from them will be $9,000 ($5,500 + $2,000 + $1,500).

Now suppose that you expect projects F, G, and H to be available next year (year 1). If other operations yield $10,000 for investments next year, you will have a total of $19,000 to invest in year 1. With this amount of money, you can invest in projects F and H, which require a total investment of $15,000 and have a combined NPV of $9,546 ($9,091 + $455). Therefore, in year 0 dollars, the total value created from investing activities over the two years will be $17,046 ($7,500 + $9,546).

While $17,046 is a lot of value for a total investment of $25,000 ($10,000 today and $15,000 in year 1), you could do better. Notice that if, instead of projects A, B, and D, you invest in projects A, C, and D today, you will have enough cash in year 1 to invest in projects F and G. This strategy would yield a total NPV of $21,955 ($5,000 + $1,000 + $500 + $9,091 + $6,364)! Ranking and selecting the projects today based on the PI

If you have a strong math background and are interested, you can learn more about linear programming from a site maintained by Northwestern University and Argonne National Laboratory: www-unix.mcs.anl.gov/otc/Guide/faq/linear-programming-faq.html.

Exhibit 12.11 Positive NPV Investments for Two Years

Project	Year 0	Year 1	Year 2	Year 3	Year 0 NPV @10%	PI
A	−$5,000	$5,500	$6,050	$0	$5,000	2.000
B	−$3,000	$2,000	$3,850	$0	$2,000	1.667
C	−$3,000	$4,400	$0	$0	$1,000	1.333
D	−$2,000	$1,500	$1,375	$0	$500	1.250
F		−$10,000	$12,000	$11,000	$9,091	1.909
G		−$10,000	$8,000	$11,770	$6,364	1.636
H		−$5,000	$4,000	$2,255	$455	1.091

Investment decision-making with capital rationing becomes more complex when multiple periods are involved. This exhibit shows the yearly free cash flows, NPV, and profitability index (PI) for the four positive NPV projects in Exhibit 12.10 and for three other positive-NPV projects that are expected to become available in year 1.

would have yielded a bundle of projects over two years with a lower NPV. This illustrates an important limitation of the profitability index. It does not tell us enough to make informed decisions over multiple periods. Solving a multiple-period problem requires the application of more advanced analytical techniques, such as linear programming, that are beyond the scope of this book.

> **Before You Go On**
>
> 1. What decision criteria should managers use in selecting projects when there is not enough money to invest in all available positive NPV projects?
> 2. What might cause a firm to face capital constraints?
> 3. How can the PI help in choosing projects when a firm faces capital constraints? What are its limitations?

Summary of Learning Objectives

1. **Explain and be able to demonstrate how variable costs and fixed costs affect the volatility of pretax operating cash flows and accounting operating profits.**

   Because the fixed costs associated with a project do not change as revenue changes, fluctuations in revenue are magnified so that pretax operating cash flows and accounting operating profits fluctuate more than revenue in percentage terms. The greater the proportion of total costs that are fixed, the more the fluctuations in revenue will be magnified. To demonstrate this, you can perform calculations like those in the hammock-manufacturing example and in Learning by Doing Applications 12.1 and 12.2.

2. **Calculate and distinguish between the degree of pretax cash flow operating leverage and the degree of accounting operating leverage.**

   The degree of pretax cash flow operating leverage is a measure of how much pretax operating cash flow will change in relation to a change in revenue. Similarly, the degree of accounting operating leverage is a measure of how much accounting operating profits will change in relation to a change in revenue. The only difference between cash flow operating leverage and accounting operating leverage is that the accounting measure treats incremental depreciation and amortization charges as a fixed cost in the calculation. These charges are excluded from the cash flow operating leverage measure because they do not reflect actual cash expenses and, therefore, do not affect pretax cash flows. Equations 12.2 and 12.3 are used to calculate these two measures.

3. **Define and calculate the pretax operating cash flow and accounting operating profit break-even points and the crossover levels of unit sales for a project.**

   The pretax operating cash flow break-even point is the number of units that must be sold in a particular year to break even on a pretax operating cash flow basis. It is calculated using Equation 12.4.

The accounting operating profit break-even point is the number of units that must be sold in a particular year to break even on an accounting operating profit basis. A project breaks even on an accounting operating profit basis when it produces exactly $0 in incremental operating profits (EBIT). It is calculated using Equation 12.6.

The crossover level of unit sales is the level of unit sales at which the pretax operating cash flows or accounting operating profits for one project alternative switches from being lower than that of another alternative to being higher. The EBITDA and EBIT crossover levels of unit sales are calculated using Equations 12.5 and 12.7, respectively.

4. **Define sensitivity analysis, scenario analysis, and simulation analysis, and describe how they are used to evaluate the risks associated with a project.**

Sensitivity analysis is concerned with how sensitive the output from a financial analysis, such as the NPV, is to changes in an individual assumption. It helps identify which assumptions have the greatest impact on the output and, therefore, on the value of a project. Knowing this helps an analyst identify which assumptions are especially important to that analysis. Scenario analysis is used to examine how the output from a financial analysis changes under alternative scenarios. This type of analysis recognizes that changing economic and market conditions affect more than one variable at a time and tries to account for how each of the different variables will change under alternative scenarios. Simulation analysis is like scenario analysis except that in simulation analysis a computer is used to examine a large number of scenarios in a short period of time.

5. **Explain how the profitability index can be used to rank projects when a firm faces capital rationing, and describe the limitations that apply to the profitability index.**

The profitability index (PI) aids in the process of choosing the most valuable bundle of projects that the firm can afford because it is a measure of value received per dollar invested that can be used to rank projects in a given period. The major limitation of the PI is that, while it can be used to rank projects in a given period, it can lead to misleading project choices in a multiperiod context.

Summary of Key Equations

Equation	Description	Formula
12.1	Op Ex in terms of incremental variable and fixed costs	$\text{Op Ex} = \text{VC} + \text{FC}$
12.2	Degree of pretax cash flow operating leverage	$\text{Cash Flow DOL} = 1 + \dfrac{\text{FC}}{\text{EBITDA}}$
12.3	Degree of accounting operating leverage	$\text{Accounting DOL} = 1 + \dfrac{\text{FC} + \text{D\&A}}{\text{EBIT}}$
12.4	Pretax operating cash flow break-even point	$\text{EBITDA Break-even} = \dfrac{\text{FC}}{\text{Price} - \text{Unit VC}}$
12.5	Crossover level of unit sales for EBITDA	$\text{CO}_{\text{EBITDA}} = \dfrac{\text{FC}_{\text{Alternative 1}} - \text{FC}_{\text{Alternative 2}}}{\text{Unit contribution}_{\text{Alternative 1}} - \text{Unit contribution}_{\text{Alternative 2}}}$
12.6	Accounting operating profit break-even point	$\text{EBIT Break-even} = \dfrac{\text{FC} + \text{D\&A}}{\text{Price} - \text{unit VC}}$
12.7	Crossover level of unit sales for EBIT	$\text{CO}_{\text{EBIT}} = \dfrac{(\text{FC} + \text{D\&A})_{\text{Alternative 1}} - (\text{FC} + \text{D\&A})_{\text{Alternative 2}}}{(\text{Unit contribution}_{\text{Alternative 1}} - \text{Unit contribution}_{\text{Alternative 2}})}$
12.8	Profitability index	$\text{PI} = \dfrac{\text{NPV} + \text{Initial investment}}{\text{Initial investment}}$

Self-Study Problems

12.1 The Yellow Shelf Company sells all of its shelves for $100 per shelf, and incurs $50 in variable costs to produce each. If the fixed costs for the firm are $2,000,000 per year, then what will the EBIT for the firm be if it produces and sells 45,000 shelves next year? Assume that depreciation and amortization is included in the fixed costs.

12.2 Hydrogen Batteries sells its specialty automobile batteries for $85 each, while its current variable cost per unit is $65. Total fixed costs (including depreciation and amortization expense) are $150,000 per year. The firm expects to sell 10,000 batteries next year but is concerned that its variable cost will increase next year due to material cost increases. What is the maximum variable cost per unit increase that will keep the EBIT from becoming negative?

12.3 The Vinyl CD Co. is going to take on a project that will increase its EBIT by $90,000 next year. The firm's fixed cost cash expenditures are expected to increase by $100,000, and depreciation and amortization will increase by $80,000 next year. If the project yields an additional 10 percent in revenue, what percentage increase in the project's EBIT will result from the additional revenue?

12.4 You are considering investing in a business that has monthly fixed costs of $5,500 and sells a single product that costs $35 per unit make. This product sells for $90 per unit. What is the annual pretax operating cash flow break-even point for this business?

12.5 You are considering a project that has an initial outlay of $1 million. The profitability index of the project is 2.24. What is the NPV of the project?

Solutions to Self-Study Problems

12.1 The calculations for Yellow Shelf are as follows:

Revenue	$100 × 45,000 =	$4,500,000
VC	$50 × 45,000 =	2,250,000
FC + D&A		2,000,000
EBIT		$ 250,000

12.2 The forecasted EBIT for Hydrogen Batteries is:

Revenue	$85 × 10,000 =	$850,000
VC	$65 × 10,000 =	650,000
FC + D&A		150,000
EBIT		$ 50,000

Therefore, total variable cost may increase by $50,000, which means that if the firm produces and sells 10,000 batteries, then the variable cost per unit may increase by $5 ($50,000/10,000) units.

12.3
$$\text{Accounting DOL} = 1 + \frac{FC + D\&A}{EBIT}$$
$$= 1 + \frac{\$100{,}000 + \$80{,}000}{\$90{,}000}$$
$$= 3$$

Therefore, a 10 percent additional increase in revenue should result in approximately a 30 percent increase in EBIT.

12.4 You can solve for the *monthly* pretax operating cash flow break-even point using Equation 12.4:

$$\text{EBITDA break-even} = \frac{FC}{\text{Price} - \text{Unit VC}} = \frac{\$5{,}500}{\$90 - \$35} = 100 \text{ units}$$

Therefore, the annual EBITDA break-even point is 100 × 12 = 1,200 units.

12.5 You can use Equation 12.8 to solve for the NPV:

$$PI = \frac{NPV + \text{Initial investment}}{\text{Initial investment}}$$

$$2.24 = \frac{NPV + \$1{,}000{,}000}{\$1{,}000{,}000}$$

Therefore:

$$NPV = \$1{,}240{,}000$$

Critical Thinking Questions

12.1 You are involved in the planning process for a firm that is expected to have a large increase in sales for the next year. Which type of firm would benefit the most from that sales increase: a firm with low fixed costs and high variable costs or a firm with high fixed costs and low variable costs?

12.2 You own a firm with a single new product that is about to be introduced to the public for the first time. Your marketing analysis suggests that the demand for this product could be anywhere between 500,000 units and 5,000,000 units. Given such a wide range, discuss the safest cost structure alternative for your firm.

12.3 Define *capital rationing*, and explain why it can occur in the real world.

12.4 Discuss the interpretation of the degree of accounting operating leverage and degree of pretax cash flow operating leverage.

12.5 Explain how EBITDA differs from free cash flows (FCF) and discuss the types of businesses for which this difference would be especially small or large.

12.6 Describe how the pretax operating cash flow break-even point discussed in this chapter is related to a break-even point that makes the NPV of a project equal to zero.

12.7 Is it possible to have a crossover point where the accounting break-even point is the same for two alternatives—that is, above the break-even point for a low-fixed-cost alternative but below the break-even point for a high-fixed-cost alternative? Explain.

12.8 In calculus we are able to determine the effect on an entire multivariable equation of a change to a single variable. We call that effect the *partial derivative*. Which is analogous to the partial derivative: sensitivity analysis, scenario analysis, or simulation analysis?

12.9 High Tech Monopoly Co. has plenty of cash to fund any conceivable positive NPV project. Can you describe a situation in which capital rationing could still occur?

12.10 The profitability index is a scaleless attribute for measuring a project's benefits relative to the costs. How might this help to eliminate bias in project selection?

Questions and Problems

BASIC

12.1 Fixed and variable costs: Define *variable costs* and *fixed costs*, and give an example of each.

12.2 EBIT: Describe the role that the mix of variable versus fixed costs has in the variation of earnings before interest and taxes (EBIT) for the firm.

12.3 EBIT: The Generic Publications Textbook Company sells all of its books for $100 per book, and it currently costs $50 in variable costs to produce each text. The fixed costs, which include depreciation and amortization for the firm, are currently $2 million per year. The firm is considering changing its production technology, which will increase the fixed costs for the firm by 50 percent but decrease the variable costs per unit by 50 percent. If the firm expects to sell 45,000 books next year, should the firm switch technologies?

12.4 EBIT: WalkAbout Kangaroo Shoe Stores forecasts that it will sell 9,500 pairs of shoes next year. The firm buys its shoes for $50 per pair from the wholesaler and sells them for $75 per pair. If the firm will incur fixed costs plus depreciation and amortization of $100,000, then what is the percent increase in EBIT if the actual sales next year equal 11,500 pairs of shoes?

12.5 Cash Flow DOL: The law firm of Dewey, Cheatem, and Howe has monthly fixed costs of $100,000, EBIT of $250,000, and depreciation charges on its office furniture and computers of $5,000. Calculate the Cash Flow DOL for this firm.

12.6 Accounting DOL: Explain how the value of accounting operating leverage can be used.

12.7 Break-even analysis: Why is the per-unit contribution important in a break-even analysis?

12.8 Simulation analysis: What is simulation analysis, and how is it used?

12.9 Profitability index: What is the profitability index, and why is it helpful in the capital rationing process?

INTERMEDIATE

12.10 EBIT: If a manufacturing firm and a service firm have identical cash fixed costs but the manufacturing firm has much higher depreciation and amortization, then which firm is more likely to have a large discrepancy between its FCF and its EBIT?

12.11 EBIT: Duplicate Footballs, Inc., expects to sell 15,000 balls this year. The balls sell for $110 each and have a variable cost per unit of $80. Fixed costs, including depreciation and amortization, are currently $220,000 per year. How much can either the fixed costs or the variable cost per unit increase in order to keep the company from having a negative EBIT.

12.12 EBIT: Specialty Light Bulbs anticipates selling 3,000 light bulbs this year at a price of $15 per bulb. It costs Specialty $10 in variable costs to produce each light bulb, and the fixed costs for the firm are $10,000. Specialty has an opportunity to sell an additional 1,000 bulbs next year at the same price and variable cost, but by doing so the firm will incur an additional fixed cost of $4,000 if it chooses to sell the additional bulbs. Should Specialty produce and sell the additional bulbs?

12.13 Cash Flow DOL: For the Vinyl CD Co. in Self-study Problem 12.3, what percentage increase in pretax operating cash flow will be driven by the additional revenue?

Use the following information for problems 12.14, 12.15, and 12.16:

Dandle's Candles will be producing a new line of dripless candles in the coming years and has the choice of producing the candles in a large factory with a small number of workers or a small factory with a large number of workers. Each candle will be sold for $10. If the large factory is chosen, the cost per unit to produce each candle will be $2.50, while the cost per unit will be $7.50 for the small factory. The large factory would have fixed cash costs of $2 million and a depreciation expense of $300,000 per year, while those expenses would be $500,000 and $100,000 in the small factory.

12.14 Accounting operating profit break-even: Calculate the accounting operating profit break-even point for both factory choices for Dandle's Candles.

12.15 Crossover level of unit sales: Calculate the number of candles for Dandle's Candles for which the accounting operating profit is the same regardless of the factory choice.

12.16 Pretax operating cash flow break-even: Calculate the pretax operating cash flow break-even point for both factory choices for Dandle's Candles.

12.17 Accounting and cash flow break-even: Your analysis tells you that at a projected level of sales, your firm will be below accounting break-even but above cash flow break-even. Explain why this might still be a viable project or firm.

12.18 Sensitivity and scenario analyses: Sensitivity analysis and scenario analysis are somewhat similar. Describe which is a more realistic method of analyzing different scenario impacts on a project.

12.19 Sensitivity analysis: Describe the circumstances under which sensitivity analysis might be a reasonable basis for determining changes to a firm's EBIT or FCF.

12.20 Scenario analysis: Chip's Home Brew Whiskey forecasts that if it sells each bottle of Snake-Bite for $20, then the demand for the product will be 15,000 bottles per year, whereas sales will be 90 percent as high if the price is raised 10 percent. Chip's variable cost per bottle is $10, and the total fixed cash cost for the year is $100,000. Depreciation and amortization charges are $20,000, and the firm is in the 30 percent marginal tax rate. The firm anticipates an increased working capital need of $3,000 for the year. What will be the effect of the price increase on the firm's FCF for the year?

12.21 Sensitivity, scenario, and simulation analysis: If you were interested in calculating the probability that your project would have positive FCF, what type of risk analysis tool would you most likely use?

12.22 Profitability index: Suppose that you faced the following projects but had only $30,000 to invest. How would you make your decision and which projects would you invest in?

Project	Cost	NPV
A	$ 8,000	$4,000
B	11,000	7,000
C	9,000	5,000
D	7,000	4,000

12.23 Profitability index: Suppose that you face the same projects as in the previous problem but have only $25,000 to invest. Which projects would you choose?

ADVANCED

12.24 Mick's Soft Lemonade is starting to develop a new product for which the fixed cash expenditures are expected to be $80,000. The projected EBIT is $100,000, and the Accounting DOL will be 2.0. What is the Cash Flow DOL for the firm?

12.25 If a firm has any reasonable fixed asset base, meaning that its depreciation and amortization for any year is positive, discuss the relationship between a firm's Accounting DOL and its Cash Flow DOL.

EXCEL

12.26 Silver Polygon, Inc., has determined that if its revenues were to increase by 10 percent, then EBIT would increase by 25 percent to $100,000. The fixed costs (cash only) for the firm are $100,000. Given the same 10 percent increase in revenues, what would be the corresponding change in EBITDA?

12.27 If a firm's costs are absolutely known (variable as well as fixed), then what are the only two sources of volatility for the firm's operating profits or its operating cash flows?

12.28 In most circumstances, given the choice between a higher fixed cost structure and a lower fixed cost structure, which of the two would generate a larger contribution margin?

12.29 Using the same logic as with the accounting break-even calculation in Problem 12.15, adapt the formula for the crossover level of unit sales to find the number of units sold where the pretax operating cash flow is the same whether the firm chooses the large or small factory.

EXCEL

12.30 You are analyzing two proposed capital investments with the following cash flows:

Year	Project X	Project Y
0	−$20,000	−$20,000
1	13,000	7,000
2	6,000	7,000
3	6,000	7,000
4	2,000	7,000

The cost of capital for both projects is 10 percent. Calculate the profitability index (PI) for each project. Which project, or projects, should be accepted if you have unlimited funds to invest? Which project should be accepted if they are mutually exclusive?

CFA PROBLEMS

12.31 An investment of $20,000 will create a perpetual after-tax cash flow of $2,000. The required rate of return is 8 percent. What is the investment's profitability index?
  a. 1.00
  b. 1.08
  c. 1.16
  d. 1.25

12.32 Hermann Corporation is considering an investment of $375 million with expected after-tax cash inflows of $115 million per year for seven years and an additional after-tax salvage value of $50 million in Year 7. The required rate of return is 10 percent. What is the investment's PI?
  a. 1.19
  b. 1.33
  c. 1.56
  d. 1.75

12.33 Operating leverage is a measure of the
  a. sensitivity of net earnings to changes in operating earnings.
  b. sensitivity of net earnings to changes in sales.
  c. sensitivity of fixed operating costs to changes in variable costs.
  d. sensitivity of earnings before interest and taxes to changes in the number of units produced and sold.

12.34 The Fulcrum Company produces decorative swivel platforms for home televisions. If Fulcrum produces 40 million units, it estimates that it can sell them for $100 each. The variable production costs are $65 per unit, whereas the fixed production costs are $1.05 billion. Which of the following statements is true?
  a. The Fulcrum Company produces a positive operating income if it produces and sells more than 25 million swivel platforms.
  b. The Fulcrum Company's degree of operating leverage is 1.333.
  c. If the Fulcrum Company increases production and sales by 5 percent, its operating earnings are expected to increase by 20 percent.
  d. Increasing the fixed production costs by 10 percent will result in a lower sensitivity of operating earnings to changes in units produced and sold.

Sample Test Problems

12.1 Steven's Hats forecasts that it will sell 25,000 baseball caps next year. The firm buys its caps for $3 from the wholesaler and sells them for $15 each. If the firm will incur fixed costs plus depreciation and amortization of $80,000, then what is the percent increase in EBIT if the actual sales next year equal 27,000 caps?

12.2 Alan's Fine Furniture will be creating custom bed frames. The fixed cash expenditures are expected to be $120,000, the projected EBIT for the project is $130,000, and the Accounting DOL will be 2.5. What is the depreciation and amortization for the firm, as well as Cash Flow DOL?

12.3 Red Cat Firecrackers is considering whether to build a large or small factory to produce firecrackers. Regardless of the production method, each bundle of firecrackers sells for $4.00. If the large factory is chosen, then the variable cost per bundle of firecrackers will be $0.50, while the fixed costs will be $300,000 and the annual depreciation and amortization amount will be $100,000. If the small factory is chosen, then the variable cost per bundle of firecrackers will be $1.75, while the fixed costs will be $100,000 and the annual depreciation and amortization amount will be $10,000. Calculate the number of firecracker bundles for which the accounting operating profit is the same regardless of the factory choice.

12.4 You are chairperson of the investment committee at your firm. Five projects have been submitted to your committee for approval this month. The investment required and the project profitability index for each of these projects are presented in the following table:

Project	Investment	PI
A	$20,000	2.500
B	50,000	2.000
C	70,000	1.750
D	10,000	1.000
E	80,000	0.800

If you have $500,000 available for investments, which of these projects would you approve? Assume that you do not have to worry about having enough resources for future investments when making this decision.

12.5 Ibrahim's Habanero Sauce Products forecasts that if it sells each bottle of NitroStrength for $10, then the demand for the product will be 85,000 bottles per year. The company expects that if it sells NitroStrength for a price that is 10 percent higher, then it will sell 75 percent as many bottles of the sauce. Ibrahim's variable cost per bottle is $4, and the total fixed cash cost for the year is $20,000. Depreciation and amortization charges are $3,000, and the firm is in the 40 percent marginal tax rate. The firm anticipates an increased working capital need of $2,000 for the year. What effect would the price increase have on the firm's FCF for the year?

CHAPTER 13

THE COST OF CAPITAL

LEARNING OBJECTIVES

1. Explain what the weighted average cost of capital for a firm is and why it is often used as a discount rate to evaluate projects.

2. Calculate the cost of debt for a firm.

3. Calculate the cost of common stock and the cost of preferred stock for a firm.

4. Calculate the weighted average cost of capital for a firm, explain the limitations of using a firm's weighted average cost of capital as the discount rate when evaluating a project, and discuss the alternatives that are available.

Mark Lennihan/©AP/Wide World Photos

Starwood Hotels & Resorts Worldwide, Inc., announced in 2005 that it would build a new hotel in Hoboken, New Jersey, just across the Hudson River from lower Manhattan in New York City. The 27-story, 200,000-square-foot hotel, scheduled to open in 2008, would be part of Starwood's luxury "W" hotel chain. The hotel would have 225 guest rooms, 36 private residences, retail shops, a full-service restaurant, a café, a bar, meeting spaces, and a parking garage. The tower's wedge shape would offer nearly all of the hotel rooms and residences commanding views of the New York skyline and harbor. As you can imagine, the cost of financing a project like this is quite substantial.

Starwood is a highly sophisticated and successful hotel developer and operator. Before the company announced the construction of the Hoboken hotel, you can be sure that the managers at Starwood carefully evaluated the financial aspects of the project. They evaluated the required investment, what revenues the new hotel was likely to generate, and how much it would cost to operate and maintain. They also estimated what it would cost to finance the project—how much they would pay for the debt and the returns equity investors would require for an investment with this level of risk. This "cost of capital" would be incorporated into their NPV analysis through the discounting process.

Doing a good job of estimating the cost of capital is especially important for a capital-intensive project such as the Hoboken "W" hotel. The cost of financing a hotel like the one that Starwood is building can easily claim $90 or $100 from every room rental. In other words, if an average room rents for $200, the cost of financing the project can amount to 45 to 50 percent of the revenue the hotel receives from renting a room!

From this example, you can see how important it is to get the cost of capital right. If Starwood managers had estimated the cost of capital to be 7 percent when it was really 8 percent, they might have ended up investing in a project with a large negative NPV. How did Starwood approach this important task? In this chapter, we discuss how businesses estimate the cost of capital they use to evaluate projects.

CHAPTER PREVIEW

Chapter 7 discussed the general concept of risk and described what financial analysts mean when they talk about the risk associated with a project's cash flows. It also explained how this risk is related to expected returns. With this background, we are ready to discuss the methods that financial managers use to estimate discount rates, the reasons they use these methods, and the shortcomings of each method.

We start this chapter by introducing the weighted average cost of capital and explaining how this concept is related to the discount rates that many financial managers use to evaluate projects. Then we describe various methods that are used to estimate the three broad types of financing that firms use to acquire assets—debt, common stock, and preferred stock—as well as the overall weighted average cost of capital for the firm.

We next discuss the circumstances under which it is appropriate to use the weighted average cost of capital for a firm as the discount rate for a project and outline the types of problems that can arise when the weighted average cost of capital is used inappropriately. Finally, we examine alternatives to using the weighted average cost of capital as a discount rate.

13.1 The Firm's Overall Cost of Capital

LEARNING OBJECTIVE 1

Our discussions of investment analysis up to this point have focused on evaluating individual projects. We have assumed that the rate used to discount the cash flows for a project reflects the risks associated with the incremental cash flows from that project. In Chapter 7, we saw that since *unique risk* can be eliminated by holding a diversified portfolio, *systematic risk* is the only risk that investors require compensation for bearing. With this insight, we concluded that we could use Equation 7.9, to estimate the expected rate of return for a particular investment:

$$E(R_i) = R_{rf} + \beta_i[E(R_m) - R_{rf}]$$

where $E(R_i)$ is the expected return on project i, R_{rf} is the risk-free rate of return, β_i is the beta for project i, and $E(R_m)$ is the expected return on the market. Recall that the difference between the expected return on the market and the risk-free rate $[E(R_m) - R_{rf}]$ is known as the *market risk premium*.

Although these ideas help us better understand the discount rate on a conceptual level, they can be difficult to implement in practice. Firms do not issue publicly traded shares for individual projects. This means that analysts do not have the stock returns necessary to use a regression analysis like that illustrated in Exhibit 7.10 to estimate the beta (β) for an individual project. As a result, they have no way to directly estimate the discount rate that reflects the systematic risk of the incremental cash flows from a particular project.

In many firms, senior financial managers deal with this problem by estimating the cost of capital for the firm as a whole and then requiring analysts within the firm to use this cost of capital to discount the cash flows for all projects.[1] A problem with this approach is

---

[1] Surveys of capital budgeting practices at major public firms in the United States indicate that a large percentage (possibly as high as 80 percent) of firms use the cost of capital for a firm or a division in capital budgeting calculations. For a discussion of this evidence, see the article titled "Best Practices in Estimating the Cost of Capital: Survey and Synthesis," by R. F. Bruner, K. M. Eades, R. S. Harris, and R. C. Higgins, which was published in the Spring/Summer 1998 issue of *Financial Practice and Education*.

that it ignores the fact that a firm is really a collection of projects with varying levels of risk. A firm's overall cost of capital is actually a weighted average of the costs of capital for these projects, where the weights reflect the relative values of the projects.

To see why a firm is a collection of projects, consider The Boeing Company. Boeing manufactures a number of different models of civilian and military aircraft. If you have ever flown on a commercial airline, chances are that you have been on a Boeing 737, 747, 757, 767, or 777 aircraft. Boeing manufactures several versions of each of these aircraft models to meet the needs of its customers. These versions have different ranges, seat configurations, numbers of seats, and so on. Some are designed exclusively to haul freight for companies such as UPS and FedEx. Every version of every model of aircraft at Boeing was, at some point in time, a new project. The assets owned by Boeing today and its expected cash flows are just the sum of the assets and cash flows from all of these individual projects plus the other projects at the firm, such as those involving military aircraft.[2] This means that the overall systematic risk associated with Boeing's cash flows and the company's cost of capital are weighted averages of the systematic risks and the costs of capital for its individual projects.

If the risk of an individual project differs from the average risk of the firm, the firm's overall cost of capital is not the ideal discount rate to use when evaluating that project. Nevertheless, since this is the discount rate that is commonly used, we begin by discussing how a firm's overall cost of capital is estimated. We then discuss alternatives to using the firm's cost of capital as the discount rate in evaluating a project.

The Finance Balance Sheet

finance balance sheet
a balance sheet that is based on market values of expected cash flows

To understand how financial analysts estimate their firms' costs of capital, you must be familiar with a concept that we call the **finance balance sheet**. The finance balance sheet is like the accounting balance sheet from Chapter 3. The main difference is that it is based on market values rather than book values. Recall that the total book value of the assets reported on an accounting balance sheet does not necessarily reflect the total market value of those assets. This is because the book value is largely based on historical costs, while the total market value of the assets equals the present value of the total cash flows that those assets are expected to generate in the future. The market value can be greater than or less than the book value but is rarely the same.

While the left-hand side of the accounting balance sheet reports the book values of a firm's assets, the right-hand side reports how those assets were financed. Firms finance the purchase of their assets using debt and equity.[3] Since the cost of the assets must equal the total value of the debt and equity that was used to purchase them, the book value of the assets must equal the book value of the liabilities plus the book value of the equity on the accounting balance sheet. In Chapter 3 we called this equality the *balance sheet identity*.

Just as the total book value of the assets at a firm does not generally equal the total market value of those assets, the book value of total liabilities plus stockholders' equity does not usually equal the market value of these claims. In fact, the total market value of the debt and equity claims differ from their book values by exactly the same amount that the market values of a firm's assets differ from their book values. This is because the total market value of the debt and the equity at a firm equals the present value of the cash flows that the debt holders and the stockholders have the right to receive. These cash flows are the cash flows that the assets in the firm are expected to generate. In other words, the people who have lent money to a firm and the people who have

---

[2]The total expected cash flows at Boeing also include cash flows from projects that the firm is expected to undertake in the future, or what are often referred to as *growth opportunities*. This idea is discussed in detail in later chapters. For our immediate purposes, we will assume that these cash flows are expected to equal $0.
[3]We will discuss how firms finance their assets in more detail in Chapters 15 and 16. For the time being, we will simply assume that a firm uses some combination of debt and equity. Here we use the term *debt* in the broadest sense to refer to all liabilities, including liabilities on which the firm does not pay interest, such as accounts payable. As is common practice, we focus only on long-term interest-bearing debt, such as bank loans and bonds, in the cost of capital calculations. The reason for this is discussed in the next section.

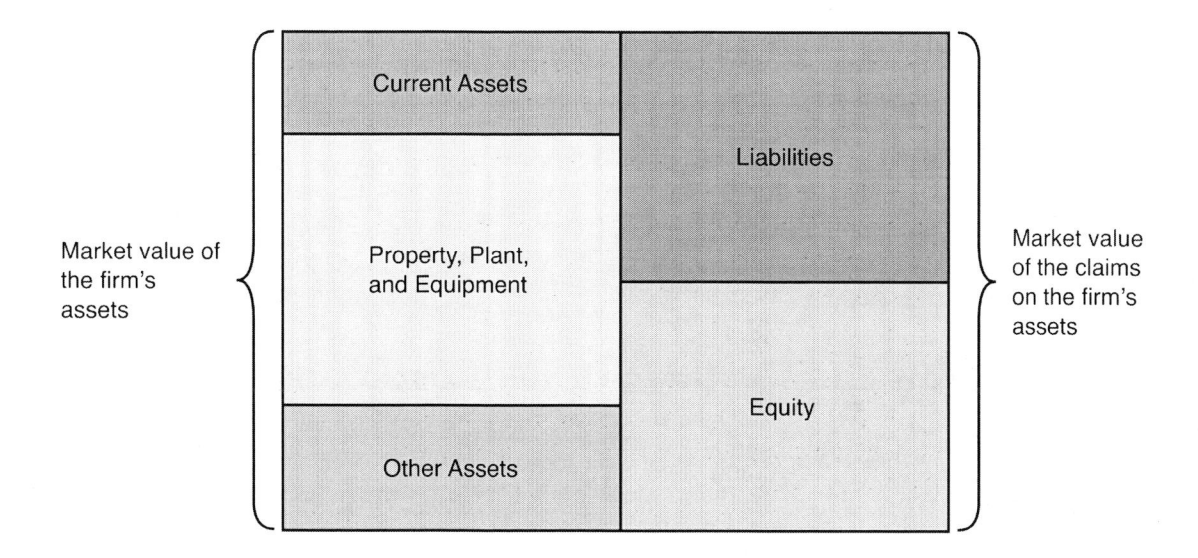

Exhibit 13.1
The Finance Balance Sheet
The market value of a firm's assets, which equals the present value of the cash flows those assets are expected to generate in the future, must equal the market value of the claims on those cash flows—the firm's liabilities and equity.

purchased the firm's stock have the right to receive all of the cash flows that the firm is expected to generate in the future. The value of the claims they hold must equal the value of the cash flows that they have a right to receive.

The fact that the market value of the assets must equal the value of the cash flows that these assets are expected to generate, combined with the fact that the value of the expected cash flows also equals the total market value of the firm's total liabilities and equity, means that we can write the market value (MV) of assets as follows:

$$\text{MV of assets} = \text{MV of liabilities} + \text{MV of equity} \qquad (13.1)$$

Equation 13.1 is just like the accounting balance sheet identity. The only difference is that Equation 13.1 is based on market values. This relation is illustrated in Exhibit 13.1.

To see why the market value of the assets must equal the total market value of the liabilities and equity, consider a firm whose only business is to own and manage an apartment building that was purchased 20 years ago for $1,000,000. Suppose that there is currently a mortgage on the building that is worth $300,000, the firm has no other debt, and the current market value of the building, based on the expected cash flows from future rents, is $4,000,000. What is the value of all of the equity (stock) in this firm? The answer is $4,000,000 − $300,000 = $3,700,000. If the cash flows that the apartment building is expected to produce are worth $4,000,000, then investors would be willing to pay $3,700,000 million for the equity in the firm. This is the value of the cash flows that they would expect to receive after making the interest and principal payments on the mortgage. Furthermore, since, by definition, the mortgage is worth $300,000, the value of the debt plus the value of the equity is $300,000 + $3,700,000 = $4,000,000—which is exactly equal to the market value of the firm's assets.

If the concept of a balance sheet based on market values seems familiar to you, it is because the idea of preparing an actual balance sheet based on market values was discussed in Chapter 3. In that chapter we pointed out that such a balance sheet would be more useful to financial decision makers than the ordinary accounting balance sheet. Financial managers are much more concerned about the future than the past when they make decisions. You might revisit the discussion of sunk costs in Chapter 11 to remind yourself of why this is true.

> **BUILDING INTUITION**
>
> ### The Market Value of a Firm's Assets Equals the Market Value of the Claims on Those Assets
>
> The market value of the debt and equity claims against the cash flows of a firm must equal the present value of the cash flows that the firm's assets are expected to generate. This is because, between them, the debt holders and the stockholders have the legal right to receive all of those cash flows.

How Firms Estimate Their Cost of Capital

Now that you understand the basic idea of the finance balance sheet, consider the challenge that financial analysts face when they want to estimate the cost of capital for a firm. If analysts at a firm could estimate the betas for each of the firm's individual projects, they could estimate the beta for the entire firm as a weighted average of the betas for the individual projects. They could do this because, as we discussed earlier, the firm is simply a collection (portfolio) of projects. This calculation would just be an application of Equation 7.10:

$$\beta_{n \text{ Asset portfolio}} = \sum_{i=1}^{n} x_i \beta_i = x_1\beta_1 + x_2\beta_2 + x_3\beta_3 + \cdots + x_n\beta_n$$

where β_i is the beta for project i and x_i is the fraction of the total firm value represented by project i.

The analysts could then use the beta for the firm in Equation 7.9:

$$E(R_i) = R_{rf} + \beta_i[E(R_m) - R_{rf}]$$

to estimate the expected return on the firm's assets, which is also the firm's cost of capital. Unfortunately, because analysts are not typically able to estimate betas for individual projects, they generally cannot use this approach.

Instead, analysts must use their knowledge of the finance balance sheet, along with the concept of market efficiency, to estimate the cost of capital for the firm. Rather than using Equations 7.10 and 7.9 to perform the calculations for the *individual projects* represented on the left-hand side of the finance balance sheet, analysts perform a similar set of calculations for the *different types of financing* (debt and equity) on the right-hand side of the finance balance sheet. They can do this because, as we said earlier, the people who finance the firm have the right to receive all of the cash flows on the left-hand side. This means that the systematic risk associated with the total assets on the left-hand side is the same as the systematic risk associated with the total financing on the right-hand side. In other words, the weighted average of the betas for the different claims on the assets must equal a weighted average of the betas for the individual assets (projects).

Analysts do not need to estimate betas for each type of financing that the firm has. As long as they can estimate the cost of each type of financing—either directly, by observing that cost in the capital markets, or by using Equation 7.9—they can compute the cost of capital for the firm using the following equation:

$$k_{\text{Firm}} = \sum_{i=1}^{n} x_i k_i = x_1 k_1 + x_2 k_2 + x_3 k_3 + \cdots + x_n k_n \qquad (13.2)$$

In Equation 13.2, k_{Firm} is the cost of capital for the firm, k_i is the cost of financing type i, and x_i is the fraction of the total market value of the financing (or of the assets) of the firm represented by financing type i. This formula simply says that the overall cost of capital for the firm is a weighted average of the cost of each different type of financing used by the firm. Note that since we are specifically talking about the cost of capital, we use the symbol k_i to represent this cost, rather than the more general notation $E(R_i)$ that we used in Chapter 7.

The similarity between Equation 13.2 and Equation 7.10 is not an accident. Both are applications of the basic idea that the systematic risk of a portfolio of assets is a weighted average of the systematic risks of the individual assets. Because R_{rf} and $E(R_m)$ in Equation 7.9 are the same for all assets, when we substitute Equation 7.9 into Equation 13.2—remember that $E(R_i)$ in Equation 7.9 is the same as k_i in Equation 13.2—and cancel out R_{rf} and $E(R_m)$, we get Equation 7.10. We will not prove this here, but you might do so to convince yourself that what we are saying is true.

To see how Equation 13.2 is applied, let's return to the example of the firm whose only business is to manage an apartment building. Recall that the total value of this firm is $4,000,000 and that it has $300,000 in debt. If the firm has only one loan and one type of stock, then the fractions of the total value represented by those two types of financing are as follows:

$$x_{Debt} = \$300,000/\$4,000,000 = 0.075, \text{ or } 7.5\%$$
$$x_{Equity} = \$3,700,000/\$4,000,000 = 0.925, \text{ or } 92.5\%$$
$$\text{where } x_{Debt} + x_{Equity} = 0.075 + 0.925 = 1.000$$

This tells us that the value of the debt claims equals 7.5 percent of the value of the firm and that the value of the equity claims equals the remaining 92.5 percent of the value of the firm. If the cost of the debt for this business is 6 percent and the cost of the equity is 10 percent, the cost of capital for the firm can be calculated as a weighted average of the costs of the debt and equity:[4]

$$k_{Firm} = x_{Debt}k_{Debt} + x_{Equity}k_{Equity} = (0.075)(0.06) + (0.925)(0.10) = 0.097, \text{ or } 9.7\%$$

Notice that we have used Equation 13.2 to calculate a **weighted average cost of capital (WACC)** for the firm in this example. In fact, this is what people typically call the firm's cost of capital, k_{Firm}. From this point on, we will use the abbreviation WACC to represent the firm's overall cost of capital.

weighted average cost of capital (WACC)
the weighted average of the costs of the different types of capital (debt and equity) that have been used to finance a firm; the cost of each type of capital is weighted by the proportion of the total capital that it represents

---

Calculating the Cost of Capital for a Firm

LEARNING BY DOING APPLICATION 13.1

Problem: You are a real estate investor who is considering investing in a new office building that will cost $2,000,000. You plan to finance the building with a $1,500,000 first mortgage at a 6.5 percent interest rate, a $300,000 second mortgage at an 8 percent interest rate, and $200,000 of your own money. You will own all of the equity (stock) in this investment. You estimate that the opportunity cost of your $200,000 investment—that is, what you could earn on an investment of similar risk in the capital market—is 12 percent with that much debt. What is the cost of capital for this investment?

Approach: You can think of the office building as a separate firm and use Equation 13.2 to calculate the WACC for this "firm." Since you are planning to finance the building with capital from three different sources—two mortgages and your own equity investment—the right-hand side of Equation 13.2 will have three terms.

(continued)

---

[4]We are ignoring the effect of taxes on the cost of debt financing for the time being. This effect is discussed in detail in Section 13.2 and explicitly incorporated into subsequent calculations.

Solution: We begin by calculating the weights for the different types of financing:

$$x_{\text{1st mortgage}} = \$1,500,000/\$2,000,000 = 0.75$$
$$x_{\text{2nd mortgage}} = \$300,000/\$2,000,000 = 0.15$$
$$x_{\text{Equity}} = \$200,000/\$2,000,000 = 0.10$$

where $x_{\text{1st mortgage}} + x_{\text{2nd mortgage}} + x_{\text{Equity}} = 0.75 + 0.15 + 0.10 = 1.00$

We can then calculate the WACC using Equation 13.2:

$$\begin{aligned} \text{WACC} = k_{\text{Firm}} &= x_{\text{1st mortgage}} k_{\text{1st mortgage}} + x_{\text{2nd mortgage}} k_{\text{2nd mortgage}} + x_{\text{Equity}} k_{\text{Equity}} \\ &= (0.75)(0.065) + (0.15)(0.08) + (0.10)(0.12) \\ &= 0.073, \text{ or } 7.3\% \end{aligned}$$

On average, you would be paying 7.3 percent per year on every dollar you invested in the office building. This is the opportunity cost of capital for the office building project. It is the rate that you would use to discount the cash flows associated with the office building in an NPV analysis.

BUILDING INTUITION

A Firm's Cost of Capital Is a Weighted Average of All of Its Financing Costs

The cost of capital for a firm is a weighted average of the costs of the different types of financing used by a firm. The weights are the proportions of the total firm value represented by the different types of financing. By weighting the costs of the individual financing types in this way, we obtain the overall average opportunity cost of each dollar invested in the firm.

Before You Go On

1. Why does the market value of the claims on the assets of a firm equal the market value of the assets?
2. How is the WACC for a firm calculated?
3. What does the WACC for a firm tell us?

13.2 The Cost of Debt

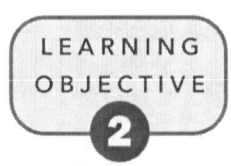

LEARNING OBJECTIVE 2

In our discussion of how the WACC for a firm is calculated, we assumed that the costs of the different types of financing were known. This assumption allowed us to simply plug those costs into Equation 13.2 once we had calculated the weight for each. Unfortunately, life is not that simple. In the real world, analysts have to estimate each of the individual costs. In other words, the discussion in the preceding section glossed over a number of concepts and issues that you should be familiar with. This section and Section 13.3 discuss those concepts and issues and show how the costs of the different types of financing can be estimated.

Before we move on to the specifics of how to estimate the costs of different types of financing, we must stress an important point: All of these calculations depend in some part on financial markets being efficient.[5] We suggested this in the last section

---
[5] Recall that we discussed the concept of financial market efficiency in Chapter 8.

when we mentioned that analysts have to rely on the concept of market efficiency to estimate the WACC. The reason is that analysts often cannot directly observe the rate of return that investors require for a particular type of financing. Instead, analysts must rely on the security prices they can observe in the financial markets to estimate the required rate.

It makes sense to rely on security prices only if you believe that the financial markets are reasonably efficient at incorporating new information into these prices. If the markets were not efficient, estimates of expected returns that were based on market security prices would be unreliable. Of course, if the returns that are plugged into Equation 13.2 are bad, the resulting estimate for WACC will also be bad. With this caveat, we can now discuss how to estimate the costs of the various types of financing.

Key Concepts for Estimating the Cost of Debt

Virtually all firms use some form of debt financing. The financial managers at firms typically arrange for revolving lines of credit to finance working capital items, such as inventories or accounts receivable. These lines of credit are very much like the lines of credit that come with your credit cards. Firms also obtain private fixed-term loans, such as bank loans, or sell bonds to the public to finance ongoing operations or the purchase of long-term assets—just as you would finance your living expenses while you are in school with a student loan or a car with a car loan. For example, an electric utility firm, such as FPL Group in Florida, will sell bonds to finance a new power plant, and a rapidly growing retailer, such as Target, will use debt to finance new stores and distribution centers. As mentioned earlier, we will discuss how firms finance themselves in more detail in Chapters 15 and 16, but for now it is sufficient to recognize that firms use these three general types of debt financing: lines of credit, private fixed-term loans, and bonds that are sold in the public markets.

There is a cost associated with each type of debt that a firm uses. However, when we estimate the cost of capital for a firm, we are particularly interested in the cost of the firm's long-term debt. Firms generally use long-term debt to finance their long-term assets, and it is the long-term assets that concern us when we think about the value of a firm's assets. By long-term debt, we usually mean the debt that, when it was borrowed, was set to mature in more than one year. This typically includes fixed-term bank loans used to finance ongoing operations or long-term assets, as well as the bonds that a firm sells in the public debt markets.

Although one year is not an especially long time, debt with a maturity of more than one year is typically viewed as permanent debt. This is because firms often borrow the money to pay off this debt when it matures.

We do not normally worry about revolving lines of credit when calculating the cost of debt because these lines tend to be temporary. Banks typically require that the outstanding balances be periodically paid down to $0 (just as we are sure you pay your entire credit card balance from time to time).

When analysts estimate the cost of a firm's long-term debt, they are estimating the cost on a particular date—the date on which they are doing the analysis. This is a very important point to keep in mind because the interest rate that the firm is paying on its outstanding debt does not necessarily reflect its current cost of debt. Interest rates change over time, and so does the cost of debt for a firm. The rate a firm was charged three years ago for a five-year loan is unlikely to be the same rate that it would be charged today for a new five-year loan. For example, suppose that FPL Group issued bonds five years ago for 7 percent. Since then, interest rates have fallen, so the same bonds could be sold at par value today for 6 percent. The cost of debt today is 6 percent, not 7 percent, and 6 percent is the cost of debt that management will use in WACC calculations. If you looked in the firm's financial statements, you would see that the firm is paying an interest rate of 7 percent. This is what the financial managers of the firm agreed to pay five years ago, not what it would cost to sell the same bonds today. The accounting statements reflect the cost of debt that was sold at some time in the past.

BUILDING INTUITION

The Current Cost of Long-Term Debt Is What Matters When Calculating WACC

The current cost of long-term debt is the appropriate cost of debt for WACC calculations. This is the relevant cost because the WACC is the opportunity cost of capital for the firm's investors as of today. Historical costs do not belong in WACC calculations.

Estimating the Current Cost of a Bond or an Outstanding Loan

We have now seen that we should not use historical costs of debt in WACC calculations. Let's discuss how we can estimate the current costs of bonds and other fixed-term loans by using market information.

THE CURRENT COST OF A BOND

You may not realize it, but we have already discussed how to estimate the current cost of debt for a publicly traded bond. This cost is estimated using the yield to maturity calculation. Recall that in Chapter 8 we defined the yield to maturity as the discount rate that makes the present value of the coupon and principal payments equal to the price of the bond.

For example, consider a 10-year $1,000 bond that was issued five years ago. This bond has five years remaining before it matures. If the bond has an annual coupon rate of 7 percent, pays coupon interest semiannually, and is currently selling for $1,042.65, we can calculate its yield to maturity by using Equation 8.1 and solving for i or by using a financial calculator. Let's use Equation 8.1 for this example.

To do this, as was discussed in the section on semiannual compounding in Chapter 8, we first convert the bond data to reflect semiannual compounding: (1) the total number of coupon payments is 10 (2 per year × 5 years), and (2) the semiannual coupon payment is $35 [($1,000 × 7 percent)/2 = $70/2]. We can now use Equation 8.1 and solve for i to find the yield to maturity:

$$P_B = \frac{C_1}{1+i} + \frac{C_2}{(1+i)^2} + \cdots + \frac{C_n + F_n}{(1+i)^n}$$

$$\$1{,}042.65 = \frac{\$35}{1+i} + \frac{\$35}{(1+i)^2} + \frac{\$35}{(1+i)^3} + \cdots + \frac{\$35}{(1+i)^9} + \frac{\$1{,}035}{(1+i)^{10}}$$

Now, by trial and error or with a financial calculator, we solve for i and find:

$$i = k_{\text{Bond}} = 0.030, \text{ or } 3.0\%$$

This semiannual rate would be quoted as an annual rate of 6 percent (2 × 0.03 = 0.06, or 6 percent) on Wall Street. However, as explained in Chapter 8, this annual rate fails to account for the effects of compounding. We must therefore use Equation 6.7 to calculate the effective annual interest rate (EAR) in order to obtain the actual current annual cost of this debt:

$$\text{EAR} = \left(1 + \frac{\text{Quoted interest rate}}{m}\right)^m - 1 = \left(1 + \frac{0.06}{2}\right)^2 - 1$$
$$= (1.03)^2 - 1 = 0.061, \text{ or } 6.1\%$$

If this bond was sold at par, it paid 7 percent when it was issued five years ago. Someone who buys it today will expect to earn only 6.1 percent per year. This is the annual rate of return required by the market on this bond, which is known as the effective annual yield on Wall Street.

Notice that the above calculation takes into account the interest payments, the face value of the debt (the amount that will be repaid in five years), and the current price at which the bond is selling. It is necessary to account for all of these characteristics of the bond. The return received by someone who buys the bond today will be determined by both the interest income and the capital appreciation (or capital depreciation in this case, since the price is higher than the face value).

We must account for one other factor when we calculate the current cost of bond financing to a company—the cost of issuing the bond. In the above example, we calculated the return that someone who buys the bond can expect to receive. Since a company must pay fees to investment bankers, lawyers, and accountants, along with various other costs, to actually issue a bond, the cost to the company is higher than 6.1 percent.[6] Therefore, in order to obtain an accurate estimate of the cost of a bond, analysis must incorporate *issuance costs* into their calculations. Issuance costs are an example of *direct out-of-pocket costs,* the actual out-of-pocket costs that a firm incurs when it raises capital.

The way in which issuance costs are incorporated into the calculation of the cost of a bond is quite simple. Analysts use the *net proceeds* that the company receives from the bond, rather than the price that is paid by the investor, on the left-hand side of Equation 8.1. Suppose the company in our example sold 5-year bonds with a 7 percent coupon today and paid issuance costs equal to 2 percent of the total value of the bonds. After paying the issuance costs, the company would receive only 98 percent of the price paid by the investors. Therefore, the company would actually receive only $1,042.65 × (1 − 0.02) = $1,021.80 for each bond it sold and the semiannual cost to the company would be:

$$P_B = \frac{C_1}{1+i} + \frac{C_2}{(1+i)^2} + \cdots + \frac{C_n + F_n}{(1+i)^n}$$

$$\$1{,}021.80 = \frac{\$35}{1+i} + \frac{\$35}{(1+i)^2} + \frac{\$35}{(1+i)^3} + \cdots + \frac{\$35}{(1+i)^9} + \frac{\$1{,}035}{(1+i)^{10}}$$

$$i = k_{Bond} = 0.0324, \text{ or } 3.24\%$$

Converting the adjusted semiannual rate to an EAR, we see that the actual annual cost of this debt financing is:

$$EAR = (1.0324)^2 - 1 = 0.066, \text{ or } 6.6\%$$

In this example the issuance costs increase the effective cost of the bonds from 6.1 percent to 6.6 percent per year.

THE CURRENT COST OF AN OUTSTANDING LOAN

Conceptually, calculating the current cost of long-term bank or other private debt is not as straightforward as estimating the current cost of a public bond because financial analysts cannot observe the market price of private debt. Fortunately, analysts do not typically have to do this. Instead, they can simply call their banker and ask what rate the bank would charge if they decided to refinance the debt today. A rate quote from a banker provides a good estimate of the current cost of a private loan.

Taxes and the Cost of Debt

It is very important that you understand one additional concept concerning the cost of debt: In the United States, *firms can deduct interest payments for tax purposes.* In other

---

[6]These types of costs are incurred by firms whenever they raise capital. We only show how to include them in the cost of bond financing and, later, in estimating the cost of preferred stock, but they should also be included in calculations of the costs of capital from other sources, such as bank loans and common equity.

words, every dollar a firm pays in interest reduces the firm's taxable income by one dollar. Thus, if the firm's marginal tax rate is 35 percent, the firm's total tax bill will be reduced by 35 cents. A dollar of interest would actually cost this firm only 65 cents because the firm would save 35 cents on its taxes.

More generally, the after-tax cost of interest payments equals the pretax cost times 1 minus the tax rate. This means that the after-tax cost of debt is:

$$k_{\text{Debt after-tax}} = k_{\text{Debt pretax}} \times (1 - t) \tag{13.3}$$

This after-tax cost of debt is the cost that firms actually use to calculate the WACC. The reason is simply that investors care only about the after-tax cost of capital—just as they care only about after-tax cash flows. Investors are concerned about what they actually have to pay for capital, and the actual cost is reduced if the government subsidizes debt by providing a tax break.

Taxes affect the cost of debt in much the same way that the interest tax deduction on a home mortgage affects the cost of financing a house. For example, assume that you borrow $200,000 at 6 percent to buy a house on January 1 and your interest payments total $12,000 in the first year. Under the tax law, you can deduct this $12,000 from your taxable income when you calculate your taxes for the year.[7]

Suppose that your taxable income before the interest deduction is $75,000 and, for simplicity, that both your average and marginal tax rates are 20 percent. Without the interest deduction, you would pay taxes totaling $15,000 ($75,000 × 0.20). However, because the interest payments reduce your taxable income, your taxes with the interest deduction will be only $12,600 [($75,000 − $12,000) × 0.20]. The ability to deduct the interest payments you made saved you $2,400 ($15,000 − $12,600)! This savings is exactly equal to the interest payment you make times your marginal tax rate: $12,000 × 0.20 = $2,400. Since you are saving $2,400, the after-tax cost of your interest payments is $9,600 ($12,000 − $2,400), which means that the after-tax cost of this debt is 4.8 percent ($9,600/$200,000). This is exactly what Equation 13.3 tells us. With $k_{\text{Debt pretax}}$ at 6 percent and t at 20 percent, Equation 13.3 gives us:

$$k_{\text{Debt after-tax}} = k_{\text{Debt pretax}} \times (1 - t) = 0.06 \times (1 - 0.2) = 0.048, \text{ or } 4.8\%$$

Estimating the Cost of Debt for a Firm

Most firms have several different debt issues outstanding at any particular point in time. Just as you might have both a car loan and a school loan, a firm might have several bank loans and bond issues outstanding. To estimate the firm's overall cost of debt when it has several debt issues outstanding, we must first estimate the costs of the individual debt issues and then calculate a weighted average of these costs.

To see how this is done, let's consider an example. Suppose that your pizza parlor business has grown dramatically in the past three years from a single restaurant to 30 restaurants. To finance this growth, two years ago you sold $25 million of five-year bonds. These bonds pay interest annually and have a coupon rate of 8 percent. They are currently selling for $1,026.24 per $1,000 bond. Just today, you also borrowed $5 million from your local bank at an interest rate of 6 percent. Assume that this is all the long-term debt that you have and that there are no issuance costs. What is the overall average after-tax cost of your debt if your business's marginal tax rate is 35 percent?

---

[7] There is a limit on the total amount of home loan interest payments that you can deduct when you calculate your taxable income. For instance, in 2006 you could deduct interest payments on loans with a total face value of $1,100,000 ($1,000,000 mortgage plus $100,000 home equity loan).

The pretax cost of the bonds as of today is the effective annual yield on those bonds. Since the bonds were sold two years ago, they will mature three years from now. Using Equation 8.1, we find that the effective annual yield (which equals the yield to maturity in this example) for these bonds is:

$$P_B = \frac{C_1}{1+i} + \frac{C_2}{(1+i)^2} + \cdots + \frac{C_n + F_n}{(1+i)^n}$$

$$\$1{,}026.24 = \frac{\$80}{1+i} + \frac{\$80}{(1+i)^2} + \frac{\$1{,}080}{(1+i)^3}$$

$$i = k_{\text{Bond pretax}} = 0.07, \text{ or } 7\%$$

The pretax cost of the bank loan that you took out today is simply the 6 percent rate that the bank is charging you, assuming that the bank is charging you the market rate.

Now that we know the pretax costs of the two types of debt that your business has outstanding, we can calculate the overall average cost of your debt by calculating the weighted average of their two costs. The weights for the two types of debt are as follows:

$$x_{\text{Bonds}} = \$25{,}000{,}000/(\$25{,}000{,}000 + \$5{,}000{,}000) = 0.833$$
$$x_{\text{Bank debt}} = \$5{,}000{,}000/(\$25{,}000{,}000 + \$5{,}000{,}000) = 0.167$$

where $x_{\text{Bonds}} + x_{\text{Bank debt}} = 0.833 + 0.167 = 1.000$

The weighted average pretax cost of debt is:

$$k_{\text{Debt pretax}} = x_{\text{Bonds}} k_{\text{Bonds pretax}} + x_{\text{Bank debt}} k_{\text{Bank debt pretax}}$$
$$= (0.833)(0.07) + (0.167)(0.06)$$
$$= 0.0683, \text{ or } 6.83\%$$

The after-tax cost of debt is therefore:

$$k_{\text{Debt after-tax}} = k_{\text{Debt pretax}} \times (1 - t) = 6.83\% \times (1 - 0.35) = 4.44\%$$

LEARNING BY DOING APPLICATION 13.2

Calculating the Cost of Debt for a Firm

Problem: You have just successfully completed a leveraged buyout of the firm that you have been working for. To finance this $35 million transaction, you and three partners put up a total of $10 million in equity capital, and you borrowed $25 million from banks and other investors. The bank debt consists of $10 million of secured debt borrowed at a rate of 6 percent from Bank of America and $7 million of senior unsecured debt borrowed at a rate of 7 percent from JPMorgan Chase. The remaining $8 million was borrowed from an investment group managed by a private equity firm. The rate on this subordinated (junior) unsecured debt is 9.5 percent. What is the overall after-tax cost of the debt financing used to buy the firm if you expect the firm's average and marginal tax rates to both be 25 percent?

Approach: The overall after-tax cost of debt can be calculated using the following three-step process: (1) Calculate the fraction of the total debt (weight) for each individual debt issue. (2) Using these weights, calculate the weighted average pretax cost of debt. (3) Use Equation 13.3 to calculate the after-tax average cost of debt.

Solution: (1) The weights for the three types of debt are as follows:

$$x_{\text{Secured debt}} = \$10{,}000{,}000/\$25{,}000{,}000 = 0.40$$
$$x_{\text{Senior unsecured debt}} = \$7{,}000{,}000/\$25{,}000{,}000 = 0.28$$
$$x_{\text{Subordinated unsecured debt}} = \$8{,}000{,}000/\$25{,}000{,}000 = 0.32$$

where $x_{\text{Secured debt}} + x_{\text{Senior unsecured debt}} + x_{\text{Subordinated unsecured debt}}$
$= 0.40 + 0.28 + 0.32 = 1.00$

(continued)

(2) The weighted average pretax cost of debt is:

$$k_{\text{Debt pretax}} = x_{\text{Secured debt}} k_{\text{Secured debt pretax}} + x_{\text{Senior unsecured debt}} k_{\text{Senior unsecured debt pretax}}$$
$$+ x_{\text{Subordinated unsecured debt}} k_{\text{Subordinated unsecured debt pretax}}$$
$$= (0.40)(0.06) + (0.28)(0.07) + (0.32)(0.095)$$
$$= 0.074, \text{ or } 7.4\%$$

(3) The after-tax cost of debt is therefore:

$$k_{\text{Debt after-tax}} = k_{\text{Debt pretax}} \times (1 - t) = 7.4\% \times (1 - 0.25) = 5.55\%$$

DECISION-MAKING EXAMPLE 13.1

Using the Cost of Debt in Decision Making

Situation: Your pizza parlor business has developed such a strong reputation that you have decided to take advantage of the restaurant's name recognition by selling frozen pizzas through grocery stores. In order to do this, you will have to build a manufacturing facility. You estimate that this will cost you $10 million. Since your business currently has only $2 million in the bank, you will have to borrow the remaining $8 million. You have spoken with two bankers about possible loan packages. The banker from Easy Money Financial Services offered you a loan for $6 million with a 6 percent rate and $2 million with a 7.5 percent rate. You calculate the pretax cost of debt for this package to be:

$$k_{\text{Loans pretax}} = (\$6{,}000{,}000/\$8{,}000{,}000)(0.06) + (\$2{,}000{,}000/\$8{,}000{,}000)(0.075)$$
$$= 6.375\%$$

Your local banker offered you a single $8 million loan for 6.350 percent. Which financing should you choose if all terms on all of the loans, other than the interest rates, are the same?

Decision: This is an easy decision. You should choose the least expensive alternative—the loan from your local bank. In this example, you can directly compare the pretax costs of the two alternatives. You do not need to calculate the after-tax costs because multiplying each pretax cost by the same number, $1 - t$, will not change your decision.

> **Before You Go On**
>
> 1. Why do analysts care about the *current* cost of long-term debt when estimating a firm's cost of capital?
> 2. How do you estimate the cost of debt for a firm with more than one type of debt?
> 3. How do taxes affect the cost of debt?

13.3 The Cost of Equity

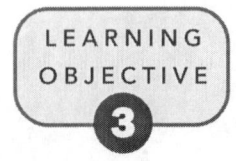

LEARNING OBJECTIVE 3

The cost of equity for a firm is a weighted average of the costs of the different types of stock that the firm has outstanding at a particular point in time. We saw in Chapter 9 that some firms have both preferred stock and common stock outstanding. In order to calculate the cost of equity for these firms, we have to know how to calculate the cost of both common stock and preferred stock. In this section, we discuss how financial analysts can estimate the costs associated with these two different types of stock.

Common Stock

Just as information about market rates of return is used to estimate the cost of debt, market information is also used to estimate the cost of equity. There are several ways to do this. The particular approach a financial analyst chooses will depend on what information is available and how reliable the analyst believes it is. Next we discuss three alternative methods for estimating the cost of common stock. It is important to remember throughout this discussion that the "cost" we are referring to is the rate of return that investors require for investing in the stock at a particular point in time, given its systematic risk.

METHOD 1: USING THE CAPITAL ASSET PRICING MODEL (CAPM)

The first method for estimating the cost of common equity is one that we discussed in Chapter 7. This method uses Equation 7.9:

$$E(R_i) = R_{rf} + \beta_i[E(R_m) - R_{rf}]$$

In this equation, the expected return on an asset is a linear function of the systematic risk associated with that asset.

If we recognize that $E(R_i)$ in Equation 7.9 is the cost of the common stock capital used by the firm (k_{cs}) when we are calculating the cost of equity and that $[E(R_m) - R_{rf}]$ is the market risk premium, we can rewrite Equation 7.9 as follows:

$$k_{cs} = R_{rf} + (\beta_{cs} \times \text{Market risk premium}) \quad (13.4)$$

Equation 13.4 is just another way of writing Equation 7.9. It tells us that the cost of common stock equals the risk-free rate of return plus compensation for the systematic risk associated with the common stock. You already saw some examples of how to use this equation to calculate the cost of equity in the discussion of the Capital Asset Pricing Model (CAPM) in Chapter 7. In those examples you were given the current risk-free rate, the beta for the stock, and the market risk premium and were asked to calculate k_{cs} using the equation. Now we turn our attention to some practical considerations that you must be concerned with when choosing the appropriate risk-free rate, beta, and market risk premium for this calculation.

The Risk-Free Rate. First, let's consider the risk-free rate. The current effective annual yield on a risk-free asset should always be used in Equation 13.4. This is because the risk-free rate at a particular point in time reflects the rate of inflation that the market expects in the future. Since the expected rate of inflation changes over time, an old risk-free rate might not reflect current inflation expectations.

When analysts select a risk-free rate, they must choose between using a short-term rate, such as that for Treasury bills, or a longer-term rate, such as those for Treasury notes or bonds. Which of these choices is most appropriate? This question has been hotly debated by finance professionals for many years. We recommend that you use the risk-free rate on a long-term Treasury security when you estimate the cost of equity capital because the equity claim is a long-term claim on the firm's cash flows. As you saw in Chapter 9, the stockholders have a claim on the cash flows of the firm in perpetuity. By using a long-term Treasury security, you are matching a long-term risk-free rate with a long-term claim. A long-term risk-free rate better reflects long-term inflation expectations and the cost of getting investors to part with their money for a long period of time than a short-term rate.

> You can find current yields on Treasury bills, notes, and bonds at the Web site of the U.S. Federal Reserve Bank at www.federalreserve.gov/releases/H15/update.

The Beta. If the common stock of a company is publicly traded, then you can estimate the beta for that stock using a regression analysis similar to that illustrated in Exhibit 7.10. However, identifying the appropriate beta is much more complicated if the common stock is not publicly traded. Since most companies in the United States are privately owned and do not have publicly traded stock, this is a problem that arises quite often when someone wants to estimate the cost of common equity for a firm.

Companies with publicly traded equity usually provide a lot of information about their businesses and financial performance on their Web sites. The Domino's Pizza Web site is a good example. Go to http://phx.corporate-ir.net/phoenix.zhtml?c=135383&p=irol-irhome.

Financial analysts often overcome this problem by identifying a "comparable" company with publicly traded stock that is in the same business and that has a similar amount of debt. For example, suppose you are trying to estimate the beta for your pizza business. The company has now grown to include more than 2,000 restaurants throughout the world. The frozen-foods business, however, was never successful and had to be shut down. You know that Domino's Pizza, Inc., one of your major competitors, has publicly traded equity and that the proportion of debt to equity for Domino's is similar to the proportion for your firm. Since Domino's overall business is similar to yours, in that it is only in the pizza business and competes in similar geographic areas, it would be reasonable to consider Domino's a comparable company.

The systematic risk associated with the stock of a comparable company is likely to be similar to the systematic risk for the private firm because systematic risk is determined by the nature of the firm's business and the amount of debt that it uses. If you are able to identify a good comparable company, such as Domino's Pizza, you can use its beta in Equation 13.4 to estimate the cost of equity capital for your firm. Even when a good comparable company cannot be identified, it is sometimes possible to use an average of the betas for the public firms in the same industry.

The Market Risk Premium. It is not possible to directly observe the market risk premium. We just do not know what rate of return investors expect for the market portfolio—$E(R_m)$—at a particular point in time. Therefore, we cannot simply calculate the market risk premium as the difference between the expected return on the market and the risk-free rate—$[E(R_m) - R_{rf}]$. For this reason, financial analysts generally use a measure of the average risk premium investors have actually earned in the past as an indication of the risk premium they might require today.

For example, from 1926 through the end of 2006, actual returns on the U.S. stock market exceeded actual returns on long-term U.S. government bonds by an average of 6.51 percent per year. If, on average, investors earned the risk premium that they expected, this figure reflects the average market risk premium over the period from 1926 to 2006. If a financial analyst believes that the market risk premium in the past is a reasonable estimate of the risk premium today, then he or she might use 6.51 percent as the market risk premium in Equation 13.4.

With this background, let's work an example to illustrate how Equation 13.4 is used in practice to estimate the cost of common stock for a firm. Suppose that it is December 27, 2007, and we want to estimate the cost of the common stock for the oil company ConocoPhillips. Using yields reported in the *Wall Street Journal* on that day, we determine that 30-day Treasury bills have an effective annual yield of 2.85 percent and that 20-year Treasury bonds have an effective annual yield of 4.66 percent. From the MSN Money Web site (http://moneycentral.msn.com), we find that the beta for ConocoPhillips stock is 0.51. We know that the market risk premium averaged 6.51 percent from 1926 to 2006. What is the expected rate of return on ConocoPhillips common stock?

Since we are estimating the expected rate of return on common stock, and common stock is a long-term asset, we use the long-term Treasury bond yield of 4.66 percent in the calculation. Notice that the Treasury bill and Treasury bond rates differed by 1.81 percent (4.66 − 2.85 = 1.81) on December 27, 2007. They often differ by this amount or more, so the choice of which rate to use can make quite a difference in the estimated cost of equity.

Once we have selected the appropriate risk-free rate, we can plug it, along with the beta and market risk premium values, into Equation 13.4 to calculate the cost of common equity for ConocoPhillips:

$$k_{cs} = R_{rf} + (\beta_{cs} \times \text{Market risk premium})$$
$$= 0.0466 + (0.51 \times 0.0651) = 0.0798, \text{ or } 7.98\%$$

This example illustrates how Equation 13.4 is used to estimate the cost of common stock for a company. How would the analysis differ for a private company? The only difference is that we would not be able to estimate the beta directly. We would have to estimate the beta from betas for similar public companies.

13.3 The Cost of Equity

LEARNING BY DOING — APPLICATION 13.3

Calculating the Cost of Equity Using a Stock's Beta

Problem: You have decided to estimate the cost of the common equity in your pizza business on December 27, 2007. As noted earlier, the risk-free rate and the market risk premium on that day were 4.66 percent and 6.51 percent, respectively. Since you have already decided that Domino's Pizza is a reasonably comparable company, you obtain Domino's beta from the Yahoo! finance Web site (http://finance.yahoo.com). This beta is 0.57. What do you estimate the cost of common equity in your pizza business to be?

Approach: Method 1 for calculating the cost of equity is to use the Capital Asset Pricing Model (CAPM). Therefore, in this example we will use Equation 13.4.

Solution:

$$k_{cs} = R_{rf} + (\beta_{cs} \times \text{Market risk premium}) = 0.0466 + (0.57 \times 0.0651) = 0.0837, \text{ or } 8.37\%$$

METHOD 2: USING THE CONSTANT-GROWTH DIVIDEND MODEL

In Chapter 9 we noted that if the dividends received by the owner of a share of common stock are expected to grow at a constant rate in perpetuity, then the value of that share today can be calculated using Equation 9.5:

$$P_0 = \frac{D_1}{R - g}$$

where D_1 is the dividend expected to be paid one period from today, R is the required rate of return, and g is the annual rate at which the dividends are expected to grow in perpetuity.

We can replace the R in Equation 9.5 with k_{cs} since we are specifically estimating the expected rate of return for investing in common stock (also the cost of equity). We can then rearrange this equation to solve for k_{cs}:

$$k_{cs} = \frac{D_1}{P_0} + g \tag{13.5}$$

While Equation 13.5 is just a variation of Equation 9.5, it is important enough to identify as a separate equation because it provides a direct way of estimating the cost of equity under certain circumstances. If we can estimate the dividend that stockholders will receive next period, D_1, and we can estimate the rate at which the market expects dividends to grow over the long run, g, then we can use today's market price, P_0, in Equation 13.5 to tell us what rate of return investors in the firm's common stock are expecting to earn.

Consider an example. Suppose that the current price for the common stock at Sprigg Lane Company is $20, that the firm is expected to pay a dividend of $2 per share to its common stockholders next year, and that the dividend is expected to grow at a rate of 3 percent in perpetuity after next year. Equation 13.5 tells us that the required rate of return for Sprigg Lane's stock is

$$k_{cs} = \frac{D_1}{P_0} + g = \frac{\$2}{\$20} + 0.03 = 0.13, \text{ or } 13\%$$

This approach can be useful for a firm that pays dividends when it is reasonable to assume dividends will grow at a constant rate and when the analyst has a good idea what that growth rate will be. An electric utility firm is an example of this type of firm. Some electric utility firms pay relatively high and predictable dividends that increase at a fairly consistent rate. In contrast, this approach would not be appropriate for use by a high-tech firm that pays no dividends or that pays a small dividend that is likely to increase at a high rate in the short run. Equation 13.5, like any other equation, should be used only if it is appropriate for the particular stock.

You might be asking yourself at this point where you would get P_0, D_1, and g in order to use Equation 13.5 for a particular stock. You can get the current price of a share of stock as well as the dividend that a firm is expected to pay next year quite easily from many different Web sites on the Internet—for example, MSN Money and Yahoo! Finance, which were both mentioned earlier. The financial information includes the dollar value of dividends paid in the past year and the dividend that the firm is expected to pay in the next year.

Estimating the long-term rate of growth in dividends is more difficult, but there are some guidelines that can help. As we discussed in Chapter 9, the first rule is that dividends cannot grow faster than the long-term growth rate of the economy in a perpetuity model such as Equation 9.5 or 13.5. Assuming dividends will grow faster than the economy is the same as assuming that dividends will eventually become larger than the economy itself! We know this is impossible.

What is the long-term growth rate of the economy? Well, historically it has been the rate of inflation plus about 3 percent. This means that if inflation is expected to be 4 percent in the long run, then a reasonable estimate for the long-term growth rate in the economy is 7 percent (4 percent inflation plus 3 percent real growth). This tells us that g in Equation 13.5 will not be greater than 7 percent. What exactly it will be depends on the nature of the business and the industry it is in. If it is a declining industry, then g might be negative. If the industry is expected to grow with the economy and the particular firm you are evaluating is expected to retain its market share, then a reasonable estimate for g might be 6 or 7 percent.

METHOD 3: USING A MULTISTAGE-GROWTH DIVIDEND MODEL

Using a **multistage-growth dividend model** to estimate the cost of equity for a firm is very similar to using a constant-growth dividend model. The difference is that a multistage-growth dividend model allows for faster dividend growth rates in the near term, followed by a constant long-term growth rate. If this concept sounds familiar, that is because it is the idea behind the *mixed (supernormal) growth dividend model* discussed in Chapter 9. In Equation 9.6 this model was written as:

$$P_0 = \frac{D_1}{1+R} + \frac{D_2}{(1+R)^2} + \cdots + \frac{D_t}{(1+R)^t} + \frac{P_t}{(1+R)^t}$$

where D_i is the dividend in period i, P_t is the value of constant-growth dividend payments in period t, and R is the required rate of return.

To refresh your memory of how this model works, let's consider a three-stage example. Suppose that a firm will pay a dividend one year from today (D_1) and that this dividend will increase at a rate of g_1 the following year, g_2 the year after that, and g_3 per year thereafter. The value of a share of this stock today thus equals:

$$P_0 = \frac{D_1}{1+k_{cs}} + \frac{D_1(1+g_1)}{(1+k_{cs})^2} + \frac{D_1(1+g_1)(1+g_2)}{(1+k_{cs})^3}$$
$$+ \left[\frac{D_1(1+g_1)(1+g_2)(1+g_3)}{k_{cs}-g_3}\right]\left[\frac{1}{(1+k_{cs})^3}\right]$$

In this equation, we have replaced the R in Equation 9.6 with k_{cs} since we are specifically estimating the expected rate of return for common stock. We have also written all

---

You can obtain recent stock prices and financial information for a large number of firms from Yahoo! Finance at http://finance.yahoo.com/.

multistage-growth dividend model
a model that allows for varying dividend growth rates in the near term, followed by a constant long-term growth rate; another term used to describe the mixed (supernormal) dividend growth model discussed in Chapter 9

of the dividends in terms of D_1 to illustrate how the different growth rates will affect the dividends in each year. Finally, we have written P_t in terms of the constant-growth model. If we substitute D_1, D_2, D_3, and D_4 where appropriate, you can see that this is really just Equation 9.6, where we have replaced R with k_{cs} and written P_t in terms of the constant-growth model:

$$P_0 = \frac{D_1}{1+k_{cs}} + \frac{D_2}{(1+k_{cs})^2} + \frac{D_3}{(1+k_{cs})^3} + \left[\frac{D_4}{k_{cs}-g_3}\right]\left[\frac{1}{(1+k_{cs})^3}\right]$$

All this equation does is add the present values of the dividends that are expected in each of the next three years and the present value of a growing perpetuity that begins in the fourth year. Exhibit 13.2 illustrates how cash flows relate to the four terms in the equation.

Note that the fourth term in Exhibit 13.2 is discounted only three years because, as we saw in Chapters 6 and 9, the constant-growth model gives you the present value of a growing perpetuity as of the year before the first cash flow. In this case since the first cash flow is D_4, the model gives you the value of the growing perpetuity as of year 3.

A multistage-growth dividend model is much more flexible than the constant-growth dividend model because we do not have to assume that dividends grow at the same rate forever. We can use a model such as this to estimate the cost of common stock, k_{cs}, by plugging P_0, D_1, and the appropriate growth rates into the model and solving for k_{cs} using trial and error—just as we solved for the yield to maturity of bonds in Chapter 8 and earlier in this chapter. The major issues we have to be concerned about when we use a growth dividend model are (1) that we have chosen the right model, meaning that we have included enough stages or growth rates, and (2) that our estimates of the growth rates are reasonable.

Let's work an example to illustrate how this model is used to calculate the cost of common stock. Suppose that we want to estimate the cost of common stock for a firm that is expected to pay a dividend of $1.50 per share next year. This dividend is expected to increase 15 percent the following year, 10 percent the year after that, 7 percent the year after that, and 5 percent annually thereafter. If the firm's common stock is currently selling for $24 per share, what is the rate of return that investors require for investing in this stock?

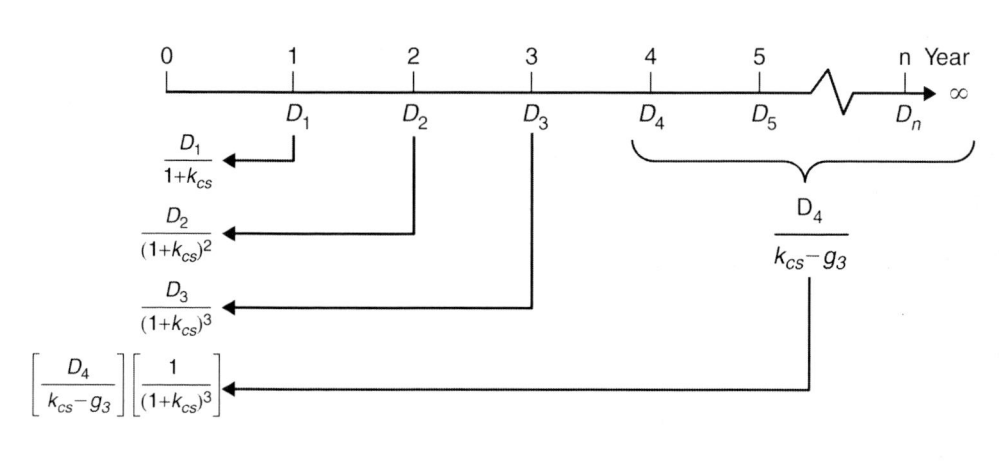

Exhibit 13.2
The Three-Stage Dividend Growth Equation
In the three-stage dividend growth model shown here, the price of a share of stock equals the present values of dividends expected to be received at the end of years 1, 2, and 3, plus the present value of a growing perpetuity that begins in year 4 and whose dividends are assumed to grow at a constant rate g_3 forever.

CHAPTER 13 | The Cost of Capital

Because there are four different growth rates in this example, we have to solve a formula with five terms:

$$P_0 = \frac{D_1}{1+k_{cs}} + \frac{D_2}{(1+k_{cs})^2} + \frac{D_3}{(1+k_{cs})^3} + \frac{D_4}{(1+k_{cs})^4} + \left[\frac{D_5}{k_{cs}-g_4}\right]\left[\frac{1}{(1+k_{cs})^4}\right]$$

From the information given in the problem statement, we know the following:

$$D_1 = \$1.50$$
$$D_2 = D_1 \times (1+g_1) = \$1.500 \times 1.15 = \$1.725$$
$$D_3 = D_2 \times (1+g_2) = \$1.725 \times 1.10 = \$1.898$$
$$D_4 = D_3 \times (1+g_3) = \$1.898 \times 1.07 = \$2.031$$
$$D_5 = D_4 \times (1+g_4) = \$2.031 \times 1.05 = \$2.133$$

Substituting these values into the above equation gives us the following, which we solve for k_{cs}:

$$\$24 = \frac{\$1.50}{1+k_{cs}} + \frac{\$1.73}{(1+k_{cs})^2} + \frac{\$1.90}{(1+k_{cs})^3} + \frac{\$2.03}{(1+k_{cs})^4} + \left[\frac{\$2.13}{k_{cs}-g_4}\right]\left[\frac{1}{(1+k_{cs})^4}\right]$$

As mentioned earlier, we can solve this equation for k_{cs} using trial and error. When we do this, we find that k_{cs} is 12.2 percent. This is the rate of return at which the present value of the cash flows equals $24. Therefore, it is the rate that investors currently require for investing in this stock.

USING EXCEL

Solving for k_{cs} Using a Multistage-Growth Dividend Model

Because trial and error calculations can be somewhat tedious when you perform them by hand, you may find it helpful to use a spreadsheet program. If you would like to use a spreadsheet program to solve the preceding problem yourself, the output from the spreadsheet below shows you how to do it using trial and error.

Once you input the indicated numbers and formulas into cells B3 through B14, you can then vary the number in cell B2 until the number in cell B5 equals $24. Once you have built the model, you can also use the "goal seek" or "solver" functions in Excel to avoid having to manually solve the problem by trial and error. See the "Help" feature in Excel for information on how to use these functions.

	A	B	C	D
1				Comment
2	k_{cs} =	0.12205		Change this number until the P_0 equals $24.00
3	g_1 =	0.15		Growth rate in year 1
4	g_2 =	0.10		Growth rate in year 2
5	g_3 =	0.07		Growth rate in year 3
6	g_4 =	0.05		Growth rate for perpetuity
7				
8	P_0 =	$24.00		Formula: =NPV(B2,B11:B14) - This formula calculates the present value of the
9				future dividends in cells B11 to B14 using the discount rate in cell B2.
10	Year			
11	1	$1.500		D_1
12	2	$1.725		D_2 = B11*(1+B3)
13	3	$1.898		D_3 = B12*(1+B4)
14	4	$31.619		D_4 = [B13*(1+B5)] + [B13*(1+B5)*(1+B6)]/(B2-B6) - This formula calculates the
15				value of D_4 plus the present value of all the cash flows after year 4 in year 4 dollars.
16				

WHICH METHOD SHOULD WE USE?

We now have discussed three methods of estimating the cost of common equity for a firm. You might be asking yourself how you are supposed to know which method to use. The short answer is that, in practice, most people use the CAPM (Method 1) to estimate the cost of common equity if the result is going to be used in the discount rate for evaluating a project. One reason is that, assuming the theory is valid, CAPM tells managers what rate of return investors should require for equity having the same level of systematic risk that the firm's equity has. This is the appropriate opportunity cost of equity capital for an NPV analysis if the project has the same risk as the firm and will have similar leverage. Furthermore, CAPM does not require financial analysts to make assumptions about future growth rates in dividends, as Methods 2 and 3 do.

Used properly, Methods 2 and 3 provide an estimate of the rate of return that is implied by the current price of a firm's stock at a particular point in time. If the stock markets are efficient, then this should be the same as the number that we would estimate using CAPM. However, to the extent that the firm's stock is mispriced—for example, because investors are not informed or have misinterpreted the future prospects for the firm—deriving the cost of equity from the price at one point in time can yield a bad estimate of the true cost of equity.

Preferred Stock

As we discussed in Chapter 9, preferred stock is a form of equity that has a stated value and specified dividend rate. For example, a share of preferred stock might have a stated value of $100 and a 5 percent dividend rate. The owner of such a share would be entitled to receive a dividend of $5 ($100 × 0.05) each year. Another key feature of preferred stock is that it does not have an expiration date. In other words, preferred stock continues to pay the specified dividend in perpetuity, unless the firm repurchases it or goes out of business.

These characteristics of preferred stock allow us to use the perpetuity model, Equation 6.3, to estimate the cost of preferred equity. For example, suppose that investors would pay $85 for a share of the preferred stock mentioned above. We can rewrite Equation 6.3:

$$PVA_\infty = \frac{CF}{i}$$

as:

$$P_{ps} = \frac{D_{ps}}{k_{ps}}$$

where P_{ps} is the present value of the expected dividends (the current preferred stock price), D_{ps} is the annual preferred stock dividend, and k_{ps} is the cost of the preferred stock. Rearranging the formula to solve for k_{ps} yields:

$$k_{ps} = \frac{D_{ps}}{P_{ps}} \quad (13.6)$$

Plugging the information from our example into Equation 13.6, we see that k_{ps} for the preferred stock in our example is:

$$k_{ps} = \frac{D_{ps}}{P_{ps}} = \frac{\$5}{\$85} = 0.059, \text{ or } 5.9\%$$

This is the rate of return at which the present value of the annual $5 cash flows equals the market price of $85. Therefore, 5.9 percent is the rate that investors currently require for investing in this preferred stock.

It is easy to incorporate issuance costs into the above calculation to obtain the cost of the preferred stock to the firm that issues it. As in the earlier bond calculations, we use the net proceeds from the sale rather than the price that is paid by the investor in the calculation. For example, suppose that in order for a firm to sell the above preferred stock, it must pay an investment banker 5 percent of the amount of money raised. If there are no other issuance costs, the company would receive $85 \times (1 - 0.05) = \$80.75$ for each share sold, and the total cost of this financing to the firm would be:

$$k_{ps} = \frac{D_{ps}}{P_{ps}} = \frac{\$5}{\$80.75} = 0.062, \text{ or } 6.2\%$$

You may recall from the discussion in Chapter 9 that certain characteristics of preferred stock look a lot like those of debt. The equation $P_{ps} = D_{ps}/k_{ps}$ shows that the value of preferred stock also varies with market rates of return in the same way as debt. Because k_{ps} is in the denominator of the fraction on the right-hand side of the equation, whenever k_{ps} increases, P_{ps} decreases, and whenever k_{ps} decreases, P_{ps} increases. That is, the value of preferred stock is negatively related to market rates.

It is also important to recognize that the CAPM can be used to estimate the cost of preferred equity, just as it can be used to estimate the cost of common equity. A financial analyst can simply substitute k_{ps} for k_{cs} and β_{ps} for β_{cs} in Equation 13.4 and use it to estimate the cost of preferred stock. Remember from Chapter 7 that the CAPM does not apply only to common stock; rather, it applies to any asset. Therefore, we can use it to calculate the rate of return on any asset if we can estimate the beta for that asset.

LEARNING BY DOING APPLICATION 13.4

Estimating the Cost of Preferred Stock

Problem: You work in the Treasury Department at JPMorgan Chase, and your manager has asked you to estimate the cost of each of the different types of stock that JPMorgan has outstanding. One of these issues is a 6.625 percent cumulative preferred stock that has a stated value of $50 and is currently selling for $51.10. Although this preferred stock is publicly traded, it does not trade very often. This means that you cannot use the CAPM to estimate k_{ps} because you cannot get a good estimate of the beta using regression analysis. How else can you estimate the cost of this preferred stock, and what is this cost?

Approach: You can also use Equation 13.6 to estimate the cost of preferred stock.

Solution: First, you must find the annual dividend that someone who owns a share of this stock will receive. The dividend rate for this stock is quoted in eighths, or units of 0.125 of a percent. Therefore, in decimal terms, this preferred stock issue pays an annual dividend (for simplicity we are assuming one dividend payment per year) that equals 6 percent + 0.625 (5/8) percent = 6.625 percent. The annual dividend equals this percentage times the $50 stated value, or 6.625 percent of $50 = $50 × 0.06625 = $3.3125. Substituting the annual dividend and the market price into Equation 13.6 yields:

$$k_{ps} = \frac{D_{ps}}{P_{ps}} = \frac{\$3.3125}{\$51.10} = 0.065, \text{ or } 6.5\%$$

Before You Go On

1. What information is needed to use the CAPM to estimate k_{cs} or k_{ps}?
2. Under what circumstances can you use the constant-growth dividend formula to estimate k_{cs}?
3. What is the advantage of using a multistage-growth dividend model, rather than the constant-growth dividend model, to estimate k_{cs}?

13.4 Using the WACC in Practice

LEARNING OBJECTIVE 4

We have now covered the basic concepts and computational tools that are used to estimate the WACC. At this point, we are ready to talk about some of the practical issues that arise when financial analysts calculate the WACC for their firms.

When financial analysts think about calculating the WACC, they usually think of it as a weighted average of the firm's after-tax cost of debt, cost of preferred stock, and cost of common equity. Equation 13.2 is usually written as:

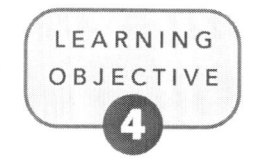

$$\text{WACC} = x_{\text{Debt}} k_{\text{Debt pretax}} (1 - t) + x_{\text{ps}} k_{\text{ps}} + x_{\text{cs}} k_{\text{cs}} \quad (13.7)$$

where $x_{\text{Debt}} + x_{\text{ps}} + x_{\text{cs}} = 1$. If the firm has more than one type of debt outstanding or more than one type of preferred or common stock, analysts will calculate a weighted average for each of those types of securities and then plug those averages into Equation 13.7. Financial analysts will also use the *market values,* rather than the accounting book values, of the debt, preferred stock, and common stock to calculate the weights (the x's) in Equation 13.7. This is because, as we have already seen, the theory underlying the discounting process requires that the costs of the different types of financing be weighted by their relative market values. Accounting book values have no place in these calculations unless they just happen to equal the market values.

Calculating WACC: An Example

An example provides a useful way of illustrating how the theories and tools that we have discussed are used in practice. Assume that you are a financial analyst at a manufacturing company that has used three types of debt, preferred stock, and common stock to finance its investments.

Debt: The debt includes a $4 million bank loan that is secured by machinery and equipment. This loan has an interest rate of 6 percent, and your firm could expect to pay the same rate if the loan were refinanced today. Your firm also has a second bank loan (a $3 million mortgage on your manufacturing plant) with an interest rate of 5.5 percent. Again, the rate would be the same today. The third type of debt is a bond issue that the firm sold two years ago for $11 million. The market value of these bonds today is $10 million. Using the approach we discussed earlier, you have estimated that the effective annual yield on the bonds is 7 percent.

Preferred Stock: The preferred stock pays an annual dividend of 4.5 percent on a stated value of $100. A share of this stock is currently selling for $60, and there are 100,000 shares outstanding.

Common Stock: There are 1 million shares of common stock outstanding, and they are currently selling for $21 each. Using a regression analysis, you have estimated that the beta of these shares is 0.95.

The 20-year Treasury bond rate is currently 4.66 percent and you have estimated the market risk premium to be 6.51 percent using the returns on stocks and Treasury bonds from the 1926 to 2006 period. Your firm's marginal tax rate is 35 percent. What is the WACC for your firm?

The first step in computing the WACC is to calculate the pretax cost of debt. Since the market value of the firm's debt is $17 million ($4 + $3 + $10), we can calculate the pretax cost of debt as follows:

$$\begin{aligned} k_{\text{Debt pretax}} &= x_{\text{Bank loan 1}} k_{\text{Bank loan 1 pretax}} + x_{\text{Bank loan 2}} k_{\text{Bank loan 2 pretax}} + x_{\text{Bonds}} k_{\text{Bonds pretax}} \\ &= (\$4/\$17)(0.06) + (\$3/\$17)(0.055) + (\$10/\$17)(0.07) \\ &= 0.065, \text{ or } 6.5\% \end{aligned}$$

Note that because the $4 million and $3 million loans have rates that equal what it would cost to refinance them today, their market values equal the amount that is owed. Since the $10 million market value of the bond issue is below the $11 million face value, the rate that firm is actually paying must be lower than the 7 percent rate you estimated to reflect the current cost of this debt. Recall that as interest rates increase, the market value of a bond decreases. This is the negative relation that we referred to earlier in this chapter.

We next calculate the cost of the preferred stock using Equation 13.6, as follows:

$$k_{ps} = \frac{D_{ps}}{P_{ps}} = \frac{0.045 \times \$100}{\$60}$$

$$= \frac{\$4.5}{\$60} = 0.075, \text{ or } 7.5\%$$

From Equation 13.4, we calculate the cost of the common equity to be:

$$k_{cs} = R_{rf} + (\beta_{cs} \times \text{Market risk premium}) = 0.0466 + (0.95 \times 0.0651)$$
$$= 0.108, \text{ or } 10.8\%$$

We are now ready to use Equation 13.7 to calculate the firm's WACC. Since the firm has $17 million of debt, $6 million of preferred stock ($60 × 100,000 shares), and $21 million of common equity ($21 × 1,000,000 shares), the total market value of its capital is $44 million ($17 + $6 + $21). The firm's WACC is therefore:

$$\text{WACC} = x_{Debt}k_{Debt\,pretax}(1-t) + x_{ps}k_{ps} + x_{cs}k_{cs}$$
$$= (\$17/\$44)(0.065)(1-0.35) + (\$6/\$44)(0.075) + (\$21/\$44)(0.108)$$
$$= 0.078, \text{ or } 7.8\%$$

LEARNING BY DOING APPLICATION 13.5

Calculating the WACC with Equation 13.7

Problem: After calculating the cost of the common equity in your pizza business to be 8.37 percent (see Learning by Doing Application 13.3), you have decided to estimate the WACC. You recently hired a business appraiser to estimate the value of your stock, which includes all of the outstanding common equity. His report indicates that it is worth $500 million.

In order to finance the 2,000 restaurants that are now part of your company, you have sold three different bond issues. Based on the current prices of the bonds from these issues and the issue characteristics (face values and coupon rates), you have estimated the market values and effective annual yields to be:

Bond Issue	Value ($ millions)	Effective Annual Yield
1	$100	6.5%
2	187	6.9
3	154	7.3
Total	$441	

Your company has no other long-term debt or any preferred stock outstanding. Both the marginal and average tax rates for your company are 20 percent. What is the WACC for your pizza business?

Approach: You can use Equation 13.7 to solve for the WACC for your pizza business. To do so, you must first calculate the weighted average cost of debt. You can then plug the weights and costs for the debt and common equity into Equation 13.7. Since your business has no preferred stock, the value for this term in Equation 13.7 will equal $0.

Solution: The weighted average cost of the debt is:

$$k_{\text{Debt pretax}} = x_1 k_{1\text{ Debt pretax}} + x_2 k_{2\text{ Debt pretax}} + x_3 k_{3\text{ Debt pretax}}$$
$$= (\$100/\$441)(0.065) + (\$187/\$441)(0.069) + (\$154/\$441)(0.073)$$
$$= 0.070, \text{ or } 7.0\%$$

and the WACC is:

$$\text{WACC} = x_{\text{Debt}} k_{\text{Debt pretax}}(1 - t) + x_{\text{ps}} k_{\text{ps}} + x_{\text{cs}} k_{\text{cs}}$$
$$= (\$441/[\$441 + \$500])(0.07)(1 - 0.20) + 0 + (\$500/[\$441 + \$500])(0.0837)$$
$$= 0.071, \text{ or } 7.1\%$$

You can see real-world applications of the WACC calculation at the New Zealand Web site for PricewaterhouseCoopers, the international accounting and consulting firm, at www.pwcglobal.com/Extweb/pwcpublications.nsf/docid/748F5814D61CC2618525693A007EC870.

Interpreting the WACC

DECISION-MAKING EXAMPLE 13.2

Situation: You are a financial analyst for the company whose WACC of 7.8 percent we just calculated in the main text. One day, your manager walks in to your office and tells you that she is thinking about selling $23 million of common stock and using the proceeds from the sale to pay back both of the firm's loans and to repurchase all of the outstanding bonds and preferred stock. She tells you that this is a smart move because if she does this, the beta of the firm's common stock will decline to 0.70 and the overall k_{cs} will decline from 10.8 percent to 9.22 percent:

$$k_{\text{cs}} = R_{\text{rf}} + (\beta_{\text{cs}} \times \text{Market risk premium}) = 0.0466 + (0.70 \times 0.0651)$$
$$= 0.0922, \text{ or } 9.22\%$$

What do you tell your manager?

Decision: You should politely point out that she is making the wrong comparison. Since the refinancing will result in the firm being financed entirely with equity, k_{cs} will equal the firm's WACC. Therefore, the 9.22 percent should really be compared with the 7.8 percent WACC. If your manager goes through with the refinancing, she will be making a bad decision. The average after-tax cost of the capital that your firm uses will *increase* from 7.8 percent to 9.22 percent.

Limitations of WACC as a Discount Rate for Evaluating Projects

At the beginning of this chapter, we told you that financial managers often require analysts within the firm to use the firm's current cost of capital to discount the cash flows for individual projects. They do so because it is very difficult to directly estimate the discount rate for individual projects. You should recognize by now that the WACC is the discount rate that analysts are often required to use. Using the WACC to discount the cash flows for a project can make sense under certain circumstances. However, in other circumstances, it can be very dangerous. The rest of this section discusses when it makes sense to use the WACC as a discount rate and the problems that can occur when the WACC is used incorrectly.

Chapter 11 discussed how an analyst forecasting the cash flows for a project is forecasting the incremental after-tax free cash flows at the firm level. These cash flows represent the difference between the cash flows that the firm will generate if the project is adopted and the cash flows that the firm will generate if the project is not adopted.

Financial theory tells us that the rate that should be used to discount these incremental cash flows is the rate that reflects their systematic risk. This means that the

WACC is going to be the appropriate discount rate for evaluating a project only when the project has cash flows with systematic risks that are exactly the same as those for the firm as a whole. Unfortunately, this is not true for most projects. The firm itself is a portfolio of projects with varying degrees of risk.

When a single rate, such as the WACC, is used to discount cash flows for projects with varying levels of risk, the discount rate will be too low in some cases and too high in others. When the discount rate is too low, the firm runs the risk of accepting a negative NPV project. To see how this might happen, assume that you work at a company that manufactures soft drinks and that the managers at your company are concerned about all the competition in the core soft drink business. They are thinking about expanding into the manufacture and sale of exotic tropical beverages. The managers believe that entering this market would allow the firm to better differentiate its products and earn higher profits. Suppose also that the appropriate beta for soft drink projects is 1.2, while the appropriate beta for tropical beverage projects is 1.5. Since your firm is only in the soft drink business right now, the beta for its overall cash flows is 1.2. Exhibit 13.3 illustrates the problem that could arise if your firm's WACC is used to evaluate a tropical beverage project.

In the exhibit, you can see that since the beta of the tropical beverage project is larger than the beta of the firm as a whole, the expected return (or discount rate) for the tropical beverage project should be higher than the firm's WACC. The Security Market Line indicates what this expected return should be. Now, if the firm's WACC is used to discount the expected cash flows for this project, and the expected return on the project is above the firm's WACC, then the estimated NPV will be positive. So far, so good. However, as illustrated in the exhibit for the tropical beverage example, some projects may have an expected return that is above the WACC but below the SML. For projects such as those, using the WACC as the discount rate may actually cause the firm to accept a negative NPV project! The estimated NPV will be positive even though the true NPV is negative. The negative NPV projects that would be accepted in those situations have returns that fall in the red shaded area below the SML, above the WACC line, and to the right of the firm's beta.

Exhibit 13.3
Potential Errors When Using the WACC to Evaluate Projects
Two types of problems can arise when the WACC for a firm is used to evaluate individual projects: a positive NPV project may be rejected or a negative NPV project may be accepted. For the tropical beverage example, if the expected return on that project was below the level indicated by the SML, but above the firm's WACC, the project might be accepted even though it would have a negative NPV.

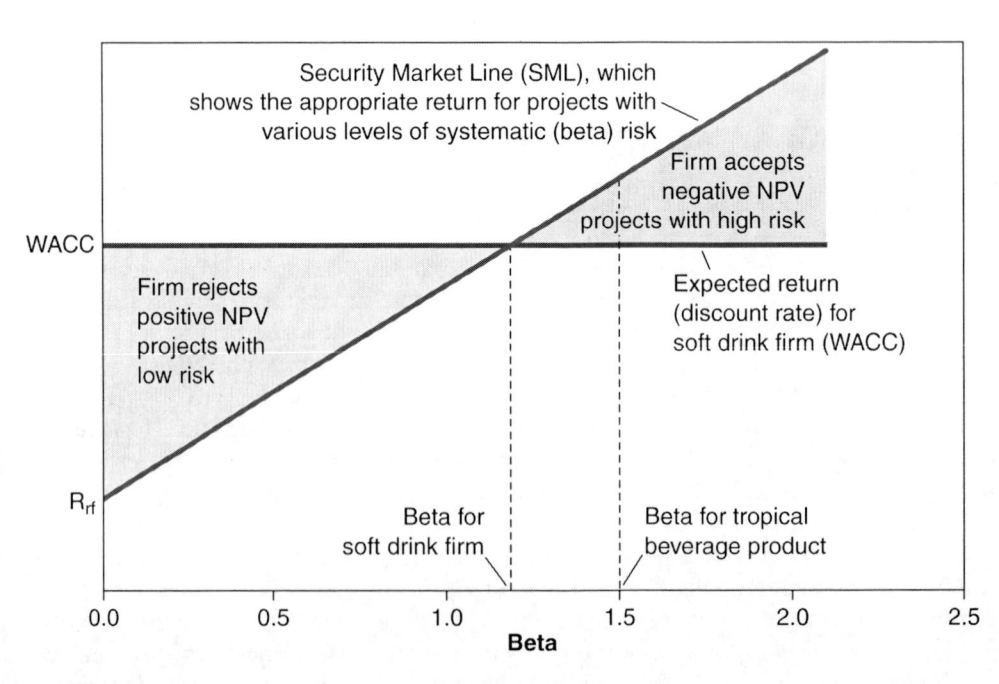

In Exhibit 13.3 you can also see that using the WACC to discount expected cash flows for low-risk projects can result in managers at the firm rejecting projects that have positive NPVs. This problem is, in some sense, the mirror image of the case where the WACC is lower than the correct discount rate. Financial managers run the risk of turning down positive NPV projects whenever the WACC is higher than the correct discount rate. The positive NPV projects that would be rejected are those that fall into the green shaded area that is below the WACC but above the SML and to the left of the firm's beta.

To see how these types of problems arise, consider a project that requires an initial investment of $100 and that is expected to produce cash inflows of $40 per year for three years. If the correct discount rate for this project is 8 percent, its NPV will be:

$$\begin{aligned} NPV &= FCF_0 + \frac{FCF_1}{1+k} + \frac{FCF_2}{(1+k)^2} + \frac{FCF_3}{(1+k)^3} \\ &= -\$100 + \frac{\$40}{1+0.08} + \frac{\$40}{(1+0.08)^2} + \frac{\$40}{(1+0.08)^3} \\ &= \$3.08 \end{aligned}$$

This is an attractive project because it returns more than the investors' opportunity cost of capital.

Suppose, however, that the financial managers of the firm considering this project require that all projects be evaluated using the firm's WACC of 11 percent. When the cash flows are discounted using a rate of 11 percent, the NPV is:

$$NPV = -\$100 + \frac{\$40}{1+0.11} + \frac{\$40}{(1+0.11)^2} + \frac{\$40}{(1+0.11)^3} = -\$2.25$$

As you can see, when the WACC is used to discount the cash flows, the firm will end up rejecting a positive NPV project. The firm will be passing up an opportunity to create value for its stockholders. (As an exercise, you might try constructing a numerical example in which a firm accepts a negative NPV project.)

It is also important to recognize that when a firm uses a single rate to evaluate all of its projects, there will be a bias toward accepting more risky projects. The average risk of the firm's assets will tend to increase over time. Furthermore, because some positive NPV projects are likely to be rejected and some negative NPV projects are likely to be accepted, new projects on the whole will probably create less value for stockholders than if the appropriate discount rate had been used to evaluate all projects. This, in turn, can put the firm at a disadvantage when compared with its competitors and adversely affect the value of its existing projects.

The key point to take away from this discussion is that it is only really correct to use a firm's WACC to discount the cash flows for a project if the expected cash flows from that project have the same systematic risk as the expected cash flows from the firm as a whole. You might be wondering how you can tell when this condition exists. The answer is that we never know for sure. Nevertheless, there are some guidelines that you can use when assessing whether the systematic risk for a particular project is similar to that for the firm as a whole.

The systematic risk of the cash flows from a project depends on the nature of the business. Revenues and expenses in some businesses are affected more by changes in general economic conditions than revenues and expenses in other businesses. For example, consider the differences between a company that makes bread and a company that makes recreational vehicles. The demand for bread will be relatively constant in good economic conditions and in bad. The demand for recreational vehicles will be more volatile. People buy fewer recreational vehicles during recessions than when the economy is doing well. Furthermore, as we discussed in Chapter 12, operating leverage magnifies volatility in revenue. Therefore, if the recreational vehicle manufacturing process has more fixed costs than the bread manufacturing business, the difference in the volatilities of the pretax operating cash flows will be even greater than the difference in the volatilities of the revenues.

While total volatility is not the same as systematic volatility, we find that businesses with more total volatility (uncertainty or risk) typically have more systematic volatility. Since beta is a measure of systematic risk, and systematic risk is a key factor in determining a firm's WACC, this suggests that the firm's WACC should be used only for projects with business risks similar to those for the firm as a whole. Since financial managers usually think of systematic risk when they think of underlying business risks, we can restate this condition as follows:

Condition 1: A firm's WACC should be used to evaluate the cash flows for a new project only if the level of systematic risk for the project is the same as that for the portfolio of projects that currently comprise the firm.

You have to consider one other factor when you decide whether it is appropriate to use a firm's WACC to discount the cash flows for a project. That is the way in which the project will be financed and how this financing compares with the way the firm's assets are financed. To better understand why this is important, consider Equation 13.7:

$$\text{WACC} = x_{\text{Debt}} k_{\text{Debt pretax}}(1 - t) + x_{\text{ps}} k_{\text{ps}} + x_{\text{cs}} k_{\text{cs}}$$

This equation provides a measure of the firm's cost of capital that reflects both how the firm has financed its assets—that is, the mix of debt and preferred and common stock it has used—and the current cost of each type of financing. In other words, the WACC reflects both the x's and the k's associated with the firm's financing. Why is this important? Because the costs of the different types of capital depend on the fraction of the total firm financing that each represents. If the firm uses more or less debt, the cost of debt will be higher or lower. In turn, the cost of both preferred stock and common stock will be affected. This means that even if the underlying business risk of the project is the same as that for the firm as a whole, if the project is financed differently than the firm, the appropriate discount rate for the project analysis will be different from that for the firm as a whole.

Condition 2: A firm's WACC should be used to evaluate a project only if that project uses the same financing mix—the same proportions of debt, preferred shares, and common shares—used to finance the firm as a whole.

In summary, WACC is a measure of the current cost of the capital that the firm has used to finance its projects. It is an appropriate discount rate for evaluating projects only if (1) the project's systematic risk is the same as that of the firm's current portfolio of projects and (2) the project will be financed with the same mix of debt and equity as the firm's current portfolio of projects. If either of these two conditions does not hold, then managers should be careful in using the firm's current WACC to evaluate a project.

Alternatives to Using WACC for Evaluating Projects

Financial managers understand the limitations of using a firm's WACC to evaluate projects, but they also know that there are no perfect alternatives. As we noted earlier in this chapter, there is no publicly traded common stock for most individual projects within a firm. It is, therefore, not possible to directly estimate the beta for the common stock used to finance an individual project.[8] Although it might be possible to obtain an estimate of the cost of debt from the firm's bankers, without an estimate of the common stock beta—and, therefore, the cost of common stock—it is not possible to obtain a direct estimate of the appropriate discount rate for a project using Equation 13.7.

---

[8]Some firms issue a type of stock that has an equity claim on only part of their business. If a project is similar to the part of the business for which "tracking stock" like this has been sold, the returns on the tracking stock can be used to estimate the beta for the common stock used to finance a project.

If the discount rate for a project cannot be estimated directly, a financial analyst might try to find a public firm that is in a business that is similar to that of the project. For example, in our exotic tropical beverage example, an analyst at the soft drink company might look for a company that produces only exotic tropical beverages and that also has publicly traded stock. This public company would be what financial analysts call a **pure-play comparable** because it is exactly like the project. The returns on the pure-play company's stock could be used to estimate the expected return on the equity that is used to finance the project. Unfortunately, this approach is generally not feasible due to the difficulty of finding a public firm that is only in the business represented by the project. If the public firm is in other businesses as well, then we run into the same sorts of problems that we face when we use the firm's WACC.

> **pure-play comparable**
> a comparable company that is in exactly the same business as the project or business being analyzed

From a practical standpoint, financial managers, such as company treasurers and chief financial officers, do not like letting analysts estimate the discount rates for their projects. Different analysts tend to make different assumptions or use different approaches, which can lead to inconsistencies that make it difficult to compare projects. In addition, analysts may be tempted to manipulate discount rates in order to make pet projects look more attractive.

In an effort to use discount rates that reflect project risks better than the firm's WACC, while retaining control of the process through which discount rates are set, financial managers sometimes classify projects into categories based on their systematic risks. They then specify a discount rate that is to be used to discount the cash flows for all projects within each category. The idea is that each category of projects has a different level of systematic risk and therefore a different discount rate should be used for each. Exhibit 13.4 illustrates such a classification scheme.

The scheme illustrated in Exhibit 13.4 includes four project categories:

1. *Efficiency projects,* such as the implementation of a new production technology that reduces manufacturing costs for an existing product.

2. *Product extension projects,* such as those in which Boeing created variations of its aircraft, such as the Boeing 737, to help meet customer needs.

3. *Market extension projects,* in which existing products are sold in new markets, such as when Texas Instruments considers selling a new version of a computer chip that has been used in digital phones to digital camera manufacturers.

4. *New product projects,* in which entirely new products are being considered.

When using the scheme illustrated in Exhibit 13.4, the financial manager would assign a discount rate for each category that reflects the beta in the middle of the indicated range of betas. Such an approach is attractive because it is not generally difficult for analysts to figure out in which of the four categories particular projects belong, and it limits their discretion in choosing discount rates. Most important, it can reduce the possibility of accepting negative NPV projects or rejecting positive NPV projects. We can see the latter benefit by comparing the shaded areas in the figures in Exhibits 13.3 and 13.4. The total size of the shaded areas, which represents the possibility of making an error, is much smaller in Exhibit 13.4.

> **Before You Go On**
>
> 1. Do analysts use book values or market values to calculate the weights when they use Equation 13.7? Why?
> 2. What kinds of errors can be made when the WACC for a firm is used as the discount rate for evaluating all projects in the firm?
> 3. Under what conditions is the WACC the appropriate discount rate for a project?

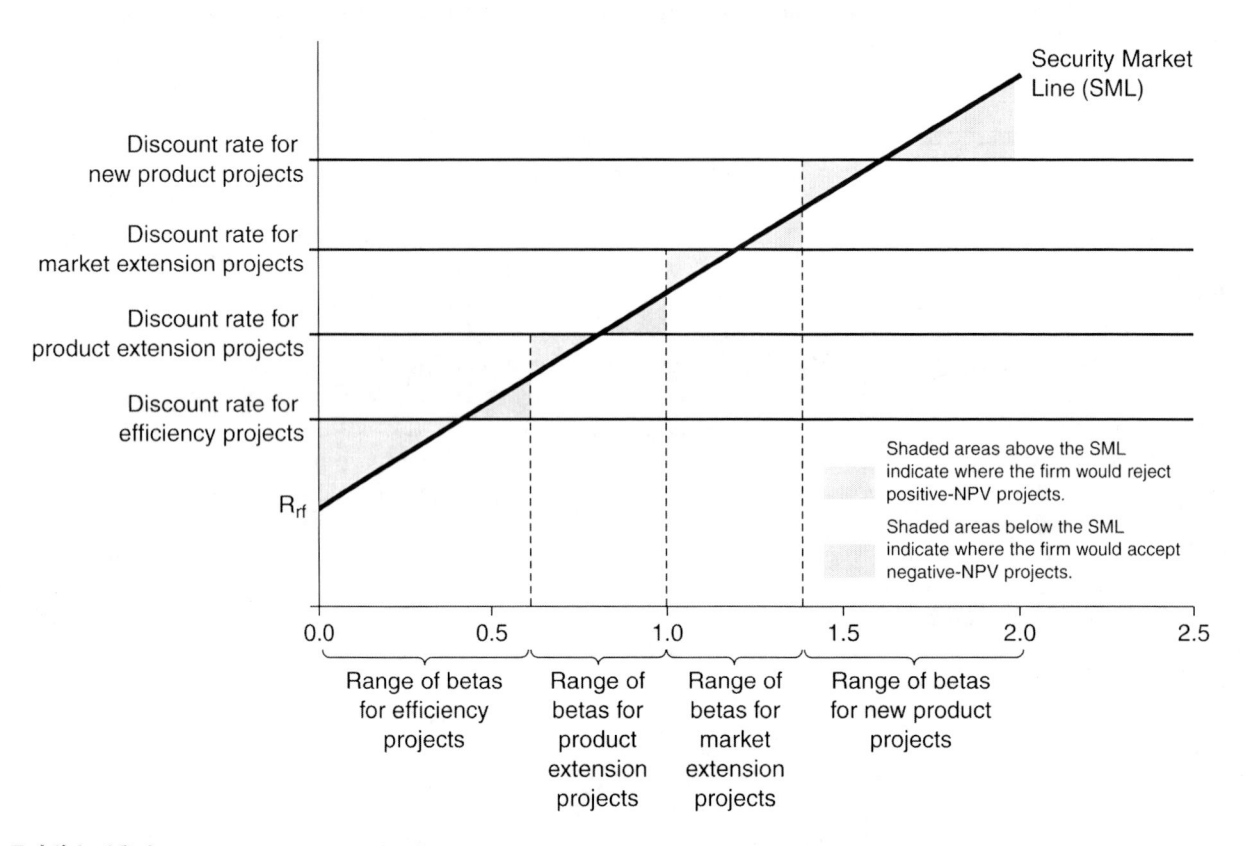

Exhibit 13.4
Potential Errors When Using Multiple Discount Rates to Evaluate Projects

The potential for errors—either rejecting a positive NPV project or accepting a negative NPV project—is smaller when discount rates better reflect the risk of the projects that they are used to evaluate. You can see this by noting that the total size of the shaded areas in this figure is smaller than the size of the shaded areas in Exhibit 13.3. In the ideal situation, where the correct discount rate is used for each project, there would be no shaded area at all in a figure like this.

Summary of Learning Objectives

1. **Explain what the weighted average cost of capital for a firm is and why it is often used as a discount rate to evaluate projects.**

    The weighted average cost of capital (WACC) for a firm is a weighted average of the current costs of the different types of financing that a firm has used to finance the purchase of its assets. When the WACC is calculated, the cost of each type of financing is weighted according to the fraction of the total firm value represented by that type of financing. The WACC is often used as a discount rate in evaluating projects because it is not possible to directly estimate the appropriate discount rate for many projects. As we also discuss in Section 13.4, having a single discount rate reduces inconsistencies that can arise when different analysts in the firm use different methods to estimate the discount rate and can also limit the ability of analysts to manipulate discount rates to favor pet projects.

2. **Calculate the cost of debt for a firm.**

    The cost of debt can be calculated by solving for the yield to maturity of the debt using the bond pricing model (Equation 8.1), computing the effective annual yield, and adjusting for taxes using Equation 13.3.

3. **Calculate the cost of common stock and the cost of preferred stock for a firm.**

    The cost of common stock can be estimated using the CAPM, the constant-growth dividend formula, and a multistage-growth dividend formula. The cost of preferred stock can be calculated using the perpetuity model for the present value of cash flows.

4. **Calculate the weighted average cost of capital for a firm, explain the limitations of using a firm's weighted average cost of capital as the discount rate when evaluating a project, and discuss the alternatives that are available.**

    The weighted average cost of capital is estimated using either Equation 13.2 or Equation 13.7, with the cost of each individual type of financing estimated using the appropriate method.

    When a firm uses a single rate to discount the cash flows for all of its projects, some project cash flows will be discounted using a rate that is too high and other project cash flows will be discounted using a rate that is too low. This can result in the firm rejecting some positive NPV projects and accepting some negative NPV projects. It will bias the firm toward accepting more risky projects and can cause the firm to create less value for stockholders than it would have if the appropriate discount rates had been used.

One approach to using the WACC is to identify a firm that engages in business activities that are similar to those associated with the project under consideration and that has publicly traded stock. The returns from this pure-play firm's stock can then be used to estimate the common stock beta for the project. In instances where pure-play firms are not available, financial managers can classify projects according to their systematic risks and can use a different discount rate for each classification. This is the type of classification scheme illustrated in Exhibit 13.4.

Summary of Key Equations

Equation	Description	Formula
13.1	Finance balance sheet identity	MV of assets = MV of liabilities + MV of equity
13.2	General formula for weighted average cost of capital (WACC) for a firm	$k_{Firm} = \sum_{i=1}^{n} x_i k_i = x_1 k_1 + x_2 k_2 + x_3 k_3 + \cdots + x_n k_n$
13.3	After-tax cost of debt	$k_{Debt\ after-tax} = k_{Debt\ pretax} \times (1 - t)$
13.4	CAPM formula for the cost of common stock	$k_{cs} = R_{rf} + (\beta_{cs} \times \text{Market risk premium})$
13.5	Constant-growth dividend formula for the cost of common stock	$k_{cs} = \dfrac{D_1}{P_0} + g$
13.6	Perpetuity formula for the cost of preferred stock	$k_{ps} = \dfrac{D_{ps}}{P_{ps}}$
13.7	Traditional WACC formula	$\text{WACC} = x_{Debt} k_{Debt\ pretax}(1 - t) + x_{ps} k_{ps} + x_{cs} k_{cs}$

Self-Study Problems

13.1 The market value of a firm's assets is $3 billion. If the market value of the firm's liabilities is $2 billion, what is the market value of the stockholders' investment and why?

13.2 Berron Comics, Inc., has borrowed $100 million and is required to pay investors $8 million in interest this year. If Berron is in the 35 percent marginal tax bracket, then what is the after-tax cost of debt (in dollars as well as in annual interest) to Berron.

13.3 Explain why the after-tax cost of equity (common or preferred) does not have to be adjusted by the marginal income tax rate for the firm.

13.4 Mike's T-Shirts, Inc., has debt claims of $400 (market value) and equity claims of $600 (market value). If the cost of debt financing (after tax) is 11 percent and the cost of equity is 17 percent, then what is Mike's weighted average cost of capital?

13.5 You are analyzing a firm that is financed with 60 percent debt and 40 percent equity. The current cost of debt financing is 10 percent, but due to a recent downgrade by the rating agencies, the firm's cost of debt is expected to increase to 12 percent immediately. How will this change the firm's weighted average cost of capital if you ignore taxes?

Solutions to Self-Study Problems

13.1 Since the accounting identity that Assets = Liabilities + Equity holds for market values as well as book values, then we know that the market value of the firm's equity is $3 billion − $2 billion, or $1 billion.

13.2 Since Berron enjoys a tax deduction for its interest charges, the after-tax interest expense for Berron is $8 million × (1 − 0.35) = $5.2 million, which translates into an annual after-tax interest expense of $5.2/$100 = 0.052, or 5.2 percent.

13.3 The U.S. tax code allows a deduction for interest expense incurred on borrowing. Preferred and common shares are not considered debt and, thus, do not benefit from an interest deduction. As a result, there is no distinction between the before-tax and after-tax cost of equity capital.

13.4 Mike's T-Shirts's total firm value = $400 + $600 = $1,000. Therefore,

Debt = 40% of financing
Equity = 60% of financing
WACC = $x_{Debt}k_{Debt}(1 − t) + x_{ps}k_{ps} + x_{cs}k_{cs}$
WACC = (0.4 × 0.11) + (0.6 × 0.17) = 0.146, or 14.6%

13.5 The pretax debt contribution to the cost of capital is $x_{Debt} \times k_{Debt}$, and since the firm's pretax cost of debt is expected to increase by 2 percent, we know that the effect on WACC (pretax) will be 0.6 × 0.02 = 0.012, or 1.2 percent. Incidentally, if we assume that the firm is subject to the 40 percent marginal tax rate, then the after-tax increase in the cost of capital for the firm would be 0.012 × (1 − 0.4) = 0.0072, or 0.72 percent.

Critical Thinking Questions

13.1 Explain why the required rate of return on a firm's assets must be equal to the weighted average cost of capital associated with its liabilities and equity.

13.2 Which is easier to calculate directly, the expected rate of return on the assets of a firm or the expected rate of return on the firm's debt and equity? Assume that you are an outsider to the firm.

13.3 With respect to the level of risk and the required return for a firm's portfolio of projects, discuss how the market and a firm's management can have inconsistent information and expectations.

13.4 Your friend has recently told you that the federal government effectively subsidizes the cost of debt (compared to equity use) for corporations. Do you agree with that statement? Explain.

13.5 Your firm will have a fixed interest expense for the next 10 years. You recently found out that the marginal income tax rate for the firm will change from 30 percent to 40 percent next year. Describe how the change will affect the cash flow available to investors.

13.6 Describe why it is not usually appropriate to use the coupon rate on a firm's bonds to estimate the pretax cost of debt for the firm.

13.7 Maltese Falcone, Inc., has not checked its weighted average cost of capital for four years. Firm management claims that since Maltese has not had to raise capital for new projects since that time, they should not have to worry about their current weighted average cost of capital since they have essentially locked in their cost of capital. Critique that statement.

13.8 Ten years ago, the Edson Water Company issued preferred stock with a price equal to the par amount of $100. If the dividend yield on that issue was 12 percent, explain why the firm's current cost of preferred capital is likely not equal to 12 percent.

13.9 Discuss under what circumstances you might be able to use a model that assumes constant growth in dividends to calculate the current cost of equity capital for a firm.

13.10 Your manager just finished computing your firm's weighted average cost of capital. He is relieved because he says that he can now use that cost of capital to evaluate all projects that the firm is considering for the next four years. Evaluate that statement.

Questions and Problems

13.1 Finance balance sheet: KneeMan Markup Company has total debt obligations with a book and market value equal to $30 million and $28 million, respectively. It also has total equity with a book and market value equal to $20 million and $70 million, respectively. If you were going to buy all of the assets of KneeMan Markup today, how much should you be willing to pay?

BASIC

13.2 WACC: What is the weighted average cost of capital?

13.3 Current cost of a bond: You are analyzing the cost of debt for a firm. You know that the firm's 14-year maturity, 8.5 percent coupon bonds are selling at a price of $823.48. The bonds pay interest semiannually. If these bonds are the only debt outstanding for the firm, what is the after-tax cost of debt for this firm if the firm is in the 30 percent marginal tax rate?

13.4 Taxes and the cost of debt: How are taxes accounted for when we calculate the cost of debt?

13.5 Taxes and the cost of debt: ProFarma, Inc., has earnings before interest and taxes equal to $500. If the firm incurred interest expense of $200 and pays taxes at the 35 percent marginal tax rate, what amount of cash is available for ProFarma's investors?

13.6 Cost of common equity: List and describe each of the three methods used to calculate the cost of common equity.

13.7 Cost of common stock: Whitewall Tire Co. just paid a $1.60 dividend on its common shares. If Whitewall is expected to increase its annual dividend by 2 percent per year into the foreseeable future and the current price of Whitewall's common shares is $11.66, what is the cost of common equity for Whitewall?

13.8 Cost of common stock: Seerex Wok Co. is expected to pay a dividend of $1.10 one year from today on its common shares. That dividend is expected to increase by 5 percent every year thereafter. If the price of Seerex is $13.75, what is Seerex's cost of common equity?

13.9 Cost of common stock: Two-Stage Rocket's common stock is expected to pay an annual dividend equal of $1.25, and it is commonly known that the firm expects dividends paid to increase by 8 percent for the next two years and by 2 percent thereafter. If the current price of Two-Stage's common shares is $17.80, what is the cost of common equity capital for the firm?

13.10 Cost of preferred stock: Fjord Luxury Liners has preferred shares outstanding that pay an annual dividend equal to $15 per year. If the current price of Fjord preferred shares is $107.14, what is the after-tax cost of preferred shares for Fjord?

13.11 Cost of preferred stock: Kresler Autos has preferred shares outstanding that pay annual dividends of $12, and the current price of the shares is $80. What is the after-tax cost of new preferred shares for Kresler if the flotation (issuance) costs for a new issue of preferred are 5 percent?

13.12 WACC: Describe the alternatives to using a firm's WACC as a discount rate when evaluating a project.

13.13 WACC for a firm: Capital Co. has a capital structure that is financed, based on current market values, with 50 percent debt, 10 percent preferred shares, and 40 percent common shares. If the return offered to the investors for each of those sources is 8 percent, 10 percent, and 15 percent for debt, preferred shares, and common shares, respectively, what is Capital's after-tax WACC? Assume that the firm's marginal tax rate is 40 percent.

13.14 WACC: What are direct out-of-pocket costs?

INTERMEDIATE

13.15 Finance balance sheet: Describe why the total value of all of the securities financing the firm must be equal to the value of the firm.

13.16 Finance balance sheet: Describe why the cost of capital for the firm is equal to the expected rate of return to the investors of the firm.

13.17 Current cost of a bond: You know that the after-tax cost of debt capital for Bubbles Champagne is 7 percent. If the firm has only one issue of five-year maturity bonds outstanding, what is the current price of the bonds if the coupon rate on those bonds is 10 percent? Assume the bonds make semiannual coupon payments and the marginal tax rate is 30 percent.

13.18 Current cost of a bond: Perpetual Ltd. has issued bonds that never require the principal amount to be repaid to investors. Correspondingly, Perpetual must make interest payments into the infinite future. If the bondholders receive annual payments of $75 and the current price of the bonds is $882.35, what is the after-tax cost of this borrowing for Perpetual if the firm is in the 40 percent marginal tax rate?

13.19 Taxes and the cost of debt: Holding all other things constant but assuming that the marginal tax rate for a firm decreases, does that provide incentive for the firm to increase its use of debt or decrease that use?

13.20 Cost of debt for a firm: You are analyzing the after-tax cost of debt for a firm. You know that the firm's 12-year maturity, 9.5 percent coupon bonds are selling at a price of $1,200. If these bonds are the only debt outstanding for the firm, what is the after-tax cost of debt for this firm if the marginal tax rate for the firm is 34 percent? What if the bonds are selling at par?

13.21 Cost of common stock: Underestimated Inc.'s common shares currently sell for $36 per share. The firm believes that its shares should really sell for $54 per share. If the firm just paid an annual dividend of $2 per share and the firm expects those dividends to increase by 8 percent per year forever (and this is common knowledge to the market), what is the current cost of common equity for the firm and what does the firm believe is a more appropriate cost of common equity for the firm?

13.22 Cost of common stock: Write out the general equation for the price of a stock that will grow dividends very rapidly for four years after our next predicted dividend and thereafter at a constant, but lower, rate for the foreseeable future. Discuss the problems in estimating the cost of equity capital for such a stock.

13.23 Cost of common stock: You have calculated the cost of common equity using all three methods described in the chapter. Unfortunately, all three methods have yielded different answers. Describe which answer (if any) is most appropriate.

13.24 WACC for a firm: A firm financed totally with common equity is evaluating two distinct projects. The first project has a large amount of nonsystematic risk and a small amount of systematic risk. The second project has a small amount of nonsystematic risk and a large amount of systematic risk. Which project, if taken, will have a tendency to increase the firm's cost of capital?

13.25 WACC for a firm: The Imaginary Products Co. currently has $300 million of market value debt outstanding. The 9 percent coupon bonds (semiannual pay) have a maturity of 15 years and are currently priced at $1,440.03 per bond. The firm also has an issue of 2 million preferred shares outstanding with a market price of $12.00. The preferred shares offer an annual dividend of $1.20. Imaginary also has 14 million shares of common stock outstanding with a price of $20.00 per share. The firm is expected to pay a $2.20 common dividend one year from today, and that dividend is expected to increase by 5 percent per year forever. If Imaginary is subject to a 40 percent marginal tax rate, then what is the firm's weighted average cost of capital?

13.26 Choosing a discount rate: For the Imaginary Products firm in Problem 13.25, calculate the appropriate cost of capital for a new project that is financed with the same proportion of debt, preferred shares, and common shares as the firm's current capital structure. Also assume that the project has the same degree of systematic risk as the average project that the firm is currently undertaking (the project is also in the same general industry as the firm's current line of business).

13.27 Choosing a discount rate: If a firm anticipates financing a project with a capital mix different than the firm's current capital structure, describe in realistic terms how the firm is subjecting itself to a calculation error if it chooses to use its historical WACC to evaluate the project.

13.28 You are analyzing the cost of capital for MacroSwift Corporation, which develops software operating systems for computers. The firm's dividend growth rate has been a very constant 3 percent per year for the past 15 years. Competition for the firm's current products is expected to develop in the next year, and MacroSwift is currently expanding its revenue stream into the multimedia industry. Evaluate using a 3 percent growth rate in dividends for MacroSwift in your cost of capital model.

ADVANCED

13.29 You are an external financial analyst evaluating the merits of a stock. Since you are using a dividend discount model approach to calculating a cost of equity capital, you need to estimate the dividend growth rate for the firm in the future. Describe how you might go about that process.

13.30 You know that the return of Momentum Cyclicals common shares reacts to macroeconomic information 1.6 more times than the return of the market. If the risk-free rate of return is 4 percent and market risk premium is 6 percent, what is Momentum Cyclicals's cost of common equity capital?

13.31 In your analysis of the cost of capital for a common stock, you calculate a cost of capital using a dividend discount model that is much lower than the calculation for the cost of capital using the CAPM model. Explain a possible source for the discrepancy.

13.32 RetRyder Hand Trucks has a preferred share issue outstanding that pays an annual dividend of $1.30 per year. The current cost of preferred equity for RetRyder is 9 percent. If RetRyder issues additional preferred shares that pay exactly the same dividend and the investment banker retains 8 percent of the sale price, what is the cost of new preferred shares for RetRyder?

EXCEL®

13.33 Enigma Corporation's management believes that the firm's cost of capital (WACC) is too high because the firm has been too secretive with the market concerning its operations. Evaluate that statement.

13.34 Discuss what valuable information would be lost if you decided to use book values in order to calculate the cost of each of the capital components within a firm's capital structure.

13.35 The cost of equity is equal to the
  a. expected market return.
  b. rate of return required by stockholders.
  c. cost of retained earnings plus dividends.
  d. risk the company incurs when financing.

CFA PROBLEMS

13.36 Dot.Com has determined that it could issue $1,000 face value bonds with an 8 percent coupon paid semiannually and a five-year maturity at $900 per bond. If Dot.Com's marginal tax rate is 38 percent, its after-tax cost of debt is closest to:
  a. 6.2 percent.
  b. 6.4 percent.
  c. 6.6 percent.
  d. 6.8 percent.

13.37 Morgan Insurance Ltd. issued a fixed-rate perpetual preferred stock three years ago and placed it privately with institutional investors. The stock was issued at $25.00 per share with a $1.75 dividend. If the company were to issue preferred stock today, the yield would be 6.5 percent. The stock's current value is:
  a. $25.00.
  b. $26.92.
  c. $37.31.
  d. $40.18.

13.38 The Gearing Company has an after-tax cost of debt capital of 4 percent, a cost of preferred stock of 8 percent, a cost of equity capital of 10 percent, and a weighted average cost of capital of 7 percent. Gearing intends to maintain its current capital structure as it raises additional capital. In making its capital-budgeting decisions for the average-risk project, the relevant cost of capital is:
  a. 4 percent.
  b. 7 percent.
  c. 8 percent.
  d. 10 percent.

13.39 Suppose the cost of capital of the Gadget Company is 10 percent. If Gadget has a capital structure that is 50 percent debt and 50 percent equity, its before-tax cost of debt is 5 percent, and its marginal tax rate is 20 percent, then its cost of equity capital is closest to:
a. 10 percent.
b. 12 percent.
c. 14 percent.
d. 16 percent.

Sample Test Problems

13.1 The Balanced, Inc., has three different product lines of business. Its least risky product line has a beta of 1.7, while its middle-risk product line has a beta of 1.8, and its most risky product line has a beta of 2.1. The market value of the assets invested in each product line is $1 billion for the least risky line, $3 billion for the middle-risk line, and $7 billion for the riskiest product line. What is the beta of The Balanced, Inc.?

13.2 Ellwood Corp. has a five-year bond issue outstanding with a coupon rate of 10 percent and a price of $1,039.56. If the bonds pay coupons semiannually, what is the pretax cost of the debt and what is the after-tax cost of the debt? Assume the marginal tax rate for the firm is 40 percent.

13.3 Miron's Copper Corp. expects its growth in common share dividends to be a very steady 1.5 percent per year for the indefinite future. The firm's shares are currently selling for $18.45, and the firm just paid a dividend of $3.00 yesterday. What is the cost of common share equity for this firm?

13.4 Micah's Time Portals has a preferred stock issue outstanding that pays an annual dividend of $2.50 per year and is currently selling for $27.78 a share. What is the cost of preferred equity for this firm?

13.5 The Old Time New Age Co. has a portfolio of projects with a beta of 1.25. The firm is currently evaluating a new project that involves a new product in a new competitive market. Briefly discuss what adjustment Old Time New Age might make to its 1.25 beta in order to evaluate this new project.

PRESENT VALUE AND FUTURE VALUE TABLES

APPENDIX A

> Table A-1
> Future Value Factors for $1 Compounded at *i* Percent for N Periods
>
> Table A-2
> Present Value Factors (at *i* Percent) for $1 Received at the End of N Periods
>
> Table A-3
> Future Value of Annuity Factors for $1 Compounded at *i* Percent for N Periods
>
> Table A-4
> Present Value of Annuity Factors (at *i* Percent Per Period) for $1 Received Per Period for Each of N Periods

Table A-1 Future Value Factors for $1 Compounded at *i* Percent for N Periods

N	1%	2%	3%	4%	5%	6%	7%	8%	9%	10%
1	1.010	1.020	1.030	1.040	1.050	1.060	1.070	1.080	1.090	1.100
2	1.020	1.040	1.061	1.082	1.103	1.124	1.145	1.166	1.188	1.210
3	1.030	1.061	1.093	1.125	1.158	1.191	1.225	1.260	1.295	1.331
4	1.041	1.082	1.126	1.170	1.216	1.262	1.311	1.360	1.412	1.464
5	1.051	1.104	1.159	1.217	1.276	1.338	1.403	1.469	1.539	1.611
6	1.062	1.126	1.194	1.265	1.340	1.419	1.501	1.587	1.677	1.772
7	1.072	1.149	1.230	1.316	1.407	1.504	1.606	1.714	1.828	1.949
8	1.083	1.172	1.267	1.369	1.477	1.594	1.718	1.851	1.993	2.144
9	1.094	1.195	1.305	1.423	1.551	1.689	1.838	1.999	2.172	2.358
10	1.105	1.219	1.344	1.480	1.629	1.791	1.967	2.159	2.367	2.594
11	1.116	1.243	1.384	1.539	1.710	1.898	2.105	2.332	2.580	2.853
12	1.127	1.268	1.426	1.601	1.796	2.012	2.252	2.518	2.813	3.138
13	1.138	1.294	1.469	1.665	1.886	2.133	2.410	2.720	3.066	3.452
14	1.149	1.319	1.513	1.732	1.980	2.261	2.579	2.937	3.342	3.797
15	1.161	1.346	1.558	1.801	2.079	2.397	2.759	3.172	3.642	4.177
16	1.173	1.373	1.605	1.873	2.183	2.540	2.952	3.426	3.970	4.595
17	1.184	1.400	1.653	1.948	2.292	2.693	3.159	3.700	4.328	5.054
18	1.196	1.428	1.702	2.026	2.407	2.854	3.380	3.996	4.717	5.560
19	1.208	1.457	1.754	2.107	2.527	3.026	3.617	4.316	5.142	6.116
20	1.220	1.486	1.806	2.191	2.653	3.207	3.870	4.661	5.604	6.727
21	1.232	1.516	1.860	2.279	2.786	3.400	4.141	5.034	6.109	7.400
22	1.245	1.546	1.916	2.370	2.925	3.604	4.430	5.437	6.659	8.140
23	1.257	1.577	1.974	2.465	3.072	3.820	4.741	5.871	7.258	8.954
24	1.270	1.608	2.033	2.563	3.225	4.049	5.072	6.341	7.911	9.850
25	1.282	1.641	2.094	2.666	3.386	4.292	5.427	6.848	8.623	10.835
30	1.348	1.811	2.427	3.243	4.322	5.743	7.612	10.063	13.268	17.449
35	1.417	2.000	2.814	3.946	5.516	7.686	10.677	14.785	20.414	28.102
40	1.489	2.208	3.262	4.801	7.040	10.286	14.974	21.725	31.409	45.259
45	1.565	2.438	3.782	5.841	8.985	13.765	21.002	31.920	48.327	72.890
50	1.645	2.692	4.384	7.107	11.467	18.420	29.457	46.902	74.358	117.390

11%	12%	13%	14%	15%	20%	25%	30%	35%	40%
1.110	1.120	1.130	1.140	1.150	1.200	1.250	1.300	1.350	1.400
1.232	1.254	1.277	1.300	1.323	1.440	1.563	1.690	1.823	1.960
1.368	1.405	1.443	1.482	1.521	1.728	1.953	2.197	2.460	2.744
1.518	1.574	1.530	1.689	1.749	2.074	2.441	2.856	3.322	3.842
1.685	1.762	1.842	1.925	2.011	2.488	3.052	3.713	4.484	5.378
1.870	1.974	2.082	2.195	2.313	2.986	3.815	4.827	6.053	7.530
2.076	2.211	2.353	2.502	2.660	3.583	4.768	6.275	8.172	10.541
2.305	2.476	2.658	2.853	3.059	4.300	5.960	8.157	11.032	14.758
2.558	2.773	3.004	3.252	3.518	5.160	7.451	10.604	14.894	20.661
2.839	3.106	3.395	3.707	4.046	6.192	9.313	13.786	20.107	28.925
3.152	3.479	3.836	4.226	4.652	7.430	11.642	17.922	27.144	40.496
3.498	3.896	4.335	4.818	5.350	8.916	14.552	23.298	36.644	56.694
3.883	4.363	4.898	5.492	6.153	10.699	18.190	30.288	49.470	79.371
4.310	4.887	5.535	6.261	7.076	12.839	22.737	39.374	66.784	111.120
4.785	5.474	6.254	7.138	8.137	15.407	28.422	51.186	90.158	155.560
5.311	6.130	7.067	8.137	9.358	18.488	35.527	66.542	121.710	217.790
5.895	6.866	7.986	9.276	10.761	22.186	44.409	86.504	164.310	304.910
6.544	7.690	9.024	10.575	12.375	26.623	55.511	112.450	221.820	426.870
7.263	8.613	10.197	12.056	14.232	31.948	69.389	146.190	299.460	597.630
8.062	9.646	11.523	13.743	16.367	38.338	86.736	190.050	404.270	836.680
8.949	10.804	13.021	15.668	18.822	46.005	108.420	247.060	545.760	1171.300
9.934	12.100	14.714	17.861	21.645	55.206	135.520	321.180	716.780	1639.800
10.026	13.552	16.627	20.362	24.891	66.247	169.400	417.530	994.660	2297.800
12.239	15.179	18.788	23.212	28.625	79.497	211.750	542.800	1342.700	3214.200
13.585	17.000	21.231	26.462	32.919	95.396	264.690	705.640	1812.700	4499.800
22.892	29.960	39.116	50.950	66.212	237.370	807.790	2619.900	8128.500	24201.000
38.575	52.800	72.069	98.100	133.170	590.660	2465.100	9727.800	36448.000	130161.000
65.001	93.051	132.782	188.880	267.860	1469.700	7523.100	36118.000	163437.000	700037.000
109.530	163.980	244.641	363.670	538.760	3657.200	22958.000	134106.000	732857.000	
184.560	289.000	450.735	700.230	1083.600	9100.400	70064.000	497929.000		

Table A-2 — Present Value Factors (at *i* Percent) for $1 Received at the End of N Periods

N	1%	2%	3%	4%	5%	6%	7%	8%	9%	10%
1	.990	.980	.971	.962	.952	.943	.935	.926	.917	.909
2	.980	.961	.943	.925	.907	.890	.873	.857	.842	.826
3	.971	.942	.915	.889	.864	.840	.816	.794	.772	.751
4	.961	.924	.888	.855	.823	.792	.763	.735	.708	.683
5	.951	.906	.863	.822	.784	.747	.713	.681	.650	.621
6	.942	.888	.837	.790	.746	.705	.666	.630	.596	.564
7	.932	.871	.813	.760	.711	.665	.623	.583	.547	.513
8	.923	.853	.789	.731	.677	.627	.582	.540	.502	.467
9	.914	.837	.766	.703	.645	.592	.544	.500	.460	.424
10	.905	.820	.744	.676	.614	.558	.508	.463	.422	.386
11	.896	.804	.722	.650	.585	.527	.475	.429	.388	.350
12	.887	.788	.701	.625	.557	.497	.444	.397	.356	.319
13	.879	.773	.681	.601	.530	.469	.415	.368	.326	.290
14	.870	.758	.661	.577	.505	.442	.388	.340	.299	.263
15	.861	.743	.642	.555	.481	.417	.362	.315	.275	.239
16	.853	.728	.623	.534	.458	.394	.339	.292	.252	.218
17	.844	.714	.605	.513	.436	.371	.317	.270	.231	.198
18	.836	.700	.587	.494	.416	.350	.296	.250	.212	.180
19	.828	.686	.570	.475	.396	.331	.277	.232	.194	.164
20	.820	.673	.554	.456	.377	.312	.258	.215	.178	.149
21	.811	.660	.538	.439	.359	.294	.242	.199	.164	.135
22	.803	.647	.522	.422	.342	.278	.226	.184	.150	.123
23	.795	.634	.507	.406	.326	.262	.211	.170	.133	.112
24	.788	.622	.492	.390	.310	.247	.197	.158	.126	.102
25	.780	.610	.478	.375	.295	.233	.184	.146	.116	.092
30	.742	.552	.412	.308	.231	.174	.131	.099	.075	.057
35	.706	.500	.355	.253	.181	.130	.094	.068	.049	.036
40	.672	.453	.307	.208	.142	.097	.067	.046	.032	.022
45	.639	.410	.264	.171	.111	.073	.048	.031	.021	.014
50	.608	.372	.228	.141	.087	.054	.034	.021	.013	.009

11%	12%	13%	14%	15%	20%	25%	30%	35%	40%
.901	.893	.885	.877	.870	.833	.800	.769	.741	.714
.812	.797	.783	.769	.756	.694	.640	.592	.449	.510
.731	.712	.693	.675	.658	.579	.512	.455	.406	.364
.659	.636	.613	.592	.572	.482	.410	.350	.301	.260
.593	.567	.543	.519	.497	.402	.328	.269	.223	.186
.535	.507	.480	.456	.432	.335	.262	.207	.165	.133
.482	.452	.425	.400	.376	.279	.210	.159	.122	.095
.434	.404	.376	.351	.327	.233	.168	.123	.091	.068
.391	.361	.333	.308	.284	.194	.134	.094	.067	.048
.352	.322	.295	.270	.247	.162	.107	.073	.050	.035
.317	.287	.261	.237	.215	.135	.086	.056	.037	.025
.286	.257	.231	.208	.187	.112	.069	.043	.027	.018
.258	.229	.204	.182	.163	.093	.055	.033	.020	.013
.232	.205	.181	.160	.141	.078	.044	.025	.015	.009
.209	.183	.160	.140	.123	.065	.035	.020	.011	.006
.188	.163	.141	.123	.107	.054	.028	.015	.008	.005
.170	.146	.125	.108	.093	.045	.023	.012	.006	.003
.153	.130	.111	.095	.081	.038	.018	.009	.005	.002
.138	.116	.098	.083	.070	.031	.014	.007	.003	.002
.124	.104	.087	.073	.061	.026	.012	.005	.002	.001
.112	.093	.077	.064	.053	.022	.009	.004	.002	.001
.101	.083	.068	.056	.046	.018	.007	.003	.001	.001
.091	.074	.060	.049	.040	.015	.006	.002	.001	
.082	.066	.053	.043	.035	.013	.005	.002	.001	
.074	.059	.047	.038	.030	.010	.004	.001	.001	
.044	.033	.026	.020	.015	.004	.001			
.026	.019	.014	.010	.008	.002				
.015	.011	.008	.005	.004	.001				
.009	.006	.004	.003	.002					
.005	.003	.002	.001	.001					

Table A-3 — Future Value of Annuity Factors for $1 Compounded at i Percent for N Periods

N	1%	2%	3%	4%	5%	6%	7%	8%	9%	10%
1	1.000	1.000	1.000	1.000	1.000	1.000	1.000	1.000	1.000	1.000
2	2.010	2.020	2.030	2.040	2.050	2.060	2.070	2.080	2.090	2.100
3	3.030	3.060	3.091	3.122	3.152	3.184	3.215	3.246	3.278	3.310
4	4.060	4.122	4.184	4.246	4.310	4.375	4.440	4.506	4.573	4.641
5	5.101	5.204	5.309	5.416	5.526	5.637	5.751	5.867	5.985	6.105
6	6.152	6.308	6.468	6.633	6.802	6.975	7.153	7.336	7.523	7.716
7	7.214	7.434	7.662	7.898	8.142	8.394	8.654	8.923	9.200	9.487
8	8.286	8.583	8.892	9.214	9.549	10.897	10.260	10.637	11.028	11.436
9	9.369	9.755	10.159	10.583	11.027	11.491	11.978	12.488	13.021	13.579
10	10.462	10.950	11.464	12.006	12.578	13.181	13.816	14.487	15.193	15.937
11	11.567	12.169	12.808	13.486	14.207	14.972	15.784	16.645	17.560	18.531
12	12.683	13.412	14.192	15.026	15.917	16.870	17.888	18.977	20.141	21.384
13	13.809	14.680	15.618	16.627	17.713	18.882	20.141	21.495	22.953	24.523
14	14.947	15.971	17.086	18.292	19.599	21.015	22.550	24.215	26.019	27.975
15	16.097	17.291	18.599	20.024	21.579	23.276	25.129	27.152	29.361	31.722
16	17.258	18.639	20.157	21.825	23.657	25.673	27.888	30.324	33.003	35.950
17	18.430	20.012	21.762	23.698	25.840	28.213	30.840	33.750	36.974	40.545
18	19.615	21.412	23.414	25.645	28.132	30.906	33.999	37.450	41.301	45.599
19	20.811	22.841	25.117	27.671	30.539	33.760	37.379	41.446	46.018	51.159
20	22.019	24.297	26.870	29.778	33.066	36.786	40.995	45.762	51.160	57.275
21	23.239	25.783	28.676	31.969	35.719	39.993	44.865	50.423	56.765	64.002
22	24.472	27.299	30.537	34.248	38.505	43.392	49.006	55.457	62.873	71.403
23	25.716	28.845	32.453	36.618	41.430	46.996	53.436	60.893	69.532	79.543
24	26.973	30.422	34.426	39.083	44.502	50.816	58.177	66.765	76.790	88.497
25	28.243	32.030	36.459	41.646	47.727	54.865	63.249	73.106	84.701	98.347
30	34.785	40.568	47.575	56.085	66.439	79.058	94.461	113.280	136.300	164.490
35	41.660	49.994	60.462	73.652	90.320	111.430	138.230	172.310	215.710	271.020
40	48.886	60.402	75.401	95.026	120.800	154.760	199.630	259.050	337.880	442.590
45	56.481	71.893	92.720	121.020	159.700	212.740	285.740	386.500	525.850	718.900
50	64.463	84.579	112.790	152.660	209.340	290.330	406.520	573.770	815.080	1163.900

11%	12%	13%	14%	15%	20%	25%	30%	35%	40%
1.000	1.000	1.000	1.000	1.000	1.000	1.000	1.000	1.000	1.000
2.110	2.120	2.130	2.140	2.150	2.200	2.250	2.300	2.350	2.400
3.342	3.374	3.407	3.440	3.472	3.640	3.813	3.990	4.172	4.360
4.710	4.779	4.850	4.921	4.993	5.368	5.766	6.187	6.633	7.104
6.228	6.353	6.480	6.610	6.742	7.442	8.207	9.043	9.954	10.196
7.913	8.115	8.232	8.536	8.754	9.930	11.259	12.756	14.438	16.324
9.783	10.089	10.405	10.730	11.067	12.916	15.073	17.583	20.492	23.853
11.859	12.300	12.757	13.233	13.727	16.499	19.842	23.858	28.664	34.395
14.164	14.776	15.416	16.085	16.786	20.799	25.802	32.015	39.696	49.153
16.722	17.549	18.420	19.337	20.304	25.959	33.253	42.619	54.590	69.814
19.561	20.655	21.814	23.045	24.349	32.150	42.566	56.405	74.697	98.739
22.713	24.133	25.650	27.271	29.002	39.581	54.208	74.327	101.840	139.230
26.212	28.029	29.985	32.089	34.352	48.497	68.760	97.625	138.480	195.920
30.095	32.393	34.883	37.581	40.505	59.196	86.949	127.910	187.950	275.300
34.405	37.280	40.417	43.842	47.580	72.035	109.680	167.280	254.730	386.420
39.190	42.753	46.672	50.980	55.717	87.442	138.100	218.470	344.890	541.980
44.501	48.884	53.739	59.118	65.075	105.930	173.630	285.010	466.610	759.780
50.396	55.750	61.725	68.394	75.836	128.110	218.040	371.510	630.920	1064.600
56.939	63.440	70.749	78.969	88.212	154.740	273.550	483.970	852.740	1491.500
64.203	72.052	80.947	91.025	102.440	186.680	342.940	630.160	1152.200	2089.200
72.265	81.699	92.470	104.760	118.810	225.020	429.680	820.210	1556.400	2925.800
81.214	92.503	105.491	120.430	137.630	271.030	538.100	1067.200	2102.200	4097.200
91.148	104.600	120.205	138.290	159.270	326.230	673.620	1388.400	2839.000	5737.100
102.170	118.150	136.831	158.650	184.160	392.480	843.030	1806.000	3833.700	8032.900
114.410	133.330	155.620	181.870	212.790	471.980	1054.700	2348.800	5176.500	11247.000
199.020	241.330	293.199	356.780	434.740	1181.800	3227.100	8729.900	23221.000	60501.000
341.590	431.660	546.681	693.570	881.170	2948.300	9856.700	32422.000	104136.000	325400.000
581.820	767.090	1013.704	1342.000	1779.000	7343.800	30088.000	120392.000	466960.000	
986.630	1358.200	1874.165	2490.500	3585.100	18281.000	91831.000	447019.000		
1668.700	2400.000	3459.507	4994.500	7217.700	45497.000	280255.000			

Table A-4: Present Value of Annuity Factors (at *i* Percent Per Period) for $1 Received Per Period for Each of N Periods

N	1%	2%	3%	4%	5%	6%	7%	8%	9%	10%
1	0.990	0.980	0.971	0.962	0.952	0.943	0.935	0.926	0.917	0.909
2	1.970	1.942	1.913	1.886	1.859	1.833	1.808	1.783	1.759	1.736
3	2.941	2.884	2.829	2.775	2.723	2.673	2.624	2.577	2.531	2.487
4	3.902	3.808	3.717	3.630	3.546	3.465	3.387	3.312	3.240	3.170
5	4.853	4.713	4.580	4.452	4.329	4.212	4.100	3.993	3.890	3.791
6	5.795	5.601	5.417	5.242	5.076	4.917	4.767	4.623	4.486	4.355
7	6.728	6.472	6.230	6.002	5.786	5.582	5.389	5.206	5.033	4.868
8	7.652	7.325	7.020	6.733	6.463	6.210	5.971	5.747	5.535	5.335
9	8.566	8.162	7.786	7.435	7.108	6.802	6.515	6.247	5.995	5.759
10	9.471	8.983	8.530	8.111	7.722	7.360	7.024	6.710	6.418	6.145
11	10.368	9.787	9.253	8.760	8.306	7.887	7.499	7.139	6.805	6.495
12	11.255	10.575	9.954	9.385	8.863	8.384	7.943	7.536	7.161	6.814
13	12.134	11.348	10.635	9.986	9.394	8.853	8.358	7.904	7.487	7.103
14	13.004	12.106	11.296	10.563	9.899	9.295	8.745	8.244	7.786	7.367
15	13.865	12.849	11.938	11.118	10.380	9.712	9.108	8.559	8.061	7.606
16	14.718	13.578	12.561	11.652	10.838	10.106	9.447	8.851	8.313	7.824
17	15.562	14.292	13.166	12.166	11.274	10.477	9.763	9.122	8.544	8.022
18	16.398	14.992	13.754	12.659	11.690	10.828	10.059	9.372	8.756	8.201
19	17.226	15.678	14.324	13.134	12.085	11.158	10.336	9.604	8.950	8.365
20	18.046	16.351	14.877	13.590	12.462	11.470	10.594	9.818	9.129	8.514
21	18.857	17.011	15.415	14.029	12.821	11.764	10.836	10.017	9.292	8.649
22	19.660	17.658	15.937	14.451	13.163	12.042	11.061	10.201	9.442	8.772
23	20.456	18.292	16.444	14.857	13.489	12.303	11.272	10.371	9.580	8.883
24	21.243	18.914	16.936	15.247	13.799	12.550	11.469	10.529	9.707	8.985
25	22.023	19.523	17.413	15.622	14.094	12.783	11.654	10.675	9.823	9.077
30	25.808	22.396	19.600	17.292	15.372	13.765	12.409	11.258	10.274	9.427
35	29.409	24.999	21.487	18.665	16.374	14.498	12.948	11.655	10.567	9.644
40	32.835	27.355	23.115	19.793	17.159	15.046	13.332	11.925	10.757	9.779
45	36.095	29.490	24.519	20.720	17.774	15.456	13.606	12.108	10.881	9.863
50	39.196	31.424	25.730	21.482	18.256	15.762	13.801	12.233	10.962	9.915

11%	12%	13%	14%	15%	20%	25%	30%	35%	40%
0.901	0.893	0.885	0.877	0.870	0.833	0.800	0.769	0.741	0.714
1.713	1.690	1.668	1.647	1.626	1.528	1.440	1.361	1.289	1.224
2.444	2.402	2.361	2.322	2.283	2.106	1.952	1.816	1.696	1.589
3.102	3.037	2.974	2.914	2.855	2.589	2.362	2.166	1.997	1.849
3.696	3.605	3.517	3.433	3.352	2.991	2.689	2.436	2.220	2.035
4.231	4.111	3.998	3.889	3.784	3.326	2.951	2.643	2.385	2.168
4.712	4.564	4.423	4.288	4.160	3.605	3.161	2.802	2.508	2.263
5.146	4.968	4.799	4.639	4.487	3.837	3.329	2.925	2.598	2.331
5.537	5.328	5.132	4.946	4.772	4.031	3.463	3.019	2.665	2.379
5.889	5.650	5.426	5.216	5.019	4.192	3.571	3.092	2.715	2.414
6.207	5.938	5.687	5.453	5.234	4.327	3.656	3.147	2.752	2.438
6.492	6.194	5.918	5.660	5.421	4.439	3.725	3.190	2.779	2.456
6.750	6.424	6.122	5.842	5.583	4.533	3.780	3.223	2.799	2.469
6.982	6.628	6.302	6.002	5.724	4.611	3.824	3.249	2.814	2.478
7.191	6.811	6.462	6.142	5.847	4.675	3.859	3.268	2.825	2.484
7.379	6.974	6.604	6.265	5.954	4.730	3.887	3.283	2.834	2.489
7.549	7.120	6.729	6.373	6.047	4.775	3.910	3.295	2.840	2.492
7.702	7.250	6.840	6.467	6.128	4.812	3.928	3.304	2.844	2.494
7.839	7.366	6.938	6.550	6.198	4.843	3.942	3.311	2.848	2.496
7.963	7.469	7.025	6.623	6.259	4.870	3.954	3.316	2.850	2.497
8.075	7.562	7.102	6.687	6.312	4.891	3.963	3.320	2.852	2.498
8.176	7.654	7.170	6.743	6.359	4.909	3.970	3.323	2.853	2.498
8.266	7.718	7.230	6.792	6.399	4.925	3.976	3.325	2.854	2.499
8.348	7.784	7.283	6.835	6.434	4.937	3.981	3.327	2.855	2.499
8.422	7.843	7.330	6.873	6.464	4.948	3.985	3.329	2.856	2.499
8.694	8.055	7.496	7.003	6.566	4.979	3.995	3.332	2.857	2.500
8.855	8.176	7.586	7.070	6.617	4.992	3.998	3.333	2.857	2.500
8.951	8.244	7.634	7.105	6.642	4.997	3.999	3.333	2.857	2.500
9.008	8.283	7.661	7.123	6.654	4.999	4.000	3.333	2.857	2.500
9.042	8.304	7.675	7.133	6.661	4.999	4.000	3.333	2.857	2.500

SOLUTIONS TO SELECTED QUESTIONS AND PROBLEMS

APPENDIX B

CHAPTER 1

1.1 The two basic sources of funds for all businesses are debt and equity.

1.3 A profitable firm is able to generate enough cash flows from productive assets to cover its operating expenses, taxes, and payments to creditors. Unprofitable firms fail to do this and therefore they may be forced to declare bankruptcy.

1.5 A firm should undertake a capital project only if the value of its future cash flows exceeds the cost of the project.

1.7 Working capital management is the day-to-day management of a firm's current assets and liabilities. The financial manager has to make decisions regarding the level of inventory to hold, the terms of granting credit (account receivables), and the firm's policy on paying accounts payable.

1.9 Advantages: easiest business type to start; least regulated; owners have full control; all income is taxed as personal income. Disadvantages: unlimited liability of proprietor; initial capital limited to proprietor's wealth; difficult to transfer ownership.

1.11 The owners of a corporation are its stockholders and the evidence of their ownership is represented by shares of common stock.

1.13 The owners of a corporation are subject to double taxation—first at the corporate level when the firm's earnings are taxed and then again at a personal level when the dividends they receive are taxed.

1.15 The most important governing body within an organization is the board of directors. Its primary role is to represent the interest of stockholders. The board also hires (and occasionally fires) the CEO, advises him or her on major decisions, and monitors the firm's performance.

1.17 Problems include: difficult to determine what is meant by profits; it does not address the size and timing of cash flows—it does not account for the time value of money; and ignores the uncertainty of risk of cash flows.

1.19 The following factors affect the stock price: the firm, the economy, economic shocks, the business environment, expected cash flows, and current market conditions.

1.21 If a firm's stock price falls sustainably below its maximum potential price, it may attract corporate raiders. These persons look for firms that are fundamentally sound but that are poorly managed, so they can buy the firm, turn it around, and sell it for a handsome profit.

1.23 Business dishonesty and lack of transparency lead to corruption, and that in turn creates inefficiencies in an economy, inhibits growths of capital markets, and slows the rate of economic growth. An example is the Russian economy until it changed its transparency rules in the mid 1990s.

1.25 Insider trading is an example of information asymmetry. The main idea is that investment decisions should be made on an even playing field. Insider trading is considered morally wrong and has been made illegal.

CHAPTER 2

2.1 The role of the financial system is to gather money from businesses and individuals and channel funds to those who need them. The financial system consists of financial markets and financial institutions.

2.3 Saver-lenders are those who have more money than they need right now. The principal saver-lenders in the economy are households. Borrower-spenders are those who need the money saver-lenders are offering. The main borrower-spenders in the economy are businesses and the federal government.

2.5 Your security seems to be marketable, but not liquid. Liquidity implies that when a security is sold, its value will be preserved, marketability does not.

2.7 Trader Inc. is more likely to go public because of its larger size. Though the cost of SEC registration and compliance is very high, larger firms can offset these costs by the lower funding cost in public markets. Smaller companies find the cost prohibitive for the dollar amount of securities they sell.

2.9 **a.** secondary; **b.** secondary; **c.** primary

2.11 **a.** $300,000; **b.** 3.05%; **c.** $9,850,000

2.13 Financial intermediaries allow smaller companies to access the financial markets. They do this through converting securities with one set of characteristics into securities with another set of characteristics that meet the needs of smaller companies. By repackaging securities, they are able to meet the needs of different clients.

2.15 Money markets are where short-term debt instruments with maturities of less than one year are bought and sold. Capital markets are where equity securities and debt instruments with maturities of more than one year are sold.

2.17 Dow Jones Industrial Index consists of the 30 largest public companies in the U.S. and it was established to gauge the performance of the U.S. economy, specifically the industrial component of the stock market.

2.19 U.S. treasury bills are short-term debt of the U.S. government. They are the most liquid money market instrument and are considered free of default risk.

2.21 Money markets allow large corporations to adjust their liquidity positions by temporarily investing idle cash in money market instruments and then selling them when cash is needed. In addition, some large firms are able to borrow money by selling commercial paper in the money markets when cash is needed.

2.23 Public markets are wholesale markets for securities open to the public to buy securities. To sell securities publicly, issuers must register their securities with the SEC. Most corporations want access to the public markets because securities can be sold there at the lowest possibly funding cost. Private markets are where securities are sold directly to individual investors. Securities sold privately do not have to be registered with the SEC and, as a result, securities can be brought to market quickly and at very low transactions cost. However, because the securities are not registered, their sale and secondary market activities are severely restricted.

2.25 The real rate of interest measures the return earned on savings and it represents the cost of borrowing to finance capital goods. The real rate of interest is determined by the interaction between firms that invest in capital projects and the rate of return they expect to earn on those investments, and individuals' time preference for consumption. The rate of interest is determined when the desired level of savings equals the desired level of investments in the economy.

2.27 The Fisher effect is the expected annualized change in commodity prices (ΔP_e). The so-called inflation premium is used to protect lenders from losses of purchasing power on their loan contracts due to inflation. It is incorporated into a loan contract by adding it to the real interest rate, as can be seen in Equation 2.2.

2.29 Yes. The CD will be worth $1,067.50 at the end of the year and the price of the trip will be $1,066.

CHAPTER 3

3.1 $97,118

3.3 FIFO makes sense during times of rising prices because it allows the firm to eliminate the lower-priced inventory first resulting in higher profit margin.

3.5 $6,655,610

3.7 $242,401.25

3.9 −$132.085

3.11 Expenses identified on income statement that did not result in cash flows. Depreciation and amortization are examples.

3.13 Marginal tax rates are appropriate because it is the rate at which the next dollar is taxed at.

3.15 $168,022

3.17 $222,764

3.19 $137,263

3.21 $1,804,545.76

3.23 $621,178

3.25 $218,364.32; 34%, 34%.

3.27 $715,719.75

3.29 $198,152

CHAPTER 4

4.1 This measure includes only the most liquid of the current assets and hence gives a better measure of liquidity.

4.3 $1,627,579

4.5 2.87 times; 127.1 days.

4.7 2.65; 0.623; 29.9%.

4.9 Time trend analysis, industry average analysis, and peer group analysis

4.11 $2.55; 21.3 times.

4.13 ($767,243)

4.15 $843,863

4.17 1.27; 2.27.

4.19 51.2%; 19.1%; 12.6%.

4.21 0.41; 36%; 18.32%; 25.92%.

4.23 34.4 times; 22.04 times

4.25 $6,473,600; 5.7%.

4.27 $10,226,559; $88,236,056; 0.82.

4.29 Current ratio = 0.77, quick ratio = 0.57, gross margin = 51.2%, profit margin = 19.1%, debt ratio = 0.70, long-term debt to equity = 0.73, interest coverage = 15.6, ROA = 11.4%, ROE = 37.5%

4.31 Profit margin = 12.61%, total asset turnover = 0.90, equity multiplier = 3.30, return on assets = 11.4%, return on equity = 37.5%

4.33 $292,756.63

4.35 Current ratio = 1.81, quick ratio = 1.19, inventory turnover = 3.50, accounts receivable turnover = 5.16, DSO = 70.76, total asset turnover = 1.23, fixed asset turnover = 7.15, total debt ratio = 1.72, debt to equity ratio = 1.72, equity multiplier = 2.72, times interest earned = 17.56, cash coverage = 37.30, gross profit margin = 0.36, net profit margin = 0.08, ROA = 0.10, ROE = 0.27

CHAPTER 5

5.1 $53,973.12

5.3 $6,712.35

5.5 $3,289.69

5.7 $154,154.24; $154,637.37; $154,874.91; $154,883.03.

5.9 $16,108.92

5.11 $6,507.05

5.13 $734.83

5.15 7.42%

5.17 92,016; 101,218.

5.19 1,045

5.21 10.42%

5.23 11 years

5.25 3.8 years

5.27 **a.** $2,246.57; **b.** $2,073.16; **c.** $2,946.96; **d.** $2,949.88

5.29 13.96%

5.31 Option 1: $26,803.77; Option 2: $23,579.48

5.33 Option C: $ 7,083,096.26

5.35 13.14%

CHAPTER 6

6.1 $74,472.48

6.3 $3,185.40

6.5 $5,747.40

6.7 $5,652.06

6.9 $247,609.95

6.11 $1,361,642.36

6.13 $4,221.07

6.15 **a.** $15,000; **b.** $6,000; **c.** $10,000

6.17 7%

6.19 $5,391,978
6.21 $1,496,377.71
6.23 $1,193,831.54
6.25 $7,000,000
6.27 a. $17,857.14; b. $114,533.97; c. $4,250.
6.29 b. 8.57%
6.31 $12,847,215.41, $11,374,540.65, and $14,519,339.52
6.33 a. $86,124.36; b. $14,156.64;
c. $71,967.72; d. $6.627.21.
6.35 $2,103.89

CHAPTER 7

7.1 Total holding period return represents the percentage return to an investor from holding an asset over a given period of time. The expected return is the probability weighted average of the future performance of an investment under all scenarios.

7.3 $78,000

7.5 Stock B

7.7 Systematic risk is risk that a security has in common with the market. Because all risky assets in the market have systematic risk, it cannot be eliminated through diversification.

7.9 Since a U.S. Treasury bill has no risk, its beta should equal 0.

7.11 The CAPM describes the relation between systematic risk and the expected return that investors require for bearing that risk.

7.13 $1,250

7.15 0.145; 0.162.

7.17 0.125; 0.168.

7.19 for $\sigma_{12} = 0.12, 0.1225; \sigma_{12} = -0.12, 0.0025$

7.21 While it has no unsystematic risk, the portfolio still will have an expected return that is higher than that for a risk-free asset if it has systematic risk.

7.23 The statement is false. Even if we could afford such a portfolio and thus completely diversify our portfolio, we would only be eliminating non-systematic risk.

7.25 0.185; 0.165.

7.27 0.19

7.29 Diversified investors are willing to pay the highest prices for assets. They drive prices to the point where investments are expected to yield the returns described by CAPM.

7.31 Risk-free asset

7.33 The first security is underpriced and the second is overpriced.

CHAPTER 8

8.1 $1,147.20
8.3 $1,008.15
8.5 $975.91
8.7 $359.38
8.9 6.58%; 6.69%.
8.11 9.52%
8.13 $1,000
8.15 $912.61
8.17 $1,079.22
8.19 12.453%
8.21 7.36%
8.23 10.57%
8.25 8.84%
8.27 a. $924.75; b. 4.33%.
8.29 a. $904.76; b. $1,086.46, $832.53; d. $1,063.42, $866.65.

CHAPTER 9

9.1 $14.24
9.3 $27.39
9.5 $8.50
9.7 $31.12
9.9 12.15%
9.11 $56.90
9.13 $2.46
9.15 $21.07
9.17 $23.35
9.19 $32.34
9.21 $25.95
9.23 $2.15
9.25 a. $35.00; b. Buy;
9.27 b. $7.87; c. $31.88; d. $24.31; e. $24.32.
9.29 a. $14.09; b. $74.80; c. $51.28.

CHAPTER 10

10.1 $62,337
10.3 Yes; $134,986
10.5 2.87 years
10.7 3.45 years
10.9 33.8%
10.11 $1,496,910; $1,084,734; Alpha 8300.
10.13 $27,222; $732,228; Both.
10.15 No; 4.33 years
10.17 Type 2; 3.6 years
10.19 20.1%
10.21 22.7%
10.23 a. 9%; b. 12.3%; c. 16.3%.
10.25 a. 10.7%; 15%; b. No to project I, Yes to project II
10.27 7.6%; 19.2%; 25.1%; 2 & 3 Only
10.29 18.8%, 20%; Both
10.31 a. 3.8 years; b. $2,189,325; c. 20.3%.
10.33 a. 3.21 years; b. 57.7%; c. $1,029,085; d. 32.5%.
10.35 a. 6 years, 8.8 years; b. $116,980; c. 12.5%.

CHAPTER 11

11.1 The main reason is that accounting earnings generally differ from cash flows and cash flows are what stockholders care about.

11.3 Subtract depreciation from EBITDA, multiply by (1− tax rate), and add back depreciation. This enables us to account for the fact that depreciation reduces the taxes that must be paid.

11.5 The average tax rate is the total amount of tax divided by total amount of money earned, while the marginal tax rate is the rate paid on the last dollar earned. Use the marginal tax rate.

11.7 Variable costs are costs that vary directly with the number of units sold. Fixed costs do not vary with the number of units sold.

11.9 $1,370

11.11 The Equivalent Annual Cost (EAC) is the annual payment from an annuity that has a life equal to that of a project and that has the same NPV as the project.

11.13 $891.84
11.15 marginal = 35%; average = 34.2%
11.17 $168,020,000
11.19 $EAC_A = -\$2,866.47$; $EAC_B = -\$2,978.44$; buy Model A
11.21 end of year 3
11.23 end of year 2
11.25 $4,558.70
11.27 yes; the NPV = $38,356
11.29 $532,089.14
11.31 −$363,805

CHAPTER 12

12.1 Fixed costs are cost which in the short term cannot be changed regardless of how much output the project produces. Variable costs are costs which vary with the number of units of output produced by the project.

12.3 Yes. EBIT is $375,000 with the new technology and $250,000 with the old.

12.5 0.392

12.7 To determine how many units are required to make up for the fixed cost we must know the additional positive cash flow or profits from each additional unit sold.

12.9 PI is the ratio of NPV plus initial investment to initial investment. It is useful in ranking projects by the value created per dollar invested.

12.11 Fixed costs could increase by $230,000 and variable cost per unit could increase by $15.33.

12.13 15.9%

12.15 340,000 units

12.17 The accounting break-even is higher because the calculation includes depreciation and amortization. This is a non-cash charge that might not accurately reflect an incremental cash flow.

12.19 Since sensitivity analysis assumes independence among variables, this analysis will be most useful when this sort of independence exists.

12.21 Simulation analysis

12.23 Choose projects A, C, and D

12.25 Cash Flow DOL will be less than Accounting DOL

12.27 Changes in revenue and operating leverage

12.29 CO = 300,000 units

CHAPTER 13

13.1 $98 million
13.3 7.7%
13.5 $395
13.7 16%
13.9 10%
13.11 15.8%
13.13 9.4%

13.15 The owners of the securities, collectively, own all of the cash flows that the firm generates. The value of these securities must equal the value of these cash flows and, therefore, the value of the firm.

13.17 $1,000

13.19 decrease

13.21 14%, 12%

13.23 If you can confidently estimate future dividends, and you believe the market is efficient, then one of the methods that rely on dividend projections might be appropriate. If not, the CAPM, which does not require dividend forecasts, would probably be best.

13.25 9.26%

13.27 Since the firm is financing the project with a different capital mix than it has historically used, then we know the weights and rates for debt, preferred, and common shares in the WACC formula will be different. Therefore, using its historical WACC can cause result in an error in the NPV estimate for the project.

13.29 Use a combination of historical growth information and available information about future growth prospects.

13.31 Under-estimating the dividend growth rate or market inefficiency in the pricing of the stock.

13.33 If the market perceives the risk of the firm to be higher than it actually is due to a lack of information, then the WACC might be too high and the firm might be able to lower it by sharing more information with the market.

CHAPTER 14

14.1 69 days
14.3 −2 days
14.5 73 days
14.7 34.72%
14.9 $626.91
14.11 11.6%
14.13 75.9 days
14.15 $1,511,918
14.17 36.5 days
14.19 16 orders
14.21 8.775%
14.23 5.54%
14.25 $9,324
14.27 28.2 days
14.29 37.1%
14.31 a. Increase, Increase;   b. Increase, Increase;
       c. No change, Decrease;   d. Increase, Increase;
       e. Increase, Unchanged.
14.33 a. 67.9 days;   b. 80.6 days;   c. 105.7 days;
       d. 148.5 days;   e. 42.8 days.
14.35 a. $30,000;   b. 63.2%;   c. 85.1%

CHAPTER 15

15.1 A description of the business and industry trends, vision and key strategies for the business, principal products or services and any innovative features or patents, the management team and their experience, market analysis and sales forecast, how the products will be marketed and sold, production costs such as materials and labor, facilities needed and estimated costs, capital required and the use of the proceeds, detailed budget with six years of projected financial statements.

15.3 Sell the business at some period, take it public, or remain a private company.

15.5 Look at comparable companies and see what they are trading for; do a discounted cash flow analysis.

15.7 $32,465,457

15.9 a. false   b. true   c. true   d. false   e. true

15.11 There are economies of scale in issuing securities, meaning that as the size of the offering increases, the total flotation costs decline.

15.13 Nalco is better off choosing to sell debt in public market, given its size.

15.15 9.43%

15.17 $1,220,000

15.19 $68,700,000

15.21 a. $130 million; b. $109 million; c. $21 million.

15.23 6.52%

CHAPTER 16

16.1 The assumption that there are no information or transaction costs.

16.3 The value of the firm is independent of the proportion of debt and equity utilized by the firm under Modigliani and Miller's Proposition 1.

16.5 20%

16.7 18%

16.9 $150,000,000

16.11 10.5%

16.13 42%

16.15 Information or transaction costs would reduce the total value that is available for the debt holders and the stockholders and, therefore, the value of the firm.

16.17 $530,000,000

16.19 Lower productivity due to lower morale and job hunting and higher recruiting costs are among the costs that the firm will incur.

16.21 Managers expect to lose their jobs in one year whether they take on the project and work hard or not. They have no incentive to take on the project. Declining it makes the shortage to the debt holders, as well as the stockholders, greater than it would be if the firm followed the rule of always accepting positive NPV projects.

16.23 Given the information in the question we would expect that an increase in the marginal tax rate will increase the value of the tax shield and increase the amount of debt in the optimal capital structure.

16.25 That internally generated equity is utilized first as a source of financing does not mean that the internally generated funds are cheaper than debt. Internally generated funds belong to stockholders and are therefore really equity financing, which we know to be more expensive than debt.

16.27 Under these conditions, the value of the firm will increase with the amount of debt financing that is used. The conservative approach will not maximize firm value.

16.29 $810,000,000

16.31 If enough debt is used to finance this firm then the challenges of ensuring that the firm produces enough cash to make interest and principal payments would provide managers of the firm with incentives to work on new positive NPV projects rather than spend their Fridays in Cancun.

CHAPTER 17

17.1 This reduction could indicate that management expects a lower level of profitability in the future (negative signal). It could also indicate that Poseidon requires additional money to invest in positive NPV projects that were not previously available (positive signal).

17.3 (1) Declaration date, (2) Ex-dividend date, (3) Record date, (4) Payment date

17.5 Any cash paid to stockholders through a dividend reduces the value of the assets that are securing the creditors' claims.

17.7 $9.75

17.9 With a stock repurchase, stockholders can decide whether to participate. If they do choose to participate, there are tax advantages for the stockholders, relative to a dividend.

17.11 Relaxing the no transaction cost assumption increases the cost of producing a homemade dividend (the cost of undoing unwanted dividends). This makes a firm's dividend policy a relevant factor when valuing its shares.

17.13 The value of dividend paying stocks should decrease relative to the value of non-dividend-paying stocks.

17.15 Reducing a dividend may indicate that a firm does not have sufficient cash, which would be a negative signal. On the other hand, when a high growth firm increases its dividend, the increase may be interpreted as indicating that the firm's growth rate will decline, which is also a negative signal.

17.17 The announcement of a special dividend is a binding commitment.

17.19 This commits a firm to returning to the capital markets periodically to raise capital, which provides managers with incentives to act in the interest of stockholders.

17.21 A Dutch auction enables a firm to repurchase the number of shares that it wants to repurchase at the lowest possible cost.

17.23 Paying a dividend reduces the value of equity and thereby increases the debt-to-total-capital ratio in a levered firm.

17.25 $15

17.27 $72,500

17.29 $150,000

CHAPTER 18

18.1 The forms of organizations discussed in this chapter include: Sole Proprietorship, Partnership (General Partnership and Limited Partnership), Limited Liability Company (LLC), and Corporation (S-Corporation and C-Corporation).

18.3 With sole proprietors and general partners there is the possibility that personal assets can be taken to satisfy claims on the businesses. In contrast, the liabilities of investors in LLCs and corporations are generally limited to the money that they have invested in the business.

18.5 Equity: friends and family, venture capitalists, or other potential investors that you know. Debt: bank loans, cash advances on credit cards, or loans from other individual investors or other businesses.

18.7 The cost of duplicating the assets of the business in their present form.

18.9 Excess cash is a nonoperating asset because this cash can be distributed to stockholders without affecting the operations of the business and therefore the value of the expected future cash flows. It makes sense to add back the value of excess cash because it represents value over and above that which the business is expected to produce.

18.11 Probably not. The private shares are relatively illiquid and the value would be discounted for this in the market.

18.13 A Limited Liability Company (LLC) is a hybrid of a corporation and a limited partnership. It has limited liability with the tax advantages of a partnership.

18.15 Break-even for TV option = 1,250 units per year. Break-even for flyer option = 150 units per year. Choose the flyer option.

18.17 $1,573.64 million

18.19 The enterprise value/EBITDA multiple is more appropriate since the capital structures of Johnson and Billy's differ considerably.

18.21 $12,675,000

18.23 It is not adequate. $9,400 or additional capital will be required up front. $89,400 is needed to maintain a $5,000 cash balance. The monthly break-even points for the firm are: 4,333.3 bottles in the initial month and 1,833.3 bottles in the following months.

18.25 See outline for a business plan in section 18.2.

18.27 The company has a short history, high investments, no sales, and highly uncertain future cash flows. The cost approach is not valid for such a young biochemical company. It is hard to value the company using multiples because of the lack of sales and negative earnings, and because of lack of comparable public companies. The transaction approach is also likely to be difficult to apply due to the difficulty of finding a comparable transaction.

CHAPTER 19

19.1 It drives all decision making within the firm and covers all areas of a firm's operations.

19.3 Identifies EFN, source of funding, target capital structure, and dividend policy.

19.5 Sales forecasts, pro forma statements, investment decisions, and financing decisions.

19.7 55%

19.9 Measures the amount of assets needed to generate one dollar in sales.

19.11 68%

19.13 6.8%

19.17 Electric utilities industry and the aluminum processing industry.

19.19 8%

19.21 8.2%

19.23 9.9%

19.25 5.2%

19.27 35.9%

19.29 9.6%

19.33 3.37%; 6.26%

19.35 **a.** 4.31%; **b.** 13.9%; **c.** $4,777,333;

CHAPTER 20

20.1 The right to buy or sell an asset at a pre-specified price on or before a pre-specified date.

20.3 $0; $15

20.5 The value of a call option increases as: (1) Current value of the underlying asset increases; (2) Exercise price decreases; (3) Volatility of the value of the underlying asset increases; (4) Time until the expiration of the option increases; or (5) Risk-free rate of interest increases.

20.7 That the value of the underlying asset will remain at or above the exercise price, thereby making it worthless to the owner (buyer).

20.9 No. The losses to the seller of a call option are only limited by the extent to which the value of the underlying asset can increase. There is no other limit.

20.11 Your option is worth very slightly more than zero. There is little chance that the stock price will move above $100 by tomorrow, but the chance is not zero, so the option still has some value.

20.13 The underlying asset of a financial option is financial asset, while the underlying asset of a real option is a non-financial asset, such as a project.

20.15 The payoff functions for lenders and stockholders are like those for different types of options. Agency costs arise because these payoff functions are different.

20.17 The purchaser of a callable bond is simultaneously buying a straight (non-callable) bond and selling the issuer a call option on that bond. The total value of the callable bond would equal the value of the straight bond minus the value of the option. It would be lower than the value for a straight bond.

20.19 Because the buyer pays them. The amount that the seller receives is known as the bond premium.

20.21 $7.01

20.23 $1.18

20.25 A golden parachute can help reduce agency problems by reducing the potential cost to a manager of making decisions that stockholders want, but that could harm the manager. For example, having a golden parachute can provide a manager with stronger incentives to invest in risky projects or approve a merger that could result in the loss of his or her job.

20.27 The payoff of these two portfolios is identical.

20.29 $5 million; $6.5 million; $3.5 million

CHAPTER 21

21.1 $209.30

21.3 **a.** MP 11.8483/$; **b.** 1.6359/£; **c.** C$ 0.0316/Rs

21.5 Same cost in both cities based on the spot rate!

21.7 $9,400

21.9 $2,861,776

21.11 0.069%

21.13 0.45%

21.15 Won 2,120.23/£

21.19 5.4% discount

21.20 3.5% premium

21.21 0.007368/¥

21.23 Rs.43.43/$

21.25 $2,055,201

21.27 $5,286.50

21.29 $7,807.35

21.31 3,685.366 million Won

21.33 2.92%, 2.95% — domestic bond issue

21.35 $62,500; $61,875 — Daiwa's offer

GLOSSARY

A

accounting operating profit (EBIT) break-even point the number of units that must be sold for accounting operating profit to equal $0

accounting rate of return (ARR) a rate of return on a capital project based on average net income divided by average assets over the project's life; also called the *book rate of return*

adjusted book value the sum of the fair market values of the individual assets in a business

agency costs the costs arising from conflicts of interest between a principal and an agent; for example, between a firm's owners and its management

agency conflicts conflicts of interest between a principal and an agent

amortization schedule with regard to a loan, a table that shows the loan balance at the beginning and end of each period, the payment made during that period, and how much of that payment represents interest and how much represents repayment of principal

amortizing loan a loan for which each loan payment contains repayment of some principal and a payment of interest that is based on the remaining principal to be repaid

angels (angel investors) wealthy individuals who invest their own money in new ventures

annual percentage rate (APR) the simple interest rate charged per period multiplied by the number of periods per year

annuity due an annuity in which payments are made at the beginning of each period

annuity a series of equally spaced and level cash flows extending over a finite number

arbitrage buying and selling assets in a way that takes advantage of price discrepancies and yields a profit greater than that which would be expected based solely on the risk of the individual investments

asset substitution problem the incentive that stockholders in a financially leveraged firm have to substitute more risky assets for less risky assets

average tax rate total taxes paid divided by taxable income

B

balance sheet financial statement that shows a firm's financial position at a point in time

bankruptcy costs, or costs of financial distress costs associated with financial difficulties a firm might experience because it uses debt financing

bankruptcy legally declared inability of an individual or a company to pay its creditors

Benchmark a standard against which performance is measured

best-effort underwriting underwriting agreement in which the underwriter does not agree to purchase the securities at a particular price but promises only to make its "best effort" to sell as much of the issue as possible above a certain price

beta (β) a measure of nondiversifiable, systematic, or market, risk

bid price the price a securities dealer will pay for a given stock

book value the net value of an asset or liability recorded on the financial statements that normally reflects historical cost

break-even analysis an analysis that tells us how many units must be sold in order for a project to break even on a cash flow or accounting profit basis

brokers market specialists who bring buyers and sellers together, usually for commission

business plan a document that describes the details of how a business will be developed over time

business risk the risk in the cash flows to stockholders that is associated with uncertainty due to the characteristics of the business itself

C

call option an option to buy the underlying asset

call premium the price that the buyer of a call option pays the seller for that option

Capital Asset Pricing Model (CAPM) a model that describes the relation between risk and expected return

capital budgeting the process of choosing the real assets in which the firm will invest

capital markets financial markets where equity and debt instruments with maturities greater than one year are traded

capital rationing a situation where a firm does not have enough capital to invest in all attractive projects and must therefore ration capital

capital structure the mix of debt and equity that is used to finance a firm

cash conversion cycle the length of time from the point at which a company pays for raw materials until the point at which it receives cash from the sale of finished goods made from those materials

chief financial officer (CFO) the most senior financial manager in a company

coefficient of variation (CV) a measure of the risk associated with an investment for each 1 percent of expected return

collection time (float) the time between when a customer makes a payment and when the cash becomes available to the firm

commercial paper short-term debt in the form of promissory notes issued by large, financially secure firms with high credit ratings

common stock an equity share that represents the basic ownership claim in a corporation; the most common type of equity security

common-size financial statement a financial statement in which each number is expressed as a percent of a base number, such as total assets or total revenues

compensating balances bank balances that firms must maintain to at least partially compensate banks for loans or services rendered.

compound annual growth rate (CAGR) the average annual growth rate over a specified period of time

compound interest interest earned both on the original principal amount and on interest previously earned

compounding the process by which interest earned on an investment is reinvested, so in future periods interest is earned on the interest as well as the principal

consumer credit credit extended by a business to consumers

contingent project a project whose acceptance depends on the acceptance of another project

control premium an adjustment that is made to a business value estimate to reflect value associated with control that is not already reflected in the analysis

conventional cash flow a cash flow pattern made up of an initial cash outflow that is followed by one or more cash inflows

corporation a legal entity formed and authorized under a state charter; in a legal sense, a corporation is a "person" distinct from its owners

cost of capital the required rate of return for a capital investment

cost of revenue the cost directly attributable to the production of the product; also known as the cost of goods sold

country risk the political uncertainty associated with a particular country

coupon payments the interest payments made to bondholders

coupon rate the annual coupon payment of a bond divided by the bond's face value

covariance a measure of how the returns on two assets covary, or move together

crossover level of unit sales (CO) the level of unit sales at which cash flows or profitability for one project alternative switches from being lower than that of another alternative to being higher

crossover point the discount rate at which the NPV profiles of two projects cross and, thus, at which the NPVs of the projects are equal

current assets assets, such as accounts receivable and inventories, that are expected to be liquidated (collected or sold) within one year

D

dealers market specialists who "make markets" for securities by buying and selling from their own inventories

declaration date the date on which a dividend is publicly announced

default risk the risk that a firm will not be able to pay its debt obligations as they come due

degree of accounting operating leverage (Accounting DOL) a measure of the sensitivity of accounting operating profits (EBIT) to changes in revenue

degree of pretax cash flow operating leverage (Cash Flow DOL) a measure of the sensitivity of cash flows from operations (EBITDA) to changes in revenue

depreciation allocation of the cost of an asset over its estimated life

derivative security a security that derives its value from the value of another asset; an option is an example of a derivative security

direct bankruptcy costs out-of-pocket costs that a firm incurs when it gets into financial distress

discount bonds bonds that sell at below par (face) value

discount rate the interest rate used in the discounting process to find the present value of future cash flows

discounted payback period the length of time required to recover a project's initial cost, accounting for the time value of money

discounting the process by which the present value of future cash flows is obtained

diversifiable, unsystematic, or unique risk risk that can be eliminated through diversification

diversification a strategy of reducing risk by investing in two or more assets whose values do not always move in the same direction at the same time

dividend discount model (DDM) approach an income approach to valuation in which all dividends that are expected to be distributed to stockholders in the future are discounted to estimate the value of the equity

dividend policy the overall policy concerning the distribution of value from a firm to its stockholders

dividend reinvestment program (DRIP) a program in which a company sells new shares, commission free, to dividend recipients who elect to automatically reinvest their dividends in the company's stock

dividend yield a stock's dividend payout divided by its current price

dividend something of value distributed to a firm's stockholders on a pro-rata basis—that is, in proportion to the percentage of the firm's shares that they own

E

earnings per share (EPS) net income divided by the number of common shares outstanding

economic order quantity (EOQ) order quantity that minimizes the total costs incurred to order and hold inventory

effective annual interest rate (EAR) the annual interest rate that reflects compounding within a year

effective annual yield (EAY) the annual yield that takes compounding into account; another name for the *effective annual interest rate (EAR)*

efficient capital market market where prices rapidly reflect the knowledge and expectations of all investors

efficient market hypothesis a theory concerning the extent to which information is reflected in security prices and how information is incorporated into security prices

enterprise value the value of a company's equity plus the value of its debt; also the present value of the total cash flows the company's assets are expected to generate in the future

equivalent annual cost (EAC) the annual dollar amount of an annuity that has a life equal to that of a project and that also has a present value equal to the present value of some cash inflows or outflows from the project; the term comes from the fact that the EAC calculation is often used to calculate a constant annual cost associated with projects in order to make comparisons

Eurocredits short- to medium-term loans of a Eurocurrency to multinational corporations and governments of medium- to high-credit quality

Eurocurrency a time deposit that is in a bank located in a country different from the country that issued the currency

Eurodollar a U.S. dollar deposited in a bank outside the United States

ex-dividend date the first day on which a stock trades without the rights to a dividend

exercise (expiration) date the last date on which an option can be exercised

exercise (strike) price the price at which the owner of an option has the right to buy or sell the underlying asset

expected return an average of the possible returns from an investment, where each return is weighted by the probability that it will occur

external funding needed (EFN) the additional debt or equity a firm must raise from external sources to meet its total funding requirements

extra dividend a dividend that is generally paid at the same time as a regular cash dividend to distribute additional value

F

face value, or par value the amount on which interest is calculated and that is owed to the bondholder when a bond reaches maturity

factor an individual or a financial institution, such as a bank or a business finance company, which buys accounts receivable without recourse

fair market value the value of a business to a typical investor

finance balance sheet a balance sheet that is based on market values of expected cash flows

financial intermediation converting of securities with one set of characteristics into securities with another set of characteristics

financial leverage the use of debt in a firm's capital structure; the more debt, the higher the financial leverage

financial option the right to buy or sell a financial security, such as a share of stock, on or before a specified date for a specified price

financial plan a plan outlining the investments a firm intends to make and how it will finance them

financial planning the process by which management decides what types of investments the firm needs to make and how to finance those investments

financial ratio a number from a financial statement that has been scaled by dividing by another financial number

financial restructuring a combination of financial transactions that changes the capital structure of the firm without affecting its real assets

financial risk the risk in the cash flows to stockholders that is due to the way in which the firm has financed its activities

financial statement analysis the use of financial statements to evaluate a company's overall performance and assess its strengths and shortcomings

firm value, or enterprise value the total value of the firm's assets; it equals the value of the equity financing plus the value of the debt financing used by the firm

firm's marginal tax rate (t) the tax rate that is applied to each additional dollar of earnings at a firm

firm-commitment underwriting underwriting agreement in which the underwriter purchases securities for a specified price and resells them

fixed costs costs that do not vary directly with the number of units sold

fixed-income securities debt instruments that pay interest in amounts that are fixed for the life of the contract

flexible current asset investment strategy current asset investment strategy that involves keeping high balances of current assets on hand

foreign exchange markets international markets where currencies are bought and sold in wholesale amounts

foreign exchange rate risk, or exchange rate risk the uncertainty associated with future exchange rate movements

formal line of credit a contractual agreement between a bank and a firm under which the bank has a legal obligation to lend funds to the firm up to a preset limit

forward rate a rate agreed on today for an exchange to take place at a specified date in the future

free cash flow from the firm (FCFF) approach an income approach to valuation in which all free cash flows the assets are expected to generate in the future are discounted to estimate the enterprise value

free cash flow to equity (FCFE) approach an income approach to valuation in which all cash flows that are expected to be available for distribution to stockholders in the future are discounted to estimate the value of the equity

future value (FV) the value of an investment after it earns interest for one or more periods

future value of an annuity (FVA) the value of an annuity at some point in the future

G

general cash offer a sale of debt or equity, open to all investors, by a company that has previously sold stock to the public

generally accepted accounting principles (GAAP) a set of rules that defines how companies are to prepare financial statements

globalization the removal of barriers to free trade and the integration of national economies

going-concern value the difference between adjusted book value and the value of a business as a going concern (the present value of the expected cash flows)

growing annuity an annuity in which the cash flows increase at a constant rate

growing perpetuity a cash flow stream that grows at a constant rate forever

H

hedge a financial transaction intended to reduce risk

I

income statement a financial statement that reports a firm's profits or losses over a period of time

incremental additions to working capital (Add WC) the investments in working capital items, such as accounts receivable, inventory, and accounts payable, that must be made if the project is pursued

incremental after-tax free cash flows (FCF) the difference between the total after-tax free cash flows at a firm with a project and the total after-tax free cash flows at the same firm without that project; a measure of a project's total impact on the free cash flows at a firm

incremental capital expenditures (Cap Exp) the investments in property, plant, and equipment and other long-term assets that must be made if a project is pursued

incremental cash flow from operations (CF Opns) the cash flow that a project generates after all operating expenses and taxes have been paid but before any cash outflows for investments

incremental depreciation and amortization (D&A) the depreciation and amortization charges that are associated with a project

incremental net operating profits after tax (NOPAT) a measure of the impact of a project on the firm's cash net income, excluding any interest expenses associated with financing the project

independent projects projects whose cash flows are unrelated

indirect bankruptcy costs costs associated with changes in the behavior of people who deal with a firm when the firm gets into financial distress

informal line of credit a verbal agreement between a bank and a firm under which the firm can borrow an amount of money up to an agreed-on limit.

information asymmetry the situation in which one party in a business transaction has information that is unavailable to the other parties in the transaction

initial public offering (IPO) the first offering of a corporation's stock to the public

insolvency the inability to pay debts when they are due

intangible assets nonphysical assets such as patents, mailing lists, or brand names

interest on interest interest earned on interest that is earned in previous periods

interest rate risk uncertainty about future bond values that is caused by the unpredictability of interest rates

internal growth rate (IGR) the maximum growth rate that a firm can achieve without external financing

internal rate of return (IRR) the discount rate at which the present value of a project's expected cash inflows equals the present value of the project's outflows

inventory carrying costs expenses associated with maintaining inventory, including interest forgone on money invested in inventory, storage costs, taxes, and insurance

investment banks firms that underwrite new security issues and provide broker-dealer services

investment value the value of a business to a specific investor

investment-grade bonds bonds with low risk of default that are rated Baa (BBB) or above

K

key person discount an adjustment to a business value estimate that is made to reflect the potential loss of value associated with the unexpected departure of a key person

L

limited liability partnerships (LLPs) hybrid business organizations that combine some of the advantages of corporations and partnerships; in general, income to the partners is taxed only as personal income, but the partners have limited liability

limited liability the legal liability of a limited partner or stockholder in a business, which extends only to the capital contributed or the amount invested

liquidating dividend the final dividend that is paid to stockholders when a firm is liquidated

London Interbank Offer Rate (LIBOR) the interest rate British-based banks charge each other for short-term loans. Also, commonly used as the base rate for Eurodollar loans that are not between two banks

long-term funding strategy financing strategy that relies on long-term debt and equity to finance both fixed assets and working capital

lumpy assets fixed assets added as large discrete units; these assets may not be used to full capacity for some time, leaving the company with excess capacity

M

marginal tax rate the tax rate paid on the last dollar of income earned

market informational efficiency the degree to which current market prices reflect relevant information and, therefore, the true value of the security

market operational efficiency the degree to which the transaction costs of bringing buyers and sellers together are minimized

market portfolio the portfolio of all assets

market risk a term commonly used to refer to nondiversifiable, or systematic, risk

market value the price at which an item can be sold

marketability the ease with which a security can be sold and converted into cash

maturity matching strategy financing strategy that matches the maturities of liabilities and assets

Modified Accelerated Cost Recovery System (MACRS) 120 the accelerated depreciation method that has been in use for U.S. federal taxes since the Tax Reform Act of 1986 went into effect

modified internal rate of return (MIRR) an internal rate of return (IRR) measure which assumes that cash inflows are reinvested at the opportunity cost of capital until the end of the project

money center banks large banks that transact in both the national and international money markets

money market a market where short-term financial instruments are traded

multinational corporation a business firm that operates in more than one country

multiples analysis a valuation approach that uses stock price or other value multiples for public companies to estimate the value of another company's stock or its entire business

multistage-growth dividend model a model that allows for varying dividend growth rates in the near term, followed by a constant long-term growth rate; another term used to describe the supernormal-growth model discussed in Chapter 9

mutually exclusive projects projects for which acceptance of one precludes acceptance of the other

N

net cash flow a firm's actual cash receipts less cash payments in a given period

net present value (NPV) method a method of evaluating a capital investment project which measures the difference between its cost and the present value of its expected cash flows

net working capital the dollar difference between current assets and current liabilities

nominal dollars dollar amounts that are not adjusted for inflation. Nominal dollar amounts from different time periods cannot be compared directly to each other

nominal rate of interest the rate of interest unadjusted for inflation

nondiversifiable or systematic risk risk that cannot be eliminated through diversification

non-investment-grade bonds bonds rated below Baa (or BBB) by rating agencies; often called *speculative-grade bonds, high-yield bonds,* or *junk bonds*

nonoperating assets (NOA) cash or other assets that are not required to support the operations of a business

normal distribution a symmetric frequency distribution that is completely described by its mean and standard deviation; also known as a bell curve due to its shape

North American Industry Classification System (NAICS) a classification system for businesses introduced to refine and replace the older SIC codes

NPV profile a graph showing NPV as a function of the discount rate

O

offer (ask) price the price at which a securities dealer seeks to sell a given stock

open-market repurchase the repurchase of shares by a company in the open market

operating cycle the average time between receipt of raw materials and receipt of cash for the sale of finished goods made from those materials

operating leverage a measure of the relative amounts of fixed and variable costs in a project's cost structure; operating leverage is higher with more fixed costs

opportunity cost of capital the return an investor gives up when his or her money is invested in one asset rather than the best alternative asset

opportunity cost the return from the best alternative investment with similar risk that an investor gives up when he or she makes a certain investment

optimal capital structure the capital structure that minimizes the cost of financing a firm's activities

option payoff function the function that shows how the value of an option varies with the value of the underlying asset

ordinary annuity an annuity in which payments are made at the ends of the periods

P

partnership two or more owners joined together legally to manage a business and share in its profits

par-value bonds bonds that sell at par value, or face value; whenever a bond's coupon rate is equal to the market rate of interest on similar bonds, the bond will sell at par

payable date the date on which a dividend is paid by a company

Glossary

payback period the length of time required to recover a project's initial cost

pecking order theory the theory that in financing projects, managers first use retained earnings, which they view as the least expensive form of capital, then debt, and finally externally raised equity, which they view as the most expensive

percent of sales model a type of simple financial planning model that assumes that most income statement and balance sheet accounts vary proportionally with sales

permanent working capital the minimum level of working capital that a firm will always have on its books

perpetuity a series of level cash flows that continue forever

per-unit contribution the amount that is left over from the sale of a single unit after all the variable costs associated with that unit have been paid; this is the amount that is available to help cover FC for the project

portfolio the collection of assets an investor owns

post a specific location on the floor of a stock exchange at which auctions for a particular security take place

postaudit review an audit to compare actual project results with the results projected in the capital budgeting proposal

preferred stock an equity share in a corporation that entitles the owner to preferred treatment over owners of common stock with respect to dividend payments and claims against the firm's assets in the event of bankruptcy or liquidation but that typically has no voting rights

preliminary prospectus the initial registration statement filed with the SEC by a company preparing to issue securities in the public market; it contains detailed information about the issuer and the proposed issue

premium bonds bonds that sell at above par (face) value

present value (PV) the current value of future cash flows discounted at the appropriate discount rate

present value of an annuity (PVA) the present value of the cash flows from an annuity, discounted at the appropriate discount rate

pretax operating cash flow (EBITDA) break-even point the number of units that must be sold for pretax operating cash flow to equal $0

pretax operating cash flow earnings before interest, taxes, depreciation, and amortization, or EBITDA

price-earnings (P/E) ratio price per share divided by earnings per share

primary market a financial market in which new security issues are sold for the first time

principal the amount of money on which interest is paid

private information information that is not available to all investors

private placement the sale of an unregistered security directly to an investor, such as an insurance company

privately held corporations corporations whose stock is not traded in public markets; also called *closely held corporations*

pro forma financial statements projected financial statements that reflect a set of assumptions concerning investment, financing, and operating decisions

productive assets the tangible and intangible assets a firm uses to generate cash flows

profitability index (PI) a measure of the value a project generates for each dollar invested in that project

progressive tax system a tax system in which the marginal tax rate at low levels of income is lower than the marginal tax rate at high levels of income

public information information that is available to all investors

public markets markets regulated by the Securities and Exchange Commission in which large amounts of debt and equity are publicly traded

public markets financial markets where securities registered with the SEC are sold

pure-play comparable a comparable company that is in exactly the same business as the project or business being analyzed

put option an option to sell the underlying asset

put premium the price that the buyer of a put option pays the seller of that option

put-call parity the relation between the value of a call option on an asset and the value of a put option on the same asset that has the same exercise price

Q

quoted interest rate a simple annual interest rate, such as the APR

R

real dollars inflation-adjusted dollars; the actual purchasing power of dollars stated in "real" terms is the same regardless of when those dollars are received

real investment policy the policy relating to the criteria the firm uses in deciding which real assets (projects) to invest in

real option an option for which the underlying asset is a real asset

real rate of interest the interest rate that would exist in the absence of inflation

realized yield for a bond, the interest rate at which the present value of the actual cash flows generated by a bond equals the bond's price

record date the date by which an investor must be a stockholder of record in order to receive a dividend

regular cash dividend a cash dividend that is paid on a regular basis, typically quarterly

repatriation of earnings restrictions restrictions placed by a foreign government on the amount of cash that can be repatriated, or returned, to a parent company by a subsidiary doing business in the foreign country

replacement cost the cost of duplicating the assets of a business in their present form on the valuation date

residual cash flows the cash remaining after a firm has paid operating expenses and what it owes creditors and in taxes; can be paid to the owners as a cash dividend or reinvested in the business

restrictive current asset investment strategy current asset investment strategy that involves keeping the level of current assets at a minimum

Rule of 72 a rule proposing that the time required to double money invested (TDM) approximately equals 72/i, where i is expressed as a percentage

S

scenario analysis an analytical method concerned with how the results from a financial analysis will change under alternative scenarios

seasoned public offering the sale of securities to the public by a firm that already has publicly traded securities outstanding

secondary market a financial market in which the owners of outstanding securities can resell them to other investors

Security Market Line (SML) a plot of the relation between expected return and systematic risk

semistrong form (of the efficient market hypothesis) the theory that security prices reflect all public information but not all private information

sensitivity analysis examination of the sensitivity of the results from a financial analysis to changes in individual assumptions

shelf registration a type of SEC registration that allows firms to register to sell securities over a two-year period and, during that time, take the securities "off the shelf" and sell them as needed

shortage costs costs incurred because of lost production and sales or illiquidity

short-term funding strategy financing strategy that relies on short-term debt to finance all seasonal working capital and a portion of permanent working capital and fixed assets

simple interest interest earned on the original principal amount only

simulation analysis an analytical method that uses a computer to quickly examine a large number of scenarios and obtain probability estimates for various values in a financial analysis

sole proprietorship a business owned by a single individual

special dividend a one-time payment to stockholders that is normally used to distribute a large amount of value

specialist the trader designated by an exchange to represent orders placed by public customers at auctions of securities; specialists handle a small set of securities and are also allowed to act as dealers

spot rate the exchange rate in the market at any given point in time

stakeholder anyone other than an owner (stockholder) with a claim on the cash flows of a firm, including employees, suppliers, creditors, and the government

stand-alone principle the principle that allows us to treat each project as a stand-alone firm when we perform an NPV analysis

standard deviation (σ) the square root of the variance

Standard Industrial Classification (SIC) System a numerical system developed by the U.S. government to classify businesses according to the type of activity they perform

statement of cash flows a financial statement that shows a firm's cash receipts and cash payments for a period of time

stock dividend a distribution of new shares to existing stockholders in proportion to the percentage of shares that they own (pro rata); the value of the assets in a company does not change with a stock dividend

stock repurchase the purchase of stock by a company from it stockholders; an alternative way for the company to distribute value to the stockholders

stock split a pro-rata distribution of new shares to existing stockholders that is not associated with any change in the assets held by the firm; stock splits involve larger increases in the number of shares than stock dividends

strategic planning the process by which management establishes the firm's long-term goals, the strategies that will be used to achieve the goals, and the capabilities that are needed to sustain the firm's competitive position

strong form (of the efficient market hypothesis) the theory that security prices reflect all available information

sustainable growth rate (SGR) the rate of growth that a firm can sustain without selling additional equity while maintaining the same capital structure

T

tangible assets physical assets such as property, plant, and equipment

targeted stock repurchase a stock repurchase that targets a specific stockholder

tender offer an open offer by a company to purchase shares

term loan a business loan with a maturity greater than one year

term structure of interest rates the relation between yield and term to maturity

terminal value the value of the expected free cash flows beyond the period over which they are explicitly forecast

time value of money the difference in value between a dollar in hand today and a dollar promised in the future; a dollar today is worth more than a dollar in the future

total holding period return the total return on an asset over a specific period of time or holding period

trade credit credit extended by one business to another

trade-off theory the theory that managers trade off the benefits against the costs of using debt to identify the optimal capital structure for a firm

transactions analysis a valuation approach that uses transactions data from the sale of businesses to estimate the value of another company's stock or its entire business

transnational corporation a multinational firm that has widely dispersed ownership and that is managed from a global perspective

treasury stock stock that the firm has purchased back from investors

trend analysis analysis of trends in financial data

true (intrinsic) value for a security, the value of the cash flows an investor who owns that security can expect to receive in the future

Truth-in-Lending Act a federal law requiring lenders to fully inform borrowers of important information related to loans, including the annual percentage rate charged

Truth-in-Savings Act a federal law requiring institutions offering consumer savings vehicles, such as certificates of deposit (CD), to fully inform consumers of important information about the savings vehicles, including the annual percentage rate paid

U

underinvestment problem the incentive that stockholders in a financially leveraged firm have to turn down positive NPV projects when the firm is in financial distress

underlying asset the asset from which the value of an option is derived

underpricing offering new securities for sale at a price below their true value

underwriting syndicate a group of underwriters that joins forces to reduce underwriting risk

V

valuation date the date on which a value estimate applies

vanilla bonds a debt security whose terms and conditions are standardized and well-known to market participants

variable costs costs that vary directly with the number of units sold

variance (σ^2) a measure of the uncertainty surrounding an outcome

venture capitalists individuals or firms that invest by purchasing equity in new businesses and often provide the entrepreneurs with business advice

W

weak form (of the efficient market hypothesis) the theory that security prices reflect all information in past prices but do not reflect all private or all public information

wealth the economic value of the assets someone possesses

weighted average cost of capital (WACC) the weighted average of the costs of the different types of capital (debt and equity) that have been used to finance a firm; the cost of each type of capital is weighted by the proportion of the total capital that it represents

Y

yield curve a graph representing the term structure of interest rates, with the term to maturity on the horizontal axis and the yield on the vertical axis

yield to maturity for a bond, the discount rate that makes the present value of the coupon and principal payments equal to the price of the bond

SUBJECT INDEX

A

Abandoning projects, 679–680
Accelerated depreciation, 61, 68
Accounts payable, 464–465
  as current liability, 59
  forecasting, 381
  as short-term financing, 482
Accounts receivable, 464
  aging, 474–475
  as current assets, 59
  forecasting, 381
  management of, 472–475
  realization principle for, 56
  terms of sale for, 472–474
Accounts receivable financing, 483–484
Accounts receivable turnover, 97
Accounting controls, internal, 18
Accounting earnings, cash flows vs., 363
Accounting firm scandals, 18, 22, 53, 129–130
Accounting operating profits, 397, 406n.4. *See also* Earnings before interest and taxes; EBIT plus depreciation and amortization
Accounting operating profit (EBIT) break-even point, 410–412
Accounting principles, 55
  GAAP, 55–56
  international, 56–57
Accounting rate of return (ARR), 331
Accounting standards:
  FASB statements, 55
  in international finance, 699
Accounting statement of cash flows, 356
Accrual accounting, 70n.6
Accrued taxes, as current liability, 59
Accumulated depreciation account, 61
Acid-test ratio, 93
Additional paid-in capital account, 61–62
Add WC, *see* Incremental additions to working capital
Adjustable-rate mortgages (ARMs), 625
Adjusted book value, 600
Adjusted book value valuation approach, 600–602
After-tax cost of debt, 436–438, 532n.4
Agency conflicts, 15–20, **16**
  and agency relationships, 15–16, 21
  aligning interests of management and stockholders, 16–18
  for different forms of business, 589
  manager-stockholder, 16
  with ownership and control, 15
  payoff functions leading to, 681–684
  in private equity firms, 517
  and regulatory reforms, 18–20

Agency costs, 16, 547–550
  of debt, 681–683
  of equity, 683–684
  ethics conflicts involving, 21
  stockholder-lender, 548–550
  stockholder-manager, 547–548
Agency relationships, 15–16, 21
Agents, 15
Aging accounts receivable, 474–475
Aging schedule, 474
American currency quote, 703
American options, 668
Amortization, 180. *See also* Incremental depreciation and amortization
Amortization expense, 68
Amortization schedule, 180–183
Amortized loans, 180
Angels (angel investors), 495
Annual percentage rate (APR), 194
  on credit cards, 208
  disclosure of, 194
Annual reports, 54–55
Annuities, 175–188
  finding monthly/yearly payments from, 178–180
  future value of, 186–188
  growing, 192–193
  interest rate for, 183–186
  loan amortization schedule for, 180–183
  ordinary, 175
  present value of, 175–186
Annuities due, 190–191
Annuity transformation method, 191
Appendixes, in business plan, 597
APR, *see* Annual percentage rate
Arbitrage, 673
ARMs (adjustable-rate mortgages), 625
Arm's-length transactions, assumption of, 55
ARR (accounting rate of return), 331
Asian stock markets, 281
Ask price, 283
Ask quotations (exchange rate), 703
Assets:
  on balance sheet, 57–58
  in balance sheet identity, 428–429
  in bankruptcy, 4
  book value of, 63–64
  capital, 5. *See also* Capital Asset Pricing Model
  cash flows associated with, 360, 528
  on common-size balance sheets, 88–89
  cost of existing assets, 386–387
  current, *see* Current assets
  current market value of, 63

  depreciation of, 372–374
  financing, 481
  fixed, 64, 71, 640, 646
  harvesting, 384–385
  historical value of, 63
  intangible, 60, 68, 360
  leverage and, 536
  long-term, 60–61, 481
  lumpy, 646
  market value of, 63–64, 429–430
  nationalization of, 709
  of new firms, 496
  nonoperating, 607
  productive, 2, 5, 6. *See also* Long-term assets
  replacing, 314, 385–386
  return on, *see* Return on assets
  salvage value of, 374–377
  short-term, 481. *See also* Working capital
  tangible, 2, 60, 360
  taxes on sale of, 377–378
  underlying options, 665, 671–672, 675
  underlying risk of, 533
  underlying value of, 13
  value of, 4
  variety of, 2–3
Asset substitution problem, 549, 682
Asset turnover:
  profit margins vs., 108–109
  total, 98, 108
Asset turnover ratios, 95–98
Asset use efficiency, 108
Assumptions:
  of arm's-length transactions, 55
  changing, in Microsoft Excel, 404–405
  going concern, 56
  in sensitivity analysis, 413
  in simplifying stock valuation, 291–301
Auction markets, 284
Audit committee, 11, 19
Audited financial statements, 11, 54, 87
  for raising new equity, 573
  in valuation of companies, 613
Auditors:
  external, 11
  internal, 10, 11
Average collection period, 97
Average tax rate, 76–77, 371–372

B

β, *see* Beta
Bacanovic, Peter, 310
"Backing in," 53

Subject Index

Balance sheet, 57–66, **58**
  book-value vs. market-value, 63–66
  common-size, 88–90
  current assets and liabilities on, 59–60
  dividends on, 569
  effect of decision making on, 5
  equity accounts on, 61–63
  finance, 428–429
  in financial planning models, 634–635, 638–644
  fixed assets on, 640
  historical trends on, 639
  liability and equity on, 641
  long-term assets and liabilities on, 60–61
  pro forma, 634–635, 638–644
  relationship of other statements and, 73–75
  stock repurchases on, 569
  working capital accounts on, 639–640
Balance sheet identity, 428–429
Banks:
  commercial, 39
  investment, 31–32
  largest, 717
  money center, 32
Banking, international, 716–719
Bank loans, 518–520
  from commercial banks, 518–519
  Eurocredit, 718–719
  international, 716–718
  pricing model for, 518–519
  prime-rate, 518, 519
  short-term, 482–483
  term, 518, 519
Bank loan pricing model, 518–519
Bankruptcy, 4, 249
  losses limited in, 682
  from mismanagement of working capital, 6–7
Bankruptcy costs, 545–547
  direct, 545–546
  indirect, 546
Base salaries, 17
Basis points, 272n.4, 519
Benchmarks, 88
  in financial statement analysis, 112–114
  of performance, 88
Bermudan options, 668
Bernanke, Ben, 27–28
Best-effort basis, 32n.4, 506
Best-effort underwriting, 504, 506
Beta (β), 236, 238
  for common stock, 430
  in estimating cost of debt, 439–441
Bid price, 283
Bid quotations (exchange rate), 703
Binomial pricing model (options), 673–675
Boards of directors, 17
  expanded powers of, 19
  independence of, 18
  shift in behavior of, 20
Bonds, 252–269
  call provisions for, 270
  corporate, 252–254, 270–272, 513–514
  cost of issuing, 513–514
  estimating current cost of, 434–435
  Eurobonds, 714–715
  foreign, 714
  general cash offers for, 512
  historical returns on, 221–224
  interest rate risk with, 266–269

issuance costs for, 435, 543
as perpetuities, 188
vanilla, 512
yields of, 262–266
zero coupon, 156
Bond markets:
  for corporate bonds, 252
  international, 714–716
Bond prices, 252–253. *See also* Bond valuation
  and interest rates, 266–267
  with semiannual compounding, 261–262
  volatility of, 267
  and yields, 258–259
Bond ratings, 271–272
Bond theorems, 266–269
Bond valuation, 254–262
  discount bonds, 257
  formula for, 255–256
  in international finance, 699
  par-value bonds, 257
  premium bonds, 257
  with semiannual compounding, 259–260
  using financial calculator for, 256–257
  for zero coupon bonds, 260–262
Bonuses, 17
Book value, 55
  adjusted book value valuation approach, 600–602
  of current assets, 63–64
  of fixed assets, 64
  of liabilities, 64
  of stockholders' equity, 64
Book-value balance sheet, 65–66
Book value rate of return, *see* Accounting rate of return
Bootstrapping:
  in business formation, 494–495
  in private markets, 515
Borrower-spenders, 30
Borrowing rates, 29
"Bottom line," *see* Net income
Break-even analysis, 408–412
  accounting, 410–412
  for cash flow, 408–410
  economic, 412
  in international finance, 699
Brokers, 34, 283
Broker markets, 283
Budgets:
  capital, 630. *See also* Capital budgeting
  cash, 592–595, 628, 629, 631
Business culture, 22, 23
Business ethics, 20–23
  and accounting firm scandals, 53, 129–130
  in company-owned life insurance, 524–525
  compensation levels, 691–692
  and compliance and ethics director, 11
  conflicts of, 21–22
  consequences of mistakes in, 22
  ethics programs, 19
  everyday ethics vs., 20–21
  and insider trading, 310–311
  manager incentives for, 17
  as part of culture, 22, 23
  and regulatory reform, 18
  and salmonella outbreak, 394–395
  and student credit cards, 207–208
  in subprime mortgage market, 624–626
Business failures, 588
Business financial companies, 40

Business formation, 587–595
  by bootstrapping, 494–495
  choosing organizational form in, 588–591
  deciding to proceed with, 588
  financial considerations in, 591–595
  initial funding for, 495
  raising capital for, *see* Raising capital
  usual process for, 494
Business growth, *see* Growth of business
Business investment, 42n.7
Business language, 696–697
Business plan, 314, **596**–597
  divisional, 630
  key elements of, 597
  for seeking venture capital, 495
  in venture capital funding cycle, 498
Business risk, 533
  financial risk, total risk, and, 534
  in international finance, 699
Business strategy, 629. *See also* Strategic plan
Business valuation, 598–616. *See also* Firm value
  approaches to, 599
  controlling interest vs. minority interest in, 615
  cost approaches to, 600–602
  fundamental principles for, 598–599
  income approaches to, 607–612
  in international finance, 699
  and investors' points of view, 599
  key person discount in, 616
  market approaches to, 602–606
  for public vs. private companies, 613–614
  as time-specific, 598
  for young vs. mature companies, 614–615
Buy-vs.-build analysis, 600, 607

C

CAGR (compound annual growth rate), 159
Call interest premium (CIP), 270
Call options, 665–667, **666**
  exercising, 668
  limits on value of, 669–671
  variables affecting values of, 671–673
Call premiums, 666–667
Call provisions, 270
Cap Exp, *see* Incremental capital expenditures
Capital:
  cost of, *see* Cost of capital
  for different forms of business, 589
  and flight to quality, 515
  net working capital, 6
  for new businesses, 590
  opportunity cost of, 316
  raising, *see* Raising capital
Capital Asset Pricing Model (CAPM), 238–242
  common stock cost of equity with, 439–441
  and controlling ownership interest, 615
  and portfolio returns, 240–242
  as preferred model, 445
  preferred stock cost of equity with, 446
  Security Market Line in, 239–240
Capital assets, 5
Capital budget, 630. *See also* Investment plan
Capital budgeting, 3, 313–344
  accounting rate of return in, 331
  asset harvesting decisions in, 384–385
  asset replacement decisions in, 385–386
  capital rationing in, 415–419
  cash flows in, 356. *See also* Future cash flows

decision making in, 3–5, 314, 384–387, 630
depreciation methods in, 372–374
importance of, 313
information used in, 315
internal rate of return in, 331–342
in international finance management, 708–712
net present value in, 317–326
opportunity costs in, 386–387
payback period in, 326–330
in practice, 342–344
process for, 313–315
project classification for, 315
for projects with different lives, 381–384
techniques used in, 313
Capital gains taxes, 573–574
Capital intensity ratio, 640
Capital markets, 6, 35
efficiency of, 250–252
global, 713–716
Capital rationing, 316, 415–419
across multiple periods, 418–419
in a single period, 416–418
Capital requirements and uses, in business plan, 597
Capital structure, 6, 527–554
choosing, 550–554
decisions on, 633
dividends in management of, 573
and financial risk, 533
in financing plan, 630
and Modigliani and Miller propositions, 528–537
optimal, 527–528, 544–545
pecking order theory of, 551, 552
for selected industries, 552
trade-off theory of, 544–545, 550–552
use of debt in, 537–550
CAPM, *see* Capital Asset Pricing Model
Carrying costs, 471–472, 475–476
Cash, 464
collection of, 477–478
as current asset, 59
forecasting, 381
management and budgeting of, 477–479
reasons for holding, 477
retained earnings vs., 62
sources and uses of, 71, 574
Cash budgets, 628, 629, 631
for new businesses, 592–595
using, 595
Cash collection cycles, 478
Cash conversion cycle, 465–466, 468–470
Cash coverage, 102
Cash dividends, 563. *See also* Dividends
Cash equivalents, forecasting, 381
Cash flows, 2–4, 70–71, 356–381
in capital budgeting vs. accounting, 356
conventional, 335
debt as incentive to focus on, 543–544
differing from net income, 533n.6
estimating, 607
expected, 378–379
free, *see* Incremental after-tax free cash flows
future, *see* Future cash flows
generation of, 3–4
importance of, 71
in international finance, 699
level, 175–191

management decisions affecting, 14–15
multiple, 168–174
net income vs., 70–71
for new businesses, 591–595
from operations, 359–360. *See also* EBIT plus depreciation and amortization
from overseas capital projects, 708–709
past, 356
present value of, 529
residual, 4
risk with, 13
sensitivity to fixed vs. variable costs, 397
that grow at constant rate, 192–194
timing of, 12
and use of dividends vs. stock repurchases, 575
Cash flow (EBITDA) break-even analysis, 408–410, 592
Cash Flow DOL, *see* Degree of pretax cash flow operating leverage
Cash flow identity, 574, 575
Cash on delivery (COD), 472
Cash reconciliation, on statement of cash flows, 73
Casualty insurance companies, 39
C-corporations, 589
capital for, 590–591
characteristics of, 589
taxes on, 591
CEO, *see* Chief executive officer
Certified public accounting (CPA) firms, 11
CFO, *see* Chief financial officer
CF Opns, *see* Incremental cash flow from operations
Changes in revenue:
EBITDA sensitivity to, 398–401
EBIT sensitivity to, 401–405
fixed costs and, 397
Chicago Board of Trade, 36
Chicago Board Options Exchange, 36
Chief accountants, 9
Chief executive officer (CEO), 9, 10, 17
Chief financial officer (CFO), 9–11
China, doing business in, 312, 693–694, 698
Chinese stock market, 281
CIP (call interest premium), 270
CLOs (collateralized loan obligations), 625
Closely held corporations, *see* Privately held corporations
Closing, of firm-commitment offerings, 505, 511
CO, *see* Crossover level of unit sales
COD (cash on delivery), 472
Coefficient of variation (CV), 225–226
COLI, *see* Company-owned life insurance
Collateral, 483
Collateralized loan obligations (CLOs), 625
Collection time (cash), 477–478
Commercial banks, 39
Commercial bank loans, 518–519
Commercial paper, 483, 503n.2
Commodity price risk, options for, 684
Common-size financial statements, 88–91
balance sheet, 88–90
income statement, 90–91
Common stock, 286
cost of equity for, 439–445
cost of issuing, 513–514
and debt-to-equity ratio, 531–537
initial public offerings of, 41

market value of, 61–62
valuation of, 287–291
Common stock accounts, 61–62
Communication, in international business, 696–697
Company overview, in business plan, 597
Company-owned life insurance (COLI), 524–525
Comparables, 453, 602–606
Compensating balances, 477, 482
Compensation:
ethics in, 691–692
excess, 613
of managers, 16–17
Competition, potential, 512
Competitive financial systems, 29
Competitive sales, 511–512
Compliance and ethics director, 11
Compliance programs, 19, 20
Compound annual growth rate (CAGR), 159
Compound growth rates, 158–160
Compounding, 134, 137
for bonds, 259–260
continuous, 144–145
frequency of, 143
and future value, 135–137
power of, 141–146
with single-period investment, 135–136
with two-period investment, 136–137
Compound interest, 137–139
Concentration account system, 478
Conflicts of interest, 2, 21
Consols, 188, 540
Constant-growth dividend model, 293–295, 441–442
Consumers, global, 695
Consumer credit, 464
Consumer price index (CPI), 47
Consumer protection acts, 197
Contingent projects, 315
Control:
and choice of capital structure, 553–554
and form of organization, 589, 590
ownership vs., 15
separation of ownership and, 591
value associated with, 606
with venture capital funding, 500
Controllers, 9–11
Controlling ownership interest, 615
Control premium, 615
Conventional cash flows, 334, 335
Convertible bonds, 254
Corporate bonds, 252–254
call provision for, 270
convertible, 254
cost of issuing, 513–514
rating system for, 271–272
risk premiums for, 272
vanilla, 253
zero coupon, 253–254
Corporate debt, 252
Corporate governance, 19
Corporations, 8–9
characteristics of, 589
financial liabilities of, 591
and financial system, 40–41
life of, 590
multinational, 695, 696
stateless, 695
transnational, 695

Correlation, 229–230
Correlation of 0, 230
Costs:
   agency, 16, 547–550
   bankruptcy, 545–546
   carrying, 471–472, 475–476
   for different forms of business, 589
   of dividends, 573–574
   equivalent annual, 382–384
   of financial distress, 545. *See also* Bankruptcy costs
   fixed, 379–380
   of general cash offers, 513–514
   of IPOs, 502, 509–510
   of projects, 320
   reorder, 475–476
   replacement, 600
   of trade credit, 473
   transaction, 34
   variable, 379–380
Cost approaches to business valuation, 600–602
Cost of assets, leverage and, 536
Cost of capital, 42, 316, 336
   determining, 320
   nominal, 369
   overall, 427–431. *See also* Weighted average cost of capital
   real, 369
   use of term, 369n.3
   in venture capital funding, 500
Cost of debt, 432–438, 532n.4, 544–550
   agency costs, 547–550, 681–683
   bankruptcy costs, 545–547
   in decision making, 438
   estimating, 433–437
   in international finance, 699
   and leverage, 532n.5, 536
   in M&M proposition 2, 532n.5
   taxes and, 435–436
   use of term, 532n.4
Cost of equity, 438–446, 532n.4
   agency costs, 683–684
   with Capital Asset Pricing Model, 439–441, 615
   for common stock, 439–445
   with constant-growth dividend model, 441–442
   in international finance, 699
   and leverage, 536
   with multistage-growth dividend model, 442–444
   for preferred stock, 445–446
   use of term, 532n.4
Cost principle, 55–56
Cost structure, business risk and, 534
Country risk, 697, 709–710, 717–718
Coupon payments, 253
Coupon rate, 253
Covariance, 229
Coverage ratios, 101–102
CPA (certified public accounting) firms, 11
CPI (consumer price index), 47
Creative accounting, 12
Credit:
   consumer, 464
   and student debt, 207–208
   terms of sale for, 472
   trade, 464–465
Credit analysis, for bank loans, 519

Credit Card Nation (Robert Manning), 208
Credit cards:
   APR calculations for, 263
   for students, 207–208
Creditors:
   financial analysis for, 86–87
   as stakeholders, 2
Credit risk:
   with bank loans, 519
   with international banking, 716, 717
Crossover level of unit sales (CO), 409
   for EBIT, 411
   for EBITDA, 409
Crossover point, 338
Cross rates, 704–706
Culture:
   of business, 22, 23
   in international business, 697
Cum dividend trades, 565
Currencies, 696, 705. *See also* Foreign exchange rates
Currency risk, with international banking, 717
Current assets, 360, 462
   on balance sheet, 59
   cash flows associated with, 360
   flexible investment strategy for, 471
   inventory, 59–60
   management of, 3
   market value and book value of, 63–64
   restrictive current asset investment strategy, 471
   and use of cash, 71
Current liabilities, 59, 463
Current market values, 63
Current ratio, 92–93
Current value of the underlying asset, 671–672
CV, *see* Coefficient of variation

D

D&A, *see* Incremental depreciation and amortization
Days' payables outstanding (DPO), 467
Days' sales in inventory (DSI), 95–96, 467
Days' sales outstanding (DSO), 97, 467–468
DDM approach, *see* Dividend discount model approach
Dealers, 34, 283
Dealer markets, 283–284
Debt:
   among students, 207–208
   corporate, 252
   cost of, *see* Cost of debt
   long-term, 64
   permanent, 433
   preferred stock as, 286
   sale of, 511. *See also* General cash offers
Debt financing, 3, 6, 526, 537–550. *See also* Capital structure
   benefits of, 537–544
   cost of, 544–550. *See also* Cost of debt
   for growth, 647
   as interest tax shield, 537–543
   tax-induced bias toward, 77
   with vanilla bonds, 512
Debt ratios, 99–101
Debt-to-equity ratio, 100
   common stock and, 531–537
   solving for unknown with, 101
Decision making:
   balance sheet affected by, 5

by boards of directors, 17
   in capital budgeting, 3–5, 314, 384–387, 630
   financial models in, 644
   for financing, 3, 6, 630, 633
   in interests of owner, 2
   for international capital projects, 708
   major factors affecting, 14
   nominal vs. real dollars in, 370
   in private equity firms, 517
   for profit maximization, 12, 13
   stock prices affected by, 14–15
   using cost of debt in, 438
   using expected returns in, 216
   in working capital management, 6–7
Declaration date, 565
Default risk, 99, 270–272
Default risk premium (DRP), 270–272, 519
Deferred revenues, 70
Deferred taxes, 70
Deficit spending units (DSUs), 30n.2
Degree of accounting operating leverage (Accounting DOL), 406–408
Degree of pretax cash flow operating leverage (Cash Flow DOL), 405–406, 408
Dell, Michael, 461
Demand curve, 702
Depletion charges, 70
Depreciation, 60–61. *See also* Incremental depreciation and amortization
   GAAP vs. IRS rules for, 372–374
   on statement of cash flows, 72
Depreciation expense, 68
Derivative securities, 665
   futures as, 36
   options as, 36, 665
Direct bankruptcy costs, 545–546
Direct costs, of IPOs, 510
Direct currency quote, 703
Direct financing, 31–33
   in flow of funds, 30
   indirect financing vs., 39
   market transactions in, 31
Direct search markets, 283
Discounts for lack of marketability, 603n.3
Discount bonds, 257
Discounted payback period, 329–330
Discount factor, 149
Discounting, 134, 149
   of future cash flows, 319
   with multiple-period investment, 149–150
   and present value, 148–150
   with single-period investment, 149
   of zero coupon bonds, 261
Discount rate, 149
   for annuities, 183–186
   and capital structure, 527
   with controlling ownership position, 615
   and cost of debt, 539
   estimating, 427. *See also* Cost of capital
   for individual projects, 452–453
   IRR as, 331
   overall cost of capital as, 428–431
   relations among time, present value, and, 153–155
   WACC as, 449–452
Distribution(s), 32. *See also* Dividends
   as investment banking service, 502, 505
   noncash, 564
   stock dividends, 577–579
   stock splits, 578–579
Diversifiable risk, 232

Subject Index

Diversification, 224–233
  limits of, 232–233
  in market portfolio, 234
  in portfolios with more than one asset, 226–232
  and risk, 232–233
  and single-asset portfolios, 224–226
Dividend discount model (DDM) approach, 611, 612
Dividend payout ratio, 638
Dividend policy, 562, 571–581
  in financing plan, 630
  and firm value, 571–577
  in international finance, 699
  setting, 579–581
  stock dividends and stock splits, 577–579
Dividend reinvestment program (DRIP), 574
Dividends, 562–571, 577–579. *See also* Stock valuation
  benefits of, 572–573
  computing future stock prices, 295–296
  constant-growth dividend model, 293–295
  costs of, 573–574
  decisions on, 633
  double taxation of, 614
  expected, 442
  extra, 563
  liquidating, 564
  mixed (supernormal) growth dividend model, 297–301
  noncash, 564
  payment process for, 564–567
  on preferred stock, 63
  residual cash flows as, 4
  as return of capital, 568n.6
  as signal of strength, 572
  special, 563
  stock, 577–579
  stock repurchases vs., 568–569, 575–577
  taxes on, 77, 568, 573–574
  types of, 563–564
  as use of cash, 71
  zero-growth dividend model, 292–293
Dividend yield, 285
Divisional business plans, 630
DJIA, *see* Dow Jones Industrial Average
Dollar value of net income, 553
Dow Jones Industrial Average (DJIA), 37, 221, 281
DPO (days' payables outstanding), 467
DRIPs (dividend reinvestment programs), 574
DRP, *see* Default risk premium
DSI, *see* Days' sales in inventory
DSO, *see* Days' sales outstanding
DSUs (deficit spending units), 30n.2
Due diligence meetings (IPOs), 504–505
DuPont equation, 107, 110
DuPont system of analysis, 107–112
  applying, 110–111
  DuPont equation, 107, 110
  and maximization of ROE as goal, 112
  ROA equation in, 107–109
  ROE equation in, 109–110
Dutch auction tender offers, 570

E

EAC, *see* Equivalent annual cost
EAR, *see* Effective annual interest rate
Earnings, choice of capital structure and, 553

Earnings before interest and taxes (EBIT), 69, 102, 103
  and Accounting DOL, 406–408
  and amount of interest expense, 539
  break-even point for, 410–412
  in FCF calculation, 362–364, 367–368
  fixed costs and fluctuation in, 403–405
  forecasting, 402–403
  sensitivity to changes in revenue, 401–408
  volatility in, 408
Earnings before taxes (EBT), 69
Earnings per share (EPS), 67, 106
EAY, *see* Effective annual yield
Ebbers, Bernard J., 22
EBIT, *see* Earnings before interest and taxes
EBITDA, *see* EBIT plus depreciation and amortization
EBITDA margin, 103
EBIT plus depreciation and amortization (EBITDA), 69, 102–103
  break-even point for, 408–412
  and Cash Flow DOL, 405–408
  in FCF calculation, 362–364, 367–368
  sensitivity to changes in revenue, 398–401, 405–406
  volatility in, 408
EBIT return on assets (EROA), 104, 105
EBT (earnings before taxes), 69
ECN (electronic communications network), 284
Economic expansions/contractions, 48
Economic growth rate, 442
Economic order quantity (EOQ), 475–476
Economic systems, foreign, 697
Economies of scale:
  with general cash offers, 513–514
  with IPOs, 509
Effective annual interest rate (EAR), 194–198
  for bonds, 434–435
  for loans from factors, 484
  for terms of sale, 472–473
Effective annual yield (EAY), 263–265, **264**
Effective DSO, 474
Efficiency projects, 452
Efficiency ratios, 94–98
Efficient capital market, 250–252
Efficient market hypothesis, 251–252
EFN, *see* External funding needed
Electronic communications network (ECN), 284
Electronic funds transfers, 478
Electronic trading, 34, 37. *See also* NASDAQ
Employees:
  attracting/maintaining, 591
  company-owned insurance on, 524–525
  as stakeholders, 2
End-of-month payment (EOM), 473
Enterprise value, 528, 604, 605. *See also* Business valuation; Firm value
Entrepreneurs, 494
EOM (end-of-month payment), 473
EOQ, *see* Economic order quantity
EPS, *see* Earnings per share
Equilibrium exchange rate, 702–703
Equilibrium rate of interest, 43
Equity. *See also* Stockholders' equity; Stocks
  on common-size balance sheets, 88–89
  cost of, *see* Cost of equity
  cost of issuing, 513–514

  in financial planning models, 641
  general cash offers for, 511, 512. *See also* General cash offers
  long-term, 71
  sale of, 511
Equity accounts, on balance sheet, 61–63
Equity financing, 3, 6, 512, 526. *See also* Capital structure; Cost of equity
Equity interest, of venture capitalists, 498
Equity multiplier, 100–101
Equity valuation, in international finance, 699
Equivalent annual cost (EAC), 382–384
  and replacement of assets, 385–386
  and use of existing assets, 386–387
EROA, *see* EBIT return on assets
Ethics. *See also* Business ethics
  everyday vs. business, 20–21
  and norms in international finance, 699
Ethics programs, 19
Eurobanks, 713
Eurobonds, 714–715
Eurocredit bank loans, 718–719
Eurocredits, 714
Eurocurrency, 713–714
Eurocurrency market, 713–714
Eurodollars, 713
Euromarkets, 713
Europe:
  bond coupon interest in, 259
  business in, 698
European currency quote, 703
European GAAP, 57
European options, 668
Excess compensation, 613
Exchanges, 34, 283
  Chicago Board Options Exchange, 36
  Chinese, 281
  foreign exchange markets, 699–708
  London, 35, 695, 700
  NASDAQ, 8, 37, 283, 579
  New York Stock Exchange, 37. *See also* New York Stock Exchange
  Tokyo, 35, 695, 700
Exchange rates, *see* Foreign exchange rates
Exchange rate risk, *see* Foreign exchange rate risk
Ex-dividend date, 565–566
Executive summary, in business plan, 597
Exercise (expiration) date, 665, 668–671
Exercise (strike) price, 666, 671, 672
Exit strategy (venture capital funding), 499
Expansion, capital expenditures for, 314
Expected cash flows, 378–379
Expected rate of inflation, 44–45, 273
Expected returns, 213–216
  compensation for risk in, 237–238
  in international finance, 699
  and portfolio risk, 241
  on portfolio with more than one asset, 227–228
Expenses:
  amortization, 68
  depreciation, 68
  extraordinary items, 68
  on income statement, 67–68
  matching revenue and, 56
  noncash, 68
  prepaid, 70
Expense accounts, 613
Expiration date (options), *see* Exercise date

756 | Subject Index

External auditors, 11
   expanded powers of, 19
   regulations for, 19
External funding needed (EFN), 636
   determining, 630
   for growth, 647–651
   mathematical model for, 649–650
Extra dividends, 563
Extraordinary items, 68

F

Face value, 253
Factors, 483–484
Failure of businesses, 588
Fair market value, 599
   in adjusted book value approach, 600
   in multiples analysis, 606
Fairness, 22
   of company-owned life insurance, 525
   and insider trading, 311
FASB, *see* Financial Accounting Standards Board
FASB statements, 55
FC, *see* Fixed costs
FCF, *see* Incremental after-tax free cash flows
FCFE approach, *see* Free cash flow to equity approach
FCFF approach, *see* Free cash flow from the firm approach
Federal Drug Administration (FDA), 310
Federal income tax, *see* Income taxes
Federal Open Market Committee (FOMC), 27–28
Federal Reserve System (the Fed), 27–28, 48
FIFO (first in, first out), 59–60
Finance balance sheet, 428–429
Financial Accounting Standards Board (FASB), 55
Financial buyers, 499
Financial calculators, 135
   for annuity interest rates, 184–185
   for bond valuation, 256–257
   for bond yields, 263
   for future value of an annuity, 188
   for future value problems, 146–148, 170
   for net present value, 322
   for present value of annuities, 178
   for present value problems, 155–156, 173
   tips for using, 148
Financial claims, 31. *See also* Securities
Financial flexibility, choice of capital structure and, 553
Financial forecasts, in business plan, 597
Financial institutions, 28, 39–40. *See also* Banks
   indirect financing by, 38–40
   services of, 39–40
Financial instruments, 31. *See also* Securities
   in capital markets, 35
   in money markets, 35
Financial intermediation, 38, 39
Financial investors, 599
Financial leverage, 99, 527, 535
   and choice of capital structure, 553
   in international finance, 699
Financial management:
   fundamental decisions in, 4–7
   goal for, 11–15
   international, *see* International finance management
   organization of financial function, 9–11

Financial managers, 2–7, 9
   agency conflict between stockholders and, 16
   fundamental decisions of, 4–7
   role of, 2
Financial markets, 28, 33–36
   capital markets, 35
   direct, 31–33
   efficiency of, 432–433
   exchanges, 34
   global, 713–716
   indirect, 38–40
   money markets, 35
   over-the-counter, 34
   primary, 33
   private, 36
   public, 35, 36
   secondary, 34
   stock market, 36–38
   transparency of, 253
Financial models, in decision making, 644
Financial options, 665–677. *See also* Real options
   American, European, and Bermudan, 668
   call, 665–673
   exchange-traded, 668
   exercising, 668
   foreign currency, 708n.2
   payoff functions for, 668
   put, 667–668, 671n.2
   in risk management, 684–685
Financial options valuation, 669–677
   binomial pricing model for, 673–676
   limits on option values, 669–671
   put-call parity in, 676
   variables affecting values, 671–673
Financial plan, 628–629
Financial planning, 628–655
   for managing and financing growth, 647–655
   models for, 631–646
   planning documents, 628–631
Financial planning models, 631–646
   advanced, 637–644
   basic, 631–637
   improving, 644–646
   sales forecast for, 631–633
Financial ratios, 91–107
   analysis using, 115–118
   efficiency ratios, 95–98
   leverage ratios, 99–102
   market-value indicators, 106
   profitability ratios, 102–105
   short-term liquidity ratios, 92–95
Financial restructuring, 530–531
Financial results, in business plan, 597
Financial risk, 533, 534
Financial Services Modernization Act (1999), 32n.3
Financial shortage costs, 471
Financial statements. *See also individual types of statements*
   accounting principles for, 55–56
   adjusting for differences in accounting principles, 57
   in annual reports, 55
   audited, 11, 54, 87, 573, 613
   balance sheet, 57–66
   comparing, 88
   current vs. historical information on, 63
   for financial planning models, 632
   income statement, 66–69

   pro forma, 634–635, 638–644
   relationships among, 73–75
   SEC requirement for, 502
   standardized, 88
   statement of cash flows, 71–73
   statement of retained earnings, 69
   for tax purposes vs. management and reporting, 68
   in valuation of companies, 613–614
Financial statement analysis, 86–119
   common-size financial statements, 88–91
   creditors' perspective on, 87
   DuPont system for, 107–112
   efficiency ratios, 95–98
   guidelines for, 87–88
   in international finance, 699
   leverage ratios, 99–102
   limitations of, 118–119
   managers' perspective on, 87
   market-value indicators, 106
   profitability ratios, 102–105
   selecting benchmarks in, 112–114
   short-term liquidity ratios, 92–95
   stockholders' perspective on, 86–87
   types of financial ratios for, 91–107
   using financial ratios, 115–118
Financial system, 28–48
   characteristics of, 29
   direct financing in, 31–33
   financial markets, 33–36
   flow of funds through, 30
   global integration of, 695
   indirect financing in, 38–40
   interest rates, 41–48
   operation of corporations within, 40–41
   stock market, 36–38
Financing. *See also* Raising capital
   short-term sources of, 481–484
   in terms of sale, 472
   trade credit as, 464–465
   for working capital, 479–484
Financing activities, on statement of cash flows, 73
Financing decisions, 3, 6, 630, 633
Financing plan, 628–630
Finished goods inventories, 464
Firm-commitment underwriting, 32, 503–504, 506
Firm's marginal tax rate (*t***), 358**
Firm's overall cost of capital, 427–431. *See also* Weighted average cost of capital
Firm value, 528–529. *See also* Business valuation; Enterprise value
   and dividend policy, 571–577
   effect of debt on, 542–543
   and tax deductibility of interest, 538–543
Fisher, Irving, 45
Fisher equation, 44–45
Fixed assets:
   in financial planning models, 640, 646
   market value and book value of, 64
   use of cash for, 71
Fixed asset turnover, 98
Fixed costs (FC), 379–380
   in calculating EBIT, 401–405
   in calculating EBITDA, 398–401
   controlling, in new businesses, 592
   and project risk, 397–405
Fixed-income securities, 253

Fixed-price tender offers, 570
Flexible current asset investment strategy, 471
Flight to quality, 515
Flipping shares, 507
Float, 477
Follow-on investments, options to make, 678
FOMC, *see* Federal Open Market Committee
Forecasts:
  of EBIT, 402–403
  financial, 597
  of free cash flows, 379–381
  of future cash flows, 319
  sales, 631–633
  SEC requirement for, 502
Foreign bonds, 714
Foreign exchange markets, 699–708
  equilibrium exchange rate, 702–703
  foreign currency quotations, 703–708
  foreign exchange rates, 700–702
  participants in, 700
  structure of, 700
Foreign exchange rate risk, 685, **696,** 700, 709
Foreign exchange rates, 700–702
  equilibrium, 702–703
  quotations of, 703–708
  spot, 703
Forms of business organization, 7–9. *See also specific forms* (e.g., Limited liability companies)
  choosing, 588–591
  corporations, 8–9
  hybrid, 9
  in international finance, 699
  limited liability partnerships, 9
  partnerships, 7–8
  sole proprietorships, 7
Formal line of credit, 482–483
Forum on Corporate Finance, 526
Forward premium/discount, 706
Forward rates, 706–707
France, business in, 698
Free cash flows, 357. *See also* Incremental after-tax free cash flows
Free cash flow from the firm (FCFF) approach, 607–611
Free cash flow to equity (FCFE) approach, 611, 612
Funds, sources of, 3. *See also* Raising capital; Working capital
  internally generated, 551
  for venture capital firms, 495–496
Funding constraints, 316
Futures markets, 36
Future cash flows, 4
  calculating, 356–364
  in capital budgeting, 356
  compared to cost of project, 6
  conventional, 334, 335
  estimating, 320, 363–379
  expected, 378–379
  forecasting, 319
  free cash flows, *see* Incremental after-tax free cash flows
  investment, 360, 380–381
  marginal and average tax rates, 371–372
  nominal vs. real, 368–370
  from operations, 359–360
  tax depreciation, 372–374
Future stock prices, 295–296

Future value (FV), 135–146
  applying formula for, 140–146
  with financial calculators, 146–148
  of multiple cash flows, 168–171
  present value vs., 134
Future value equation, 137–140, 151
Future value interest factor (future value factor), 136, 140
Future value of an annuity (FVA), 186–188
FV, *see* Future value
FVA, *see* Future value of an annuity

G
GAAP, *see* Generally accepted accounting principles
Gates, Bill, 561
Gault, Stanley, 691
General cash offers, 511–514
  competitive or negotiated sales, 511–512
  cost of, 513–514
  shelf registration, 512–513
General dividend model (stock valuation), 290–291
Generally accepted accounting principles (GAAP), 55–57
  fundamental accounting principles in, 55–56
  international, 56–57
  for salvage value, 374n.5
  for tax depreciation, 372–373
General partners:
  in limited partnerships, 8
  in private equity firms, 516, 517
General partnerships, 8
  characteristics of, 589
  financial liabilities of, 591
Georgetown University, 208
Germany, business in, 698
Gerstner, Lou, 298
Global financial markets, 713–716
Globalization, 694–695
Goals of firms, 12–15
  in business plans, 596
  for financial management, 11–15
  growth rate as, 654–655
  maximization of ROE as, 112
Going concern assumption, 56
Going-concern value, 600–601
Golden rule, 20
Goodwill, 60, 68
Governance, 19
Government. *See also* Regulation
  new business investment by, 494
  as stakeholders, 2
Graham, John, 540
Grasso, Richard A., 691–692
Greenberg, Maurice R., 692
Greenspan, Alan, 281
Gross profit margin, 102–103
Gross working capital, 463. *See also* Working capital
Growing annuities, 192–193
Growing perpetuities, 193–194
Growth of business, 647–655
  external funding for, 647–650
  graphical view of, 650–651
  growth rates and profits, 654
  internal growth rate, 651–652
  opportunities for, 428n.2
  as planning goal, 654–655

sustainable growth rate, 652–654
valuation of rapidly-growing companies, 614–615
Growth rates:
  internal, 651–652
  and profits, 654
  sustainable, 652–654
Growth stock pricing, 291, 297–301

H
Harvesting assets, 384–385
Hedge, 707
Hedging, 684, 707
High-yield bonds, 271
Historical cost, 55–56, 63
Historical market performance, 221–224
Historical trends, in financial planning models, 639
HKIBOR (Hong Kong Interbank Offer Rate), 714
Holding period, 211
Holding period returns, 211–212
Hong Kong Interbank Offer Rate (HKIBOR), 714
Hybrid forms of business organization, 9

I
Identity, 58n.3
IGR, *see* Internal growth rate
Impairment test, 68
Incentives:
  alignment of, 573
  for different forms of business, 589
  for ethical behavior, 22
  for managers, 17, 683–684
  in private vs. public companies, 613–614
  for stockholders to pay dividends, 681, 682
Income, *see* Net income
Income approaches to business valuation, 607–612
  dividend discount model, 611–612
  free cash flow from the firm, 607–611
  free cash flow to equity, 611
  market approaches vs., 607
Income statement, 66–69
  common-size, 90–91
  in financial planning models, 634–635, 638
  pro forma, 634–635, 638
  relationship of other statements and, 74–75
Income taxes, 75–77
  average vs. marginal rates, 76–77
  corporate rates, 75–76
  and cost of debt, 537–543
  for different forms of business, 589
  on dividends, 77, 573
  on interest payments, 77
Incremental additions to working capital (Add WC), 358, 360, 463n.1
  in FCF calculation, 361–364, 367–368
  forecasting, 380–381
  in terminal-year FCF, 374–377
Incremental after-tax free cash flows (FCF), 357–364
  accounting earnings vs., 363
  calculation of, 357–363
  and capital structure, 527
  estimating, 363–379
  expected, 378–379
  general rules for calculating, 365–368
  tax rates and depreciation, 371–374
  terminal-year, 374–378

Incremental capital expenditures (Cap Exp), 358, 360
   in FCF calculation, 361–364, 367–368
   forecasting, 380
   in terminal-year FCF, 374–377
Incremental cash flow from operations (CF Opns), 358–360
   in FCF calculation, 367–368
   forecasting, 379–381
   in terminal-year FCF, 374–377
Incremental depreciation and amortization (D&A), 358
   in Accounting DOL, 406–407
   in accounting operating profit break-even point, 410–411
   in cash flows from operations, 359
   in EBIT calculation, 401
   in FCF calculation, 361–364, 367–368
   forecasting, 379, 380
Incremental net operating profits after tax (NOPAT), 359–360, 362–364, 367–368
Incremental net revenue (Revenue), 379
Incremental operating expenses (Op Ex):
   in FCF calculation, 361–364, 367–368
   fixed and variable costs in, 398
   forecasting, 379–380
Independent parties, 55
Independent projects, 315
Index funds, 221
Indirect bankruptcy costs, 546
Indirect currency quote, 703
Indirect financing, 38–40
   direct financing vs., 39
   financial institutions in, 39–40
   in flow of funds, 30
   market transactions in, 38–39
Industry analysis, 113
Inflation, 41
   and economic growth rate, 442
   expected rate of, 44–45, 273
   impact on loans, 44–46
   and long-term interest rates, 47–48
   realized rate of, 45
Informal line of credit, 482
Information:
   for capital budgeting, 315
   private, 251
   public, 251
Informational efficiency, 250
Information asymmetry, 22
   ethics conflicts involving, 22, 525
   with start-up companies, 496–497
Initial public offerings (IPOs), 41, 501–510
   advantages of, 501–502
   cost of, 502, 509–510
   disadvantages of, 502
   distribution of shares, 505
   investment banking services for, 502–503
   origination of, 503
   proceeds from, 505–506
   underpricing of, 507–509
   underwriting for, 503–505
   as venture capitalists' exit strategy, 499, 500
Inside directors, 17
Insider trading, 310–311
Insolvency, 92
Institutional investors, 572
Insurable interest, 524, 525
Insurance companies, 39

Intangible assets, 2, 60, **360**
   amortization of, 68
   cash flows associated with, 360
Interest:
   deferred payment of, 545
   on Eurocredit loans, 719
   as tax deduction, 435–436
   as tax shield, 537–543
Interest expense:
   in financial planning models, 645
   tax treatment of, 77
Interest on interest, 137–139, 142
Interest rates, 41–48
   annual percentage rate, 194
   for annuities, 183–186
   for bank loans, 518–519
   and bond prices, 257–258
   caps on, 624
   comparing, 195–196
   cyclical and long-term trends in, 47–48
   disclosure of, 197
   effective annual interest rate, 194–198
   equilibrium, 43
   Fed's role in setting, 27–28
   finding, 156–157
   impact of inflation on loans, 44–46
   lending and borrowing, 29
   nominal, 42
   planning ahead for variation in, 48
   and prices of bonds, 267–268
   prime, 518
   quoted, 195
   real, 41–44, 272, 273
   risk-free rate of interest for options, 672–673
   structure of, 269–274
   term structure of, 272–274
Interest rate per period, 195
Interest rate risk, 266
   with bonds, 266–269
   options in management of, 684
Interest tax, 552
Intermediation, financial, 38, 39
Internal accounting controls, 18
Internal auditors, 10, 11
Internal growth rate (IGR), 651–652
Internally generated funds, use of, 551
Internal rate of return (IRR), 331–342
   agreement of NPV and, 334–336
   calculating, 332–334
   disagreement of NPV and, 336–340
   modified, 340–341
   NPV vs., 341–342
   as practitioners' method of choice, 343
International banking, 716–719
International bond markets, 714–716
International finance management, 694–719
   basic principles of, 698–699
   capital budgeting in, 708–712
   factors affecting, 695–697
   foreign exchange markets, 699–708
   and globalization, 694–695
   goals of, 698
   international banking, 716–719
   and rise of multinational corporations, 694, 696
   use of global money and capital markets in, 713–716
International GAAP, 56–57
Intrinsic (true) value, **250,** 607

Inventory, 464
   accounting for, 59–60
   as current asset, 59
   forecasting, 381
   just-in-time, 477
   management of, 475–477
   profitability and, 7
Inventory carrying costs, 471
Inventory turnover, 95, 96
Investing activities, on statement of cash flows, 73
Investments:
   by entrepreneurs, 498
   evaluating opportunities for, 635–637
   follow-on, 678
   in multinational corporations, 695
   options to defer, 677–678
   real investment policy, 528
   through private equity funds, 516
Investment banks, 31–32
   distribution by, 32, 505
   origination by, 32, 503
   in private placements, 515
   services of, 32–33, 502
   and subprime mortgages, 626
   underwriting by, 32, 33, 503–505
Investment cash flows, 360, 380–381
Investment funds, 40
Investment-grade bonds, 271
Investment period, 211
Investment plan, 628–630
Investment policy decisions, 633
Investment projects:
   classification of, 315
   with different lives, 381–384
Investment strategies, for working capital, 470–472
Investment value, 599, 606
Investors:
   accurate assessment of risks/returns by, 416
   benefits of dividends for, 572
   business plan for, 596
   importance of cash flow to, 4
   and need for dividends, 571–572
IPOs, *see* Initial public offerings
IRR, *see* Internal rate of return
Issuance costs:
   for bonds, 435, 543
   for stock, 543

J

"Janitor's insurance," 524
Japan, business in, 698
Jobs, Steve, 493
Jones, Barbara S., 22
Junk bonds, 271
Just-in-time inventory management, 477

K

Keiretsu, 698
Key person discount, 616

L

Labor market, managerial, 17
Langone, Ken, 691
Laws. *See also* Regulation
   for business ethics, 22
   and managers' decision making, 18
Lease financing, 39
Lee, Spike, 495

Legal systems, foreign, 696
Lenders. *See also* Loans
  mortgage, 624–626
  stockholder-lender agency costs, 548–550
  venture capitalists, 495, 498–500
Lender-savers, 30
Lending margin, 719
Lending rates, 29
Level cash flows, 175–191
  annuities, 175–188
  annuities due, 190–191
  perpetuities, 188–189
Leverage:
  and choice of capital structure, 553
  and cost of assets, 536
  and cost of debt, 532n.5, 536
  and cost of equity, 536
  financial, 99, 527, 535, 553, 699
  and interest tax shield, 538, 540
  operating, 405–408, 534–535
Leveraged buyouts, 2, 516
Leverage ratios, 94, 99–102
Liabilities, 58
  on balance sheet, 58
  in balance sheet identity, 428–429
  on common-size balance sheets, 88–89
  current, 59, 463
  current market value of, 63
  for different forms of business, 589
  in financial planning models, 641
  limited, 8
  long-term, 61, 71
  market value of, 64
LIBOR (London Interbank Offer Rate), 714
Life insurance companies, 39
Life of a business:
  cycles in, 297–298
  for different business forms, 589, 590
  in valuation of business, 607
LIFO (last in, first out), 59, 60
Limited liability, 8
Limited liability companies (LLCs), 9, 589
  capital for, 590
  characteristics of, 589
  financial liabilities of, 591
  life of, 590
  partnership agreements in, 590
  private equity funds as, 516
  taxes as C-corporations, 591n.1
Limited liability partnerships (LLPs), 9
Limited partners:
  in limited partnerships, 8
  in private equity firms, 516
Limited partnerships, 8
  capital for, 590
  characteristics of, 589
  financial liabilities of, 591
  life of, 590
  private equity funds as, 516
Line of best fit, 235–237
Lines of credit, 482–483
Lintner, John, 579–580
Liquidating dividend, 564
Liquidation value of a business, 601–602
Liquidity, 34, 464
  marketability vs., 34
  in money markets, 35
  net working capital as measure of, 59
  of public markets, 501

of seasoned vs. unseasoned stocks, 502
in secondary markets, 34
Liquidity discounts, 603n.3
Liquidity position, 92
Liquidity ratios, 92–95
Listed stocks, 37
LLCs, *see* Limited liability companies
LLPs (limited liability partnerships), 9
Loans:
  amortized, 180
  from banks, *see* Bank loans
  estimating current cost of, 435
  from factors, 484
  from family and friends, 495
  impact of inflation on, 44–46
  mortgage, 624–626
  pricing model for, 518–519
  prime-rate, 518
  short-term, 482–483, 519
  term, 518
  true cost of, 196–197
  when starting a business, 495, 518–520
Loan pricing model, 518–519
Lockbox systems, 478–479
London Interbank Offer Rate (LIBOR), 714
London Stock Exchange, 35
  as foreign exchange market, 700
  foreign firms on, 695
Long-term assets:
  on balance sheet, 60–61
  funding of, 481. *See also* Raising capital
Long-term debt:
  book value and market value for, 64
  cost of, 432–438
  financing with, 481
  as source of cash, 71
Long-term equity, 71
Long-term funding strategy, 480
Long-term liabilities:
  on balance sheet, 61
  as source of cash, 71
Long-term solvency ratios, 99. *See also* Leverage ratios
Lowest-cost method of sale, 512
Lumpy assets, 646

M
MACRS, *see* Modified Accelerated Cost Recovery System
Management. *See also* Financial management
  of current assets, 3
  venture capitalists' involvement in, 500
Management team:
  in business plan, 597
  and private equity investment, 517
Managers. *See also* Financial managers
  agency relationship of stockholders and, 15–16
  aligning interests of stockholders and, 16–18, 573
  compensation of, 16–17
  competition among, 17–18
  control of firm by, 15, 16
  financial analysis for, 86–87
  incentives for, 17
  payoff function for, 683–684
  shift in behavior of, 20
  as stakeholders, 2
  and stockholder-lender agency costs, 549

and stockholder-manager agency costs, 547–548
  stock price affected by decisions of, 14–15
  waste of money by, 543
Managerial labor market, 17
Mandatory contingent projects, 315
Manning, Robert, 208
Marginal tax rate, 75–76, 371–372
  average tax rate vs., 76–77
  forecasting, 379, 380
Markets:
  bond, 252, 714–716
  efficiency of, 283, 432–433
  foreign exchange, 699–708
  historical performance of, 221–224
  informal, 700
  public, 8
  stock, 36–38, 234, 282–286
  unstable, 515
Marketability, 34, 269–270
  in business valuation, 614
  liquidity vs., 34
  with PIPE transactions, 517
Marketability discount, 603
Marketability risk premium (MRP), 270
Marketable securities, as current assets, 59
Market analysis, in business plan, 597
Market approaches to business valuation, 602–606
  income approaches vs., 607
  multiples analysis, 602–606
  transactions analysis, 602, 606
Market economies, 697
Market extension projects, 452
Market informational efficiency, 250, 251
Marketing and sales, in business plan, 597
Market operational efficiency, 250–251
Market portfolio, 234
Market risk, 234–235. *See also* Systematic risk
Market risk premium, 238, 427, 440
Market value (MV), 55, 56, 63
  of assets, 63–64, 429–430
  of common stock, 61–62
  of liabilities, 64
  of stockholders' equity, 64
  in WACC, 447
Market-value balance sheet, 65–66
Market-value ratios, 94, 106
Marking to market, 63
MAT (term to maturity), 519
Matching maturities, *see* Maturity matching strategy
Matching principle, 56
Mature companies, valuation of, 614–615
Maturity date (bonds), 258
Maturity matching strategy, 479–481
Maximizing shareholder wealth, 13, 699
MBSs, *see* Mortgage-backed securities
MDH, *see* Minnesota Department of Health
Mega Millions lottery game, 132
Michigan State University, 208
Microsoft Excel, 146
  calculating IRR in, 334
  and changes in assumptions, 404–405
  leverage model, 535
Miller, Merton, 528
Minneapolis Fed, 518
Minnesota Department of Health (MDH), 394, 395
Minority ownership interest, 615

MIRR, *see* Modified internal rate of return
Mixed (supernormal) growth dividend model, 297–301, 442–443
M&M propositions, *see* Modigliani and Miller propositions
Modified Accelerated Cost Recovery System (MACRS), 373–376
Modified internal rate of return (MIRR), 340–341
Modigliani, Franco, 528
Modigliani and Miller (M&M) propositions, 528–537
   proposition 1, 528–531
   proposition 2, 531–537
Money, value of, 44*n*.9. *See also* Foreign exchange rates; Time value of money
Money center banks, 32
   in foreign exchange market, 700
   in private placements, 515
Money markets, 35, 713–716
Mortgage-backed securities (MBSs), 624–626
Mortgage market:
   decline in, 209
   subprime, 624–626
MRP (marketability risk premium), 270
Multinational corporations, 695, 696. *See also* International finance management
Multiples analysis, 602–606, 614
Multiple cash flows, 168–174
   future value of, 168–171
   present value of, 171–174
Multistage-growth dividend model, 442–444
Mutual funds, 40
Mutually exclusive projects, 315
   with different lives, 381–384
   IRR vs. NPV methods for, 337–340
MV, *see* Market value

N

NAICS (North American Industry Classification System), 113
NASD (National Association of Securities dealers), 37
NASDAQ, 8, 37, 283, 579
NASDAQ Composite Index, 38, 221
National Association of Insurance Commissioners, 525
National Association of Securities dealers (NASD), 37
Nationalization, 709
National Venture Capital Association (NVCA), 496
NCF, *see* Net cash flow
NCFOA, *see* Net cash flow from operating activities
Negative correlation, 230
Negotiated sales, 511, 512
Net cash flow (NCF), 70, 319, 320. *See also* Incremental after-tax free cash flows
Net cash flow from operating activities (NCFOA), 70–71
Net income, 66, 67, 69
   and decrease in revenue, 534
   differing from cash flows, 533*n*.6
   dollar value of, 553
   net cash flow vs., 70–71
   and operating leverage, 534–535
Net plant and equipment, 60
Net present value (NPV):
   agreement of IRR and, 334–336
   calculation of, 321–325

   disagreement of IRR and, 336–340
   in international finance, 699
   IRR vs., 341–342
Net present value (NPV) method, 317–326
   calculation of NPV, 321–325
   for financial vs. real assets, 317
   framework for, 319–320
   as practitioners' method of choice, 343
   and value creation, 318–319
   and value of options, 678–680
Net proceeds (bonds), 435
Net profit margins, 103
   of airlines, 85
   in DuPont system of analysis, 108
Net sales, 90
Net working capital (NWC), 6, 59, 463, 470–471
Net worth, *see* Stockholders' equity
New businesses, *see* Business formation
New product projects, 452
New York Board of Trade, 36
New York Stock Exchange (NYSE), 8, 37, 283
   as auction market, 284
   as capital market, 35
   financial market classifications for, 33
   as foreign exchange market, 700
   overcompensation by, 691–692
   as public market, 35, 36
   and reverse stock splits, 579
   Wall Street Journal listings for, 284–285
New York Stock Exchange Index, 37
NOA (nonoperating assets), 607
No-documentation (no-doc) loans, 625–626
Nominal, use of term, 45*n*.10
Nominal cost of capital, 369
Nominal dollars, 368–370
Nominal rate of interest, 42, 699
Noncash expenses, 68
Noncash items, 70
Nonconvertible bonds, cost of issuing, 513–514
Nondiversifiable risk, 232. *See also* Systematic risk
Noninvestment-grade bonds, 271
Nonoperating assets (NOA), 607
NOPAT, *see* Incremental net operating profits after tax
Normal distribution, 218, 220
Normal trading range, 579
North American Industry Classification System (NAICS), 113
Notes payable, as current liability, 59
Not-for-Profit Corporation Law (New York), 691
NPV, *see* Net present value
NPV method, *see* Net present value method
NPV profile, 335–337
NVCA (National Venture Capital Association), 496
NWC, *see* Net working capital
NYSE, *see* New York Stock Exchange

O

Odd lots (of shares), 578
Offer (ask) price, 283, 504
One-period model (stock valuation), 287–288
Ongoing reviews of projects, 343–344
Open-market repurchases, 569–571, 575
Operating activities, on statement of cash flows, 72

Operating cycle, 466–468, **467**
   accounts receivable in, 472–475
   inventory management in, 475–477
Operating leverage, 405–408, 534*n*.7
   Accounting DOL, 406–407
   Cash Flow DOL, 405–407
   in international finance, 699
   and net income, 534–535
Operating profit margin, 103
Operating shortage costs, 471
Operations:
   in business plan, 597
   options to change, 678–679
Operational efficiency, 250–251
Op Ex, *see* Incremental operating expenses
Opportunity cost, 255, 316
   in FCF calculation, 365–366
   overall average, 432
   with underpriced IPOs, 507
Opportunity cost of capital, 316
Optimal capital structure, 527–528, 544–545, 699
Options, *see* Financial options; Real options
Options markets, 36
Optional contingent projects, 315
Option payoff function, 665, 666, 668
Ordinary annuities, 175
Organizational form, *see* Forms of business organization
"Organized" markets, 34. *See also* Exchanges
Origination, 32, 502, 503
OTC, *see* Over-the-counter market(s)
Otellini, Paul, 312
Out-of-pocket costs, 435
   direct bankruptcy costs as, 545–546
   economies of scale in, 513–514
   with IPOs, 509
Outside directors, 17
Overall cost of capital, 427–431. *See also* Weighted average cost of capital
   estimating, 430–431
   and finance balance sheet, 428–429
Overcompensation, 691–692
Over-the-counter (OTC) market(s), 34
   corporate bonds transactions in, 252
   NASDAQ as, 37
Owners:
   agency conflict between managers and, 16
   decisions in interest of, 2
   double taxation of, 8
Owners' equity, *see* Stockholders' equity
Ownership:
   control vs., 15
   separation of control and, 591
   transfer of, 589
Ownership interest:
   controlling vs. minority, 615
   selling/transferring, 590–591
Ownership rights, with common stock, 61
Ownership structure, in business plan, 597

P

Partnership agreements, 590
Partnerships, 7–8
   characteristics of, 589
   life of, 590
   limited liability, 9
   maximizing stock value for, 13
   taxation of, 9
Par value, 61, 253
Par-value bonds, 257

Payables, *see* Accounts payable
Payable date, 567
Payback period, 326–330
   in capital budgeting, 328–329
   computing, 326–328
   discounted, 329–330
   limitations of, 330
Payments, cash collection cycles for, 478
Payoff functions:
   and agency conflicts, 681–684
   for options, 665, 666, 668
PCs (professional corporations), 9
Pecking order theory, 551, 552
Peer group analysis, 113–114
Pension funds, 39
P/E (price-earnings) ratio, 106
Percent of sales model, 634–637
Performance analysis, 115–118
Permanent debt, 433
Permanent working capital, 479–481
Perpetuities, 175, 188–189
   common stock as, 286
   growing, 193–194
   preferred stock as, 303
Perpetuity model (stock valuation), 288–290, 445
Personal computers, 493
Personal investment, by entrepreneurs, 498
Per-unit contribution, 408–**409**
PI, *see* Profitability index
PIPE (private investments in public equity), 517
Plant and equipment, net, 60
Popeil, Ron, 628*n*.1
Portfolios, 224
   CAPM and returns on, 240–242
   market, 234
   with more than one asset, 226–232
   replicating, 673–675
   risk and diversification of, 224–233
   single-asset, 224–226
Positive correlation, 230
Posts, 284
Postaudit reviews, 343
Potential competition, 512
Preferred stock, 62–**63, 286**
   cost of equity for, 445–446
   as debt vs. equity, 286
   with fixed maturity, 302
   as perpetuities, 188, 303
   valuation of, 301–303
   for venture capitalists, 498
Preliminary prospectus, 503
Premium bonds, 257
Prepaid expenses, 70
Present value (PV), 148–156, **149**. *See also* Net present value
   applying formula for, 151–153
   of cash flows, 529
   with financial calculators, 155–156
   future value vs., 134
   of multiple cash flows, 171–174
   relations among time, discount rate, and, 153–155
   Present value equation, 150–151, 171–172
   Present value factor, 149, 186*n*.5
Present value of an annuity (PVA), 175–186
   for annuities due, 191
   interest rate, 183–186
   loan amortization schedule, 180–183
   monthly/yearly payments, 178–180

Pretax cost of debt, 436, 437, 532*n*.4
Pretax earnings, 366
Pretax operating cash flow, 398. *See also* EBIT plus depreciation and amortization (EBITDA)
Pretax operating cash flow (EBITDA) break-even point, 408–412
Price-earnings (P/E) ratio, 106, 285, 602–604
Price/revenue ratio, 602–604, 606
Price risk, 34, 283
   options in management of, 685
   and underwriting, 503
Pricing:
   of bank loans, 518–519
   of IPOs, 507–509
Pricing call, 505
Primary markets, 33
Prime-rate bank loans, 518, 519
Prime rate of interest, 518
Principal (agency), 15, 547
Principal (amount), 137, 253
   deferred payment of, 545
   in future value analysis, 136, 137
Private equity firms, 516–517
Private equity funds, 516
Private information, 251
Private investments in public equity (PIPE), 517
Privately held companies:
   business valuation for, 613–614
   dividend payment process for, 567
   financial statements of, 613–614
   transactions analysis for, 606
Privately held corporations, 8–9, 13
Private markets, 36
   private equity firms, 516–517
   private investments in public equity, 517
   private placements, 36, 515–516
   public markets vs., 515
   raising capital in, 514–518
Private placements, 36, 515–516
Products and services, in business plan, 597
Product extension projects, 452
Production, globalization of, 695
Productive assets, 2. *See also* Long-term assets
   financing of, 6
   purchasing, 5
   for venture capital funding, 496
Productivity ratios, 92
Professional corporations (PCs), 9
Professional partnerships, 9
Profits, 654. *See also* Net income
Profitability:
   and amount of debt, 552
   and inventory level, 7
Profitability index (PI), 416–419
   for ranking investment alternatives, 418
   for ranking projects, 417
Profitability ratios, 94, 102–105
Profit margins, asset turnover vs., 108–109
Profit maximization, 12, 13
Pro forma financial statements, 634–635
   balance sheet, 634–635, 638–644
   income statement, 634–635, 638
Progressive tax system, 371
Project costs, 320
Project economics, 397–415
   break-even analysis, 408–412
   cost structure and project risk, 397–405

   operating leverage, 405–408
   risk analysis, 412–415
Project risk, 397–405
   analysis of, 412–415
   determining, 320
   for projects with real options, 680
   scenario analysis, 414–415
   sensitivity analysis, 413
   sensitivity of EBIT to revenue changes, 401–405
   sensitivity of EBITDA to revenue changes, 398–401
   simulation analysis, 415
   variable and fixed costs' effect on, 397–405
Promissory notes, 482, 483
Pro-rata basis (dividends), 562
Public accounting firm scandals, *see* Accounting firm scandals
Public Accounting Reform and Investor Protection Act (2002), 18*n*.7
Public companies. *See also* Initial public offerings
   business valuation for, 613–614
   dividend payment process for, 564–567
   dividend payments and stock repurchases by, 576
   financial statements of, 613
   new regulations for, 18–19
   PIPE transactions by, 517
   transparency of, 502
Public corporations, 8. *See also* Corporations
Public information, 251
Public markets, 8, **35**, **36**. *See also* Initial public offerings
   general cash offers, 511–514
   liquidity of, 501
   private markets vs., 515
   as wholesale markets, 514
Public offerings, 501. *See also* Initial public offerings; Securities
   registered, 511. *See also* General cash offers
   seasoned, 501, 502
Pure-play comparables, 453
Put-call parity, 676
Put options, 667–668
   early exercise of, 671*n*.2
   exercising, 668
   as "insurance," 684
Put premium, 668
PV, *see* Present value
PVA, *see* Present value of an annuity

Q

Quick ratio, 93
Quoted interest rate, 195

R

r (real cost of capital), 369
Raising capital, 494–520
   with bank loans, 518–520
   by bootstrapping, 495
   business plan in, 596
   for cash-constrained companies, 592
   with general cash offers, 511–514
   with initial public offerings, 501–510
   in private markets, 514–518
   from venture capitalists, 495–501
   when starting business, 494–495
Rapidly-growing companies, valuation of, 614–615

Subject Index

Rate of return:
  accounting, 331
  internal, 331–342
  modified internal, 340–341
  and risk, 211
  risk-free, 237–238, 439
Raw materials inventories, 464
Real, use of term, 45*n*.10
Real cost of capital (r), 369
Real dollars, 368–370
Real investment policy, 528
Realization principle, 56
Realized rate of inflation, 45
Realized yield (bonds), 265–266
Real options, 677–680
  to abandon projects, 679–680
  to change operations, 678–679
  to defer investment, 677–678
  to make follow-on investments, 678
Real rate of interest, 41–44, 272, 273
Receivables, *see* Accounts receivable
Recessions, 48
Record date, 566
Redemption (bonds), 258
Registered public offerings, 511. *See also* General cash offers
Regression analysis, 235
Regular cash dividends, 563
Regulation, 18–20. *See also* Laws
  consumer protection acts, 197
  managers' decisions influenced by, 18
  of private equity firms, 517
  reforms in, 18–19
  requiring capital expenditures, 314
Reinvestment of residual cash flows, 4, 340
Renewal of assets, 314
Reoffer price, for general cash offers, 511
Reorder costs, 475–476
Repatriation of earnings restrictions, 709
Replacement cost, 600
Replacement cost valuation approach, 600
Replacement of assets, 314, 385–386
Replicating portfolios, 673–675
Reporting practices, 55
Required return, 532*n*.4. *See also* Cost of debt; Cost of equity
Resale of securities, with private placements, 515–516
Residual cash flows, 4
Resource constraints, 316
Restricted securities, 517
Restrictive current asset investment strategy, 471
Restructuring, financial, 530–531
Retained earnings:
  cash vs., 62
  events affecting, 69
Retained earnings account, 62
Retention ratio, 638
Return on assets (ROA), 104, 105
  in DuPont system of analysis, 107–109
  for multiple-asset portfolios, 226–232
  in performance analysis, 115–118
  for single-asset portfolios, 224–226
Return on equity (ROE), 91, 104–105
  in DuPont system of analysis, 109–110
  maximization of, 112
  M&M proposition 2 in calculation of, 535–536
  in performance analysis, 115–118

Return on investment, 211–216. *See also* Rate of return
  accurate assessment of, 416
  on bonds, 440. *See also* Yields, bond
  calculating, 212
  and historical market performance, 221–224
  on IPOs, 508, 510
  quantitative measures of, 211–216
  and rate of interest, 42
  for single-asset portfolios, 224–226
  on stocks, 285, 302–303, 440
  for venture capitalists, 500
Revenue(s):
  changes in, *see* Changes in revenue
  deferred, 70
  on income statement, 66
  incremental net revenue, 379
  matching expenses and, 56
Revenue recognition, 56
Reverse stock splits, 579
Review of projects, 343–344
Revolving credit, 482
Risk:
  accurate assessment of, 416
  avoiding, 12
  business, 533–534
  with cash flows, 13
  and choice of capital structure, 553
  commodity price, 684
  country, 697, 709–710, 717–718
  credit, 519, 716, 717
  currency, 717
  with debt financing, 6
  default, 270–272
  diversifiable, 232
  and diversification, 224–233
  exchange rate, 685, 696, 709
  and expected return, 241–242
  financial, 533–534
  and flight to quality, 515
  foreign exchange rate, 685, 696, 700
  interest rate, 266–269, 684
  with international bank lending, 716–718
  market, 234–235. *See also* Systematic risk
  measures of, 216–221
  nondiversifiable, 232
  with portfolio having more than one asset, 228–231
  price, 34, 283, 503, 685
  project, *see* Project risk
  and rate of return, 211
  with seasoned vs. unseasoned securities, 502
  with single-asset portfolios, 224–226
  and stockholder-manager agency costs, 547–548
  and structure of interest rates, 269–272
  systematic, 233–238
  total, 234
  total equity, 533, 534
  with underwriting, 32
  unique, 232
  unsystematic, 232–234
  with venture capital funding, 496, 498–499
Risk analysis, 412–415
Risk-free rate of interest (options), 672–673
Risk-free rate of return, 237–238, 439
Risk Management Association, 112, 113
Risk management options, 684–685
Risk managers, 10, 11

ROA, *see* Return on assets
Road show, 504
ROE, *see* Return on equity
Rollover pricing, 718–719
Round lots (of shares), 578
Rule 144A, 516
Rule of 72, 157–**158**
Russia:
  corruption in, 21
  inflation and real interest rate in, 47–48

S

σ, *see* Standard deviation
σ^2, *see* Variance
Sakhalim II partnership, 664–665
Sales forecasts, 631–633
Sale of assets, taxes on, 377–378
Salmonella outbreak, 394–395
Salvage value, 374–377
Sarbanes-Oxley Act (2002), 18, 20, 53
Savings and loan industry, 549
Scaling, 88, 92
Scandals, *see* Accounting firm scandals
Scenario analysis, 414–415
Schumer, Charles E., 624
Schwan, Marvin, 394, 395
Schwartz, Frederick August Otto, 627
S-corporations, 589–590
Seasonal working capital, 479–481
Seasoned public offerings, 501, 502. *See also* Securities
SEC, *see* Securities and Exchange Commission
Secondary markets, 34, 282
  corporate bonds transactions in, 252
  efficiency of, 283
  transactions in, 282
  types of, 283–284
Securities. *See also* Bonds; Stocks
  cost of issuing, 513
  derivative, 36, 665
  in direct financing, 31–33
  fixed-income, 253–254
  historical returns on, 221–224
  marketability of, 269–270
  public offering of, 501–502. *See also* Initial public offerings
  restricted, 517
  seasoned vs. unseasoned, 502
  and types of financial markets, 33–36
  unregistered, 36, 515–517
  U.S. government, 237
Securities and Exchange Commission (SEC), 8, 55
  and Arthur Andersen scandal, 130
  compliance and ethics directors required by, 11
  cost of compliance with, 502
  establishment of, 36*n*.5
  external auditors required by, 11
  financial statements in documents filed with, 372
  general cash offer registration statements for, 511
  IPO requirements for, 502
  PIPE registration with, 517
  private placements limited by, 515, 516
  public markets regulated by, 36
  registering securities with, 32, 503, 505
  shelf registrations allowed by, 512–513

and Martha Stewart trading case, 310, 311
Securitization of mortgage loans, 624
Security Market Line (SML), 239–240, 450, 673
Seed money, 495
Selling groups, 504
Semiannual compounding (bonds), 259–260, 434
Semistrong-form (of the efficient market hypothesis), 251
Sensitivity analysis, 413
Settlement date (bonds), 258
SGR, *see* Sustainable growth rate
Shareholders' equity, *see* Stockholders' equity
Shelf registration, 512–**513**
Shortage costs, 471
Short-term assets, 481. *See also* Working capital
Short-term financing sources, 481–484
Short-term funding strategy, 480
Short-term liabilities, book value and market value for, 64
Short-term liquidity ratios, 92–95
Short-term solvency ratios, 92. *See also* Liquidity ratios
SIBOR (Singapore Interbank Offer Rate), 714
SIC (Standard Industrial Classification) System, 113
Simple interest, 137–**139**
  for annual percentage rate, 194
  for quoted interest rate, 195
  total, 138
Simulation analysis, 415
Singapore Interbank Offer Rate (SIBOR), 714
Single-asset portfolios, returns for, 224–226
Sinking fund provisions, 286
Size factor, 92
Small-issue exemption, 503n.2
SML, *see* Security Market Line
Social language, 697
Sole proprietorships, 7
  capital for, 590
  characteristics of, 589
  financial liabilities of, 591
  life of, 590
  taxation of, 9
S&P 500, *see* Standard & Poor's 500 Index
Special dividends, 563, 575
Specialists, 284
Speculative-grade bonds, 271
Spin-offs, 548
Spitzer, Eliot, 691, 692
Spot rate, 703
Spreadsheet programs, 146
SSIs (surplus spending units), 30n.2
Staged funding (venture capital), 498
Stakeholders, 2
Stand-alone principle, 358–**359**
Standard deviation (σ), 217–**221**
Standard Industrial Classification (SIC) System, 113
Standardized financial statements, 88
Standard & Poor's (S&P) 500 Index, 37–38, 221, 223, 235
Starting a business, *see* Business formation
Stateless corporations, 695
Statement of cash flows, 71–**75**
Statement of retained earnings, 69, 74–75
Stewart, Martha, 310, 311
Stillwagoner, Peggy, 525

Stocks:
  common, 286. *See also* Common stock
  cost of equity for, *see* Cost of equity
  cost of issuing, 513–514
  dividends from, 577–579
  growth, 291
  historical returns on, 221–224
  issuance costs for, 543
  listed, 37
  odd lots vs. round lots of, 578
  preferred, 188, 286. *See also* Preferred stock
  prices of, *see* Stock prices
  Treasury, 62
  valuation of, *see* Stock valuation
Stock dividends, 577–579
Stock exchanges, *see* Exchanges
Stockholders:
  agency conflict between managers and, 16
  agency relationship of management and, 15–16
  aligning interests of management and, 16–18, 573
  cash flows available to, 611
  FCF as focus of, 358
  financial analysis for, 86–87
  limited liability of, 8
  manager monitoring by, 18
  for S-corporations, 589–590
Stockholders' equity, 58
  on balance sheet, 58
  in balance sheet identity, 428–429
  book value and market value of, 64
  and changes in cash flow expectations, 65
  maximizing, 13
Stockholder-lender agency costs, 548–550
Stockholder-manager agency costs, 547–548
Stockholder of record, 566
Stock market, 36–38, 282–286
  as benchmark for systematic risk, 234
  reading listings for, 284–285
Stock market indexes, 37–38, 221–224
Stock prices. *See also* Stock valuation
  after stock splits, 579
  current listing of, 442
  and dividend announcements, 565, 574–575
  ex-dividend date and drop in, 565–566
  future, 295–296
  growth stocks, 291, 297–301
  and management decisions, 14–15
  in market valuation approaches, 602
  maximizing, 13–14
  and ownership vs. control of firm, 16
  and size of dividends, 572
  and stock splits, 579
Stock repurchases, 568
  dividends vs., 568–569, 575–577
  managers' views on, 580
  process for, 569–571
  taxes on, 568, 569
Stock splits, 577–579, **578**
Stock valuation:
  common stock, 287–291
  computing future stock prices, 295–296
  constant-growth dividend model, 293–295
  in international finance, 699
  mixed (supernormal) growth dividend model, 297–301
  preferred stock, 301–303
  relationship between R and g, 297
  of seasoned vs. unseasoned stocks, 502

  simplifying assumptions in, 291–301
  zero-growth dividend model, 292–293
Straight-line depreciation, 61, 68
Strategic buyers, 499
Strategic investors, 599
Strategic plan, 313, 619, 628–629
Strategic planning, 619, **629**
Strike price, *see* Exercise price
Strong-form (of the efficient market hypothesis), 251
Student debt, 207–208
Subchapter S corporations, 8n.2
Subprime mortgage market, 624–626
Sunk costs, 366
SuperDOT trading system, 284
Supernormal growth dividend model, *see* Mixed growth dividend model
Suppliers, as stakeholders, 2
Supply curve, 702
Surplus spending units (SSUs), 30n.2
Sustainable growth rate (SGR), 652–**654**
Syndicates, underwriting, 504, 505
Syndication, 499
Synergies, value of, 599, 606
Systematic risk, 232–**238**
  associated with stock, 440
  beta, 236, 238
  compensation for bearing, 237–238, 427
  on financial balance sheet, 430
  line of best fit, 235–237
  measuring, 234–237
  nature of business and, 451
Systematic volatility, 452

T
t (firm's marginal tax rate), 358
Takeovers, 18
Tangible assets, 2, **60**, **360**
  cash flows associated with, 360
  depreciation of, 60
Targeted stock repurchases, 570, 571
Taxes:
  accelerating depreciation for, 68
  accrued, 59
  capital gains, 573–574
  and cost of debt, 435–436, 537–543
  deferred, 70
  and depreciation, 372–374
  for different forms of business, 589
  on dividends, 568, 573–574, 614
  in foreign countries, 696
  income, 75–77, 537–543, 573, 589
  and interest as tax shield, 537–543
  in international finance, 699
  on life insurance policies, 524–525
  on limited liability companies, 591n.1
  on limited liability partnerships, 9
  and organizational form, 591
  on owners of corporations, 8
  on partnerships, 9
  on sale of assets, 377–378
  on sole proprietorships, 9
  on stock repurchases, 568, 569
  on Subchapter S corporations, 8n.2
Tax rates:
  marginal and average, 371–372
  progressive, 371
Tax Reform Act (1986), 76, 373
Tender offers, 569–**570**
Terms of sale, 472–474

Terminal value (TV), 340–341, **607**
Terminal-year FCF, 374–378
Term loans, 518, 519
Term structure of interest rates, 272–274
Term to maturity (MAT), 519
Thin market, 252
Tillman, Anthony, 525
Tillman, Felipe, 525
Time interest earned, 102
Time lines:
 for calculating NPV, 319
 for time value of money, 133–134
Time preference for consumption, 132–133
 positive, 43, 132
 and rate of interest, 43
 and time value of money, 132–133
Time value of money, 132–160
 applying future value formula, 140–146
 applying present value formula, 151–153
 compound growth rates, 158–160
 compounding, 141–146
 finding interest rate, 156–157
 future value, 135–146
 future value equation, 137–140
 future value factor, 140
 future value vs. present value, 134
 in international finance, 699
 and positive time preference for consumption, 132–133
 present value, 148–156
 present value equation, 150–151
 and profit maximization, 12
 relations among time, discount rate, and present value, 153–155
 Rule of 72, 157–158
 time lines illustrating, 133–134
Tokyo Stock Exchange, 35
 as foreign exchange market, 700
 foreign firms on, 695
Total asset turnover, 98, 108
Total cash flow, 356
Total debt ratio, 99–100
Total equity risk, 533, 534
Total holding period return, 211–212
Total risk, 234
Total simple interest (TSI), 138
Total volatility, 452
"Tracking stock," 452n.8
Trade credit, 464–465
 cost of, 473
 as short-term financing, 482
 terms of sale, 472–474
Trade-off theory, 544–545, **550**–552
Trading range argument, 578–579
Transactions analysis, 602, 606
Transaction costs, 34, 250
 direct bankruptcy costs as, 545–546
 indirect bankruptcy costs as, 546
 for shares in public vs. private companies, 614
Transaction costs argument (stock splits), 578–579
Transfer of ownership, forms of business and, 589
Transnational corporations, 695. *See also* International finance management
Transparency:
 of COLI programs, 525
 of public companies, 502
Treasurer, 10–11

Treasury securities:
 cost of equity for, 439
 term to maturity for, 519
Treasury stock, 62
Trend analysis, 87, 112–113
Trial-and-error IRR calculation, 332–334
True (intrinsic) value, 250, 607
Truth-in-Lending Act (1968), 194, **197**
Truth-in-Savings Act, 197
TSI (total simple interest), 138
TV, *see* Terminal value
Two-period model (stock valuation), 288

U
U.K. GAAP, 57
Uncertainty, *see* Risk
Unconventional cash flows, 336–337
Underinvestment problem, 550, 692–693
Underlying assets (options), 665
 current value of, 671–672
 volatility of the value of, 672, 675
Underpricing, 507–509, 514
Underwriting, 32, 33
 for competitive vs. negotiated sales, 511–512
 as investment banking service, 502–505
Underwriting spread, 32, 503–504, 509, 513–514
Underwriting syndicates, 504, 505
Unique risk, 232
United States:
 bond coupon interest in, 259
 corporate tax system in, 371–372
 inflation and real interest rate in, 47–48
U.S. Department of Commerce, 113
U.S. Treasury bills, 221–224, 270
U.S. Treasury bonds, 254
United States Saving Bonds, 254
Unit sales:
 in break-even analysis, 408–412
 in EBIT, 401–405
 in EBITDA, 398–401
 as variable cost, 397
University of Tennessee, 208
Unregistered securities, 36, 515–517
Unsecured loans, 483
Unsystematic risk, 232–234

V
Vacek, Steve, 249
Valuation:
 of bonds, *see* Bond valuation
 of business, *see* Business valuation
 of financial options, 669–677
 of inventory, 59–60
 of stocks, *see* Stock valuation
Valuation date, 598
Value:
 book, *see* Book value
 dollar value of net income, 553
 enterprise, 528, 604, 605
 face, 253
 fair market, 599, 600, 606
 of firm, *see* Firm value
 future, *see* Future value
 going-concern, 600–601
 intrinsic (true), 250, 607
 investment, 599, 606
 liquidation, 601–602
 market, *see* Market value

 of money, 44n.9. *See also* Time value of money
 net present, 321–325, 699. *See also* Net present value method
 par, 61, 253
 present, *see* Present value
 salvage, 374–377
 of synergies, 599, 606
 terminal, 340–341, 607
 of underlying assets, 671–672
Value creation, 132, 313, 318–319
Value proposition, 498
Vanilla bonds, 253, 512
Variable costs (VC), 379–380
 in calculating EBIT, 401–405
 in calculating EBITDA, 398–401
 and project risk, 397–405
Variance (σ^2), 216–220, **217**
 in international finance, 699
 for portfolios with two assets, 228–232
VC, *see* Variable costs
Venture capital, 495–501
 advice from lenders of, 499–500
 cost of funding, 500
 funding cycle for, 497–499
 in private markets, 515
 traditional funding vs., 496–497
Venture capital industry, 496
Venture capitalists, 495
 advice from, 499–500
 risk reduction by, 498–499
Volatility:
 in EBIT, 408
 in EBITDA, 408
 and nature of business, 451
 total vs. systematic, 452
 underpricing to reduce, 507
 of the value of the underlying asset, 672

W
WACC, *see* Weighted average cost of capital
Waksal, Sam, 310, 311
Wall Street Journal, 106, 251, 281, 284–285, 440, 547, 603, 604, 694, 703, 704, 706
Walton, Sam, 693
Weak-form (of the efficient market hypothesis), 252
Wealth, 2
Wealth transfer, 548, 576
Webb, Dan, 692
Weighted average cost of capital (WACC), 431–454
 alternatives to using, 452–454
 calculating, 447–449
 and capital structure, 527
 cost of debt in, 432–438
 cost of equity in, 438–446
 effect of debt on, 541–543
 in FCFF approach, 608–609
 in international finance, 699
 limitations as a discount rate, 449–452
 minimizing, 537
 and M&M proposition 2, 532
Weighted average first-day return (IPOs), 508
Welch, Jerry, 627
Whistleblower programs, 11
Working capital, 463
 incremental additions to, *see* Incremental additions to working capital
 net, 6, 59, 463, 470–471

permanent, 479–481
seasonal, 479–481
on statement of cash flows, 72
and use of cash, 71
use of term, 462
Working capital accounts, in financial planning models, 639–640, 645
Working capital efficiency, 466
Working capital management, 3, 462–484
accounts and trade-offs in, 464–465
accounts receivable, 472–475
cash conversion cycle in, 465–466, 468–470
cash management and budgeting, 477–479
decisions in, 6–7
financing working capital, 479–484
in international finance, 699
inventory management, 475–477
investment strategies in, 470–472
operating cycle in, 466–468
terms and concepts in, 462–464
Working capital trade-offs, 464, 471–472
Wozniak, Steve, 493

Y
Yarbrough, Jon, 396
Yields, bond, 258
effective annual yield, 263–265
realized yield, 265–266
yield to maturity, 254, 262–263, 265
Yields, stock, 285, 302–303
Yield curve, 272–274
Yield to maturity (bonds), 254, **262**–263, 265
Young companies, valuation of, 614–615

Z
Zero coupon bonds, 156, 253–254, 260–262
Zero-growth dividend model, 292–293

COMPANY INDEX

A
AAR Corp., 284–285
ABM AMRO, 284–285, 717
ABM Industries, Inc., 284–285
ACA Capital Holdings, Inc., 284–285
Accenture, 129
ACCO Brands Corp., 284–285
ACE Ltd., 284–285
Advantage Medical Services, 525
AES Corp., 284–285
Aflac, 284–285
AGCO Corp., 284–285
AGL Resources, 284–285
AIG Corp., 691, 692
AirClic, 586–587
Airgas, Inc., 526
AirTran, 85
AK Steel Holding Corp., 284–285
Amazon.com, 714
AMB Property Corp., 284–285
AMCOL International Corp., 284–285
AMD, 224–227
American Airlines, 85
American Bancorp, Inc., 721
Ameriquest Mortgage Company, 625–626
AMR Corp., 284–285
Apple Inc., 31, 365, 493, 494
APT Satellite Holdings Ltd., 284–285
Archer Daniels Midland Company, 391
Arthur Andersen LLP, 129–130
AT&T, 282
AXA Group, 696

B
Banco Santander, S.A., 717
Banco Santiago, 724
Bank of America Corp., 29, 31, 32, 52, 437, 717, 723, 725
Bank of India, 723
Barclays, 717, 723
Bell Mountain Vineyards, 391
Berkshire Hathaway, Inc., 579
Best Buy, 476
Blue Ridge Company, 486
BMW, 55, 151–152, 315, 714, 723
BNP Paribas, 717
Boeing Company, 5, 59, 88, 428, 453, 678, 724
Boston Chicken, Inc., 647, 654
Boston Market Corp., 647
Boston Scientific Corp., 167
Bremer Financial Corp., 723
Bristol-Myers Squibb, 310
BP plc, 695, 696
Burger King Brands, Inc., 647

C
Cargill, Inc., 515
Carlson, 515
Caterpillar, Inc., 724
Chevron Corp., 696
Chipotle Mexican Grill, 499
Chrysler LLC, 131, 620
Cisco Systems, Inc., 125, 298, 342
Citibank, 718, 720, 723
Citigroup, 32, 691
Citigroup, Inc., 696, 717
CM Holdings, Inc., 525
Coca-Cola Enterprises, 526
Colonial Realty, 129
Columbia Industries LLC, 721
Compaq, 695
ConocoPhillips Company, 440, 696
Continental Airlines, Inc., 526
Cooper Industries, Inc., 57
Countrywide Financial Corp., 209–210
Credit Agricole, 717
CSX Corp., 228–232, 564

D
DaimlerChrysler, 620, 696
AM.D.Q. Corp., 33
Daiwa Bank Holdings, Inc., 723, 725
Datsun, 212
Dean Foods, 521
Dearborn Bancorp, Inc., 577
Dell, 212, 214, 220–221, 315, 359, 461–463, 466–469, 477, 488, 678, 695
Deloitte Development LLC, 129
Delphi Corp., 526
Delta Air Lines, Inc., 98
Deutsche Bank, 724, 725
Domino's IP Holder LLC, 440, 441
The Dow Chemical Company, 525
Dow Jones & Company, Inc., 37
Dun & Bradstreet, 113
DuPont, 107

E
Enron Corp., 18, 20–22, 63, 129–130, 249–250, 654
Enron Creditors Recovery Corp., 249
Ernst & Young, 129
Exxon Mobil Corp., 227, 342, 695, 696

F
FAO Schwarz Inc., 627, 628
FedEx, 428
Fidelity Investments, 271
First Safety Bank, 482–483
First USA Bank, 208
FITCO, 393
FPL Group, Inc., 433, 572
FMC Technologies, 114
Ford Motor Company, 88, 114, 332–335, 341, 391, 620, 630, 640, 668, 696, 714

G
Gazprom, 664
GE Capital Corp., 29, 483
General Electric Company, 235–237, 239, 696, 722
General Motors Corp., 16, 88, 473, 543, 695, 696
Global Crossing, 18, 20, 654
GMAC, 473
Gold Company, 280
The Goldman Sachs Group, Inc., 692
Goodwill Industries International, Inc., 392
The Goodyear Tire & Rubber Company, 691
Google, 620
Guidant Corp., 167

H
Halliburton, 114
Harrods Ltd., 722
Hartford Life, 525
HBOS plc, 717
Hewlett-Packard Company, 33, 62, 135, 147, 476, 615, 715
Highland Corp., 275
Honda Motor Company, 203
Hoover's, Inc., 632
H&R Block, 94–95, 98, 101
HSBC Group Holdings, 717
Hydril Pressure Control, 114
Hyundai Motor, 392

I
IBM, 5, 51, 160, 298, 665–667, 672, 714, 724
ImClone Systems, Inc., 310
Infosys Technologies Limited, 165
ING Group, 696
Intel Corp., 224–227, 298, 312, 343
Investopedia ULC, 176

J
J&J, *See* Johnson & Johnson
JMI Equity, 586
Johnson & Johnson Services, Inc., 167, 395
JPMorgan Chase & Co., 437, 446, 717

Company Index | 767

K
Kellogg Co., 342
Kia Motors, 724
Kirby Manufacturing, Inc., 484
Kmart, 56
Kohlberg Kravis Roberts & Co. (KKR), 1
KPMG International, 129
Krispy Kreme Doughnuts, 493, 494, 507

L
Larry's Ice Cream, 333–334
Laurel Electronics, Inc., 124

M
Marriott International, Inc., 548
MBNA Corp., 208
McDonalds, 499, 647
Mellon Bank Corp., 711
Merrill Lynch & Co., Inc., 29, 31, 500
Microsoft, 298, 348, 355, 552, 561, 563
Mitsubishi, 664, 698
Mitsubishi UFJ Financial Group, 717
Mitsui Group, 664, 698
Moody's Investors Service, 271–272
Morgan Stanley, 41
The Motley Fool, 287
Motorola, Inc., 586
MSN Money, 440, 442

N
Nalco Holding Company, 523
Nestlé, 525
New York Life Insurance Company, 175
Nike Inc., 235, 236
Nissan Motor Company, 212, 392
Nordstrom, Inc., 108, 109, 113
North Sails Group, LLC, 110
Northwest Airlines, 303, 304, 640

O
Oakley, Inc., 521
Orbea USA, Llc, 186–188

P
Pfizer, Inc., 526
Piper Aircraft, Inc., 88

Pitney Bowes, Inc., 525
Polo Ralph Lauren Corp., 108, 109
PricewaterhouseCoopers International Limited, 5, 129, 449
Procter & Gamble Company, 7, 125, 227, 296–297, 525

R
Regatta, Inc., 278
The Right Start Stores, 627
Rockwell Industries International Corp., 275
Ronco Corp., 628
The Royal Bank of Scotland International Limited, 717
Royal Dutch Shell plc, 664, 695, 696

S
San Diego Gas and Electric Company (SDG&E), 302
Schwan Food Company, 394–395
Sealed Air Corp., 563–564, 571
Sharp Electronics Corp., 135, 147
Shearson Lehman Hutton, Inc., 268
Shell Corp., 722
Shell Oil Company, *See* Royal Dutch Shell plc
Shimano, Inc., 186
Siemens AG, 719
Societe Generale Group, 717
Southwest Airlines Company, 85, 128
S&P, *See* Standard and Poor's
Spear, Leeds, and Kellogg Specialists LLC, 692
Standard & Poor's, 37, 113, 271–272
Starwood Hotels & Resorts Worldwide, Inc., 426–427
State Bank of India, 723, 724
State Farm Mutual Automobile Insurance Company, 29
Stride Rite Corp., 521
Sumitomo Corp., 698
Sunbeam Corp., 129

T
Target Corp., 433
Texas Instruments, Inc., 135, 147, 223, 453

Texas Pacific Group (TPG Capital), 1
Thomson Reuters, 514
3M Corp., 40, 41
Total S.A., 696
Toyota Motor Corp., 88, 114, 477, 696, 725
Tricolor Industries, Inc., 724
TXU C., 1, 516
Tyco International, Ltd., 18, 20

U
United Parcel Service of America, Inc. (UPS), 428

V
Varco International, Inc., 114
Verizon Communications, Inc., 342
Video Gaming Technologies, Inc. (VGT), 396

W
Wachovia Corp., 717
Wal-Mart Stores, Inc., 94–95, 98, 109, 113, 125, 228–232, 525, 567, 693–696
The Walt Disney Studios, 5
Waste Management, Inc., 129
Weatherford International Ltd., 114
Weil Gotshal & Manges LLP, 249
Wells Fargo & Company, 717
Weyerhaeuser Company, 68
Whole Foods Markets, Inc., 109, 578
Wikimedia Foundation, Inc., 668
Winn-Dixie Stores, Inc., 525
WorldCom, 18, 20–22, 53, 543

X
Xerox Corp., 52

Y
Yahoo! Inc., 355
Yahoo! Finance, 106, 441, 442

Z
Zephyr Sales Company, 165
Zon Capital Partners, 586

Building Intuition

Throughout the book important finance principles and concepts are identified and emphasized in *Building Intuition* boxes. These boxes restate an important finance concept that has been discussed in the main text, such as the importance of cash flows, and provide an intuitive example or explanation of the concept. The Building Intuition boxes and the pages on which they appear are as follows:

	Page
Cash Flows Matter Most to Investors	4
Sound Investments are Those Where the Value of the Benefits Exceeds Their Costs	6
Financing Decisions Affect the Value of the Firm	6
The Timing of Cash Flows Affects Their Value	12
The Riskiness of Cash Flows Affects Their Value	13
The Financial Manager's Goal Is to Maximize the Value of the Firm's Stock	14
The Value of Money Changes with Time	133
Compounding Drives Much of the Earnings on Long-Term Investments	142
More Risk Means a Higher Expected Return	211
Diversified Portfolios are Less Risky	232
Systematic Risk Is the Risk That Matters	234
Investment Decisions Have Opportunity Costs	316
Capital Budgeting Is Forward Looking	356
Incremental After-Tax Free Cash Flows Are What Stockholders Care About	358
We Discount *Expected* Cash Flows in an NPV Analysis	379
High Fixed Costs Mean Larger Fluctuations in Cash Flows and Profits	402
Revenue Changes Drive Profit Volatility Through Operating Leverage	408

	Page
The Market Value of a Firm's Assets Equals the Market Value of the Claims on Those Assets	**430**
A Firm's Cost of Capital Is a Weighted Average of All of Its Financing Costs	**432**
The Current Cost of Long-Term Debt Is What Matters When Calculating WACC	**434**
Investors View Seasoned Securities as Less Risky Than Unseasoned Securities	**502**
The Optimal Capital Structure Minimizes the Cost of Financing a Firm's Activities	**528**
Capital Structure Does Not Affect Firm Value If It Does Not Affect Total Cash Flows to Securityholders	**529**
The Cost of Equity Increases With Financial Leverage	**533**
People Behave Differently toward a firm in Financial Distress, and This Increases Bankruptcy Costs	**547**
Dividends Reduce the Stockholders' Investment in a Firm	**563**
Dividend Announcements Send Signals to Investors	**565**
The Value of a Business Is Specific to a Point in Time	**598**
The Value of a Business Is Not the Same to All Investors	**599**
A Firm's Strategy Drives Its Business Decisions	**629**
Payoff Functions for Options Are Not Linear	**668**
The Basic Principles of Finance Apply No Matter Where You Do Business	**698**